Paul Topinard

Anthropology

Paul Topinard

Anthropology

ISBN/EAN: 9783742820174

Manufactured in Europe, USA, Canada, Australia, Japa

Cover: Foto ©Thomas Meinert / pixelio.de

Manufactured and distributed by brebook publishing software
(www.brebook.com)

P. R. RYAN AND CO., LIMITED, IMPERIAL PALACE, S.K.

ANTHROPOLOGY

BY

DR. PAUL TOPINARD,

PROFESSOR OF ANTHROPOLOGY AT THE ÉCOLE DES HAUTES ÉTUDES,
CURATOR OF THE MUSEUM OF THE ANTHROPOLOGICAL SOCIETY OF PARIS,
ETC.

With Preface
BY
PROFESSOR PAUL BROCA.

TRANSLATED FROM THE FRENCH.

FOURTH THOUSAND.

With Forty-nine Woodcuts.

LONDON: CHAPMAN AND HALL, Ld.
1894.

Paul Topinard

Anthropology

AUTHOR'S PREFACE.

ANTHROPOLOGY, of all branches of natural science, was the last to be developed; nevertheless it is one which now lays claim to hold the first place in the attention of the scientific world. For fifteen years this science, whose title even was not settled, had but few adherents. Since 1740, the date at which it was inaugurated by Buffon, there have been, in every generation, a certain number of learned men who have directed their attention to it, and among these have figured many distinguished anatomists and naturalists. But these men, devoted to studies whose utility was not as yet appreciated, formed, as it were, a staff without an army, and if they had a few select readers we may safely say they had not the public at large.

A new era manifested itself in 1859, in consequence of the foundation of the Société d'Anthropologie de Paris. The Ethnological Societies of Paris, and of London and New York, which had preceded it, had not been able to extend their influence beyond a very limited area; some valuable works had been published, but the majority of the members

remained indifferent. When, in 1848, the Société Ethnologique de Paris ceased to hold its meetings, no notice was
taken of it; and when, eleven years later, some of its
members resolved to found a society for the special study
of Man, and of the races of mankind, it was with difficulty,
after six months of parleying, that nineteen of the pro-
moters could be brought together, of whom many were
only members in name.

This new society, founded with so much difficulty,
obtained, however, rapid and unexpected success. Enlarging all at once the programme of ethnology, by grouping
around the study of the human races the medical sciences,
comparative anatomy, and zoology, prehistoric archæology,
palæontology, linguistics, and history, and designating under
the title Anthropology the science whose domain was thus
largely extended, the new society opened its portals to all
those who cultivated these numerous branches of human
knowledge.

Ethnology had remained, up to this period, a speciality
prosecuted but by few; anthropology, on the contrary,
addressed itself to learned men of every class. It attracted to
it physicians, naturalists, archæologists, linguistics, happy to
be able, each in his sphere, to lend his aid; and soon these
valuable auxiliaries manifested their desire to become pro-
ficient by an assiduous devotion to its study. To the rapid
accession of learned men to its ranks, and of others who
became interested in it, are we to attribute the rapid diffusion
of anthropological knowledge.

This movement, which had its origin in France, rapidly
extended to other countries. On all sides anthropological
societies sprang up, which were founded on the same basis

and worked on the same general plan. Anthropological conferences were organised, and in the greater number of general meetings for the advancement of science, anthropology has now its section the same as other sciences. These conferences have been remarkable from the number of members who have taken an active part in them, and from the still larger number of their adherents. The latter are no longer to be computed by hundreds but by thousands. For example, the only society of anthropology in Paris has now on its roll upwards of four hundred native members, while the members comprising the two English societies is nearly double that number. There is now a large and distinguished body of persons who fully estimate the importance of the science, who approve its objects, and who naturally interest themselves in them. This is the happy outgrowth of the extension of the general scheme of anthropology. Other results, still more fortunate, have been brought about. Works have become multiplied in proportion to the number of workers. Many questions of altogether a novel character have arisen; many others have changed their aspects; all have been elucidated by constant and patient research. Innumerable facts have been observed, discussed, verified; and in the brief period of sixteen years greater progress and more important discoveries have been made in anthropology than at any period since its foundation.

But the rapidity with which the development of anthropology is proceeding is a source of considerable difficulty to those who are desirous of studying this science. No one can pretend to become conversant with all the subjects of general knowledge which it lays under contribution; to

master them with the depth and precision which imply a
thorough acquaintance with them, he must abandon the
idea of becoming a *perfect* anthropologist.   Division of
labour is more necessary here than anywhere else.   In this
vast domain each one pitches his tent in the spot where his
special tastes, his peculiar bias, and his particular knowledge invite him.   But in order that these researches, so
multiform, may not run the risk of becoming discursive,
and may be directed to one and the same end, it is necessary
that all labourers in the work should early become acquainted with the general principles of anthropology, with
its tenets, and with the whole of the facts which it has
established.   This want has been sensibly felt for some
years.   From all sides a demand has sprung up for an
elementary treatise on anthropology—a systematic résumé
where questions might be studied which are the subject of
discussion in our societies or treated of in original papers;
a work, in short, which should be at the same time a guide
for students and a manual of reference for others.   Such a
work has not appeared up to the present time.   The
remarkable "Leçons sur l'Homme," by Carl Vogt, embraced
only the subject in a general way: they were published,
moreover, twelve years since, and do not give the latest
information on the science.   The excellent little treatise of
Omalius d'Halloy, "Sur les Races Humaines," is purely
ethnological; it embraces only one special part of anthropology, and does not supply the want to which we refer.

An important gap had to be filled up.   The founders of
the Bibliothèque des Sciences Contemporaines have felt it
incumbent upon them to step in, and have confided to
Dr. Topinard the difficult task of elucidating, in a single

volume, a science of vast dimensions in process of rapid development, and one which hitherto has not received sufficient attention. More than one had shrunk from attempting it. An individual devoting himself to original research, and engaged in duties to which he is anxious to give his undivided attention, is generally little disposed to employ his time in writing a work of a popular character. But M. Topinard is one who is thoroughly equal to the task. An appeal was made to his ardent love for anthropology, which appeal has not been made in vain. He has been most unwearied in his efforts, and has brought his work to a successful issue. He has rendered signal service to anthropology, for which, on behalf of the friends of the science, I cordially thank him.

PAUL BROCA.

TRANSLATOR'S PREFACE.

Whilst endeavouring faithfully to execute the task of clothing in English garb Dr. Topinard's work on Anthropology, the translator wishes it to be understood that he does not necessarily endorse all the views of its talented author. Himself a pupil of the illustrious Prichard, he early became acquainted with that great man's arguments in favour of Monogenism, so forcibly advanced in his work "Researches into the Physical History of Mankind." Subsequent thoughtful study has only tended to confirm him in the truth of those arguments; and in an entire belief in the authenticity of the Mosaic Records, which no sophistry on the part of the advocates of Polygenism has been able to shake. One or two matters of detail contained in the original have been omitted, with a view to render the work more acceptable to the general reader, from whom, as well as from the professional reader, indulgence is craved for many conscious defects in the translation.

ROBERT T. H. BARTLEY.

November 20, 1877.

CONTENTS.

PART I.

OF MAN CONSIDERED IN HIS ENSEMBLE, AND IN HIS RELATIONS WITH ANIMALS.

CHAPTER I.

PHYSICAL CHARACTERS.

CHAPTER IX.

CHAPTER X.

CHAPTER XI.

CHAPTER XII.

PART III.

ON THE ORIGIN OF MAN.

CHAPTER I.

ANTHROPOLOGY.

INTRODUCTION.

The word *Anthropology* is of ancient date, and has always signified the study of Man; originally, of Man moral, and, later on, of Man physical. At the present time it comprehends both. We may almost say that Aristotle was the originator of it. He termed those *Anthropologists* who carried on dissertations upon Man. The word is found for the first time in the title of a work of Magnus Hundt, in 1501. It is frequently to be met with subsequently as synonymous with "a description of the soul," or of "a description of the body and soul, and of the laws which govern their union." In 1772, Diderot and D'Alembert defined it as "a treatise on Man." In 1778, Kant wrote a work on psychology, entitled "An Essay on Anthropology." Blumenbach takes it in the acceptation we give it at the present day. In 1838, Serres assumed, at the Museum, the title of Professor of Anthropology, or of the Natural History of Man; and M. Edwards, in 1839, defined it as the knowledge of Man in his physical and moral relations. Here and there, however, we find it more or less misinterpreted. Physicians have published, under this title, encyclopedias embracing at the same time anatomy, physiology, pathology, and hygiene. A

B

chapter in Professor Karl Schmidt's "Lettres Anthropologiques," written in 1853, is entitled "The Anthropology of the New Testament, or Jesus Christ." Three years ago an author in the "Revue des deux Mondes" employed it as a synonym for the "Reproduction of the human figure on Grecian vases." But such differences of signification are no longer allowable. The word has a meaning, stamped upon it by the whole of Europe, which cannot be ignored; it designates a science as well recognised and as definite as chemistry, astronomy, or social economy.

Definition.

Anthropology is the branch of natural history which treats of Man and of the races of Man. It may be summed up in the following definitions:

"Anthropology is a science which has for its object the study of the human race, considered as a whole, in its separate individuality, and in its relations with the rest of nature."—*Broca.*

"Anthropology is a science pure and concrete, having for its aim the thorough knowledge of the human group, considered: (1) In each of the four typical divisions—as to variety, race, species —compared with each other, and in relation to their respective external conditions. (2) In its *ensemble*, and in its relations with the rest of the animal world."—*Bertillon.*

"Anthropology is the natural history of Man, considered monographically, as a zoologist studying an animal would understand it."—*De Quatrefages.*

Such is an outline of the subject for our consideration. It comprehends all the points of view from which the enlightened naturalist would look, who desired to give a complete history of any animal, and of its settled varieties. He examines (1) its external form, and its internal organs after death. (2) The functions of these organs during life. He notes how the heart beats, the lungs respire, the brain thinks. He ascertains whether the animal is a biped or a quadruped; how its functions of reproduction are performed, what are the influences by which it is governed, what the character of its food, what its habits, its instincts, its passions. (3) Its particular mode of associating with those of its own species, such as the wandering life of the dingo of Australia, and the bison of America, or the sedentary life of the beaver and the ant. (4) Its method of conveying its meaning to a distance by more or less articulate sounds, as by the rapid friction of the wing-covers, or by the simple vibrations of the larynx. (5) Its migrations, whether voluntary or forced, periodical or spontaneous, owing to the pursuit of an enemy, or in consequence of a flood, or from change of climate. (6) Its numerous records. Archæology indeed gives us an insight into the habits of animals in bygone times, their migrations, the period at which they became domesticated by Man, and those species which have become extinct.

The naturalist, in this way, is enabled to give some sort of description of each group, and of each of its divisions, and to distinguish them from those to which they are the most closely allied. Then, by synthesis, he establishes their respective position in the classification of animated beings, and the family, genus, species, or variety to which they belong. Having made himself acquainted with the relations which his object of study bears to the rest of the animal kingdom, he proceeds to enter upon the higher path of philosophical inquiry.

Programme.

The course which the anthropologist takes is equally clearly defined. His aims are the same, his method of proceeding is identical. His subject is a twofold one: (1) Man considered in himself, so far as the group to which he belongs differs from, or is analogous to, contiguous groups in the class of mammalia with which he is in nearest relation. (2) The varieties of mankind, commonly called races, a word which has but little present significance as compared with that which will be accorded to it at a later period. All the traits and characters with which the naturalist is occupied equally engage his attention, and even with greater intensity.

B 2

Certain characters of his embryo state, of but trifling interest in the animal, possess in him a very high degree of importance. These characters may be classified under four principal heads, viz. (1) Physical, whether studied on the dead body or on the living. (2) Physiological, which have a particular name assigned to them, according as they have references to the brain, or to the intellectual faculties and phenomena. (3) Characters resulting from the social condition. (4) Those having reference to history, archæology, language, &c. The mode of pursuing the investigation is precisely the same for Man as for animals. If our inquiries respecting the latter require the most rigid scrutiny, what shall we say when the subject of them is ourselves? Intuitive reasoning, à priori reasoning, and other methods of a similar nature, should be altogether excluded. Whether we are determining Man's position on our planet, and the part which he plays at the head of organized beings; whether he is the sole representative of a kingdom—the human kingdom—or is only the first of the order of Primates, the same processes of scientific investigation must be put in operation. M. de Quatrefages, one of the strongest defenders of human prerogatives, expressly tells us this: Man is an animal; he comes into existence, reproduces his own species, and dies. *Memento te hominem esse!* was an exclamation to the conqueror of old.

Method of Investigation.

Man in his entirety—that is to say, in his physical and moral relations, to quote W. Edwards—is the subject of anthropology. No zoologist would dream of dividing the study of an animal into two portions, and of entrusting them to learned men of different orders, some limiting themselves to the anatomical and physiological characters of certain organs, others directing their attention only to the brain and nervous system. Neither should the study of Man, under the pretext that one portion possesses supreme importance over another, be divided between men of science and philosophers. Each would look at Man or animal from his

own particular point of view; but the anthropologist and the
naturalist should take a comprehensive view of the whole. To
understand the working of a machine, one must study its system of
wheels, and make ourselves acquainted with the mechanism and
structure of similar machines. The organisation, whether animal
or human, simple or complex, is governed by the same general laws,
is constituted of the same elements, and performs similar functions.
Man's mode of life, of thought, and of association, is as important
to know as their mode of walking or breathing. The cerebral manifestations, in their infinite variety, are as much characteristic of
races as the volume and quality of the brain distinguish man from
the brute: they are two orders of facts which are inseparable. If
the structure of the organ indicates its function, so the function
and its various manifestations indicate the organ. The body and
the mind are as indissoluble as matter and its activity, or, as it
used to be called, its properties.

The field of anthropology, then, is immeasurably vast, and might
be defined as "the science of Man and of mankind," according
to James Hunt; or "the biology of the human species," according
to M. Broca. Numerous and varied are the subjects of general
knowledge which it lays under contribution!

Its more immediate domain is the comparative anatomy and
morphology of Man and animals; then the history of animals, and
of mammalia in particular, and especially of the anthropoid apes;
then the different branches of medical science, notably physiology,
of which psychology in health and disease forms part; then that
which has reference to nations, and consequently to travel, as
ethnography, geography, history, language, and, lastly, prehistoric
archaeology. This is not all—law, the arts, literature, equally contribute their share. Léon Guillard, barrister and anthropologist,
who died at Buzenval, demonstrated, eight months previous to his
death, its intimate connection with the science of comparative law,
a subject taken up by M. Acollas in 1874.*

* "L'Anthropologie et l'Étude du Droit comparé," by L. Guillard, in
"Bull. Soc. d'Anthrop.," 2nd series, vol. v.; "L'Anthropologie et le
Droit," by E. Acollas, in "Bull. Soc. d'Anthrop.," 2nd series, vol. ix.

The year previously, M. Cènt Daly had shown, before the
Société d'Anthropologie, that architecture, in its elementary forms,
varies according to the distinctive character of each race. Fétis, in
1867, suggested a classification of races, based upon their musical
systems.* Dances, songs, and national poems, like the heathen
mythologies, serve to trace out their origin and affinities. The
first attempts at anthropometry, for the purpose of determining the
proportions of the human body, and craniometry, for analysing
the physiognomy, are due to artists.

We see, then, that anthropology appeals to all willing workers,
whatever the direction of their studies or the nature of their professional occupations may be. All, with scarcely any preparatory
study, may contribute to its progress; it is sufficient to indicate to
them its aim—the knowledge of Man. The mere word "anthropology" frightens many people, who imagine that it has to do with
medicine.

Medicine.

The study of Man, relegated at first to the dissertations of
philosophers, on assuming a real basis naturally became shared both
by physicians and naturalists; the former, however, had but little
leisure to deal with the special questions which it involved, while
the latter were reluctant to regard it in the same light as they did
that of the brute creation, which was the special subject of their
investigation. It was necessary that anthropology should be un-
constrained. Both at the Museum and in the Faculty of Medicine
of Paris, it has its representatives and its classes, but it holds a
thoroughly independent position there. While medicine has
especial reference to the individual—to the human machine—
anthropology studies the human group and its varieties. The
former has but one aspiration, one aim—the prevention and cure of
disease; the latter studies Man, his origin, and his relations with
other animated beings, without troubling himself about the manner

* "La Classification des Races," by Fétis Son., in "Bull. Soc. d'Anthrop.,"
2nd series, vol. ii., 1867.

in which society in general may treat the question. Their method of looking at things is altogether different. Is it a question of anatomy? Medicine looks at the organ in relation to adjoining parts, as it bears upon surgical operations, or at its structure, the better to understand whether its performance is regular or disturbed. Anthropology finds in it only elements of comparison with animals or between races. Is it a question of physiology, of pathology, of hygiene, or of therapeutics? They still diverge. The one seeks in the brain the method by which thought is elaborated, and how it is transformed into action; the other sees in it only different manifestations, varying according to race. Diseases are not alike in all latitudes. When it is a question of climate, it is specially in the province of medicine; when of race, it is for anthropology to step in. So with respect to the action of remedies, each regards the question from its own particular point of view. Lastly, hygiene has a bearing upon anthropology, owing to the part which it plays, or its influence on external circumstances, acclimatisation, or crossing.

An acquaintance with the medical sciences, without being indispensable to every anthropologist, gives him a marked advantage. Reciprocally, a knowledge of anthropology invests the physician with a certain pre-eminence. It augments his interest in anatomical and physiological studies, and is the climax of academic study. We are surprised, therefore, that instruction in it does not form part of the regular course in our principal faculties. Looking at it in connection with the healing art, it is indispensable that the medical men in our navy and mercantile marine, called upon, as they are, to practise among races the most diverse, should know how to distinguish them, as well as to recognise the varieties of local circumstances under which disease present themselves.

Ethnography.

The word "ethnography" was employed at the commencement of the present century as synonymous with a description of nations.

It was made use of in 1826 in the "Atlas Géographique" of M. Balbi, and was ratified under the influence of what was subsequently termed linguistics. Wiseman, in 1836, defined it as "the classification of races by the comparative study of languages;" M. Broca, as simply the description of each nation in particular. The word "ethnology" had its origin in the title of the Society of Ethnology of Paris, in 1839. It embraces, as set forth in the statutes of that society, "the physical organisation, the intellectual and moral character, the language, and historical traditions which serve to distinguish races." It is used in the same sense in England by Prichard, Lubbock, Logan, Brace, &c. In 1866, M. Broca extended its meaning as follows: "The particular description and designation of these races, the study of their resemblances and dissimilarities as regards physical constitution, as well as intellectual and social condition. The inquiry into their actual affinities, their distribution in the present and in the past, their history, their more or less probable, more or less doubtful relationship, and their respective position in the human series. Such is the purpose of that division of anthropology which we designate by the name of ethnology; the sources whence it gathers its inquiries are numerous, it borrows from ethnography, or a description of peoples. . . ." *

Ethnology.

M. Littré confines the term "ethnology" to its etymological meaning. "Ethnology," he says, "treats of the origin and distribution of peoples, and ethnography of their description. According to M. Frédéric Müller, anthropology has reference to the study of races, ethnology to that of peoples. Latham had already described ethnology as the speculative, and ethnography as the descriptive part of the science of peoples.

For ourselves, we regard anthropology and ethnology as two different aspects of the study of Man; two distinct sciences, each

* Lecture by James Hunt at the Anthropological Society of London, January 8, 1866; Article, "Anthropologie," in the "Dictionnaire Encyclopédique des Sciences Médicales," by M. Paul Broca, vol. v. Paris, 1866.

having its own adherents, enjoying an independent existence, but always having a unity of design. The former occupies itself with Man and the races of mankind, which it succeeds in minutely unfolding. The latter only concerns itself with such peoples and tribes as geography and history hand over to us, and is divided into two parts—ethnography, which is the description of each people, of its manners, customs, religion, language, physical characteristics, and origin in history ; and ethnology, properly so called, which looks at these in their *ensemble*, and as applying to all or to many peoples.

It is the province of ethnology, then, to be engaged with constituent elements, with the origin and descent of peoples, and even to make a classification of them based upon their language. It makes use of the term "races" somewhat carelessly. But it is not within its province to determine the characteristics or to make a correct classification of the races of mankind. It does not possess the qualifications for such a task, which requires the combination of all the active powers of anthropology, and especially anatomical appliances and zoological experience, to which it is a stranger.

The expression "races," as used by the ethnologist, is a permissive one. To the anthropologist, it is one of deep meaning. He looks upon it as synonymous with the natural divisions of the human group, however remote the period at which they were constituted. Cynology being the natural history of the dog, the inquiry into the primitive races which have produced its innumerable cross breeds would belong to cynology; so the inquiry into the various human races constitutes anthropology, and not ethnology. Ethnology then, as its etymology signifies, is the general science of nations.[*]

Nationality.

The study of anthropology requires a calm and vigorous judgment, free from prejudice, with but one aspiration—that of truth. There is no more delicate subject to handle. We have all been

[*] "Anthropologie, Ethnologie, et Ethnographie," in "Bull. Soc. d'Anthrop," by Paul Topinard. 1876.

brought up with preconceived notions, which have saturated our
brain substance, at a period when it was becoming fully developed,
and was the better fitted to retain impressions.* Now anthropological facts at times clash with certain matters of faith, which
religious teachers have ever considered necessary for the best
interests of mankind. On the other hand, our pride is ruffled; it
is not willing to descend from the pedestal on which it has reposed,
intends to have nothing in common with the animals, and clamours
when we tell it that there is no great gulf between them and ourselves. What we do, what we think, is ever the high, the noble,
the good, the true. Our physical type, as Europeans, is the nearest
approach to perfection. Those who have the round head, or who
imagine that they have it, affirm that it is the most intellectual.
With the Chinese, the flat face, the oblique eyes, and the
hairy upper lip, are the very perfection of beauty. The negro
looks upon black as the most beautiful of colours. In the intellectual world, our moral condition, our civilisation alone merit
the title of beautiful. Our customs alone are dictated by reason,
those of other nations are barbarous. The political passion misleads
us in the same way. Nationality, according to the Germans, is
determined by language, a doctrine purely ethnographic and
radically false; as M. Abel Hovelacque has so forcibly put it, this
is only "a social cause." Brought into being by a fortuity of circumstances, rather than by the geographical disposition of places,
it is afterwards maintained by a community of interests, of suffering, and of glory. Blood poured out in a common cause cements
it; hearts throbbing in unison with it from one end of a territory
to the other are its characteristics.†

Applications.

It is asked if anthropology has any application to real life, and

* We shall have frequently to revert to this point, more particularly in
our description of races.
† "Langues, Races, Nationalités," by A. Hovelacque, editor of the
"Revue de Linguistique." Paris, 1872.

what is its pretended aim? But had Aristotle, Linnæus, Buffon no object in view when describing the animal kingdom? Newton, when pondering over the problem of gravitation, and Cuvier, when investigating the characters of fossil species? Did Pasteur, when refuting the theory of spontaneous generation, contemplate the advantages which patient industry would deduce from it? No, true science, that which leads to the most brilliant results, is essentially disinterested. To know how to enlarge the field of human thought, and to satisfy a legitimate curiosity, such are its actuating principles.

Anthropology, more than any other science, is capable of exercising an influence on our social organisations. Is not its object to lay open to our view Man as he really is, to unfold to us the secret of his acts, his passions, and his wants in the past, and possibly in the future?

The first English society having any relation to anthropology was founded with a view to help forward the abolition of slavery, and did in fact powerfully contribute to this result. The first of any note in France had for its object to give currency to an idea which M. Edwards had gathered from the writings of Sir Walter Scott and of the two Thierrys—namely, that men and their temperaments play an important part in the existence of nations. History, elucidated by anthropology, thus assumes a new aspect; causes and effects are more readily explained, and the anthropological replaces the theological in our conceptions of past ages.*

Civilised peoples are everywhere taking the place of savage races, or substituting for them races less warlike in character. To this end governments have to choose between two courses of action, either to destroy or to bring them together. The former, spite of certain recent examples, is not admissible; the latter is only realisable by understanding the distinctive character of the vanquished nation, its capabilities, and the nature of its race. Our method of action

---

* W. F. Edwards, "Des Caractères Physiologiques des Races Humaines considérées dans leur Rapports avec l'Histoire." Letter to M. Amédée Thierry, in 1829, in "Mém. Soc. Ethnol.," vol. i.

cannot be too deeply penetrated with this truth, if we would give
its right position to the native race of Algeria, which is the
Barbary, and ought not to be considered as the Arab race. Anthropology teaches us how to recognise them.

Man inures himself to almost every climate, but only by dint
of perseverance. One race dies out in a country, while another
thrives in it. By following certain principles, the difficulties are
more or less surmounted. The science of acclimation, therefore,
is one department of anthropology. It has been said that races
may be compared to countries in which diseases are variously
developed, and which require different hygienic treatment. It is
as necessary to be able to distinguish races as in medicine to
diagnose the arthritic, the herpetic, or the nervous temperament.
In the sad expedition to Mexico the knowledge of one of the
characteristics of the negro race led to a most happy result. Vera
Cruz, where at first there was considerable mortality among the
French troops from yellow fever, was afterwards garrisoned by black
soldiers from Upper Egypt, who possessed an immunity from that
disease.

We are not now living in the time of Albert Dürer and of
Rubens, when artists were satisfied with delineating the forms and
features of those around them to represent those of foreign nations.
Our annual exhibitions testify the progress which has been made
in this direction. In the galleries of the Museum we sometimes
meet with painters studying the varieties of the human head, and
at the École des Beaux-Arts, the professor of anatomy knows that
he must teach the different forms of the beautiful, as seen in every
country and under every climate, and, therefore, must be an anthropologist.

Whether we accept the modern doctrine or not, it is undeniable
that Man, by a certain method of high breeding and well-managed
crossing, is capable of being changed in successive generations,
in his physical as well as in his moral character. According
to the modes adopted, he will go on either degenerating or
improving. Anthropology comes in here with the highest, and at
the same time most practical aim, and its utility in this alone

should secure for it the encouragement and patronage of our learned
societies.

Anthropology, be it observed, is far from being a science of
luxury. At this very moment it is leading to most important
results, and is throwing new light upon all the sciences bearing
upon Man. Naturalists, physicians, men of letters, artists, philosophers, lawyers, diplomatists, travellers, archæologists, and linguists,
are all carrying the material wherewith to build the edifice. To
those who apply themselves closely to its study it is a somewhat
arduous task, but to the great majority it is a recreation.

History.

This may be recited very briefly. The study of nature, and of
Man in particular, may be traced back to the period of the earliest
efforts of the human mind; but anthropology as a special science,
separate from natural history, is but of yesterday. Unknown up
to the close of this last century, it has only started into life towards
the latter half of the nineteenth century. Its rudiments are found
scattered up and down in the writings of physicians and naturalists. The former by observing Man under all climates, the latter
by placing him as the type of the perfectly organised being,
accomplished for anthropology what M. Jourdain did for prose.

Such were Hippocrates, who describes in his book, "On Water,
Air, and Place," the character of "the Scythians and other nomadic tribes," as well as the cranial malformations of the Macro-
cephali on the other side of Palus-Mæotis; Aristotle, who compares apes with Man, and speaks of human hybrids and of
Ethiopians; Pliny, whose frequently fantastic recitals have been
justly criticised by Isidore Geoffroy Saint-Hilaire; Galen, who,
while dissecting monkeys, prepared the way for human anatomy
founded by Mundinus and Vesalius (1544). As to philosophers,
they have had nothing to say with respect to Man's history. No
doubt some, like Lucretius, have shown their acuteness of appre-
hension of its facts; but those who long afterwards proclaimed

the true method of observation have the greatest claim on our
gratitude.

Natural History took its rise with Aristotle, and made no
further progress. Belon, in 1555, was the first to compare the
skeleton of Man with that of another animal—namely, a bird. Up
to the eighteenth century, the *chef-d'œuvre* of creation, to use a
classical expression, was only studied by physicians. Linnæus, in
1755, restored him to his place in his classification, and by applying
to him his binary nomenclature, under the title of *homo sapiens*,
obliged naturalists to accept him as belonging to them. About
the same period Buffon devoted two volumes to the "Variétés
Humaines" (1749).

The way was open. Almost simultaneously Daubenton, in 1764,
published his memoir on "La Situation du trou Occipital dans
l'Homme et les Animaux;" Blumenbach, in 1775, his inaugural
thesis on "Les Variations du Genre Humain;" Sœmmering, in
1785, his "Mémoire sur les Nègres;" Camper, in 1791, his posthumous dissertation, "Sur les Différences que présente le Visage
dans les Races Humaines;" White, in 1799, his work on "The
regular gradation of Man and Animals."

Many notable travels were undertaken about this period. On
land we may mention those of Byron, Bruce, Levaillant, Pallas,
Barrow; on the sea, those of Bougainville, Cook, La Pérouse,
Péron. The Museum of Paris shone out in all its full lustre;
natural history made gigantic strides; observations were going on
quietly. By degrees, two rival schools sprang up: the one called
the *classique*, represented by Cuvier, which confined itself to facts;
the other called the philosophical, or *des idées*, which Lamarck and
Étienne Geoffroy Saint-Hilaire represented. Lamentable prejudices
unfortunately came to be mingled with their wranglings. Linnæus
and Blumenbach had spoken of mankind without attaching any
definite importance to it. Lamarck maintained that species vary
and are transformed. So far orthodoxy was not affected, but
the danger appeared serious; the younger men were carried away
with the eloquence of Étienne Geoffroy Saint-Hilaire. A watch-
word seemed to be sent forth: "The world was created in six

days; Adam and Eve are the progenitors of all living races; the universal deluge utterly destroyed everything but the privileged pairs saved with Noah." Science must bend before these articles of faith.

The first assault was conducted to the detriment of Lamarck, who was too modest in presence of the imposing authority of Cuvier. The second was unfavourable to Etienne Geoffroy Saint-Hilaire; the transformation theory appeared to be vanquished. The third had all sorts of revolutions of fortune, and was prolonged up to about the year 1859, after the discovery of Boucher de Perthes: the ground was apparently shaken. The classical or orthodox school, then known by the name of monogenist, pleaded in favour of the unity of the human species, and of the variability of races under the influence of external circumstances and of crossings. The opposite, or polygenist school, maintained, on the contrary, the plurality of races, and the non-influence of external circumstances. In France, the former took shelter under the great name of Cuvier; Virey, Bory de Saint-Vincent, and A. Desmoulins were the partisans of the latter. But about the year 1813, a vigorous champion came forward in favour of the monogenists, in the person of Prichard. His most important arguments occupy five volumes, and are full of instruction, while they constitute, at the present moment, a veritable vade-mecum for the anthropologist.* The work of Prichard was exclusive. Another, after the model of Virey's "L'Histoire Naturelle de l'Homme," in 1801, but more comprehensive in its character, appeared in London in 1817. It was entitled, "Lectures delivered before the College of Surgeons on the Natural History of Man," by Lawrence, and rather advocated the plurality of the human species, although pretending to uphold the monogenistic doctrine. These two works, to which we may add that of M. Desmoulins on "Les Races Humaines," in 1826, prove that the researches on Man had lost nothing on an appeal to

* The first edition of "Researches into the Physical History of Man," by Prichard, appeared in 1813, and was in one volume; the second, in two volumes, appeared in 1826; and the third and last, in five volumes, from 1836 to 1837.

principles. Linguistics and ethnography, originally almost synonymous terms, and human comparative anatomy, were in course of
development. From Klaproth and Abel de Rémusat to Rénan,
Chavée, and Frederic Müller, the number of persons won over
to anthropology by the study of the comparative structure of
languages was immense.[*]

The first ethnographical society of which there is any record was
instituted in Paris in 1800, under the title of the "Société des
Observateurs de l'Homme," and died of inanition during the war.
The second was instituted in London in 1838, and was of an
exclusively philanthropic character. The fact of the polygenists
having declared that the black races are inferior to the white, was
used as an argument in favour of slavery. The society should have
set its face against this doctrine, and it suffered the penalty for not
doing so. The following year, M. Edwards founded the Société
Ethnologique de Paris, which has furnished some excellent works,
at the fore-front of which is to be mentioned a pamphlet by its
founder, "Sur les Caractères Physiologiques des Races Humaines
considérées dans leur Rapports avec l'Histoire." Some admirable
works soon appeared, both in France and elsewhere, having similar
ethnographical views, among which we may mention, "L'Homme
Américain," by Alcide d'Orbigny.[†]

In comparative anatomy, the skull, to which the labours of the
first anthropologists had been directed, continued to attract their
attention. The "Décades" of Blumenbach were followed by
others. In 1830, Sandifort published the first volume of his
"Tabulæ Craniorum Diversarum Gentium." In 1839 appeared
the best work of its kind, the "Crania Americana," by Morton;
and in 1844, his "Crania Ægyptiaca." In 1846, the "Atlas de
Craniscopie," by Carus; in 1856, the first volume of "Crania
Britannica," by Davis and Thurnam; in 1857, the "Crania
Selecta," by Von Baer, &c. Many others might be mentioned.

---

[*] "La Linguistique," by M. Abel Hovelacque. 2nd edition, Bibliothèque
des Sciences Contemporaines. Paris, 1876.

[†] "L'Homme Américain de l'Amérique Méridionale," by Alcide d'Orbigny.
Two vols. Paris, 1839.

At Heidelberg, Tiedemann, known by his incomplete cubic measurements of the skull; in Sweden, Retzius, by his division of skulls into long and short; in Holland, Van der Hoeven; in Germany, Wagner, Huschke, Lucæ, &c. The influence of such authorities as these somewhat encouraged anatomists in France to enter upon so unpopular a path of study; and, besides Daubenton, we may mention Dureau de la Malle, Dubreuil, Foville, Malkneur-Lagémoord, Parchenan, Lélut, Parchappe, Serres, Jacquart, Joulin.

Anthropology, up to this time, did not exist as a separate science; its efforts were of a restricted character; it had no programme; its name was mentioned only casually. It became of the utmost importance to centralise all the studies bearing upon the natural history of Man and his races. This was the task of the Société d'Anthropologie, which was founded in Paris in 1859, under the direction of Dr. Paul Broca, a professor of the Faculty of Medicine, by a few savants, among whom may be mentioned Isidore Geoffroy Saint-Hilaire, De Quatrefages, Gratiolet, Davesne, Ernest Godard, Charles Robin, Béclard, &c. The society, conceived in the most liberal spirit, was composed of scientific men of every denomination, whether literary men or those devoted to the study of art, so that, if any question arose, it could be discussed by the highest authorities. Anthropology, which, in 1855, gave to the Museum the chair of the Natural History of Man, started on a new basis.

Following the example of Paris, other cities founded societies bearing the same name: viz. London, in 1863; New York, St. Petersburg, and Moscow, in 1865; Manchester, in 1866; Florence, in 1868; Berlin, in 1869; Vienna, in 1870; Stockholm and Tiflis, in 1874.

The date of the foundation of the society of Paris was coincident with two events of the highest importance: the public confirmation of the discovery of Boucher de Perthes, who traced back the antiquity of Man to a remote period; and the publication of a work by Darwin on the "Origin of Species," which has contributed so much to give to the science of Man the impetus of which we are now the witness. It marks with distinguished significance the

c

commencement of a new era.   It is with the facts and established opinions generally received at the present time that we propose to deal in this volume.   Many names have been omitted in this brief historical outline, which we shall hope to have an opportunity of supplying as we proceed.

Plan of the Work.

The plan of this work is a necessary sequence from what has been stated.   Of the two branches of the study of Man—the one anthropology proper, which has to do with Man and his races, the other ethnology, which treats of nations—the former will alone occupy our attention.

Our subject naturally divides itself into two parts.   (1) The study of Man considered as a zoological group.   (2) The study of human races as divisions of that group.   In the first part we shall consider the three series of characters—the physical, the physiological, and the pathological—upon which natural history depends; and in the second part, more particularly those to be deduced from archæology, linguistics, and ethnography.

In the first part we shall endeavour to show the relations which subsist between Man and animals, and shall consider a number of questions which have reference to medical studies, regard Man in his ensemble, and have an especial bearing on our subject.

In the second part, after describing the characteristics which serve to distinguish races, we shall give a summary of the various physical types which the present improved state of science exhibits to us, and upon which the determination of races depends.

In the third part we shall detail the various theories as to Man's origin.

It will be necessary for us to say a few words, by way of introduction, as to the methods of zoological classification, and to give a description of the animals to which we shall frequently have to refer.

Zoological Classification.

When the naturalist looks off from matters of detail, and contemplates the animal kingdom in its entirety, he is struck with the

small number of agencies at work to obtain the most diverse
forms. He observes that in a general way there is a continual progression from the simplest to the most complex organisms. He
speaks of it, in other words, as "the general harmony of nature,"
"the plan followed by nature," "unity of type, of agreement in
form, or of organic likeness." He compares the succession of
beings to a ladder (Bonnet), to a chain, or to a tree with many
branches. He has an intuitive impression, whether formulated or
not, that there is a succession and gradation in the different types
of animals, as if some organic force were incessantly in operation,
modifying and increasing the number and variety of species.
Cuvier, who feared to soar above facts, maintained, on the contrary,
the doctrine of successive creations. He then abandoned it, and
finally maintained, with Isidore Saint-Hilaire, that existing species
are not descended from those of a bygone age.[*]

Whatever may be the secret of the origin of animated beings, it
is certain that appearances seem to favour the idea that they sprung
originally from one another. Many gaps exist between them;
but their number is daily decreasing, owing to unexpected discoveries in the bowels of the earth, in the depths of the
ocean, or in some hitherto unexplored corner of the globe. It
has been repeatedly said; "Nature does not make sudden jumps."
There is a successiveness observable throughout, especially in
minutiæ.

M. Ch. Martins and M. Durand (de Gros) have furnished us with
examples of this.[†] The method by which the fin is transformed
into the bent limb, having one direction, as in the tortoise, or on
opposite one, as in Man; how it becomes divided into a longitudinal shaft, which is enlarged or reduced in size, according as it
goes to form the leg of the dog, the wild boar, the horse, or the
gorilla, is truly marvellous.

Agassiz used to demonstrate to his audience at New York how

[*] "Vie et Doctrine de E. Geoffroy Saint-Hilaire." Paris, 1847.

[†] "Création et Transformisme," by J. P. Durand (de Gros), in "Bull. Soc.
d'Anthrop," 2nd series, vol. v., 1870; "Hommes et Singes," by L. Agassiz,
in the "Revue Scientifique," 2nd series, vol. III. p. 818, 1874.

"by twisting this, and elongating that," one might form a fish, a reptile, a mammifer, or an ape, &c.[*]

Hence the difficulties which naturalists experience in exactly circumscribing the limits of the divisions upon which their classifications rest, and of giving to each the proper name which belongs to it. That which is *family* in one becomes *order* in another; that which is *genus* becomes *species*, and *vice versâ*. All depends upon the point of view from which they are regarded, and the particular opinion formed as to their characteristic features.

In order to account for the disputes which are going on about Man, and the place which he occupies relatively to other beings, it is necessary that this should be thoroughly understood. In some, classifications depend upon clearly defined natural groups, which are recognised, though they cannot be strictly demonstrated. In others they are based upon certain groups shading off into contiguous groups. "Methods of classification," writes Daubenton, "have one principal defect which it is impossible to avoid, namely, that art takes a larger share in their arrangement than nature." "Classifications," says Lamarck, "are artificial methods; nature has not really formed either classes, orders, families, genera, or unvarying species—but individuals only." Geoffroy Saint-Hilaire, on his return from Egypt, alluded to them in these terms: "A useful method doubtless, but necessarily imperfect in its resources, and incomplete in its aim; true science ought to have higher aspirations." The illustrious opponent of Cuvier, who was about to publish a catalogue of the Museum, which was a veritable classification, gave it up, although the proof-sheets were in the press.

Nevertheless, classifications are valuable, and, indeed, indispensable. They assist study, bring together animated beings, generally in a natural way, and mark the measure of progress accomplished. In natural history we understand classification to mean the grouping together of beings according to their degree of probable relationship, based on the number and importance of their common characters.

Thus, throughout the whole of the animal kingdom, one observes

[*] "Hommes et Singes," by L. Agassiz, in the "Revue Scientifique," 2nd series, vol. iii. p. 519, 1874.

one principal special feature whereby to establish a primary division
of four branches. From the presence or absence of a skeleton,
whether internal or external, we distinguish Zoophytes, Mollusca,
the Articulata, and the Vertebrata. We may remark, before going
farther, that zoophytes approximate in their inferior forms to
cryptogams of the vegetable kingdom, but that now a new kingdom
has been placed between them, formed of organisms still more
elementary, under the name of règne de protistes (Haeckel). From
many characters, derived principally from the external covering,
Vertebrata have been divided into four classes, viz.: Reptiles,
Fishes, Birds, and Mammalia. Mammalia, again, are divided—
according to the existence or non-existence of an external abdominal
pouch, in which the young pass through the second phase of
their development—into two sub-classes—the Didelphia and the
Monodelphia.

So far, the chief characteristics present modifications so fundamental in the arrangement of the principal apparatus of the
organism that, by virtue of the law of subordination of characters,
it is easy to confine oneself to a single one. The presence of an
internal skeleton is proof of a special arrangement of the nervous
system no less characteristic. Indeed we have no other choice than
to divide Vertebrata in this way, and it is no less necessary as
regards those next in the series. The more we descend in the subdivisions of the former, the more the difficulty increases. We then
have to consider many features in combination, and are not compelled to adopt any fixed plan. At each step the same uncertainty
presents itself. What is the general characteristic of the group?
And is it really the proper one? Have we not created it ourselves,
according to the distinctive feature we may fix upon?

All scientific classification is provisional and arbitrary, so long as
a science is in course of development. Its province is chiefly to
introduce some order into the medley of individuals it has under
its immediate notice, to set up beacons, the correctness of whose
guidance time will either establish or annul. Two groups being
given, it is easy by laying hold of individuals the most dissimilar
to distinguish two opposite types. But a certain number of indi-

viduals will always more or less deviate from them, and will be blended with contiguous types altogether dissimilar.

There are few secondary divisions in natural history which can be regarded as settled, and which might not be changed to-morrow. Thus, to the four classes of Vertebrata, many have added a fifth under the name of *Batrachians*, making them a distinct class from reptiles. So the Didelphs, one of the most correctly defined of the sub-classes, from being based on their *habitat*, have been displaced and abolished, most of them being classed with the *Edentata* or the *Rodents*, the remainder becoming a distinct order under the name of *Pedimana*.

Species is the convenient zoological unit. We will define it in due course. On the one side we have varieties; on the other, genera, families, &c. A genus is the assemblage of many species presenting certain points of connection; a family, the assemblage of many genera, and so on. Between the genus and the species we sometimes have sub-genera; between the genus and the family, the particular tribe we are in search of; between the family and the order, the sub-order, &c. The number of genera in a family, or of species in a genus, is indeterminate.

Mammalia.

Now, in the class of Mammalia, the Didelphs include the *Marsupials* (kangaroo, opossum) and the *Monotremes* (echidna, ornithorhynchus). The Monodelphs include (1) The *Cetacea* and *Amphibia*. (2) The *Pachydermata* and *Ruminantia*. (3) The *Edentata*, the *Rodentia*, the *Carnivora*, the *Cheiroptera*, the *Quadrumana*, and the *Bimana*—the Orders according to Cuvier. We cannot enlarge further on this subject. In a special work on Zoology, published in the Bibliothèque des Sciences Contemporaines, will be found what the general opinion is as to these divisions. We have to do with the last two, and we shall discuss them according to their relative importance.

Linnæus associated Man, the monkey, and the bat, in one and the same order, under the name of Primates. This purely zoological arrangement, which placed Man at the head of the series of animated beings, greatly disturbed Blumenbach, Lacépède, Daubenton, and Cuvier; and in a spirit of reaction, as it would seem, Cuvier proceeded to isolate Man in a distinct order, and placed the monkey in another order, the bat in a third, &c.

Two principal classifications are before us, in which the distance which separates Man from his nearest zoological connections is estimated differently. In one, Man forms a distinct order, in the same category as the ape or one of the Carnaria; in the other, he forms merely one family in the order of Primates, the various divisions of the monkey tribe coming afterwards. Thus:

Primates.

First system of classification.—*First Order*: Man. *Second Order*: Apes. *Third Order*: Bats. *Fourth Order*: Dogs, Bears, &c.

Second system of classification.—*First Order*: Primates. *First Family*: Man. *Second Family*: The higher Apes, or Anthropoids (the gorilla, the chimpanzee, the orang, and the gibbon). *Third Family*: The Monkeys of the Old Continent, or Pithecians (semnopithecus, guenon, magot, cynocephalus [baboon]). *Fourth Family*: The Monkeys of the New Continent, or Cebians (howling monkey, atele [spider monkey], sajou, ouistiti [marmoset]). *Fifth Family*: The Lemurs, Macauco, Galeopithecus.*

---

* We draw attention to the various names in this list, to which we shall frequently have to refer. In current language we sometimes speak of the Anthropoids as the great apes or monkeys, and the Pithecians and Cebians as the common or true monkeys. Frequently the epithet "Simian" will occur in like manner, as synonymous with monkey-like, particularly those of the first three families.

Lesson united the Pithecians and the Cebians, under the name of Simiades; so that he had in the first order, or Primates, five families: the Hominiens, the Anthropomorpha, the Simiadæ, the Lemuriens, and the False Lemuriens. Huxley divides his families into seven—namely: the Anthropini (man), the Catarrhini, the Platyrrhini, the Arctopithecini, or Marmosets, the Lemurs, the Cheiromyini, and the Galeopitheci, or flying monkeys. Two of these appellations originated with Geoffroy Saint-Hilaire, the Catarrhini, or monkeys of the Old Continent; and the Platyrrhini, or

Second Order : The Cheiroptera, or Bats.

Third Order : The Carnacia. *First Family :* The Plantigrades. *Second Family :* The Digitigrades, &c.

Anthropoid Apes.

We notice that the Lemurs, or inferior monkeys, form the transition between the common monkey and various genera scattered through the succeeding orders. For example, between the family of Anthropoids, the Gibbon forms the connecting link with the Pithecinæ; and some of the Cebinæ have a similar relation to the Lemurs. It is from these intermediate forms that we fill up the gaps in question.

Which of these two systems of classification is the better? If we consulted only our own wishes, the answer would be an easy one. Each of us has the consciousness of being vastly superior to the highest class of apes, and would desire that the separation should be as wide as possible; but this is only a matter of feeling. It is a question of fact. Let us proceed then. The question resolves itself into the following terms :

monkeys of the New Continent, which are distinguished by the structure of the nose. Others have understood the word "Catarrhini" to mean those without a tail (Anthropoids), or with a tail (Pithecians). The second classification which we have above enumerated is that which M. Brocu has adopted in his memoir, "Sur l'Ordre des Primates," in 1869.

Among the Anthropoids, the genus Gorilla is limited to a single species, the Gorilla Savagii, whose habits have been described by Paul du Chaillu.—(" Voyages et Aventures dans l'Afrique Equatoriale." Paul du Chaillu. Paris, 1863. And " A Journey to Ashango Land," by the same author. London, 1867.) Of the Chimpanzee, or Troglodytes, there are at least six species: the black, the most common; the Aubryi, a specimen of which was brought to France by Count Aubrey; the Calvus, or bald; and the Koolakamba, mentioned by M. du Chaillu; the Schweinfurthii, from the rivers of the White Nile; and the Livingstonii, or Soko, from the banks of Lake Benguela. With the exception of the last two, all are to be found from the Gambia to the 15th degree of south latitude. The Orang-outang, or Simia, or Satyrus, includes two species: the Rufus, or red-haired, of Borneo; and the Bicolor, of Sumatra. Lastly, the Gibbon, or Hylobates, has numerous species, of which about ten have been described. The largest is the Siamang, or Hylobates Syndactylus.

What is the value of the characteristic points of difference between Man and monkeys, and especially the anthropoid apes? Are these differences as great as those which separate two families or two orders?

The nature of the reply will be dependent on the facts we are about to set forth in the following chapter, and which M. Broca proposes to call *anthropologie zoologique.**

* M. Broca, in the article in the "Dictionnaire Encycl. des Sciences Médicales," mentioned at page 8, divides anthropology as follows: (1) Zoological anthropology, or the study of the human group considered in its relations with the rest of organised nature; (2) Descriptive anthropology, or the study of the human group considered in its individual relations; (3) General anthropology, or the study of the human group considered as a whole. On one occasion our esteemed master relettered to us his views somewhat as follows: Medicine studies individuals; ethnography, peoples; ethnology, races; and general anthropology, man in his ensemble, and in his relations with animals—this last constituting a particular section as zoological anthropology. Our objection is, that the denomination "zoological" relates as much to the part which treats of the human races as to that which treats of Man in general, and that we proceed by the same methods in both, the pre-eminence attaching to anatomical characters. We wish that ethnology were taken, according to its etymological sense, to express the general science of peoples, according to Frederic Müller's method, and that the study and description of primitive races, regarded as natural divisions of the human group, were left to anthropology proper. (See page 8.) M. Broca in his system has considered ethnology as merely a branch of anthropology, which consequently should enter into the plan of this work; whilst in ours, ethnology, though furnishing numerous materials to anthropology, preserves an entire independence, and requires a distinct volume.

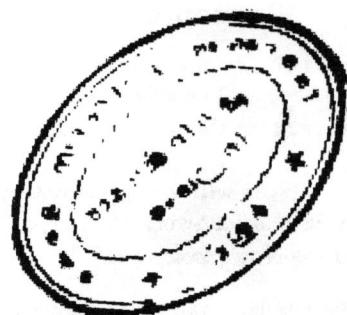

PART I.

OF MAN CONSIDERED IN HIS ENSEMBLE, AND IN HIS RELATIONS WITH ANIMALS.

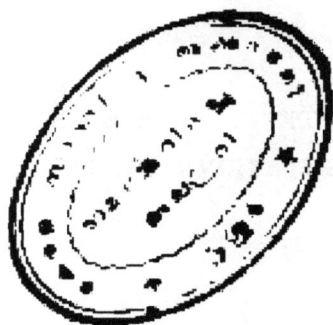

CHAPTER I.

PHYSICAL CHARACTERS.

SKELETON AND SKULL IN GENERAL—ZOOLOGICAL FACIAL ANGLE—
CRANIAL CAPACITY—SITUATION AND DIRECTION OF THE OCCIPITAL
FORAMEN—OCCIPITAL AND BIORBITAL ANGLES.

THE characters of the human group are of two orders: some
organic, to be studied on the skeleton and on the dead body;
others physiological, on the living. Among the former, those to be
drawn from the skeleton occupy the first rank; the skeleton, in
fact, determines the general form of the body, serves for the
attachment of muscles, and marks out the boundaries of the
visceral cavities.

Osteological Considerations.

The skeleton of Mammalia—the class of Vertebrata which will
alone engage our attention—is composed (1) Of a central axis, constituted by the bodies of the vertebræ; (2) Of a series of neurnas
arcs directed backwards, to form, by their aggregation, a large
canal, in which are contained the brain, the cerebellum, and the
spinal cord; (3) Of a series of arcs directed forwards, bounding
certain cavities which are occupied, above by the organs of
vision, smell, and taste—then by the central organs of circulation
and the lungs—lower down by the digestive apparatus—and lower
still by the organs of reproduction; (4) Of the appendages to
various segments called extremities, the anterior serving, in a
general way, for prehension, the posterior for locomotion.

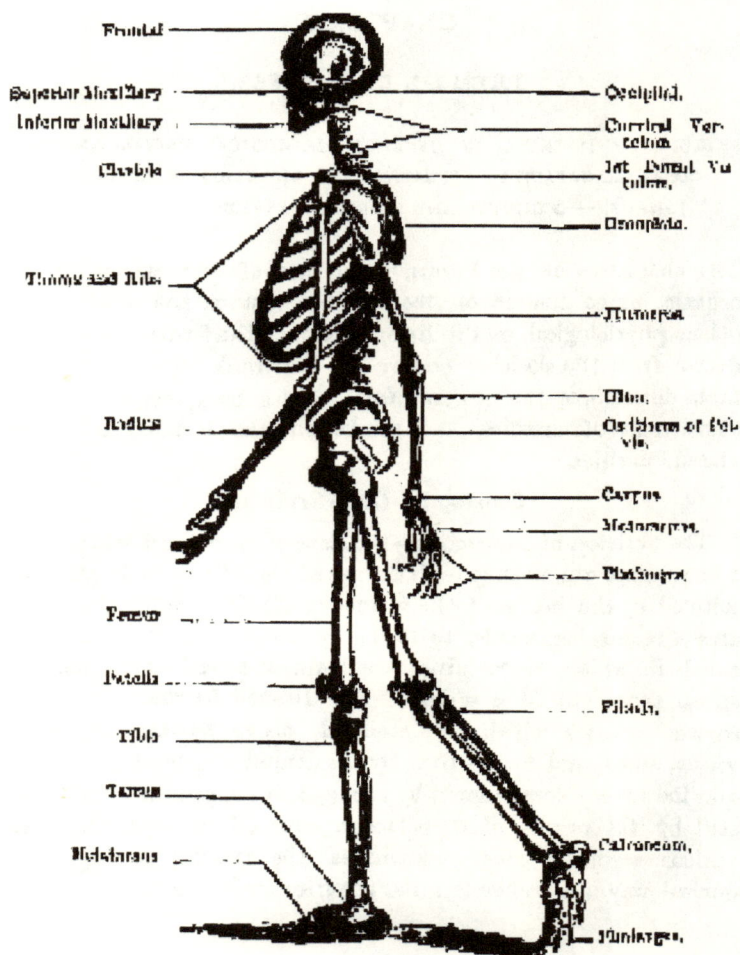

Frontal

Superior Maxillary
Inferior Maxillary

Clavicle

Thorax and Ribs

Radius

Femur

Patella

Tibia

Tarsus

Metatarsus

Occipital.

Cervical Vertebra

1st Dorsal Vertebra.

Omoplate.

Humerus

Ilium.

Os (Bone) of Pelvis.

Carpus

Metacarpus.

Metatarsus

Fibula.

Calcaneum.

Phalanges.

Fig. I.

The skeleton is composed in Man of one hundred and eighty-eight bones, exclusive of the patella, a small bone developed in the thick part of the tendons of the principal extensor muscle of the thigh; that is to say, twenty-six for the vertebral column, eight for the cranium, fourteen for the face, thirty-two for each of the superior extremities, and thirty for each of the inferior, &c.

The twenty-six bones of the vertebral column are divided thus: seven cervical vertebræ; twelve dorsal; five, and sometimes six lumbar; five or six sacral bones, which, being anchylosed, form the sacrum; and four or five caudal, which, more or less welded together, form the coccyx. To speak correctly, the cranium is formed of three modified vertebræ, and is the true commencement of the vertebral column.

Every vertebra, whether cervical, dorsal, or lumbar, consists (1) In the centre, of a foramen, through which the cord passes; (2) Anteriorly, of a body, which is articulated to those of the vertebræ above and below by a fibro-cartilaginous disc, called the intervertebral; (3) Posteriorly, of a spinous process, bifurcated in the cervical region, simple in the rest of the column, the bases of which are called laminæ; (4) Of two transverse processes, attached to the body by two pedicles; and (5) Of four articular processes, which serve to attach the vertebra to those above and below.

The eight bones of the cranium consist of four middle and symmetrical—the occipital, the sphenoid, the ethmoid, and the frontal; and two lateral pairs—the parietal and the temporal.

The middle portions of the occipital, the sphenoid, and the ethmoid represent the body of each of three vertebræ. The large flat portion of the occipital, temporal, and frontal is called the squamous portion, or écaille (shell). These bones come under the denomination of flat bones. They have an internal surface, which looks towards the cranial cavity, called by M. Broca *endocrâne*, and an external surface.

The body of the occipital (O, Fig. 2) is formed by the basilar process, which is united to the body of the sphenoid by an important articulation, the basilar suture. Its surface is transversely divided by a semicircular ridge, for the attachment of the muscles of the neck, the middle portion of which is occupied by the *inion*, or external occipital protuberance; the portion above, or sur-occipital, is separated during a part of intra-uterine existence, and exceptionally in the adult, and is designated the interparietal, or sub-occipital bone. The portion below has a second curved line, also for the attachment of muscles.

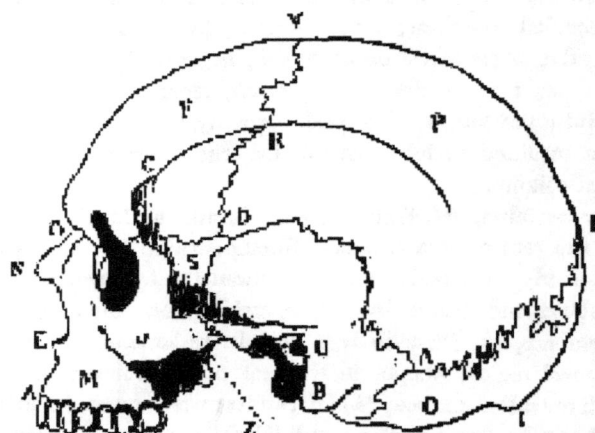

FIG. 2.—F, Frontal bone; P, Parietal; O, Occipital; T, Temporal; S, Greater wings of the sphenoid; the body of the bone is unobserved; M, Superior maxilla; J, Malar or jugal bone; N, Bones of the nose, or nasal bones; A, Median portion of the arch, or superior alveolar border, called *point aréolaire*; E, Nasal spine, or *point nasonné*; H, Root of the nose, the bottom of which is occupied by the naso-frontal suture, or *point nasal*; V, Position of the centre of the cranium, or fronto-parietal suture of the cranium, or *bregma*; L, Point where the parieto-occipital suture is united to that of the opposite side, and to the sagittal, or biparietal suture (not seen in the plate), or *lambda*; I, External occipital protuberance, or *inion*; B, Mastoid process; V, External meatus of the auditory canal, also called *iter*, or *point auriculaire*; Z, Zygomatic arch, formed, in front, by the malar bone, behind, by a process called the *zygoma*, arising from the temporal bone; D, Point where the four sutures unite—the coronal, the fronto-sphenoid, the temporo-sphenoid, and the temporo-frontal, or *pterion*; C, Curved line or temporal ridge; R, Point where this line crosses the coronal suture, or *stephanion*. All the portion situated below the temporal ridge, marked by the letters R B T constitutes the temporal fossa.

At the union of the basilar process and the squamous portion is the occipital foramen, or foramen magnum of foreign authors, the middle, anterior, and posterior portions of which bear the names of basion and opisthion, the internal portions being occupied by the occipital condyles, by which it is articulated with the first cervical vertebra, or atlas. Two irregularities in the bone sometimes exist, namely, in front of the basion, an eminence which has been called the third condyle of the occipital; and on the external part of the ordinary condyles, an eminence called the jugular process.

The parietal bones (P) present nothing to particularise but a projection in the centre, which marks the centre of ossification, and takes the name of parietal eminence. The frontal bone (F) is divided externally into two portions—the superior and the inferior. The superior, or squamous, has at the sides two curved lines, termed temporal ridges, which give insertion to the temporal muscle; and, nearer the median line, two projections, termed the frontal eminences. The inferior, or sub-cerebral, belongs to the face, and presents from without inwards. (1) The external orbital processes, by which it is articulated with the malar bones, their sharp lower border forming the superior border of the orbits; (2) Ridges, or superciliary arches, which correspond with the position of the eyebrows, and have a similar direction; (3) A projection, or glabella, on the median line. The median point, answering to the point of separation of the two cerebral and sub-cerebral portions, is called the *point sus-orbitaire*, or ophryon.

The surface of the temporal (T) is divisible externally into three portions: a mastoid portion, forming the mastoid processes (B), to which powerful muscles are attached; a squamous portion; and a zygomatic portion. The zygomatic is simply a horizontal process, which arises by a root, or longitudinal crest, surmounting the auditory or auricular opening. A fourth portion is especially seen on the inferior and internal surface, called the hard or petrous portion, in which is enclosed the auditory apparatus.

The sphenoid (S), so called on account of its being wedged in between the bones at the base of the skull, consists of a body, which at birth is formed of two portions, called anterior sphenoid and posterior sphenoid; of two descending wings, or pterygoid processes, which form the boundaries of the posterior nares; of two large ascending wings, of which the highest external portion is seen at S, Fig. 2; and of two lesser horizontal wings, which form part of the cranial cavity, where they separate the middle and anterior cerebral fossæ. Viewed from above, that is to say from

D

the side of the cranial cavity, the body of the sphenoid presents
an excavation, the sella turcica (I, Fig. 6), a transverse fissure, the
optic fissure, and between the two a slight ridge, to which the
Germans have given the name of ephippium.

The ethmoid has special relation to the nasal fossæ, and only
has interest to the anthropologist from the side of the cranial
cavity, where it impinges upon the median line between two portions

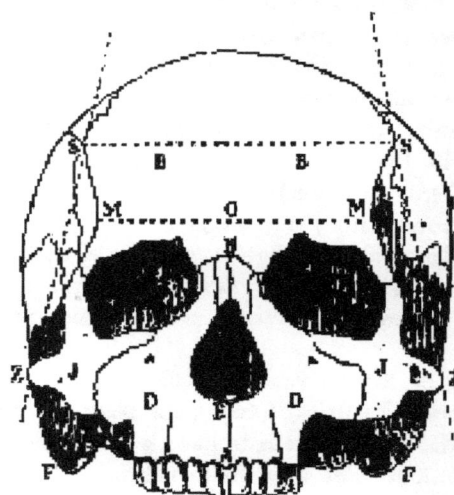

FIG. 3.—O, Supra-orbital, or supra-nasal point, in the centre of the midmost frontal
   width MM ; N, Nasal point in the centre of the naso-frontal suture ; E, Nasal spine,
   or sub-nasal point ; A, Middle point of the anterior alveolar arch, or superior
   alveolar point ; S, Point of junction of the temporal ridge and the coronal suture,
   or stephanion ; B, Position of the frontal eminences ; D, Maxillary bones ; J, Malar
   bones ; O, Anterior nares ; Z, Zygomatic arches ; F, Mastoid processes.

of the frontal, by giving attachment to the crista galli and the
cribriform lamella, through which the filaments of the olfactory
nerve pass from the cranial cavity into the nasal fossæ.

The principal bones of the face are the nasal bones (N, Fig. 3),
which unite with the frontal to form the naso-frontal suture at
the root of the nose ; the superior maxillary bones (D), a prolongation of which, called the ascending process, is articulated with the
frontal at the sides ; the palate bones, which enter into the formation of the roof of the palate behind ; the malar, or jugal bones (J),

which project backwards, and at the side, at the junction of the temporal, to form a sort of bridge, called the zygomatic arch; and the inferior maxillary bone. The superior maxillary bones are the principal bones of the face. At the sides they are articulated with the malar bones; above, they form the inferior wall of the orbits; internally they are united to the bones proper of the nose, and form the boundary of the anterior nares; below, they form, by their union, the superior alveolar arch. At the point where the posterior border of the ascending process joins the frontal and the os unguis, is the particular spot for the application of the craniometer, or dacryon. On the median line of the part adjacent to the anterior nares, are two other important points—the sub-nasal, which corresponds with the border of the nostril, occupied by an osseous point called the nasal spine, and the alveolar point, situated in the middle of the alveolar arch, at its anterior and inferior portion.

The inferior maxillary bone is composed altogether differently—of a body, of a vertical and posterior ramus, which forms an angle with it, and of a border or alveolar arch. As a matter of detail, we may mention the coronoid process and the articular condyle, which terminate, the one in front of, the other behind, the superior border of the posterior ramus; then the mental eminence, and behind it, internally, the tubercles géni.

The thorax comprises, besides twelve dorsal vertebræ, which close it in behind, the sternum in front (Fig. 1) and twelve ribs on each side. Seven, called the true ribs, are directly connected with the sternum by cartilages; and five false are only united to it indirectly, the last two bearing the name of floating.

The abdomen has no bone, in the proper sense, belonging to it, but at certain points of its parietes are seen thick fibrous bands, which are the vestiges of ribs to be found in some mammalia, and especially in reptiles.

The pelvic cavity, or pelvis (Fig. 10), is composed of bones which equally appertain to other parts, namely, to the vertebral column and the inferior extremities.

Each extremity is composed (1) Of a base, which is the shoulder in the one and the haunch in the other. The bones which compose it form, by uniting with those of the opposite side, an osseous

cincture at each extremity of the trunk.   At the superior extremity
these are the clavicle and scapula ; and at the inferior, the iliac, or
coxal bone, formed of three primordial bones—the pubis, the
ischium, and the ilium.   (2) Of a first segment, the arm, formed
by the humerus ; and the thigh, by the femur.   (3) Of a second
segment, the forearm, formed by the radius and ulna ; and the
leg, by the tibia and fibula.   (4) Of a third segment, the hand,
made up of eight bones for the carpus, five for the metacarpus,
and three for each finger, except the first, which has only two ;
and the foot, made up of seven bones for the tarsus, five for the
metatarsus, and three for each toe, except the first, which has only
two.   Of the bones of the tarsus, the calcaneum, or bone of the
heel, merits particular notice.

The femur, which we select as an example of a long bone, consists of (1) a shaft, or diaphysis, formed on its outer surface of a
layer of compact tissue, and on its inner of a medullary canal ; and
(2) of extremities, or epiphyses.   At the upper extremity are the
greater and lesser trochanter—processes for the insertion of
muscles ; the neck, which is very long, and takes an oblique outward direction ; and the articular head.   The lower extremity
consists of an internal and external condyle, and an articular
surface.   The humerus consists, in like manner, of a shaft, two
tuberosities at the upper extremity, a very short neck, and a head ;
inferiorly, of two processes—an external and an internal condyle.

The bones, whether long, short, or flat, are covered by inequalities, tubercles, eminences, or processes, all having the same
object—namely, to furnish points of attachment for muscles and
ligaments.   It is to these several points we apply our instruments,
as well as to certain edges and prominences, when making osteo-
metric measurements.   We ought to mention also the styloid
process, at the outer side of the lower extremity of the radius ;
and the internal malleolus, on the inner side of the lower extremity
of the tibia, &c.   The flat bones of the cranium are united together
by sutures, the long bones of the extremities by articulations.
The most interesting of these latter, as far as we are concerned, is
(1) The scapulo-humeral, in which the head of the humerus is
received into the glenoid cavity of the scapula, a sort of ligamentous

bag, in which the two surfaces are kept in contact, and at the same time are permitted to glide easily the one upon the other. (2) The coxo-femoral articulation, in which the head of the femur is received into the cotyloid cavity of the ilium. (3) The hinge-like articulations of the elbow and the ankle-joints, which only permit the movements of flexion and extension. (4) The superior articulation of the radius, so marvellously adapted for free rotation in every direction, &c.

Bones, when first formed, consist of cartilage, the osseous matter being deposited at certain points, which afterwards coalesce. Later on, when the entire bone has become fully formed, and old age begins, those with sutures become soldered together edge to edge. Thus we have two orders of phenomena—the fusion of osseous points in one and the same bone, and the fusion of distinct and contiguous bones, which we must be careful not to confound, and upon which we shall have more to say presently.

Variations of the Skeleton.

The number of bones slightly varies in the mammalian series. All have seven cervical vertebræ, except the ai, or sloth, which has nine, and the lamantin, or sea-cow, eight. Among long-necked quadrupeds, as the giraffe, they only increase in height. The number of dorsal vertebræ, and of pairs of ribs which they support, is less constant—from eleven in the bat, they attain to nineteen or twenty in the elephant. The number of the lumbar vertebræ deviates but little, and varies generally from four to seven. The lamantin, however, has but one, while the dolphin has eighteen. These inconstancies do not, however, appear to have the importance which we might imagine. Genera far removed from one another have the same number of ribs or dorsal vertebræ: as the orang, the hare, the camel, the rat, and the kangaroo, which have twelve; while contiguous species have a different number, as the ox of Europe, which has thirteen; the aurochs, or wild ox, fourteen; and the bison, fifteen—all three of the genus bos. Often the difference is merely that a lumbar vertebra becomes dorsal, or vice versâ. When, in the human subject, there is a thirteenth rib on one side only, or thirteen on both, a lumbar vertebra is the point of articulation. The number of caudal or coccygeal vertebræ varies in the monkey tribe—not including the anthropoid apes—from one to four in the magot to twenty-nine to thirty-one in the baboon and some of the ateles; and among the rest of mammalia, from two in the Egyptian tapir to sixty in the Cape rorqual.

The bones of the head are constructed in animals after the same model as in Man; certain parts of them are more or less developed; the cells or sinuses interposed between their laminæ are more or less large; some sutures, by closing slowly, leave certain portions of the bone isolated; while others, owing to their becoming consolidated early, diminish the number of bones. Hence the cause of the differences met with between them. Man, at his full development, has the smallest number of bones, and the rodents, at birth, the greatest number. Among the latter, the squamous portion of the occipital bone is divided into two, while the parietal and frontal are cemented together into one.

The anterior and posterior sphenoids, united in Man, are distinct in the greater number of mammalia. The squamous and petrous portions of the temporal, on the contrary, remain distinct in the latter, and perhaps, with one exception, are united in Man and the monkey tribe.[*] Moreover, we frequently observe in Man, as an anomaly, the reproduction of normal arrangements in other animals, as if by a sort of reversion towards certain states which his own organisation might have gone through previously. Thus the fusion of the parietals into one—as among the rodents—the division of the frontal into two separate bones—common among mammalia—the persistence of an interparietal bone, &c. The early fusion of the two bones proper of the nose, especially in the inferior races, and the tardy consolidation, on the contrary, of the intermaxillary with the maxillary, are other examples of the same kind.

Bones of the Nose.

The bones of the nose proper remain separated on the median line up to an advanced age in the white; their union is frequently

[*] "Traité d'Anatomie Comparée," &c., by J. F. Meckel. Translated into French by Th. Schuster. Ten vols. 8vo. Paris, 1868.

completed at twenty or twenty-five years in Hottentots. Of twenty-seven skeletons of adult men, taken at random by M. Broca, the fusion existed in five, all in negroes. In the chimpanzee they appear united at two years of age ; in the gorilla and the pithecians even sooner. But in the cabians their fusion is slow, so that these resemble Man in this respect more than the anthropoids.

Camper has forgotten the tardy union of the intermaxillary with the maxillary bones, and having made their constant absence to be distinctly characteristic of Man, we must speak of them more at length.

The intermaxillary bones, to the number of two, appear to be united in the form of a wedge, enclosed between the two superior maxillary, supporting the incisor teeth, and having above two processes which partly close in the anterior opening of the nasal fossæ. Though easily seen up to the third month, their independent existence is brief, they commence to consolidate at that period at their external side, and become united with the maxillary about the third year. Nevertheless their palatine sutures do not entirely disappear till towards twelve or fourteen years of age, according to M. Sappey, and were still visible in one hundred and four out of two hundred French skulls examined by M. Husny. All the phases of their solidification would be retarded in the negro races.

Intermaxillary Bones.

In the majority of mammalia the intermaxillary bones continue, on the contrary, beyond adult age, and remain distinct. The elephant, the dolphin, and the sheep are an exception, and resemble Man in this respect ; so do the anthropoids—their intermaxillary suture should disappear about the end of the first dentition, according to M. Vogt. In descending the scale in monkeys, the intermaxillary generally partakes of the characters which it has in the generality of quadrupeds.

In the extremities the general type of Man and mammalia varies but little, and is unimportant. Some bones, for example, which, owing to the habits of the species, are superfluous, become atrophied, or anchylosed together. Thus the clavicles are reduced to mere

vestiges in some carnivora, and disappear altogether in ruminants
and amphibious mammalia. Sometimes one of the bones of the
forearm or the leg becomes reduced in size, or anchylosed to the
adjoining one. The same phenomenon is observed even more frequently at their extremities. The metatarsal or metacarpal bones
are four in number in the sloth, two in the stag, and one, called
the cannon bone, in the horse. There is some relation between
this number and that of the digits or toes. Thus the pig has only
four digits, the rhinoceros three, the greater number of ruminants
two, and the horse but one, called the hoof. In the horse the
atrophy of other digits is manifest, the vestiges of them remaining
at the sides in the form of needle-like roughnesses.

An analogous absence, as if from want of use, occurs in the bones
of the pelvis of amphibious mammalia, whose hinder extremities
have become of little importance, or are wanting. The pelvis is
only represented by certain osseous styles which are amalgamated
with the soft parts, or is altogether wanting. This is to be noticed
in the dugong, the porpoise, the whale, &c.

Relations of the Cranium to the Face.

The cranium is formed of two portions in all mammalia—the
cranium proper, the receptacle of the brain; and the face, the
receptacle of the principal organs of sense and of the masticatory
apparatus. Their development is in an inverse ratio, and their
respective situation in relation to that development. In Man the
cranium is large and placed above the face; in quadrupeds it becomes less, and recedes more and more backwards; in monkeys the
size and situation of the cranium and face are intermedial. These
two characters thus assume a considerable importance, and are the
point de départ of other subordinate characters, which, in their
turn, assist in distinguishing man and animals. It is natural,
therefore, that anthropologists should early have bethought them of
some decided methods of estimating their value. Various methods
have been proposed; the one most in vogue is that of the facial angles.

This was one of the first attempts of craniometry. This branch
of anthropology, so cultivated at the present time, has been hitherto

studied especially with reference to the comparison of races, and will consequently be treated at length in the second part of this work, which is specially set apart for that purpose. We will not now anticipate the subject further than by mentioning a few of the more striking characters which distinguish Man in general from animals.

Facial Angles.

The facial angles are four in number. The most ancient is the angle of Camper. It is formed by two lines, one called the hori-

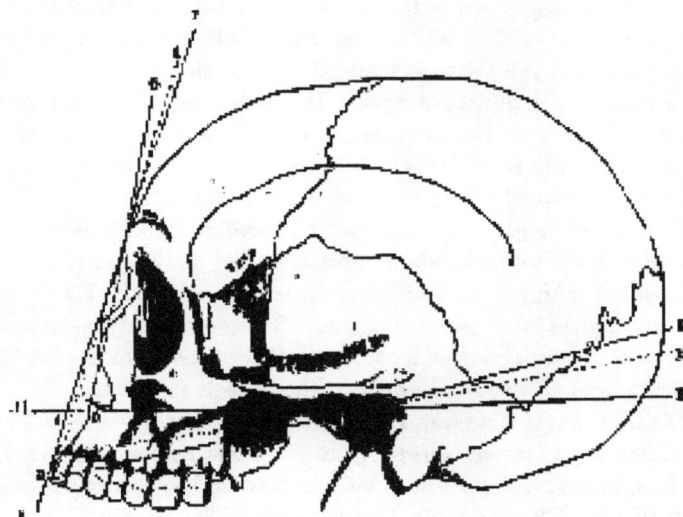

FIG. 4.—H H', Horizontal of Camper; F F', Facial line of Camper; F A H', true angle of Camper; F D E, Angle of Geoffroy Saint-Hilaire and Cuvier, its vertex at the edge of the incisors; T O M, Angle of Jules Cloquet, its vertex at the alveolar border; O D H', Angle of Jacquart, the sub-nasal point; O D, Facial line of Jacquart.

The most useful angle is that of Cloquet, with the vertex at C, for whose facial line, C I, indicates, not at the most projecting point of the forehead, but immediately above the superciliary arches.

zontal, H H', Fig. 4, which its author marked as a principal guide, over the auditory opening, and the inferior border of the nose; the other, called the facial, F F', tangent to the two most prominent points of the face—the glabella, or central point of the forehead, above; the surface anterior to the incisor teeth, below.

The original intention of Pierre Camper* was to give to artists
a method of comparing the heads of living persons with the skulls
of different races and of different ages; but in another work he
extended its use to animals

Camper's Angle.

Its apex was situated at the intersection of these two lines, at
a point, A, Fig. 4, placed sometimes in front of the superior
maxillary, as in negroes; sometimes behind, as in many animals
—the dog, for example; or at the nasal spine, as in the white
races.   "The angle which the facial or characteristic line of the
face makes," says Camper, "varies from 70 to 80 degrees in the
human species.   All above is resolved by the rules of art, all below
bears resemblance to that of apes. If I make the facial line lean
forward, I have an antique head; if backward, the head of a
negro. If I still more incline it, I have the head of an ape; and
if more still, that of a dog, and then that of an idiot."

The second angle was suggested by Geoffroy Saint-Hilaire and
Cuvier in 1795, and afterwards abandoned, no doubt owing to the
difficulty of taking it with accuracy on certain animals. The facial
line of Camper was maintained, but the horizontal line became
oblique, K D, passing across from the auditory opening to the border
of the incisors, B, where the apex of the triangle is situated.

The third angle is a mean between the two preceding ones. The
facial line rests tangent superiorly at the most prominent part of
the face, but slope short below, on a level with the superior alveolar
border, I G. The horizontal line descends obliquely, like that of
Geoffroy Saint-Hilaire and Cuvier, but terminates at the same
alveolar border, G, which becomes the apex of the triangle. Jules
Cloquet adopted it in 1821.

The fourth angle, which moreover has enjoyed very considerable
repute, was the result of a misconception. M. Jacquart, in adopt-
ing it in 1856, thought to follow in the footsteps of Camper, or

* "Dissertation sur les Différences réelles que présentent les Traits du
Visage chez les Hommes de différents Pays et de différents Ages," by
Pierre Camper. Posthumous work published by his son. Paris, 1791
(written in 1786).

rather in the principles which had guided Morton in the construction of his goniometer.* One of these two lines is the facial line of Camper, terminating at the nasal spine, O D, the other the horizontal line, but stopping short also at this point, D H'. Its apex therefore is always formed at the nasal spine, D.

Our own measurements, made on more than eleven hundred human skulls, and on about a hundred skulls of animals, enable us to form a judgment as to the value of these four facial angles.†

Jacquart's Angle.

The angle of Jacquart, at its apex at the nasal spine, varies under five influences. (1) The degree of prominence of the nasal spine, very strongly marked, as M. Broca has observed, in the white races, often not observable in negroes; (2) The degree of prominence of the glabella, which, about one hundred and ninety-nine times out of two hundred, is the superior point of the facial line; (3) The difference of height of the auditory foramen relatively to the base of the skull; (4) The more or less marked elongation of the face, that is to say, the degree of prognathism; (5) The amount of development forward of the anterior portion of the brain, as shown by calculations made among the hydrocephali, in whom the brain-case is very much enlarged, and among the microcephali, in whom it is very much diminished in size. Under all these various influences, it is very difficult to determine which has the greatest predominance, and consequently which represents the angle of Jacquart.

The angle of Camper diminishes or increases for the same reasons, except that it has no reference to the prominence of the nasal spine. It takes account, however, of the elongation of the face in its sub-nasal portion, which has by far the most influence

* "Mensuration de l'Angle Facial et Goniométrie," by H. Jacquart, in "Mém. Soc. de Biologie," 1856; "De la Valeur de l'Os Épactal" (measurements of sixteen facial angles), by the same author, in "Journal Anat. et Physiol.," 1865; "Crania Americana," by S. G. Morton, Philadelphia, 1839.
† "Études sur Pierre Camper et sur l'Angle Facial dit de Camper," by Paul Topinard, in "Revue d'Anthropologie," vol. ii., 1874.

on prognathism in Man, and which the angle of Jacquart altogether leaves out of consideration.

Angles of Geoffroy and Cuvier.

The angle of Geoffroy Saint-Hilaire and Cuvier also sets aside the nasal spine, and takes in, in the same way, the sub-nasal region of the face; but at the same time exhibiting it in a more complete manner. Hence we shall accord to it the preference. Why, indeed, should we preserve the pretended horizontal line of Camper? It does not exist in Man, and still less in animals. By intersecting with the facial line it more frequently has but one virtual apex, which gives an unfavourable impression. The auriculo-dental line of Saint-Hilaire and Cuvier is, on the contrary, rational; it passes along at the same extremity of the face, and does not lose one of the two portions which one desires to measure—the development of the face. Apart from these objections, which appertain to all the facial angles, the angle of Geoffroy Saint-Hilaire and Cuvier has one specially belonging to it, namely, the impossibility of accepting the line of the teeth as the extremity of the face. In a great many animals, in fact, the front teeth are either curved downwards, immoderately elongated into offensive weapons, or are altogether wanting; frequently, also, they fall out during life, or are lost after death.

Cloquet's Angle.

The angle of Jules Cloquet has all the advantages of the preceding, without this latter objection; we consider, therefore, that it should have the preference.

The principal objection which attaches to all the facial angles is the adoption of, not the most logical point for the superior extremity of the facial line, but the most prominent, which is always found to be, with the angle of Jacquart, and almost always with the others, the glabella, or the centre of the superciliary ridges. The differences of prominence of these parts causes the facial angle in Man to vary several degrees; that is to say, there is as much difference as there is between the natural faculties of races the most opposite. In animals it is even more so; and Cuvier

made up his mind, under all circumstances, to abide by the
principle of Camper. What he very properly sought was the
anterior limit of the brain at the lower part of the forehead—the
point sus-orbitaire of M. Broca. In a gorilla, for example, by
taking the most prominent point, which lies over the superciliary
arches, the facial angle, at its apex at the nasal spine, would be
about 40 degrees; whereas in reality, that is to say at the supra-
orbital point, it is only 37 degrees. Consequently it is always the
anterior limit of the cranial cavity, whichever angle is preferred,
and not the most prominent point, which should be taken for the
facial line superiorly. It is in this way that the following angles
have been measured, for the purpose of showing the difference
between the most divergent human crania we have met with, an
anthropoid and a carnivorous animal.

FACIAL ANGLES (FACIAL LINE AT THE SUPRA-ORBITAL POINT).*

	Geoffroy Saint-Hilaire.	Cloquet.	Jacquart.	Camper.
Native of Lower Brittany...	68·5	72·0	85·0	81·5
Namaquois negro ...	54·0	56·0	62·5	59·0
Male gorilla...	29·0	31·0	32·0	31·5
Newfoundland dog...	25·0	24·5	25·0	25·0

The facial angle adopted for the comparison between Man and
animals is that of Cloquet, the superior extremity of the facial line
being transferred to the supra-orbital point. We shall give it the
name of "*angle facial zoologique.*" The following table gives some
examples of its division:

ANGLE OF CLOQUET (ITS VERTEX AT THE ALVEOLAR BORDER AND THE FACIAL
LINE AT THE SUPRA-ORBITAL POINT).

White man, maximum	...	...	...	...	72·0
Namaquois negro, minimum...	...	...	...	54·0
2 male chimpanzees ...	...	...	...	38·0
1 „ „ 1st dentition	...	...	...	51·5
5 male gorillas	...	...	...	32·2
3 female gorillas	...	...	...	31·5
1 male orang ...	...	...	...	28·5
1 „ „ 1st dentition ...	...	...	...	50·5

* The angles in this and the following table have been taken principally
by projection, from drawings made with the craniograph of M. Broca.

1 magot (pithecians)	...	...	...	...	...	30·5
2 macaques	,,	...	...	...	...	37·4
3 baboons	,,	...	...	...	...	32·8
8 howlers (cebinae)	...	...	...	...	...	31·7
1 maki (lemurians)	,,	...	...	...	...	26·5
2 badgers (plantigrades)	...	...	...	...	...	82·0
1 bear	...	...	...	...	...	30·6
2 elephants (proboscidians)	...	...	...	...	30.2
1 seal (amphibia)	...	...	...	...	...	28·0
1 phascolomys (marsupialia)	...	...	...	...	25·0
2 horses (equidae)	...	...	...	...	...	24·0
6 dogs (carnivora)	...	...	...	...	...	24·6
2 foxes	...	...	...	...	...	22·5
2 lions	,,	...	...	...	...	22·6
2 pacas (rodentia)	...	...	...	...	...	22·2
2 sheep (ruminantia)	...	...	...	...	...	21·5
2 kangaroos (marsupialia)	...	...	...	...	20·4
1 wild boar (pachydermata)	...	...	...	...	10·0

It follows from this (1) That between the narrowest facial angle of an adult man, which is 56 degrees, and the widest angle in an adult anthropoid (one of our chimpanzees), which is 48 degrees, there exists an interval as great as these two extremes are exceptional; (2) That between anthropoid apes, next in order, there is no such line of demarcation; (3) That by this characteristic, man is separated in the most remarkable manner from the rest of the mammalia, including the anthropoids. It has been argued, from the enormous angle in young anthropoids, that one must make the comparison in the child and not in the adult man, and then the distance is quite as great.

The facial angle, then, furnishes a primary characteristic of Man in relation to animals. But it expresses less the relation of the size of the face to the size of the cranium, than the absolute development of the former. It attains seventy-two degrees in Man, because the face is small and short, and only ten degrees in the wild boar, because it has considerable length and flatness.

Method of Cuvier.

Other methods lead to the same result. The most simple consists in estimating the importance of each part, and of compating them afterwards. Cuvier estimated, upon sections, that the cranium, in proportion to the face, was as follows:

White man	...	...	...	...	...	1 : 1
Negro	...	...	...	...	...	4 : 1·26
Chimpanzee	...	...	...	...	...	8 : 1
Gibbon, sapajou, and macaque			...		...	9 : 1
Hedgehog	...	...	...	...	...	1 : 1
Porcupine	...	...	...	...	...	1 : 2
Hare	...	...	...	...	...	1 : 3
Horse	...	...	...	...	...	1 : 4
Whale	...	...	...	...	...	1 : 15 or 20

Method of Segond.

M. Segond has proposed to measure, upon antero-posterior sections, the various angles formed at the level of the anterior border of the occipital foramen, by lines drawn from the principal points of the middle circumference of the head. On these sections he applies a graduated circle, whose centre corresponds to the basion (D, Fig. 6), and upon which needles, or movable radii, are directed towards the points desired. The face is thus found interrupted by two lines, the one separating it from the cranial cavity, and which meets at the supra-orbital point; the other going to the inferior border of the jaw; the cranium being included between the same line of separation and the long axis of the occipital foramen. These two angles have given us the following results, which satisfactorily exhibit the relative development of the cranium and of the face:

	Cerebral angle.	Facial angle.
2 European infants	178°	22°
8 " adults	150°	47°
3 adult negroes	152°	41°
1 chimpanzee	116°	50°
1 gorilla	105°	51°
4 orangs	108°	47°
Otter	115°	24°
Viscacha	100°	41°
Dog	97°	32°
Rat	125°	27°
Fox	89°	28°
Hippopotamus	76°	46°

The process of Cuvier does not seem to have been applied but very approximately ; that of M. Segond gives only one of the elements of comparison. It would be better to measure directly the base of the triangles, of which M. Segond only notices the angles, and to calculate their area ; or to obtain, on one side, the volume of the face by a sort of triangulation ; and on the other, of the cranium by the ordinary cubic measurement of its cavity. M. Assezat has commenced that part of the study which relates to the face in his "Récherches sur les Proportions de la Face," communicated, in 1874, to the French Association for the Advancement of Science ; it rests with him to extend it to animals. The question as regards the cranium is not yet settled.

Capacity of Cranial Cavity.

The capacity of the cranial cavity is arrived at, as we shall see presently, by filling this cavity with grains of different sorts, and preferably with small shot, in accordance with certain directions. The figures giving the height, volume, or weight of the human body, as compared with the volume of the brain in the mammalian series, would form a very instructive table, if observers had taken more care to give us either one of these three elements. Our object, however, being to give more particularly the comparison of Man with the anthropoid apes, the following data will suffice :

	Cubic millimètres.
Man, European male, in round numbers	1500
16 gorillas, males	531
5 „ females	472
1 gorilla, 2nd dentition	440
1 „ 1st „	415
5 orange, males	430
1 orang, female	413
1 „ 2nd dentition	404
1 „ 1st „	425
7 chimpanzees, males	421
3 „ females	404
1 chimpanzee, 1st dentition	338
2 lions	321
1 bear	265
1 wild boar	207
1 rain	150
1 Newfoundland dog	106

Thus we perceive that the capacity of the cranial cavity, and consequently the volume of the organ it encloses, increases slowly and gradually in animals, but suddenly and to a prodigious extent as we pass to Man. Now all the animals except the last two or three are obviously of the same size as Man. If the three anthropoids are a little less in stature, their limbs, head, chest, and especially their abdomen, are much larger; the gorilla, especially, is enormous, and ought, other things being equal, to have greater cranial capacity than man. The chimpanzee, however, has only 38·06 per cent.; the orang, 29·28; and the gorilla, 35·40, as compared with Man, while the extreme proportions among gorilla males are from 31·60 to 41·58 per cent. Moreover, the difference between the sexes is as in Man: the cranial capacity of the anthropoid male exceeds that of the female by about 50 cubic centimètres.

M. Vogt has tabulated a number of cubic measurements of the skull, obtained by various methods other than our own, and amongst them that by the use of millet. They cannot be directly compared with ours, but their mutual relations merit consideration. Thus:

	Cubic centimètres.
German skull, male	1480
1 gorilla, male	500
2 gorilla, females	425
8 orang, males	448
7 „ females	378
8 chimpanzee, males	417
1 chimpanzee, female	370

The conclusions deduced from these agree with preceding ones. By taking the mean, on the one hand, of all the anthropoid males of M. Vogt, and, on the other, that of all of ours, and comparing them with the corresponding mean in Man, we arrive at the following result:

	Vogt's 18 cases.	Topinard's 26 cases
Mean absolute capacity of anthropoids ..	444 cub. cent.	490 cub. cent.
Its proportion to that of man	30·03 per cent.	32·05 per cent.

It is very evident from this that the three anthropoids in question have, cæteris paribus, three times less cranial cavity than Man. We do not hesitate to say that, taking into account the

E

bulk of the body, it is not three, but four and even five times less
than is here stated. There seems to us to be a very fundamental
distinction between Man and the animal most nearly resembling
him. We have three or four times more brain—three or four times
more thinking matter! The supremacy which our very exalted
intellectual faculties secure to us, is confirmed to us by the existence
of an exceptional development of the organ which is its seat.
Anatomy furnishes us, at the outset, with powerful characters
sufficient to satisfy the most jealous defenders of human prerogo-
tive, and to console them under the difficulties they will meet with
in matters of minor importance. We shall consider, shortly, the
minimum and maximum variations observed in the capacity of the
human cranium, and in the weight of its contents. But it may be
useful to notice here these variations in the three great anthropoid
apes. The three following series refer only to adults, and are the
most significant that we have been able to bring together. In the
first, the cubic measurement has been made by one and the same
process—that of filling the skull with small shot; in the two others-
the processes were different.*

					Capacity in cubic centimetres.
16 gorillas, males	...	...	...	...	473 to 633
5 „ females	...	...	...	...	395 „ 540
3 orangs, males	...	...	...	...	413 „ 478
7 chimpanzees, males	...	...	...	...	392 „ 452
3 „ females	...	...	...	...	367 „ 425

VOGT, ETC.†

3 gorillas, females	...	...	...	370 to 490
5 orangs, males	...	...	...	390 „ 400
7 „ females, and doubtful	...	...	335 „ 485
8 chimpanzees, males	...	...	...	300 „ 410

WYMAN, ETC.

10 gorillas, males	...	...	...	424 to 535
4 „ females	...	...	...	385 „ 391
7 chimpanzees	...	...	...	381 „ 424

* The anthropoid apes and other animals we have measured were procured from the Museum, and also from the Institut Anthropologique. We
are also indebted to M. Traouet, the preparator of natural history at the
Institut Anthropologique, and to M. Bouvier, special preparator, for the
loan of a number of specimens, for which we beg to express our obligation.
"Mémoire sur les Microcéphales," by Charles Vogt. Geneva, 1867.

The cranial characters in Man and animals, which we are about to examine, are partly the result of the difference of volume of their cranial cavity, and partly, and more especially, of the difference of their natural posture. Man alone stands perfectly upright;

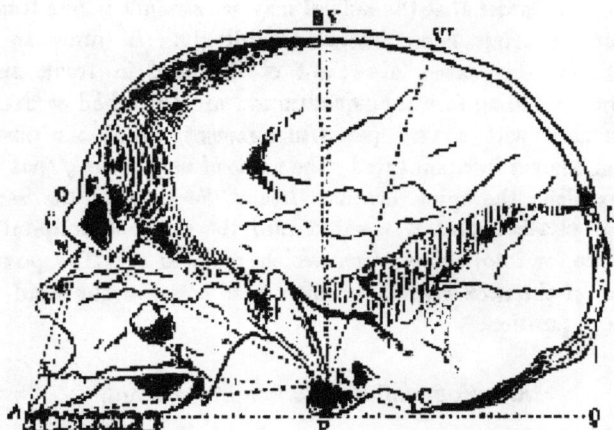

FIG. 5.—B, Anterior border of the occipital foramen or basion; C, its posterior border, or opisthion; X C, Side view and plane of the occipital foramen; A, Alveolar point; P, Inferior surface of an occipital condyle (articulating with the first cervical vertebra, or atlas); A P G, Horizontal plane of the base of the skull, or alveolo-condylean; L, Inion; L, Lambda; B, Bregma; O, Supra-orbital point, or ophryon; G, Glabella; N, Nasal point; E, Sub-nasal point; A, Alveolar point.

the anthropoid apes have an oblique or side movement in progression; the other mammalia have a horizontal attitude; hence their name—quadrupeds.

Attitude of the Body.

The head, in all the mammalian series, is articulated with the vertebral column by means of the condyles of the occipital, which rotate from before backwards, and from behind forwards, in cavities formed in the bodies of the first cervical vertebra, or atlas. Between and behind these condyles is the occipital foramen, through which the spinal cord enters the skull; its middle and anterior point is the basion, and its posterior point, the opisthion, of which we have already spoken. In quadrupeds, the occipital foramen and its condyles are situated very far backward, and in some, as the horse, they no longer occupy the base of the skull, whose posterior surface

F 2

becomes vertical. The muzzle is at the same time more or less
elongated, as the zoological facial angle showed us just now. It
follows (1) That the head is no longer in equilibrium upon the
vertebral column, but falls forwards. (2) That its position has to
be mixed, in order that the animal may see straight before him, the
axis of the orbits being altered accordingly. In order to com-
pensate for this excess of weight of the head in front, and to
prevent its falling forwards, quadrupeds are furnished at the nape
of the neck with a very powerful ligament, called the posterior
cervical, known in ruminants by the name of *nerf de bœuf* (paxwax).
It runs along the spine, becomes free at the level of the seventh
cervical vertebra, and is inserted into the external occipital protuberance, or into a depression which replaces it. The powerful
muscles of the neck contribute, with it, to preserve the head more
or less in position.

Conditions of Equilibrium of the Head.

In Man, on the contrary, the head is naturally in equilibrium
upon the vertebral column. The occipital foramen occupies the
middle of the base of the skull; the weight of the portion in front
of the basion, and that of the portion behind it, are sensibly equal,
and the posterior cervical ligament is wanting, or is only represented
by a simple aponeurotic interlacing. His position with regard to
seeing, on the other hand, is horizontal; the axis of the orbits
is directed forwards, and the back of the retina is anatomically
arranged in accordance with this. Special physiologists demonstrate in the same way that man's organisation is such that he sees
better in the erect posture. Another result of the position of
the head is a certain horizontality of the plane of mastication of
the molars as well as the incisors, as may be shown by inserting
between the teeth a flat rule, placed parallel to the horizon.

Situation and Direction of Occipital Foramen.

The occipital foramen is situated in the European at an equal
distance between the anterior and posterior portion of the entire

cranium. In the negro, it is a little more backward; in the anthropoid ape it is considerably so; in the various quadrupeds it again recedes, and still more in the horse and the hippopotamus, in which it no longer forms part of the base of the skull. Its plane looks downwards and forwards in the white man, directly downwards in the negro, notably downwards and backwards in the anthropoid ape, and still more so in quadrupeds. The fundamental characteristics of the occipital foramen are its situation and direction. The portion of the occipital which is behind the foramen is very nearly horizontal, if not concave downwards, in Man; whereas in animals it is more or less elevated from before backwards, and from below upwards. The foramen cannot therefore be removed backwards, without its posterior border being elevated at the same time; when still farther back, this part of the occipital shell is transformed, as it were, into another posterior and altogether vertical wall of the skull, which is the boundary above of a strong horizontal crest, situated upon the superior semicircular line. These excessive modifications of posture are oblique as compared with those of the biped, or, properly speaking, quadrupedal. The more the foramen is carried backwards, the more the equilibrium is disturbed, and the more the weight of the anterior part increases to the detriment of the posterior.

It will be sufficient to measure one of the two terms; for example, the inclination of the plane of the occipital foramen; that is to say, the angle which it makes with a given line being taken as a term of comparison, to find the other, namely, the amount of displacement of the foramen. This is what was done by Daubenton, in 1764, by choosing the line O D (see Fig. 6), passing from the posterior border of the occipital foramen to the inferior border of the orbit. The angle D O A, looking forwards, thus determined was 0 to 3 degrees in Man, 34 degrees in an orang-outang, 47 degrees in a maccaco, about 80 degrees in the dog, and 90 degrees in the horse. But Daubenton has never mentioned how he measured this angle; he appeared to be satisfied with a very doubtful approximation, to judge by his drawings. This measurement, the first attempt at craniometry, necessarily engaged the attention of M. Broca. By means of his occipital goniometer, he at once demonstrated that the prolonged plane of the occipital foramen was elevated occasionally, in the white man, above the line adopted by Daubenton, which gave an inverted or negative angle, which the latter had not foreseen. M. Broca was thus led to substitute for the line of Daubenton another passing from the same point, the opisthion, to the root of the nose, and at a later period

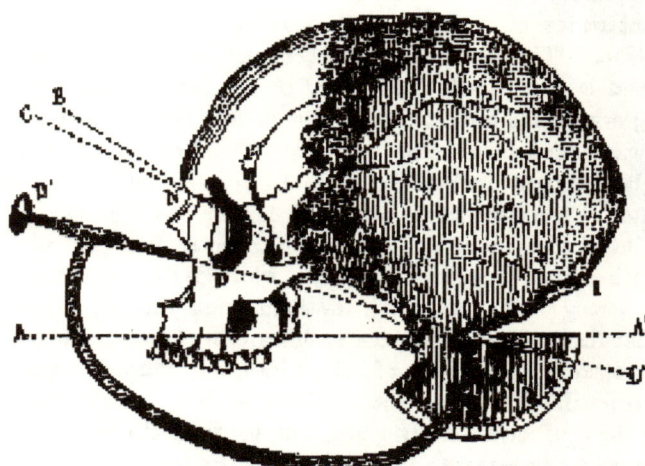

Fig. 8.—The anterior half represents the skull intact, in order to show the inferior border of the orbit; the posterior half represents the skull open for the purpose of showing the occipital foramen and its two median points, anterior and posterior. O, Opisthion, or posterior border of the occipital foramen, hidden by the centre of the disk of the gonimeter; B, Basion; D, Inferior border of the orbit, or anterior terminating point of the line of Daubenton; N, Nasal point preferred by M. Broca; D O D', Line of Daubenton; A B b A', Plane of occipital foramen prolonged both ways; A O B, Occipital angle of Daubenton; A O C, Occipital angle of Broca; A B E, Basilar angle of Broca; F, Basilar groove; G, Sella turcica; I, External occipital protuberance, or inion; J, Internal occipital protuberance.

to measure a second angle by transferring the apex of the first to the basion.

Now we have three angles relating to the occipital plane. A first, D O A, or occipital of Daubenton, has its apex at the opisthion, and its sides formed by the occipital plane and by the opisthio-suborbital line; a second, N O A, or occipital of Broca, has this same apex, and for its sides the same plane and the opisthio-nasal line; and a third, A B E, or basilar of Broca, has its apex at the hasion, and its sides formed by the occipital plane and the basio-nasal line.   The following table exhibits the results:

—	Occipital angle of Daubenton.	Occipital angle of Broca.	Basilar angle of Broca.
25 human series from...	1°5 to 2°3	10°8 to 30°1	14°8 to 26°5
4 chimpanzees	26°3	36°4	45°5
5 orangs	31°5	45°4	55°2
6 gorillas	34°5	44°4	58°2
9 gibbons	51°5	40°6	51°6
12 pitheciens	19°6 to 23°8	33°8 to 38°8	46°6 to 46°0 *

Thus the direction of the occipital foramen changes somewhat abruptly in passing from Man to the anthropoid apes, and forms a line of demarcation between them which corresponds with their difference of posture.   Between anthropoid apes and some others of the monkey tribe and the strictly mammalian quadrupeds, as the horse or the elephant, the deviation is still greater.   The plane of the foramen is raised backwards to 90 degrees.

Horizontality of Vision.

Horizontality of vision in the living subject, and of the axis of the orbit in the skeleton, depends more exclusively still on the upright posture.   M. Broca, to whose labours we shall have so frequently to refer, is now prosecuting this subject.

Alveolo-condylean Plane.

Of all the lines, or planes, used in craniometry, the most convenient, and, at the same time, the most physiological, is the alveolo-condylean plane, determined by three readily accessible points, viz. the alveolar, or middle point of the superior alveolar arch, and the most sloping points of the inferior surface of the occipital condyles.   It is represented in Fig. 5 by the line A P Q, and in Fig. 7 by the line C C.   It is in relation to this alveolo-condylean plane, which is also called the natural plane of the base of the skull, that M. Broca measures the degree of inclination or of straight direction of vision, or, rather, of the plane passing through the two orbital axes.

* We refer to the memoir of M. Broca, "Sur les Angles Occipitaux," "Revue d'Anthropologie," vol. ii. p. 193, for the second decimals.   How-ever, we purpose in this volume confining ourselves generally to the first.

The dihedral angle which they form by being prolonged is called positive, or ordinary, when the plane of vision is raised, and the meeting of the two takes place backward; and negative, when

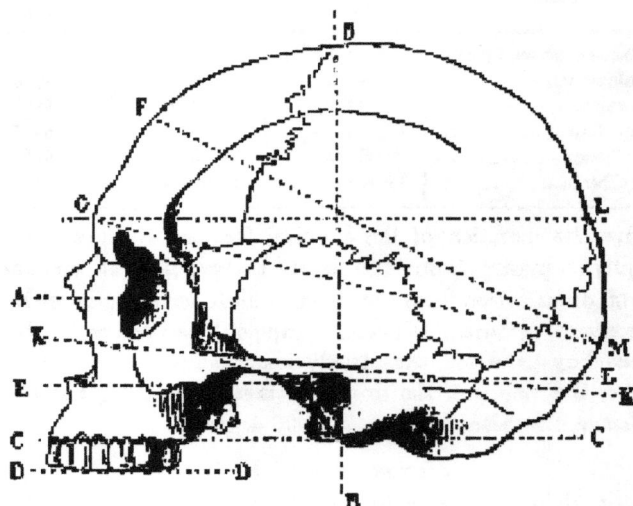

Fig. 7.—A, Horizontal axis of the orbit passing through the centre of the optic foramen behind and through the centre of the line of the orbit in front; O O, Alveolo-condylean plane, or plane of Seres (see A F B, Fig. 6). The other references are the same as in that figure.

it is depressed, and the meeting is in front. In the following table the former has no sign before it; the latter is accompanied by the sign −. The second column refers to another character which will come afterwards. In Fig. 7, the alveolo-condylean plane, C C, is parallel, as we see, to the plane of vision, A.

				Orbito-alveolo-condylean angle.	Biorbital angle.
43 men	...	...	...	− 0·01	47° 47
5 gorillas	...	...	...	19° 31	39° 04
1 orang	...	...	...	28° 53	46° 90
4 pithecians	...	...	...	15° 41	52° 24
5 cebidae	...	...	...	7° 22	41° 90
1 maki	...	...	...	23° 58	73° 72
3 dogs	...	...	...	24° 94	70° 51
3 rabbits	...	...	...	31° 15	143° 43
2 horses	...	...	...	30° 00	168° 10
1 wild boar	...	...	...	47° 41	98° 94

Thus we find that the vision of Man is sensibly horizontal in relation to the alveolo-condylean plane, since it is not depressed even one degree in a mean of forty-three skulls, while it is raised in all the mammalia, including the anthropoid apes, from a mean of 7 degrees in cubiuns to 36 in the horse, and 47 in the wild boar.

Biorbital Angle.

The divergence of vision furnishes another differential character to which M. Broca has given his attention, in his memoir "Sur le Plan Horizontal de la Tête," to which we refer the reader for the figures. The second column above gives some of them, under the head of 'biorbital angle.' It is the angle, open in front, which the two visual axes form between them, or, in other words, their degree of divergence. It varies from 40 degrees to 50 degrees in Man, and from 33 degrees to 62 degrees in the monkey tribe ; is raised to 74 degrees in the lemur, increases enormously in quadrupeds, and attains 143 degrees in the rabbit. This is how Man is commingled with the generality of monkeys as far as the lemurs, and is separated from the races of quadrupeds. The anthropoid apes, however, share his lot ; like him they have their orbital axes a little divergent.

Temporal Fossa.

Of all the mammalia, Man has the least development of the muscles of the jaw, and the smallest extent of surface for insertion of these muscles. What a difference between his small temporal fossa, bounded above by a curved line, which is at times clearly marked, and the deep fossa of the anthropoid apes! Not only does the whole of the lateral surface of the skull in these latter give insertion to the fibres of the temporal—the masticatory muscle par excellence—but also on the median line in the male there is besides a large elevated crest, which allows of these fibres being increased to any extent. The elevation, too, of the temporal line, the extent of its curve, and its nearness to the median line, are, in the human group, marks of inferiority. In certain prehistoric skulls from Florida, and modern ones from New Caledonia, the two lines distant normally from 8 to 10 centimètres, do not deviate but about 3 to 4 centimètres, thus showing a marked resemblance to the female anthropoids.

The condyles of the inferior maxillary, and the glenoid cavities in which they are received, are directed transversely in the carnivorous mammalia, from before backwards in rodentia, and are flat in the herbivora. In Man they have an intermediate direction, thus bearing testimony to his omnivorous functions.

Teeth.

The teeth, divided into incisors for cutting, canines for tearing, and molars for grinding and triturating, show still more clearly this aptitude of Man. Of his immediate zoological neighbours, the orang and the chimpanzee resemble him the most in this respect, particularly in their molars; the gorilla, on the contrary, differs from him, and in the arrangement of his teeth somewhat resembles the carnivora.

The canines are larger in the anthropoid apes, and have a length and size which entitle them to be regarded as offensive weapons, particularly in the gorilla. Between the canines and the upper lateral incisors may be noticed, among adult anthropoid apes, as in the greater number of the monkeys next in order, a gap, called diastema. This is, in great part, for the reception of the inferior canine, while the superior canine presses between the inferior canine and the first premolar, and so wears itself a place mechanically. Another characteristic of the teeth of anthropoid apes is the projection of the anterior incisors, which is more exaggerated than in the lowest races of the human group.

Man, at least the white, has vertical teeth; the canines, as well as the molars and incisors, are close together and smaller. His small permanent molars have two tubercles, and the larger four; in this respect there is no difference between him and the anthropoids. There are twenty temporary and thirty-two permanent teeth, exactly as in the four anthropoid apes, the pithecians, and the greater number of the lemurs. In the cebians, a small molar is added on each side, which raises their total number to thirty-six. Some monkeys have a different dental formula; the macauco, for example, has thirty-eight.

The progress of the eruption of the teeth in monkeys, and their periods of succession, are but imperfectly known. It is certain that the eruption is more rapid (*cæteris paribus*) in the anthropoid apes than in Man.*

The superior alveolar arch in Man is generally in the form of an hyperbola, with relatively short branches; that of the three

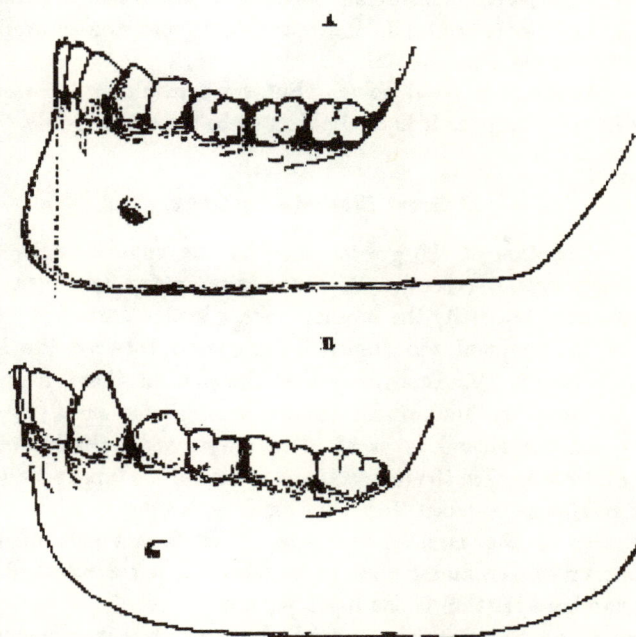

FIG. 8.— A, Jaw of the European; B, Jaw of the Chimpanzee.

principal anthropoid apes takes the form of a U with long and exactly parallel branches; that of the sajou and the macaque is elliptical—(*Owen*). Other characters have been given as peculiar to Man; for example:

* See "L'Homme et les Singes Anthropomorphes," by M. Magitot, in "Bull. Soc. d'Anthrop.," 2nd series, vol. iv. p. 113. Paris.

The presence of a chin—that is to say, of a small triangular surface, more or less projecting above the inferior border of the jaw. But this character has lost its value since its absence has been noticed in a certain number of human specimens, among them the prehistoric jaw of the Naulette, and some contemporaneous ones represented by MM. Quatrefages and Hamy.

The existence of the tubercles géni, on the posterior surface of the inferior maxillary bone, which are replaced by a depression in monkeys. But exceptions of an opposite kind are met with continually, such as tubercles in the anthropoid apes, the depression on the jaw of the Naulette, &c.

The presence of a nasal spine. But some monkeys have one, whilst in many negroes it is so slight as to be almost invisible.

Different Cranial Characters.

The articulation of the greater wing of the sphenoid directly with the parietal.—(Owen). But in a great many specimens of different races, especially the inferior ones, a bridge formed by the union of the temporal and frontal is interposed between the two preceding bones. M. Broca describes the first of these arrangements as usual in Man, under the name of ptérion en H (see D, Fig. 2), and the second as usual in monkeys, under the names of ptérion retourné, when the temporal and sphenoid are largely united, and of ptérion en K when they only touch each other.

The size of the mastoid processes. This is a result of the development of the sterno-mastoid muscles which are attached to them, and have relation to the biped posture.

There is no one cranial or facial character, however strongly marked, which can be drawn as a line of demarcation between Man and animals, but numerous cases will arise to efface or to weaken it. In the head, the transition to the anthropoid apes would be inappreciable, but for the five following characters of Man: (1) The increase of volume of his cranial cavity; (2) The relatively inverse diminution of the face; (3) The increase of the facial angle which arises from it; (4) The situation of the occipital foramen below, and at the centre of the base of the skull, and the

horizontality of the two orbital axes, both dependent on the bipad
posture. But the first is of such pre-eminent importance that we
would sum up by saying : The head of Man is only distinguishable
from the head of animals by a single important character—the
capacity of the brain-case.

CHAPTER II.

VERTEBRAL COLUMN — SACRUM — PELVIS — THORAX — STERNUM —
PARALLEL BETWEEN THE SUPERIOR AND INFERIOR EXTREMITIES
—THE HAND AND FOOT—PROPORTIONS OF THE SKELETON.

Vertebral Column.

THE cervical region, which is in continuation with the head, does
not materially differ in the mammalian series, except in the height
of the vertebræ as before stated.   M. Broca has, however, described
certain variations in it. The spinous processes, bifurcated in Man,
are simple in the anthropoid apes and in monkeys ; but in some
human skeletons of an inferior race they have been found simple ;
and in the chimpanzee two of them are bifurcated, which establishes
a transitional link between them.   In the second place, the anthropoid apes and Man have the superior surface of each vertebra
bounded by two projections, which are wanting in the inferior
monkeys, whilst they have no little appendix with transverse
processes, as in the lemurs and carnivora. Their types, in consequence, have been disarranged by being separated from that of
the next zoological groups.

Conditions of the Equilibrium of the Trunk.

The differences which the dorso-lumbar region presents are very
characteristic. Normally composed in Man of twelve dorsal
vertebræ and of five lumbar, it has sometimes thirteen dorsal and
only four lumbar, as in the gorilla and chimpanzee. There is not,

therefore, any very serious differences in this respect between these
two and ourselves. The orang, on the contrary, loses one lumbar
vertebra, and the gibbon gains one dorsal, which brings up the
total number of dorso-lumbars to sixteen in the one and eighteen
in the other. In the pithecians generally, and in most of the
celians, there are nineteen, there being more lumbar in the former
and more dorsal in the latter. In lemurs there is an increase in
both regions, but especially in the lumbar. The slender loris has
altogether twenty-three or twenty-four dorso-lumbar vertebra.

The dorso-lumbar region presents other differences much more
important, which have relation to the three kinds of posture or
attitude of mammalia—the vertical, the oblique, and the horizontal.

The human head is in natural equilibrium on the spine—well
and good; but the weight of the viscera contained in the thoracic
and abdominal cavities tends to throw the whole trunk forward.
To counteract this, two anatomical arrangements come in. Elastic
ligaments, called yellow, are interposed between the vertebral
laminæ, and, by virtue of their structure, keep the body erect
without fatigue. A number of ligaments and muscles, almost
always more or less fixed at a right angle—that is to say, under
the most favourable incidences, at the extremity of the spinous
and transverse processes throughout the entire length of the column
—conduce to the same end. In the second place, the vertebral
column presents three alternative curvatures, which tend to preserve
the line of gravity of the head and trunk in the axis of sustentation
passing through the pelvis. By the first of these curvatures, the
cervical, whose convexity looks forwards, the weight of the head
is brought backwards; the second, or dorsal, being directed the
reverse way, brings the centre of gravity forwards; while the third,
or lumbar, with an anterior convexity, serves the purpose of keeping
the whole column erect.

In quadrupeds, on the contrary, there are only two curvatures,
the one cervical, as in Man, the other dorso-lumbar, with the convexity looking backwards, like the dorsal region in Man—or rather
looking upwards.* It follows that, if by any contrivance one

---

* It is well to remark that in the vertical posture of Man, the posterior
part of the column, and of the whole trunk, looks backwards, and the

compelled the individual to stand upright, the line of gravity would be forcibly brought forwards, and the weight of the viscera would come to bear against the anterior wall of the thorax, or the inferior wall of the abdomen.

Curvatures of the Vertebral Column.

Monkeys, in this respect, are divided into two groups: the pithecians, the cebians, and the lemurs, which have the dorsolumbar curvature only, conformably with their quadrupedal attitude; and the anthropoids, which appear under various aspects, more approaching, however, the human arrangement. Many gibbons have three very marked curvatures. In the chimpanzee, the lumbar curvature, distinctive of the human group, is only over the last two vertebræ, and in the orang, over the last. The gorilla, with his straight lumbar column, is farthest removed from Man, without, however, presenting the absolute organization of the quadruped.

The division of the trunk and of the vertebral column in mammalia in general into two series—the one anterior, the other posterior—and the absence of all distinction of this kind in Man, is more characteristic. Let us explain this, according to the views of M. Broca.

A muscle is a fleshy mass, elongated, and more or less attached at its two extremities, which approach each other when the muscle contracts under the influence of the will. The more movable extremity is displaced, drawing along with it the lever to which it is attached, whilst the other, rendered immovable by other muscles, remains stationary. In any movement, then, we must consider the action of a whole system of muscles, and not of one only.

In Man, the muscles which indirectly contribute to locomotion,

anterior part forwards; whilst in the horizontal posture of quadrupeds, the former looks upwards and the latter downwards. In the same way the upper extremities of Man become anterior in quadrupeds, and the lower posterior. The anthropoid apes passing continually from one posture to the other, both orders of arrangement can be applied to them.

"L'Ordre des Primates: Parallèle Anatomique de l'Homme et des Singes," by M. Broca, "Bull. Soc. d'Anthrop.," 2nd series, vol. iv. p. 228, 1869.

by fixing the pelvis and the successive portions of the vertebral
column which furnish the *point d'appui*, are attached to the
spinous and transverse processes of the vertebræ, and tend throughout their whole length to draw or bend them downwards in a direct
ratio to the limited mobility of the whole column. The dorsal
processes yield considerably, are bent down and imbricated; those
of the lumbar yield less.

In quadrupeds the traction of the process is exerted, on the
contrary, in the direction of the anterior extremity in the lumbar
vertebræ, and of the posterior in the dorsal. These processes are
inclined, then, in a contrary direction—the lumbar upwards and
the dorsal downwards. The spot where the change of direction
takes place establishes the division between the anterior and the
posterior series. It is situated in the carnaria, between the last
dorsal vertebra but one—which is attached to the thorax by a costal
cartilage—and the last, which only supports one of the floating
ribs. The spinous process of the one is inclined upwards, that of
the other downwards, and it is there that the two series become
independent.

Anteversion and Retroversion.

Thus, by the appearance alone of a vertebral column, we recognise
the habitual attitude of the individual. In Man, the processes are
all oblique below, or in retroversion; he has but one series. In
quadrupeds, the dorsal processes are descending, except the last,
and the lumbars ascending, or in anteversion; they have two
series.

All the monkeys proper are in the latter category, generally in a
very marked way in lemurs, less in cebians, less still in the higher
species—the pithecians. "The scene suddenly changes as regards
the anthropoid apes. All the characters indicating the functional separation of the series in front, and of that behind, have
completely disappeared. The dorsal spinous processes, by their
length, their great obliquity, and their imbrication, approximate to
the human type much more than to that of the pithecians and other
apes; those of the false dorsal are obliquely inclined towards the

pelvis, as in Man; and those of the lumbar have not the least
tendency to anteversion; far from it, for often they are rather
inclined towards the pelvis."—(Broca).

In the semnopithecus (Fig. 9), belonging to the family of
pithecians, are represented the single dorso-lumbar curvature, with
its convexity looking upwards; the retroversion of the spinous
processes of the dorsal vertebræ (except the last two), the anteversion of the lumbars, and the scarcely visible processes of the

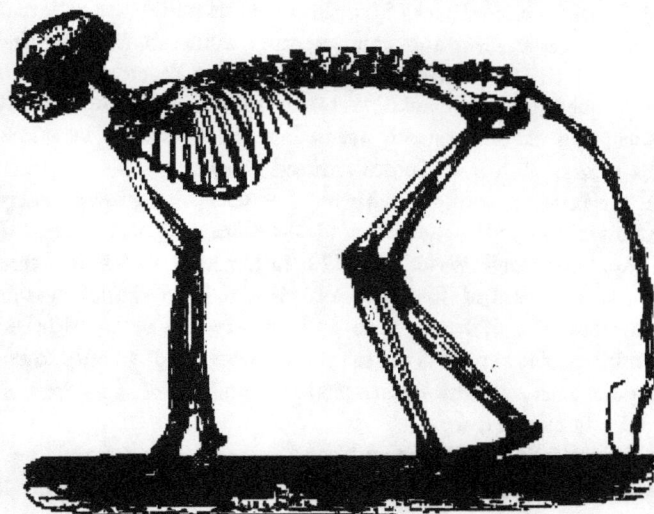

FIG. 9.—Skeleton of Semnopithecus Entellus, one of the Pithecians.

last two dorsal, answering to the separation of the trunk into two
series—the one anterior, the other posterior.

Styloid Processes of Vertebræ.

The consolidation of each series into one compact whole is
the last distinctive character of quadrupeds. The ribs and the
sternum are the intermediary of this consolidation in the anterior
series, which is a reason for the last dorsal with an independent

rib being excluded from it. A special system of processes, called
styloid, detached from the lumbar vertebræ, and which does not
exist in Man, nor in the anthropoid apes, has the same design in
the posterior series.

Sacrum and Coccyx.

The mode of termination of the vertebral column—below in
bipeds, behind in quadrupeds—has been the object of careful study
by M. Broca. According to him, the vertebræ which are articulated
with the coccyx form the true sacrum, while all the remainder
appertain to the tail, which is divided into two segments; the one
basic, formed of true caudal vertebræ, in which the spinal canal
remains; the other terminal, formed of false caudal vertebræ—
that is to say, with their bodies reduced in size.

All the inferior monkeys, with but few exceptions, have a sacrum
of three vertebræ, all articulating at the sides with the ilium—that
is to say, true sacral vertebræ. The tail, which forms the termination, is composed of five true and twelve false caudal vertebræ
in the macaque; of seven true and twenty-two or more false in
the ateles paniscus; of five to seven true, and twenty-four to
twenty-six false, in the cynocephali generally; of five true and
four false in the lori, &c.

In the so-called tailless monkeys, the sacrum is formed, as in
those above mentioned, of three anchylosed vertebræ; but the
remainder is either reduced in size in each of its two kinds of
vertebræ—as in the cynocephalus niger, which is reduced to three
true and three false caudals; or more or less atrophied from the
extremity to the base, as in the magot, which has no trace of false
caudals, and has from one to four true.

In Man the type is altogether different. His sacrum is composed
of two parts, the one consisting of three vertebræ, as in the monkeys
mentioned above, which articulate with the ilium and constitute the
sacrum nécessaire; the other of two or three vertebræ, free at their
external borders and having a spinal groove, and which represent
a *sacrum supplémentaire*, anchylosed with the former. The coccyx
consists of four or five vertebræ—all false. Man, then, has a tail

formed of six or eight pieces, the first being at the basic segment and the last at the terminal segment, as in mammalia generally. The justice of this interpretation is confirmed by studying the extremity of the vertebral column in the fœtus.

To what type do the anthropoid apes approximate? " In all, the true caudal vertebræ are anchylosed with the sacrum, as in Man, and the coccyx is composed of false vertebræ only, similar to those of the coccyx of Man—that is to say, more developed in width than in height, and flattened from before backwards."—(Broca). The supplementary sacrum of Man is formed, four times out of six, of three vertebræ, instead of two; and that of the anthropoid ape varies from two to four. Ought we to look upon this as a difference? Other morphological variations in the coccyx, of less importance, equally present themselves in both.

In a word, Man and the higher apes resemble each other in the conformation of the tail, at the same time that they differ in this respect from monkeys proper.

The Pelvis.

The pelvis exhibits considerable differences between Man and quadrupeds, which arise from their different attitude. It is formed of two halves which originally consisted of three distinct bones—the ilium, the ischium, and the pubis, at the junction of which, externally, is the cotyloid cavity (c, Fig. 10). It is divided by a circular crest, called the superior brim, into two portions, termed the greater and lesser pelvis. The fœtus lies, and is matured, in the former, and passes into the latter a short time previous to birth.

In Man, the iliac bones are expanded, laterally, into two great wings, thin in the centre, and concave—admirably constructed to support the mass of the viscera, and in the female the weight of the fœtus. Their external surface, or external iliac fossa, is, in consequence, convex, to give insertion to the muscles of the buttock. In quadrupeds, on the contrary, the iliac bones are closer together, are elongated on each side of the lumbar portion of the column, and

F 2

convex on their internal surface, the external becoming inversely concave.

The iliac bones in Man therefore have somewhat the form of valves, which are composed of flat bones. They rapidly become long and tapering, on the contrary, in quadrupeds, as in the equidæ, the hare, and the kangaroo, and are converted, as it were, into long bones. Between these two arrangements are seen all kinds of intermediary ones.

The measurements which we have made upon two hundred and

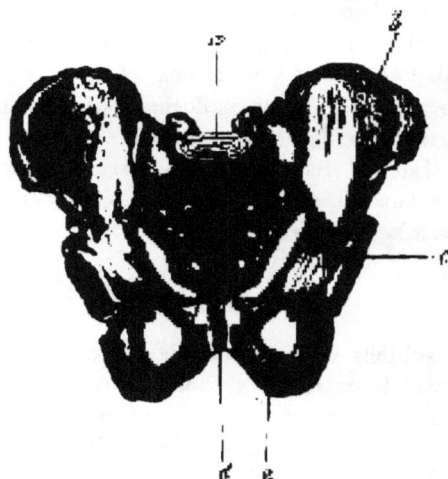

FIG. 11.—The pelvis in Man : *a*, Portion of the bone of the sacrum, which is articulated with the last lumbar vertebræ : *b*, Iliac crest, or superior border of the ilium : *c*, Cotyloid cavity, in which is received the head of the femur : *d*, Symphysis pubis, or articulation of the two bones of the pubis : *e*, Point where the ischium, which is to the outside, is united to the pubis, which is to the inside.

seven different pelves, serve to throw light upon this subject, and may be thus summed up :[*]

The maximum length, taken from the point of the ischium to the farthest point of the iliac crest, exceeds the maximum breadth taken from one iliac crest to the other in 23 per cent. of the ruminants examined, thirty-two of the carnivors, thirty-

[*] "Sur les Proportions Générales chez l'Homme et les Mammifères," by Paul Topinard, in "Bull. Soc. d'Anthrop.," 2nd series, vol. x., 1875.

three of the rolentia, thirty-seven of the marsupialia, and thirty-
eight of the edentata. It is the reverse in Man—the breadth is =
28·77 per cent. to the length. The anthropoids vary, but they
come nearer to Man than to quadrupeds. The gibbons, like the
other monkeys, have still the length greater than the breadth.
In chimpanzees, the two are nearly equal. The gorillas and orangs
are very nearly allied to Man. The breadth exceeds the length
in 24 per cent. in the former, and in 16·50 in the latter. For
certain physiological reasons peculiar to their group, the elephants
and the mastodons have the pelvis of similar conformation to that
of Man.

Consequently the sacrum of quadrupeds is straight, elongated,
a little hollow on its internal surface, and is in contrast with
that of Man which is wide at the base, thick, conical, and curved
at the point. The sacrum of anthropoid apes holds a middle
position, and frequently resembles that of some of the inferior
races of Man, as the Hottentot, dissected by Jeffries Wyman, or
the Boojeswoman, by Cuvier.

At the same time that the human pelvis becomes wider and
diminishes in height, its antero-posterior diameter becomes shortened,
relatively to that of the anthropoid ape and other mammalia. The
promontory—that is to say, the projecting angle in front which
the curve of the loins makes with the curve of the sacrum, is, on
the other hand, stronger, in accordance with the requirements of the
biped attitude. We may add that the tuberosities of the ischium
are shorter, less widely separated, and less marked than in the
anthropoid, and that the symphysis pubis is shorter.

That which we remark in the pelvis may also be found at the
other extremity of the trunk.

The Thorax

The thorax, in Man, is more developed transversely; that of
quadrupeds, on the contrary, is more so from before backwards, or
from the sternum to the spine. The arms in the former have to
move in all directions, and especially outwardly, and to this end

are kept wide apart by the arches, which are the clavicles. In the quadrupeds proper, they only serve for locomotion, but in a parallel way downwards, and remain apart. Thus the clavicle disappears, and the thorax becomes flattened sideways. Monkeys, in this respect, hold an inferior position to quadrupeds, a superior one to Man. The lemurians, the sebians, and the pithecians have the thorax compressed laterally, the anthropoid apes rather from before backwards.

The volume of the chest could not furnish any special character. Its development is enormous in the three great anthropoid apes. Whilst the circumference was about ninety-four centimètres in a thousand and eighty Englishmen measured by Mr. Hutchinson,

Fig. 11.—Anterior portion of the sternum in Man: St, Sternum, showing the three divisions—the upper or handle, the middle or body, and the lower or xiphoid appendix; R, Ribs; R', Costal cartilages.

it attained one hundred and fifty-seven in an immense gorilla measured by Du Chaillu.

The Sternum.

The sternum in the same way, while broad and flat in Man, is narrow and developed antero-posteriorly, or rather from below upwards, in quadrupeds. In this respect the anthropoid apes come nearer to Man.

The sternum is composed, speaking philosophically, of seven portions, corresponding to the seven ribs which are directly articulated with it, and of a xiphoid appendix. These are distinctly seen in the fœtus, but at birth are reduced to two—exclusive of the appendix—namely, the handle and the body, the latter being formed by the anchylosis of the six lower portions. The handle, or upper separated portion, exists in all the mammalia with clavicles; the appendix also. The body is entire in Man; in the greater number of the monkeys proper it is composed of six distinct parts; in one of the anthropoids, the gibbon, it is entire, as in Man, and in the other three it is divided into three or four. Thus we see that in this respect the anthropoid apes, and notably the magot, are between Man and the pithecians.

The extremities, four in number in the majority of mammalia, are reduced to two, the anterior, in the whale and the porpoise. Their terminal segment bears the name of foot or hand, a denomination upon which Blumenbach and Cuvier based their division of the order of Primates of Linnæus into Bimana, comprehending Man, and Quadrumana, embracing the monkey tribe, a name which Tyson had given them in 1699.

The Hand and Foot.

What then is to the hand and foot, and especially the hand? Cuvier says that which constitutes the hand is the faculty of opposing the thumb to the other fingers for the purpose of taking hold of the smallest objects. Agassiz terms the hand, "a limb having a certain number of fingers bending one way, another finger being opposed to them." He defines a foot as, "a limb terminated by digits all on the same level, and all having the same direction."

The hand is recognised, according to Huxley, by the disposition of the bones of the carpus and of the metacarpus; the foot by the presence of short flexor muscles, a short extensor of the digital appendices, and a long peroneal. All these definitions look only to one side of the question. M. de La Palisse's maxim is that it is their use which distinguishes the foot from the hand.

The Foot.

M. Broca, with greater breadth of view, says: "A foot is an extremity which serves chiefly for standing or walking; a hand is an extremity which serves principally for prehension and touch." We might add that the fin is an extremity which serves principally for notation, &c. The hand is perfect when it answers the end for which it was exclusively intended. The foot is perfect when it is only constructed for walking. Both are imperfect when they encroach on the functions which do not specially belong to them. An anterior extremity may lose all its functions of prehension, and it would be only a foot. Various physiological variations, and of different degrees, are noticed in the mammalian series.

But if the sole of the foot bears directly on the ground, or if the palm of the hand grasps objects, the whole extremity is, in reality, applied to its general function, all its parts are made conformable to the purposes for which it was designed. It is not, then, the foot or the hand only, but the extremity as a whole, which we must examine to discover its function of prehension or locomotion. This has been already done by M. Broca.

The anatomical conditions, which secure to the inferior extremity its function of locomotion, "may be reduced," says M. Broca, "to three: (1) The root of the extremity—that is to say, the head of the femur;* should be received into a deep hemispherical cavity, looking downwards and outwards, which allows the limb to move freely from before backwards, and from behind forwards, to execute the two movements of progression, whilst the other movements, and, in particular, adduction, are very limited; (2) The two bones of the leg should be immovable the one on the other, and more or less united together as a single bone, in order to bear the weight of the body, and so that the foot may not turn; (3) The articulations immediately above the part touching the ground should only allow two movements—those of flexion and extension—and should be bent at a more or less right angle, in order to present to the ground a flat surface, formed at the expense of the posterior surface of the extremity, now become inferior."

Man, who exclusively rests on his two feet, realises all these conditions in the highest degree. His femur, retained in the

* We refer the reader to page 30 and following for the anatomical expressions employed here, and elsewhere, with respect to the skeleton.

cotyloid cavity by a virtual vacuum, is moved as a balance in two directions. The articulations of his knee and instep are hinge-like. His tibia and fibula are immovable, and fall perpendicularly on the

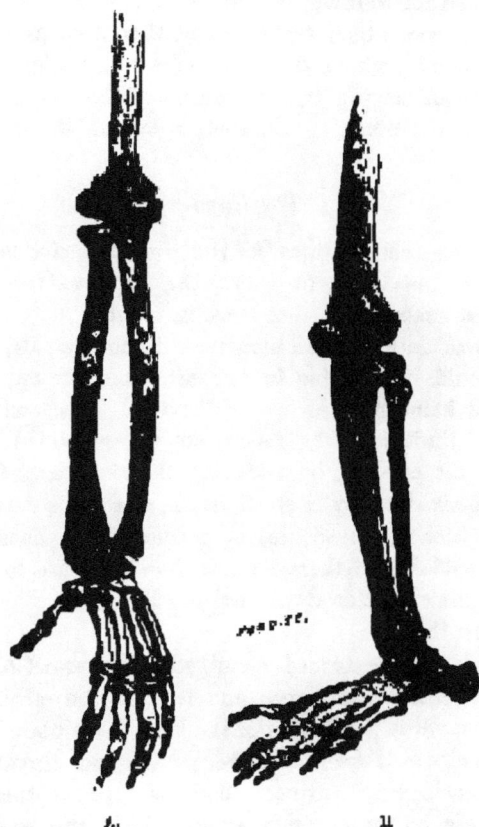

Fig. 13.—A, Skeleton of the hand, the forearm in supination (the radius outside, on the side of the thumb, the ulna inside), and a part of the humerus of the gorilla. B, Skeleton of the foot, leg (fibula outside, tibia inside), and part of the femur of the gorilla.

crown of an elastic arch, which rests on the ground by the calcaneum behind and the metatarsus in front.

In the majority of mammalia, these arrangements are identical,

or analogous. Whether the constituent columns of the foot amount
to four, three, or two; whether the individual bears on his
phalanges, his metatarsus, or the entire sole of the foot, they are
always adapted for walking and for support.

The cheiropters, which make use of their foot as a hook, and
perhaps kangaroos, which are able to grasp in a slight degree, are
the only animals having free movement of the two bones of the
leg one upon the other.   We shall speak of the monkey tribe
presently.

The Hand.

The indispensable qualities for the regular performance of acts
of prehension and touch, of which the upper extremity of Man
offers the best example, are also three in number.

(1) The articulation of the humerus with the scapula, or scapulo-
humeral, should be movable in two directions, in order to allow
the arm and hand play in every direction. Circumduction and
adduction, if limited in the femur, are not neglected here. The
presence of the clavicle, by widening the shoulders, favours the
latter; the glenoid cavity is small, ovoid, and looks outwards; the
axis of the humeral head lies perpendicularly. These last two
features are sufficient of themselves, in doubtful cases, to enable one
to recognise the character of the upper extremities. We are now
about to show this.

The arm is a thigh turned round, says Professor Ch. Martins.[*]
The articular line of the knee and that of the elbow are both
transverse, but while the flexion of the knee takes place backwards,
that of the elbow is forwards; the patella and olecranon, which
are analogues, occupy inverse positions. In reptiles the two
extremities are, on the contrary, symmetrical; and, as M. Durand
(de Gros) says, isomerous, flexion being exerted in the same direction.   How is this difference in mammalia to be explained? In a
very simple way. The part of the arm which is above the middle
third has undergone, in the former, a twisting from behind for-

---

[*] "Nouvelle Comparaison des Membres Pelviens et Thoraciques," by
Ch. Martins, in "Mém. Acad. de Montpellier," 1857.

wards, and from within outwards, as if the bone had been turned round.
Proofs of this are visible upon the humerus in the shape of a
groove of torsion. This is why the thumb, which is inwards in
the foot, has become outwards in the hand. But this twisting or
rotation, has not the same extent in bipeds and quadrupeds, or
rather in the humeri of the limbs, whether designed for prehension
or for locomotion.

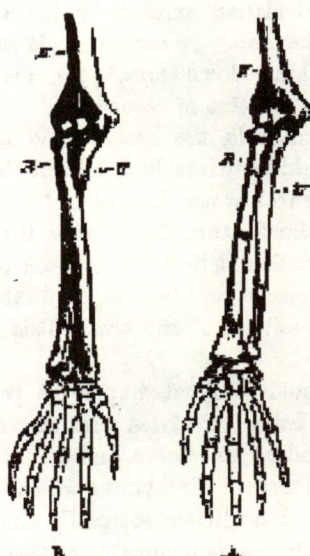

Fig. 10.—Skeleton of the forearm: A, in supination; B, in pronation; H, Humerus;
R, Radius; U, Ulna.

In the former case it is about 180 degrees, in the latter about
90 degrees. Moreover, in bipeds, as in quadrupeds, the forearm
is bent upon the arm in a similar way relatively to the body. It is
because the glenoid cavity of the scapula describes, in the latter,
a complementary arc of a circle, equally from behind forwards and
from without inwards, that so much of it is spared for the
humerus; consequently it looks forwards relatively to the axis of
the body in these, and downwards in quadrupeds. The 90
degrees for the humerus and the 90 for the glenoid cavity, thus

give the 180 degrees which make of the arm a "thigh turned round." The degree of rotation varies sometimes in both, and the part which the humerus takes in it is measured by the angle which the vertical plane of its head makes with the vertical and transverse plane of its inferior extremity.

Thus an angle of torsion of the humerus of 180 degrees, and a glenoid cavity looking outwards, are the characters which the scapulo-humeral articulation exhibits in the extremities destined principally for prehension. A similar angle of 90 degrees, and a glenoid cavity looking downwards,[*] are, on the contrary, the characteristic of the function of locomotion. If the cavity, in this case, had looked outwards, the head of the humerus, instead of resting upon it, would be driven back against the articular capsule, which by the least shock would be ruptured.

(3) The radius should turn freely over the ulna, so that the hand, placed in pronation at its extremity, can be put in supination and lay hold of objects readily. Fig. 13 shows the difference between these two positions of the arm. This rotation in Man is about 180 degrees.

(4) The hand should be situated upon the prolonged axis of the forearm, the carpus being articulated with the radius in such a way as to have every kind of movement, and especially the most complete flexion and extension. Everything which adds to the mobility of the phalanges, and facilitates especially the opposition of the thumb to the other fingers, is favourable to this end.

Thus mobility of the member in all its parts is that which characterises the hand, solidity that which marks the foot. The details of configuration is only a question of relative perfection in either case.

Hand and Foot.

The anterior extremities of Man exhibit all the attributes above mentioned, which go to make up a perfect organ of prehension. Those of the carnivora and pachydermata differ from them entirely,

---

[*] Downwards, because we are thinking of quadrupeds; but if we suppose the trunk vertical, it is forwards.

and are adapted in all their parts for locomotion. We find all terrestrial mammalia inclining towards one or other of these two types. In the kangaroo, the movement of pronation and supination, the axis of his hand being in continuation with that of the forearm, the conformation of his five digits, everything, except that the glenoid cavity looks forward,* goes to show that his anterior extremity is formed for prehension. In the dog, the anterior extremity, on the contrary, is better adapted for progression, and, therefore, the two bones of his forearm move one upon the other. It is scarcely necessary to enumerate the many rodentia, carnivora, and edentata which employ their front paws as hands to seize their prey, to carry it to the mouth, to burrow in the ground, to caress their young, to carry them, &c.

In the common monkeys the anterior extremities hang loosely at the sides of the body; their angle of humeral torsion is that of quadrupeds. In the lemurs, the ouistiti, the stele, and the sapajou it is as high as 95 or 100 degrees; in the magot, 105 degrees; in the semnopithecus, 110 degrees. The amount of rotation of the radius is variable; in some cebians and pithecians it does not exceed 90 degrees; in the mona it attains to 100 degrees. When the common monkeys use the hand as a foot, it is held at an angle more or less approaching a right angle, and leans on the ground by the whole palmar surface, with the digits extended; it has then all the character of a foot. But if they use it for seizing objects, or the limb is left to itself, as in the dead body, the axis of the hand is continued in a straight line with that of the forearm. It is, then, to all intents and purposes, a hand.

With regard to their posterior extremity, it possesses all the characters which render it adapted for locomotion; its terminal extremity is set at a right angle, and rests on the ground by the whole plantar surface. The digits are nevertheless longer, and the thumb more loosely attached and more spreading, than in Man; the thumb is not opposed to the other digits, as we have said, but by its span it plays the part of one leg of a cramp-iron or pincers,

* We say forwards because the kangaroo holds himself most frequently in the standing position.

the four other digits forming the other leg.   It is by this means
that monkeys hang on to the boughs of trees as well by their feet
as by their hands.   In a word, the common monkeys have feet
behind and hands in front, but they employ them subordinately,
the former for climbing and the latter for walking.   Properly
speaking they neither belong to quadrupeds nor to the quadrumana.

In anthropoid apes all the characters proper to the organ of
prehension are developed in the same degree as in Man : there is
the same independence of the limb—greater in the gibbon perhaps ;
the humeral angle of torsion is about 150 degrees, whilst that of
the negro is 154 degrees, and that of the white man 163 degrees,
according to M. Gegenbaur ; the movement of pronation and of
supination of the radius is from 140 to 180 degrees, whilst that of
Man is 180 degrees ; the axis of the hand is in continuation of that
of the forearm ; the power of extension, that is to say, the movement which would, when required, make it serve for a foot, is less
than in Man ; the configuration of the bones of the hand is
identical with that of Man, except that the orang and some gibbons
have an additional bone in the carpus, called the intermedium,
and that the thumb has greater span in the gorilla, and is somewhat atrophied in the orang, and perhaps in the chimpanzee.   As
to the inferior extremity, the resemblance to that of Man is still
more close, except that the orang has the great toe much smaller,
and much more behind.   In fine, the gorilla most nearly approaches
to Man in the shape of his hand and foot, while the chimpanzee
comes next.

The anthropoid ape seizes the smallest objects with the thumb
and fingers of his hand, which he opposes perfectly.   In the foot
the opposition is nil—it is not greater than that of Chinese
oarsmen, Nubian horsemen, or painters without arms, who lay
hold by bending the toes all together, or by making the second toe
act as a thumb.   His thumb and digits can only clasp the two sides
of a bough, like the two legs of a cramp-iron, in the act of climbing.
His ordinary method of progression is in an oblique direction, the
legs close together, the arms extended and somewhat separated

when making a step; the forearms in pronation, and the hands closed, resting altogether upon the inner border and the dorsal surface of the phalanges. The orang which we have had an opportunity of seeing, walked with the toes turned under, and with the external border of the foot resting on the ground. It seems, nevertheless, that other anthropoids sometimes rest on the entire flat surface of the sole of the foot, and that they keep the toes extended. With regard to the erect position, the anthropoid ape assumes it frequently, but only by accident. Thus we have seen gibbons run along in the upright position, the arms elevated above the head, and thrown backwards, evidently in order to place their centre of gravity in a more favourable position. The gorilla generally runs away from Man, but if he suddenly finds himself in his presence, or has to cover the retreat of the female, he faces his enemy with the greatest bravery, holds up his head, strikes his chest, and comes forward in an upright position with the head erect. The chimpanzee frequently straightens himself in the same manner. The orang is so apathetic that he almost always walks along crawling.

In a word, the anthropoid ape is a biped, but he possesses an arrangement of the feet which allows him to walk upon the branches of trees. He is bimanous, but he has the assistance of his hands in walking, as we ourselves should have if, with longer arms, we wished to imitate him. His attitude in progression is more nearly the vertical than the horizontal, and is sometimes that of Man and sometimes that of quadrupeds.

To return to terrestrial mammalia. Their posterior extremities are always adapted for progression, the anterior sometimes for prehension, sometimes for progression, frequently for both. The four extremities should, in the main, be simply for support. The more or less perfect adaptation of the anterior to the act of touch and prehension is a characteristic of gradual development, and if one must establish a graduated scale in reference to this matter, the series would succeed each other as follows: the pachydermata and ruminantia, carnivora in general, kangaroos, ordinary monkeys, anthropoid apes, Man.

Stature.

Having considered the skeleton in detail, it remains for us to examine it in its *ensemble*. Height and size in comparative anatomy have a secondary value, the largest animals go side by side with the smallest in contiguous genera. Among the gibbons, for example, the siamang reaches 1·16 mètre; the entelloïd, 80 centimètres. The other anthropoids come nearer to Man than that. The chimpanzee is about 1·30 mètre; the two or three species of orang from 1·10 mètre to 1·60 mètre; the gorilla from 1·40 mètre to 1·73 mètre, and more. Now the height of an adult man (France) is about 1·65 mètre, and this varies in every part of the globe from 1·30 mètre to about 2 mètres. Among pithecians, the cynocephali are generally the tallest; the nasicus measures 1·10 mètre, the miotheus, 30 centimètres; the cebians vary from 60 centimètres in the brachyuri to 20 centimètres in the ouistiti; the lemurs are small. So much for the approximate measurements. How can we compare animals, some of which go on all-fours, and others in a semi-inclined attitude, with Man, who is perfectly erect?

Their general forms have more interest. Man varies so far as to merit the epithets tall and thin, or short and stout; he is lean or fat, his neck is long or short, his abdomen drawn in or prominent. In the anthropoid apes the differences are also great. The gibbon is slender, long in the body, and made for agility, in this respect approaching to the semnopitheci; he only wants a tail to make him resemble them in his movements. The orang, on the contrary, is dull, apathetic, and squat; he walks with measured steps. The gorilla is remarkable for his athletic figure; he is said to wrestle even with the leopard, and to have the best of it. Both the orang and the gorilla have monstrously prominent bellies, which belongs to their herbivorous or granivorous mode of feeding. The chimpanzee, though less muscular in his limbs, and not so stout, has, like the gorilla, considerable strength. Among the Gaboon species we would mention the koolokamba, which, to judge by his skeleton, ought to have slender limbs.

Proportions of the Skeleton.

The proportions of the skeleton have also much interest. Their study having hitherto afforded more results in the comparison between man and animals than in that of races between themselves, we shall speak of them here in a general way.

Osteometry.

Osteometry, one of the most promising branches of anthropology, and one having an intimate connection with craniometry, is a study which has especial reference to the measurement of the facial angle and the direction of the occipital foramen, matters already considered. Osteometry itself is only a part of what should be called zoometry, which has to do with animals, in contradistinction to anthropometry, which has Man for its object of study. Are we to seek for the proportion of the body on the skeleton or on the living subject? This is the question which governs all osteometry.

On the living subject one has the advantage of being able to refer each particular measurement to a unit of comparison, as stature, if we are dealing only with Man, or length of trunk or of the vertebral column, if we extend our examination to animals. But in spite of the greatest skill on the part of the preparator who mounts the skeleton, there is always somewhat of arbitrariness in the mode of articulating the bones, and of replacing the intervertebral substance with discs of leather. The bones are not found at all in the same condition when dry and when in the fresh state; in the former case the cartilages are dried up, and so reduced in size that it is impossible to form any proper comparison between one skeleton and another. If we take a single articular extremity, the retraction of its investing cartilage is slight, but if we take the twelve surfaces of the entire hand, which are found between the tip of the fingers and the wrist, it amounts to something considerable. On the living subject, it is true, the measuring points are sometimes difficult to recognise, or are altogether inaccessible.

To take the length of a femur, for example, as it is exhibited in
the upright position, we place the two condyles flat on the table,
the bone takes its natural direction, and the length required is the
projection comprised between the plane of the table and the plane
which is parallel to it, passing through the highest point of its
head. On the living subject we have no means of obtaining anything of the kind; the head of the femur is out of view in the
cotyloid cavity. Under these circumstances we are obliged to be
satisfied with a different length, and we have recourse to other
points of measurement—below, to the external side of the inter-
articular space; above, to the point of the great trochanter, which
is covered by a thick cushion of cellulo-adipose tissue, and the mass
of fibrous tissue and tendons which have insertion in this tuberosity, and whose consistence can scarcely be distinguished by the
finger from the resistance of the osseous tissues. The same
difficulties, although less in amount, are met with in the wrist, the
elbow, and the shoulder.

In a word, on the living subject we are enabled to make com-
parisons of differences arising from stature, but from bad measuring points; on the skeleton, to take perfect measurements, but to
have no certain term of comparison. Another advantage of the
measurements in the living subject is that they can be taken, by
those interested in the study, in foreign countries, and upon a large
number of individuals.

Anatomists employ both methods. Some, taking care that the
skeleton is properly mounted, give the particular length of each
bone relatively to its height, or to the vertebral column. Others
compare the bones directly together, without taking into account
the height. For our own part we think the arbitrary mode in
which the skeleton is mounted is exaggerated. The disposition of
the articular processes of the vertebræ obliges the preparator to give,
almost unconsciously, the proper thickness to the intervertebral
discs; his sources of error arise entirely from the drying up of the
cartilages on the articular surfaces of these processes, amounting to fifty in the entire column. The skeleton of a gorilla,
one of the tallest ever seen, mounted in America, was 1·650

mètres in height; the animal measured, immediately after death,
1·727 mètres.   Four gorillas were dissected in the Laboratory of
Anthropology, and their skeletons, which were afterwards mounted
by M. Tramont, were less by three centimètres.

These remarks have no reference either to the head or to the
pelvis, whose internal proportions alone we generally study, but
simply to the trunk, the extremities, and their segments.   Let us
now proceed to results, referring the reader to Chapter IV. of
Part II. for a description of the usual methods of proceeding in
taking measurements.

Proportions of the Trunk.

The first element of comparison which it is necessary to know,
is the relative proportion of the trunk to the height of the body.
The length of the trunk can only be measured on the living subject,
but the measuring points differ.   The Americans, in their measurements made on a million individuals during the War of Secession,
chose as boundaries the spinous, or prominent process of the
seventh cervical vertebræ, and the perinæum.   In their four series
of measurements, which were taken with the greatest care, in from
207 to 1,064 individuals, the mean length was from 362 to 394-
thousandths of the stature.   Quételet takes from the clavicles above,
and from the perinæum below ; his mean is about 354-thousandths
of the stature.   In M. Scrizia's statistics, we have taken the interval
between the biacromial line, or width of the shoulders, and the
biischiatic line, or width of the seat; the mean was 352-thou-
sandths.   The length of the trunk in Man would then be more
than one-third, and less than two-fifths of the stature.   In the
anthropoid apes there are less indications.   In a gorilla killed by
Du Chaillu, the distance from the seventh cervical vertebra to the
point of the sacrum was about 440-thousandths of the stature.
In M. Broca's laboratory, we have compared the length from the
seventh cervical vertebra to the point of the sacrum in eleven
skeletons of men, and one of the gorilla.   Its relation to the stature
was 360 in the latter, and varied from 293 to 340-thousandths in

                                                        H 2

the former. The trunk of Man thus estimated would be shorter, but only relatively, because his lower extremities increase his height. We are precluded, from want of space, from giving here the proportions of the thorax, and especially its circumference in Man and the animal.

Grande Envergure.

The relation of the *grande envergure* to the stature deserves our consideration. By the name *grande envergure* we understand the distance from the middle finger of one hand to the middle finger of the other, with the arms extended at full length like a cross. This distance is about six centimetres shorter than that of the sum of the biacromial diameter, and the length of the two extremities, taken in the ordinary way, from the acromion to the middle finger, because, in measuring the limb in an extreme state of abduction, the head of the humerus is buried in the armpit, and the limb is thereby shortened. The *envergure* exceeds the stature, in Man, variously from 0 to 89 parts in the thousand. In a series of 10,876 American soldiers it was as 1·043 to 1·000. In the anthropoid apes, especially the gibbon and the orang, it is considerably greater. Its relation to the height was 1·054 in a gorilla, measured immediately after death, and about 1·428 in a chimpanzee of the bald species. We see in a moment the enormous differences between these and Man.

The proportions of the extremities have been studied by White, Humphry, Lebarzic, Broca, Huxley, Hamy, Weisbach, Quételet, and Gould, in the adult man, and in some animals. We may now proceed to consider them both on the living subject and on the skeleton, but with the drawbacks we have mentioned. The first method for ascertaining the dimensions of the upper extremities, which exhibit the greatest difference between Man and the ape, is the *grande envergure* previously alluded to. The second, still more simple, consists in noticing the exact point to which the extremity of the middle finger reaches in the position of the soldier standing at "attention." This extremity was separated from the upper border of the patella by an interval of from seven to twelve centimetres in the mean results obtained on soldiers of different races in the American army.   According to Mr. Huxley, the hands reach the middle of the thigh in Man, below the knee in the chimpanzee, the middle of the leg in the gorilla, the ankle-bones in the orang, and the ground in the gibbon.   The direct measurements which we are about to mention are preferable.

Proportions of the Extremities.

The relation of the superior to the inferior extremities is different in Man and the anthropoid apes.   It is easily obtained by measurements taken on the living subject, but the measuring points sadly vary among different observers.   It is obtained still better on the dry bones, whose length is added, leaving out the hand and foot, which do not appear the same in the upright posture, the one giving its long axis, and the other only its thickness.   The first figures we quote are those of Mr. Huxley, which have no reference to the stature, but to the entire vertebral column from the atlas to the point of the sacrum = 100.   This is very useful for making the comparison with animals, and especially quadrupeds.[*]   The two men are a European and a Bosjesman, the extremes of the group.

			Superior extremity less the hand.			Inferior extremity less the foot.
2 men	...	...	— 79 ...	...	... 113
1 chimpanzee	...	...	90 ...	...	90
1 gorilla	...	...	... 115 ...	...	... 96
1 orang	...	...	... 113 ...	...	... 89

From this it appears : (1) That the upper extremity is shorter and the lower longer than the vertebral column, while this is the reverse in the anthropoid apes, with the exception of the upper extremity of chimpanzees; (2) That of the two extremities, the upper is shorter and the lower longer in Man, whilst this is the reverse in anthropoids.   But the cases before us are not sufficiently numerous, and the measurement was made upon the mounted skeleton.

[*] " Man's Place in Nature," by T. H. Huxley ; translated into French by E. Dally.   Paris, 1868.

Dr. Humphry[*] has taken his measurements independently, and has made them bear relation, not to the column, but to the entire height of the individuals examined. Of his fifty men half are Europeans and half negroes. His figures show the following results, which exhibit the relation of the added lengths of the humerus and radius to the added lengths of the femur and tibia, the latter being taken as = 100:

						H + R : F + T.
50 men						69·1
4 chimpanzees						103·5
2 gorillas						117·1
2 orangs						141·1

The result is similar to the preceding : the anthropoid apes have the upper extremities longer, and the inferior extremities shorter than Man, but we may still raise the objection that the height taken on the skeleton is not exact. Then we must compare the absolute length of the additional bones directly with each other.

To this end we have measured eighteen anthropoid apes, the largest number upon which any one observer has practised. We will give their measurements together with those made on Man, published by M. Broca.[†] The following table shows the relation of the sum of the humerus and radius to the sum of the femur and tibia, the latter being taken as = 100:

						H + R : F + T.
30 men						69·0
5 gorillas						100·9
9 chimpanzees						108·2
1 orang						140·4

The deductions are the same. Whether, therefore, we compare the measurements in relation to the vertebral column to the height

[*] "A Treatise on the Human Skeleton," by G. M. Humphry. Cambridge, 1858.

[†] "Sur les Proportions du Bras, de l'Avant-Bras, et de la Clavicule, chez les Nègres et les Européens," in "Bull. Soc. d'Anthrop.," vol. iii., 1862 ; and "Sur les Proportions Relatives des Membres Supérieurs et des Membres Inférieurs chez les Nègres et les Européens," in "Bull. Soc. d'Anthrop.," 2nd series, vol. ii., 1867, by Paul Broca ; see also the article "Membres," in "Encycl. des Sciences Médicales," by M. E. Dally, Paris, 1872.

or the absolute measurements, the result is the same. The upper extremity, from the wrist to the shoulder, is shorter in Man, longer in the anthropoid ape, than the lower extremity from the instep to the articulation of the hip. The respective proportions of the two segments which enter into the constitution of each will throw further light on the matter.

Relation of the Radius to the Humerus.

The relation of the radius to the humerus, or of the forearm to the arm, first received attention in 1795, by White, who thus became the founder of osteometry as applied to Man. By measurements made on the living subject, and on the skeleton, he proved that the forearm of the negro is longer than that of the white races. His researches, which had long passed out of notice, were revived by Lawrence in 1817. Mr. Humphry again took up the question in 1858, embraced the lower extremities in his measurements, and extended the comparison between Man and the anthropoid apes. Lastly, in 1862 and in 1867, M. Broca casually touched upon the subject in the two memoirs before referred to.*

There are more or less marked shades of difference in the relative dimensions of the bones of the extremities, and before inquiring into them it is well to bear in mind the general fact. The radius is always smaller than the humerus, and the tibia smaller than the femur in the human skeleton. It is the same in the gorilla and the chimpanzee. The same may be noticed in the tibia of the orang, while the radius is perceptibly equal to the humerus, which proves that the proportions are not the same in all the anthropoids, and differ as in the human races.

The following table gives the relative proportion of the radius to the humerus, 100 being taken as the length of the latter. The first column has been calculated with the measures of Mr. Humphry

* References to books occupy so much space that we can only give the more important ones. The researches of White are to be found in his memoir, p. 14; in Lawrence's work, p. 14; that of Humphry, p. 86; and that of M. Broca, p. 50.

upon the 50 men and the 8 anthropoid apes previously alluded
to, and the second with those of M. Broca upon 30 men of all
races, and with our own upon 18 anthropoid apes:

				Humphry.				Broca and Topinard.
Man	...	...	...	75·1	...	...	...	70·1
Gorilla	...	...	...	77·1	...	...	...	70·8
Chimpanzee	...	...	...	90·1	...	...	...	90·2
Orang	...	...	...	100·0	...	...	...	85·7

Setting aside some differences of detail pertaining to individual
varieties, arising from the mode of proceeding, the general results
agree in both columns. The difference between Man and the ape is
not great, looking at the proportion between the upper and lower
extremity, but it is not the less certain. In questions of proportion
a slight matter materially alters the result. The radius is shorter
compared with the humerus in Man than in the anthropoid ape.
As the number of gorillas and chimpanzees in the two lists amounts
to 22, the question may be regarded as settled so far as they are
concerned. It is less so as regards the three orangs, which, taken
together, show the relative length of the radius to be 95·2, pre-
suming that we regard this bone as longer than in the two other
kinds of anthropoids.

The relative proportion of the tibia to the femur, the latter being
taken as = 100, is given in the following table, in the same subjects
as in the one preceding:

				Humphry.				Broca and Topinard.
Man	...	...	...	83·6	...	...	...	80·6
Gorilla	...	...	...	84·7	...	...	...	77·6
Chimpanzee	...	...	...	84·5	...	...	...	78·7
Orang	...	...	...	86·6	...	...	...	83·7

The results appear to contradict each other. According to those
of Mr. Humphry, the tibia would be shorter than that of the apes.
According to ours, looking at the greater number of gorillas and
chimpanzees, which makes the matter still more decisive, the
human tibia would, on the contrary, be longer, our single orang
being left out of consideration. Some of the differences in these

two lists are probably attributable to the method of calculating, M. Broca and myself having left out the internal malleolus, and Mr. Humphry having probably included it. The main point is that each of us has proceeded in the same way in all the series. We admit that the second segment of the lower extremity is generally shorter in the anthropoid ape, whilst that of the upper is longer. Might not the two conditions be explained in the same way? The leg would be shortened in the ape because his lower extremity is less exclusively employed in progression; his forearm would be lengthened, on the contrary, because the upper extremity, in addition to its function of prehension, contributes to progression.

The relative proportion of the humerus to the femur, the latter taken as = 100, has also been a subject of study. Our figures and those of Mr. Humphry represent it as follows:

	Humphry.	Broca and Topinard.
Man	71·7	70·7
Chimpanzee	90·8	107·5
Gorilla	110·2	118·4
Orang	131·6	123·6

With some minute shades of difference the conclusions arrived at are similar. The humerus is shorter in proportion to the femur in Man, and longer in the anthropoid apes. We may hence infer, by taking into consideration the greater length of the upper arm in the anthropoids, and the greater length also of the radius, that the two bones contribute, each in its degree, to the lengthening of the whole limb in these animals.

Thus a long humerus, a still longer radius, a short femur, a still shorter tibia, such are simian characters, the more human being the very reverse.

The relation of the foot and the hand to the stature, or to the rest of the corresponding limb, can only be examined on the living subject. Later on we shall give their relative lengths in the human races, the term of comparison failing us as regards the anthropoid apes. But, for want of a better, we shall give the

measurements relatively to stature taken on the skeleton by Mr.
Humphry :

				Hand.				Foot.
Man	...	...	...	11·82	...	...	...	16·86
Gorilla	...	...	...	14·54	...	...	...	20·50
Chimpanzee	...	...	...	18·00	...	...	...	21·00
Orang	...	...	...	20·88	...	...	...	26·00

The foot and the hand are thus shown to become larger as we
pass from Man to the anthropoids, and progressively so in the three
mentioned above. We shall say nothing of the relation of the
clavicle to the humerus, concerning which but little has been
recorded.

Such are the primary results with regard to the comparative
proportions of Man and anthropoids. Can we say anything further
as to the near affinity of one of them to Man?

The question is only doubtful as between the gorilla and the chimpanzee. In every instance recorded in our list the orang occupies
the most remote position, except as regards the tibia in the single
case in our list which the two cases of Mr. Humphry nullify. The
gorilla has the whole of the upper extremity, including the radius
and the hand, more human, while in the chimpanzee the resemblance
is only as regards the humerus and tibia. In considering only the
two upper segments, each seems to have an advantage in its
way, the gorilla by his shorter forearm, the chimpanzee by his
shorter arm. The length of the upper extremity and of the hand
have, however, the greater weight in the balance, and we should give
it in favour of the gorilla. But in the long bones, as well as in
the vertebral column and skull, there are characters besides the
dimensions which as yet have been but little studied. Only to take
one example : the greater obliquity of the femur, the greater angle
which its neck makes with the diaphysis, and the comparative
slenderness of the entire bone give the advantage to the chimpanzee
and especially to the koolokamba species. It is indisputable that
the proportions of the skeleton are very different in the four kinds
of apes, although in their general type there may be much similarity.
We will say more: they differ even in the species of one and the

same genus; which it behoves us to consider, when, during the
prosecution of these studies, we shall have more subjects at our
command. We shall consider this relation of the anthropoid apes
in general, as well as of men in general at a future time.

CHAPTER III.

MUSCLES—ORGANS OF SENSE—VISCERA—LARYNX—GENITAL ORGANS
—NERVOUS SYSTEM—BRAIN : ITS STRUCTURE, CONVOLUTIONS,
WEIGHT—RUDIMENTARY ORGANS AND REVERSIVE ANOMALIES.

THE study of the muscles naturally follows that of the skeleton.
Their arrangement throughout the whole mammalian series is
dependant on configuration, and on the various functions of
movement. In no part of the organism is there to be found a
more palpable demonstration of the great physiological law that
" use makes the organ," than in the wasting away of those parts
which are not in use, and the hypertrophy of those constantly at
work. Nevertheless the type varies somewhat : the muscles are
the same, but at one part a muscular fasciculus becomes strong or
is reduced to a mere vestige ; at another a portion is detached, or
subdivided, or its insertions are a little nearer or a little farther off.
The muscles of the monkey are so like those of Man, that up to
the fifteenth century, descriptions of them absolutely took the place
of the latter. We are indebted to André Vesalius for having
shown that the dissections of Galen were never carried on but upon
monkeys. The resemblance is still more perfect in the anthropoid
apes.

We shall confine ourselves to mentioning some of the differences
which we find among anthropoids. The cutaneous muscle which
is so developed in the majority of mammalia, as well as in the
ordinary monkeys, for the purpose of contracting the skin, is
concentrated in the cervical region in the anthropoid apes, where

Its size is almost equal to that of Man. The whole of the cervical muscles, whose development in quadrupeds and in the inferior monkeys is in proportion to the necessity of maintaining the head in the horizontal position, have merely an importance in the anthropoid apes and in Man, commensurate with the oblique attitude in the former and the upright in the latter.

The trachelo-acromialis muscle of Cuvier, which is met with in many of the mammalia, and especially in monkeys, is wanting in Man, as well as in the gorilla and the chimpanzee; it seems to be merely a supplement to the elevator scapulæ, which Man possesses also.

The great rectus abdominis muscle, which has generally four aponeurotic intersections in mammalia (Cuvier), and seven in the cynocephali, has but five in man, in the chimpanzee, and in the gorilla. It is said that the anthropoid apes have a long abductor of the great toe more than Man, but it is merely a fasciculus of the tibialis anticus muscle. It is also said that they have a short extensor of the great toe, and an extensor digitorum with three tendons instead of four as in Man; but it is a misinterpretation of the same fact. The extensor of monkeys is in reality the counterpart of the same muscle so irregular in Man. So with regard to the black chimpanzee. It is said to have no proper extensor indicis. Two chimpanzees in M. Brown's laboratory, however, had it.

Nevertheless, between Man and the anthropoid apes there are differences, though they are but slight. The situation and the insertions of the pectoralis minor vary in the two groups, and in that of the inferior monkeys; but these variations are less recognised between the two former than between the anthropoid apes and the group next to them. The short flexor of the thumb, so powerful in Man, in anthropoids is atrophied, and blended with the deep flexor of the fingers, which is connected with the index. A tendon of this last, in the gorilla, is inserted into the thumb, and assists in the movement of flexion. The same tendon in the orang and the gibbon is furnished by the adductor of the thumb.

In place of the proper extensor of the index and of the extensor of the little finger, the orang and the ordinary monkeys have only one muscle, with four tendons supplying the four fingers, not taking into consideration the common extensor of the fingers in either case.

In the foot the differences are not so great. The great toe, on whose pretended movement of opposition an entirely erroneous system has been based, is supplied by the same muscles as in Man. Nevertheless, owing to its more lateral insertion into the metatarsus, it is found that the long lateral peroneal muscle contributes partially to its flexion.

The transverse adductor of the great toe, rudimentary in Man, is well developed in monkeys. The flexors of the toes differ somewhat in Man, and in the anthropoids; but what the movements gain in force and extent in the latter, they lose in independence and precision in the former. In the orang the long flexor of the great toe is entirely wanting.

The sole muscular peculiarity by which the anthropoid is really separated from Man and is brought into closer affinity with the ordinary monkeys, is the existence in the arm of a fasciculus called the accessory of the latissimus dorsi, which does not exist in Man, and is inserted superiorly into the tendon of the latissimus dorsi, and inferiorly into the head of the humerus. It has also been observed in a rudimentary state in some negroes. Two features of the muscular system have been noticed as distinctive of Man and animals, especially monkeys. These are the prominence of the buttocks and of the calves of the legs, owing to the development of the gluteal muscles and of the triceps, to which is due the strength of the tendo achillis. Such is the fact, and is a result of the biped attitude. The use of the gluteal muscles especially is to keep the thigh extended upon the pelvis. But in both respects the gorilla, casts of whose muscles have been taken from the subject, and reproduced in pasteboard by M. Auzou, is unquestionably more favoured than some negroes.

Moreover all the minute, or at least the more important points, which seem peculiar to the anthropoid, are found from time to time in Man, and especially in the negro race. M. Chudzinski, preparator to the laboratory of the École des hautes Études, has already published two excellent memoirs upon this subject.[*]

Organs of Sense.

In these is included the cutaneous envelope which surrounds the body, protects it against external agencies, and is the seat of the function of touch.

One of the characters which distinguish the class of mammalia from that of birds, fishes, and reptiles, is the presence of hair upon the body. De Blainville proposed to substitute for his designation that of *pilifera*. Some, however, have the skin naked, as certain cetacea. The characteristic of man proposed by Linnæus, therefore, is anything but a correct one: *homo nudus et tacrnts*. Man really has hair not only on the head, on the face, under the armpits, and on the pubis, but over the whole of the body, and in certain races quite a thick crop on the chest, behind the shoulders, and on the limbs, resembling down, and masking the colour of the skin. The history of Esau is a most probable one. Compared with the majority of mammalia, and in particular of monkeys, Man is the least hairy; the palms of his hands and the soles of his feet are alone without hair, which is to be accounted for by its having worn away.

The smooth and indurated surfaces on the buttocks, called *callosités fessières* in the pithecians, are wanting in the anthropoid apes, with the exception of certain gibbons, as well as in the cebians and lemurs.

The nails, claws, and hoofs of mammalia are a secretion from the skin, like hair and horns. The presence of flat nails, not bent round, on the fingers and toes, has been given as a characteristic of Man. We must, therefore, associate the anthropoids with him. The orang alone forms a partial exception, having no nail on the great toe. Flat nails are found in the pithecians; they are bent

---

[*] "Contribution à l'Anatomie du Nègre et Nouvelles Observations sur le Système Musculaire du Nègre," by T. Chudzinski, in the "Revue d'Anthropologie," vols. ii. and iii.

round into claws in the cynocephali; the flat nail and the transition to the claw are seen simultaneously in others. The ouistitis, some other cebians, and the arctopithecians have claws, except on the great toe. In lemurs it is the reverse; the claw is found on the great toe, and nails on the other toes.

The arrangement of the wrinkles and of the corpuscles of Paccini in the palm of the hand has reference to the function of touch.

In Man, there are two principal wrinkles in the hand, one produced by the flexion of the last three fingers, the other by the flexion of the thumb, and passing round the eminence, *thénar*; a third, which is variable, and between the two, is joined at its external extremity with the latter, and is free, and nearly parallel with the former at its internal extremity. According to M. Alix, the fold of the thumb is wanting in the monkey tribe, and the other two are united to form one. The fact is evident in the three inferior groups, but doubtful as regards the first. If some anthropoids exhibit in consequence of this an inferior simian arrangement, Man is exceptionally in the same position. The corpuscles of Paccini, or tactile corpuscles, are little bodies situated in the direction of the nervous filaments of the palmar surface of the hand and fingers, and of the plantar surface of the foot. M. Nepveu has shown that their appearance under the microscope is alike in Man and the chimpanzee, whilst it is somewhat different in the common monkey, the baboon, and the sajou.

The organ of vision is similar in Man, the anthropoid apes, the pithecians, and the cebians. But in many lemurs, the fundus of the eye assumes a glittering appearance, which in the cat and the ox has received the name of tapetum. A little muscular fasciculus also exists, analogous to the musculus choanoides found in the majority of quadrupeds.

The nose, anatomically the same in Man and the monkey tribe, presents merely morphological changes. Sometimes projecting in the former, in a less degree however than in the nasices, one of the pithecians, it is at other times more or less flat, as in the generality of monkeys. The nostrils are usually directed downwards, as in the anthropoid apes and pithecians, and sometimes sideways, as in cabines; two arrangements which have suggested to Geoffroy Saint-Hilaire his division of monkeys into catarrhini and platyrrhini. The septum is comparatively thin in the catarrhini, and thick at the anterior triangular border in the platyrrhini. The cartilage of the ear, whose form and length are so variable in different mammals, is monkeys is usually strong, having no fold behind; it is sometimes square above, and rounded off, and is without a lobule. These arrangements are occasionally found in Man. On the other hand, the ears of the gorilla and the chimpanzee are often as well folded as those of Man.

The pithecians have two pouches, named abajoue, which open in the mouth — the anthropoids, like Man, having nothing of the kind.

Viscera.

The length of the alimentary canal is about six times the length of the body, or about eleven mètres, according to M. Sappey. In carnivora it varies from two to eight times, and in solipeds and ruminants from ten to twenty-eight times; in monkeys it is from five to eight times, in the gibbon about eight.

The stomach of all the monkey tribe is simple as in Man. The semnopithecians and the colobians are exceptions; their stomach if not multiple, is at least multilocular, resembling the herbivora in this respect. The commencement of the large intestine, or caecum, lies in the right iliac fossa, as in Man, and is covered in front by the peritoneum. In pithecians, the caecum is, on the contrary, enveloped by the peritoneum, which forms one of the folds of the mesentery behind, and is designed for the purpose of facilitating the mobility of that part of the intestine. In the anthropoid the peritoneum surrounds the caecum, as in Man.

An appendix, the vermicular, is annexed to the human caecum. It exists also in anthropoid apes, but is wanting in the monkeys below them, with the exception of some lemurs.

The liver of Man has, properly speaking, only two lobes; in anthropoid apes it is similar. In the other monkeys, on the contrary, it is very much subdivided, as in the lion and the rabbit.

M. Broca in his memoir, "Sur les Primates," has drawn attention to the variations of the peritoneum, the serous membrane which is reflected round the organs in the abdominal cavity, and has for its object to isolate them, and to allow them to glide smoothly upon one another. His opinion is, that the arrangement of the peritoneum does not perceptibly differ in Man and the anthropoid apes, whilst in passing to the pithecians it immediately exhibits marked differences.

The distinction of mammals into bipeds and quadrupeds may to a certain extent be recognised by the arrangement of their internal organs. The marked peculiarity of the peritoneum in its relation to the cæcum may be specially mentioned. In the chest we see differences of the same description.

The pericardium, or membrane surrounding the heart, is to this organ what the peritoneum is to the intestines. In Man it is altogether separated from the sternum and is attached to the diaphragm, a transverse muscular septum which separates the thorax from the abdominal cavity. In quadrupeds it is firmly fixed to the sternum and to the articulations of the ribs, and is not attached to the diaphragm. In the former, indeed, the heart lies on the diaphragm, in the latter on the sternum, in accordance with the attitude of the animal. In monkeys the arrangement is intermediate; in lemurs the pericardium does not adhere to the diaphragm except to a very limited extent; in cebians and pithecians the surface attachment increases in size. In the anthropoid apes the pericardium is as in Man. Similar changes occur in the direction of the heart, in the length of the vena cava inferior, and in the curve of the aorta near its origin.

In quadrupeds a result of the non-attachment of the heart to the diaphragm, is the interposition between the two of a lobule of the right lung. This lobule, known by the name of impar, exists throughout the whole mammalian series, from the marsupialia to the carnivora, and is wanting in Man. In the lemurians and the cebians it is also developed. In the pithecians it becomes less; in the gibbons it is almost nil; in the orang, the chimpanzee, and the gorilla there is not the slightest trace of it.

H

From the viscera we now pass to the vessels, where we shall always find a confirmation of the same fact—namely, that the organisation of anthropoids is a counterpart of that of Man, and differs widely from that of the other simian groups. We shall say a few words respecting the larynx and the organs of reproduction before entering upon a study of the very highest importance—that of the brain.

The Larynx.

The larynx, or organ of voice, is at the upper extremity of the windpipe, where the glottis is situated, through which the air is respired. It is composed, like the trachea, of cartilages, though much larger. The two principal ones are the cricoid below and the thyroid above. It is closed at certain moments by another cartilage, which acts like a valve, and is called the epiglottis. In all essential points this little apparatus is identical throughout the entire mammalian series, and notably in that of monkeys.

Upon four points of its extent—that is to say, below the cricoid, between it and the thyroid, between the thyroid and the epiglottis, and between the vocal chords—are seen occasionally dilatations or ampullæ, which have considerable importance in anthropoid apes; some median and single—giving rise to three primary anatomical varieties — others lateral and double, forming a fourth. The first, or tracheal variety of dilatation, is observed in the horse, the ass, and in the conito, one of the monkeys of the cebian group; the second in two other kinds of cebians; the third in a lemur, a cebian, two pithecians, and a gibbon. The fourth variety exists in a rudimentary state in Man under the name of *arrière-cavité*, or ventricle of the larynx,* and attains with age, in the three higher anthropoids, an enormous development, especially in the male, and is known in them under the name of air sac. In a young chimpanzee dissected by M. Broca, it formed

* M. Sappey described it under the name of *portion verticale* of the ventricles of the larynx. It is situated, he says, at the upper border of the thyroid cartilage, close to the hyoid bone, and in rarer instances reaches to the base of the tongue, and extends under its mucous membrane.

two little lateral projections about the size of a pea, which over-
lapped above the superior border of the thyroid. In the adult
gorilla and orang the projections become larger, and run under
the sterno-mastoid muscles, under the trapezius, envelop the

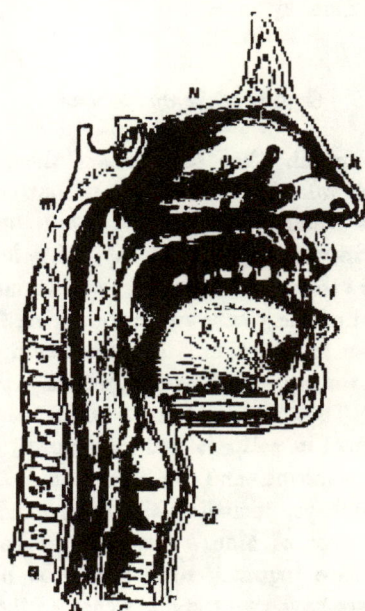

Fig. 24.—Vertical and antero-posterior section of the face and neck : a, Bodies of the
cervical vertebræ : n, Basilar process, or body of the occipital bone ; u, Floor of
the anterior cerebral fossæ ; o, p, q, Superior middle and inferior shells of the nasal
fossæ ; t, Arch of the palate ; f, Velum of the palate ; k, Genio-glossi muscles of
the tongue, attached in front to the tubercles genii, situated at the posterior surface
of the lower jaw ; b, Œsophagus ; e, Trachea ; d, Thyroid cartilage ; c, Epiglottis ;
r, Os hyoides, serving as a point of attachment for important muscles of the tongue
and larynx. The transverse slit which is seen in the latter, and whose borders form
the vocal chords, is the ventricle of the larynx, into which the ventricle of
Morgagni opens

clavicle, and reach down to the armpits. They are, in fact,
veritable hernia. In a morphological point of view, these singular organs establish an important difference between Man and
the anthropoids in question ; but, in an anatomical point of
view, the difference is nil ; it is the same organ, only of a dif-

ferent size. We may add, lastly, that the true air sac is absolutely wanting in all the other apes, so that this, which appears to establish a character between Man and the anthropoid, shows, on the contrary, their relationship, and the distance of the latter from others of the monkey tribe.

Organs of Reproduction.

The characters which they furnish are those to which we attach the greatest value in the various departments of natural history; the class mammalia is, indeed, based upon them. All mammalia are viviparous—that is to say, bring forth their young alive—and all have teats. These glands vary in number, generally being equal to that of the young which they bring forth at a birth, and they vary also in situation. The cat has 8; the bitch, 10; the agouti, 14; woman, 2, although generally she has but one child at a birth. They are abdominal in the carnivora and the marsupialia; inguinal in solipeds and ruminants; and pectoral in the woman, the elephant, and the lamantin. In this twofold point of view, monkeys, including the anthropoid apes, are constructed after the type of Man. Many lemurs have four teats—two pectoral and two inguinal, some macaucos having four pectoral; all the others have two teats, attached to the breast.

Among mammalia, a few, as the marsupials, have no placenta—that is to say, an intermediate fleshy substance between the embryo and the uterus; others have one, called *en zone*, when it occupies a considerable surface of the internal parietes of the uterus, or *en disque* when it occupies only a small portion. Man, the monkey tribe, the rodentia, the insectivora, and the cheiroptera belong to this category. There is some difference between them however. In Man the placenta is single, and the umbilical cord is composed of one vein and two arteries. In ceblans it is still single, but it is furnished with two veins and two arteries. In pithecians it is double; it has, however, only one cord, formed of one vein and two arteries. In which arrangement do the anthropoids approach to them? The gibbon, which usually holds the transitional position between them and the pithecians, has, like them, a double placenta. In the chimpanzee, on the contrary, it is single, as in Man (Owen). The orang and the gorilla have not been examined on this point.

After the descent of the testis into the scrotum in Man, the peritoneal communication is obliterated; in other mammalia it is persistent. Nothing is yet known as to this in anthropoids. The same may be said with regard to quadrupeds generally. The uterus in them has two cornua, and is divided into two cavities. That of woman is, as a rule, unilocular; that of ordinary monkeys holds a middle position.

Nervous System.

In the Invertebrata it is composed of little masses of gray substance interspersed through the viscera, and attached to them by nervous filaments. In the Vertebrata there is, in addition, another and a symmetrical apparatus, consisting of an axis, called the cerebro-spinal, of centrifugal nerves for movements, and of centripetal for impressions. The essential differences between them are to be found at the superior or anterior extremity of the axis or encephalon, which we shall first describe as it exists in Man.

The spinal cord, called medulla oblongata at the level of the first cervical vertebra, passes through the occipital foramen, beneath the transverse fibres which unite the two lobes of the cerebellum under the name of pons varolii, and divides into two fasciculi called the cerebral peduncles, one to the right the other to the left; they then spread out into two fan-like expansions of white fibres, pass upwards and outwards, bend down at the borders like a mushroom about its stalk, and go to form the cerebral hemispheres, on the surface of which is a layer of gray substance. The white portion is the conducting matter, the gray the sentient and reacting. At the internal contiguous borders of the hemispheres the white transverse fibres become bound together to form the corpus callosum. Each is surrounded by a canal, forming a series of cavities, of which the principal are the lateral ventricles, which exhibit three cornua : the anterior or frontal cornu, the inferior or temporo-sphenoidal, and the posterior or occipital—the last presenting an elevation on its floor called hippocampus minor.

The encephalon consists of (1) The cerebellum ; (2) The portion lying between its two lobes connecting the medulla oblongata with the brain—the pons varolii, or protuberantia annularis ; (3) The brain proper, formed by the peduncles and the series of expansions which proceed from them—viz. the tubercula quadrigemina, the optic thalami, and the corpora striata—by the ventricles, and by the cerebral hemispheres, the surface of which exhibits sinuosities.

The principal sinuosities are called convolutions, and the secondary ones, folds. The external surface of the brain occupied by these is divided into distinct portions or lobes by fissures, and the convolutions of which these lobes are composed, by sulci. The communications between the lobes are called transition convolutions (plis de passage), and those between one convolution and another in the same lobe, anastomoses.

From the base of the encephalon arise the first twelve pairs of nerves, or encephalic nerves. The first are the olfactory, the bulbous portion of which—called the olfactory bulb—lies longitudinally in a depression on the surface of the anterior lobe ; the second are the optic, whose decussation at the median line is called the chiasma.

When we place the encephalon on its upper or convex surface, and remove the cerebellum and pons varolii by a transverse section passing between the junction of the latter with the cerebral peduncles, the whole inferior surface of the two hemispheres is exposed to view (Fig. 15). At the junction of the anterior third with the posterior two-thirds is seen a deep transverse fissure, with its concavity looking backwards. This is the fissure of Sylvius (A, Fig. 15). The portion in front is the inferior surface of the frontal or anterior lobe ; that behind is the inferior surface of the posterior lobe, which is separated into two well-marked and unequal portions, the one with its convexity looking forwards and outwards, which is the inferior region of the tempora-

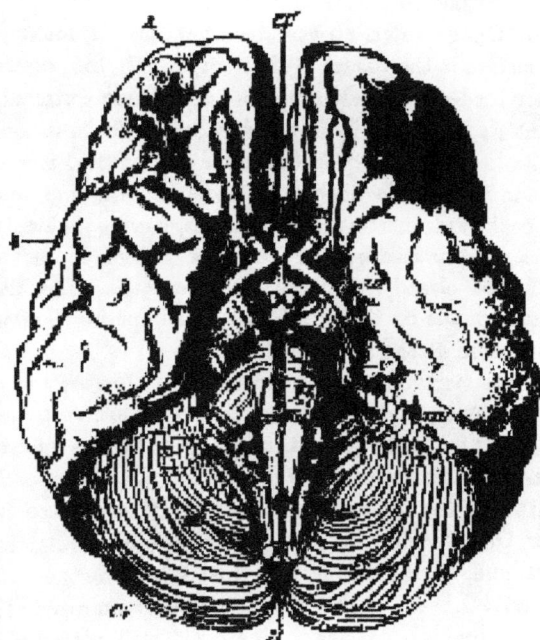

Fig. 16.—Inferior surface of the encephalon: A, Anterior or frontal lobe; B, Temporo-sphenoidal portion of the posterior lobe: A and B are separated by a fissure with its convexity looking backwards—the fissure of Sylvius; C b, Cerebellum; M, Section of the spinal cord, where it joins the medulla oblongata; VI, Annular protuberance—at its anterior border are seen the two cerebral peduncles; CC, Corpus callosum—the dotted line is on the median or inter-hemispherical line; I to XII, The twelve pairs of encephalic nerves at their origin; I, Olfactory nerve with its bulb; II, Optic nerve, the union of which with that of the opposite side forms the chiasma; III, IV, VI, Nerves of motion of the globe of the eye; V, Trigeminal, or fifth, supplying the muscles of expression; XII, Hypoglossal nerve, the nerve of motion of the tongue.

sphenoidal lobe, the other, posterior or concave, upon which the cerebellum lies.

The superior or convex surface of the hemisphere may be viewed from above or laterally, the plates sometimes representing them

under one aspect, sometimes under another. We prefer the latter
method. Each hemisphere has an internal surface, which looks
towards the median line, and an external.

The first thing which strikes the attention on looking at the
external surface is the fissure of Sylvius, which has passed round
the inferior border of the hemisphere, and whose external surface
is shown at A, Fig. 16. It is divided into two branches, which
unite in the form of a V. The anterior and vertical is very short,
and is lost in the anterior lobe; the posterior is longer, and passes
obliquely backwards and a little upwards, having below it a large
elongated and very distinct cerebral lobe, which is the temporo-
sphenoidal lobe already seen from underneath. The fissure of
Sylvius corresponds on the skull with the superior border of the
squamous portion of the temporal (*Broca*).

There is no mark of equal importance to this on the external
surface of the brain, and it is asked how we contrive to make any
other fundamental division. It is, however, in the midst of the
sulci, apparently so complicated, that we take the fissure of Rolando
(B, Fig. 16) as the line of separation of this surface into the
anterior or frontal, and the posterior or parieto-occipital lobe. It
is constant, and, in the fœtus, the most clearly defined after the
fissure of Sylvius. Its situation and direction are nearly the same
in all healthy brains. It commences some millimètres above the
fissure of Sylvius, and passes vertically, or rather a little obliquely,
backwards, reaching to within a few millimètres of the superior
border of the hemisphere. Its obliquity and its situation are
indicated by the two following relations: The total length of the
brain being reckoned as 100, the portion in front is to that behind
as 43·0 to 57·0 at the inferior extremity of the sulcus, and as 56·3
to 43·7 at its superior. It follows from this that the middle portion should be equidistant from the two extremities of the
hemisphere. M. Hamy calculates that the inclination of the
sulcus in the adult is about 70 degrees.

Gratiolet thought that the fissure of Rolando corresponds exactly,
on the skull, with the coronal suture. M. Broca was the first to
notice that, in the European, it is always from 40 to 56 millimètres

behind it at its upper part, 47 in the middle, and 15 at the lower part.[*]

A second fissure marks another division of the external surface of the hemispheres—namely, the external perpendicular fissure (E E, Fig. 10). It separates the posterior lobe into two, the parietal and the occipital lobe, and on the skull answers to the lambdoidal suture, being distant from it about two millimètres. In order to discover it, the student should look for it from its prolongation on the floor of the hemisphere, to a few centimètres from the posterior extremity, where it takes the name of internal perpendicular fissure. It is so called because it exactly separates, from below upwards, the most remote part of the hemisphere, to form of it an occipital lobe.

We have then (1) An anterior or frontal lobe, bounded behind by the fissure of Rolando; (2) A middle or parietal lobe, included between the latter and the external perpendicular fissure; (3) A posterior or occipital lobe, situated behind the perpendicular fissure; and (4) An inferior or temporo-sphenoidal lobe, subjacent to the long branch of the fissure of Sylvius. Such are the important divisions on the external surface of the hemispheres. We shall now describe those of the internal surface, as well as its convolutions.

Convolutions.

The acts of transmission in the brain, which have reference to altogether voluntary movements, to certain reflex movements, to sensations, or to certain phases of intellectual operations, have for their seat the fibres of which the central white mass of the hemispheres is formed. The initiative acts of thought pass, on the contrary, through the gray substance which constitutes the cortical portion of these hemispheres. Consequently, the greater the amount of gray substance, and of surface upon which it can be developed in a continuous layer, the more power the truly intellectual phenomena acquire. To this end, the surface is folded and

[*] "Sur la Déformation Toulousaine de Crâne," by Paul Broca, in "Bull. Soc. d'Anthrop.," 2nd series, vol. vi., 1871.

contorted, so as to increase its extent. Such is the office of the convolutions, elongated and tortuous swellings, separated by sulci more or less deep. It was long thought that their arrangement was inextricable and the result of mere chance. This is an error: the complexity is only apparent. They consist of fundamental parts, or convolutions, properly so called, whose type is constant throughout the human series; and of secondary parts or folds, which exhibit variations between one individual and another, similar to those which the features of the countenance present. The brain of the fœtus at the beginning is smooth. The fissures appear first, then the sulci. At the seventh month the convolutions are simple but formed; at birth it is the same with the folds. At a later period the whole is completed. The convolutions become enlarged and more complex as age advances, in proportion to the activity which the organ exhibits. A convolution would be rectilinear in a subject of tolerable intelligence, as in the patient of Bicêtre, whose brain we have now before us. In another subject of superior intelligence it would be tortuous, double, and altered in form, by the pressure of neighbouring redundant convolutions. The sulci would be hidden, and the anastomosis between one convolution and another, in a rudimentary state in the former, while in the latter it would be considerable, and would cause a change in the configuration of the primary convolution. This, which is called the richness of the convolutions—that is to say, their development in number and tortuosity, causes not only an absolute increase in the quantity of these convolutions, but also a reduction in size of each of them taken singly. Large and simple convolutions are thus a sign of idiocy, or of weak intellect, in any man. Small convolutions with numerous foldings are a sign of large intellectual capacity.

However, by carefully studying the brains of monkeys, of the fœtus, of infants, and of idiots with simple convolutions, all this is explained. Desmoulins first drew attention to this subject.[*] The imaginative fancies of phrenologists, and some recent results in reference to the localisation of the faculties, have given it a

* "Anatomie du Système Nerveux," by A. Desmoulins, vol. ii., 1825.

new direction. Now, thanks to the labours of Gratiolet, Owen, Turner, Bischoff, Broca, and Ecker, it has been made clear. All that we must do is to turn it to account in studying the science of comparative intellectual phenomena.*

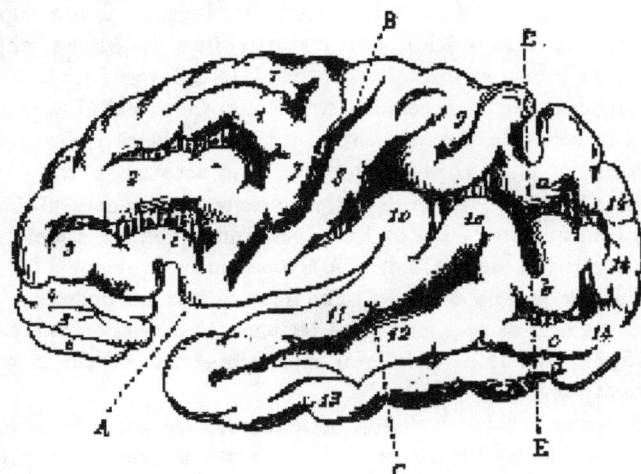

FIG. 16.—Diagram of the external surface of the brain: A, Fissure of Sylvius; B, Fissure of Rolando; C, Parallel sulcus; D, Interparietal sulcus; E, External perpendicular fissure.

1, First antero-posterior frontal convolution, double; 2, Second frontal convolution; 3, Third frontal convolution; 4, 5, 6, Convolutions of the orbital region of the frontal lobe; 7, Ascending frontal, or ascending anterior convolution; 8, Ascending parietal, or ascending posterior convolution; 9, Superior parietal convolution; 10, Inferior parietal convolution, or curved fold; 11, 12, First and second temporo-sphenoidal convolutions; B, Third temporo-sphenoidal convolution in continuation with the third temporo-sphenoidal of the internal surface; 14, The three stages of the occipital lobe; a and b, First and second plis de passage, uniting the two parietal convolutions with the occipital lobe; c and d, Third and fourth plis de passage, uniting the last two temporo-sphenoidal convolutions with the occipital lobe; e, Gyrus, belonging to the third transverse frontal convolution.

The external or convex surface of the brain (Figs. 16 and 18), looked at in profile, is that from which we shall commence our description of the convolutions. We shall consider first the fissure

* "Sur la Structure des Circonvolutions." See "Recherches sur la Structure de la Couche Corticale des Circonvolutions," by M. Baillarger, in "Mém. Acad. de Médecine," 1840, vol. viii, and the article "Cerveau," in the "Dictionnaire Encycl. des Sciences Médicales."

of Sylvius—that is to say, its base, and the parts below and above.
The base only deserves mention as regards the point of the V.
By separating the two lips at this point we discover a well-marked
tubercle, called insula of Reil, and also central lobule, because it is
situated in the exact line of the cerebral peduncles; it is occupied
by five or six shallow folds, which radiate from its inferior angle.
The region below, or temporo-sphenoidal lobe, forms a large mass,
obliquely directed from below upwards, and from behind forwards,
and is traversed in the same way by a sulcus, which is parallel to
the fissure of Sylvius, and which on that account is called the
parallel sulcus (C). From its posterior extremity a small *cul-de-sac*
passes to the centre of the parietal lobe, and sometimes a prolongation towards the occipital lobe. A second sulcus is observed below,
but of much less importance. The intermediate enlargements are
termed the first, second, and third tempero-sphenoidal convolutions
(11, 12, 13), the third or inferior appertaining also to the inferior
surface of the brain.

The region above includes both the frontal and the parietal
lobes, separated by the fissure of Rolando, whose two lips form two
of the most distinct convolutions of the whole system of the
external surface. Having the same direction as the sulcus which
separates them, one belongs to the frontal lobe and takes the name
of anterior ascending convolution (7), the other to the parietal lobe,
and is called the posterior ascending convolution (8).

The frontal lobe, so important in Man, since it is in it that
his highest faculties reside, consists of three regions; one, which
we shall find on the external surface; a second, which is seen
on the inferior; and a third, the most important of all. The
second rests upon the roof of the orbit, and comprises three or four
small convolutions of but little interest: one bound up between
the sulcus of the olfactory nerve and the internal border of the
hemisphere, and which forms the termination of the first frontal
convolution; the other two being in continuation, in the same
way, with the two frontals on the external surface.

The frontal region proper of the anterior lobe comprises four
convolutions: an anterior or frontal ascending, already mentioned,

and three longitudinal and parallel, superposed in three storeys.
The first, or superior frontal convolution, arises by one, and sometimes by two roots from the superior extremity of the ascending,
becomes double, skirts the superior border of the hemisphere, and
is lost in the orbital region.   The second, or middle frontal convolution, arises also behind, by one root, and bifurcates occasionally
to give an anastomosis to two adjoining frontal convolutions.   The
posterior part of the sulcus, which separates it from the third, corresponds, according to M. Broca, to the curved temporal line of the
parietal.   The third, or inferior frontal convolution, commences in
the most sloping portion of the ascending frontal, forms a large
gyrus round the small branch of the fissure of Sylvius, and loses
itself in front.

M. Broca's way of looking at it is somewhat different.   He
merely brings in the ascending frontal convolution to assist in the
description.   According to him there are only three frontal convolutions, all antero-posterior and parallel, including, at the back, the
portion of the ascending convolution where each takes its origin,
which must not be forgotten when discussing the localisation of the
faculty of language.   We know indeed that there is aphasia—that
is to say, loss of speech; or aphemia—that is to say, loss of speech
with preservation of the intellect, whenever an acute lesion occurs
at the posterior part of the third frontal convolution of Broca when
this lesion is on the left side.   The faculty of language has its seat
on both sides, but it is put in exercise from this side in the greater
number of cases.   Its surface has a vertical extent of about four
centimètres, and an antero-posterior of from two to three and a half.
Its form is that of a quadrilateral, bounded in front by the small
branch of the fissure of Sylvius, and behind by the base of the
fissure of Rolando.   Its centre corresponds, on the external part of
the skull, with a point situated about one centimètre and a half
behind the coronal suture, and three centimètres above the pterion.*

* "Sur le Siége de la Faculté du Langage Articulé," by P. Broca, in
" Bull. Soc. d'Anthrop.," Paris, 1861 ; and " Sur la Topographie Cérébrale,
ou sur les Rapports Anatomiques du Crâne et du Cerveau," by the same, in
" Revue d'Anthrop.," vol. v., 1876.

The next, or parietal lobe, included between the border of the hemisphere above, the fissure of Sylvius, and the temporo-sphenoidal lobe below, and the perpendicular fissure behind, is formed by three convolutions. The first, or posterior, ascending, has been described. The second, or superior parietal convolution (9), commences by one or two roots towards the middle and superior portion of the posterior ascending, describes a number of vertical flexures which reach to the superior border of the hemisphere, and form a small lobule, which is very easily recognised. The third is below, and is separated from it by a transverse sulcus, called the interparietal sulcus (D); it arises at the inferior part of the posterior ascending, in the angle which it makes with the fissure of Sylvius, turns round the end of this and ends in a group of vertical flexures, which anastomose, sometimes with the first, sometimes with the second temporo-sphenoidal convolution, and sometimes with both. This is the inferior parietal convolution, or curved fold of Gratiolet (10), so called because the fold embraces in a simple or complex gyrus, not only the termination of the fissure of Sylvius, but also that of the parallel sulcus. Another arrangement is found. The termination of this parallel sulcus is bifurcated, and its posterior branch reaches the external perpendicular fissure, which it leaps over to become one of the transverse sulci of the occipital lobe. In this case, the gyrus which the curved fold forms is persistent; but it goes to form what we shall presently call the second transition convolution, without anastomosing with the second temporo-sphenoidal convolution. M. Gratiolet has described on the side of the inferior parietal convolution, a superior marginal fold, and an inferior marginal fold, which are merely the folds bordering the extremity of the fissure of Sylvius. The former, indeed, is the part of the inferior parietal convolution, which extends from its junction with the posterior ascending convolution, to the end of the fissure, and the latter is the continuation of the first temporo-sphenoidal convolution. The increased size of the flexures is of little importance, inasmuch as they constantly vary.

The occipital lobe, the smallest of all, is formed of three storeys, which are bounded by two antero-posterior sulci. The external perpendicular fissure separates it from the parietal lobe, and from the temporo-sphenoidal lobe; a fissure somewhat difficult to trace out in Man, because it is partly filled up, or hidden by four folds of communication with the adjoining lobes, whose study affords considerable interest under the name of *plis de passage*, or transition convolutions (*a, b, c,* and *d*). The first, or superior, of Gratiolet, comes from the superior parietal convolution; the second, or inferior, from the inferior parietal; the third, lower down, from the second temporo-sphenoidal convolution; and the fourth, concealed at the inferior border of the brain by the third temporo-sphenoidal convolution.

We shall say but little as to the internal surface of the hemisphere, which is in apposition with the falx cerebri on the median line (Fig. 17). When we harden and dry a brain by M. Broca's process (nitric acid),[*] the organ shrinks more in the transverse direction, and that which formed the concave part of the interior surface behind, appears, when looking at it sideways, to form part of the internal surface. We shall study in this way the two surfaces united.

In the centre is seen the corpus callosum, an elongated vault which covers in the ventricles, and is terminated in front by a swelling called *genou* (knee), the most slanting point of which is the *bec* (beak), and behind by another swelling called the *bourrelet* (cushion). Towards its anterior extremity is then seen a slit rendered gaping by the preparation, which is the internal perpendicular fissure already described. On this surface is a triangular lobule, forming a portion of the occipital lobe, looking from this side, and which bounds the sulcus of the hippocampi below. All the portion situated beneath, and to the left of this sulcus in the figure, is the internal surface (at the lower part) of the temporo-sphenoidal lobe. A primary and well-defined transverse sulcus, and a smaller faint one which is parallel to it, divide this region into three convolutions (6, 7, and 8); the superior bending round

[*] "Procédé pour la Momification des Cerveaux," by M. Paul Broca, in "Bull. Soc. d'Anthrop.," vol. i., 1865.

in a gyrus at its anterior extremity, to form the outline of the circumpolmicular fissure, and the inferior forming one with the third temporo-sphenoidal on the external surface.

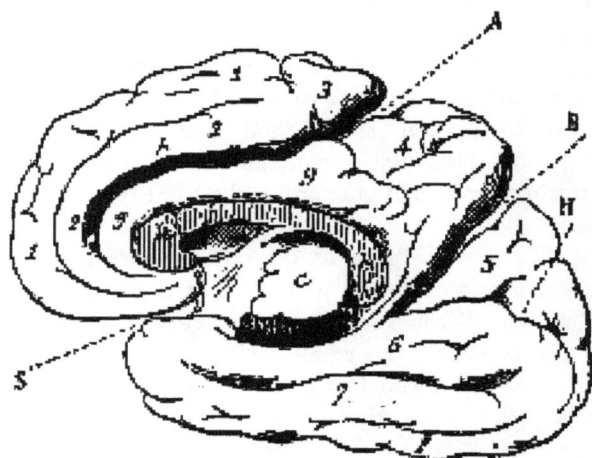

FIG. 17.—Diagram of the internal surface of the brain. a, Genou of the corpus callosum; b, Bourrelet of the corpus callosum; c, The crura cerebri cut across; A, Fronto-parietal fissure; B, Internal perpendicular fissure; S, Fissure of Sylvius; H, Sulcus of the Hippocampi; 1, 2, and 3, Internal frontal convolutions; 1, Portion in continuation with the first frontal of the external surface; 3, The oval lobule; 4, Quadrilateral, or internal parietal lobule; 5, Triangular, or internal occipital lobule; 6 and 7, First and second internal temporo-sphenoidal convolutions; 8, Third internal temporo-sphenoidal convolution in continuation with the third on the external surface; 9, Convolution of the corpus callosum, or hem.

In front of the triangular lobule is a well-marked quadrangular lobule (Foville), which is simply the internal side of the superior parietal lobe, lengthened out below as far as the corpus callosum, and bounded behind by the perpendicular fissure, and in front by a small oval lobule (Pozzi)—which we may leave for the present—which is situated in front of the quadrangular lobule, close to the superior border of the hemisphere. This lobule is formed by the junction, looking from the internal surface, of the two anterior and posterior ascending convolutions of its external surface.

The remaining portion of the internal surface is divided into two parts, the one superior and anterior, which forms part of the frontal lobe; the other inferior, and resting on the corpus callosum, to which we must consider it as attached. A fissure, however, divides them, which is called festonnée, or calloso-marginal, in its anterior four-fifths, and fronto-parietal towards its termination. It commences below the beak of the corpus callosum, turns round its knee, passes horizontally behind, and, separating the oval from the quadrilateral lobule, reaches obliquely the superior border of the hemisphere. A single convolution, called the convolution of the corpus callosum, is concentric to it, and continues to follow this organ, to form the base of the quadrilateral lobule, and to anastomose with the first internal temporo-sphenoidal convolution. Another convolution, called the internal frontal, is eccentric to it, and has the form of an italic S. Its anterior gyrus is separated from the knee of the corpus callosum by the convolution and the fissure just mentioned, and its posterior gyrus forms the oval lobule. In the greater part of its length it is divided by an interrupted sulcus into two storeys, of which the first is in direct continuation with the first frontal convolution on the external surface. The number and distribution of the primary convolutions may be summed up as follows:

EXTERNAL SURFACE.

Frontal lobe	Orbital region .	3 convolutions in form of a star.
	Frontal region	1 ascending convolution.
		3 antero-posterior convolutions.
Parietal lobe	1 ascending convolution.	
	2 convolutions	1 superior.
		1 inferior.
Occipital lobe	3 antero-posterior convolutions.	
Temporo-sphenoidal lobe .	3 parallel convolutions.	

INTERNAL SURFACE.

Frontal lobe	...	...	...	1 convolution.
Parietal lobe	...	...	...	1 quadrilateral lobule.
Temporo-occipito-sphenoidal lobe				1 triangular lobule.
				3 parallel convolutions.
Lobe of the corpus callosum	...			1 convolution.

One point in reference to the convolutions upon which M. Broca lays stress, is their want of symmetry on both sides in the best

selected individuals. Simple convolutions, developed uninterruptedly, and alike in both hemispheres, are characteristic of
inferiority in Man, as well as throughout the mammalian series.
Bichat then was wrong when, influenced by a statement of
Tiedemann, he attributed intellectual aberrations to the asymmetry
of the brain; his own autopsy proved the contrary.[*]

The difference between the encephalon of mammalia and that of
Man is in the relative volume of the principal parts, in certain
internal structural arrangements, in the absence or in the number of
the convolutions, and in the weight of the organ.

On viewing the whole encephalic system on its superior surface,
we notice that the hemispheres in the marsupialia and monotremata
exhibit in front certain swellings called olfactory bulbs, which, in
the majority of mammalia, have the importance of lobes, and behind
the greater portion of the tubercula quadrigemina, or optic lobes,
and the cerebellum. In other animals, as the ant-eater, the rat, the
hare, and the bat, the optic lobes cease to be visible, but the
olfactory lobes and the cerebellum are more exposed to view. In
others, and as far as monkeys exclusively, the former are concealed,
while a more or less considerable portion of the cerebellum is
visible. In lemurians, the cerebellum slightly projects beyond the
hemispheres; in pithecians and cebians it is more generally on a
level with them. In the anthropoid apes and in Man, not only is
it out of sight, but the hemispheres in their turn more or less pass
beyond it.

[*] On the subject of the convolutions, see "Traité de l'Anatomie Physiolo-
gique et Pathologique du Système Nerveux Cérébro-Spinal," by Foville, 1st
part, Paris, 1844; "Mémoire sur les Plis du Cerveau," by M. Bischoff, in
"Bull. Soc. d'Anthrop.," 2nd series, vol. iv., 1860; "Mémoire sur les Plis
Cérébraux de l'Homme et des Primates," by Gratiolet, Paris, 1856, a memoir
already mentioned in "Les Primates," by M. Broca, 1869; "The Convolutions
of the Human Cerebrum topographically considered," by Turner, Paris,
1866; "Zur Entwicklungsgeschichte der Furchen und Windungen der
Grosshirn-Hemisphären in Fötus der Menschen," by Ecker, in "Archiv für
Anthrop.," 1869; "Études sur les Circonvolutions chez l'Homme et les
Singes," by J. Gromier, Paris, 1874; Article "Circonvolutions," in "Dict.
Encycl. des Sciences Médicales," by S. Pozzi, 1st series, vol. xvii., 1873.

The brain is modified also as to form. In Man it is more or less elongated as a whole, and ovoid at its anterior extremity; its frontal region is contracted occasionally, as though squeezed together, globular, and acquires its maximum of fulness. The last traces of this contraction are seen in front, at the point of the internal anterior and inferior angle of each hemisphere. It is more or less strongly marked in pithecians, less so in the anthropoid apes, and commonly not at all in Man.

In these two relations, the anthropoids more nearly approach to Man than to the other monkeys.

As regards internal structure, the first difference is the absence of the corpus callosum in the marsupialia and the monotremata, as well as in the classes of vertebrata below, whilst it exists in all the other mammalia. The aqueduct of Sylvius, a simple canal perforating the corpora-quadrigemina in Man and the majority of the mammalia, is a cavity, or rather a supplementary ventricle in the kangaroo. The anterior and middle cornua of the lateral ventricles exist in all the mammalia; the posterior or occipital cornu is peculiar to Man, to the monkey, the seal, and the porpoise. Professor Owen thought that the absence in anthropoids of this cornu, of the hippocampus minor belonging to it, and of the occipital lobe in which it is hollowed, constituted a distinct characteristic separating the ape from Man. On more careful examination, however, he altered his opinion. Man and the anthropoid ape in this respect are alike.

A characteristic of Man has also been sought for in the presence of the mammillary tubercles, little round bodies situated at the base of the brain, and whose use is unknown. Vain hope! The chimpanzee, the orang, the gibbon, and the mône possess them.

The convolutions are wanting in fishes, reptiles, and birds. They are absent in a considerable number of mammalia, are tolerably developed in others, and very much so in many, as the porpoise and the elephant. Mr. Owen has proposed to make them the basis of a fourfold classification: (1) Lyencephala, having the brain smooth and the optic lobes exposed; (2) Lissencephala, having the

I 2

brain smooth, but with the optic lobes concealed ; (3) Gyrencephala, with but few convolutions ; and (4) Archencephala, in which Man alone is placed. But the other features of the organisation do not move in parallelism with these characteristics, and the fourth class is only hypothetical.*

Erasistratus of old wrote that the convolutions are more numerous in Man, because he is supreme as the possessor of a mind and reasoning power. A. Desmoulins, in 1825, maintained that the number and perfection of the intellectual faculties in species as in individuals, are in proportion to the extent of surface of the hemispheres, and that this is in direct ratio to the number and depth of the convolutions. M. Dareste started another proposition: that the convolutions were developed in a direct ratio to the stature, and that the smaller species most frequently have the brain smooth. Gratiolet took upon himself to refute him. Man, and then the orang, the chimpanzee, the seal, the bear, the dog, the elephant, have the most complex convolutions ; whilst in the insectivora, the rodents, and the marsupials, generally less intelligent, they are scarcely visible. Neither the stature nor the volume of the body has anything to do with the question ; the smallest dog has more convolutions than the most gigantic kangaroo, the seal more than the ox. There are exceptions, but these are easily explained. The increased amount of the gray cortical substance of the hemispheres is what we must look for as evidence of a larger amount of activity. We must look for (1) The increase of the cerebral mass, and consequently, cæteris paribus, of its surface ; (2) The increase of the number of folds and windings, which allow of a much greater proportion of the gray substance being deposited in a given space; (3) The increase of the latter in thickness, and its improvement in quality. Unless we take account of all these elements we must not be surprised if there are exceptions, but the general fact remains—the amount of intelligence in mammalia is in proportion to the development of the convolutions.

The consideration of the monkey tribe will now engage our

* "The Anatomy of Vertebrates," vol. iii., "Mammals," by R. Owen. London, 1868.

attention.   From the ouistiti, the lowest of the celians, which has
the brain smooth and only a trace of the fissure of Sylvius, to Man,
every variety is to be met with.   In the sapajous, some convolutions are visible.   Their number increases rapidly in the highest
celians and the pithecians.   In anthropoids, suddenly and almost
without transition, they have a similar appearance to those of Man.
All the principal convolutions are there, the type is the same, the
difference is only in parts of a subordinate character, and in the degree of convolutions, which varies also in Man and is peculiar to him.

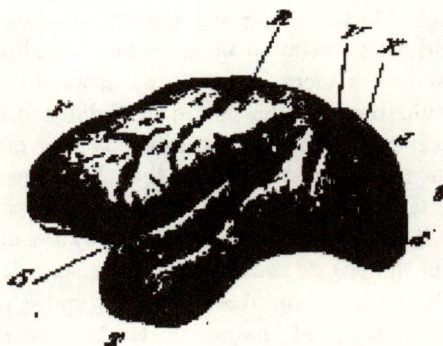

FIG. 19.—Brain of pithecian—the guenon or cercopithecus—seen on the external surface.
F, Frontal lobe ; T, Temporo-sphenoidal lobe ; O, Occipital lobe ; S, Fissure of
Sylvius ; R, Fissure of Rolando ; V, External perpendicular fissure   A A, Ascending
frontal convolution ; a1, a2, a3, First, second, and third antero-posterior frontal
convolutions ; P, R, Ascending parietal convolution, giving origin behind to the
superior parietal and the inferior parietal at curved fold, the latter turning round
the fissure of Sylvius and the parallel sulcus, as in Fig. 16 ; c1 and c2, First and
second external temporo-sphenoidal convolutions, separated by the parallel sulcus.

"Between the smooth brain of ouistitis and the marvellously
complicated brain of chimpanzees and orang, there is a gap," says
M. Broca, "while there are but faint shadows of difference
between the latter and that of Man ;" and further : "The enormous
and complex mass of convolutions in Man . . . . . is composed
of the same fundamental folds, united by the same connections, and
separated by the same sulci.   These primary convolutions, these
essential parts, common and only common to all human brains, are

found without exception in the brains of the orang and the chimpanzee." That of the gorilla is but little known.[*]

A few words as to the changes which are exhibited as far as the inferior orders of cobians.

The orbital region of the frontal lobe, which is flat in Man, is depressed in pithecians; the sulcus of the olfactory nerve is wanting; the angle which terminates the third frontal convolution behind is rectilinear, which has interest with regard to the faculty of language. The first frontal convolution is simple, as in the Hottentot Venus of Cuvier, and the idiot studied by Gratiolet, while it is double in the orang and the chimpanzee, as in Man. The inferior parietal convolution should rather be called the curved fold, as it commences more in front and more distinctly curves round the terminations of the fissure of Sylvius and the parallel sulcus. The superior parietal convolution is very much reduced, particularly in the cynocephali. In the chimpanzee it forms a lobule as important as in Man. The external part of the perpendicular fissure is more open and more visible by the absence or the greater depth of the plis de passage of this region. It follows that the occipital lobe throws up above it at its upper part an operculum, whose amount of projection is less characteristic of inferiority. The central lobule, very smooth in Man, slightly so in the orang and chimpanzee, is smooth in the majority of pithecians and cobians, and is wanting in lemurs, as also in the other mammalia.

The occipital lobe deserves especial notice. Its volume is generally in an inverse ratio to the number of the sulci and convolutions. Almost entirely smooth in cynocephali, its uniform surface contrasts so strongly with the rest of the cerebral surface in the macacque and the guenon, that Gratiolet compared it to a cap covering the posterior extremity of the brain. The contrast is less in some semnopitheci; some gashes are seen, which are well marked in the gibbon, and become in the chimpanzee and the orang very nearly as complex as in Man.

* Memoir already quoted, "Sur les Primates."

Owen discovered a cerebral characteristic of Man in the structure of his occipital lobe; Gratiolet, in his second *pli de passage*, from the parietal to the occipital lobe.

It is not a question of two inferior *plis de passage*, they always exist. Thinner in gibbons and pithecians, they are thick in Man and the great anthropoid apes, and entirely fill up the inferior (or external) portion of the external perpendicular fissure. It is otherwise as regards the two superior *plis de passage*. They are superficial, deep, or altogether wanting, according to four types. (1) In Man and the atoles—the highest in the order of cebians—they are both superficial, hence the difficulty that students have in discovering the external perpendicular fissure which they traverse. (2) The first is superficial and the second deep in the orang, the gibbon, and the semnopitheci. (3) The first is wanting and the second is deep in the chimpanzee, the macaque, and the cynocephalus (the gorilla has not been studied in this respect). (4) Both are deep in the guenons. The three anthropoid apes which have been studied differ, then, from Man, in that the second fold is deep. There is some doubt as to the first fold being absent in the chimpanzee; it was present in the subjects studied by Rolleston, Marshall, and Turner. Notably, in two, the first fold was present on one side and not on the other; while, by way of compensation, the second was deep on one side but superficial on the other: according to M. Broca it should always exist on one side or the other. Moreover, in Man, even in individuals of sound mind, one of the superior *plis de passage* may be deep on one side or wanting, and the other at the same time be feebly developed. Does not all this prove that these are only changes or gradations of development from the healthy man to the anthropoids, the cebians, and the pithecians? Relative to anthropoids we can only come to one conclusion, namely, that they are not more separated from Man by the character of their *plis de passage* than from the monkeys next in order, and that in this, as well as in everything relating to the convolutions, they are found to take their place with Man at the head of the series.

If the differences hitherto established in the morphology and anatomy of the brain of Man, as compared with that of animals, are not such as we should have desired, what we are about to say with respect to its weight and mass, and what we have already said on the subject of the cranial capacity, will be sufficient to satisfy the warmest advocates of human supremacy.

The weight of the encephalon varies in the adult man of sound mind from 1,830 grammes, which was the weight of Cuvier's brain, to 872, which is that of a Bosjeswoman studied in England by Mr. Marshall: but these are exceptional cases. According to Huschke, its mean weight, at the age of 30 or 40 years, in the white race, and when the organ has attained its full growth, is about 1,410 in men, and 1,272 in women. The weight varies, moreover, according to height, sex, age, intelligence, and occupation. Let us rapidly run over the principal results obtained on these points, in order that we may not have again to recur to them.*

The encephalon is heavier in tall persons than in short. In five men having a mean stature of 1·74 mètre, the brain was 96 grammes heavier than in five other short men, whose mean stature was 1·63 mètre. The difference of weight was 6 per cent., and corresponded exactly with the difference of stature. The same result has been obtained in reference to women.

The brain is lighter in the woman than in the man : the former weighing 100, ceteris paribus, the latter would weigh 112, according to Huschke. This difference is only attributable to the fact that usually she is less in height. Parchappe has shown that the height of the woman is to that of the man as 92·7 to 100; whilst the weight of her brain would be as 90·9 to 100. The brain, then, is lighter in the woman, and we may add, that it is so at all ages.

The tables constructed by Broca, with materials furnished by

* "Sur le Poids du Cerveau," by Lélut, in "Journal des Conn. Médico-Chirurg.," vol. v., Paris, 1837 ; "Recherches sur l'Encéphale," by Parchappe, Paris, 1836 ; "Ueber die Typischen Verschiedenheiten der Windungen der Hemisphären und über die Lehre vom Hirngewicht," by Rud. Wagner, Göttingen, 1860 ; "Discussion sur le Cerveau," by Broca, Gratiolet, Daresta, &c., in "Bull. Soc. d'Anthrop.," vol. ii., 1861.

Wagner, of the weight of 347 healthy brains, prove that this organ goes on increasing up to 40 years of age, that it remains stationary up to 50, and decreases afterwards. After the age of 60 years men had lost from 5 to 7 per cent. of maximum weight, and women from 4 to 7. Gratiolet has shown that the cranium of the infant is more elongated at birth, that it enlarges subsequently in the temporal regions, and that it goes on developing in front: it ought to be the same with the brain.

The brain increases, *cæteris paribus*, in proportion to the vascular activity of which it is the seat. This is the reason that the brain of certain criminals and lunatics is so large. But of all the kinds of activity, that which has reference to the special design of the organ has the most influence. Such is physiological activity, of which intelligence is the result. The weights taken by Lélut, Parchappe, and Wagner, clearly show this. The labouring men studied by Parchappe had the head longer than his "distinguished men." So with the *internes* of the hospital of Bicêtre measured by M. Broca, relatively to the officers of the institution. The cranial capacity of Parisians from the twelfth to the nineteenth century, has increased to such an extent that we may be allowed to attribute it to the progress of civilisation. The cranial capacity is greater, *cæteris paribus*, in the white race, less generally in the negro races, less still in the lowest among them. The brains of idiots, and of the insane in lunatic asylums, are smaller and lighter than those of the *employés* and ordinary sick, or of persons suffering from acute mania. The enormous weight of Cuvier's brain is in itself an argument. No less remarkable, though less largely developed, were the brains of Abercrombie, of Broca, of Duportron, and other eminent persons, as recorded by Wagner. The reason that the brain of the woman is lighter than that of the man is that she has less cerebral activity to exercise in her sphere of duty. In former times it was relatively larger in the department of Lozère, because there the woman and the man mutually shared the burden of their daily labour. The truth is, that the weight of the brain increases with the use which we make of that organ, with the exercise of certain professions; in a word, with the degree of intelligence. The absolute mean weight

of the brain at its maximum of growth, in men, is, in round
numbers, about 1,400 grammes, in women about 1,250. With
some few exceptions it is the heaviest of the mammalian series.
We will give the figures farther on.

They would, however, be of little value as regards the majority
of mammalia if we did not take account of the stature or weight
of the body. M. Sappey estimates the weight of the brain of
the elephant to be from 1,500 to 4,000 grammes, and that of
the dolphin about 1,800; and then it would be in proportion
to the weight of the body as 1 to 1,500 in the former, and
1 to 100 in the latter; while in Man it is as 1 to 36, according to Cuvier, and 1 to 52 according to Colin. This may
be so, but we do not think these figures are to be thoroughly
relied on; for the brain of a young Asiatic elephant in M. Broca's
laboratory weighed double, that is to say, 3,060 grammes; the
greater reason why we should take into our calculation the stature
of the animal. In the list published by Cuvier, the weight of the
brain being 1, that of the body is from 48 to 105 in the ordinary
monkeys; from 97 to 365 in the carnivora; from 530 to 800 in
marsupials; from 700 to 800 in two oxen. In a gibbon, according
to M. Leuret,[*] it was 48, and in another, in M. Broca's laboratory,
18·7. Most fortunately, we are able to make a direct comparison
between Man and the three higher anthropoids. If, on the average,
they are a little less in stature, they are, on the other hand, stouter,
so that the body, taken as a whole, agrees as nearly as possible.
The anthropoid is generally a little more bulky, which, ceteris
paribus, would necessitate his having rather a larger brain. It is
true that we have not had an opportunity of weighing the brains
of the great apes in a fresh state, but we may estimate the weight
sufficiently accurately by the cranial capacity.[†]   Mr. Huxley thinks
that the weight of the brain of the gorilla may reach 567 grammes,
and M. Broca found that the weight of the one the cubic measure-

[*] See "Anatomy of the Nervous System," by Leuret, vol. i., 1839, and
the table at page 124.
[†] Mr. Owen, however, weighed the fresh brain of a gorilla; it was 15
ounces = 425·19 grammes.

ment of whose cranium he made with M. Alix, was 540 grammes.
We ourselves should estimate that the mean, without reference to
sex, would be below 475 in the gorilla, and much lower still in the
orang and chimpanzea.

Proportions of different Parts of the Encephalon.

M. Baillarger has attempted to estimate the absolute extent of
surface of the convolutions which is covered by the grey substance.
He found it to be 1,700 square centimètres in Man, and 24 in the
rabbit. M. Hermann Wagner calculated the amount of superficies
in each lobe relatively to the total superficies of the brain. It is to
be feared that the result of these efforts has not been of much importance, though they should be encouraged. The following are
the mean proportions obtained by M. Wagner :

			Man.			Orang
Frontal lobe	...	...	48·5	...	...	36·8
Parietal lobe	...	...	16·9	...	...	25·1
Temporal lobe	...	...	21·8	...	...	19·6
Occipital lobe	...	...	17·7	...	...	18·3
Total surface	...	...	100·0	...	...	100·0

We have more to expect from the relation of the cerebellum to
the hemispheres. The weight of the former in the man is about
179 grammes, and in the woman 147 grammes, according to Parchappe, and 176 in Man, according to Lélut. This weight being
expressed by 1, that of the hemispheres would be 15·5 in the man,
and 13·9 grammes in the woman, according to Parchappe, and 15·5
also in the man, according to Lélut. It is the same with animals ;
in the saïmiri it is 14 ; môns, 8 ; mangot, papion, and coïta, 7 ; ouistiti,
6·2 ; macauco, 4·5 ; gibbon, 4·4 grammes, among apes : and the
hedgehog, 12 ; hare, 14·3 ; ox, 9 ; horse, 7 ; sheep, 5 ; mouse, 2,
among the mammalia (Leuret). It follows from this that the
human cerebellum is lighter in proportion to the weight of the
brain, and if we put aside three of the 44 examples of Leuret,
that Man would be found to have the advantage in this respect, as

well as with regard to the entire weight of the encephalon. Attempts have been made to compare the weight of the encephalon with that of the spinal cord = 1·10, but the comparison has not been carried out in Man. The following figures, borrowed from M. Colin, have been drawn up in reference to this question, and to those preceding us to domestic animals:

	Weight of the encephalon.	Weight of the body. Encephalon = 1.	Weight of the two hemispheres. Cerebellum = 1.	Weight of the encephalon. Spinal cord = 1.
15 stallions	553	648	6·0	2·3
15 mares	595	645	7·4	2·8
17 dogs	83	212	8·5	4·7
5 cats	29	106	6·1	3·6
8 oxen	659	649	6·3	2·4
4 asses	308	353	7·2	2·0
8 hogs	123	659	7·5	2·9

One of M. Colin's conclusions deserves to be considered side by side with that arrived at by M. Dareste. He says the smaller species of animals have the brain more developed than the larger. The mouse, for example, has, in proportion to his body, more brain than Man, and thirteen times more than the horse, and eleven times more than the elephant. M. Dareste infers that the smaller species generally have the brain smooth. The two propositions mutually agree. The convolutions have less tendency to be developed in the smaller species, supposing the fact proved: because their brain is larger, this was superfluous. Thus the same result is arrived at by different methods of proceeding.

Lastly, Sœmmering has conceived the idea of comparing the brain with the nerves which proceed from it. The relative volume of the former would be considerably greater in Man; the apes would come next. "The largest horse's brain that I have weighed," says he, "was one pound and seven ounces, and the smallest man's, two pounds five ounces and a quarter, notwithstanding that the nerves at the base were ten times larger in the former, although the difference in weight between the two brains was at least fourteen ounces and a quarter."

Measurement of the Brain.

This has not yet been practised to any extent except on animals. Semmtouring and Ebel have compared the width of the medulla oblongata, at its union with the protuberantia annularis, with the maximum width of the brain. Leuret has taken the relative dimensions and situation of the corpus callosum and the cerebellum. Cuvier has given the width, the height, and the maximum length of the brain in 38 mammals. Leuret applied himself to the width in relation to the length, taking his measurements, not on the brain, but on the interior of the cranial cavity. We can speak highly of this method, when we employ the special instruments invented by M. Brom, which allow of all the details being measured without injuring the skull by making a section. In a first group, including the kangaroo, the guinea-pig, and the beaver, the two diameters are equal; in a second, consisting of the majority of the rodents, the elephant, the porpoise, and the whale, the transverse diameter is greater than the antero-posterior; in a third, embracing the monkey tribe, the carnivora, the solipeds, and the ruminants, the antero-posterior diameter is the longer, as in Man.

The relation of these two diameters, the transverse and the antero-posterior, is worthy, in our opinion, to have a place assigned to it in Zoological Anthropology, under the name of cerebral index. A few calculations from Leuret's tables are subjoined.

Papio (mandril)	...	...	...	...	75·6	
Macaque	...	...	...	...	80·3	
Mandril	...	...	...	...	83·2	
Maccaco (maki)	...	...	...	...	86·3	
Horse	...	...	...	...	84·5	
White bear	...	...	...	...	84·5	
Guinea-pig	...	...	...	...	100·0	
Phascolomys (wombat)	...	...	...	102·5	
Porcupine	...	...	...	...	125·1	
Whale	...	...	...	...	148·7	
5 dogs	...	...	...	...	75·0 to	89·9
8 kangaroos	...	...	...	...	86·2 „	100·0
2 seals	...	...	...	...	97·5 „	112·5
8 bats	...	...	...	...	122·2 „	126·0
2 elephants	...	...	...	...	136·9 „	166·7

Three forms of brain, then, would find place in the mammalian series, as there are three sorts of human crania—viz. the long, the intermediate, and the broad. But here the lines of demarcation between each form would be changed. Those which we should call dolichocephali (long heads) would be below 90, the mesaticephali (middle heads), from 90 to 110, and the brachycephali (short heads), above 110.

Rudimentary Organs and Reversive Anomalies.

In the necessarily rapid examination which we have just made of the characters by which Man differs from or approaches to animals, we have only taken into consideration those which are constant and exist in all individuals. But there are others which unexpectedly make their appearance in all the races of Man, and more frequently in those reputed inferior, concerning which we ought to say a few words. We refer to what are called the rudimentary organs, and anomalies. In the hypothesis of a transformation by a certain process from forms relatively inferior into those of a higher and more perfect character, they take the name of reversions, which is meant to convey the idea of a relationship in the past between organisms now divergent, and bearing upon the question of the affinity of Man with the other mammalia.

As examples of rudimentary organs in animals we may mention the germs of teeth in the foetus of the whale, and those of the upper incisors in ruminants, although these organs are never developed, and appear to be useless; the teats of all male quadrupeds; the eyes of sightless animals, or those species which pass their lives in dark caverns, or inhabit the fathomless depths of the ocean; the two needle-like ossicles on the sides of the single metacarpal or metatarsal bone of the horse, which represent the other metacarpals or metatarsals which have disappeared; &c.

Examples are numerous in Man. The semilunar fold at the internal angle of the eye, so marked in some persons, would represent the remains of the third eyelid of marsupials, the walrus, &c.

The vermicular appendix of the large intestine, which seems useless, and is occasionally the cause of death, is the representative of an organ which is enormous in herbivorous animals, and in the koala attains a length three times that of the body. The muscles of the ear, equally useless, although sufficiently developed in some individuals to enable them to move the cartilage, are merely vestiges of a very well-marked apparatus in animals. The sub-vomerine bone of Rambaud, in like manner, is the remains of the organ of Jacobson, and is very much developed in the horse, as also in some apes, &c. Anomalies are still more frequent in Man. We may mention the bifid, and even the double uterus; the former repeating the horned uterus of the rodent, or the elongated and angular uterus seen in some ordinary monkeys and lemurs; the latter the double uterus with two orifices of marsupials. We may mention the persistence in the adult of the suture which divides the malar bones into two, as in some apes and other mammalia; that of the median frontal suture, as in the majority of the lower mammalia; the appearance, once in a hundred times, according to Mr. Turner, of the supra-condylean humeral foramen peculiar to various animals, through which the principal nerve and artery of the limb pass; the altogether simian conformation of the cartilage of the ear; &c.

In the muscles especially reversions are common. Traces of the cutaneous muscle are seen in the armpits and on the scapula, as well as on the head and face; the sternal muscle of mammalia was seen in 18 out of 600 men; the ischio-pubic muscle, constant in the majority of male animals, was noticed in 19 out of 40 men, and in 2 out of 30 women; the elevator claviculae of most apes in 1 out of 60. M. Chudzinski, in the "Revue d'Anthropologie," has given many examples of simian arrangements in Man. Mr. J. Wood found in one individual as many as seven examples of muscles peculiar to certain apes.

Whatever interpretation may be given to these facts, they establish a link between the type of organisation of Man and that of animals. A third order of facts has been brought together, namely, those which we term teratological, and of which we shall speak by-and-by.

CHAPTER IV.

HITHERTO we have been engaged with anatomical characters, that
is to say, with those relating to the organs as seen after death.
We shall now consider the physiological, or those exhibited in the
living subject, the result of the growth and development of those
organs. Their history commences from the period when the first
lineaments of organisation were planned, continues through the
various phases of existence, and exhibits to us Man moving and
thinking, up to the period when motion and thought cease.

Development—Age.

Our first entrance into life is unostentatious, and in no way
differs from that of animals. Enclosed in an ovum of the same
character as that of all the oviparous or viviparous mammalia,
nothing then distinguishes the future monarch from the humblest
pariah—the lord of creation from the ape or the kangaroo. The
researches of Wolf in 1759, of Oken in 1806, of Bäer in 1819,
of Coste, &c., have put this beyond contradiction.

The ovum at first is a simple cell, a microscopic point, which is
composed of an albuminous substance, or vitellus, and of a nucleus,
or germinal vesicle, enclosing within it a nucleolus, or germinal
spot. Under this form it is thrown off from the ovaries, traverses
the oviduct, passes into the uterus, and, if it becomes fecundated,
is there developed. The cell then becomes divided into two, into
four, and gradually into an infinite number of cells, which increase
at the periphery and assume the form of a hollow sphere. At one

point there afterwards appears an opacity, which becomes elongated and divided into three leaflets. This is the rudiment of the future being, whether man or dog. The external leaflet will become the skin and cerebro-spinal axis, the internal the digestive mucous membrane, the middle the parenchyma from which the various organs are formed. The multiplication of cells continuing, a primitive line is drawn, which has at one of its extremities an enlargement, upon which before long are seen five ampullæ. The line is the spinal cord, the enlargement is the brain, the anterior ampulla will be the hemispheres, the second the optic thalamus, the third the tubercula quadrigemina, the fourth the cerebellum, and the fifth the medulla oblongata.

According to the variable development of these rudiments, results, by degrees, the special genus or species. At the fourth week the difference between the Man and the dog is inappreciable. The divergence only commences in earnest at the eighth week. In the human fœtus the anterior ampulla becomes larger, in the fœtus of the dog the caudal extremity elongates.

At birth the infant weighs from 3 to 4 kilogrammes, and is 50 centimètres in length; his pulse is 140 in the minute; a fine down covers his body; his pupils are generally open as soon as respiration becomes fully established; the thymus gland, an organ exclusively fœtal, atrophies. He takes the breast up to the second or third year, or rather until the sixteen or twenty milk teeth have appeared. During the period of infancy the pulse ranges from 100 to 110, the respiration becomes proportionately slower, its movements being in relation to the heart's pulsations as 1 to 3. At about 14 years, in our climates, puberty takes place in the boy; his features become altered, the voice changes, the beard developes, and most important modifications take place in the genital organs. At the same time, in the girl, the breasts increase in size, the menses make their appearance. At 20 years adult age is attained; growth still goes on; the brain continues to be developed in proportion to its exercise, and attains its maximum of activity at or before 35 years. Soon decadence commences; the faculty of reproduction in the man becomes diminished. In woman

the hair turns white and falls off; the teeth become loosened from
their sockets; the crystalline lens is flattened, causing the eye to
become presbyopic; the senses become dull; the lung is emphy-
sematous, the heart hypertrophied; the arteries become ossified;
fat is infiltrated through the tissues, and death takes place naturally,
without any struggle, from the moment that one of the three principal organs of organic life—the heart, the lung, or the digestive
tube—loses the power to perform its function.*

Except in some trifling particulars, this is the same as regards all
mammalia. The organisation of Man, of the anthropoid ape, or of
the carnivora, obeys the same physiological laws, and passes through
three similar periods: one of growth, one of full development—
during which the process of reproduction goes on—and one of
decay. These periods are of longer or shorter duration—that is the
only difference. Of all these phenomena, those which are exhibited
on the skeleton have the greatest amount of interest for the anthropologist. It is by a thorough acquaintance with them that we
determine with accuracy the age of bones, a problem not less important for the anthropologist in his laboratory than for the
archæologist who is desirous of ascertaining the date of his fossils.

A few words, however, as to the head. Its proportions relatively
to the body during the earliest periods of embryonic existence, or
even at birth, are not what they are at a later period. At the
second month of intra-uterine life the head forms one-half, at
birth one-quarter, and at adult age one-eighth part of the entire
body. The same may be said as regards the contents of the brain-
case.

Growth of the Brain.

Throughout the whole of the mammalian series this organ is

* M. Broca divides the periods of human life as follows: First infancy
from birth to the end of the sixth year, when the first large permanent
molar is cut; second infancy, from 7 to 14 years, on the eruption of the
second molars; youth, from 14 to 25 years, when the basilar suture is
ossified, or the wisdom tooth is cut; adult age, from 25 to 40, when the
cerebral sutures begin to ossify; ripe age, from 40 to 60; old age, beyond
60 years. In craniometry, we designate, in a general way, under the name
of adult, crania in which the basilar suture is closed.

smaller relatively to the rest of the body at birth than at the period of its complete development. In the newly-born marsupial, Mr. Owen says it is less large in proportion than in the upper classes of mammalia.

The following figures of M. Welcker exhibit the cranial capacity in Man at different ages, and consequently the progressive volume of his brain :

				Man. Centimetres.			Women. Centimetres.
New-born infant...	...	...	...	400	...	...	360
At 2 months	...	...	...	640	...	...	610
At 1 year	...	...	...	900	...	...	850
At 6 years	...	...	...	1080	...	...	1010
At 10 years	...	...	...	1860	...	...	1250
From 20 to 60 years	...	...	1450	...	...	1800

In anthropoids the development is less rapid : we are ignorant as to their cranial capacity at birth, but during the first dentition, in eight orangs, it was found to be 322 cubic centimetres, while in 16 adults of the same species it was 413. Supposing, then, that their first dentition takes place at the mean age of two years, the cranial capacity would increase 31 per cent. in Man from this period to adult age, and 22 per cent only in the orang.

To obviate the numerous disorders to which so considerable a development of the brain would give rise, owing to the resistance of the walls of the cranium, the sutures which unite the bones preserve their softness a much longer time in Man, and do not begin to ossify until a late period, when there is no longer any probability of the increase of the contents, and when cerebral activity is becoming less. This leads us to speak of the action of the sutures, and of the chief means of ascertaining the age of a cranium.

Ossification of the Cranial Sutures.

The bones pass through three phases, corresponding to the three periods of life. In the first, the bone is soft, then cartilaginous; in the second, it is osseous, and continues so in every part; in the

K 3

third, or senile period, it becomes more dense, although lighter and more fragile, the diploë in the flat bones is more spongy, the medullary canal in the long bones is of greater diameter, and the cells at their extremities are larger. Between the first and second period there is one of transition, during which points or centres of ossification appear in the middle of the cartilage, which gradually become larger and larger, and at last occupy the entire bone. These points are of two descriptions—the principal ones for the body, or diaphysis; the secondary for the extremities, or epiphyses, and the prominences or processes.

In the skull, the points of ossification first appear in the centres which correspond with the bodies of the three cranial vertebræ—the basilar process of the occipital, the posterior sphenoid and the anterior sphenoid, then in the lateral bones and in those of the vault. It is well to know the period at which the secondary portions become united, so as to be enabled to judge, in certain circumstances, if the development has proceeded regularly. Thus :

At the third month of fœtal life the two superior points of the occipital shell become united to the two inferior. What we call the interparietal suture is closed.

At the eighth or ninth month of fœtal life the body of the anterior sphenoid is united to the body of the posterior sphenoid.

About two months after birth, the false suture which separates the basilar portion of the occipital from the two condyloid portions is closed.

About the fifth or sixth months the body of the posterior sphenoid is united to the greater wings.

About a year, the three portions of the temporal—the petrous, the mastoid, and the squamous—become anchylosed. The two halves of the frontal also. The suture which they form when they are persistent in the adult, is called the medio-frontal, or metopic. We have noticed this abnormal persistence in 58 out of 611 Parisian skulls which we have examined = 1 in 9·66.

About the third or fourth year, the styloid process becomes united to the temporal, unless it continues separated from it during the remainder of life.

About the fifth or sixth year, the suture which separates the external occipital portion of the occipital shell is closed.

The true sutures are the coronal, the sagittal, the lambdoidal, the temporal, and the spheno-parietal, spaces being formed at their junction, which are designated by the name of fontanelles. The exact period at which the process of ossification is completed at their edges is doubtful. The sagittal and coronal sutures close very soon after birth, and before those of the base. The bregmatic fontanelle, except in cases of disease, is always closed before two-and-a-half years of age according to M. Bouvier, and sooner according to M. Broca.

The suture which unites the occipital to the sphenoid is sometimes wanting in animals, sometimes it remains persistent through the whole of life; in Man it passes immediately from the cartilaginous to the osseous state at from 18 to 22 years of age.

All these data serve to determine the age, but it is at their third phase, when other parts of the body fail to give us any information, that the examination of the sutures becomes valuable.

At this moment the serrations become obliterated, the bones which are in contact become anchylosed, the suture is synostosed. This synostosis, one of the first signs of age in the skeleton, may in some cases be produced more quickly by disease. There is, then, no adult or stationary condition of the suture, and the younger the individual the more serious the disorders which result from it as regards the development of the cranium and the brain. We shall consider this subject further when speaking as to pathological characters. The spot where synostosis first appears during the progress of age varies. The most frequent is at a point on the sagittal, at the union of its posterior fifth with its anterior three-fifths, where the suture is clearly marked, *obelion*. At other times it is at the extremities of the coronal, near the temporal ridge, or lower down, at the junction of the four sutures, in the form of the letter H. The second or third spot is on the lambdoidal suture, the synostosis appearing at first in the middle of one of its branches, or as an extension of the sagittal ossification. The fourth point is the coronal suture, close to the bregma. The fifth is on the squamous suture of the temporal.[*]

In a word, if the suture is entire, the individual is about 35 years of age or less. If the posterior sagittal point is commencing to close he is about 40 years. The ossification of the coronal suture close to the bregma would show that he was 50 or more. If the temporal suture is closed he would be 60 or more. As regards intermediate and subsequent ages we examine as to the extent to which complete closure has taken place at each spot, and also as to other matters, of which we are about to speak.

The definite period of ossification of the sutures moreover varies very considerably. It sometimes takes place partially and very early in life; at others it is retarded. The more the brain is exercised the more it is postponed, according to M. Broca. In idiots it takes place early. It varies according to race. In the white races the ossification generally proceeds from behind forwards. In the negro races it is the reverse, according to Gratiolet, that is to say from before backwards. This latter statement is somewhat hasty; and without going so far as to deny it, we should say it cannot be looked upon as universally the case.

If the brain-case at the period of birth is very large, the face, on the other hand, is small, and makes increase, especially in the maxillary region, as is shown by the enlargement of the facial angle and of the angle of prognathism, from infancy to adult age. The development for the most part takes place in the alveolar arches, at the part corresponding with the molars of the second dentition; they become elongated from behind forwards, and increase in height and thickness.

A phenomenon the reverse of this takes place when the teeth fall out naturally in the progress of age; the edges of the alveoli come nearer together and become absorbed, and the alveolar border loses its height and thickness. Two anatomical results are the consequence: (1) The mental foramen, situated in the adult at an

[*] See "Recherches sur l'État Sénile du Crâne," by R. Sauvage. Paris, 1870.

equal distance from, or a little nearer to, the two borders of the
bone, appears in the old man gradually to come nearer to the
superior, a circumstance of which M. Broca has taken particular
notice in his interesting memoir, published in 1848, on the bones
of Celestines.   (2) The angle which the horizontal makes with the
posterior branch of the lower jaw becomes widened, and has a
tendency to return to that which it was in infancy. This angle at
birth is from 170 to 160 degrees; it descends to 150 and 130
during the first dentition; then to 115 degrees during the second
dentition; approaches a right angle during the adult period, and
returns to 130 and 140 degrees in old age (*Humphry*).   Thence a
series of characteristics which, even in solitary maxillæ, enables us
to ascertain approximately the age of the individual. Besides
those furnished by the cranial sutures, there are others drawn from
the eburnification, or the unequal atrophy of the malformed
cranium, as well as those from the teeth: all appearances on the
head, so probably indicative of the same fact as regards age, as to
be looked upon as certainties.

The maxillary apparatus is not the only portion of the face which
assumes various alterations of place during life. The brain cavities
do the same in a less degree. Thus the frontal sinuses connected
with the olfactory apparatus are rudimentary in the infant, very
largely developed in the adult, and become atrophied in old age.
All the sinuses of the face, moreover, including the mastoid cells,
obey the same law—they do not arrive at their full development
until after puberty.

Evolution of the Teeth.

Of all the methods in use for the purpose of determining the age
of a cranium, particularly before the adult period, those derived
from the examination of the teeth are the most satisfactory. Their
evolution is divided into two periods, the more important to define,
in that we have no other data from which to form an idea as to the
relative age of the monkeys imported into Europe. The duration
of the first period in Man is about 24 months, when the whole of
the milk or temporary teeth are cut; that of the second is six

years, when the permanent teeth appear. The wisdom teeth we do
not take into consideration, as often they are not cut at all. The
following table shows the mean period of the eruption of each
tooth. It thus appears that from three to five years Man has the
minimum number of 20 teeth; from seven to twelve, 24; from
fourteen to sixteen, 28; and later on, the maximum number, 32,
not reckoning anomalies in the shape of supernumerary teeth.

Eruption of the Teeth in Man.

TEMPORARY OR DECIDUOUS TEETH = 20.

		Cruveilhier.			Magitot.
Incisors, middle lower	...	4th to 10th month	...	...	6 months.
„ „ upper	...	A little after ...	...	...	10 „
„ lateral lower	...	8th to 16th month	...	...	16 „
„ „ upper	...	A little after ...	...	...	20 „
Molars, first small, lower	...	15th to 24th month	...	...	24 „
„ „ „ upper	...	—	...	...	26 „
Canine	...	...	20th to 30th month	...	30 to 32 „
Molars, second small, lower		28th to 40th month	...	...	23 „
„ „ „ upper		—	...	...	30 „

PERMANENT TEETH = 32.

		Cruveilhier.			Magitot.
Molars, first large	...	7 years	...	5 to 6 years.
Incisors, middle, lower	...	6 to 8 „	...	7 „
„ „ upper	...	7 „ 9 „	...	—
„ lateral	...	8 „ 10 „	...	8½ „
Molars, first small	...	9 „ 11 „	...	9 „ 11 „
„ second small	...	11 „ 12 „	...	11 „
Canine	...	10 „ 11 „	...	11 „ 12 „
Molars, second large	...	12 „ 14 „	...	12 „ 13 „
„ third large, or dentes sapientiae	...	18 „ 30 „	...	16 „ 25 „

With the skull before us it is generally easy to determine the
age before 18 years. Sometimes, in the interval between the two
periods of eruption, search must be made at the bottom of the
alveolus, or we must judge from the projection of the anterior surface of the alveolar border, as to the time when the tooth is about
to make its appearance. In old age, when the teeth naturally fall

out, we should look to see how far the alveolus is closed or filled up.   The molars fall out first   We may guess the probable age on the inferior maxilla by the number of empty alveoli, by the amount of absorption of the alveolar arches, and by the senile indications already mentioned.

There is another method of ascertaining the age, namely, by examining the amount of wear and tear of the teeth.   The deciduous as well as the permanent teeth wear out, but the latter more so, on account of their much greater length of use.   The molars and canines are generally the most worn, but in the inferior or prehistoric races the incisors are frequently worn down one-half or four-fifths of their height.   M. Broca lays down four degrees of wear : in the first, the enamel is alone worn ; in the second, the tubercles of the crown have disappeared and the ivory is exposed ; in the third, some portion of the height of the tooth is reduced ; in the fourth, the wear has extended to the neck.   The last is seen in old age, but it is more often the result of particular habits, as that of chewing the betel-nut, among the Malays, or working with the teeth on skins, among the Esquimaux.   The tubercles of the first molar are soon worn down, occasionally by the commencement of adult age ; those of the second molar are more persistent.

In a word, the determination of the age of a cranium is reduced to a balancing of probabilities : the condition of the sutures deciding the question in one way, the wearing away of the teeth or the character of the jaw in another : we should take the mean.   At two or five years one can scarcely be deceived ; taking the period from 22 to 35 years it is more difficult to decide.

Distinctive Characters of the Teeth.

We cannot conclude this chapter without stating the principles by the guidance of which the archæologist or the anthropologist may discover the alveolus to which any isolated tooth belongs. The teeth of the second dentition interest us most in this respect. The four kinds may be recognised as follows : the incisors are sharp at the edges, the canines have a single and conical point, the small and large molars a flat and tuberculated crown. The difficulty is to know to which jaw and to which side of the jaw they belong.

In a general way, the teeth of the upper jaw are larger than those of the lower, with the exception of the large molars, where it is often the reverse. The incisors may be recognised in the same way; the middle incisors of the upper jaw, and the lateral of the lower, are the largest. The upper canines are not only larger but longer.

The second character has a certain value. The curve which the superior dental arch describes is wider than the inferior, and its posterior branches are turned outwards, while those of the inferior arch are turned inwards. It follows from this that the two arches do not exactly agree, the upper incisors passing a little in front of the lower, and the crown of the upper molars overlapping, on the outside, the crown of the lower. The wearing away, then, of any one or more molars begins on the inner side on the upper jaw, and on the outer on the lower. Hence, also, the plane of this wearing down is considerably oblique inwardly as regards the upper teeth, and oblique outwardly as regards the lower. For the same reason the sharp border of the lower incisors is worn slopingly on the anterior surface, which causes them to be easily recognised.

The third character has reference to all the teeth, but especially to the incisors and canines, and then to the small molars. Of the two lateral surfaces of the tooth, the internal—when we are speaking of the front teeth—or anterior, when speaking of the side teeth—is relatively plane and vertical; the other, external or posterior, is swollen and convex, and slightly mammillated close to the crown.—(Oligrom).

The fourth character has sole reference to the molars, and is derived from the tubercles on their crowns—two on the small and four on the large molars. The largest tubercle on the small molars is on the outside; the groove which separates them is somewhat deep in the upper, and is occasionally interrupted by the vestige of a third tubercle in the lower. The four tubercles of the large molars are separated by a cross-shaped sulcus, and sometimes a fifth tubercle is noticed. The wisdom tooth has usually only three tubercles—two external and one internal; or its crown presents the form of the letter S, the posterior branch of which commences on the inside, and the anterior branch terminates on the outside by doubling upon itself. In reality, its tubercles exhibit the same arrangement as the adjoining great molar, but are less definite, and, as it were, rudimentary.

The fangs furnish the last characters of which we shall speak. The small molars have usually but one, except the second upper, which has frequently two. The large lower molars have two fangs, an anterior and a posterior, which are curved slightly the one towards the other, and converge at the point. The upper have three fangs, one internal and two external, which diverge, because the inferior border of the maxillary sinus passes between them (Broca). In the large lower molars, the fang which is behind is by far the largest; in the upper, the intermediate one is the longest. The wisdom tooth has the same number of fangs as the adjoining molars, but they are generally consolidated into one or two. Lastly, the fangs of all the teeth, but especially those of the incisors, the canines, and the small molars, have their points curved outwards or backwards in the direction crossing the arch.— (Coligmon).

We may add that the crown of the first large molar bears sometimes a resemblance to that of a small molar, and the first small molar to a canine. The first large molar is the strongest, the third has the lowest crown. The milk teeth may be recognised by the following marks: they are bluish-white in colour, and not of the yellowish-blue tint of those of the second dentition. The incisors and canines are smaller, and have shorter fangs. The two milk molars are larger than the two small permanent molars; they are multicuspidate, and not bicuspidate, having three tubercles on the outside and two on the inside. They have more the appearance of large molars than of the small molars which succeed them. If we take, then, the head alone, it is easy to determine the age; if the rest of the skeleton, with the exception of one or two bones, we arrive at the same result. The indications are still derived from the evolution of certain parts.

Ossification of the Long Bones.

At the end of the fourth week of intra-uterine life, the points of ossification of the clavicle make their appearance; then those of the lower jaw; from the thirty-fifth to the fortieth day those of the femur, the humerus, the tibia, the superior maxilla, the vertebræ, and the ribs; about the fiftieth day those of the sacrum; and then—of which there is some doubt—of the scapula, &c. Ossification continues to go on; the points of the extremities, or epiphyses of the long bones, become united to one another, and then to the body or diaphysis. Of course the length of the bone furnishes some evidence of the age, but the following data are preferable. The periods indicated represent the mean of the variations observed and recorded by authors:

About 5 years, the scaphoid, the latest formed of the bones of the tarsus, is ossified.

  „   12   „   the pisiform, the latest formed of the bones of the carpus, is ossified.

  „   14   „   the three portions of the iliac bone are united.

  „   14   „   the inferior extremity of the radius is united to the body of the bone.

  „   15   „   the superior extremity of the ulna is united to the body of the bone.

  „   15   „   the lesser trochanter of the femur is united to the greater.

  „   16   „   the coronoid process is united to the scapula.

  „   16   „   the calcaneum is ossified throughout.

  „   17   „   the greater trochanter is united to the head of the femur.

  „   17   „   all the points of the inferior extremity of the humerus are united.

  „   17   „   the epiphyses of the phalanges of the fingers are united to the body of the bone.

  „   18   „   the superior extremity of the femur is united in its entirety to the shaft.

  „   18   „   the inferior extremity of the humerus is united to the body of the bone.

  „   18   „   the inferior extremity of the tibia is united to the body.

  „   18   „   the inferior extremity of the fibula is united to the body.

  „   18   „   the epiphyses of the metatarsal bones are united to the body.

About 19 years, the superior extremity of the humerus is united to the
     body.

"   20   "   the epiphyses of the metacarpal bones are united to the
     body.

"   20   "   the inferior extremity of the femur is united to the body.

"   20   "   the inferior extremity of the radius is united to the body.

"   20   "   the inferior extremity of the tibia is united to the body.

"   20   "   the inferior extremity of the ulna is united to the body.

"   20   "   the body of the sphenoid is united to the body of the
     occipital.

"   20   "   the patella is completely ossified.

"   20   "   the sacral vertebræ are anchylosed together.

"   45   "   the xiphoid cartilage is anchylosed to the sternum.

"   60   "   the coccyx is anchylosed to the sacrum.

It is said that during fœtal life the body is developed more
rapidly than the head. The extremities, M. Sappey says, are
formed from their free extremity to their root; the greater part of
the hand and foot appears in the form of buds attached to the
trunk; then the fore-arm and the leg, the arm and the thigh,
successively make their appearance; the divisions into fingers and
toes appear the last. When first fully formed the various segments
have not the proportions which they have at a later period. The
femurs, small at first in proportion to the body, afterwards become
relatively large. The same with the humerus. M. Hamy, taking
the measurements of Sue, Gunz, Liharzic, and others, has shown
that about the fourteenth day of intra-uterine life, the fore-arm of
the European is longer than the humerus; while from about two
months and a half it gradually becomes smaller. At this period the
length of the fore-arm, in proportion to that of the humerus, is
as 88 to 100; at birth this relation is 77; and from 5 to 13
years reaches 72, which it henceforth preserves. In the adult
Negro this relation is higher; from which M. Hamy concludes that
the proportions of the fore-arm, relatively to the arm, are at first
of the Negro character in the European, and assume their true
character at a later period.

Other modifications, some connected with evolution, others with
the biped attitude, are exhibited in the inferior extremities.

The pelvis at birth is relatively narrow, and, as a consequence, the great trochanters appear more projecting. The angle which the neck of the femur makes with the body of the bone is very wide, and the two femurs fall almost perpendicularly. At adult age the pelvis enlarges; the trochanter femoris is less projecting; the angle of the neck is less open—from 125 to 130 degrees in the man, and approaching a right angle in the woman (*Humphry*); the shaft of the bone is very oblique, owing to the inferior extremity making an angle with the perpendicular, looking from above, of about 15 degrees. In old age the angle of the neck is still diminished, and in the man reaches about 110 degrees; the pelvis appears larger, and the great trochanters are less prominent; lastly, the curve, with its concavity looking backwards, is increased.

We may add, incidentally, that the angle of the neck is smaller, and the obliquity of the femur more pronounced in short men: it is the same in woman, according to Humphry. These two anatomical conditions of the femur—the obliquity estimated by the angle which its extremity makes with the vertical, and the angle of its neck with the diaphysis—have been the subject of special study by our colleague, Dr. Kuhff. His researches have been carried out upon twenty-four femurs, and the following are the mean results obtained in reference to these two points :

	Number.	Angle of obliquity.	Angle of neck.
Cavern of La Loubre	5	9.7	125°
Dolmens of La Lozère	5	11	122
Grottoes of La Marne	19	11	129
Gallo-Romans	6	12	132
Carlovingians	4	12	118

His maximum and minimum degrees of obliquity are 14 and 8 respectively, and of the angle of the neck, 140 and 117 degrees. The results agree very closely with those of Mr. Humphry.

One of the causes of the diminution of the stature at an advanced age is the sinking of the neck. Another, still more important, is the subsidence of the intervertebral discs, which takes place for the most part anteriorly, whereby the whole of the trunk is bent forwards. Osseous vegetations are thrown out between the body of one vertebra and that of another, which tend to strengthen the column and to limit the incurvation.

If the first task of the anthropologist, when called upon to give his opinion upon human remains, is to determine their age, his second is to ascertain the sex. Both studies concern Men in his *ensemble*, and not Man in his ethnic varieties. It is of the latter therefore that we shall speak in this place.

Sexual Differences in the Skeleton.

There is no appreciable difference in the skeleton in infancy, and up to puberty; its features are rather of a feminine character. At puberty, the line of demarcation commences, but the characters are not thoroughly defined until 20 years of age and upwards. At about 45, or upwards, the distinctions of sex become less marked, and at advanced age are but trifling, though the general character of the skeleton is rather masculine.

The principles which govern the sexual differences in adult age may be summed up in a few words. All the parts of the female skeleton are lighter and more frail; the general contour is more soft and graceful; the eminences, processes, or tubercules, are smaller and less marked. If there is one well-established physiological fact, it is this: that the asperities which serve for the insertion of muscles are developed in proportion to the activity of those muscles. Less marked in the studious man than in the labourer, these asperities are still less so in the woman, especially in women residing in towns. This law is so exact that we can tell by the degree of prominence of the crests and processes, what muscles the individual was most in the habit of using, and hence judge as to his profession or calling. As a sequence of these prominences, the depressions, grooves, and marks are more distinct in the man. So the temporal ridge, which serves superiorly for the insertion of the temporal muscle, and the transverse ridges, which divide the internal surface of the scapula, and serve for the insertion of the subscapularis muscle, are more marked in the male; the

groove of torsion of the humerus is more visible, and the two S-like
curvatures of the clavicle are stronger. In the woman, on the
contrary, the external protuberance of the occipital, and the two
subjacent curved lines which serve for the insertion of the muscles
of the nucha—the anterior tubercle of the tibia to which the triceps
femoris is attached—the tuberosity of the radius which gives
insertion to the biceps of the humerus, are less prominent—the
curved alveolar borders are more regular—the borders of the malar
bone are less thick—the canine fossa is less deep. In a word, it is
tolerably easy to determine the sex by the appearance of a bone; in
the case of a long bone, we are rarely in doubt; in a short bone, as
the calcaneum, it is still possible to do so. But we must not be
surprised if we are occasionally at fault; by making a comparison
between one bone and another, the difficulty will be cleared up.
Suppose we took the clean-shaved head of any individual, the beard
being removed, or the hand, or foot, the rest of the body being
concealed, anyone, particularly after a little practice, would be able
to tell whether the part belonged to a man or a woman, though it
might be sometimes difficult to do so. Both, whether spontaneously
or by reason of the work in which they had been engaged, or owing
to exposure to the air, would have all the appearances of the
opposite sex. On the skeleton, a woman who had worked hard all
her life would have the bony prominences and the processes for the
articulations of muscles more developed, probably, than a man who
had not worked at all.

Let us consider two organs only. The woman has the crests of
the ilia larger and wider, in other words, the lips more prominent;
the subpubic foramen is of a triangular shape, while in the man it
is irregularly oval; the symphysis pubis is shorter, the subjacent
arch is broad-pointed, while in the man it forms a very acute angle,
and the cotyloid cavities are more expanded. In a word, all the
transverse diameters of her pelvis are increased, while in the man
the vertical are the more so. In 113 male pelves, the maximum
width to the length, or maximum height, was as 125·5 to 1000,
and in the woman, as 136 to 1000. The mean relative width to
the height of the individual in each sex, is as 160 to 1000 in the

man, and as 174 in the woman; that is to say, fourteen-thousandths more in the latter.

The head of the woman is smaller and lighter, its contours more delicate, the surfaces smoother, the ridges and processes not so marked. The superciliary arches are but little prominent; the external half of the superior orbital border is thin and sharp (*Broca*). The forehead is vertical below, projecting above. The occipital condyles are small, as also the mastoid and styloid processes. The zygomatic arches are slender. The cranium in its *ensemble* is less high and longer. The subnasal portion of the face is more prognathous in the white races, less so in the black. The inferior maxilla is smaller, its posterior angles having no projecting roughnesses. The frontal sinuses are less developed, &c.

Of all these characters the most important and the only ones easy to measure are the smallness of the head, the less capacity of the cranial cavity, and the relative lightness of the brain. Then the obliteration of the glabella, the throwing outwards of the superior orbital border, the smallness of the inion, the slight projection of the occipital curved lines, and, lastly, the more abrupt angle, more nearly approaching a right angle, of the forehead at the level of the frontal protuberances. Five times out of six we may decide the question with certainty; M. Mantegazza says nine times out of ten.[*] It may be asked, What skulls should be preferred upon which to study the races of Man? With Van der Hoeven, we reply, those of men. No one would be so bold as to say that ethnic characters are best exhibited in the cranium of the infant; but the skeleton of the woman is intermediate between that of the infant and the adult man. Having considered the skeleton, we must take a brief glance at other questions in relation to age and function in Men and animals.[†]

[*] P. Mantegazza, "Dei Caratteri Sessuali del Cranio Umano," in "Archivio per l'Antrop.," vol. ii., 1872; A. Dareste, "Des Caractères Sexuels du Crâne Humain," in "Revue d'Anthrop.," vol. ii., 1873.

[†] See Colin, "Traité de Physiologie Comparée des Animaux." Two vols. Paris, 1871.

The Temperature of the Body.

Some degrees above zero (centigrade) in most animals termed cold blooded, as reptiles and fishes, is some degrees higher in birds and mammalia, which are both warm blooded. Moreover, it varies but little in the latter. The temperature of Man (in the axilla) is 37·8 centigrade; that of the hare and squirrel is the same; that of the horse is 38; of the ox, 38·5; of the bat and the whale, 36·6; of the tiger and panther, 39; of the ordinary monkeys, 39·7 (*Noguès*); of the wolf, 40·5.

The Pulse.

Varies considerably. It is from 70 to 80 in the minute in the adult man; from 25 to 28 in the elephant; from 36 to 40 in the horse; from 45 to 50 in the ox; from 70 to 80 in the pig, the sheep, and the goat; from 90 to 100 in the dog; from 120 to 140 in the cat; 175 in the dormouse; 200 in the mouse.

Phenomena of Reproduction.

These exhibit still more marked differences. Three points here demand our attention, viz. the duration of gestation, the number of young, and menstruation. Generally speaking, in the mammalian series, the circumstances which are favourable to reproduction are in direct ratio to the shortness of life. The smaller species carry their young a shorter period than the larger, and have a greater number of young at a birth. In the following list we see the place occupied by Man. He has two at a birth more frequently than the monkey tribe, and exceptionally he has three or four.

	Period of Gestation, Weeks.			Number of young.
Mouse	...	...	... 3	... 10 to 16
Hare	...	...	... 4	... 3 or 4
Parrot	...	...	... 6	... 6 to 8
Dog	...	...	... 9	... 5 or 6
Lion	...	...	... 14	... 4 „ 5

	Period of Gestation. Weeks.	Number of young.
Roebuck	24	2
Macacus	16	1
Macacus Rhesus	20	1
Macacus Maimon	31	1
Stag	26	1
Seal	39	1
Woman	39	1
Cow	41	1
Mare	42	1
Camel	43	1
Giraffe	61	1
Elephant	100	1

Menstruation is not confined to woman, nor to the pithecian monkeys. The phenomenon is identical with that called "rut" in animals.

Duration of Life.

The mean duration of life in Man is at the present time, in France, about 40 years,[*] and the ordinary duration from 70 to 80. Some individuals, exceptionally, live beyond 100 years. Bérard says, one in 3100 in England. Prichard mentions that in the year 1799, Easton had collected together 1712 cases of centenarians : of this number, 277 had attained from 110 to 120 years; 117 from 120 to 150; and eight from 150 to 180. He also gives a great number of other equally well-authenticated and not less extraordinary cases. With some exceptions, Man is the most highly favoured of the mammalia as regards longevity; the reproductive faculty continues longer, and he enjoys a long old age. But is not this due to the care which he takes of himself? The average duration of life in Europe is increasing, while in countries where the people go about naked it is decreasing.

Among animals, longevity is generally less in the smaller species. The pig lives to the age of 9 years, the dog from 15 to 18, the

* "Sur la Prétendue Dégénérescence de la Population Française," by M. Broca, in "Bull. Acad. Méd." 1867.

bear from 20 to 25,* the horse and the ox to 20, the camel to 45, the elephant from 150 to 200 years. As regards the three higher anthropoids, the average duration of life is from 40 to 60 years.

General Functions and Psychical Manifestations.

Man inhabits every region of the globe, and inures himself to all climates and to all conditions of life. Whether at the pole or the equator, on the highest mountains or in the deepest valleys, in arid deserts or unhealthy swamps, nothing seems to daunt him. The Esquimaux are to be met with up to 80 degrees north. There are those who live and thrive in the Andes and the Himalayas, at an altitude of 4000 or 5000 mètres and upwards; and we find inhabitants even in those vast regions in which Livingstone travelled up to his middle in water. From 47 degrees cent. (= 116·6 Fahr.) in the shade, as observed in Senegal, to 56 below zero (= 100 degrees Fahrenheit below freezing-point) at the poles, are the extremes of temperature which he is able to support. Some animals readily adapt themselves to the most opposite conditions of climate, as the dog; others are unable to bear such changes, as the reindeer, the bear, the lion, the whale. This is how the disappearance of certain geological species, as the megatherium, the mastodon, and the mammoth, is to be accounted for. The anthropoid apes live in communities in certain circumscribed regions; the gorilla and the chimpanzee on the west coast of Africa, at about 15 degrees north and south of the equator; the orang in Borneo and Sumatra; the gibbons in India, bordering on China and Malacca. M. Schweinfurth has discovered a new species of chimpanzee on the banks of the Upper White Nile. Other species have been described, belonging to the tertiary epochs, in different parts of the globe, especially in France. We may remark that the anthropoids are only to be met with in hot countries. This power which Man possesses, of more or less readily accustoming himself to any climate, is to be accounted for from the fact (1) That he is omnivorous;

* A bear cubbed in one of the pits in Berne, is said to have reached the age of 47 years.

and (2) that he knows how to clothe himself and to manufacture weapons and implements. The Esquimaux subsists on oil and the flesh of seals; the Todas of the Nilgherries on milk and pulse. Some tribes live on fish and shell-fish, and take sea water as a beverage. Others mix clay with their food, while civilised nations obtain their supplies from all sources. Man cooks his food, but he does not despise the raw mollusk, or undressed fish, or the raw flesh of the mammalia. Unlike any other animal, he rears cattle and devotes himself to agriculture. He makes use of various animals, as the dog, the cat, the camel, and the reindeer, to subserve his own purposes; and even his fellow-creatures, be they black or white, are equally under his dominion. In this respect some animals imitate him—as the red ants in their treatment of the black ants.

The majority of animals possess natural means of protection and defence. The gorilla has a far peculiar to himself, powerful canine teeth, and a muscular system of extraordinary strength. Other mammalia possess agility and swiftness in running, which enables them to escape from enemies. Man has nothing of the kind. "Naked and without weapons," such is Linnæus's definition of him. All his various methods of operation he owes to his industry. From the remotest period he has made use of fire, and has manufactured flint implements. The anthropoid ape has never known how to make use of a staff, to put up a fence, to make a fire, nor to construct a habitation which can be dignified by a higher title than that of a nest.[*] The negroes of the islands in the Indian Ocean, who live in trees, or sleep under bundles of sticks laid against a rock, do so from indolence or indifference, rather than from incapacity. The lowest savages known have some notion of drawing; they know at least how to make a cross or a round in imitation of objects which they see around them; and, for our part, we attach but little credence to the statement made by Oldfield, that the aborigines of Western Australia are unable to

[*] Livingstone saw one of these enormous nests constructed by the actor, one of the chimpanzees. M. du Chaillu saw a sort of circular roofing in trees, constructed by another chimpanzee, the troglodytes calvus.

distinguish the figure of a tree from that of a ship. In the same region other travellers have observed, on the contrary, that they possess a certain amount of intellectual capacity. It would have been well if Oldfield had given some case in verification of his statement.

Among all races of mankind there exists the desire to please, or the love of dress. In civilised countries it is more developed in the woman, among barbarous tribes it is more so in the man. Some tattoo themselves, or suspend various ornaments to their ears, or to the septum of the nose, while others dye their hair, or sharpen their front teeth into points. Something analogous has been observed in domestic monkeys. Many tribes cannot count above two, and are less favoured in this respect than the magpie, which can count up to three, some say up to twelve. But all have some notion of number. A Boajesman, however, although intelligent in other respects, was incapable of adding one and one together.

Man is not to be distinguished from animals as regards his family relations. He is monogamous or polygamous, and the woman is similarly polyandrous. The gorilla and the chimpanzee are monogamous, very jealous of the fidelity of their partners, and very devoted in their attentions to them. Man, likewise, attaches himself without hesitation to those of his own kindred. He lavishes his care and love on his offspring beyond the period of lactation, and up to that when they are able to look after themselves. If this period should be prolonged beyond puberty it is owing to the customs of society. The ceremonies which among all savage tribes mark the progress from infancy to manhood also mark the period at which Man acquires his independence. Maternal affection, with all its evidences of blind devotion, is, with rarest exceptions, universal. The father exercises authority over the life of his children; he practises infanticide openly at his will and pleasure, in the same way as the son, at a later period, disencumbers himself from his parents who have become a burden to him. The Todas destroy in the cradle all their female children beyond a certain number, as being useless, in the same way as they kill all their male buffaloes but one, because they do not give milk. In a state of nature Man considers utility first, and refers everything to his wants, his family, and so on. It must be confessed that in the social condition there is much of this sort of thing under a less rough exterior. Selfishness is well known to be the moving principle almost universally, and is only limited in its action by a fear of the law, or by education.

Man lives in society because he is compelled to do so, like many other animals. Being endowed with the faculty of language, and with exalted intellectual powers, he wants to exercise them, having in view also the more ready satisfying of his material wants, and the realisation of a larger amount of comfort. Emulation, which results from this, is the most powerful cause of progress in the physical, moral, and intellectual world. The larger the community, the greater the amount of rivalry; and the more fierce the contest, the more rapid the progress.

A great number of animals also seek the society of their fellow-creatures, and work in company, as the beaver, the buffalo, the Australian dog, the horse, the swallow, the bee, the ant. The soko, an anthropoid ape, lives in a troop of ten individuals on the banks of the river Lualaba. Many species of monkeys, like Man, select a chief, who directs their operations and to whom they submit. The howlers, or mycetes, belonging to the cebian family, hold meetings in which one of them speaks for hours at a time in the midst of general silence, succeeded by great excitement, which comes as soon as the speaker gives the word of command. Other monkeys combine together to plan an incursion; divided into detachments, some plunder and tear up roots, others make a chain for the purpose of carrying them from hand to hand; others are placed as sentinels to keep watch. In unexpected danger, the sentinel gives the alarm and all decamp. It has been remarked that if it happens that the troop is surprised, owing to the fault of the sentinel, there is a grand hubbub in the neighbouring forest during the night, and on the morrow the body of one of the plunderers is found, to all appearance having been put to death by his companions.

It has been said that one of the characteristics of man is religiousness, that is to say, "the faculty of belief in something above human understanding." Would it not be better to define it as an internal impulse, which prompts us to individualise the unknown and to make him the object of adoration.† *

Be it as it may, many, even among the most civilised, have neither this belief nor this impulse, and are satisfied to live without troubling themselves as to that which they do not comprehend; they have neither fear, nor reverence, nor gratitude—the three essences of religious conceptions. There are nations and tribes without religion and without any mode of worship, and who believe only in wizards or fetich. It is true they make every form of superstition to subserve their religiousness. But some African or Melanesian tribes have not even superstitions.†

Neither good luck nor misfortune affects them in any way. If,

---

* It is impossible to take religion in its strict sense as the faculty of believing in a god; if so, half of the population of the globe would be destitute of it. Taking Buddhism alone, there are three or four hundred million votaries of this "religion without God," founded on charity amounting to madness."—Laboulaye.

† Nothing requires such calm and impartial judgment as the inquiry into the moral and religious condition of savage tribes. Burchell, through his interpreter, addressed two or three questions to Bojesmans, and immediately came to the conclusion that "they were brutes, because they did not answer the simple question : What is the difference between a good and a bad action?" Cases of this kind are very common. Other travellers, less impulsive, perseveringly inquired into their beliefs and superstitions, and came to the conclusion that they had no conception of anything outside themselves, and were persuaded that they die in the same condition. Which are we to believe? Such a thing is rare as a rule. All missionaries, to whatever church they belong, are impressed with the conviction that savages believe in a god, in the existence of a soul, and in the deluge; while independent travellers arrive at altogether different conclusions. The fact is, the savage endeavours to please those from whom he is likely to gain something. He understands the wishes of the missionaries and satisfies them. It is absolutely undeniable that the absence of all abstract ideas is a very common characteristic of savage tribes; hence causes them to see evil spirits everywhere, and to create for themselves fetich, but the opposite feeling, the recognition of that which does them good, induces them to conceive of beneficent spirits.

after long abstinence, they get a windfall, they eat and think of nothing further. In this respect Man is inferior to the dog, which maintains a devoted attachment to the hand that brings him his daily food, to the master, who is to him as a God. Assuredly this animal has a belief in something above him. Say it those birds which warble their songs at the rising of the sun are not moved by an internal impulse to praise nature for the infinite pleasure which she bestows upon them? This is but little removed from adoration.

Man alone has an idea of duty—a morale. Is this certain? And of what kind of morality are we to speak first—of that of the peasant or of the noble—of the morality of the laws or of natural morality? A very remarkable English work* mentions that morality is essentially variable, progressive, and perfectible; that it is a reflex of wants, of usages, and of circumstances; what is good here, is bad elsewhere—as to take care of one's infirm parent, or to bury him alive. Its radius, he says, has gone on enlarging for ages, from the inferior to the superior races; at first consisting only of the family, it has since extended to the whole tribe; that which was evil in one was good in other tribes. Thence it has spread far and wide and has become international. "Morality or ethics," says Mr. Tylor, "signifies the act of conforming to the manners (mores, ἔθη) of the society to which we belong. There are not two races in the world which have exactly the same code of morality, but each has its own, which is sanctioned by public opinion." At the present moment throughout Europe do not the rules of morality change in the event of war? Tylor's most approved criterion, "Do not to another that which you would not have done to yourself," applies to animals as well as to man. The dog knows that in order not to be bitten he must not bite, and acts accordingly: he has also his morality.

Man possesses consciousness of that which philosophers call le moi, that is to say of himself, of his personality. It would be

---

* "Primitive Culture," by E. B. Tylor. Second edition. London, 1873. Translated into French; Reinwald and Co.'s edition. Paris, 1876.

strange if animals had it not also. Man has the sense of the
noble, of the just, though he has many ways of expressing it. He
grasps the relations of cause to effect; the animal does the same.
He possesses spontaneity, will, the power of balancing probabilities
but is it not so with animals? Madness even is not peculiar to
man.[*]

M. Houzeau has worked out this subject in a masterly manner
in his two volumes on "The Mental Faculties of Animals." But
Prichard, the most orthodox of anthropologists, had previously
devoted a long chapter to the consideration of their psychical en-
dowments (*facultés psychiques*). There is also a work in the
"Bibliothèque des Sciences Contemporaines," which treats of all
these questions.[†]

But to the anthropologist, or the unprejudiced naturalist, the
inference is obvious. Between Man and most animals there is no
absolute radical difference in intellectual arrangement. All the
faculties of Man are to be found, without exception, in animals,
but in a rudimentary state; some are very highly developed, others
more so even than in ourselves. It is not the exclusive possession
of special faculties which gives us our supremacy, our judgment,
our intelligence, our correctness of observation; but the measure of
these, and, better still, our holding them in perfect equilibrium. In
a madman we continually notice a faculty of rising to a higher
state than that which the sane man possesses. Keep this well in
view, and the madman would appear to you to be a genius; but at
the same time other faculties are debased, there is a loss of balance,
and consequently a less amount of reason. The intellectual
characteristic of Men in general, and especially of the man of
wisdom, is the exact equilibrium of all his faculties, and not the
increase or exaltation of any.

Another physiological character connected with the function of
the brain, which anthropologists look upon as peculiar to man, is

* See "Traité de la Folie des Animaux et de ses Rapports avec celle de
l'Homme," by Pierquin. Two vols. Paris, 1839.

† See also "L'Anatomie Comparée du Système Nerveux," by Leuret and
Gratiolet, vol. i., chap. "Facultés des Mammifères." Paris, 1839.

the faculty of language, or that of uttering articulate sounds. According to the doctrine of the derivation of Man from less perfect animal forms, Man would have taken his origin from the moment that he was put in possession of this faculty.

Faculty of Language.

Many, if not all, animals communicate to one another their thoughts relating to their usual life; they have intonations and modulations of voice, each of which has a distinct and definite meaning. They variously express fear, joy, suffering, and hunger. They make themselves understood by those of their own species, of their own family, of their own young; they warn them of the approach, of the nature, and of the amount of danger. But, as a general rule, they do not articulate. Some of them join together a few consonants to vowels, but they repeat them without change. In this respect the notes of birds would better deserve the name of language.

Let us explain. There exists in Man and animals, and common to them both, a general faculty called that of expression (expression), or the faculty of connecting an idea with a sign. Its various manifestations are the faculties of mimicry and of speech; probably also music and drawing. The mimic faculty evidently exists in animals. The dog which stands at game, and runs back to see if his master is in pursuit, or which scratches at the door to be let in, is a proof of this. It is not surprising that the animal does not possess the faculty of delineation, seeing that it has not the perfect hand of Man, nor has it been instructed. We can simply allude to the hum of insects produced by the friction of their elytra, and pass on to the vocal faculty. There is not the slightest doubt that animals express their ideas in this way. M. Couderau has taken great pains to analyse the language of the hen, and the numerous intonations corresponding to each order of ideas, which are provoked by the small number of feelings and wants in connection with its humble existence. But in this, and probably in that which is uttered by the howling monkey, are there not articulate

sounds, or syllables more or less jumbled together, which deserve
the title of language? We must remember that the primitive
languages spoken by Man were monosyllabic. All philologists tell
us so, and that very few elementary syllables were sufficient at
first to constitute an articulate language. The question then
resolves itself into this: How many articulate sounds or simple
syllables would be required to constitute a language, and where is
the line to be drawn between the relatively perfect language of
some species of animals, and the primitive language of the
lowest type of our own progenitors? Of course we are not referring
to the parrot, which attaches no meaning to its utterances, but to
monkeys, which make use of different syllables, each having a
distinct meaning.

We will now analyse the mechanism of human speech. The
air expired from the lungs enters into vibration in the larynx,
where the voice is formed, and passes through the mouth, where
articulation takes place. The muscles of the larynx modify the
former, the muscles of the vault of the palate, of the tongue, of the
cheeks and lips, have to do with the latter. But these also contract
for other purposes, and are supplied by different nerves. The
stimulation of these nerves at their origin would only produce
irregular contractions having no definite object. There are then
besides special centres, having distinct functions, in which the
appropriate movements are co-ordinated, and to which the mental
impressions are conveyed. Thanks to the experience with which
nature favours us in the living body, the centre, in relation not
only with articulation in general, but with each particular system,
is well known. When the quadrilateral* indicated by M. Broca,
at the posterior extremity of his third frontal convolution, especially on the left side, is affected by an acute lesion, the faculty of
articulating is disturbed or altogether suppressed.†

* See page 109 on the Seat of the Faculty of Language.
† In microcephales, who have never been able to learn to speak, the
third frontal convolution has been found atrophied. It has been asked why
the faculty of language should appear to be localised, or rather is the more

The phenomenon reduced to its most simple expression is termed aphemia. The individual preserves his intellect, expresses his ideas by gestures or by writing, moves his tongue and lips, and has power of voice, but is unable to articulate; his general faculty of expression remains, but he has lost the power of speech. At other times the lesion is more extensive; he has still ideas, but is incapable of committing them to writing or otherwise. Sometimes the lesion is still more considerable, and the intellect itself is affected.

We see then the series of operations which language requires, and to which so many more or less distinct organs lend their aid: (1) Thought and will; (2) The general faculty of expression; (3) The particular faculty of articulating; (4) The transmission by nerves; (5) The execution by muscles. These functions are thoroughly in accord, and largely developed in Man, but is it not so in the animal? The animal has ideas, he possesses the faculty of expression and of articulating sounds, but all this is in a rudimentary state. In Man, on the contrary, all have assumed gigantic proportions; his ideas have become multiplied in the course of ages; his faculty of articulating has become perfected by use; his nerves and muscles have learnt to obey him absolutely. And in the same way as an instrument gives out more harmonious sounds according as the fingers which play upon it acquire greater expertness, and the musical power which directs them greater force, so human language is the result of progressive development in the

oftener exercised from the left side. Two explanations have been given; that of M. Broca is the one generally admitted. We are not right-handed, he says, by accident, but because the left hemisphere, which presides over the movements of the right side by the decussation of the nerves near their origin, has from the first a greater amount of activity. This excess of activity extends to all the functions of which this hemisphere is the seat, and possibly of that of articulation. There are exceptions, nevertheless; that is to say, there are persons who originally, or after a lesion in the left hemisphere, speak with their right; in the same way as there are some people originally left-handed, and others who have become left-handed in consequence of having lost their right hand.

course of ages from efforts at first weak and unpretending. But is
it the multiplication of ideas which originally gave birth to
language, or language which has given development to ideas?
This is the question.[*]

CHAPTER V.

PATHOLOGICAL CHARACTERS—DISEASES—FACTS OF TERATOLOGY—
MICROCEPHALCS—HYDROCEPHALUS—PREMATURE SYNOSTOSES—
ARTIFICIAL DEFORMATIONS OF THE SKULL—CONCLUSION AS TO
MAN'S PLACE IN THE CLASS OF MAMMALIA.

PATHOLOGICAL conditions are merely deviations from the physiological state. They affect living organs, and have reference also
to man's life generally. The chapter on pathological characters,
although important, is only a sequel of our general division on
physiological characters. The points on this horizon which interest the anthropologist, only looking at the comparison of Man
with the other mammalia, are of three orders: (1) The number
of diseases common to Man and animals, and the few peculiar to
the one or the other; (2) The disturbances in the regular development of the body, when they can throw any light on the
problem of the origins of organisation; (3) Particular alterations in
the skeleton being capable of being confounded with the normal
condition.

The laws of pathology are the same throughout the whole
mammalian series as those of physiology, upon which they depend;
their effects, too, are generally identical. Animals, like Man, are
subject to accidents, to faults of development, to diseases of an
acute and transient nature, and to those which are chronic and of
long duration. They have the troubles of youth as well as those

---

[*] See "La Linguistique," by M. Abel Hovelacque, 2nd edition, Paris, 1876,
' Bibliothèque des Sciences Contemporaines."

of old age. In both are observed inflammatory and rheumatic
affections, eruptive fevers, typhus, the neuroses; the only difference
is in the country in which these diseases manifest themselves,
and in the symptoms resulting from this. There is as great a
difference between the diseases which attack Europeans and those
seen in Negroes, as between the diseases of Man and those of
animals.*

Thus the *eaux aux jambes* (grease) in the horse is the same disease
as the cow-pox of the cow and the small-pox of Man. Experiments
by inoculation have clearly proved this. The scab of sheep is
doubtless something of the same kind; the pig, too, is subject to a
form of small-pox. The congestion of the spleen of the sheep
species becomes the *charbon* in horned cattle, and the malignant
pustule in Man. It is unnecessary to say that affections of the
skin are not the same on the thick skin of the horse and on the
delicate skin of the European. Between the latter and that of the
Negro there are also differences in this respect. So the nervous
system being less impressionable in animals, the reaction is less
strong, and the fever less apparent. Like ourselves, the animal is
dyspeptic, asthmatic, tuberculous, scrofulous, or cancerous. Like
ourselves, the constituent elements of his blood—the globule, the
albumen, and the fibrin—increase or diminish, producing anæmia,
dropsy, or scurvy. Food other than the milk provided for their
use, produces in their young diarrhœa, as in Man. They have the
same swelling of the glands during the eruption of the teeth. A
young orang died under our own observation owing to disorders of
dentition, which arose while we were treating it as we should have
done a human being. The *acarus* which produces the itch may
differ in kind, but its effects are identical. Parasites in general,
such as entozoa, vary, as in Man, according to climate, but in the
same way as those which infest vegetables. Hydrophobia is met
with in the dog, the cat, the wolf, the fox, the cow, and the horse,
as in Man (*Trousseau*). Syphilis exists among apes. A *macacus
sinicus* which was the subject of a communication to the Anthropo-

* "Dictionnaire de Médecine Vétérinaire," by Bouley and Reynal. Two
vols. 1866.

logical Society of London, in 1865, presented the three series of
phenomena—the ulceration of the sexual organs, the falling off of
the hair, and the affection of the bones.   The diseases of the brain
themselves are not peculiar to Man.   Animals exhibit many forms
of delirium; but they are more frequent in Man, owing to the importance of the organ which is their seat, as well as to the activity
and delicacy of its manifestations.

In a word, the pathological types are the same throughout the
whole mammalian series, and are only modified according to species.
The diseases peculiar to one or many species are rare, as glanders,
which appears peculiar to Man and solipeds.   Moreover, animal
pathology has advanced but little, and has scarcely reached beyond
that of our domestic species.

Anomalies of development are, according to our idea, of four
kinds.   Some exhibit themselves physiologically during life: for
example, giants and those afflicted with polysarcia; others are congenital, but can be modified or removed after birth; a third kind
are congenital and irremediable, except occasionally by surgical
means, and are called monstrosities, or teratological phenomena; a
fourth are the organic anomalies described at page 126, under the
name of Perversions.

Among giants we may mention a Finlander, who was 2·85 mètres
in height, and a Kalmuck, whose skeleton is in the Museum Orfila,
2·53 mètres.   Then we have dwarfs, but these are for the most
part affected with rickets.   The height of the celebrated Bébé
of King Stanislas of Poland was 89 centimètres; another, 25
years of age and 56 centimètres in height, was presented to
Henrietta of France in a pie.

The ordinary weight of the man is 63 kilogrammes, according to Quételet, and that of the woman, 54.   We have seen
dwarfs who only weighed from 4 to 8 kilogrammes.   In
polysarcia, or obesity, the weight is often more than 150 kilogrammes.   Two Englishmen, brothers, weighed, the one 233
kilogrammes, the other 240 (Sappey).   Another Englishman, in
1724, measured 1 mètre 72 centimètres round the body, and was
1 mètre 86 centimètres in height.   Barrow mentions a half-caste

from the Cape of Good Hope, who lived twelve years in his bed,
and was burnt alive in it; the house having taken fire, neither the
door nor the window was found large enough to enable him to get
out.

Albinos are individuals in whom the pigmentary matter is so
far deficient that the skin and hair are colourless, the iris is transparent, and the choroid coat destitute of the dark pigment for the
absorption of redundant rays of light. In consequence of this,
they are unable to bear bright sunlight, and see better at night than
during the day. Their eyeballs are affected with a perpetual
oscillating movement, their skin and hair are colourless, or of a
dull white, the eyes reddish, the transparency of the tissues showing the blood circulating through the capillaries. They are often
indolent, and without muscular vigour. There are partial albinos,
in whom all the above symptoms are observed, but in a less degree.
They may easily pass unnoticed among the white races, but are
very observable among the black; their hair is flaxen or red, their
skin coffee-coloured or speckled, their eyes are light blue or
reddish.

Both are met with among all races and under all climates. In
some of the native courts on the west coast of Africa, especially in
Congo, they are an object of veneration, and go by the name of
"dondos." Dr. Schweinfurth has seen a great number of them with
the king of the Monbuttous on the banks of the Bahr-el-Ghazel.
From their presence among the blackest populations, Prichard
framed an important argument in favour of the influence of
external circumstances, and of the derivation of the human race
from one primitive pair. He delighted to reiterate it, and moreover he was the first to establish the fact that their hair was as
woolly and their features were as negro as those of their fellow-
countrymen of the same tribe. We say again, albinism is only a
monstrosity, a pathological condition which has been cured, and
we must take care how we place implicit reliance on the confused
accounts given of it by travellers. A cutaneous affection called
pityriasis versicolor is seen in whites, as a partial loss of colour of
some portions of the skin, while the accumulation of pigment upon

M

other portions causes them to appear of a deeper colour. The eyes
are not at all affected in these cases.

Our opinion is that what has been called in negroes piebald,
and described as an example of partial albinism, is the same thing.
The scaly affection called ichthyosis, often of a marked hereditary
character, to which Mr. Darwin frequently alludes, and the subjects
of which deserve the title of porcupine men, has no interest for the
anthropologist.

Two individuals, Russians by birth, were recently exhibited in
Paris, called dog-men, whose bodies were covered with a quantity of
long coarse hair ; they were also said to have exhibited a defective
development of the teeth.   Similar cases in Burmah and India have
been described, which were hereditary through three generations.

Monstrosities, of which there are many varieties,* are produced
during embryonic or fœtal life, either in consequence of hereditary
predisposition, of some accident to the mother, or from some disease
of the fœtus.   They arise either from arrest, excess, or perversion
of development.   Some are incompatible with life, others do not
interfere with it. We are not about to give an explanation
respecting the two theories—either the one as to the pre-existence
of germs, as maintained by Winslow, but now abandoned, and
which means that the embryo represents from the very first the
future being in his entirety ; or the other, that of Serres and Isidore
Geoffroy Saint-Hilaire, called epigenesis, which we have described
at page 128, and which admits progressive development. Among
these monstrosities, we may mention polydactylism, or the existence
of from four to seven fingers, which has been noticed as having
occurred through many generations ; inversion of the viscera, in
which the heart is found only on the right side, or where all the
viscera are inverted ; the absence of one or more limbs ; hermaphroditism ; hypospadias ; imperforate anus ; hare-lip ; spina bifida ;
microcephalus, &c.   One of the most curious of the teratological
groups is diplogenesis, in which the whole body is more or less
double, as if there had been a fusion of two germs, or a duplication
of a single one.   The Siamese twins, and the two Zambo girls

* Isidore Geoffroy Saint-Hilaire. "Traité de Tératologie." Paris, 1832.

exhibited in 1874 in Paris were of this kind. Perhaps we ought
to speak of them as examples of supplementary limbs, as that of a
girl of 14 or 15 years of age, exhibited the same year before the
Anthropological Society by Dr. Ball.

Monstrosities are not peculiar to Man; they are frequent also
among animals. We shall only speak of those which are specially
interesting to us as taking place in the head, as microcephalus and
hydrocophalus. Under the name of mental alienation we include
all the various functional disorders of the brain. These may be
reduced to three : (1) Mania properly so called, which breaks out
in individuals hitherto sane, has two forms—the one of excitement,
the other of depression—and is general or partial ; (2) Dementia,
which is a general and progressive feebleness of all the faculties,
and is of two kinds—accidental, or senile; (3) Idiotcy, in which
the faculties have never attained their full development. In the
three forms, the volume of the brain is increased or diminished
according to the amount of disease, and according to the greater or
less amount of blood which it contains. In ordinary mania there
is rather an increase, and in dementia, sooner or later, a decrease.
The lesion affects the entire organ, its central portions, its convolutions, and sometimes solely the gray substance covering them, and
the functional disorder becomes permanent. It is impossible to be
deceived, and true human superiority consists in knowing how to
look the truth in the face. The most beautiful of our intellectual
manifestations—those of which we are so justly proud—are the
product of a material organ, in the same way as bile is the
product of the liver, and the circulation is the product of the contractions of the heart. A sound and healthy brain produces sound
judgment and understanding ; a diseased, bloodless, and impaired
brain produces the reverse. That which distinguishes Man from
the brute is the quality and quantity of the organ—the quality and
quantity of the product.

If mania and dementia only concern medicine, idiotcy has an
interest for anthropology ; it exhibits the brain sometimes less
developed, more simple, more or less stunted in growth, and
approaching more to that of animals.

There are many direct causes of idiotcy. Sometimes the volume
of the brain is normal, but its convolutions are very large, generally
less flexuous, or decidedly imperfect at some particular point.
Sometimes it is hypertrophied, and its convolutions, though simple,
are, as it were, piled upon one another, and tend to produce impressions on the internal surface of the cranium. Sometimes it is
altogether atrophied, or only so on one side, in its frontal, parietal,
or occipital lobes, in its central portions, or in a group of convolutions which we have seen replaced by cellular tissue, or transformed into a serous cyst. In a case shown to us by Dr. Mierze-
jewski, the parietal and occipital lobes were so shrunken, that the
cerebellum was completely uncovered, as in the kangaroo. These
apparently contradictory lesions explain why the weight of the
brain of lunatics generally has not uniformly exhibited the diminution which we might have expected, as compared with the
brains of men of sound mind. It is the same with the cubic
measurements of the cranial capacity. The cranium, at the termination of infancy, may remain small, but at adult age and later it
is unable to follow the retraction of its contents, and to become less
in size. After inspecting 520 crania of insane persons, collected by
Esquirol, which form part of the museum of the Anthropological
Institute of Paris, and setting aside the probable cases of hydrocephalus, we may safely say that their mean cranial capacity is
below the mean in men of sound mind. If one could obtain those
of idiots—that is to say, those who have been insane from birth—
there cannot be a doubt that we should find it the same in them.
Cretins, which are to be found under various names in almost all
mountainous parts of the globe, may be placed in the same category
as idiots. The immediate cause of cretinism is by no means certain.
But how singular that this widespread malady should take place under
the influence of external circumstances acting upon the brain of the
infant even during intra-uterine life! The head is generally large, the
figure that of an aged person, and the nose deeply sunk at the root,
which has given rise to a theory of which we shall speak presently.[*]

---

[*] See "Treatise on Mental Diseases," by Greisenger. Translated into
French by M. Baillarger. Paris, 1864.

Microcephalus.

All in whom the brain has not attained a certain degree of development, or the cranial cavity a given capacity at adult age, are termed microcephales, whether such be really idiots or have only a general diminution of intellect similar to that of young infants. M. Broca divides them into demi-microcephales and microcephales proper.

He says all the non-deformed crania of adult Europeans whose capacity is below 1150 cubic centimètres, and the horizontal circumference less than 480 millimètres, if a man, and 475 if a woman, are demi-microcephales. The length and width are less positive; moreover, we may consider crania to be demi-microcephales whose length is 163 millimètres and under, in the man, or 160 and under, in the woman, and whose width is 133 in the man and 137 in the woman.* But the diminution continues still further, which brings us to the consideration of the true microcephales.

Microcephalus is owing to a general or partial arrest or perversion of development in one part of the brain, which manifests itself at various periods of intra-uterine life. It is merely an anatomical variety of idiocy. The organ, in the absence of complication, continues to grow, but irregularly and slowly. Its weight, at puberty, reaches from 400 to 500 grammes, according to M. Delasiauve; it has been known to be 360 and even 240 grammes (*Marshall*). The cerebellum, Gratiolet states, is larger in proportion to the brain proper, and the convolutions are those of a fœtus of five months. Atrophy is most frequently seen on the anterior lobes, and sometimes on the posterior. The cranium has a capacity of from 300 to 600 cubic centimètres, a circumference of from 330 to 370 millimètres, and a length of from 100 to 118. Two microcephales, of the ages of 10 and 15 years, mentioned by Vogt, had a mean of 333 cubic centimètres, and seven adults, a mean of 493. The mean, in six cases of all ages, from M. Broca's museum and laboratory, measured by M. Montané, was 440, and that of three of them

* See Chapters II. and III. for the measurements of normal crania.

of from 20 to 30 years of age, measured by M. Broca himself, 414.*

The body remains dwarfed or continues to be developed; it
reaches puberty, and presents all the characteristics of that period
without the power of procreation; such was the case in the microcephales exhibited twice in Paris under the name of Aztecs, on
account of their supposed origin. The man, who was 33 years of
age, was 1·36 mètre in height, the woman, who was 29, 1·32 mètre.
Their intellectual capacity was scarcely that of a child of three years
of age; their language consisted of about fifteen words, which they
uttered in jerks. (Fig. 19.)

As a result of the defective development of the brain, there is

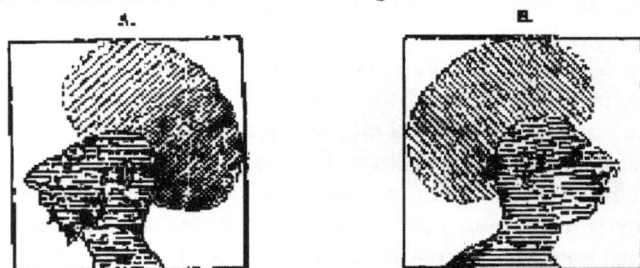

Fig. 19.—A, Maximo: B, Bartola; two microcephales from Central America, the hair
growing like a nimbus all round(?), in the Ofrians, a variety of mixed breed between
the Indian and the Negro.

smallness of the cranium, especially in the frontal region, as seen
in the above figures of two Aztecs. The facial region, which
grows regularly, at least more so than the cranium, appears large.
The eyeballs, in consequence of the atrophy of the forehead, project
above, and are slightly hidden under the lower lid; the nose, at
least in these two cases, is very projecting. They are very prognathous, their lower jaw is smaller than the upper, so that the
alveolar arch recedes about 25 millimètres.†

* "Instructions Craniologiques de la Société d'Anthropologie," drawn up
by M. Broca, p. 147—a pamphlet of 200 pages, with plates, Paris, 1875;
"Sur les Microcéphales," by Carl Vogt, Geneva, 1867; "Étude Anatomique
du Crâne chez les Microcéphales," by L. Mondard, Paris, 1874.

† See the discussion on the microcephales on the occasion of our introducing
these two Aztecs to the Anthropological Society in "Bull. Soc. d'Anthrop.,"
2nd series, vol. ix. 1874, vol. x. 1875.

The third series of pathological characters has reference to morbid deformities, or those following upon morbid conditions. They affect especially the skeleton, bones deformed by disease being mistaken for sound bones. These morbid conditions either affect all the bones or only those of the cranium; the former include rickets, inflammations of the bones, syphilis, old sores, and fractures. We refer the reader to works on pathology for the majority of these, and shall confine ourselves principally to rickets, and to some diseases peculiar to the cranium.

Rickets.

Rickets is a disorder of nutrition, in which the process of ossification is arrested at the period when the osseous tissue is about to become thoroughly organised (*Brun*). It is less a disease than a state of suffering, symptomatic of an impoverished condition of the system. It exhibits itself from the third month of intra-uterine life, up to 18 or 25 years of age, when the skeleton has done growing (*L. Tripier*), but it is more frequent about two years of age. The softened bones become deformed and incurved, in consequence of the weight of the body, of the contraction of the muscles, and of accidental pressure. It is at the weakest point of the natural incurvations that the bending usually takes place. A character common to all these deformities is the following: By making a section of an old rickety long bone, the compact osseous tissue is thicker on the diaphysis at the concavity of the curve, and thinner at the convexity. Another effect of the disease is this: the epiphyses, owing to the stage of ossification being accelerated, are found anchylosed to the diaphysis before the bone has arrived at its full size, so that the child ceases to grow, and remains a dwarf and deformed ever afterwards. We cannot therefore depend upon any important measurement if made upon bones affected with rickets. The following are certain indications by which they may be recognised:

In the clavicle the two curvatures are increased, especially the internal, which makes an abrupt bend.

In the ribs the flatness and thinness are increased.

In the humerus the curve takes place below the middle portion, its convexity looking forwards, forwards and outwards, or outwards.

In the fore-arm the bend is in both bones, or in one only, about the middle, and is from behind forwards, being accompanied by a certain amount of torsion.

In the femur the angle of the neck is diminished, and the natural torsion of the bone is increased, the lower half becoming arched forwards or outwards.

In the leg both bones are affected. The deformity never occurs in the upper part of the tibia, but at its middle and inferior portion. The most common is the curvature internally, which M. Brom compares to a yataghan; the bone is flattened from before backwards, its anterior border is more or less sunk in; its external concave border is sharp; the internal, to which is attached the interosseous aponeurosis, is thick. The next form is that of an antero-posterior curvature, the section of which is triangular, and the anterior border is convex from above downwards, and sharper than usual; it has the appearance of a sabre, but in an opposite direction. The curvature outwards or backwards is also met with, but less frequently. Numbers 2 and 3, Fig. 30, copied from the memoir in which M. Broca had to contradict M. Pruner-Bey relative to the pretended rickety deformities in the bones of the Eyzies, exhibit the two most common forms.

Rickets exhibits its effect on the cranium in a very decided way. It causes the process of ossification to be suspended, and at a later period it accelerates and perverts it. Two absolutely opposite results are produced, the one retarding the evolution of the sutures, the other hastening it. It is evident that rickets sometimes exists during the period of intra-uterine life. All do not allow this, but it is certain that some analogous disorder passes at this period into the bones, traces of which remain during the whole of life. If this condition is cured spontaneously by an acceleration of the process of ossification, like true rickets, we should have in it a simple explanation of a series of cranial deformities depending on the development of the bones, for which the usual theories would not account. The effects of rickets which it unexpectedly comes on

after birth are better understood.   Giving warning of its approach
before the fontanelles and the fibro-cartilaginous laminæ which give
form to the bones during the process of ossification are sufficiently
consolidated, rickets causes them to become soft, lessens their
resistance, leaving the cranium to struggle against the continual
growth of its contents. Here and there the osseous parietes become
thinned and even perforated; bulgings are formed from the moment
that the work has a tendency to begin again, new and independent
points of ossification make their appearance, which later on produce
the ossa Wormiana.   M. Bouvier says, " when the bregmatic fontanelle is not closed at two-and-a-half years of age, it is caused by
rickets."   Should the disease unexpectedly make its appearance at

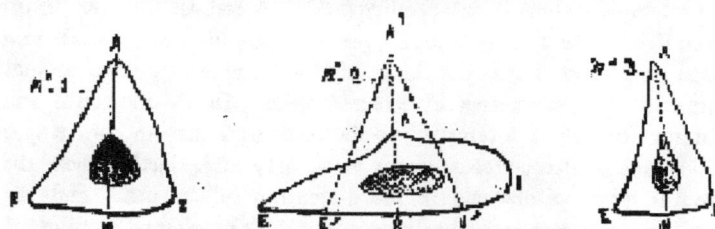

Fig. 20.—Section of the tibia at the union of the upper fourth with the lower three-fourths.
No. 1, Normal triangular tibia : 2, Rickety tibia, at its lateral curvature ; 3, Rickety
tibia at its antero-posterior curvature : 1, Internal border : E, External border ; A,
Anterior border or crest of the tibia : A¹ E T, Ex. 2, shows the way in which the
deformity is produced.

a later period, when the sutures are more advanced, the effects are
different. Subsequently a cure takes place by a kind of porous or
condensed callus, ossification proceeds with undue energy, especially
in the sutures, and a condition of things is brought about in one
or several of the sutures which ought only to exist naturally at or
beyond 40 years of age—premature synostosis.

A loss of balance between the resistance of the parietes of the
cranium and the increasing development of its contents is the principal cause of its pathological deformities.   It is sufficient that one
of these causes should be at work for the bones and even for the
brain to become diseased.   The parietes become softened, or at a
later period prematurely consolidated, whereas the brain remains
sound and goes on increasing naturally; deformity is making its

appearance. If the parietes are passing through their regular phases of development while hydrocephalus or hypertrophy of the brain is going on, the same result may be produced. The causes of the phenomena are simple while their results are complex.

Hydrocephalus.

Hydrocephalus is dropsy, or an increased secretion of fluid, in the cranial cavity, whether this fluid has its source in the ventricles or between the membranes.

It is acute or chronic, the chronic form being either very serious in amount, moderate, or slight. If the acute form exists to any considerable extent it is speedily fatal. A certain Cardinal, however, lived to be twenty-three (?) years of age; his head resembled a large ball, and from the base of the forehead to the occiput measured 87 centimètres in circumference. In its moderate and chronic form it is interesting to the anthropologist in two ways: either the hydrocephalus comes on shortly after birth, when the sutures offer no obstacle to the distention of the head, and the skull on recovery is easily distinguished by its generally spherical shape; or it makes its appearance at a later period, when the membranous spaces between the sutures are more or less ossified or serrated, and then the arched projections are more limited in extent, and only appear at certain points. We may also mention, but with some reserve, a condition of partial hydrocephalus, in which, owing to adhesions between the membranes, the fluid accumulates at particular spots in the form of cysts, or the bones give way, or become altered, as in the preceding case, at some special point.

The principal causes of hydrocephalus are the bad constitution of the parents, or hereditary predisposition. Franck mentions the fact of seven infants following, and Gralis of six, being attacked with this disease. Its symptoms are easily recognised: the sutures are wide and very slow in closing; the bones become thinned, ossification is arrested, and a species of local rickets, confined to the cranium, comes on as a complication.

General hydrocephalus, which comes on after birth, and is subsequently amenable to treatment, is recognised at once by the globular form of the cranium.   That of the second or third kind is more difficult to diagnose, owing to the existence in both of the following characters : The frontal protuberances are projecting, or rather the whole forehead is so ; the temporal shells present at their centre a rounded arching, or the superior border is detached from the parietal.   The supra-occipital region forms an ovoid projection, which communicates with the parietal surfaces by an abrupt inclined plane, in the thick portion of which we see a number of ossa Wormiana.   The retro-mastoid sutures are complicated ; the sagittal and coronal, as well as the union of the greater wings of the sphenoid with the parietal, are thickened, or raised, or interrupted by ossa Wormiana.   Frequently a transverse channel, from one surface of the greater wing of the sphenoid to the other, and which is not readily found, passes across the bregma, and seems to divide the cranium into two parts; each of which is increased in size ; the orbital vault is pressed downwards.   M. Broca mentions as important signs—when they exist—a primary circumscribed arching at the anterior border of the temporal shell, encroaching upon the adjacent portion of the pterion, and another arching at a point which he calls the dacrion, that is to say at the internal surface of the orbit at the union of the frontal, the ascending process of the maxillary and the os unguis.

Hypertrophy.

Hypertrophy as well as atrophy of the brain are disorders of development of the substance of that organ, which generally produce their effects upon the parietes of the brain-case.   It assumes the form of an acute or chronic disease, or of a sub-physiological condition, and is frequently induced by excessive work which parents exact from their children before they are fully developed. That which comes on during life or at its close does not concern us here ; that which appears during intra-uterine life, or soon after birth, has a most important influence on the evolution of the cranium.   M. Baillarger has seen a case of hypertrophy in which the body weighing 35 kilogrammes, the brain weighed 1160 grammes; and another in which at four years of age this organ weighed 1306 grammes. Hypertrophy is general, or partial; it affects the whole encephalon, the brain, a single hemisphere, a single lobe, the corpus callosum, or a group of convolutions. The causes which produce it are such as produce hydrocephalus or rickets, and the effects of the three diseases are similar. The inflammation which more particularly causes hypertrophy or hydrocephalus sometimes passes to the parietes of the cranium through the membranes, producing porous or condensed callus, and an arrest in the ossification of the sutures or their premature obliteration, although the natural effect of each of these maladies is distention of the cranium.

Premature Synostoses.

Deformities of the most varied description result from all the above-mentioned causes, and from the unequal method in which they exercise their influence upon the sutures. The arrest of the ossification of the sutures is, however, less serious than their premature obliteration. The temporary sutures of intra-uterine life, as the interparietal and metopic, persist for an indefinite period without resulting in any appreciable deformity; and moreover this persistence is regarded by some persons as the probable indication of some disorder in the new-born infant. Stahl has seen the bregmatic fontanelle open in a man of 50 years of age, but he does not say whether he presented any other peculiarity. The result of an arrest of the ordinary ossification at the edges of the sutures is that there is an increase of the volume of the cranium, which is not sensibly deformed. The effects of premature synostoses are more serious, but they vary according to the period at which they are produced. Of a grave character when the synostosis takes place in early infancy, their gravity diminishes subsequently, and gradually disappears when the brain has arrived at or near its full term of development.

M. Virchow* has attempted to formulate a general law: "At the end of the synostosis of a suture," he says, "the development of the cranium stops short in a direction perpendicular to that of the closed suture"—that is to say, the sagittal suture being closed, the cranium remains narrower and developes in length. His second proposition is that "of all the parts of the cranium, the base, and notably the basilar vertebræ, attain the largest amount of development."

Two other statements of the same author ought to be recorded. Cretinism, according to him, is due to the synostosis of the tri-basilar bone—that is to say, of the spheno-basilar suture and the suture of the body of the anterior sphenoid and the posterior sphenoid. This is why cretins have the occipital shortened, and the base of the nose sunk in. Neither the one nor the other is proved to demonstration. Cruveilhier has refuted by anticipation the explanation given as to microcephalus; the facts collected by M. Vogt do not establish it, and the specimens in the laboratory of M. Broca contradict it.

Let us give some examples of our own.

Should the spheno-frontal suture be synostosed, the forehead not having the power to become further enlarged, will remain contracted while the rest of the cranium continues to increase. Should the sagittal and coronal sutures be ossified, the lambdoidal and inferior lateral remaining free, the vault of the cranium will become lifted up en masse (acrocephalus), and the increased development will be at the expense of the occipital portion. We are acquainted with two examples of this kind. In another cranium we witness the contrary: the sagittal and the lambdoidal are synostosed, and it is the frontal which is driven forwards, the vault of the cranium being at the same time raised. Another cranium exhibits better still what is taking place: all the lateral, posterior, and anterior sutures are welded together, with the exception of the anterior two-thirds of the sagittal, and the internal two-thirds of the coronal on the left side. What is the result?

* Virchow, "Gesammelte Abhandlungen," Frankfort, 1856; and "Untersuchungen über die Entwickelung der Schädelgrundes," Berlin, 1857.

The anterior and internal half of the left parietal is lifted up above the level of the neighbouring surfaces. It is unnecessary to proceed farther. What we always notice is an internal pressure at one point, exerting its influence at the part in the immediate vicinity where it meets with the least resistance, and producing at the first point an arrest of development, and at others one or more compensatory archings (*courbures de compensation*). What frequently surprises us is to notice a similar synostosis in two different skulls, and one only to be deformed. This depends on the age at

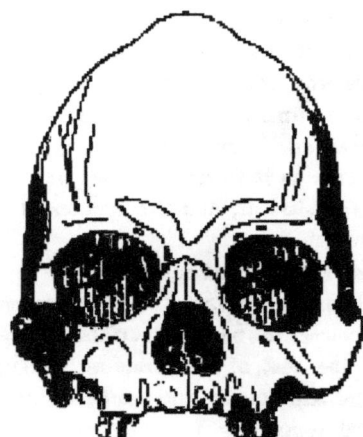

Fig. 21.—Scaphocephalic cranium of a Negress from Senegal.

which the lesion is produced. Dr. Thulié has presented to the Société d'Anthropologie a cranium which possesses considerable interest in this respect. An accidental bony callus was present on one of the parietals, and had synostosed the sagittal and coronal suture on one side only, notwithstanding which the cranium was perfectly uniform; this, as well as other indications, showed that the welding had taken place at 15 or 20 years of age. We must also remember that we are only looking at the external surface of the cranium, and that in certain unaccountable deformities there may exist on the internal surface incomplete synostoses which escape observation. We will conclude by giving a classical example of synostosis.

Scaphocephalus signifies a deformity peculiar to the cranium, and is characterised by its contraction transversely, its antero-posterior elongation, and its increase in height. The skull turned upside down has the form of a boat, from which its name is derived; the forehead is straight, bulging, and narrow; the occipital is globular and conical, and projects backwards from the lambdoidal suture. An horizontal crest reaches from one to the other on the anterior half, the sides shelving like the roof of a house, which the obliteration of the parietal protuberances renders still more prominent. In two specimens presented to the Société d'Anthropologie, the length was to the width as 56 : 100 in one, and as 60 : 100 in the other. These are the faintest cephalic indices hitherto observed on the human cranium.

Four opinions are put forward in explanation of this pheno-menon :* (1) According to M. Virchow, it is due to synostosis, during infancy, of the sagittal suture, the other sutures remaining open. (2) According to MM. Minchin and Von Baër, it proceeds from there being but one point of ossification for both parietals—an hypothesis which has but few supporters. (3) According to M. Morselli, there are two distinct parietals, but their two points of ossification are so near together that their fusion quickly takes place. (4) M. Calori thinks that it is the result of an original elongation and narrowness of the cranium. The four may be reduced to two, namely, the fusion of the two parietals and peculiar formation from the first. Mr. Bernard Davis is opposed to the former from the fact that in his collection, out of 27 crania with the sagittal suture closed, there are only four scaphocephali. In the laboratory of M. Broca there are many examples of pre-mature obliteration of the sagittal suture, without scaphocephalus. In a Tartar skull belonging to Mr. Huxley, which is one of the largest known, the sagittal suture is closed, and the others are open. But there is an easy reply to objections: the synostosis of

* See "Revue d'Anthropologie," vol. III., p. 700 ; "Bull. Soc. d'Anthrop," meeting of May 7. 1874; and "Instructions Craniologiques."

the sagittal only produces an arrest of development of the vault in
a transverse direction and compensatory increase in length, that is
to say scaphocephalus, before the age of from 8 to 12 years (Broca).
At two years of age its effects are almost inevitable. A case is
mentioned in which the deformity existed even at birth. No case
of scaphocephalus has been published up to the present time in
which obliteration of the sagittal had not taken place.

Pathological Deformities.

Various terms, chiefly of foreign origin, have been employed to
designate the principal cranial forms produced by the causes just
mentioned. Similar names are given to certain physiological
forms which are met with as characteristic of certain races. Here,
from the physiological to the morbid condition, as with respect to
so many disorders and other affections of the brain, the transition
is scarcely perceptible. In how many skulls, looked upon as
sound, is there not present this globular supra-bains projection of
the occipital, which is sometimes a characteristic of race, and at
others an evidence of hydrocephalus or of premature synostosis?
One of the Esquimaux skulls in the museum, regular otherwise, at
least in appearance, deserves the epithet of scaphocephalus. The
term has been similarly applied to the normal skulls of Australians,
Polynesians, and African negroes. The following are some of the
terms just referred to, with their signification :

Acrocephalic, oxycephalic, hypsocephalic, pyrgocephalic, elevated skull.
Platycephalic, tapeinocephalic, with the vault of the skull flattened,
elliptical.
Eurycephalic, large skull.
Stenocephalic, narrow skull.
Trochocephalic, very round skull.
Trigonocephalic, skull triangular at the top anteriorly, supposed to be
owing to the medio-frontal synostosis.
Megalocephalic, skull of very large capacity.
Kephalon, large skull, great (Virchow).
Sphenocephalic, nelencephalic, small skull.
Macrocephalic, elongated skull.

Plagiocephalic, an obliquely-oval deformity (Virchow), large skull with forehead flattened (Linnæus, Beck).

Cylindrocephalic, elongated cylindrical skull.

Klinocephalic, skull with vault in form of a saddle.

Gymbocoophalic, cumbocephalic, an exaggeration of the preceding, or skull en dôme.

Scaphocephalic, sphenocephalic, boat-shaped skull.

Pachycephalic, skull with thick hypertrophical parietes.

Many of these are frequently associated together. Van der Hoeven, for example, says that the skulls from the Caroline Archipelago, certain of the Hebrides, and New Caledonia, are hypsistenocephalic; Barlow, that a certain deformed skull found in Silesia is oxyklinocephalic. As we proceed we shall find other names, equally derived from the Greek, which are more generally in use.

There are not only pathological deformities; there are others with which the anthropologist ought to be acquainted, which he frequently meets with in certain skulls in the course of his craniometrical studies, and which he is obliged to put aside.

Posthumous, Platybasic, and Plagiocephalic Deformities.

The first, or posthumous, is easily recognised. It is produced in more or less moist argillaceous soils, by the pressure of the earth which has been exerted upon the softened skull at intervals for ages. The skull is said to have the consistence of soft wax, being variously shaped according to the nature of the soil in which it is enveloped.[*] One wall might be more or less depressed or sheared round, while the opposite wall might be exactly the reverse. Or the pressure might be local. Sometimes an entire bone might be irregularly furrowed. Its principal characteristic is the absence of regularity and symmetry.

The second has been called plastic by Mr. B. Davis, a term more conformable with the preceding, and platybasic by M. Ænea. It makes its appearance unexpectedly at all periods of life, but princi-

[*] "Fouilles d'un Cimetière Bourguignon du Cinquième Siècle," by Paul Topinard, in "Bull. Soc. d'Émulation de l'Ain." Bourgandy, 1874.

N

pally during infancy and old age, owing to a defective consistence
of the bones at the circumference of the occipital foramen. The
weight of the head is the immediate cause of it; the articular
condyles, the circumference of the occipital foramen, and the
adjoining portion of the basilar apophysis become bent, and
penetrate into the cranial cavity about one centimètre or less.
M. Broca considers that it is shown to exist in white races when
the negative angle of Daubenton is more than eight degrees.

The third takes place during infancy, but accidentally, either
owing to the infant being constantly carried on the same arm,
or by the pressure which the weight of the head exerts upon the
entire occipital or upon one side of it when the infant is lying on
its back. In the one case a median flattening, in the other a
lateral depression of the whole of the nucha, is produced; the skull
continuing to develope, a compensatory arching (*voussure de compensation*) is formed on the opposite side, and the maximum
antero-posterior length of the skull becomes oblique or diagonal.
This is termed the obliquely oval or plagiocephalic deformity.
Other results also follow. Thus the synostosis of one-half of the
sagittal and lambdoidal suture, certain chronic forms of torticollis,
rickets, partial hydrocephalus, &c.

Artificial Deformations.

These are also due to pressure exerted during life. Sometimes
they are produced involuntarily by badly - constructed head-
dresses, sometimes voluntarily in order to conform to accustomed
usage or to submit to certain rites. Man is an intelligent animal,
but also a very whimsical one. The structure of his brain incites
him to the noblest deeds as well as to the most ridiculous practices,
such as cutting off the little finger, scorching the soles of the feet,
extracting the front teeth, or deforming the head, because others
have done so before him.

Artificial deformations of this kind are simply customs, and consequently might have been treated of in our second part when considering ethnic characters; but it is difficult to separate them

from deformities produced by other causes, and we ought to be
acquainted with them before commencing to practise craniometry
on normal skulls.

They are met with in both hemispheres. Hippocrates and
Herodotus were the first to describe them among the Macrocephalos,
a people to the east of the Palus-Maeotis, to which custom they
owe their name. Aristotle, Strabo, and Pliny also make mention
of them. Within the last few years there have been discovered
in the Caucasus, in the Crimea, in Hungary, in Silesia, in Belgium,
and in various parts of France, ancient and contemporaneous
deformed skulls, agreeing in type with those which have been
mentioned. We conclude, therefore, in comparing these data with
those with which history furnishes us, that the Aryan notions
with one of their tribes having this custom have passed over the
Volkes-Tretosages of the Caucasus under the name of Cimmerii,
through Europe into France, where the processes of disfigurement
have become modified in the way we have mentioned. Other
skulls, however, have been met with in Europe, as the Helveto-
Burgundian skull of Voiteur in the Jura, in the form of a sugar-
loaf; and perhaps that of Bel-Air, near Lausanne, in Switzerland,
the nature of whose deformity is different, which leads us to
believe that all the European peoples disfiguring their heads have
not had the same origin. Deformations of the skull have been
discovered in Polynesia, especially in Tahiti, in Malacca, and in
different parts of Asia as far as Syria.

But the classic country in which these deformations are found is
America. From a period prior to the Christian era, we see a nation,
the *Nahuas*, leaving Florida, according to Brasseur de Bourbourg,
to settle in Mexico, and quitting it in the year 174 to disperse,
some to the north, along the Mississippi, others to the south, across
the Isthmus of Panama, and there disseminating the custom of
flattening the head from behind forwards. Other deformations of a
different type are met with in the same country, which it seems
reasonable to refer to another primitive people. From these deviations from one and the same custom, we may infer that its origin
dates back to a very remote period. They practised it during

infancy on both sexes, and sometimes on the male only, by very different methods. Sometimes the infant was fastened on a plank, or a sort of cradle with leather straps; or they applied pieces of clay, pressing them down with small boards on the forehead, the vertex, and the occiput, according to the particular object they had in view. Sometimes the head was kneaded with the hands or the knees, or, the infant being laid on the back, the elbow was pressed on the forehead. Circular bands were sometimes employed to support the sides of the head. Sometimes they had recourse to some other method, which they carried out in another way. Each people, each tribe, each family had its various methods by which they might be recognised. In Vancouver's Island and the neighbouring islands, three very different types have been noticed side by side.

The infant sometimes dies during the process, and when it survives, it does so to the detriment of the intellectual faculties. The intellect, however, does not seem generally to be so much affected as we might have supposed. Even the cranial capacity is not diminished, because the brain, if it does not accommodate itself when pressure is forcibly exerted on it, is capable of resisting slow, partial, and progressive pressure. It has been asked whether in the course of time these deformations become hereditary. The question has generally been answered in the negative, notwithstanding which we would not assert that certain brachycephales did not originate in this way.

M. Gosse has described sixteen species of artificial deformation, ten of which were in American skulls, which he afterwards reduces to five. M. Lunier admits seven species.[*]

We shall reduce the most interesting and the most common of them to two, the one *dressé*, the other *couché*, comprising each of the species and the varieties. Moreover, there are but few of these which can be taken apart from the rest; all of them seem to have

* Gosse, "Essai sur les Déformations Artificielles du Crâne," Paris, 1855; and "Présentation d'un Crâne Déformé de Nation," in "Bull. Soc. d'Anthrop.," vol. II., 1871; Lunier, Article "Déformations Artificielles du Crâne," in "Nouv. Dict. de Méd. et Chirurg. Pratiques," 1869.

gradations of form of the most opposite character, and it would be difficult to determine what name to give to them.

It is, however, from their being so characteristic, and of forms with which we have become so familiar, that they enable us to recognise the people to which the skull belongs.

In the first kind, more or less forcible pressure and counter-pressure, varying also in height and in extent, have been exerted at the two extremities of the skull, thus shortening the antero-posterior and lengthening the vertical and frequently the transverse diameter.

In the second kind, the length is, on the contrary, increased. Whether the deformations be symmetrical or asymmetrical is immaterial; sometimes we should expect the latter, but most frequently this would be involuntary and the result of a badly-conducted operation.

When in the first kind, the *direct*, the most continuous pressure was exerted on a great extent of the occipital, while at the forehead there was only slight counter-pressure, the result was simple occipital deformation, or a vertical occiput. This is observed on the coasts of Peru, among some Fuegians, in one of the tribes of the Vancouver Archipelago, in Malacca, and even in France. If the sides of the skull were at the same time compressed or supported, we should get the quadrangular deformation met with in South America, and among the Paws mentioned by Morton. The pressure on the occipital being increased, and that of the forehead being continued, we should arrive at the mixed cuneiform deformation (*déformation cunéiforme relevée*) of Gosse, which is characteristic of the Nahuas, their descendants the Natchez, certain of the Chinooks, and, in another part of the world, the Tahitians. The most celebrated variety is the *déformation trilobée*, in the form of a trefoil, of the Island of Sacrificios, in the Gulf of Mexico, which is produced by a supplementary band beginning at the occiput, passing up over the median line, and bifurcating in the middle of the sagittal suture to reach the temporal fossae. Things remaining thus, if the frontal pressure is made higher the middle lobe disappears, and we have the cuneiform deformity and not the bilobed, because it would become amalgamated with another of which we shall speak presently.

In the laboratory of M. Broca there are sixteen beautiful specimens of this from Ancoun, Peru, &c.

In the second kind, or *couché*, the frontal pressure was greater, it being exerted over the whole surface of the bone, while the occipital counter-pressure was exerted lower, was very slight, or none at all (the *point d'appui* then passed through the vertebral column) ; the skull therefore became elongated behind without obstruction. In the generality of cases, however, a supplementary pressure was made on the vertex. Hence we find on the upper surface of these skulls, from before backwards ; (1) a frontal depression or flattening ; (2) a bregmatic projection ; (3) a post-bregmatic depression ; (4) a swelling formed by the whole mass of the receding skull. The flattening of the forehead—which is sometimes immoderately receding, as in Fig. 19, representing the Aztecs—took the name, among certain peoples, of deformation of courage (*déformation du courage*). In the kind termed *dressé*, the forehead was more frequently widened and more elevated ; in this, it is usually narrower, longer, and lower. One of the consequences of this is that the roof of the orbits is depressed, and that the eyeballs are raised by being made to project. There are three species of this deformation or distortion ; (1) The cuneiform deformation (*déformation cunéiforme couchée*) of Gosse, which is very marked in the Caribs of the Antilles, the northern Guaranis, and some North American tribes near Vancouver's Island. The majority of Chinooks and other flat-heads (*têtes plates*) from the Columbia river, described by Morton, are in the same category. (2) The elongated symmetrical deformation (*déformation symétrique allongée*) of Morton, in use among the ancient Aymaras. (3) The macrocephalic deformation (*déformation macrocéphale*) of Europe, which in France has given origin to the annular (*annulaire*) variety of Foville,[*] and the bilobed (*bilobée*) of Lunier—observed in the departments of the Lower Seine and the two Sèvres—and to the simple frontal or Toulousian (*Toulousaine*) variety, so named from the country in which it has been specially noticed. (Fig. 32.) In the annular, the band extends from a point behind the bregma,

[*] See also " La Déformation allongée et cylindrique " of Foville, of which the annular is a variety, in " Anat. Syst. Nerveux " of Foville. Paris, 1844.

vertically below the chin, by crossing a circular furrow which divides the head into two portions; these being less decided in the annular than in the bilobed variety. In the Toulousian, the line starts from the occiput, reaches the forehead obliquely, and then exerts its principal pressure.[*] The macrocephalic unites the two systems, so that the frontal depression of the Toulousian and the post-bregmatic depression of the annular exist there, the two being separated by a bregmatic projection.

We must say it is often difficult to distinguish certain macrocephalic skulls of the Crimea from certain elongated crania from

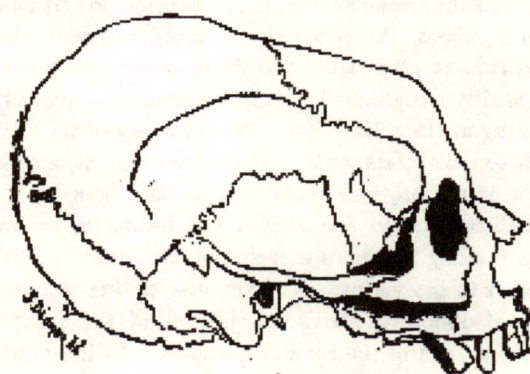

Fig. 21.—Artificial deformation of the skull, called Toulousaine.

the country of the ancient Aymaras. Among the deformations not included with the two preceding kinds, and which Gosse describes, we may mention the nasal deformation (*déformation nasale*) or flattening of the bones of the nose, practised by the Botocudos of America, and the naso-parietal (*déformation naso-pariétale*) or Mongolian, peculiar to the ancient Huns and to certain Kirghis.

We have said that the types of ethnic deformations of the skull present gradations, whereby they are at times insensibly transformed into other types, although their general character remains

[*] "Sur la Déformation Toulousaine du Crâne," by M. Broca, in "Bull. Soc. d'Anthrop.," 1871.

The skulls which are met with in Upper Peru and Bolivia, and are generally attributed to the Aymaras, are proofs of this. Their varieties may be reduced to three. In the first, almost the entire skull is thrown backwards, and has the appearance of being recumbent (*couché*) horizontally. The most striking example of this which has been under our notice, and which belonged to M. Brom's laboratory, projects 89 millimètres backwards behind the opisthion, while in 20 Europeans', taken at random, the same projection is 68 millimètres; but the skull in this species is not always so *couché*, and we have noticed in others that the sub-occipital region is better supported. In the second species, the most common and most classic among the Aymaras, the sub-occipital counter-pressure is a little higher, and is more perceptible, and the more compact lateral bands, which are readily recognised by their impression, prevent the skull from spreading at the sides. Thus the extremity of the skull which corresponds to the obelion, or to the interval which separates it from the lambda, is conical, and constricted at the base by a circular furrow which starts from the occiput and bifurcates on each side, one portion tending towards the region of the frontal protuberances and the other to the vertex. The varieties of this species differ in the degree of obliquity, above and behind, of the great posterior axis of the skull and of the cone in question. In the most oblique form the recumbent deformation (*décsuchée*) has become raised. In the example which we have seen lately, the projection behind the opisthion is not more than 68 millimètres, that is to say, it is as much diminished as in the preceding case it was increased. In order to account for the difference in these two cases, we must compare together the following measurements, viz.: their post-opisthine projection, their maximum vertical projection, and their maximum antero-posterior diameter. The first, which shows the elongation, and the second, the straight character of the skull, are expressed in hundredths of the antero-posterior diameter. In the first example, the index of the projection backwards is 44·6 and that of the height 77·6; and in the second, the one is 34·3 and the other 92·9. This proves that the deformation gains in horizontal projection in the former case what it loses in vertical in the latter. In the

third species, which varies as to inclination, all the lands which
compressed the sides have disappeared, or at least are scarcely perceptible. The lateral furrows are wanting, traces of the frontal
pressure alone remain; the skull is swollen above and behind the
auditory foramina, and the whole deformation has the appearance of
an egg with its larger extremity posteriorly. This most resembles
the macrocephalic deformity of the Caucasian skulls. Notwithstanding these varieties, we discover in the three species that a
similar method of proceeding has been employed, and for a similar
object, which is characteristic of the Aymara race, and which
distinguishes it at once from the race of Ancona and also from
that of Peru, in which the head is plainly raised up by a flattening
from behind forwards. From this fact alone we should conclude
that the peoples of Ancona belonged to the conquering race, which
in Florida bore the name of Nahua, and of which the Toltecs of
Mexico, the Natchez of the Mississippi, and the Totonacks of
Sacrificios are other representatives.

Conclusion.

Our first part being completed thus far, in which we have considered Man zoologically in his *ensemble*, and having taken special
notice of his varieties, it remains for us to give an answer to the
question propounded at the close of our preliminary remarks:
What place does Man occupy in the class of mammalia? Is he to
be classified in an order or in a family? We cannot too frequently
reiterate that Man, owing to his intellectual powers, occupies the
first place in creation, and is its culminating point as a marvel of
organisation; he therefore exercises upon the planet of which he is
an inhabitant a rightful dominion over all living beings. But we
must also remember that there does not seem any radical difference
between him and those most nearly related to him—the anthropoid
apes. Anatomically, they possess the same organs, constructed and
arranged in the same way, there being only secondary shades of
differences between them. The feet, the hands, the vertebral
column, the thorax, the pelvis, the organs of sense—all have the

same configuration. The brain also in its structure and its convolutions is identical. Physiologically, the various functions are exercised in a similar manner; even their diseases are alike. All the important differences between them reside in the volume of the brain, which is three times more developed in Man, and in his faculties, the due adjustment and co-ordination of which give him the judgment, the reason, and the understanding, which are the noblest if not the brightest gems in his crown. An Emeritus professor relates that one day finding himself alone on Mont Blanc, at the halting-place of the Grands Mulets, he cast his eye over the depth of the abyss which separated him from Chamounix, and which the Glacier des Bossons rendered impassable. Some intelligent guides, however, had discovered a number of invisible paths, which connected these two points, and so assured their communication. Such, said he, is the nature of the abyss which separates Man from animals.

The comparison is ingenious, but scarcely correct. The characters which Man and animals possess in common are manifest to all, and no one would have had any doubt on the subject if their serenity had not been disturbed by biblical legends or by philosophical speculations. The modes of transition, the anomalies which produce in one that which is normal, in others a strict identity in the majority of the organs, only slightly differing as to form, all indicate that unity of arrangement of which Geoffroy Saint-Hilaire speaks. What should we say if, instead of their being reduced to the human and simian forms which time had bequeathed to us, we had to arrange those which were intermediate, and which had escaped us?

Whatever his past may have been, Man now appears before us as forming a circumscribed zoological group, to which it is proper to give a name in our classification. What is it to be?

In the preceding pages, we have been led to recognise the existence of particular types in each zoological division or subdivision. First, we found a general type proper to all mammalia, that is to say, an ensemble of characters common to men and animals, which, whilst distinguishing them collectively, unites them with birds and reptiles, as if all had been formed in one and the same mould, and

diversity had supervened subsequently. Then, laying aside that
which is foreign to our purpose, a general type common to all the
monkey tribe, and to which Man assimilates infinitely more than to
that of the carnivori or ruminants. Lastly, in this simian group we
found a succession of dissimilar types: first, that of lemurs, but
slightly homogeneous, ill-defined, and showing a preference on the
one side to certain cheiroptera and insectivora, and on the other to
some species of cebinæ, or monkeys of the new continent; a second
type, better defined and brought to greater perfection; then a third
type, that of pithecians, or monkeys of the old continent, divorcing
itself from the second, and in which the particular traces of
resemblance to Man are more apparent.

Up to this point, the three simian types follow each other in a
regular gradation of succession. But after the third there is a
bound; the pithecians have less resemblance to the anthropoid
apes than to the cebinæ. The general type of the anthropoids is
indeed altogether different and very marked, but it bears the closest
resemblance to that of Man. The conclusions we formed at each
step were, that many a characteristic so similar in monkeys of the
three inferior groups, and in quadrupeds, is different in the anthropoid; and the physiognomy assumes a resemblance to that which it
presents in Man. In a word, the type of character changes as we
pass from the pithecians to the anthropoids; their degree or their
quantity alone varying as we pass from the anthropoids to Man.
The real differences between these last may be reduced to two,
which are not of equal value: (1) Man always stands erect. The
anthropoid ape sometimes holds himself erect and sometimes goes on
all-fours; and in the latter case he makes use of his anterior
extremities as hands—as we should do in that attitude—and not as
feet. The variations in their respective skeletons, muscles, viscera,
as well as their direction of vision, depend on it. (2) The brain
of Man is three times as large; hence the development of his
intellectual faculties, of his faculty of language, and of his facial
angle.

Apart from these two points, and from everything which they
involve, we can only discover resemblances between Man and the

anthropoids, and the following question naturally arises : Among the four classes of anthropoids, is there one more than another which approaches to Man ?

The gibbon may be set aside. In respect to his cerebral convolutions and the vertebral column, taken as a whole he is really superior; but as regards the proportions of his extremities, the narrowness of his pelvis, the arrangement of his muscles, the callosities on his buttocks, and his habits of living, he establishes the transition to the pithecians.

The orang occupies an equally unfavourable position, by reason of certain anatomical characteristics which are proper to him, by the proportions of his skeleton, and by his defective feet and hands; but he recovers it owing to his cerebral convolutions, his facial angle, the number of his ribs, his teeth, and perhaps also his intelligence.

The chimpanzee is remarkable for the richness of his cerebral convolutions, the proportions of his skeleton, the disposition of his femurs, and the general physiognomy of his skull.

Lastly, the gorilla has the volume of his brain in his favour; the direction of his vision, his height, the general proportion of his limbs, the arrangement of his muscles, his hand, his foot, and his pelvis; but he has thirteen pairs of ribs, a defective vertebral column, laryngeal sacs, a diastema, and very large canines. For our part we rather decide in favour of the chimpanzee, and particularly of certain of his species; but it is necessary that these should be better known.

The elements upon which the leading arrangement of the zoological divisions should be based are: (1) a general type, common to all the mammalia; (2) a general sub-type, common to all monkeys proper, to the anthropoid, and to Man; (3) a particular type, common to these last two; (4) the human type. The most striking fact in relation to this was brought forward at a remarkable discussion which took place in 1860, at a meeting of the Société d'Anthropologie. The question of doctrine having been carefully avoided, the conclusion was arrived at that *the anthropoid apes more nearly approach Man anatomically than the monkeys next in order to them.*

Consequently the separation to be made at the extreme of the series, between the inferior monkeys and Man, cannot be logically placed between the anthropoid and the so-called common monkeys. This leads us to Mr. Huxley's classification: (1) Man and the anthropoid apes; (2) the monkeys of the old and new continents; (3) lemurs.

But we must necessarily draw a strong line of demarcation between Man and the anthropoids. Although the type common to both differs only in degree, that which concerns the brain has so considerable a range that division becomes inevitable. But, to be logical, we must in the same way separate the monkeys of the old continent from those of the new, which have an equal claim to differ by reason of other characteristics; and this leads us definitely to adopt the classification of M. Broca: (1) Man; (2) the anthropoid apes; (3) pithecians; (4) cebians; (5) lemurs.

Now these five groups have nearly the same zoological value, and are separated from each other by equal intervals. United, they present an *ensemble* of common features, which separates them *en masse* from the carnivora as much as these are separated from the marsupials or the cetacea. We must then give to each of them equivalent leading titles, and to the whole collectively a title similar to that of carnivora, of marsupialia, or cetacea. They thus form five families in one and the same order—that of Primates. Consequently, Man forms one FAMILY; the first in the ORDER of Primates, the first in the CLASS of Mammalia.

It remains for us to inquire whether the divisions of this family are to be arranged as genera, as species, or as varieties. We shall decide this question after having examined the elements of the problem in our second part.

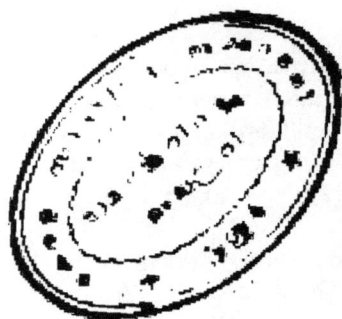

PART II.

OF THE RACES OF MANKIND.

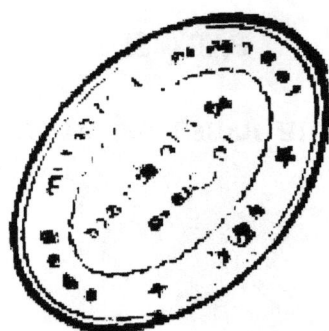

CHAPTER I.

THE divisions and subdivisions of the human family are designated
in current language by the name of races; and as such their study
would not present greater difficulties than that of all other analogous divisions of natural history, but for the intrusion of questions
of doctrine. Have these races the value of species, of varieties, or
even of genera? This is the question. Before giving a reply we
must pass in review: (1) the accepted definitions of all these terms;
(2) the classification of races; (3) the particular characteristics upon
which they rest; (4) the principal physical types which we may
take for granted exist among mankind in general.

Of Species.

The main point of the dispute lies in the sense attached to
this word, and to its exact limitation; which necessitates our
bringing in a certain number of definitions, and these have the
advantage of drawing the questions closer together. In determining
the first series of definitions we shall be met at the very threshold
with inherent difficulties. In the second is sketched out a principle
pregnant with consequences — species are variable, without any

o

precise limits, and become transformed in the course of time. In the last the contrary principle is maintained, namely, that species are immutable, and changes in them never pass beyond certain boundaries.

"Under the denomination of species," Robinet writes in 1768, "naturalists embrace the aggregate of individuals which possess an amount of appreciable difference."

"Species," says Agassiz, "is the last division of classification at which naturalists pause; and this division is based upon the least important characteristics, such as form, colour, and proportions."

"Species," according to Lamarck, "is the aggregate of individuals like each other, whose offspring is perpetuated in the same condition, *as long as circumstances of situation are not changed* to such a degree as to alter their habits, their disposition, and their forms."

"Species," says Geoffroy Saint-Hilaire subsequently, "is an aggregation or succession of individuals characterised by a uniformity of distinctive features, whose transmission is natural, regular, and unlimited *in the present state of things.*"

"Species," says Cuvier, "is the aggregate of all organised beings, descended from one original parentage, or from those which resemble them as far as they resemble each other."

In the following definition of Prichard, in which especial reference is made to the position assigned to Man, we perceive the dominance of orthodox ideas, and, at the same time, some amount of vagueness attributable to the influence of Lamarck. "Species," he remarks, "is an aggregate of individuals resembling each other, whose slight differences are explained by the influence of physical agencies, and who are descended from a primitive pair." This is the ancient monogenetic creed.

M. de Quatrefages considers that the elements of the definition may be reduced to two, viz.: "the resemblance of individuals to each other, and their uninterrupted descent from a primitive group." It is not until subsequently that he admits, as a practical criterion of species, the result of inbreeding "Individuals of the same species," he remarks, "are alone capable of producing prolific offspring." This idea is precisely that of the old botanists Ray and De Candolle. What are we to think of these divergences? That species might really be nothing more than one of those "products of art" of which Lamarck speaks, and not a definite and absolute zoological association. Its most zealous partisans declare that it has but one criterion by which it may be recognised—the fecundity of individuals *inter se*, and their sterility with those of contiguous species. But this criterion has undergone many assaults of late years. Many species, admitted incontestably to be diverse from one another, have produced prolific offspring, unquestionably very prolific. Naturalists generally denied it at first, and held to the denial with pertinacious grasp, declaring that they were deceived, and that the pretended species were simply varieties. Be it so. The hare and the rabbit, the dog and the wolf, the camel and the dromedary are of the same species. But the distance between the goat and the sheep is greater; they are genera, and by descending only one step they would only become species. Now their cross-breeds succeed well in Chili. The wild goat and the domestic goat are also different genera; nevertheless, in the Pyrenees they produce mixed breeds, which have been described by Count de Bouillé. It appears that even the union of a heifer and a stag produced a hybrid, which was exhibited at an agricultural meeting in the department of Aisne.

But it is not sufficient that there should be a cross-breed and progeny; the criterion of species is that this progeny itself and its descendants should be fertile, and that the mongrels left to themselves should never revert either to the paternal or maternal type. However, this is only one step in the mode of manifestation of an organic property, which we shall describe later on under the name of homogenesis, and which is the faculty that two germs of opposite sexes possess in different individuals of becoming reciprocally prolific, however great their zoological distance may be. Simple fecundity is the first step. The union of the hare and the rabbit furnishes an example of the most advanced step. The different species produce offspring of an intermediate character, termed

o 2

leporides, which after twenty generations are still fixed, after repeated experiments both in France and Germany.

The perpetuity of the type of species is secured, under these circumstances, by the faculty of individuals to intercross more successfully and to produce offspring, which in their turn continue to propagate those resembling themselves. No one disputes this. It is equally the rule that crossings outside the species are sterile, but in both cases there are exceptions which do not confirm the rule, and which increase in number the more closely we look at the matter; exceptions which, reasoning by analogy, could not be foreseen, and which are only learnt from experience. This more or less potent affinity between genera and species, and the more or less favoured varieties of mongrels resulting in consequence, prove at least that the barriers of species are not inviolable, and that the pretended criterion has nothing positive about it.

Later on, when we are considering the degree of homogenesis of races in human cross-breeds, we must beware of gathering from them an argument either for or against their quality of species or variety.

Of Variety.

Under this name, devoid of all qualification, we usually understand an assemblage of individuals presenting common characteristics, and thereby distinguished from contiguous groups having other common characteristics, or those of a more general type. It is transient and accidental, or permanent. Teratological variety, and variety the result of the influence of external conditions, belong to the former. Apropos of the permanent variety, all kinds of difference of doctrine are observable. In the transformation schools of the present day no distinction is made between them and species. In the opposite school of olden time, that of Frichard for example, the two so far approach each other that their characteristics are altogether hereditary; but whilst the permanent variety is merely an accidental one which is fixed and determined, species had always existed, or at least had descended from a single pair.

Of Race.

The word has many acceptations, according to the particular
doctrine embraced or the absence of doctrine. In the one case it
corresponds to the permanent and secondary variety of Prichard,
in the other it expresses so well-marked a zoological limit, that one
is compelled to ask whether it is not confounded with species. In
current language indeed it has a vague meaning, leaving all the
questions *sub judice*.

"Races are hereditary varieties," remarks Adrien de Jussieu;
and M. de Quatrefages says: "When the accidental characteristics
which distinguish a vegetable or an animal variety are transmitted
by generation and become hereditary, then we have a race."
"Zoologists and botanists are unanimous on this point," he goes on
to say; and further: "The race is the ensemble of individuals like
each other, belonging to one and the same species, having received
and transmitted by generation the characteristics of a primitive
variety." Does M. de Quatrefages mean to say that it is quite
primitive? for, the disputed criterion of fecundity being set aside,
how are we to distinguish primitive variety from species? The
accidental origin is pointed out precisely in this other definition.
"Race," says Isidore Geoffroy Saint-Hilaire, "is a succession of
individuals springing from one another, and marked distinct by
undeviating characteristics."*

M. G. Pouchet gives the word another acceptation, which is that
of the ancient polygenists: "The word 'race' designates the different
natural groups of mankind." According to him they are so many
species. There is a radical difference between this, not admitting
that certain races represent species, but that others are only permanent varieties.†

* "Revue des Cours Scientif., 1867-68;" "Leçons" of M. de Quatrefages,
"Histoire Nat. Gén. des Régions Organiques," by Isidore Geoffroy Saint-
Hilaire, 3 vols., Paris, 1859.
† "De la Pluralité des Races Humaines," by Georges Pouchet. Second
edition. Paris, 1864.

Another way in which the word "race" is understood, or rather employed, is that set forth in the following definition of Prichard: "Under the name of races we include all assemblages of individuals presenting *more or less* common characteristics, transmissible by succession, *the origin of these characteristics being an unsettled question.*" The term may thus be used indifferently and taken in its widest sense. It applies as well to more or less thoroughly-defined human varieties, or sub-varieties, as to species. Under its shadow every variety of opinion may recline; negroes in general may be looked upon as a race in the same way as Kaffirs or natives of the Gold Coast. We shall speak as a matter of convenience of pure, cross, mixed, primary, and secondary races. There will be anthropological and historical races, as well as those determined according to language. Some are lost in obscurity, and will only be found by a diligent examination of every possible species of evidence; others will be seen under our very eyes, as the living races of Australia and America. At the moment when we ought to decide as to the number and value of races, we shall come to an orderly arrangement inspired by the teachings of our master, M. Broca, who says, "The varieties of mankind have received the name of races, which gives the idea of a more or less direct relationship between individuals of the same variety, but does not decide either affirmatively or negatively the question of the relationship between individuals of different varieties." *

Races thus included, that is to say, the more or less generally accepted divisions and subdivisions of the human family, are well-nigh infinite; we are compelled therefore to group them. Those of the most striking character we place first; then those which are less and less determined; and, lastly, those which we make a guess at, or which are to be discovered by the help of geography, history, and linguistics.

Classification of Races.

The first attempt at classification was made in the year 1772, by F. Bernier, a French traveller, who made out that there were

* Article "Anthropologie," in " Dict. Encycl. des Sciences Médicales," vol. v.

four races : the white in Europe, the yellow in Asia, the black in Africa, and Laplanders in the north.

The second was that of Linnæus. His genus *Man* includes three species : *homo sapiens, homo ferus,* and *homo monstruosus*. His *savage* man is dumb, covered with hair, and walks on all-fours. Among his *monstrous* men he includes the microcephales and the plagiocephales. His *homo sapiens* includes four varieties : the European, with flaxen hair, blue eyes, and light skin ; the Asiatic, with blackish hair, brown eyes, and yellowish skin ; the African, with black woolly hair, black skin, flat nose, and thick lips ; and the American, with tawny skin, long black hair, and beardless chin.

Buffon did not classify—he described. He recognised more particularly a northern race, a Malay race, and made a distinction between Hottentots and other African negroes. The first classification which possessed a certain amount of prestige was that of Blumenbach. The Göttingen professor described five human varieties : the Caucasian, the Mongolian, the Ethiopian, the American, and the Malay. He was the originator of the title of Caucasian, which is now in use, and which he employed because the Caucasus is near Mount Ararat, upon which the ark rested after the flood. But a period soon arrived when a reaction took place among a certain number of naturalists. Three pairs alone having survived the universal deluge, as a matter of course all the races of mankind now living upon the earth descended from them.

Cuvier admits three races—the white, or Caucasian, the Mongolian, and the negro. Désormais divides the first into three—the Indo-Pelasgian, the Armenian (Semitic), and the Scytho-Tartarian ; and includes in the second the Kalmucks, the Mantchds, the Chinese, the Japanese, the Coreans, and the inhabitants of Micronesia (the Marianne and Caroline Isles). He does not speak of the divisions of the negro race ; but, not knowing where to find a place in his classification for the Malays, Papuans, Lapps, Esquimaux, and Americans, he rejects them altogether from his category. "The real colour of the Indians of America," however, he does " not consider sufficient ground for placing them in a distinct race."

The authority of Blumenbach, however, counterbalanced that of
Cuvier, and classic authors, with some dissentients, divided them
between the five races of the one and the three races of the other.
Lacépède, Prichard, Jacquinot, and Flourens were in favour of
three, the last-named recognising about thirty-three different types.

The first opposition came from Virey, in 1801, who gave out
that the human family was composed of two species, the white and
the black, each being divided into six races, and these in their
turn into families.

Bory de Saint-Vincent and A. Desmoulins were of the same
opinion. The former, taking up the propositions of La Peyrère,
declared that Adam was "the father of the Jews only, and that the
differences between the human races are sufficiently great to merit
the designation of species." He admitted fifteen, many of which
in their turn included many races, namely, the Japhetic or
European, the Arabian, the Hindoo, the Scythian (Turks), the
Sinican (Chinese), the Hyperborean, the Neptunian (Malays,
Polynesians, and Papous), the Australian, the Columbian and
American, the Ethiopian, the Kaffir, the Melanesian, and the
Hottentot. Among the secondary races a few deserve to be
mentioned : the Arabian species, comprising the Adamic Jews and
Arabians, and the Atlantic race (Berbers).

A. Desmoulins at the same time as, or rather before, Bory de
Saint-Vincent, raised the number of human species to sixteen.
He mentions two which had escaped Bory, namely, the Kurilian
and the Papuan. The Caucasian species is taken in a different
acceptation to that of Blumenbach and Cuvier; it merely designates a particular group of the Caucasus, including the Mingrelians,
the Georgians, and the Armenians. His division of the Mongolian species into the Indo-Sinican, the Mongol, and the Hyperborean race is equally worthy of attention. It is to be regretted
that A. Desmoulins should have brought into his Scythian or
European species the Finnish race. But in his arrangement are
found unforeseen affinities which science has not confirmed, but
which perhaps will deserve to be one day taken again into consideration. It would be impossible to enumerate all the methods

of classification which have been proposed, from the four races of
Leibnitz, the four varieties of Kant, the five groups (divided
into twenty-six families) of Morton, or the nine centres of Agassiz,
to the more recent classifications of M. Fr. Müller and M. Hæckel.
These only will engage our attention before we close this subject:
the method of Isidore Geoffroy Saint-Hilaire, which was the first
to make classification depend exclusively on the methodical arrangement of a certain number of physical characteristics; that of Mr.
Huxley, which has a certain amount of originality; and that of
M. de Quatrefages, which examines into the whole of nature in
accordance with the principles of the natural method.

The classifications of Isidore Geoffroy Saint-Hilaire are two in
number. In the first he distributes his eleven principal races
according to the character of the hair, the flatness or projecting
form of the nose, the colour of the skin, the shape of the eyes, and
the size of the lower extremities. In the second he admits the
following human types: the first, or Caucasian, with the face oval
and the jaws vertical (orthognathous); the second, or Mongolian,
with the face broad in consequence of the prominence of the cheek-
bones (eurygnathous); the third, or Ethiopian, with projecting
jaws (prognathous); and the fourth, or Hottentot type, with wide
cheek-bones and projecting jaws (eurygnathous and prognathous).
This division has not been settled finally, but the bases of it are
excellent.

The classification of Mr. Huxley includes two primary divisions:
The ulotrichi, with woolly hair, and the leiotrichi, with smooth
hair. (1) Ulotrichi. Colour varying from yellow-brown to the
jettest black; the hair and eyes dark, and with only a few exceptions they are dolichocephales (elongated head). Example: the
negroes of Africa and the Papous. (2) Leiotrichi. These are
divisible into four groups: the australoid group, with dark skin,
hair, and eyes; the hair long and straight, prognathous skull,
with well-developed superciliary ridges. Example: the blacks
found in Australia and in the Deccan, and perhaps the ancient
Egyptians. The mongoloid group: yellowish brown to reddish-
brown skin, dark eyes, long, black, and straight hair, mosti-

cephalic skull. Example: the Mongols, Chinese, Polynesians, Esquimaux, and Americans. The xanthochroic group: pale skin, blue eyes, and abundant fair hair, skull mesaticephalic. Example: the Slavonians, Teutons, Scandinavians, and the fair Celtic-speaking people. The melanochroid group: pale-complexioned, dark eyes, hair long and black. Example: Iberians and black Celts and the Berbers.

There are many objections to this classification. The form of the head, for example, is not always exact. If the Chinese and the Polynesians of the third group are mesaticephalic, the Esquimaux are the most dolichocephalic to be found on the globe, and the Mongols among the most brachycephalic.

The best classification, apart from the monogenistic principle upon which it is based, is that of M. de Quatrefages. The eminent professor at the Museum of Paris regards the whole of the human races, "pure or regarded as such,"[*] as a single stem with three trunks—the white, the yellow, and the black—which are divided into branches, and these again into boughs, upon which the families divided into groups are grafted. The branches of the white trunk are the Aryan, the Semitic, and the Allophyle (Esthonians, Caucasians, Ainos); those of the yellow trunk are the Mongolian or meridional, and the Ougrian or boreal; and those of the black trunk, the Negrito, the Melanesian, the African, and the Sunh (Hottentots). As examples of the boughs we may mention the three of the Aryan branch—the Celt, the German, and the Slav; the two of the Semitic branch—the Semitic and the Libyan; the two of the Mongolian branch—the Sinican (Chinese, &c.); and the Turanian (Turks). As examples of families: the

---

[*] The monogenistic theory does not recognise the existence of really pure races. All being derived from a single individual, and being gradually produced by the influence of external conditions, the epithet is not absolutely applicable to them at any period of their existence. In the ancient polygenistic doctrine a definite number of races have existed from the first, with characteristics such as we now find them to possess, and consequently have remained pure. In the transformation theory also races are never stationary, or at least are not so far as our finite vision can make out; their purity therefore is always relative, as in the monogenistic theory.

Chaldean, the Aralée, and the Amhara of the Semitic bough; the first furnishing the Hebrew group, the second the Hymyarite and Arabian groups, and the third the Abyssinian group. M. de Quatrefages admits besides, "the great races belonging more or less" to one of the three trunks. So among those of the yellow trunk, races "à éléments juxtaposés" (the Japanese), and the races "à éléments fondus" (the Malayo-Polynesians).* In fact, the majority of classifications go on progressing. We see them commencing thickly, then multiplying their divisions, and then descending to details. Questions as to geographical boundaries are the first to attract attention, then physical characteristics, language, and subsequently records of every kind, both ethnic, historical, and archæological. The defect of many is their exclusive character, as the classification of M. Fr. Müller, which is essentially linguistic. M. de Quatrefages, on the contrary, draws from all sources, and well weighs every question. Perhaps, however, he does not lay sufficient stress on physical characteristics, which ought in his eyes as a naturalist to take precedence of every other. Ethnology, which classes peoples, naturally leaves them out of consideration; anthropology, which has to do with the distribution of races—like botany, which makes divisions and subdivisions of the vegetable kingdom—takes them as its principal basis.†

Before resuming this question, let us consider first the physical characteristics of races, and then the physiological, which flow from them. We shall also speak of ethnic, archæological, and linguistic characteristics, but only to a limited extent, inasmuch as

* We must not allow the name of M. de Quatrefages to pass without expressing our sense of the liberality with which he has for many years placed at our disposal the magnificent anthropological collections of the Museum. Without endorsing all his views, we must admire the clear and sensible mode in which he expresses them in his lectures and published works. His examination of the doctrine of Darwin has particularly struck us, and demands very serious and thoughtful attention.

† See "Systema Naturæ," by Ch. Linnæus, Leyden, 1735; "Dissertatio Inauguralis de Generis Humani Varietate Nativâ," by J. F. Blumenbach, Gœttingen, 1775, in 4to; "Le Règne Animal," by Baron Cuvier, 5 vols., vol. i., Paris, 1829; "Species des Mammifères Bimanes et Quadrumanes," by R. P. Lesson, Paris, 1840, in 8vo.

there are volumes published in the "Bibliothèque des Sciences Contemporaines," specially devoted to these subjects.[*]

The Physical Characteristics.

The physical characteristics which separate races are of two orders: anatomical, which are to be studied in the laboratory; and external, to be observed on the living subject.

The two are far from possessing the same value in the present phase of anthropological science. In the laboratory, everything is done carefully and methodically, as far as can be done, with the compass and the balance. Observations are conducted with calmness, and every available source of information is brought into requisition. In a foreign land, that is to say on the living subject, it is quite otherwise. The traveller has generally other objects which occupy his attention. He sets out with certain erroneous opinions, allows himself to be influenced by the events of the day and his own preconceived notions; or he ignores what he ought to observe, and passes by facts which possibly might clear up questions long in dispute. Thus the observations which reach us from afar, sometimes from a source looked upon as a most favourable one, have never the same degree of exactness about them which facts

* "Histoire Naturelle de l'Homme," by J. J. Virey, 2 vols., Paris, 1801; "Dictionnaire Classique d'Histoire Naturelle," arts. "Bimaner," "Homme," "Orang," by Bory de Saint-Vincent, vol. viii., 1825, and vol. xii., 1827; "Histoire Naturelle des Races Humaines," by A. Desmoulins, 8vo, Paris, 1826; "Manuel de Physiologie," by J. Müller, translated into French, 2 vols., Paris, 1845; "Cours de Physiologie," by P. Bérard, vol. i., Paris, 1848, &c. &c.; "The Races of Man and their Distribution," by Charles Pickering, 1 vol., 4to, Boston, 1848 and 1854; "Types of Mankind," by Nott and Gliddon, p. 618, Philadelphia, 1 vol., 1854; table of the first classification of Isidore Geoffroy Saint-Hilaire in "Études sur l'Histoire Naturelle," by Camille Dalville, Paris; "Sur la Classification Anthropologique," by Isidore Geoffroy Saint-Hilaire, in "Mémoires de la Société d'Anthropologie," vol. i., 1860; "Comparative Anatomy of Vertebrated Animals," by T. H. Huxley, translated into French, Paris, 1875; "Dict. Encycl. des Sciences Méd.," article "Races Humaines," by De Quatrefages, 1873; "Allgemeine Ethnographie," by F. Müller, Vienna, 1873, &c.

of a much more unpretending character possess when collated in
the silence of the study.

The information published by our learned societies is intended
to supply this want of inexpertness which we find in ordinary
travellers, and to make them understand the desiderata of science,
and how to conduct their observations. But the observation of
minor characteristics presents the greatest difficulty. A scholar
like Dr. Beddoe will draw up very instructive tables as to the
colour of the hair; an ordinary observer will appropriate the tables
drawn up by the Société d'Anthropologie; another, like Quételet,
and every physician familiar with anatomy, will carefully notice
the proportions of the body, but we cannot expect this from the
generality of travellers. They fancy they have done great things
if they take note of a certain date when they met with a native
having the elongated face, the curly hair, the flat nose, or the dark
complexion. But such observations are generally insufficient.
The expeditions such as those of the Novarra in Oceania, or of
Petermann in the North, in which certain men were selected to
make special observations, are rare. In France we may mention
the Pérons, the Pickerings, the D'Orbignys, the Humboldts, the
Fritschs; but how few these are! It is doubtful if the travels of
Livingstone have helped forward in any way the science of anthropology. In natural history what we want most particularly is to
have specimens of plants and animals, which those specially
learned in each department may arrange at their leisure. In
ethnology we want to note the manners and customs, and to
ascertain the distribution of each tribe as well as its history. Such
men as Pallas, Barrow, and Eyre are not wanting; but all the
work of anthropology has to be done at a distance, with such
assistance as is to be obtained from bones, hair, and photographic
drawings. Hence the relatively low ebb at which we find the
physical study of the living subject, as compared with the flourishing results obtained in the laboratory. But among these there are
those which in the very nature of things have obtained special
pre-eminence. The thing of primary importance in a laboratory is
to have specimens, and the commonest among them are those which

give the least trouble and can best be preserved, as the bones, and especially skulls. For some time, however, the laboratory of M. Broca has been enriched with brains, preserved in alcohol, which have been sent from all parts of the world.

Bones, on the other hand, have the inestimable advantage of presenting to us all that remains of ancient peoples of which there are no longer any living representatives; some extending back to one and two thousand years, others to ten and twenty thousand, when the various types had become less changed.

When making a comparison of races, therefore, it should not be matter of surprise that such importance is attached to the study of the bones, and particularly of the skull—that noblest part of the human animal.

Craniology.

Craniology thus forms the first chapter of the anthropology of the human races.

Some of the differences which skulls exhibit are slight, others are considerable; some are more readily appreciable by their general appearance, others by measurement. The particular type of each skull, or the general type of the group to which it belongs, is to be ascertained by carefully studying their *ensemble*. Some of these differences moreover are sufficiently striking of themselves to characterise the race, and to enable us to recognise at once the source from whence the specimen was derived. For example, the excessive length and height of the Esquimaux skull, or the keel-shaped vertex associated with great depth of the root of the nose in the Tasmanian skull. There are exceptions, however; craniology, in its present phase, is a science of analysis and of patience, and not yet a science of synthesis. There are two general methods, each of which claims pre-eminence, which however are equally useful and mutually perfect. In one, cranioscopy, the eye, or simple means which one has always at hand, are sufficient. In the other, craniometry, we have recourse to proceedings requiring accuracy. We shall term the characteristics ascertained by the former descriptive, and those by the latter craniometrical.

Descriptive Characteristics.

A skull being submitted to examination, the first thing is to determine the age and the sex, and to notice whether it presents any deformity, whether posthumous, platybasic, artificial, or pathological. We should especially direct our attention, with a view to after examination, to the small skulls which M. Broca has called demi-microcephales, and to those manifestly affected with old hydrocephalus. We should afterwards notice if the skull presents any anatomical anomalies, such as a supplementary suture dividing one of the parietal or malar bones ; the persistence of the inter-maxillary, the metopic, or the interparietal sutures ; the welding together of the bones of the nose ; the exceptionally large ossa Wormiana—an epactal, for example ; the enlargement of the two vascular foramina, occasionally absent, called parietal foramina, and situated about two centimètres outside and on each side of the sagittal suture, at the junction of its anterior four-fifths with its posterior one-fifth ; an enlargement of about two centimètres in diameter, to which M. Broca has drawn attention ;[*] a third condyle ; a jugular apophysis, &c. What we have mentioned in the first part respecting all these peculiarities will suffice. One word, however, with respect to the epactal bone.

It is simple or multiple, and varies in size from that of a mere triangular Wormian bone enclosed within the point of the V which is formed by the lambda below, to one almost having the appearance of an interparietal bone. It is distinguished from this latter in that the true interparietal suture leads directly from one asterion to the other, passing below the inion, while the suture of the epactal is always above, and ends more or less high up on the branches of the lambdoidal suture. The epactal has been called os Incae by Rivero and Tschudy, who improperly look upon it as an almost constant characteristic of the three races of Peru. In 47 Aucanian skulls in M. Broca's laboratory (the others have still the skin and

[*] " Sur la Perforation Congénitale et Symétrique des deux Pariétaux," by P. Broca, in " Bull. Soc. d'Anthrop.," 1875.

hair on them) it was present, of greater or less size, eleven times, which is oftener than usual.

Among the most important characteristics to establish are:

(1) The state of the cranial sutures, the serratures of which are very complex in the superior races, usually simple in the inferior.

(2) The projection of the inion or external occipital protuberance, the degree of development of which M. Broca expresses by five figures, the 5 corresponding to the maximum development, and the 0 to its complete obliteration.

(3) The disposition of the pterion like an H or a K. The former is the more usual, in which the greater wings of the sphenoid are directly articulated with the parietal to a variable extent, which M. Broca measures with the compasses; the latter is exceptional, where the temporal touches the frontal to a variable extent, pushing back the sphenoid and parietal above and below.

(4) The part of the face where the plane of the artificially lengthened occipital foramen comes to. In the white races this spot is situated at the superior half of the skeleton of the nose; in blacks, it comes down close to the nasal spine or below it. M. Broca indicates the different points thus met with by the vowels A, E, I, O, U. A indicates the alveolar point; E, the nasal spine; I, the spot corresponding to the position of the inferior turbinated bone; O, where the inferior border of the orbit ends on the median line; U, the median point situated at the top of the os unguis.[*] In some cases the plane reaches the root of the nose at a point which he then indicates by N. A simple rule or a knitting-needle placed on the plane of the occipital foramen, gives in a moment this element of appreciation of the skull, which is merely the inclination of the plane of the occipital foramen, the angle of which is taken more accurately with the occipital goniometer. The letter N corresponds to an angle of Daubenton from − 11 to − 13 degrees; U, from − 5 to − 7; O, to 0; I, from + 2 to + 5; E, from + 7 to + 11; and A, from + 13 to + 17. For further details, see p. 64, and Chapter III., Part II.

We shall see that the direction or inclination of the plane of the

[*] Memoir already quoted on the occipital angles.

occipital foramen, estimated rapidly by this proceeding or strictly with the goniometer, is one of the most important characteristics by which we distinguish the negro from the European.   M. Broca has invented for use in the laboratory, and as a good substitute for the rule to which we have referred, a curved stem, the curve of which passes underneath the superior maxillary bone, and which is termed *crochet occipital.*   (Fig. 29.)

The following peculiarities, which are very difficult to define, and which have hitherto defied all attempts at measurement, assist us in characterising the physiognomy of the skull, and are occasionally sufficient to enable us to recognise it.

(1) The flatness of the lateral parietes of the skull, as well as their

Fig. 29.—Occipital crochet of M. Broca, for the purpose of determining the part of the face where the prolonged plane of the occipital foramen meets.

vertical character, so remarkable in certain negroes of Africa, and especially of Oceania; while at other times, as among the Lapps and the Auvergnians, these parietes are very much bulged.

(2) The curve of the temporal line, its height, and its prolongation behind as far as the mastoid region, showing the extent of the temporal fossa and the importance of the temporal muscle, which is inserted upon the whole of its surface.   This line usually extends from the median line at the base of the forehead, but sometimes, in altogether inferior types, it approaches to about two centimètres of the sagittal suture.   This very simian character has been observed in some ancient skulls from Florida, in some from New Caledonia, in an Usbeck skull in M. Broca's laboratory, &c.

(3) The projection of the glabella and the superciliary arches. Not visible in children, the glabella makes its appearance at about

P

15 years of age and upwards, and, as we have said, is scarcely perceptible in women; generally faint in the negroes of Africa, the Malays, and in all the yellow races, even in men, it is very much developed in some prehistoric races, in Europeans, particularly in Auvergniaus, but especially in Australians, Tasmanians, and New Caledonians. The projection of the sides of the superciliary arches follows the same law, and is less wanting in women.

(4) The form of the forehead, divided into two planes united at a more or less obtuse angle at the level of the frontal eminences. These eminences are high or low, projecting, obliterated, or exceptionally united into one at the median line. When the angle is very open, as in the microcephales, in the prehistoric race of the Neanderthal, and in the negroes of Oceania generally, the forehead is termed receding (*fuyant*). When it is much less—as in women, in Malays and Chinese, the negroes of Africa, and particularly in the beautiful series of Nubian skulls which M. Broca has disinterred from the banks of the Nile—the forehead is termed straight. The increased projection and height of the eminences, and a too straight forehead, should make us suspect that there had been hydrocephalus during infancy.

(5) The curve of the vault. In reputedly well-formed skulls, as the skull of the Arab, it gradually rises from the frontal eminences, reaches its culminating point behind the bregma, and begins to descend at two or three centimètres farther, as far as the line which unites the two parietal eminences, where the descent becomes more rapid. A too great or a too slight curve in one particular part of its extent, the falling back of the culminating point, or the flattening of the quadrilateral space included between the frontal and parietal eminences, are so many less satisfactory characteristics.

The median line is not usually in relief. Sometimes it is even slightly hollowed at the commencement of its descent, between the parietal eminences. But at others it is bulged out, and gives origin to an antero-posterior crest, which extends from the bregma, from the frontal eminences, or lower down, as far as the obelion, and is occasionally cleft for the lodgment of the depressed sagittal suture. At the sides of the median line are then seen two out-

wardly-inclined planes, either straight, convex, or concave, which
end at the curved temporal line and the parietal eminences, at one
part obliterated, at another enlarged, turning round, or by a rapid
fall, at the sides of the skull.   Hence the three configurations of
the vault are called *en toit*, or roof-shaped; *an ogive*, or like a
sugar-loaf; and *en carène*, or keel-shaped. The first is very common
in Oceania, the second has been improperly said to be peculiar
to the skulls of Mongols, the third is very characteristic of the
Polynesian and especially of the Tasmanian skulls.

(6) The posterior curve of the skull from the line crossing
between the parietal eminences as far as the inion. It consists
of two portions separated by the lambda. The former commences
more or less in front, and is more or less inclined downwards and
rounded off.   The latter is vertical and bulged out, and has
received the name of occipital protuberance, and by the English of
probola. Continuous with the preceding in skulls of a superior type,
this is frequently as if raised and separated, and forms a globular
projection, which when moderate in size appears to be a characteristic of race, as in the tribes of Cro-Magnon and of l'Homme Mort,
in the Esquimaux and Patagonians, &c.; and when considerable
ought to be regarded as a sign of unusual cerebral pressure from
within, or of hydrocephalus in infancy. Many human types
exhibit, to a greater or less extent, a more or less marked flattening
of the posterior curve. Most frequently, as in the ancient
Tchudclahan, it does not pass beyond the lambda; at other times
it goes beyond, as in many Auvergnians. At other times again it
impinges upon the supra-iniac region, and in extreme cases surrounds
it entirely, as in the Malays and Americans. Morton, indeed, made
this falling of the skull backwards one of the characteristics of the
entire American race.

(7) The curve of the sub-iniac region or receptaculum cerebelli is
very variable. Its bulging out frequently passes beyond the plane
of the occipital foramen, and then prevents the condyles from
touching the table when the skull is laid on its base.

(8) Various other characteristics, such as the singular depression,
mentioned by M. Bröca, in the middle of the parieto-occipital

suture in the skulls of Orrouy, at the Polished Stone epoch; the size of the mastoid processes, which, allowance being made for differences of sex, are large in certain races and small in others; a peculiar supra-mastoidean projection situated at the junction of the posterior prolongation of the temporal line and at the posterior root of the zygomatic process, and particularly developed in Esthonian skulls.

In the face, characteristics to be discovered by simple inspection are not wanting. In the first line is to be noticed whatever has reference to the malar bones, the methods for whose measurement are by no means satisfactory; the absence of marks in places where we have most need of them is very much to be regretted. These bones are small and lank in European races, massive and projecting outwards in the Mongol races. In the Esquimaux, their external, anterior, and inferior angle is so thrown outwards and forwards that by this feature alone we are able to recognise the skulls of that race. Then come the prominence of the extremity of the bones proper of the nose and their projection at a very acute angle, two characteristics belonging to human races; their flattening, or the contrary, in the negro races of Africa and especially the yellow races; the depth of the hollow at the root of the nose, slight in Arabians, less still in the negroes of Africa and in all the yellow species; well marked in Europeans generally, but especially so in Australians, New Caledonians, and Tasmanians. We have already mentioned in the Tasmanian race a see-saw motion of the superior maxilla, by virtue of which its upper part plunges beneath the cranium, while its lower projects forwards. We have also described the differences, five in number, which the inferior border of the nares presents on the skeleton. Thus in Europeans it has the form of a heart, such as we see on playing-cards, the nasal spine of which represents the median point and presents only a sharp lip. In the negroes of Africa the border is blunt, spread out, and becomes horizontal by the progressive obliteration of the nasal spine. In the Chinese and some other yellow races it is replaced by two digital depressions, which in Melanesians are transformed into two channels. It has been observed in rare

instances, especially in New Caledonians, that the whole line of
demarcation between the nasal fossæ and the anterior surface of
the alveolar arch has disappeared. In this latter respect certain
negroes resemble the anthropoid apes. In the general configuration
there are other characteristics of a similar kind. M. Pruner-Bey
has laid much stress on the various harmonious relations or otherwise of the cranium to the face. A cranium elongated from before
backwards, and at the same time elevated, is already in harmony
by itself; but if the face, on the other hand, is elongated from
above downwards, and narrows, the harmony is complete. Such
are the Esquimaux and Kymri skulls. The Lapp and Auvergnian
skulls, on the contrary, are short from before backwards and from
above downwards, and wide both in the cranium and face. Among
skulls of an opposite character we find the celebrated Cro-Magnon
skull of the Stone period, which is elongated from before backwards, while the face is contracted from above downwards. The
same with the Tasmanian skull. There are other characteristics
which run parallel with these; for example, the arch of the
palate is somewhat elongated in long skulls, and widened in wide
skulls; the occipital foramen in the same way.

All craniologists, or, rather, cranioscopists, have spoken of grace-
fully-formed skulls, with smooth contours and regular outlines,
and of those with "*beastly*" features, of sombre, stern aspect, and of
brutish appearance. Between the two are to be seen soft, undefined
forms, destitute of character. Those of Europeans, New Caledonians,
and Chinese are of these descriptions. But we ought not to set too high
a value upon such appearances. These forms, whether pleasing or
brute-like, are to be met with in all races, in the European as well as
in the negro. In what respect, for example, is the prominent and
narrow-shaped nose of the European handsomer than the small but
broader nose of the Chinese? Let different persons compare the
skull of the man and the woman, those of Cro-Magnon and of the
Cavern de l'Homme Mort, opinions will be divided respecting them;
it is simply a matter of custom, of education, or of prejudice.

The best example of erroneous views resulting from the abuse of
cranioscopy is to be seen in a memoir of last year.

M. Mantegazza and two friends placed two hundred skulls in a series, according to the ideas which they had formed of the beautiful. They took as their model the Jupiter Olympus, in which the proportions are conventional, and which has a facial angle such as is only met with among hydrocephali. They brought together, confusedly, the skulls of both sexes and of all ages, and found that the measurements as given with the craniometer did not accord with their æsthetic notions. That M. Mantegazza was discouraged by the unsatisfactory result obtained by certain measurements, notably Camper's facial angle, we can easily believe, but this is no reason why the scientific method should be abandoned. Before we can obtain one satisfactory measurement we must be prepared to sacrifice several of them. The illustrious anthropologist regrets that craniometry does not exhibit the relative superiority of races in the way in which he conceived it. But does craniometry reject this superiority? No, it is content that each one should stand on its own merits. Let us relegate sentiment to artists, it is an essential part of their nature, and let us take care that our observations are made with rigid strictness, without which there would be an end to science; we shall move less quickly, but surely.

The method of studying the aspect of skulls from different points of view originated almost simultaneously with craniometry, but was the one generally in use until lately. It is convenient, inasmuch as one forms a judgment at once, in the same way as one would form one of a picture—certain lines, certain colour, by such a master. Blumenbach was the originator of this method, which was termed the vertical view (norma verticalis). He placed a series of skulls with the malar bones in the same horizontal line as they would have taken had the lower jaws been attached, and then viewed them in succession, fixing the eye above the vertex of each. In this way he estimated the breadth or narrowness of the contour of the vault, its length, its general form, and the projection of the frontal bone. He noticed whether the zygomatic arches and the jaws were visible, and to what degree. In white races these parts are generally out of view, in the black they more or less project. He also gives the skulls of a Georgian, a Tungusian, and a negro of Guinea as specimens

of the three varieties of form. The *norma verticalis* has continued
to be the method usually employed when we wish to make a rapid
estimate of the general form of the skull, as well as the cephalic
index, without the assistance of an instrument. But instead of the
skull being placed on its base, after Blumenbach's fashion, it should
be held at a distance, so that the eye can take into view the
extremities of its antero-posterior and its maximum transverse
diameters. The view ought to be made perpendicularly to the
horizontal plane passing through the glabella and a point situated

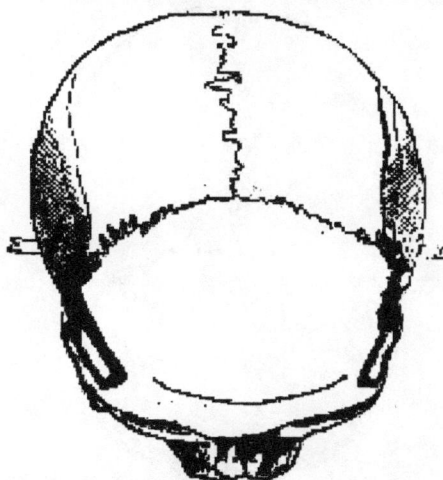

Fig. 24.—*Norma verticalis* of Blumenbach, taken with the stereograph. Brachycephalic
skull of Auvergnat. Cephalic index, 85·10.

at about two centimètres above the inion. Figs. 24 and 25 show
the two principal forms of the skull which we may distinguish in
this way.

Contemporaneously with Blumenbach, Camper adopted the
method of studying the skull in profile; and later on, Owen, being
desirous of comparing the anthropoid apes with Man, supplemented
it with the view from below. This last then took into account the
position of the occipital foramen relatively to the anterior and
posterior extremities of the skull, the segment described by the
zygomatic arches, the form of the arch of the palate, &c.

Prichard combined these three methods, and added that of the face, but made no reference to the view from behind. He recognised three principal forms of the skull: the oval, the pyramidal, and the prognathous, a division since adopted by M. Pruner-Bey.

The first, or oval, corresponds to our European type. The forehead is well developed, the maxillary bones and the zygomatic arches being so formed as to give the face an oval shape. The forehead and malar bones are nearly on a plane with these, the alveolar borders and the incisor teeth are vertical.

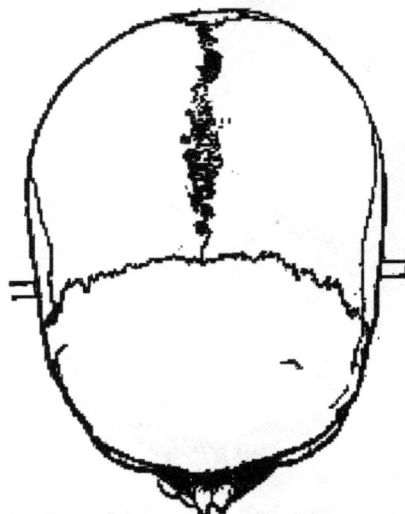

Fig. 25.—Norma verticalis of Blumenbach, taken with the stereograph. Dolichocephalic skull of Spanish Basque (province of Guipuscoa). Cephalic index, 74·19.

The second, or pyramidal, he says, is to be noticed in the Mongols, and more so in the Esquimaux. Its most striking character is the outward projection of the zygomatic arches. "The cheek-bones project from under the middle of the orbit, and turn backwards in a large arch or segment of a circle, the lateral projection of the zygomas being so considerable, that if a line drawn from one to the other be taken as a base, this will form with the top of the forehead a nearly triangular figure. The upper part of the face is remarkably plane and flat, the nose being flat, and the nasal bones, as well as the spaces between the eyebrows, nearly on the same plane with the cheek-bones. Lastly, at the point of the pyramid is the fronto-sagittal crest," &c.

The third, or prognathous, corresponds to the negro type. The skull is compressed laterally, the temporal muscles are inserted very high up, producing the effects of lateral elongation and flattening. The cheek-bones project rather forwards than outwards (prognathism).* This is one of the most valuable portions of Prichard's work.

However striking certain characteristics furnished by the eye and the forms thus recognised may be à priori, both are insufficient to lay the foundation of an exact science, and craniology thus limited would be of little avail. The traits of character so judged of are entirely individual in the majority of cases, and their estimate depends upon the mental disposition of the observer, as well as upon the accurate recollection of his latent visual impressions. These can only be committed to writing in a very imperfect way. According to the way in which the light falls upon the skull so do appearances vary, and M. Broca is daily exhibiting to his pupils the fallacies to which any one of the characteristics, looked upon by craniology as of the highest importance, may be exposed. According as the skull is looked at at a height or on the ground, so the estimates vary; so many millimètres of greater or less inclination will give the appearance of prognathism or not. In Blumenbach's method the skull rarely remains in the same position; the variable size of the mastoid processes, the presence or absence of the teeth; the swelling or depression behind the occipital foramen cause it to fall forwards or backwards, sometimes in one way, sometimes in another. It is not less important to have some fixed method of holding the skull, and Prichard himself, by relying too much upon his draughtsman, has unwittingly shown what errors may be committed in this way. Craniology as a science would scarcely exist but for the really scientific methods of examination which it possesses, and the characteristics which it is capable of expressing

* "Researches into the Physical History of Mankind," by J. C. Prichard. Five vols. 1846–47.

with precision. The process is a long and laborious one, but the results arrived at are certain; they may need interpretation, but they never deceive. This part of craniology is termed craniometry and is merely one branch of anthropometry.

Anthropometry is the study of the human body by mathematical modes of procedure; osteometry is its application to the skeleton in general; craniometry to the skull in particular; pelvimetry to the pelvis.

Craniometry.

The first attempts at measurement upon the human subject, excluding those artists who up to the last century had not settled any definite distinction between races, were made by Daubenton, Camper, Sœmmering, and White. Craniometry, however, did not soar aloft until the time of Morton. Since this period it has been practised in all parts of the civilised world. It has its adepts in Patagonia, in the person of Dr. Moreno, and in the Caucasus in that of Professor Snirnow. The works, on the skull, of Thurnam, B. Davis, Busk, and Carter Blake in England are well known, as also in Italy those of Mantegazza, Calori, Nicolucci; in Eastern Europe, Wagner, Van der Hoeven, Von Bäer, Lucae, Baker, Virchow, Welcker; in France, Gratiolet, Broca, De Quatrefages, Bertillon, Hamy. Collections of skulls have been made in all directions. Among the most celebrated we may mention the collection of Morton at Philadelphia, which in 1857 consisted of 1,045 specimens; of Bernard Davis at Shelton, Staffordshire, which at the present time amounts to about 1,700; and those of Paris, which altogether number upwards of 7,000.

Craniometrical Characteristics.

One is necessarily compelled when practising craniometry, in order to make oneself thoroughly acquainted with a race, to study a number of its representatives and to take their average, in order that there may be no preponderance of any special characteristic. You arrive in a town and see an individual of fair complexion; do you jump to the conclusion at once that all the inhabitants are fair?

No.   You pass from one quarter of the town to another, make a certain number of observations, and from them draw your inferences. So with craniometry ; a single skull may by chance exhibit the type of the race, but it may also be an exception and lead to error.   The characteristics of the type sought can only be correctly expressed in their *ensemble* upon different skulls.   The first thing, then, which is requisite for craniometrical study is a sufficient number of specimens.   The type being once recognised, one, two, or more skulls will be found necessary in order to furnish further information, and we must wait.   The archæologist, therefore, should collect together the most likely specimens he can find, and not take any he may lay hold of and bring them to the laboratory with the question : Are these the skulls of Franks, Burgundians, Saracens, or Romans ?

Moreover, few of the series collected in one and the same place are examples of an unmixed type.   Most frequently they are only a medley of different races more or less nearly allied to one another, with quite opposite characteristics, some corresponding to one of the ancient types, others to another ; they include cases of atavism, and even stray examples obtained from various sources.

Twenty skulls of the same sex are sufficient in general to remove all questions of difficulty, but this number is necessary ; and here arises a serious question : What is the extent of individual variations admissible in a race reputed pure, as in the Andamans for example ?   It is only possible to answer this question as regards each particular case.   First, it depends on the extent of the maximum and minimum deviations observed throughout the whole human series.   The less considerable these deviations and the better understood, the greater the value of the characteristic.   There are characteristics which, *cæteris paribus*, vary enormously when expressed in one way and vary slightly when in another.   This is so with prognathism, which is estimated sometimes by the relation of the horizontal projection to the height of the region, sometimes by the angle at the culminating point of the upper jaw.   M. Broca has recognised variations in the cephalic index in one and the same race to the number of 10 per cent ; it is only when they reach

15 to 18 per cent. that we can say with certainty that they are due to mixture of race.

The figures expressing each individual measurement being arranged in a progressive series, the most divergent are placed at the two extremities, while those which are most frequently alike are grouped in the middle. Sometimes, however, there are two maxima of concentration, separated by an interval in which the numbers are clearly distributed. M. Baelitton attributes this to a commingling of two races of opposite characters, and has deduced some valuable conclusions therefrom.

The measurements taken in centimètres and millimètres are added, and divided by the number of subjects measured. The quotient is the mean; it expresses the characteristic directly, such as the breadth of the forehead for example, or is only valuable when compared with some other measurement. A skull is broad in certain cases, not from the number of centimètres which it measures, but in proportion to its volume, that is to say, its length. We therefore convert its breadth into centimètres of its length. It is thus an index or relation, a far superior method to that of directly estimating the absolute measurements. The mode of calculating this index is by no means unimportant. There are three ways of proceeding: (1) We calculate each index separately and take the mean (*moyenne des indices*); (2) We add each of the series of factors, we take their means, and from these we calculate the index (*indice des moyennes*)—this mode is preferable, and avoids the losses arising from decimals omitted; (3) We again add the factors, and with their sum obtain the index directly. This has the advantage of economy in working, and is that which we usually adopt.

The means have reference to the straight measurements, to the curves, the angles, and even to the marks which M. Broca expresses by certain figures, as the projection of the inion from 0 to 5.

The first condition of a good measurement is to be determined by certain fixed anatomical marks, so that two observers at a distance from each other may not deviate from them in the slightest degree under any circumstances. In this point of view the maximum and minimum measurements are excellent. Those which pass from some definite point of the base and lead to any optional part, as the vertex, not determined by projection, are bad, such as those which meet at the parietal or frontal eminences. We can never succeed twice following in placing their culminating point at the same spot, consequently they only furnish approximative dimensions. It would be better to give up any preconceived notion than to deviate from certain defined marks, or at any rate as little as possible; and observers who publish measurements without giving a precise description of their method of working, run the risk of having little attention paid to them.

Every measurement should be made with a definite object. Craniometrical characteristics under this aspect are of two kinds: rational, that is to say, related to some physiological opinion; or empirical, having no apparent design.

If we take two skulls resembling each other but of different capacity, we shall find the largest to be, cæteris paribus, the one with the more developed frontal bone, the more rounded vault, the posterior part more ample, the occipital foramen more elevated, the distance of this foramen from the bregma more considerable. Gratiolet has divided the human races into frontal, parietal, and occipital, according as the skull is more or less developed at the expense of this or that part. Hence we have one of the first series of characteristics subordinate to one and the same idea, viz. the variable development of the characteristic organ in the human family.

Other characteristics are looked upon, whether rightly or wrongly, as dominant. They have an affinity in degrees to those which they exhibit in apes, and establish the transition between these and Europeans. Thus both on the skeleton, in the muscles and in the viscera, there are certain arrangements having respect to a sideling attitude, as that of anthropoids. The mind is then led to consider these more or less considerable variations as proof of a gradual approach of the organism to perfection, and that all the human races sprung from one and the same inferior type. The Bosjesmans, in several respects, are at the bottom of the scale;

the Melanesians, the negroes of Guinea, the Caffres, the yellow races, &c., would be next to them. But this, although true as to certain characteristics, does not hold good as regards others. Some have only a negative character, such as the width between the cheek-bones, the flatness of the face, the elliptical or hyperbolical form of the alveolar arches, the projection of the superciliary ridges, the sinking in at the root of the nose, the keel-like form of the top of the head, &c. Many characteristics which we usually, though wrongly, place in the series are of this kind, of which the skeleton furnishes numerous examples. Their frequency does not surprise us, and we may add that it is in this more than in the variations of the brain-case that we discover the best marks of difference between races. The nasal index of M. Broca, among others, is a proof in point.

An erroneous idea has prevailed that Man being distinguished from animals more particularly as regards the brain, we ought to find in the skull the fundamental characteristics whereby we may separate races. It is rather the reverse. Evidently Man is essentially characterised by the brain and its osseous envelope. But in natural history, when a characteristic intervenes to separate one group from another, the more natural, palpable, and important it is, the less does it vary in the divisions and varieties. In botany, it is not even in the characteristic of a family, a tribe, or a genus that we must seek for shades of difference with a view to establish secondary divisions, it is in other parts of the plant. One of the labiatæ is recognised at once by its inflorescence, as Man is by his cranium. In both it is apart from their essential characteristic feature that differences are found which lay the foundation of permanent varieties.

Empirical characteristics derived from craniometry are opposed to the monogenetic creed, inasmuch as they witness in favour of the original plurality of the principal groups.

Sometimes, when having to make choice of craniometrical measurements, we are guided by the development and growth of the skeleton. The brain and its envelope increase according to one law, the cavities of the senses and the maxillary apparatus according to another; whence a possible antagonism, an influence capable of giving origin to peculiarities in races which, by being often repeated, may be considered as characteristic.

But throughout the entire range of craniometry we must not lose sight of the subordination of characteristics. Thus the development of the anterior portion of the brain cavity causes the occipital foramen to be driven backwards. The increase of the maxillary bone in front, whence prognathism is caused, gives rise to a similar result. *Cæteris paribus*, an elongated and at the same time contracted skull is proportionably increased in height. A round skull, on the contrary, appears to be decreased vertically. It is well also to consider the correlation of characteristics. An example on the living subject will explain what we mean. Blue eyes are usually accompanied by light hair. So in the skull, the flattening of the entire face, including the cheek-bones, usually causes the obliteration of the glabella and the superciliary arches, and the crushing in of the root of the nose; this forms part of the harmonious characteristics of which we spoke just now. In reality, it is from this agreement of character that the idea of type has taken its origin.

Bernard de Palissy maintained that the human skull is the most irregularly-formed figure in nature, and gives expression to a sentiment in which all must agree, who are commencing craniometrical researches. "I have a desire," he says, "to measure the head, in order directly to know its dimensions, and it appears to me that the sauterelle, the rule, and the compass would be very proper instruments to employ for that purpose, but the fact is I can never be sure of my measurements." [*] Bernard de Palissy used exaggerative language in reference to these matters. Separate, in thought, the cranium from the face, and consider the former as an egg with its larger extremity posteriorly, the diameters and circumferences of which we want simply to measure; and the latter as a pyramid, the base of which corresponds to the face, and the point to the anterior border of the occipital foramen; and the thing becomes as simple as possible. Then recollect that the cranium is the pre-

* Bernard de Palissy, "Œuvres." 16mo. Paris, 185[ ]

longation of the vertebral column, the axis of which is bent at the level of the anterior border of the occipital foramen, giving origin to three cranial vertebræ and that consequently there exists in the cranium a central point—the lesion—around which all the various modifications of development are taking place. Lastly, remember that the head possesses a natural attitude, to which, at the base of the skull, there corresponds a horizontal plane which is determined in a moment, and that in consequence we can always take the position of any point by referring to it or to the vertical median plane. Such is the basis of craniometry. The systems which apply certain measurements to the auditory foramina, or to any other point, and the gauging of the cavities only complicate it.

There is great danger of exaggeration in making craniological measurements. Everyone at first is anxious to carry out his own method of proceeding, without the help of a guide or some manual indicating all the most approved measurements. The tendency to run into minutiæ is especially predominant here; and we recollect seeing a memoir in which we counted 193 different dimensions or indices, and in another as many as 200. It is evident that craniology is an illimitable science, and it is the duty of every inquirer to make it the subject of diligent investigation. One measurement, which appears valueless, is found to have considerable importance; while another, which we have fought hard to verify, leads to no practical result.

It happens with craniology as it does almost constantly at the dawn of every new science. We have difficulties to contend with at the very onset with regard to the description of the series of skulls. We take into consideration, in a word, their characteristics as witnessed in their pathological, physiological, or accidental variations. This is a bad method. We must set out with craniometry generally. Above all, it is necessary to lay down certain bases, to ascertain facts, to determine *seriatim* the value of each characteristic, to know which to preserve and which to reject, and so to arrange the plan and method of proceeding that the labours accomplished on one side of a frontier line may be available on the other.

In America, in Italy, in England, and in France, the methods of measurement in general use differ but slightly. In Germany it is not so, notwithstanding the efforts of the congress at Göttingen and more recent congresses to bring the various systems into harmonious action. M. Welcker, in particular, is far from being in accord with the majority of his colleagues. By his works, from which we have largely drawn supplies, he has deserved well of anthropology; but his cranial net, its horizontal circumference, and its antero-posterior diameter are not well expressed. The frontal and parietal eminences cannot serve as marks for important measurements. We are sure that we have determined the position of the former thousands of times, and we declare that the results have been most unsatisfactory.

The Germans, if we may venture an opinion on the subject, do not go straight to the point. Under the pretext of anatomical philosophy, they take the detail for the essential, and frequently even distort ideas from their simple acceptation. The methods followed by M. Ecker and M. Wiesbach are probably most in accordance with the French mode of proceeding.

Without too much slighting the measurements extolled by foreigners, we very much prefer those which our learned master considers the best—at least those of which he has published abundant records. When anyone has the advantage, such as we have had, of seeing M. Broca at work in his laboratory, comparing all the measurements upon thousands of skulls, rejecting those upon which he appeared to set especial value, recommencing upon and examining entire series which he regarded as at all doubtful, a thought crosses the mind, Is it certain that everywhere else so much scrupulous care has been bestowed? We may be pardoned, then, if we give the highest place to his instructions, whether public or private.[*]

* See especially "Mémoires d'Anthropologie," by Paul Broca, vols. i. and ii., published by Ch. Reinwald & Co., Paris; "Bull. Soc. d'Anthrop." 1860-75, 15 vols.; "Mémoires d'Anthrop." 3 vols.; and "Revue d'Anthrop." edited by M. Paul Broca, 1872-75, 4 vols.

CHAPTER II.

MEASUREMENT OF THE CRANIAL CAVITY—STRAIGHT AND CURVED
MEASUREMENTS—CEPHALIC, VERTICAL, FRONTAL, NASAL, ORBITAL
INDICES—FACIAL TRIANGLE.

THE cranium is measured : (1) In any position, whether as regards
its ensemble, its cerebral or facial portion taken separately, its
interior or its exterior ; (2) In a position conformable with that
which it affects on the living subject.   Hence a series of measurements or operations may be ranged under five heads : (1) Gauging
and cubic measurements ; (2) Straight and curved measurements ;
(3) Projections ; (4) Angles ; (5) Special systems of measurement.

Measurement of the Cranial Capacity.

The importance of the cerebral cavity in man, and its influence
on the external configuration of the skull, early engaged the
attention of anthropologists, with a view to determine its capacity.
But the substance employed was objectionable, the methods of
proceeding were of an irregular character, and soon fell into dis-
repute.   Revived by Morton, the measurement of the cranium has
become, in the hands of M. Broca, a mathematical operation upon
which we can now depend.   The operation consists of two parts :
gauging, in which we fill the skull with some substance ; and cubic
measurement, by which we determine its volume.   Gauging has
been practised with water by Sœmmering, Virey, Treadwell ; with
mercury by M. Broca, in a skull which he made use of as a
standard ; with sand by Hamilton and Mr. Barnard Davis ; with
millet by M. Tiedemann and M. Mantegazza ; with white mustard
seed by Philipps ; with pearl barley by M. Welcker ; and with
shot by Morton and M. Broca.   Many other things have been

tried : water in a caoutchouc bladder, an arrangement with intra-cranial casts, with a view to ascertain the quantity of water which they displaced. Glass and earthenware beads have also been suggested, &c. Fluids are out of the question.* Of other substances, some get with difficulty into the cavities, or adhere to the parietes ; all arrange themselves unequally according to the way in which the observer, whose patience is frequently put to the test, manages matters. Some operators tap the parietes gently, others ram down the substances employed. The method of filling the cavity may also lead to error. In taking the dimensions also there are frequently mistakes made. Wyman having taken the cubic measurement of the cranial cavity eight times on the same skull, with different materials, found the result varied as follows :

With Peas	...	...	...	...	...	1198·0
„ Shot	...	...	...	...	...	1201·8
„ Haricot beans	...	...	...	...	...	1206·2
„ Rice	...	...	...	...	...	1220·2
„ Linseed	...	...	...	...	...	1247·5
„ Coarse sand	...	...	...	...	...	1267·5
„ Fine sand	...	...	...	...	...	1313·0

It is a matter of importance, therefore, to be exact in every detail of the operation, whether of gauging or of cubic measurement. Then again, certain substances answer better than others—shot, for example—which M. Broca prefers and has generally employed ; or millet, or mustard seed, which he uses when the skull is fragile.

The circumstances which most influence the result in the case of shot are the way in which it is rammed in, the rapidity with which it is poured down the funnel, and the diameter of the funnel employed, as well as the height from which the shot is allowed to

* We do not understand Dr. Beddoe's recommendation to travellers to " measure the capacity in cubes of fine sand, or, what is better (if possible), of water."—" Notes and Queries on Anthropology for the Use of Travellers and Residents in Uncivilised Lands," London, 1874.

full into the measuring vessels. If the litre is full, and placed
down on the table with some little force, the shot should not sink
lower than the original level. Consequently M. Broca has endeavoured to determine the conditions of the operation which give
the most constant result, and with some amount of success. The
following is his mode of proceeding, to the minutest details. The
orbit being filled with cotton wool and the vault of the cranium
placed in a wooden bowl, the first litre of shot is poured into its
cavity; then, the skull being grasped with both hands, is shaken
so as to allow the shot to pass into the anterior part of the cavity.
It is then turned about, and at the same time a wooden spindle is
used to ram down the shot, until the cavity can hold no more.
Then pressing hard with the thumb, the shot is rammed in until it
is on a level with the occipital foramen. The contents are then
emptied into a vessel, and from this turned quickly into a the litre,
the surface of which is levelled with a flat rule. The remainder is
passed into a glass gauge, graduated in cubic centimètres, through
a funnel, the neck of which is fixed in a wooden disc fitted to the
gauge like a cover. If the quantity is beyond the 500 centimètres
marked on the gauge, the surface is made level as before, and
the surplus is measured in the same way afterwards with the
gauge.

The four special instruments, then, are the rammer, the litre, the
gauge, and the funnel. The first is a conical piece of wood 10
centimètres in length and 2 in breadth. The litre is 80 millimètres in internal diameter and 175 in height. The gauge, of a
cylindrical form, has a cubic capacity of 500 centimètres, is 35 to 40
centimètres in height and 4 in width on the inside. The funnel
is 10 centimètres in diameter at its base, 10 centimètres in height,
with a neck 1 centimètre long and 2 wide. The size of the shot
is that known as No. 8, each grain measuring two millimètres and
two-tenths in diameter.[*] Broken skulls, or those in which the

* All these instruments are to be procured of Mathieu, surgical instrument maker, manufacturer of apparatus to the Institut Anthropologique.

sphcno-basilar suture has not ossified, are previously bound together
with leather straps.*

By scrupulously following out these instructions, the results do
not vary in one and the same skull more than five cubic centimètres,
although obtained by different individuals. In the course of an
hour a person, with the help of an assistant, may easily measure
20 skulls. Let us see the results.

The inferior races have a less capacity than the superior.
Australians are the lowest in the scale in this respect, having,
according to our measurements, a mean capacity of 1324 cubic
centimètres. The skulls of Americans, whether normal or distorted, have also a small cranial cavity. The capacity increases
in the yellow races, and attains its maximum in whites. The
Auvergnians have 1523, and the 384 Parisians of M. Broca, 1437
cubic centimètres of capacity. The difference is so great between
the two sexes, that it is absolutely necessary to examine them
separately. In races now living this difference varies from 145 to
220 cubic centimètres. It is a curious circumstance that it is not
more than 99·5 in the only skull of the immense series which we
possess of prehistoric date (Troglodytes of La Lozère). The greatest
cranial capacity with which we are acquainted is 1900 cubic centimètres, in a Parisian, and the smallest in a native of the Andaman
Islands, namely, 1093. But if this latter appears physiological,
we cannot say the same of the former. The highest maximum
limit of capacity of a cranial cavity, according to M. Welcker, is
1650; we think this too small. But we must beware lest we
exaggerate. Some of the averages of Morton and D. Davis ought
to be rejected, as, for example, the Irish skull of 1903 cubic centimètres. The mean capacity of four adult hydrocephalic skulls
from the Museum Dupuytren, was found by M. Broca to be 3727
cubic centimètres, and of three adult microcephali 414.† The
cranial capacity seems to vary according to intellectual endow-

* "Sur la Mensuration de la Capacité du Crâne," by M. Broca, in "Mém.
Soc. d'Anthrop," vol. ii., 2nd series, 1873.
† See page 165, on demi-microcephali.

ment. The skulls of Parisians of the 19th century are more capacious than those of the 12th; those from the Morgue more so than those from certain cemeteries. The following are some of M. Broca's examples of mean capacity:

	Men. Cub. cent.		Women. Cub. cent.
55 Auvergnians	1598	...	1445
62 Gauls from Brittany ...	1599	...	1426
63 Lower Brittany ...	1564	...	1406
124 Parisians	1558	...	1337
18 Caverne de l'Homme Mort	1606	...	1507
20 Gascons	1567	...	1369
60 Spaniards (Basques) ...	1574	...	1406
26 Corsicans	1552	...	1367
64 Merovingians	1501	...	1301
22 Chinese	1518	...	1383
18 Esquimaux	1539	...	1406
64 New Caledonians	1440	...	1310
85 Negroes of Western Africa	1430	...	1251
7 Tasmanians	1368	...	1201
18 Australians	1347	...	1181
21 Nubians	1329	...	1298

We repeat that in the present state of the science the process with shot, provided the instructions are rigidly carried out, gives the most uniform results. M. Broca has been engaged in making very careful experiments with millet and mustard seed, but he has not yet given us an opportunity of judging of their relative value. To show how important the matter is, we may mention that after a skull had been measured very carefully with millet by a foreign craniologist, on our repeating the process we discovered a difference of 100 cubic centimètres.

However, we may make use of the tables already published of cubic measurements with other substances, provided we do not compare them with those of a similar kind. The figures of an operator who follows his own particular method of working have a relative value of their own. The most important are those of Morton, Welcker, Barnard Davis, and Mantegazza. The following are some of the principal averages of Morton:[*]

[*] "Thesaurus Craniorum; or, Catalogue of Skulls of various Races of Men," by Barnard Davis. One vol. London, 1867.

						Cranl. capacity.
38 Europeans	...	...	...	...	...	1534
15 Mongols	...	...	...	...	...	1421
79 Negroes of Africa	...	...	...	...	...	1364
10 „ of Oceania	...	...	...	...	...	1284
152 Peruvians	...	...	...	...	...	1234
25 Mexicans	...	...	...	...	...	1390
164 Americans (other)	...	...	...	...	...	1234

In Mr. Davis's method the sand made use of is from the seashore near Calais, and thoroughly well dried. The skull is weighed when empty and again when full, and the calculation made accordingly. The actual weight of the sand, which is supposed to be invariable, being 1425, we deduct from it one ounce, avoirdupois (English), representing a volume of one cubic inch and 215-thousandths (English), or 19 cubic centimètres and 802-thousandths (French). To convert Mr. Davis's ounces and tenths of ounces it is sufficient to multiply them by 19·892. The following are some of his cubic measurements so converted: [a]

						Cub. cent.
146 Ancient Britons	...	...	...	...	...	1624
10 Anglo-Saxons	...	...	...	...	...	1417
19 Saxons	...	...	...	...	...	1488
81 Irish	...	...	...	...	...	1473
18 Swedes	...	...	...	...	...	1600
23 Netherlanders	...	...	...	...	...	1406
9 Lapps	...	...	...	...	...	1410
31 Chinese	...	...	...	...	...	1462
118 Knonkas	...	...	...	...	...	1470
27 Marquesan Islanders	...	...	...	...	...	1442
7 Mauris	...	...	...	...	...	1446
12 Dahoman Negroes	...	...	...	...	...	1452
9 New Hebrideans	...	...	...	...	...	1492
16 Australians	...	...	...	...	...	1296

Cephalo-Orbital Index.

The brain-case is not the only cavity of the skull of which cubic measurements have been made. The cavities and sinuses communicating with the nasal fossæ have also been measured. M. Mau-

[a] "Crania Americana," by S. G. Morton. Folio. Philadelphia, 1839.

tegazza has made the orbits his special study in this respect. He
closes the orifices with wax, and fills the cavities with mercury,
the volume of which he afterwards measures. The sum of the
volumes of both orbits thus obtained he compares with the cerebral
capacity. This is the cephalo-orbital index. His mean upon 200
orbit skulls from various sources was 27·2, and the extremes 22·7,
and 36·5, not taking into account an index, evidently abnormal, of
33·8 in an American skull. But it is important to be able to

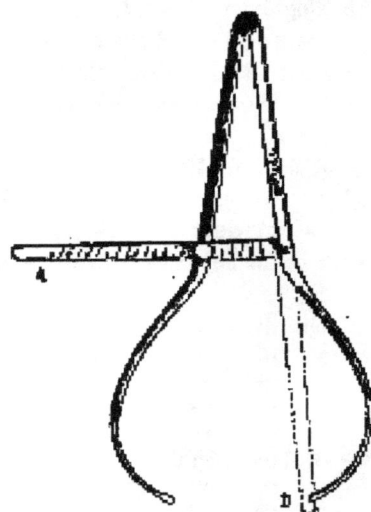

FIG. 26.—The Callipers (Compas d'Épaisseur).

distinguish between one race and another. To this end we have
taken from M. Mantegazza's measurements of these 200 skulls
recently published, 30 Italians and 12 Negroes and Oceanians, and
the following are their cephalo-orbital indices :*

20 Italians	...	...	...	...	...	27·73
2 Australians	...	...	...	...	...	26·61
3 New Zealanders	...	...	...	...	...	33·19
6 Negroes	...	...	...	...	...	27·19

* "Dei Caratteri Gerarchia del Cranio Umano," by Paolo Mantegazza, in
"Archivio dell' Anthropologia e la Etnologia." Florence, 1875.

The number of each series, except the first, is unfortunately too few for us to be able to form any conclusion respecting them. The New Zealanders appear to have larger orbital cavities than the Australians in proportion to the cerebral cavity.

This result should be considered, according to M. Mantegazza's proposal, by comparing Man with the anthropoid apes, namely, that the orbital capacity is smaller relatively to the cranial capacity, that the dominant place is less elevated in the organic series; this however wants confirmation.

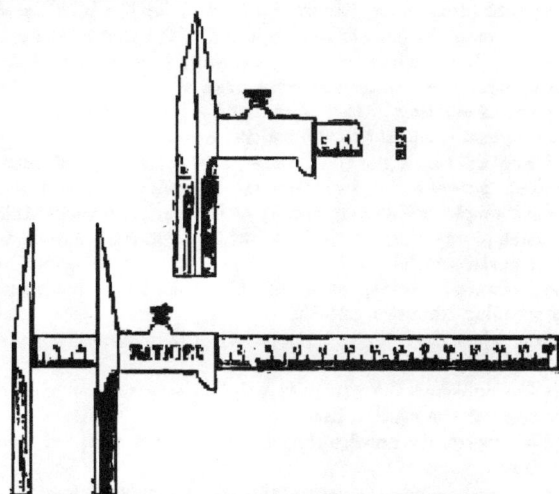

FIG. 27.—Sliding Compass (Compas Glissière).

Craniometrical Measurements.

The first to engage our attention will be the straight ones, which are taken with the callipers and sliding compass (see Figs. 26 and 27), and the curved with the ordinary measuring tape. We shall consider successively those of the cranium proper and those of the face, first in their *ensemble* and then in their separate regions.

The cranium, when separated from the face, as we see it in many specimens from old graves, has the form of an ovoid, with the larger extremity looking backwards and the smaller flattened

slightly at the side. It is this ovoid which we have to measure by
means of its three principal circumferences and diameters. Before
proceeding farther, however, we must briefly explain a number of
terms which we have already employed, having reference to the
principal marks (*points de repère*). Some are single and median,
others lateral and in pairs. (See Figs. 2, 3, and 4.)

Glabella, a swelling sometimes replaced by a depression between the two
superciliary arches.

Supra-orbital point, or *supra-nasal*, or *ophryon* (from ὀφρύς, an eyelid),
is the middle of the transverse line of the frontal bone, which corresponds
to the prolongation of the base of the skull and to the root of the orbits.

Metopic point (from μέτωπον, the forehead), a point situated on the
median line between the two frontal eminences.

Bregma, point of meeting of the coronal and sagittal sutures.

Vertex, the highest point of the vault of the cranium.

Obelion (from ὀβελός, a dart; in Latin, *sagittalis*, *sagittal suture*), the
region situated between the two parietal foramina, where the sagittal
suture becomes simple, which is generally at its fourth posterior fifth.

Lambda, place of meeting of the sagittal or biparietal suture with the
lambdoidal or parieto-occipital.

Maximum occipital point, spot on the maximum antero-posterior
diameter proceeding from the glabella.

Inion (from ἰνίον, the nape of the neck), the external occipital protuberance.

Opisthion (τὸ ὀπίσθιον, the posterior point), the posterior border of the
occipital foramen at the median line.

Basion (from βάσις, the base), anterior border of the occipital foramen at
the median line.

Stephanion (from στέφανος, a crown, the coronal suture), spot where the
coronal suture crosses the temporal ridge.

Pterion (from πτερόν, a wing; wings of the sphenoid), the region where
the frontal parietal, temporal, and sphenoid bones meet, in the form of an H.

Asterion (from ἀστήρ, a star), point behind the mastoid process, where
the parietal, occipital, and temporal bones meet.

Nasal point, middle of the naso-frontal suture at the root of the nose.

Sub-nasal point, middle of the inferior border of the anterior nares, and
if this point cannot be found, the base of the nasal spine.

Alveolar point, superior alveolar border in front of the median line.

Mental point (*point mentonnier*), inferior border of the inferior maxillary
bone in front of the median line.

Auricular point, centre of the external orifice of the auditory canal.

Supra-auricular point, above the preceding at the longitudinal root of
the zygomatic process.

Dacryon (from δάκρυον a tear), a point on the sides of the root of the nose where the frontal, the os unguis, and the ascending process of the superior maxillary bone meet.

Jugal point, point situated at the angle which the posterior border of the frontal branch of the malar bone makes with the superior border of its zygomatic branch.

Malar point, point situated on the tubercle on the external surface of the malar bone; and when this does not exist, the point at the junction of a horizontal line going from the inferior border of the orbit to the superior border of the zygomatic arch, and a vertical line going from the external lip of the fronto-malar suture to the tubercle which is situated at the border of the inferior external angle of the malar bone.

Gonion (from γωνία, an angle), the region of the angle of the lower jaw.

We shall also give a table of the principal measurements, as obtained by M. Broca on 77 men and 41 women from his series of contemporary Parisian skulls.*

Diameters.	Men.	Women.
Antero-posterior, maximum	182·7	174·4
Transverse, maximum	146·2	139·5
Vertical or basilo-bregmatic	132·0	125·1
Transverse Frontal, minimum or inferior	100·0	93·2
" " stephanic or superior	121·7	113·1
" occipital, maximum	112·5	106·6

Curves.	Men.	Women.
Median frontal, sub-cerebral	18·1	16·6
" cerebral	110·9	101·1
parietal	126·2	121·4
occipital supra-iniac	71·6	68·5
" cerebellar	47·0	46·1
Transverse, supra-auricular	312·4	291·6
total	445·1	415·6
Horizontal, anterior	251·2	243·8
posterior	273·4	254·4
total	525·6	498·0

Face.	Men.	Women.
Length	87·7	80·6
Width, bizygomatic	133·0	122·5
Length, skeleton of nose	51·3	48·3
Width	24·1	22·7

* "Mémoire sur la Race Celtique," by M. Broca, in "Revue d'Anthropologie," vol. ii., 1873.

Indices.					Men.	Women.
Cephalic	...	...	...	...	...	79·6	...	77·7
Frontal	...	...	...	...	...	65·9	...	66·8
Stephanic	...	...	...	...	...	82·4	...	83·0
Vertical	...	...	...	...	...	73·2	...	71·3
Facial	...	...	...	...	...	65·9	...	65·9
Orbital	...	...	...	...	...	86·7	...	89·2
Nasal ...	...	...	...	...	...	46·8	...	47·0
Occipital foramen	...	...	...	...	84·0	...	84·5

Cephalic Index.

The first measurements on the skull which should be taken, when we have no time to take more, are its greatest length, or maximum antero-posterior diameter, and its greatest breadth, or maximum transverse diameter. They are of the greater value from the fact that, with one or two exceptions, the same methods of proceeding are usually followed, and the same marks (*points de repère*) made use of by all craniologists. The relation of one cephalic index to another is the same for all, an index which M. Gratiolet calls the horizontal, in contradistinction from another less important —the vertical. He expresses the general form of the skull very much according to Blumenbach's *norma verticalis.*

The antero-posterior diameter extends from the glabella to the farthest point of the skull behind, at that point which we have called maximum occipital, and which we mark with a pencil for ulterior proceedings. Morton, Retzius, Thurnam, and Davis, Von Baer, Broca, Virchow, Ecker, and Wieloch, are unanimous on this matter. M. Welcker alone dissents; his corresponding diameter extends from the interval between the frontal eminences to the same maximum occipital point. This is the diameter which M. Broca selects, with another object in view, under the name of antero-posterior metopic. The maximum transverse diameter is taken, as its name indicates, transversely and maximum, whatever the spot may be where it falls, by Morton, Retzius, Von Baer, Broca, Ecker, Wiesbach. We must avoid going too low, where we sometimes meet with the supra-mastoidean projection mentioned at page 212. Precaution must be taken to hold the two legs of the compass perfectly horizontally, in order that the diameter may not be oblique in the slightest degree. The method of Welcker slightly differs from this: he places the points of the instrument at the junction of the two vertical and horizontal circumferences, about which we shall have more to say presently. M. Virchow at one time had also his particular mode of proceeding; his mark (point de repère) was situated a little above the middle portion of the superior border of the temporal. But neither of the transverse diameters of these observers was the maximum.

M. Virchow, however, in his " Memoir on the Skulls of Copenhagen," in 1872, appears decidedly to have come round to the French method. It appears from the " Crania Britannica," that the authors of that work have not recognized the maximum transverse diameter, but on referring to the " Thesaurus Craniorum," by Mr. Barnard Davis, it is evident that in this respect they are at one with most craniologists.

It follows that the cephalic index, that is to say the relation of the maximum transverse diameter to the maximum antero-posterior diameter, of which the formula is $\frac{\text{Tr. diam. } \times 100}{\text{Ant. post. diam.}}$, presents itself under precisely the same conditions to Morton, Retzius, Thurnam, Von Baer, Broca, Davis, Ecker, Weisbach, Pruner-Bey, as well as to the Italian anthropologists, that it was diminished at the expense of the transverse diameter by the original method of Virchow, and that it only differs from that of M. Welcker.

This index varies in the human races from 71·40 in Greenlanders to 85·63 in Lapps, in the averages of the series; and from 69·62 in a New Caledonian to 92·77 in a Slav (Wend) in particular instances. The difference is greater if we include the distorted skulls. A scaphocephalus in the Laboratory of Anthropology has an index of 56·33, and a Peruvian skull of an Inca, one of 103. The extreme indices are found in the long or dolichocephalic skulls of Retzius, and in his round or brachycephalic.*   Between the two a term was wanted to designate the medium skulls, and M. Broca has

* "Ethnologische Schriften," by A. Retzius.   Stockholm, 1864.

called them mesaticephali. But from the fact that in practice there exists a vast variety between the extremes of the groups, M. Broca gave the name of sub-dolichocephali to the skulls which were less long, and sub-brachycephali to those which were less round. Hence he makes five divisions, as follows:

CEPHALIC INDICES.

Dolichocephali	...	...	...	75·00 and under
Sub-dolichocephali	...	...	...	75·01 to 77·77
Mesaticephali	...	...	...	77·78 „ 80·00
Sub-brachycephali	...	...	...	80·01 „ 83·33
Brachycephali	...	...	...	83·34 and above

This nomenclature is universally adopted in the present day, as being most generally useful, except by Thurnam, Huxley, and Welcker.

In Thurnam's system the dolichocephali are 71 and under; the sub-dolichocephali from 72 to 73; the orthocephali, which replace M. Broca's mesaticephali, from 74 to 76; the sub-brachycephali from 77 to 79; and the brachycephali 80 and above. The system of M. Welcker differs slightly from this. His orthocephali are from 74 to 78; his sub-brachycephali from 79 to 80; and his brachycephali 81 and above. In Mr. Huxley's system the terms themselves are altered. His mecistocephali are 69 and under; the mesocephali 71 to 74; the orthocephali 74 to 77; the sub-brachycephali from 77 to 80; the eurycephali from 80 to 83; and the brachystocephali 83 and above. The term "orthocephalon" in the three systems is given from the belief that such an average is more satisfactory and more suitable than others. These differences of terms and limits of groups, moreover, lose all their interest to the foreigner, inasmuch as we are in the habit of expressing the form of a skull simply by the index figure.

In the course of this work we confine ourselves to M. Broca's nomenclature.

The cephalic index of Welcker being the only one which fundamentally differs from ours, that is to say in the method of taking the two diameters, we have endeavoured to determine in what that difference consists. The following is a résumé of the

comparative results of our own and M. Welcker's measurements of
25 Auvergnians and 25 negroes; they express the difference in
plus or minus by M. Welcker's method ·

	Auvergnians	Negroes
Individual variations, from	+1·22 to - 5·39	From +1·37 to - 6·49
Mean	- 1·58	+ 0·23

The two means are contradictory, which is not surprising, considering the like variations in plus and minus. On the one hand
the transverse diameter of Welcker is always smaller, and his
antero-posterior sometimes longer, sometimes shorter, according as
the frontal eminences are projecting or not. On the other, our
antero-posterior diameter varies with the projection of the glabella.
It is admitted, however, that the indices of Welcker are weaker
by two units, and his averages are really smaller than those of other
observers. But two units would be too much; and for our part
we have come to the conclusion that there is no possible advantage
in making a comparison between the results of the two systems.

One of the first effects of the methodical arrangement of the form
of the skull, on an examination of a large number of specimens, was
the reversal of a celebrated doctrine of Retzius. He stated that
the aboriginal races of Europe, which were then represented by the
Fins and the Basques, are brachycephalic, while the races next
in order are dolichocephalic. The discovery that the Basques are
dolichocephalic gave the first blow to this belief; that of the
ancient fossil skulls, all of which were dolichocephalic, completed it.
It was subsequently established that the negro races are generally
very dolichocephalic, and the greater number of the Mongol races
brachycephalic. It is only lately that a brachycephalic race has
been discovered among the blacks of Oceania. The Hyperborean
race, indeed, was separated as soon as it was ascertained that in
point of number the Lapps and Esquimaux, which were both included under this title, are, the former the most brachycephalic,
and the latter the most dolichocephalic in the world. Considering
the importance of the cephalic index, which however is one of
those empirical characters to which we have already alluded, we
shall give tables of it derived from various sources.

The first is that of M. Broca.*

(1) DOLICHOCEPHALIC.

27 Australians	71·49
21 Esquimaux of Greenland	71·71
54 New Caledonians	71·79
18 Hottentots and Bushmen	72·42
6 Kaffirs	72·54
85 Negroes of Western Africa	73·40
6 Cro-Magnon and Paris diluvium (Stone period) ...	73·34
19 Troglodytes of La Lozère (Polished Stone epoch) ...	73·28
22 Nubians of the Elephantine Isle	73·72
19 Arabians of Algeria...	74·06
18 Pariahs of Calcutta	74·17
11 Berbers	74·68

(2) SUB-DOLICHOCEPHALIC.

54 Dolmens at the north of Paris (Polished Stone epoch)...	75·01
25 Cemeteries of Avapress (19th century)	75·35
20 Usbechs of the Oxus	75·53
81 Ancient Egyptians	75·58
20 Dolmens of La Lozère (Polished Stone epoch)	75·86
10 Tasmanians	76·11
41 Polynesians	76·50
81 Merovingians	76·56
12 Modern Egyptians, Copts	76·59
60 Spanish Basques (Guipuzcoa)	77·68
26 Chinese	77·00

(3) MESATICEPHALIC.

44 Troglodytes de la Marne (Baye, Polished Stone epoch)...	76·00
86 Gauls	78·00
36 Mexicans (not distorted)	78·12
53 Normands of the 17th century (St. Arnould, Calvados)	78·77
49 Hollanders	78·90
10 Troglodytes of l'Oise (Orrouy) (Polished Stone epoch)	79·50
364 Parisians from the 12th to the 19th century	79·46
27 South Americans (not distorted)	79·10
30 North Americans „	79·26

* "Sur la Classification et la Nomenclature d'après les Indices Céphaliques," by Paul Broca, in "Revue d'Anthrop.," vol. i. p. 896, 1872.

(4) SUB-BRACHYCEPHALIC.

57 French Basques (St. Jean-de-Luz)	...	...	...	80·25
4 Æthiopians	...	...	...	...	10·39
63 Bretons (Low) from the north coast (Canteus Breévennes)	81·25
11 Mongols, various	...	...	...	...	81·40
11 Turks	...	...	...	...	...	81·49
20 Javanese (Fradik collection)	...	...	...	81·81
73 Bretons (Low) from the north coast (Canteus Gulluts)	82·05
11 Alsatians and Lorrainians	...	...	...	82·08

(5) BRACHYCEPHALIC.

10 Indo-Chinese	...	...	...	...	...	83·51
22 Savoyards	...	...	...	...	...	83·03
6 Finns	...	...	...	...	...	83·69
88 Auvergnians (St. Nectaire-le-Haut)	...	...	84·57
11 Croats	...	...	...	...	...	84·83
6 Bavarians and Swabians	...	...	...	...	84·97
11 Lapps	...	...	...	...	...	85·07
12 Syrians of Gebel-Obeikh (slightly distorted)	...	...	85·45

The following table is taken from the "Thesaurus Craniorum" of Mr. Barnard Davis, and from the supplement to the same work. We wish especially to direct attention to the three series of Esquimaux, and the four of the savage tribes of India:

148 Ancient Britons	...	...	...	...	...	77·0
36 Anglo-Saxons	...	...	...	...	75·0
80 English	...	...	...	...	...	77·0
31 Irish	...	...	...	...	...	76·0
12 Swedes	...	...	...	...	76·0
14 Prussians	...	...	...	...	...	76·8
10 Finns	...	...	...	...	...	82·0
14 Esquimaux of Greenland, or Eastern	...	...	71·4
6 " " Central	...	...	73·1
6 " " Western	...	...	76·3
110 Kanakas of the Sandwich Islands	...	...	80·0
34 Marquesan Islanders	...	...	...	...	77·4
7 Maoris of New Zealand	...	...	...	...	76·8
17 Tasmanians	...	...	...	...	...	76·6
35 Australians	...	...	...	...	...	71·8
7 Keshgars and Yarkandiah	...	...	...	70·1
10 Afghans	...	...	...	...	...	78·0
11 Birmese	...	...	...	...	...	80·6

R

8 Assam tribes	...	...	...	...	78·4
45 Tribes of Southern Himalaya	...		...	...	78·0
12 ,, Central India ...	...		...	...	73·3
8 ,, the coast of Coromandel (India)				...	73·5

The following list of M. Wiesbach relates entirely to one special group of peoples :

30 Ruthenians (Slavs of the North)			...	...	82·3
40 Poles	,,	,,	...	...	82·9
20 Slovacians	,,	,,	...	...	82·5
40 Tchecs	,,	,,	...	...	82·1
72 Croats (Slavs of the South)			...	...	84·4
19 Slovenes	,,	,,	...	...	81·3
41 Roumanians	...	...	...	...	82·2
40 Magyars	...	...	...	...	84·3
180 Austrians (German)		...	...	...	82·0
40 Italians (North)	...	...	...	...	81·6

The following is a series collected from various sources. The Veddahs ought to be included with those of India in the preceding tables, and the Aleutians with the Western Esquimaux of Mr. Davis's list :

101 Esquimaux (Bessels)	...	...	...	...	71·37
12 Veddahs of Ceylon (various authors)	...		...	71·76
6 Tehuelches of Patagonia (Topinard)	...		...	72·22
5 Ainos (various authors)	...	...	...	...	70·00
12 Bulgarians (Kopernicki)		...	...	...	76·60
9 Tsiganians (Hovelacque)		...	...	...	77·46
20 ,, (Kopernicki)		...	...	...	77·40
16 Aleutians (Bessels)	...	...	...	...	75·00
8 Andamans (various authors)	...	...	...	81·87
12 Magyars (Lenhossek)	...	...	...	...	82·90
100 Germans, Southern (Ecker)	...	...	...	88·00
10 Roumanians (Hovelacque)	...	...	...	84·06
80 Lapps from Scandinavian museums (Hamy)	...	84·99

The Vertical Index.

The vertical index, or index of height, is less important. It gives the form of the skull according to an antero-posterior section, which divides the cranial ovoid into two lateral halves, in the same way as the cephalic index, or the index of breadth gives the form of the skull such as is shown by the *norma verticalis* of Blumenbach. It is the relation of the vertical diameter to the before-mentioned maximum antero-posterior diameters. Its formula is $\frac{\text{Vert. diam.} \times 100}{\text{Ant. post. diam.}}$

But there is a want of unanimity here; in France there is only one way of taking the vertical diameter; in other countries there are several different ways. There is not the slightest doubt that its inferior extremity should commence at the occipital foramen, and, for greater precision, at the basion. But where are we to make its superior extremity meet? What we look for first is the

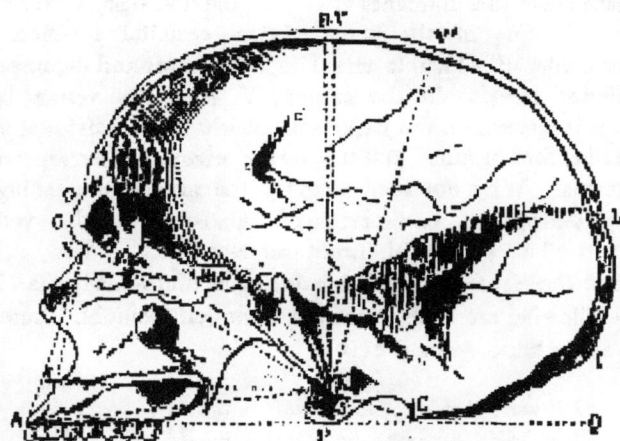

Fig. 59.—A PQ, Alveolo-condylean plane; K V, True vertical diameter in relation to this plane; E C, Plane of the occipital foramen; K V, Vertical diameter of Mr. B. Davis in relation to this plane; K B, Vertical or basilo-bregmatic diameter of M. Broca; K N, Naso-basilar line; A A, Alveolo-basilar line; A N, Naso-alveolar line; K N A, Facial triangle of Virgil; K E, Basilo-sub-nasal line; S E, Naso-sub-nasal line; E N E, Facial triangle of Welcker. For the other lines, &c., see Fig. 5.

culminating point of the vertex. How are we to determine it? Some guess it; others make it have relation to one of the natural planes at the base of the skull. Now, if, following the example of Mr. B. Davis, we make it have relation to the plane of the occipital foramen, it falls generally about three or four centimetres behind the bregma, while if it has relation to the real plane of the base, the alveolo-condylean, it corresponds as nearly as possible to the bregma. The following shows the situation of the vertex in four

(+) or behind (−) the bregma in either case. V′ when it is determined by the plane of the occipital foramen, K C., as in Fig. 28; V, when by the alveolo-condylean plane A P Q.*

		V′. mill.		V. mill.
12 Caverne de l'Homme Mort	...	− 42	...	0
21 Auvergnians	...	− 61	...	− 1
21 Bretons (Low)	... ...	− 49	...	− 1
16 Mongols and Chinese	... ...	− 33	...	+ 3
21 Nubians	... ...	− 26	...	− 9
31 Negroes of Africa	... ...	− 32	...	−10

Whence does this difference arise? In the first case, V′, from the angular deviation of the plane of the occipital foramen, the anterior border of which is raised in white races and depressed in the inferior races. In the second, V, from the vertex being placed as it appears on the living subject when the individual looks straight in front of him. But this vertex perceptibly corresponds to the bregma. Why not then simplify the manual proceeding by directly taking the basilo-bregmatic diameter as the vertical diameter? This is what M. Broca has done.

In 250 Parisians, the vertical index, thus understood, was 71·8.

The following are some examples borrowed from M. Broca, in which sex is taken account of:†

				Men.	Women.
63 Bretons (Low)	...	...	...	71·5	... 70·8
29 Corsicans	...	...	...	71·5	... 73·3
125 Parisians (19th century)	...	...	72·2	... 71·7
13 Basques	...	...	...	72·9	... 73·4
56 Auvergnians	...	...	...	73·0	... 73·8
62 Negroes of Africa	...	...	...	73·4	... 75·5
54 New Caledonians	...	...	...	73·7	... 74·6
27 Chinese	...	...	...	77·3	... 76·8
16 Caverne de l'Homme Mort	...	...	68·9	... 78·0

This table is rather favourable to M. Virchow's view; his own figures indeed cannot express it more strongly. He puts the

* "Examen des Mesures Craniométriques du 'Thesaurus Craniorum,'" by Paul Topinard, in "Revue d'Anthrop.," vol. ii. p. 99.

† "Les Crânes Anciens d'Origine Septentrionale à Copenhague," by Rud. Virchow, in "Arch. für Anthrop.," vol. iv., 1871.

vertical index in the first line among his craniometrical measurements.

The following are those which he published some years ago. The first column gives the ordinary vertical index; the second the relation of its height, not to the length, but to the breadth of the skull :

				Height to length.	Height to breadth.
6 Lapps	...	...	...	74·0 ...	... 80·2
5 Greenlanders	...	...	...	71·0 ...	... 103·0
8 Fins	...	...	...	73·2 ...	... 91·1

This table also shows the defective side. Esquimaux have one of the most, if not the most, elevated skulls in existence ; Lapps, at least those in the museum, have, on the contrary, one of the least so. According to the foregoing table it is the reverse. It is because in every index there are two factors. In the ordinary cephalic, the one by increasing, the other by diminishing, or the reverse, contribute to the same end. In this there is nothing of the kind. The vertical index of the first column is small in the Esquimaux, because the length of the skull in proportion to its height is enormous ; it is large in the Lapps because this length is reduced to a minimum. The second index appears more to the point ; the same objection, however, is applicable to it, except that it has reference more to the breadth. In our opinion, by adding together the two indices, and taking the mean, the result would be more correct. We should thus have a mixed index of height of 88·5 in the Esquimaux, of 82·5 in the Lapp, and of 82·1 in the Fin ; which is in accordance with what we should expect from the appearance of these skulls. This new index would enable one to distinguish, otherwise than by the view, the acrocephalic, or elevated, from the platycephalic, or low skulls. In the 384 Parisians of M. Broca it is 77·2.

The three foregoing diameters, and the three circumferences of which we are about to speak, are the fundamental measurements by means of which the cranial ovoid is recognised in its *ensemble*.

The various sections of the antero-posterior circumference are taken with the tape as follows: (1) The sub-cerebral, or that subjacent to the brain, from the nasal to the supra-orbital point. (2) The cerebral or frontal, from this point to the bregma. (3) The parietal, from the bregma to the lambda. (4) The occipital, from the lambda to the inion. (5) From the inion to the opisthion. The length of the occipital foramen and the naso-basilar line, in a direct line from the basion to the naso-frontal suture, the *point de départ* of the circuit, completes the circumference. Its different parts are more in use, indeed, than its *ensemble* for the purpose of comparing the development of each portion of the skull. Logically, the sub-cerebral, which belongs to the face, should be excluded from it, and we should substitute for the naso-basilar line, the ophryo-basilar line; but custom has decided otherwise.

The transverse circumference consists of two portions—one, the supra-auricular, going from a point situated above the auditory foramen, on the line passing from the longitudinal root of the zygomatic process to the analogous point on the opposite side, passing through the bregma; the other, but little used, connecting the same two points by passing beneath the skull. It is customary, with a view to ulterior operations, to mark with a pencil on the sides of the skull the outline of this curve, which divides it into two parts, viz. the anterior and the posterior. The horizontal circumference commences at the supra-orbital point, crosses the temporal ridge at the spot where the minimum frontal diameter is taken, reaches the maximum occipital point, and returns to its point of departure on the opposite side. The maximum antero-posterior diameter represents its great axis. It naturally divides itself into two parts, the one anterior the other posterior to the before-mentioned transverse curve. By comparing each of these parts to the whole, = 100, we at once have an idea of the relative development of the anterior and posterior craniam, and determine whether the subject is to be included among the frontal or occipital races of Gratiolet. The following are some examples of the horizontal circumference:

			Men.			Women.	
Auvergnats ...	...	...	43	524·6	...	39	502·8
Contemporary Parisians	...	77	525·6	...	41	496·0
Lapps ...	...	...	...	6	512·2	...	2	504·0

	Men.		Women.	
Chinese	21	511·6	...	7	495·9
Negroes of Africa	54	512·0	...	24	499·1
New Caledonian	29	510·0	...	23	484·4
Hottentots and Boschmans...	10	500·7	...	5	453·6

Some craniologists discard the transverse circumference, but all accept the other two.   M. Welcker alone deviates from the method of measuring the horizontal circumference by taking it round the frontal eminences in front, and the maximum occipital point behind.   The difference between the measurement made in this way was three millimètres less than that by the ordinary method

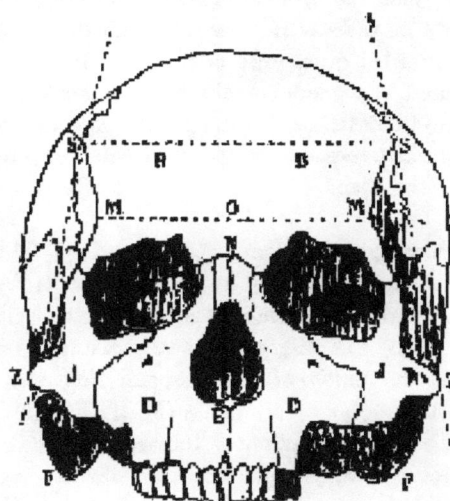

Fig. 9.—M M, Minimum frontal diameter; S S, Superior frontal or bi-stephanic diameter of Broca; B B', Oblique line of M. de Quatrefages determining the parietal angle; G, Width of the nasal orifice, one of the factors of the nasal index; in the orbital cavity are the two lines showing the orbital index; O, Supra-orbital point; N, Nasal point; B, Sub-nasal point; A, Alveolar point, &c.   See Fig. 3.

in 25 Auvergnians, and 18 more in 35 Negroes; which proves that the region of the frontal eminences was less developed in the former, and exceptionally very projecting and very elevated in the latter.

The utility of the horizontal circumference may be noticed,

especially when we have to determine certain extraordinary pathological conditions, such as microcephalus and hydrocephalus. The
following, taken upon adults only, show :

4 Microcephali	...	...	...	840
21 Demi-microcephali	...	...	...	438 to 450 (about)
1 Moderate hydrocephalus		...	...	566
4 Exceptional	...	...	...	640

The same circumference, by M. Welcker's method, was 654 in
the last four, the excess being owing to the projection of the
metople point, and the frontal eminences in front of the supra-
orbital point. The cases of negroes in which the circumference of
M. Welcker exceeded ours, were attributable to the same cause.
Having measured the cranial oval in its ensemble, we now proceed to measure its details. To the parietal measurements already
indicated of the antero-posterior and horizontal circumferences, we
will add here the transverse diameters of the frontal and the
occipital.

Many measurements are taken on the frontal : (1) The chord of its
antero-posterior curve, as well as of its other curves ; (2) The
transverse diameters. M. Broca makes two : The superior transverse,
or stephenic (S S, Fig. 29), whose two measuring points are the
stephanions at the union of the temporal ridge and the coronal
suture ; and the inferior or minimum (M M, Fig. 29). M. Ecker
and Mr. Davis take a maximum transverse frontal, but on the
coronal, wherever it may happen to be. Morton takes one only,
namely at the inferior and anterior angle of the parietals.
Welcker and Virchow take the distance from one frontal eminence
to the other. The most important, undoubtedly, is the minimum
frontal, and Broca, Ecker, Bogdanoff, Mantegazza, &c., are of the
same opinion. We say little of M. Pruner-Bey, because he has
never indicated exactly his method of proceeding. In his tables
the inferior frontal of 30 negroes is 100 millimètres ; this evidently
cannot be their minimum. The minimum transverse frontal, M M,
is measured from the two points of the temporal ridge which most

nearly approach each other, above the external orbital processes.
It generally corresponds, in white races, with the transverse line,
marking the separation of the cranium from the face; the supra-
orbital point is then situated in its centre. In the inferior races it
has a tendency to be elevated, and in some exceptional cases it
ascends as high as the vertex. It is, nevertheless, usual to take
it above the superciliary arches, so that the epithet "inferior" would
be a better one. The following are some examples of this
measurement:

						Millimètres.
354 Parisians	...	...	...	...	...	96·7
28 Auvergnians	...	...	...	...	...	97·7
60 Basques (Spanish)		...	...	...	...	96·1
88 „ (French)	...	...	...	...	...	90·2
60 Gallo-Bretons	...	...	...	...	...	96·0
69 Bretons (Low)	...	...	...	...	...	97·8
18 Caverne de l'Homme Mort		...	...	...	92·0
8 Lapps	...	...	...	...	...	100·0
28 Chinese	...	...	...	...	...	92·5
16 Esquimaux	...	...	...	...	...	94·1
82 Negroes of Africa	...	...	...	...	94·2
23 Nubians	...	...	...	...	...	93·2
54 New Caledonians	...	...	...	...	93·6
8 Tasmanians	...	...	...	...	...	94·0
12 Australians	...	...	...	...	...	92·7

To be sure there are marked differences between one sex and the
other. For example: In 54 negroes, the diameter was 95 millimètres, and in 24 negresses, 90; 23 New Caledonian men, 95,
24 women, 91; 43 Auvergnians, males, 108, 39 females, 95, &c.
The narrowest forehead observed by M. Broca is 83 in a female
Parisian of the same period, and the widest, 122, in a male Parisian.
But what is probably of greater importance is the relation between
this minimum breadth and the maximum breadths of the parts of
the cranial envelope, situated in front and behind. M. Broca compares this minimum frontal diameter (1) To the superior and
maximum frontal, or stephanic diameter upon the temporal ridge;
(2) To the transverse maximum diameter of the skull. Hence a

stephanic index, the averages of which vary in different races from
79 to 92, and a frontal index, of which the following are some
examples :

384 Parisians	...	...	...	...	...	69·0
99 Bretons (Low)	...	...	...	...	...	67·7
28 Auvergnats	...	...	...	...	...	66·6
15 Esquimaux	...	...	...	...	...	69·8
29 Chinese	...	...	...	...	...	86·5
29 Javanese	...	...	...	...	...	64·8
85 Negroes	...	...	...	...	...	70·5
8 Tasmanians	...	...	...	...	...	67·0
12 Australians	...	...	...	...	...	71·2

The maximum transverse occipital diameter extends from
one asterion to the other. M. Abel Hovelacque made this the
subject of a paper at the last meeting of the French Association for
the Advancement of Science, at Lille.* The following complete the
series of transverse straight measurements, which are taken at
pleasure on the several regions, according to the object we have in
view : (1) The asym-auricular chord of the transverse curve, already
indicated ; (2) A maximum biparietal diameter, which is generally
confounded with the ordinary maximum transverse ; (3) A bitem-
poral diameter, its maximum taken at the surface of the temporal
shell ; (4) A bimastoidean diameter, which extends from the
middle of the line, passing from the summit of the mastoid process
to the posterior extremity of the squamous suture of the temporal
of the other side, according to Thurnam, Davis, and Ecker; and
from the same summit of one mastoid process to the other, according to Morton, Welcker, and Virchow ; (5) The distance from one
parietal eminence to the other, so extolled by M. Welcker. Various
projections, angles, and radii contribute to our knowledge of each
of these several regions.

We may add that after the ordinary longitudinal diameter,
M. Broca usually takes the longitudinal metopic, from the metopic
point to the maximum occipital point, and the longitudinal iniac
from the glabella to the inion, which, compared to the former,

* See the Report of the session 1874.

enables us to know, the one the degree of projection of the forehead, the other, with certain limits, how far the cerebral region overlaps the cerebellar. We may add that it measures the breadth and the length of the occipital foramen also, and establishes its relation, the latter being = 100. M. Broca's methods of measurement not having yet been published, we shall give a summary, as to this latter point, of the researches of M. Mantegazza.

This eminent anthropologist has directed his whole attention to the occipital foramen. In the first place he has taken its index according to M. Broca's method, and has concluded from it that there is no relation between its form and that of the cranium. A narrow cranium may have either an elongated, a moderate, or a narrow occipital foramen. In the second place, he has measured its superficies by the aid of little wooden cubes, and, in the interspaces, with little metallic needles, and has compared it, expressed in square millimètres, to the cranial capacity, expressed in cubic centimètres. This last being taken as 100, he thus obtains the cephalo-spinal index. In 200 skulls of all kinds, his mean was 18·8, the two greatest indices were 39·64 and 37·46, and the two smallest 12·60 and 13·07. In anthropoids the index is still less, the highest being 8·36. In the memoir of M. Mantegazza, already mentioned, the same series have given us the following mean cephalo-spinal index :

10 Indians	...	...	...	...	...	19·2
9 Negroes	...	...	...	...	...	16·8
3 New Zealanders	...	...	...	...	...	17·4
2 Australians	...	...	...	...	...	17·3

These series are too limited, and moreover, the three inferior races occupy a position in them more nearly approaching the anthropoids than the superior race represented by the Indians, which it is well to notice.

Measurements of the Face.

They are general, or special, some having reference to the proportions as a whole, others to details. The former concern the breadth, the length, and the thickness, or median antero-posterior section. The maximum breadth is not situated at the cheek-bones, even in the yellow races, but at the zygomatic arches. It is here that the maximum transverse or bizygomatic diameter of the face is taken; craniologists are unanimous on this point. A bimalar diameter, however, would have been one more meriting consideration, from the fact that upon it depends the physiognomy of the Esquimaux; but the difficulty to find upon it definite marking points of any value, has caused it to be looked upon with disfavour. The maximum length is taken in different ways, which it is important to point out precisely. It must be remembered, in the first place, that on the living subject the face extends from the line of the hair at the top of the forehead to the chin, while on the skeleton it only commences at the line of separation of the cranium, that is to say, at the supra-orbital point. In the second place, and considering how rarely we find skulls with the lower jaw attached, and the difficulty of replacing the latter in its articulation exactly as in the living subject, it is usual to study the lower jaw separately, and only to employ the word "face" for the portion above the superior alveolar border, which we have elsewhere called "the superior face." We have, then, three lengths, which must not be confounded; namely, the length of the entire face; the total length of the face from the supra-orbital point to the point of the chin; and the simple length from the supra-orbital to the alveolar point. The following is an extract from M. Pruner-Bey's tables; the figures in the first column show the total length of the face, those of the second its bizygomatic breadth:

	Length. Mill.	Breadth. Mill.
18 Esquimaux	136	135
12 Chinese	134	137
10 Scandinavians	129	132
6 Germans (South)	127	131
80 New Caledonians	126	137
80 Negroes of Africa	124	130
5 Hottentots	116	125
6 Lapps	109	130

The part of the face, then, subjacent to the eyebrows is longest in the Esquimaux and Chinese, and shortest in the Lapps. On the other hand, the Chinese and the New Caledonians have the broadest face, and the Hottentots the narrowest.

The simple, or ophryo-alveolar, length of the face should no longer be confounded with the naso-alveolar line, which goes from the nasal to the alveolar point, nor with the height of the face, which is the perpendicular falling from the supra-alveolar point upon the alveolo-condylean plane. The first two, always oblique, are taken with the compass, the last is the vertical projection of the face in the normal attitude of the head, and is taken as we see in Fig. 33.

M. Broca compares this length to the bizygomatic diameter, under the name of facial index, with this formula $\frac{\text{Ophry.-alveo. L.} \times 100}{\text{Bizygomatic diam.}}$

The following are some examples :

13 Esquimaux ...	...	73·1
90 Negroes ...	...	68·6
69 Gallo-Bretons	...	68·5
89 Auvergnats	...	67·8
49 New Caledonians	...	66·2
125 Parisians	...	66·9
12 Australians ...	...	65·6
8 Tasmanians ...	...	62·0

The median section of the face (Fig. 28) has the appearance of a triangle, whose base is represented by a line passing from the basion, K, to the alveolar point, A, and whose two other sides are the naso-basilar line, N K, extending from the basion to the nasal point, and the naso-alveolar line, of which we have just spoken. This last gives the anterior profile of the superior maxilla, and produces prognathism ; later on we shall study its inclination. The first, or basio-alveolar, is interesting in so far that its elongation or shortening causes the naso-alveolar line to be straightened or placed farther backwards. With regard to the third, or naso-basilar line, as to which it is doubtful whether it forms a constituent part of the antero-posterior circumference of the skull, the Germans have laid considerable stress upon it. They consider it as the philosophical base of the cerebral skull ; as the chord of the curve which the bodies of the three cranial vertebræ describe ; as the axis around which the skull, on the one hand, and the face, on the other, revolve.

The following are its absolute lengths, according to M. Welcker :[*]

							Millimetres.
3 Papuans, 2 Birmese ...	...	...	...	...	...	...	96
13 Burghese, 2 Lapps, 3 Brazilians	...	...	...	...	...	97
6 Jews ...	...	...	...	...	...	...	98
2 Hungarians, 6 Tsiganians, 6 Madamas, 2 Hottentots	...	...	99
30 Germans, 12 Russians, 5 Cossacks, 5 Tartars, 16 Chinese,							
2 Mexicans, 20 Negroes ...	...	...	...	...	...	100
3 Scotch (Highlanders), 5 Boskirs ...	...	...	...	101
8 French, 6 Hollanders, 6 Malays of Sumatra	...	...	...	102
9 Finn, 7 Moluccans ...	...	...	...	...	...	103
5 Australians, 8 Ancient Greeks	...	...	...	...	104
11 Esquimaux ...	...	...	...	...	...	...	106
2 Kaffirs	...	...	...	...	...	...	107

We may add that the naso-basilar line is generally shorter in the brachycephali than in the dolichocephali, which may easily be imagined.

MM. Welcker and Virchow, who have given special study to the facial triangle, compare the naso-basilar line to the rest of the antero-posterior circumference of the skull, of which it forms an arc. In the following table, this line being = 100, the circumference in the various races would be :

2 Hottentots	...	...	...	...	...	...	418
16 Chinese	...	...	...	...	...	...	407
30 Germans	...	...	...	...	...	...	404
9 Kalmucks	...	...	...	...	...	...	403
20 Javanese	...	...	...	...	...	...	403
20 Negroes	...	...	...	...	...	...	402
5 French	...	...	...	...	...	...	398
5 Australians	...	...	...	...	...	...	395

There is no great amount of instruction to be derived from this. The same authors have since compared the naso-basilar line, not to the line proceeding from the basion to meet at the alveolar border, but to that which, proceeding from the same point, crosses the

[*] "Untersuchungen über Wachsthum und Bau des Menschlichen Schädels," by H. Welcker. Leipsic, 1862.

vault of the palate, and terminates at the sub-nasal point. We are at a loss to understand their reason for thus leaving out the alveolar arch. The following are the results, the naso-basilar line being as previously = 100, the palatine line in question would be:

4 Egyptians, 2 Ancient Greeks	...	...	...	67
9 Scotch, 0 Turks	...	...	...	91
8 French, 6 Jews, 5 Taiganians, 4 Lapps, 6 Tartars, 9 Kalmucks, 16 Chinese, 7 Moluccans	...	...	92
11 Esquimaux, 6 Madurans, 12 Negroes, 2 Hottentots	...	...	...	98
20 Germans, 13 Russians, 20 Javanese,...	...	...	94
6 Cossacks, 6 Malays of Sumatra	...	...	96
2 Kaffirs	...	...	...	97
5 Australians, 5 Ancient Romans	...	...	98

There is nothing to be deduced from this; it would however denote prognathism, according to M. Virchow. The angle which the naso-basilar line makes, not with the naso-alveolar line, as it should be, and as M. Vogt makes it, but with the naso-sub-nasal line terminating at the sub-nasal point where the preceding palatine line meets, has been studied by MM. Welcker and Virchow, under the name of naso-basal angle (K N E, Fig. 28.)

The following are some results:

6 Turks	...	...	...	...	...	64 2
8 French	...	...	...	...	...	65 1
8 Kalmucks	...	...	...	...	...	65 8
16 Chinese	...	...	...	...	...	65 9
20 Germans	...	...	...	...	...	66 7
11 Esquimaux	...	...	...	...	...	68 7
8 Hottentots	...	...	...	...	...	67 4
20 Negroes of Africa	...	...	...	...	...	71 1
5 Australians	...	...	...	...	...	72 0

This angle also professes to give the measurement of prognathism, but it leaves out the sub-nasal portion of the maxilla, the most important in this respect, and only concerns itself with its superior or nasal portion. These figures are, in other respects, more eloquent than words. The Germans are certainly less prognathous than the Chinese, as one glance at a Chinese skull would show in a moment

The measurements which the median facial triangle gives of Germans do not tend to anything of a decisive character, which appears to us owing to the unfortunate selection of one of its points, the subnasal. The true facial triangle ought to have its apex at the alveolar point, as M. Vogt desires it to have. In the next chapter we shall speak of another way in which M. Assézat has understood the facial triangle, and of the results which he has obtained.

The straight or curved measurements belonging to particular regions of the face are more numerous than those of the cranium. There is but one organ in the latter, while there are many very distinct organs belonging to the face. Each bone, each cavity varies in its configuration, and furnishes certain elements by which to distinguish races. The measurements which have been most studied are those which give the nasal and the orbital indices.

The Nasal Index.

The nasal index is the relation of the maximum breadth of the anterior orifice of the nose (G, Fig. 29) to its maximum length, taken from the nasal spine, F, to the naso-frontal suture, N. This character, in a certain point of view, is included in the category of those establishing a transition from Man to the ape, but more still among those the rationale of which has not as yet been explained. While the negroes of Oceania are for the most part inferior to the negroes of Africa, as regards this index they are their superiors. It substantiates what we stated, that the most rational characters in craniometry, as the facial angle, do not always lead us to form a real distinction between races; while one which à priori would be looked upon as indifferent, may be of the utmost importance. It shown that qualities derived from the conformation of the organ characteristic of the zoological human groups, are sometimes surpassed by those deduced from peculiarities in the conformation of secondary parts. M. Broca has, in fact, discovered that the nasal index is one of the best for the purpose of distinguishing the various races of mankind, although he does not arrange them in a regular scale conformably to the exalted idea that we ourselves form of these races. The following extracts from his tables show this:

10 Hottentots	...	...	...	...	...	60·86
8 Tasmanians	...	...	...	...	...	60·02
80 Negroes of Africa	...	...	...	...	...	51·78
29 „ Nubia	...	...	...	...	...	60·17
14 Australians	...	...	...	...	...	53·39
60 New Caledonians	...	...	...	...	...	53·66
29 Javanese	...	...	...	...	...	51·47
11 Lapps	...	...	...	...	...	50·29
45 Peruvians	...	...	...	...	...	50·23
26 Polynesians	...	...	...	...	...	49·95
11 Mongols	...	...	...	...	...	48·66
27 Chinese	...	...	...	...	...	48·58
128 Parisians (modern)	...	...	...	...	...	45·81
53 Basques (French)	...	...	...	...	...	45·60
38 „ (Spanish)	...	...	...	...	...	44·71
17 Guanches	...	...	...	...	...	44·25
14 Esquimaux	...	...	...	...	...	43·83

The individual figures in M. Broca's tables vary from 72·33 in a Bosjesman, to 36·71 in a Russian. This interval is divided into three groups, the platyrhinians, with the nasal skeleton wide, from 53 to 58; the mesorrhinians, with the nasal skeleton moderate, from 48 to 53; and the leptorhinians, with the nasal skeleton elongated, from 42 to 47. The black races are all in the first group; the Mongols and Americans, with the exception of the Esquimaux, in the second; and the white races in the third.

The orbital index is the relation of the vertical diameter of the base of the orbit to its horizontal diameter; the latter going from the dacryon to the opposite point of the great axis of this base, the former starting from the spot where the malo-maxillary suture meets the inferior orbital edge, and cutting perpendicularly the horizontal diameter. The two diameters are perceptibly equal at birth; the vertical then becomes gradually shorter; but the true relation is not established until after puberty, the woman always retaining, however, a less short vertical diameter, and in this, as in many other particulars, resembling the infant. Individual orbital indices vary from 60·9 in a Tasmanian, or from 61·3 in the old man of Cro-Magnon belonging to the Ancient Stone period, to 100 in a New Caledonian, as recorded by M. Broca, 104 in a negress of the Sahara, and 107 in a Chinese. In these latter cases the ordinary condition is reversed ; the two diameters are equal, the orbit appears circular, especially when the angles are rounded off, or, if anything, the vertical is rather greater than the horizontal. Everyone knows the opposite conformation in the Cro-Magnon skull, the orbits being rectangular, with the angles almost right-angles, and the vertical diameter short. The averages of the series of course vary within narrower limits : from 90·0 to 77·0 in white races, from 95·4 to 66·2 in the yellow races, and from 85·4 to 79·3 in the black races. M. Broca has created three general terms for all the craniometrical characters, bearing reference to this index, whose variations have not as yet received other specific designations ; namely, mégasème when the index is large ; mésosème when it is moderate ; and microsème when it is small ; the limits of the corresponding groups varying according to each particular character.* In the present case the mégasèmes of the orbital index are 89 and above, the mésosèmes from 89 to 83, and the microsèmes 83 and under. Among the indications which the study of the orbital index gives, we may mention the following : It does not arrange the races in a graduated series, according to the opinions which may be formed of each ; and the form of the base of the orbit might be regarded as empirical, if, within certain limits, it did not apply to the general structural plan of the cranium and of the face. All the prehistoric races of France are microsèmes, the height of the orbit increases when we come to the Gauls, but it is not until after the Merovingians that it assumes the present mésosème type. The Guanches approach our prehistoric populations by this character. The mégasème, on the other hand, connects all the yellow races, or those derived from the yellow races, except the Esquimaux, who by this as well as by the nasal index, and by so many other points, are separated from them

---

* Memoir of M. Broca, "Sur l'Indice Orbitaire," in the "Revue d'Anthropologie," vol. iv, 1875.

completely, in spite of certain evident features of resemblance. Negroes are removed from the yellow races in this respect, especially the negroes of Oceania, which here favour the Australians, as if to repudiate all alliance with them.

The following are some examples:

27 Chinese	...	93.8
39 Peruvians (not distorted)	...	95.1
40 Polynesians	...	92.0
43 Javanese	...	91.1
96 North-American Indians	...	90.7
17 Indo-Chinese	...	90.2
87 Auvergnians	...	86.6
10 Kymris (?) of Paleaux	...	80.2
122 Contemporary Parisians	...	81.4
11 Croats	...	84.3
50 Basques (Spanish)	...	88.9
84 Negroes of Africa	...	85.4
24 „ Kordofan	...	85.0
16 Hottentots	...	83.8
14 Caverne de l'Homme Mort (Polished Stone period)	...	81.9
5 Grenelle (Ancient Stone period)	...	81.2
55 Merovingians of Chelles	...	81.2
62 New Caledonians	...	80.0
12 Dolmens of the North of France	...	80.5
27 Australians	...	80.4
8 Troglodytes	...	79.6
11 Guanches	...	77.0

Some other useful measurements are applied to the region of the orbits, such as (a) The relative superficies of the base of the orbits, which is obtained, as if it were a true rectangle, by multiplying the length by the breadth before mentioned; (b) The capacity of the orbital cavity, studied by M. Mantegazza; (c) The depth of the orbits, given by a line extending from the optic foramen to the inferior and external angle of the base of the orbits. In its immediate vicinity are also taken (a) The external biorbital diameter, from the external lip of the fronto-malar suture on one side to that on the opposite (it is this which M. Virchow takes for the inferior frontal) ; (b) The orbital interval, or from one decryon to the other; it is broad in the most marked yellow races, rather so in the negro races, and narrow in Europeans; (c) The length and breadth of the bones proper of the nose, the narrowness of which is of such great importance in Esquimaux ; (d) The angle made by the two great axes of the orbits taken together. Under all circumstances it is very obtuse, and open below, but sometimes, as in the Chinese race, the two lines are raised so as to become horizontal. Never, as far as we know, does this go, in these races, so far as to produce an angle open above, as we should be led to suppose by the position of the palpebral apertures in the living subject. With regard to the molar bones, M. Broca is satisfied with two principal measurements; the bijugal and the bimalar diameter, each going from one point of the same name to the other.

The Superior Maxilla.

The superior maxilla plays a considerable part in the architecture of the face. The part which it takes in the irregular enlargement of the face in Tasmanians, or in its increase in height in Esquimaux, demands consideration. In order to this we measure the height of the bone : (1) The maximum, from the point of its ascending process ; (2) The mean, from the inferior border of the orbit ; (3) The minimum, from the nasal spine to the alveolar border in each case. Then we take the breadth : (1) The maximum, at the inferior part of the maxillo-malar suture; (2) The maximum, at the level and outside of the alveolar arch. We may ascertain the form of this arch by its inner side, and consequently that of the palate. It is presented to us under four aspects : (1) Hyperbolic, when the branches of the arch go or diverge in a backward direction ; (2) Parabolic, when they still diverge, but somewhat less so, and in such a manner as, that if prolonged they would eventually return upon themselves and meet ; (3) In the form of the letter U when they are exactly parallel ; and (4) Elliptical, when they converge, whatever the degree of such convergence may be. The first two and noblest forms are common in the white races; the third and fourth are rare, and are especially seen in black races; the form of the letter U is that of anthropoid apes; the elliptical is seen in the négro and the macaque. The following is an example of the measurements which M. Broca makes use of to determine them; they have reference to his celebrated series of troglodytes of La Lozère:

				7 men.	5 women.
Internal curve, width at	Behind	...	...	34·2	... 32·7
the internal lip of the	At the first molar			23·4	... 41·2
alveolar arch ...	„ incisor		...	20·2	... 20·3
Vault of the palate, total length		...	...	47·0	... 49·7

Whence it follows that in this example the breadth at the posterior extremity of the arch is greater than at the level of the first molar, that this extremity goes on diverging, and consequently that the alveolar arch is hyperbolical. In fact it is rather the form of the vault of the palate which is thus measured, and it is to be noticed that the line of the teeth themselves does not always convey to the eye exactly the same impression. M. Broca again takes account of the relation of the maximum breadth of the vault of the palate to its maximum length, in making comparison of races. This is the palatine index.

The dimensions common to the cranium and to the face will be found in the following chapters. Here we shall merely mention, among the right lines, the line of Virchow, going from the root of the nose to the lambda; a second, going from the root of the nose to the maximum occipital point; and a third, extolled by Morton, adopted by the Germans, and improperly called the alveolar line by M. Vogt, which extends from the alveolar point to the maximum occipital point. Compared together, these two diameters have been employed for the purpose of recognising prognathism, orthognathism, and opisthognathism. The alveolar line would be longer in the first case, equal in the second, and shorter in the third. This is a bad method.

The Inferior Maxilla.

The inferior maxilla is not generally studied as much as it deserves. The form of its alveolar arch is to be examined. Then the following principal measurements are to be taken: namely, the distance across from one angle to the other; the distance obliquely from the same angle to the point of the chin; the height of the bone at the symphysis, and its height at the level of the coronoid process. Two angles are specially to be noticed: the angle of the jaw, properly so called, which varies according to age (p. 185) and race, and the angle which the symphysian line or profile makes with the plane of the inferior border of the body of the bone; this latter bears the name of the symphysian angle. The direction of the front teeth, whether vertical or oblique—this latter constituting inferior dental prognathism—and the projection or absence of the chin are to be noticed. This projection passes beyond the perpendicular from three to five millimètres in European races. It is replaced in anthropoids by a recession backwards, amounting to one centimètre. In negro races the chin is still in front of the perpendicular, but from time to time there have been noticed, as upon some prehistoric jaws, examples which exhibit all the intermediate gradations between Man and the anthropoid ape. In the example where this recession of the chin was the most marked, namely, on the ancient jaw of La Naulette, it reached three millimètres. It is here that the symphysian angle is measured, and which must be regarded as prognathism of the body of the lower jaw.[*]

Before concluding this chapter, we shall reproduce a table published by M. Broca in the "Instructions Craniologiques" of the Société d'Anthropologie, which was prepared at the same time as the first edition of this volume, and of which we had previously made a résumé, with the exception of Chapter I., On the Récolte et Conservation des Crânes et Ossements, and Chapter VIII., On the

[*] See "Les Caractères Anatomiques de l'Homme Préhistorique," by M. Broca, in "Mém. d'Anthrop.," vol. ii. p. 146.

Mise en Œuvre des Séries. This table alone was omitted. It gives for each index, other than the cephalic and the nasal (1) The minimum mean and the maximum mean, that is to say the extreme means presented by the series in all the races measured by M. Broca; (2) The extent of each of the three groups—the micro- series, the mésosèmes, and the mégasèmes (see p. 258), into which they are divided. The basilar index will be described in the next chapter. According to our custom, we shall omit a decimal.

Nomenclature of indices other than the cephalic and nasal:

Indices.	Means. Min. Max.	Microsèmes.	Mésosème.	Megasèmes
Vertical...	... 80 ... 78 to 71·9	... 78 to 74·9	... 75 and beyond.	
Transverso-vertical	... 86 ...101 ,, 91·9	... 92 ,, 97·9	... 98 ,, ,,	
Frontal ...	... 63 ... 79 ,, 65·9	... 66 ,, 66·9	... 00 ,, ,,	
Stephanic	... 79 ... 92 ,, 82·9	... 83 ,, 86·9	... 87 ,, ,,	
Basilar ...	... 46 ... 54 ,, 48·9	... 49 ,, 50·9	... 51 ,, ,,	
Of the occipital foramen	77 ... 80 ,, 81·9	... 82 ,, 85·9	... 86 ,, ,,	
Facial ...	... 61 ... 79 ,, 65·9	... 80 ,, 69·9	... 69 ,, ,,	
Orbital ...	... 77 ... 95 ,, 82·9	... 88 ,, 88·9	... 89 ,, ,,	
Palatine ...	... 63 ... 84 ,, 70·9	... 71 ,, 76·9	... 77 ,, ,,	

CHAPTER III.

PROJECTIONS—HORIZONTAL ALVEOLO-CONDYLEAN PLANE—AURICULAR RADII—PROGNATHISM—CRANIOMETRICAL ANGLES OF JACQUART, DE QUATREFAGES, BROCA, WELCKER.

Method of Projections.

THE method of projections is daily assuming greater importance. Under the name of projections, in geometry, is understood the representation on a plane of a figure situated without the plane, by means of the trace which is described by the intersections of all the straight lines which can be drawn from every point of the

figure upon the plane of projection. The projection is orthogonal,
or geometrical, when all these lines are parallel, and central when
they converge towards one and the same point. The images which
are delineated on the retina are central projections; it is the same
with photographs—in both, the objects are described according to
the laws of perspective. Orthogonal projections are the only ones
which give exact measurements applicable to craniometry. There
are two ways of taking them: directly, on the skull, by various
modes of proceeding; and indirectly, on drawings. The latter is
the more ancient, and apparently the more simple. It was in this
way that Camper proceeded for his facial angle. When Blumenbach fixed his eye at a certain distance above the vertex, according
to the *norma verticalis*, the view which he obtained of the vault
of the skull was a projection in the horizontal plane, but it was a
central projection, consequently giving rise to an illusion.

The figure of the skull may be projected on a screen in three
different planes: the view from above and from below, in the
horizontal plane; the view from before and from behind, in the
transverse vertical; and the profile view, in the antero-posterior
vertical. When on a drawing, or directly on the skull, we measure
the projection which the alveolar arch makes with relation to the
supra-orbital point, the two points are supposed to be in the same
plane, which in this case is the horizontal. But, according as the
head is more or less leaning forwards, the projection increases or
diminishes. Hence the fundamental principle of the method of
projections. The head ought always to be placed in one definite
position, agreed upon by all anthropologists anxious that their
results may be arranged and compared; the slightest violation of
the rule occasions the most serious errors.

It is therefore absolutely necessary that all should be agreed as
to this *ne varietur* position relatively to the three planes upon
which the skull may be placed.

As to the antero-posterior median plane, provided that the skull
does not incline either to the right or to the left, the orientation is
easy. We have only to take care that the two sides are symmetrical,
and that the two zygomatic arches, for example, are mathematically

at the same height. As to the transverse plane, provided the whole front of the face looks exactly forwards, it is equally easy. But with the horizontal plane, in order that neither the front nor the back of the skull may be raised or depressed at the caprice of the observer, a rule must be made use of at the measuring points, a horizontal plane, or at least a horizontal line. Such indeed have been the matters which have occupied the attention of anthropologists from Camper to the present time. The task was undertaken

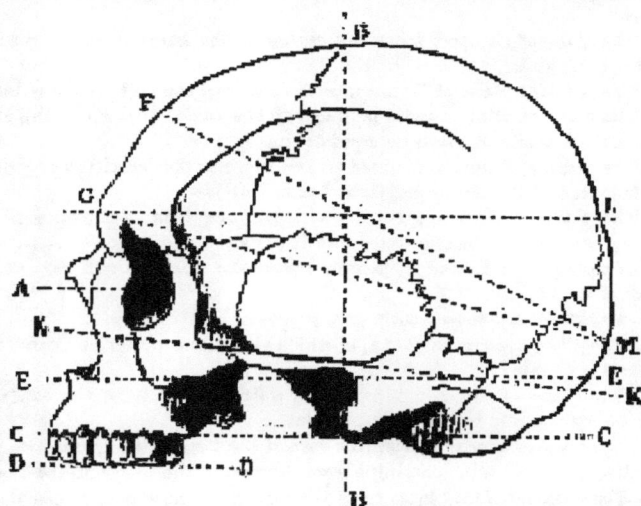

Fig. 30.— A, Plane of the axis of the orbits; C C, Alveolo-condylean plane; D D, Auriculo-bregmatic line, determining the plane of Bush, which is perpendicular to it; G L, Glabello-lambdoidean plane of Hamy; D D, Plane of mastication; E E, Plane of Camper; K K, Plane of Bär; G M, Ordinary maximum antero-posterior diameter; F M, Antero-posterior diameter of Welcker.

by a congress assembled in Germany, but with little success. The theory is that the skull rests, if it can be made to do so, absolutely in its natural attitude, as in the living subject. Some observers therefore have taken up a fixed vertico-transverse plane, the horizontal being necessarily perpendicular to it. Thus Charles Bell sought to represent the natural axis of the skull by a spindle which passed through the occipital foramen, was applied to the roof of the cavity beneath the vertex, and kept the skull in equilibrium by a point. It is in this way that Mr. Busk takes the plane passing across the bregma and the auditory openings. Others have fixed their attention directly on the horizontal plane, being moved by physiological, artistic, or empirical considerations, or simply as a matter of convenience. In short, fifteen different planes have been suggested, namely :

1. The planes of Bell and Busk above alluded to.

2. The plane of mastication, determined principally by the surface of the molars.

3. The plane of Camper, from the centre of the auditory opening to the inferior nasal spine.

4. The palatine plane of Barclay, or the plane of the arch of the palate.

5. The plane of Blumenbach, or plane of the table upon which the skull, without the lower jaw, takes its equilibrium.

6. The plane of Barr, determined by the superior border of the zygomatic arch (adopted at the Göttingen Congress in 1861).

7. The plane of Meckel, given by a line drawn from the centre of the auditory canal to the inferior border of the orbit.

8. The plane of Daubenton, passing across the opisthion and the inferior border of the orbits.

9. The glabella-lambdoidean plane, proposed by M. Hamy.

10. The glabello-occipital plane, in which the antero-posterior diameter of the skull is situated.

11. The plane of Bolle, determined by a line drawn from the centre of the auditory opening to the alveolar point.

12. The naso-inion plane, from the root of the nose to the inion.

13. The plane of Aeby, passing across the root of the nose and the basion.

14. The naso-opisthion plane, from the root of the nose to the opisthion.

15. The alveolo-condylean plane of M. Broca.

The last alone starts from a physiological conception. The head is in its natural position when its two visual axes in the living subject, or its two orbitar axes in the skeleton, are directed towards the horizon, a direction which is the result of Man's perfectly upright attitude. For this reason this plane deserves our favourable consideration, but still more so because it has the three-fold advantage (1) Of being accessible, so that without any special contrivance a skull can rest or be readily suspended on the plane ; (2) Of being in the middle in the different races, and sensibly parallel to the plane of vision ; (3) Of exhibiting the minimum

amount of oscillation which can be obtained. The alveolo-condylean
plane is determined by three points : namely, the inferior surface of
the two condyles of the occipital, and the median point of the
alveolar arch, and does not bear comparison with any other for
convenience.   With respect to the two other advantages, they
may be judged of by the following comparative table. The first
column indicates the degree of elevation or depression of the
plane relatively to the plane of vision, the second the maximum
divergence in individual cases. The planes are arranged in the
order of their importance, according as they more or less realise
these two indications:

Planes.	Mean.	Deviation.
Alveolo-condylean	+ 0·68	12·63
Hamy	+ 0·07	23·63
Busk	− 1·61	18·61
Martinson	+ 1·85	20·21
Camper	+ 4·65	19·69
Barclay	+ 6·18	22·01
Blumenbach	+ 8·09	22·65
Baer	− 6·51	17·87
Meckel	− 7·98	17·49
Glabello-occipital	− 12·96	20·61
Daubenton	− 15·11	16·59
Rolle	+ 15·81	18·53
Naso-inian	− 15·68	24·84
Naso-opisthion	− 26·76	17·46
Aeby	− 31·26	16·38

M. Broca is of opinion that, next to the alveolo-condylean plane,
and in default of measuring points, as in skulls without the face or
occipital foramen, the best are those of Hamy and Busk.

The following table shows the maximum, the minimum, and the
mean which the alveolo-condylean plane has presented when taken
by itself, in three series subjected to examination :[*]

	Maximum.	Minimum.	Mean.
18 Auvergnese	+ 8·20	− 9·41	− 0·60
12 Mongols	+ 8·63	0·00	+ 3·85
12 Negroes	+ 9·44	− 4·02	− 0·16

[*] "Sur le Plan Horizontal de la Tête," by M. Paul Broca, in "Bull. Soc.
d'Anthrop.," 2nd series, vol. vii., 1872.

Before entrusting a skull to a draughtsman to delineate its contours geometrically with the aid of special instruments, or to set off its projections in a direct manner, the first thing is to place it in such a way that all the parts are symmetrical, and that it rests on the horizontal plane passing across the inferior surface of the occipital condyles and the inferior border of the alveolar arch. The drawings of Blumenbach and many others are almost valueless,

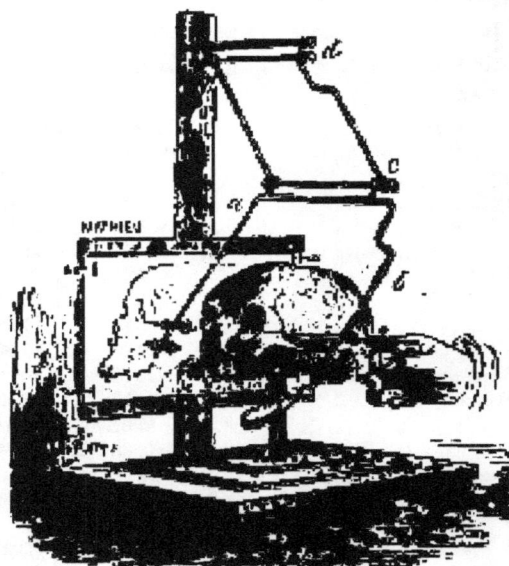

FIG. 31.—Stereograph of M. Broca. The skull is placed on the craniophore in the position shown in the drawing. The same support, if turned, serves for the views in front and behind. A special support is substituted when we wish to have drawings according to the same methods of the superior or inferior surface of the skull.

owing to the want of this precaution. Those of Prichard are frequently in contradiction to his text, for the same reason.

Among the instruments by the help of which drawings by projection are obtained, some are only capable of giving the principal points, the operator completing the figure as well as he can. Such are the apparatus of Camper and Leach. Others require scarcely any skill on the part of the operator, as the diopter of Lucæ, the *dessinateur horizontal*, the diagraph of Gavart, the craniograph and stereograph of Broca. The last three are to be preferred. The diagraph requires some amount of precision. In using the other two it is only necessary to have a light hand. The craniograph is very exact, but it only gives the outlines of the profile, and the situation of the auditory meatus. The stereograph represented by Fig. 81 gives, on the contrary, all the visible details, as well as some inaccessible to the eye, and is applied to each of the five surfaces of the skull which it is useful to reproduce. On the outlines which it delineates we measure the straight lines, curves, and angles to a millimètre, more readily than on the skull itself; the curves alone require a special instrument—the *roulette millimétrique*. It is however recommended to take the projections, as much as possible, in a direct manner. The first which M. Broca was concerned with, were made upon the part situated behind the basion, or posterior cranium, and upon that in front of it. At that time he only made use of Blumenbach's plane. The head being placed on a small board graduated from before backwards and from behind forwards, commencing from a pin which passes through the occipital foramen, and is arrested at its anterior border, he placed a square on a level with the necks on the one hand and the alveolar border on the other, and read off the two distances indicated. He then took the same two projections on the profiles, obtained with the craniograph, but taking care to let fall a perpendicular from the supra-orbital point upon the alveo-condyloan plane or line previously traced, which gives the projection separately from the whole of the face in front of this point, and consequently allows of its being cut off from the projection of the entire head, or of that portion in front of the basion. He thus had three projections: one posterior for the posterior cranium, a middle one for the anterior cranium, and an anterior one for the face.[*]

Each portion being then compared to the total projection of

[*] "Sur les Projections de la Tête," by Paul Broca, in "Bull. Soc. d'Anthrop.," vol. iii., 1862.

the head = 1000, he obtained the following proportions (see Fig. 32):

		Europeans.	Negroes.	Difference in + or − in Negroes.
Projections of the face	... ...	64·8	... 137·5	... ... + 72·7
" " anterior cranium	408·9	... 801·0	... ... − 48·9
" " posterior "	625·2	... 501·3	... ... − 23·8

M. Broca concludes from this: (1) That the face of the negro occupies the greater portion of the total length of the head—which no one disputes; (2) That his anterior cranium is less developed than his posterior, relatively to that of the white; (3) That his occipital foramen is situated more backwards in relation to the total projection of the head, but more forwards in relation to the cranium only. The negro, in other words, has, cæteris paribus, the cerebral cranium less developed than the white, but its posterior portion is more developed than the anterior. It comes, therefore, within the occipital races of Gratiolet, and the European in his frontal races. M. Broca has established, besides, a basilar index (p. 263) which is the relation of the projection of the part anterior to the basion to the projection of the entire skull.

The auricular radii are only projections in the antero-posterior vertical plane of the skull; their imaginary centre is situated in the middle of the line passing from one auditory meatus to the other. M. Broca sets them off upon his drawings, made either with the craniograph or the stereograph (see Fig. 32).

In the following table each radius bears the name of the cranio-metrical point at which it meets on the median line.*

					155 Parisians.	Negroes.
Alveolar	radius	...	...	...	90·0	... 112·7
Nasal	"	...	...	...	89·8	... 98·7
Supra-orbital	"	...	...	...	98·8	... 108·0
Bregmatic	"	...	...	...	111·8	... 109·8
Lambdoidal	"	...	...	...	104·6	... 101·2
Iniac	"	...	...	...	78·9	... 76·0
Opisthiac	"	...	...	...	43·8	... 42·0

* See his article, "Sur les Crânes Basques," in "Bull. Soc. d'Anthrop.," 1st series, vol. iv. p. 51, 1863.

These radii may also be taken in a direct manner with the instrument of Mr. Barnard Davis, a sort of frame which turns round the skull, having for its centre two steel pins, which are inserted in the auditory meati. The authors of "Crania Britannica" made use of it more particularly to take the three maximum radii—the frontal, the parietal, and the occipital, whatever the point in each bone on

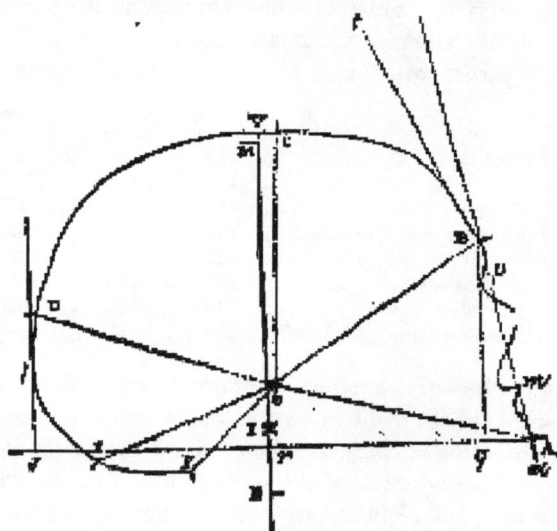

FIG. 32.—Profile taken with M. Broca's craniograph. O, Auricular point, or centre of the auditory meatus ; O A, Auriculo-alveolar radius ; O D, Auriculo-supra-orbital radius ; O e, Auriculo-bregmatic radius ; O b, Auriculo-lambdoidal radius ; O E, Auriculo-iniac radius ; e F, Auriculo-ophthalmic radius ; A S, alveolo-condylean line, or giving the total projection of the skull ; D g, Perpendicular falling from the supra-orbital point, and dividing the facial portion (A g) ; T e, Perpendicular passing through the basion (I) and separating the cranial projection proper into two parts, one (e y) projection of the anterior maximum, the other (y t) the projection of the posterior ; O A, Oculo-occipital length of the face ; B g, Height of the face.

which that maximum might be. By slightly modifying it we are able to take the three additional radii of Mr. Busk : namely, the nasal, at the nasal point ; the alveolar or maxillary ; and the bregmatic or vertical ; and consequently all those of M. Broca, as well as the three of M. Ecker, meeting at the glabella, at the vertex, and at the maximum occipital point. M. Ecker has an instrument of his own for taking projections, which possesses all the advantages of that of

Mr. Davis, and allows the skull to be more accurately fixed in position according to the plane which may be preferred. In Germany a preference is given to Baer's or Meckel's plane. M. Ecker thus measures the projection of the anterior cranium with relation to the auricular axis, and not, as we do, with relation to the basion. The following are some of the results obtained by Mr. Davis with regard to his three maximum auricular radii—the frontal, the parietal, and the occipital. We must not confound them with those of M. Broca, which go to particular points. All the subjects are males:

	Frontal radius.	Parietal radius.	Occipital radius.
21 English	119	121	106
9 Fins	119	122	104
17 Chinese	116	121	106
7 Esquimaux of Greenland	127	128	107
60 Negroes	118	126	107
18 Australians	109	116	101
9 New Hebrideans	116	119	104
64 Kanakas (Sandwich Isles)	124	127	104

The applications of the method of projections are infinite, such as: (a) The height of the auditory meatus above the alveolo-condylean plane, or, deducting the height of the condyles, the height above the basion; (b) The projection of the superior border of the orbit with relation to its inferior border—in front in many of the Melanesians, behind as a general rule; (c) The vertical or more or less oblique direction of the forehead; (d) The total height of the head as observed on the living subject, or only that portion above the mouth; (e) The height of the cheek-bones and their projection, whether forwards or outwards; (f) The different kinds of prognathism; (g) The height of the inion, &c., not including the ordinary horizontal projections of the head, the face and the anterior and posterior cranium.

Under all circumstances the process is the same, namely, that of the double square; the methods alone vary, and are done impromptu. Two squares, graduated in centimetres and millimetres, are essential: the larger consists of two pieces, one of which is graduated; the other, being heavy, rests in equilibrium on the table: the smaller is the common one.

Suppose we want to take the height of a point with relation to the alveolo-condylean plane. The skull being placed on this plane in its natural position, the larger square is put upright on the plane close to the point required. On its vertical portion, graduated so that zero corresponds to the alveolo-condylean plane, we slide at a right angle the second square, until the sloping side of its point touches the point in question. We have then only to read off the height required. But without moving, the same operation gives

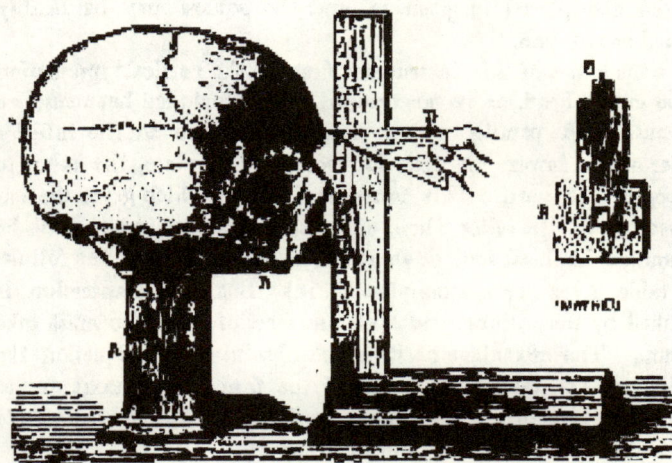

Fig. 81.—Topinard's Craniophore. A, Pedestal; B, Skull; C, Sliding piece and small blade; D, Small square. The other is the large square. The apparatus is in position for measuring the height of the supra-orbital point, and its horizontal projection behind the alveolar point.

the horizontal projection of the same point with relation to any other spot that we desire at the periphery of the skull. The vertical portion being placed upright, for example, in contact with the alveolar border, the distance indicated on the smaller square from the supra-orbital point to this vertical portion, will be the horizontal projection of that point with relation to the alveolar point.

Such is the object of the craniophore, of our own invention, and which is now in common use. It consists of two pieces—a pedestal

T

and a shelf—the two, when adjusted, being exactly 10 centimètres in height; the shelf sliding in a groove, so as to allow of its being lengthened and adapted for different-sized skulls, and at its extremity there is a steel blade, which is inserted between the incisor teeth at the alveolar point. The large square has its zero placed at the height of 10 centimètres, or rather it is graduated from the base for other purposes, but we reckon the zero at this height instead of ten. In this way, as seen in Fig. 99, the skull is isolated and placed in position, and the square may be readily applied at any part.

We made use of this instrument first for the vertical* projection of the entire head, or its maximum height, included between two horizontal and parallel planes, tangent, the one to the inferior border of the lower jaw with its teeth, and in place, the other to the top of the head. This projection is that which gives the impression to the traveller when, on looking a person in the face, he pronounces his head long or short. (The first column of the following table gives some examples of it.) But this impression is modified by the variable width of the face, of which he must take account. The advantage of it is the obtaining by projection the relation of the maximum height of the face to its maximum or bizygomatic breadth. We propose to call it l'indice générale de la tête osseuse: the second column expresses it.

				Total projection of the head.		Its width = 100.
7 Esquimaux	...	...	...	198·8	... ...	108·7
0 Chinese	...	...	...	198·3	... ...	168·1
5 Arabs	...	...	...	196·2	... ...	156·6
5 Kaffirs	...	...	...	196·8	... ...	143·1
10 Malays	...	...	...	194·2	... ...	142·9
10 Negroes (various)	...	...	...	190·7	... ...	149·5
19 Bretons (Low)	...	...	...	190·0	... ...	146·7
8 Australians	...	...	...	187·5	... ...	148·0
6 Alsatians	...	...	...	186·0	... ...	184·8
10 Hottentots	...	...	...	182·8	... ...	144·8
8 Tasmanians	...	...	...	182·0	... ...	133·9
3 Lapps	...	...	...	177·0	... ...	129·6

* "Presentation of a new craniophore, an instrument for taking all the cranial projections," by Paul Topinard, in "Bull. Soc. d'Anthrop.," 2nd series, vol. vii. p. 563, 1872.

This shows—(1) That Esquimaux, and the yellow races generally, have unquestionably the longest head; Lappa, Tasmanians, and Hottentots the shortest. (2) That this length is greatest relatively to its bizygomatic breadth in Arabs, and least again in Lappa. All the variations in the second column are readily understood. The Esquimaux have descended in the scale because their face grows wide, as in all the yellow races, disproportionately to the elongation of the head. The Arabs have ascended in the scale for the opposite reason, narrowness of the face being characteristic of the white races. In our opinion this absolute height of the head, the jaw included, whether relatively to its breadth or not, is a craniometrical character of the highest importance, and the more

FIG. 81.—Example of the straight forehead, with high and projecting protuberances.

useful in that it is one of the indications which travellers are most inclined to note. It is not however included in the scale in the series of races, and is only characteristic by itself. Thus travellers, when contrasting the Kaffir with the Hottentot race, speak of the former as having a long and the latter a short head. So Australians are distinguished from Tasmanians, the former being classed among long heads, the latter among short heads.

Another purpose for which the craniophore is used, is to determine the degree of inclination of the forehead, or rather the situation of the frontal protuberances which form its culminating point. When we put aside the breadth of the forehead measured by the two transverse diameters, the minimum and the stephanic, and seek to take account of its vertical development on the median line, we are sometimes struck with the difference which it presents in different races, which seem à priori at variance with prevailing notions. What is termed a fine forehead—that is to say, straight or projecting—seems to be met with frequently among the negro races of Africa. M. Broca's series of Nubians, so negroid when we look at the skull, is specially remarkable for the projection of the frontal protuberances. In this region there are many craniometrical elements to be taken into consideration; but the principal one, after the breadth, is the position of the tubers in relation to the glabella, which is its most sloping and its most anterior point. Above it, the plane becomes vertical or oblique as far as the tubers, or bends round to reach the bregma, forming a more or less obtuse angle. When it approaches a right angle, we have the straight forehead; and when the angle is very obtuse, we have the receding forehead. It is this height of the tubers above the glabella, and their position more or less behind it, which we have taken with the double square. Its results are given in the following table. The first column indicates the height of the tubers; the second, their horizontal distance behind the glabella; the third, the relation of these two factors, the height being = 100; the fourth, the same converted by trigonometrical calculation into an angle, the point of which is at the glabella, and which expresses the degree of obliquity of the forehead as far as the tubers relatively to the horizontal:

	Vertical projection. Mill.	Horizontal projection. Mill.	Relation. Mill.	Angle
43 Auvergnians	50·4	14·2	35·2	72·07°
20 Nubians	29·0	7·7	26·8	75·27
42 Negroes of Africa	30·7	8·5	27·0	74·41
28 Mongols and Chinese	50·8	13·9	42·6	66·68

Whence it follows that the Auvergnians have the highest and most posterior frontal tubers, and the Nubians the lowest and most anterior. This circumstance accounts for the conformation of the forehead of the latter, which we should scarcely have expected. From the combination of these two elements, as regards the relation of the horizontal to the vertical projection, the result is that the frontal tubers are in a measure more conformable to the cerebral organ which they protect in the European than in the negro, and especially the Asiatic. The Asiatic, it is true, gains in breadth what he loses in projection and in height, and is in consequence above the negro. Craniometry thus confirms the prevailing opinion that a well-developed forehead specially belongs to the white races and is a mark of beauty.

Moreover, the angular measurement exhibits this conformation still more strongly, showing the deficient forehead of the Mongols and Chinese. The contrast would be still more striking if the Auvergnians, our term of comparison, did not possess an enormous glabella, owing to which the inferior extremity of the frontal line is brought forward, and the angular aperture is diminished to their

Fig. 35.—Example of the receding forehead, with the brain low and almost obliterated.

prejudice; while in the yellow races, the glabella being almost obliterated, it is increased to their advantage.

The measurement of prognathism is another purpose to which the craniophore is applied.

Prognathism.

Prognathism has always since the time of Prichard been understood to mean the elongation and prominence, or obliquity, of the jaws, common in the black races of Africa and Oceania, accidental in some Europeans. It is in profile that we at once recognise it, whether in the living subject or on the skull. An imaginary perpendicular is let fall from the root or anterior spine

of the nose, and according as the portion in front is more or less
considerable, so we say the subject is, or is not, prognathous.
Nothing is more simple, and yet we meet with the term among
authors in various acceptations. Some speak of the prognathism
of the face, others of that of the jaws; others go so far as to
exclude all that portion of the face below the nares, taking in only
that part of the maxilla between the root of the nose and the
inferior nasal spine. Two expressions intended to be in opposition
to that of prognathism have tended to complicate the question.
Oblique teeth, they say, are prognathous; teeth in an upright
position, orthognathous. So far so good; but the word has been
transferred to the face, in which the profile line is never straight.
The word "opisthognathous," which has been applied to those cases
in which the line is inclined backwards, is still more objectionable.
The various methods or processes which have been employed for
measuring prognathism will enable us to form an idea of the difference of opinion which has prevailed on the subject. We shall
only mention the principal ones.

1. The facial angle of Camper. It measures, indeed, the degree of elon-
gation of the face, but not very accurately. The angles of Cloquet, Geoffroy
Saint-Hilaire, and Cuvier are preferable in this respect. The angle of
Jacquart does not express it at all.

2. The naso-basal angle of Welcker (see page 256).

3. The same angle modified by M. Vogt, by its anterior side being prolonged as far as the alveolar point.

4. The palatine and vomerine angles of Vogt.

5. The relation of two lines proceeding from the basion, the one to the
nasal the other to the sub-nasal point. This is M. Virchow's latest method
(see page 256).

6. The relation of two lines extending from the maximum occipital
point, one to the glabella the other to the alveolar point. This is the old
German method.

7. The relation of the facial radii of Mr. Busk, proceeding from the
auditory meatus, or even of the auricular radii of M. Broca.

8. The method employed by M. Broca for taking the projection of the
face, and which is also applied to each of its parts (see page 271).

9. The method of Lucae. In his drawing he lets fall a perpendicular
from the naso-frontal suture on the horizontal line, slightly modified, of the
Germans (passing straight through the imaginary axis of the zygomatic
arch), and on this perpendicular, ordinates proceeding from the sub-nasal
point, alveolar point, &c. The last two alone go directly to the mark; they

rest on the same principle—the necessity, in order to get at prognathism, of placing the head in its natural position, as it is in the living subject; they only differ as regards the horizontal plane. The table, page 267, will show which is to be preferred.

10. The last is our own method. It differs from that of M. Broca only from the fact that it is applied directly to the skull, and takes account of the variations of the height of the face. It was by M. Broca's advice that we made use of it as regards this latter. The same horizontal projection will be weak in a high skull, and very considerable in a low one.

The following are the various kinds of prognathism which may be admitted:

Superior facial ... ... { In its entirety.
{ Superior maxillary.
{ Alveolo-sub-nasal.
{ Superior dental.

Inferior facial ... ... { Inferior dental.
{ „ maxillary.

The teeth, being independent organs, should be excluded. Whether upright or oblique in both jaws, or only in the upper, which is the rule, their arrangement is generally conformable to that of their sockets. Their special prognathism, if it really exists, has yet to form a subject for investigation. Of the prognathism of the body of the lower jaw we have already spoken. It remains for us to refer to the three other kinds.

Each corresponds to the inclination, on the alveolo-condylean plane, of a line extending from the alveolar point to one of the special points of the face, the sub-nasal, the nasal, or the sub-orbital. These lines represent the diagonal of a quadrilateral figure, the equal sides of which are the height or vertical projection of the region, and its antero-posterior length or horizontal projection. The relation of the latter to the former expresses this diagonal, or the projection of the region. It is thus that, in 1872, we spoke of the index of such or such prognathism; but, acting upon M. Broca's advice, we have since thought that it ought to be converted by the trigonometrical method into an angle at the alveolar point, which has the advantage of exhibiting in a direct manner the angle of inclination of the profile lines on the horizontal plane. Let us take an example of sub-nasal prognathism. The skull is that of a Namaquan in the Museum, and is the most prognathous known. The height of the nasal spine or subnasal point above the horizontal plane is 20 millimètres; the horizontal projection from the same point to the perpendicular line in contact with the alveolar border is 16 millimètres. The relation then of the latter to the former, or index, is 80, and the angle at the alveolar point according to the calculation, 51·35°.

		Prognathism.	
		Facial.	Maxillary.
Extreme Individual variations	...	86·5° to 63·8° ...	87·1° to 69·6°
Average variations {	White races...	82·0 „ 77·0 ...	81·5 „ 75·2
	Yellow „	79·8 „ 74·9 ...	77·0 „ 74·8
	Black „ ...	79·7 „ 74·9 ...	77·2 „ 68·0
14 Guanches	... ...	80·48°	...	79·80°
360 Parisians	... ...	79·00	...	78·13
76 Auvergnats	... ...	78·21	...	77·00
9 Esquimaux	... ...	70·71	...	75·51
53 Negroes of West Africa	...	78·15	...	79·33
53 New Caledonians	... ...	75·48	...	78·15
7 Bushjesmans and Narongonas		74·11	...	69·00

The first table has reference to prognathism of the face (upper) in its entirety, and to prognathism of the maxilla, also in its entirety. The extreme variations observed in about 1000 skulls, the limit of the averages in about 60 of all races, and some examples of these averages, have been recorded. We refer the reader to our treatise for a separate description of prognathism of the nasal region, of which M. Virchow has made measurements, though it possesses but little interest.[*]

The results have not answered our expectations respecting those two kinds of prognathism. Anthropologists have been wrong, up to the present time, in giving so much importance to the projection of the whole maxilla, or of the whole face. Craniometry proves that the imaginative method was an erroneous one. The variations are frequently determined by anatomical considerations foreign to the character sought for. There is no fixedness of result in one and the same series, and most flagrant contradictions are met with between averages in contiguous races. There is, however, a certain

---

[*] "Des Diverses Espèces de Prognathisme," by Paul Topinard, in "Revue d'Anthrop.," vols. i. and ii., 1872 and 1873.

conformity with usually-received notions in the general distribution
of their angles, which arises from the part which the particular
prognathism of the sub-nasal region bears in the general prognathism
of the face or of the maxilla. Prognathism of the face is to be
altogether discarded as an important character. That of the
maxilla, as a whole, occasionally gives us some information.

True Prognathism.

We must consider alveolo-sub-nasal prognathism in an entirely
different way, affecting as it does both the portion of the maxilla
subjacent to the nasal spine which corresponds to the palatine arch,
and that next to it in which the alveoli are situated. It is to it
that the term prognathism should be strictly confined. It is to this
sub-nasal region that we must look when endeavouring to find out
the source whence a skull has been derived. It furnishes of
itself the differential character of the various races of mankind.
Subjoined are examples of this.

TRUE OR SUB-NASAL PROGNATHISM.

Individual variations, maximum and minimum ...	88° to 51·3°
Average variations { White races ...	... 82 „ 70·5
Yellow „ ...	... 76 „ 68·5
Black „ ...	... 69 „ 59·6
14 Genackes	81·86°
16 Corsicans	81·98
28 Gauls	80·67
14 Caverne de l'Homme Mort	79·77
560 Parisians	75·18
10 Tonbouctous	76·50
76 Auvergnians	77·18
48 Merovingians	74·54
7 Fins and Esthonians	75·58
6 Tasmanians	78·26
10 Tahitians	75·00
14 Chinese	75·00
10 Esquimaux	71·46
46 Malays	69·48
50 New Caledonians	68·87
11 Australians	68·24
86 Negroes of West Africa	65·91
7 Namaquas and Boojesmins	59·68

We gather from this—(a) That the angle of prognathism never reaches a right angle; the sub-nasal line is always more or less inclined on the natural plane of the base of the skull, consequently neither orthognathism nor opisthognathism has any existence. (b) All races, all individuals are prognathous, the difference between them being only in degree. (c) The races of Europe are slightly so, the yellow races and Polynesians much more so, the negro races more still. (d) The least prognathous of Europe are the inhabitants of the Polished Stone period—the Gauls, Corsicans, and Guanches; the most prognathous, the Finno-Esthonians. (e) At the Merovingian period prognathism increased among the higher classes, and diminished subsequently. (f) Among the yellow races, prognathism appears to be less in the Mongols of the West; it increases in the Chinese and Esquimaux, and attains its maximum in Malays. (g) The Polynesians of purest blood, and (we hardly venture to say) the Tasmanians which we have measured come nearer to the white races in this respect than the yellow races of the East, or the negro races of Africa. (h) The negroes of the east coast of Africa are less prognathous than those of the west; the negroes of Oceania less than the negroes of Africa: the purest Hottentots reach the highest maximum of the whole human race.

Setting aside the Finno-Esthonians and some Mongols of the East, the difference between the white and yellow races is very great; there is an insensible transition, on the contrary, from the latter to negroes. Taking the word in its ordinary sense, we may say that the white races are never prognathous, and that the yellow and black races are so in various degrees. In all the races, however, there are exceptions. There are negroes as little prognathous as whites, as shown in a Bambarra skull, and whites excessively prognathous, as seen in the skull of Lemaire the assassin; but in our opinion these are cases of atavism or of hybridity, and sometimes cases of disease. In fine, alveolo-sub-nasal prognathism is one of the best craniological characteristics. Before concluding our remarks on projections, we would say a word respecting the researches of M. Asséez on the general proportions of the face. He has studied—(a) The relation of its height, or rather of a perpendicular let fall from the nasal spine, or root of the nose, on the alveolo-condylean plane—its maximum or bizygomatic breadth. (b) The area of the median and anterior triangle included between the nasal point, the alveolar point, and the point where the basion is projected on the alveolo-condylean plane. The facial height which we adopt varies, in the first place, as to its absolute measurements, from 77 millimètres in Esquimaux to 61 in Tasmanians, which justifies the impression which the skull of each of these gives. The same height, compared to its maximum breadth satisfactorily shows that Basques have the longest face, and Lapps the shortest. But in every question of this kind there are two factors, and it is well to observe that in Basques the diminution of the transverse diameter plays the principal part. (See p. 253.) The study of the area of the triangle is equally instructive: there is no need of explanation, the figures speak for themselves. In Esquimaux the surface is 28 per cent. larger than in Lapps, which is an additional characteristic to those which already separate these two races formerly included under one and the same name. In Auvergnians it is 15 per cent. larger than in Merovingians, and 11 per cent. more than in Basques; which tends to distinguish our ancient Celtic race from the other indigenous races of France.

Craniometrical Angles.

Craniometrical angles are obtained in the same way as projections, in two ways; either directly with the assistance of particular instruments, or on geometrical drawings by means of the protractor. There is a third, which is indirect—the trigonometrical method, of which M. Broca has given formulæ for certain cases: as the biorbital angle, the parietal angle of M. de Quatrefages, the angle of prognathism of which we have just spoken, the angle which is formed by the prolongation of the two sides of the superior cranial trapezium of M. Welcker, which unite the parietal to the frontal eminences.[*] The angle of Daubenton, having its point at the opis-

[*] "Sur le Plan Horizontal de la Tête, et sur la Méthode Trigonométrique," by Paul Broca. Paris, 1873.

thion, and for its sides the plane of the prolonged occipital foramen, and the line going from the opisthion to the level of the inferior orbital border, is the most ancient known. It has been described at page 53, as well as the two other occipital angles, the one to the opisthion and the other to the basion, which M. Broca has added to it. All three are taken almost at one operation, with the occipital goniometer, with the arc in the position as represented in Fig. 6.

The centre of the dial being fixed at the opisthion by a little pin, the index-needle is applied first on the anterior measuring point (*point de repère*) of the line of Daubenton, and then on that of the line which M. Broca prefers—viz. the nasal point. Two angles are thus indicated which can be read off. The centre being then carried forward upon the basion, and the needle placed at the nasal point, we get the third or basilar angle.

In the generality of cases, the angle of Daubenton is positive (+); that is to say the prolongation of the occipital foramen ends at the face above the line which unites the inferior border of the two orbits. More rarely it is negative (–), which Daubenton had not noticed; that is to say the prolongation of the foramen ends above the inferior border of the orbits. The second occipital angle of Broca is always positive; once only has the basilar angle been found negative.

The variations observed in the races of Mankind with regard to the angle of Daubenton are from – 16 degrees in an Auvergnian to + 19 in a Hottentot; but M. Broca has found that in the majority of cases above – 12 degrees, the skull was affected with the plastic deformation described by Mr. B. Davis, and he thinks that this +19 is a mistake of from one to two degrees, so that the physiological deviation between the extremes of this angle should be about 29 degrees. The – 3 which Daubenton attributed to Man in general is far from being settled. These variations are due to the influence of race, and average from – 1·50° in Auvergnians to + 9·34° in Nubians.

In M. Broca's table all the races of Europe are grouped at the top from – 1·53° to + 2·06°, while the last three races at the

bottom from + 7·86° to + 9·34° are negroes. Whence the conclusion that the lowering of the plane of the occipital foramen,
which increases the angle of Daubenton, constitutes a mark of
inferiority; and this conclusion is confirmed by the angle of
+ 11·37° obtained in four microcephali, and these still stronger
than any we have described in the mammalian series. (See page
95.) Some races, as that of the Tasmanians, are far removed from
this reckoning; but in other respects have we not already seen this
singular race separated from the negro group in which, from their
woolly hair and black skin, they had been included? In reference
to the angle of Daubenton, the conclusion we have come to is this:
that the character which it expresses, in spite of its value, is out of
the series. Like the form of the head, the orbital index, or the
facial angle, it has no regular gradation, and is rather favourable to
the monogenistic theory. The dimensions of the occipital and
basilar angles of Broca similarly vary. The averages of the occipital are from + 10·83° in Auvergnians to – 20·12° in Nubians;
and of the basilar from + 14·36° in Slavs of Austria to – 36·33°
in Nubians also; the minimum and maximum individual dimensions of the basilar being from – 2 in an Auvergnian to + 37 in a
West African. In order not to be tediously prolix, we shall confine ourselves to some examples of the angle of Daubenton and of
the basilar angle of Broca.

					Angle of Daubenton.	Basilar angle.
60	Basques (Spanish)	...	...	...	– 1·62°	15·29°
59	Auvergnians	...	...	...	– 1·50	14·72
62	Bretons (Low)	...	...	...	– 0·80	16·03
126	Parisians of the 19th century	...	– 0·17	17·38
114	„ „ 12th „	...	...	+ 1·46	17·69
6	Tasmanians	...	...	...	+ 2·58	10·49
11	Mongols	...	...	...	+ 2·72	20·09
29	Chinese	...	...	...	+ 5·86	24·51
14	Eskimaux	...	...	...	+ 6·63	24·42
18	Hottentots	...	...	...	+ 6·54	21·57
9	Australians	...	...	...	+ 6·87	21·48
61	New Caledonians	...	...	...	+ 7·65	29·69
44	Negroes (Western)	...	...	...	+ 8·47	25·97
22	Nubians	...	...	...	+ 9·34	36·33

The facial angle had its origin subsequently to that of Daubenton. We have seen (page 41 and Fig. 4) that there are four varieties of it : (1) The original angle of Camper, the vertex of which varies, is often vertical, and always on the prolonged horizontal line of Camper ; (2) The angle of Jacquart, the vertex of which is at the nasal spine ; (3) The angle of Cloquet, the vertex of which is at the alveolar border ; and (4) The angle of Geoffroy Saint-Hilaire and Cuvier, the vertex of which is at the centre of the incisors. We have shown that all have for their posterior point the auditory meatus, or rather a virtual point in the middle of the biauricular line, and for the superior the culminant point of the forehead, which is almost always the glabella, or the place of convergence of the two superciliary arches. We may remark that this latter point is a bad one, and that the bulgings of the glabella and of the arches occasioned by the development of the frontal sinuses are to be avoided. For the comparison of Man with animals we prefer the angle of Cloquet, modified according to circumstances. For the comparison of the human races we are of the same opinion, but measurements of them to any extent have not yet been made.

The following table, extracted from No. 11 in our treatise upon the facial angles, has reference to the angle of Jacquart taken in two ways only : the ordinary one at the glabella ; the other higher up, generally at the supra-orbital point, in order to avoid the glabella or superciliary projection. M. Broca calls the latter angle the ophryo-spinal.

FACIAL ANGLE OF JACQUART.

Men.		Glabella.	Sup.-orb. point.	Difference.
9 Auvergnians...	...	81·25°	... 75·11°	... 6·14°
28 Bretons (Low)	...	75·13	... 73·51	... 1·62
86 Gallo-Bretons	...	77·12	... 74·42	... 2·70
29 Basques (French)	...	78·24	... 75·41	... 2·83
48 ,, (Spanish)	...	77·30	... 75·18	... 2·18
13 Esquimaux ...	...	70·32	... 74·43	... 1·89
29 Chinese ...	...	76·04	... 72·57	... 3·47
85 Malays ...	...	75·64	... 74·12	... 1·52
135 Negroes of Africa	...	75·03	... 74·81	... 0·22
69 New Caledonians	...	74·73	... 72·09	... 2·64

FACIAL ANGLE OF JACQUART.

Worms.		Glabella.	Suprancis. point.	Difference.
88 Auvergnians ...	...	76·00'	... 76·05"	... 1·05"
25 Bretons (Low)	...	74·56	... 75·52	... 1·04
23 Gallo-Bretons	...	76·08	... 76·51	... 0·47
19 Basques (French)	...	76·96	... 71·91	... 1·44
17 „ (Spanish)	...	77·89	... 70·84	... 1·05
4 Chinese	... ...	73·60	... 72·95	... 1·80
5 Malays	... ...	74·31	... 73·96	... 0·36
58 Negresses of Africa		75·73	... 75·08	... 0·95
28 New Caledonians	...	75·29	... 74·91	... 1·08

The individual limits of the first angle vary in these series from 87·2° to 66·2°, which leaves a certain margin for the distribution of mean; but their averages are not more than from 79·5 in the Auvergnians of both sexes to 74·4 in a special series of negroes of Cape de Verd. Looking only at the two great divisions, the general averages fall to 77·6 in the 687 individuals of the white men, 75·6 in the 140 of the yellow, 75·2 in the 118 of the negro race of Oceania, and 76·0 in the 90 of the negro races of Africa—the difference in this case not being more than two degrees. If we take the second angle—that is to say making allowance for the projection of the glabella or the superciliary ridges—the interval is not more favourable. In the averages of the series it was nine degrees in men and 4·3° in women; at the present time it is 9·7° in the former and 2·4° in the latter. Whence we come to the conclusion that the true angle of Jacquart, as well as his modified angle, may be useful for the differentiation of individuals, but they are not so for that of races. The facial angles, moreover, do not measure the relation of the development of the cranium and face, as was once thought, but the obliquity of the line of profile of the face; we must then prolong this line as far as the alveolar border, and not conclude it at the nasal spine. We must consequently await the results which the angle of Cloquet gives according to race. The angle of Jacquart is taken directly with the goniometer of that name, that of Camper with the goniometer of Morton, and that of Jules Cloquet with the median goniometer of M. Broca; all on plans by orthogonal projection.

The parietal angle, which will now engage our attention,[*] was devised by M. de Quatrefages with a view to controvert two statements of Blumenbach and Prichard, and is taken with the instrument represented at Fig. 30. When we carry two lines (S Z, Fig. 29) across the extremities of the transverse maximum, or bizygomatic diameter of the face, and the extremities of the maximum transverse frontal diameter, which in that case is commonly looked upon as identical with the transverse stephanic, these lines generally meet either at a variable point at a distance above the head, are parallel, or meet at a point below. In the first case the angle is positive: this is the pyramidal angle of Prichard; in the second there is none; in the third the angle is negative. When the angle is positive, the zygomatic arches are called phenozygous—that is to say, visible by the norma verticalis method of Blumenbach; when negative, the arches are cryptozygous, or concealed.

The following table shows the maximum and minimum, and the means in some of the human series:

		Averages.		Variations.		
26 Auvergnians	...	... + 2·5°	...	− 6°	to +	6°
10 Roumanians	...	... + 8·0	...	− 0·5	„ +	18
18 Guanches	...	... − 10·1	...	+ 5	„ +	17
10 Lapps	...	... + 5·5	...	− 5	„ +	15
13 Esquimaux	...	... + 15·7	...	+ 4	„ +	23·5
12 Chinese	...	... + 11·2	...	+ 4	„ +	18
10 Mongols	...	... + 10·1	...	+ 5	„ +	17
6 Uzbecks	...	... + 8·0	...	− 6	„ +	18
4 Telinchas	...	... + 11·5	...	+ 5	„ +	16
10 Negroes of Africa	...	... + 7·0	...	+ 2	„ +	18
12 New Caledonians	...	... + 20·3	...	+ 15	„ +	30

From these data it follows—(a) That the individual limits of the parietal angle vary from − 5 to + 30, and the means in ones the most divergent from + 2·5 to 20·3; (b) That the angles from 35 to 39 degrees, represented in the figures which accompany Prichard's description, and which led him to give the title of pyramidal to the Mongolian skull, are never seen; (c) That the

[*] "De l'Angle Pariétal," by M. de Quatrefages; "Comptes Rendus de l'Académie des Sciences," meeting of April 25, 1856.

most oval skull, to use his own expression, that in which the
zygomatic arches are the most visible by the method of Blumenbach, is met with among the negroes of Oceania, and not among
Mongols ; (d) That inversely, the most negative angle—viz. that in
which the zygomatic arches are the least projecting—is noticed
among Auvergnians, Lapps, and African negroes.

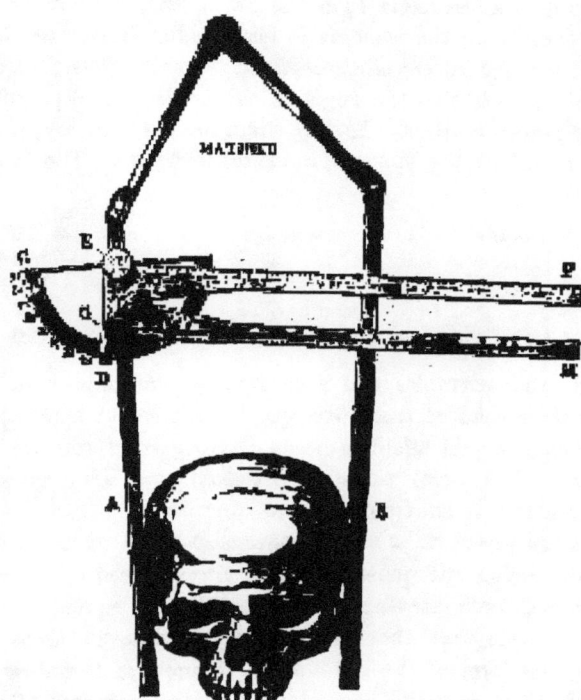

Fig. 30.—Parietal goniometer of M. de Quatrefages. The branches A and B ought to
touch the coronal suture. They show, notwithstanding, that if prolonged they would
meet below the skull—the angle would be negative.

This angle is the resultant of two frequently contradictory conditions; viz. the widening of the cheek-bones, and the degree of
swelling of the temples at the fronto-parietal suture. In default
of an instrument, the relation of the two diameters, the bizygomatic and the bistephanic, might be substituted for it. Thus the

Auvergnians have scarcely any parietal angle, and occasionally a negative one, because their brachycephalic character is associated with a feeble widening of the cheek-bones and zygomatic arches. The New Caledonians, on the contrary, have a very acute angle, because in them a considerable dolichocephalism is accompanied by a wide separation of the cheek-bones. If the true Mongols and Usbecks have a less angle than the Esquimaux, the breadth of the cheek-bones being the same, it is because the former are brachycephalic and the latter dolichocephalic. Another thing we deduce from this table is, that the angle in the adult is always, with but few exceptions, positive. In the child, on the contrary, it is constantly negative; the younger it is, the more so. The following figures show this :—

2 children of 15 to 16 years of age	...	...	—	7·6°
3 ,, ,, 6 ,, 8 ,, ,,	...	...	—	15·3
2 ,, ,, 3 ,, 4 ,, ,,	...	...	—	15·0
4 ,, ,, 16 ,, 18 months old	...	...	—	21·7
1 child ,, 4 ,,	...	...	—	24·0

From other examples, and even from one of those which have swelled the second of these averages, we are led to think that the parietal angle would afford a means of recognising anterior hydrocephalus. The usual mean at a certain age being given, any considerable deviation from it would be its index.

It has surprised us to see pathological cases in which, while the zygomatic arches still preserved their normal breadth, the anterior cranium was prominent or depressed. It will be noticed in the subjoined table that the variations are similar to those which age and the form of the head ought to produce according to the foregoing opinions. We have also given some measurements taken upon anthropoid apes; here again the principle with regard to age is confirmed in the case of the young orang.

4 hydrocephali, adults	...	...	...	— 31·6°
2 microcephali, ,,	...	...	...	+ 33·0
2 ,, ,, (brachycephalic)	...	...	+ 21·0
1 microcephalus, 7 years of age	...	...	...	— 2·0
2 staphocephali	...	...	...	+ 13·0

1 young orang	...	...	...	...	...	+ 17·0
1 adult orang	...	...	...	...	...	+ 80·6
4 „ gorilla	...	...	...	...	...	+ 77·1
1 „ chimpanzee	...	...	...	...	...	+ 69·0

In a word, the parietal angle of M. de Quatrefages affords an excellent character for craniometrical study, but it has no part in the series, and contradicts the views put forth by Blumenbach and Prichard. The auricular angles, of which we have already spoken (page 271), having their vertex on the biauricular vertex, and crossed by the radii going from this axis to particular points of the head, as taken with the craniograph, have given rise to the following arrangement of M. Broca:

	315 Parisians.	60 Basques.	35 Negroes.
Facial angle: arc passing from the supraorbital to the alveolar point	61·5°	49·6°	46·2°
Frontal angle: arc passing from the supra-orbital point to the bregma ...	60·4	64·2	64·1
Parietal angle	80·9	81·4	68·2
Total occipital angle	71·2	78·0	73·2
Frontal angle in hundredths of the total cranial angle: the arc from the supra-orbital point to the opisthion	30·9	28·3	27·0

This comparison shows the share of development which each portion of the head takes. We see that the frontal region is larger in the Parisians than in the Basques, and less in the negroes. It appears à priori that the face of Parisians is larger, but it must be remembered that the face in the negro is developed in length, which, instead of increasing, diminishes the angle.[*]

The angle of prognathism has been already described. There are besides: (a) The metafacial angle of Serres, which the pterygoid processes form with the base of the skull. It seems to us to vary with the prognathism, but not very much. (b) The corona-facial angle of Gratiolet, formed by the meeting of the plane passing across the coronal suture of both sides and the facial line of Camper. (c) The naso-basal angle, described at page 255. (d) The

---

[*] "Sur les Crânes Basques de Zaraus," in "Mém. d'Anthrop.," by Paul Broca, vol. ii. p. 28.

sphenoidal angle of Welcker, (e) The angle of Barclay. (f) The
cranio-facial angle of Huxley, which differs somewhat from the
cranio-facial angle of Ecker, &c. It has been a matter of
dispute as to the naso-basilar line, as well as to the chord (N B,
Fig. 37), measuring the extent of inflection which the bodies of the
cranial vertebræ describe, from the basion where they commence to
the naso-frontal suture looked upon as their termination. This
inflection is divided, in reality, into two parts; viz. a line, B S,

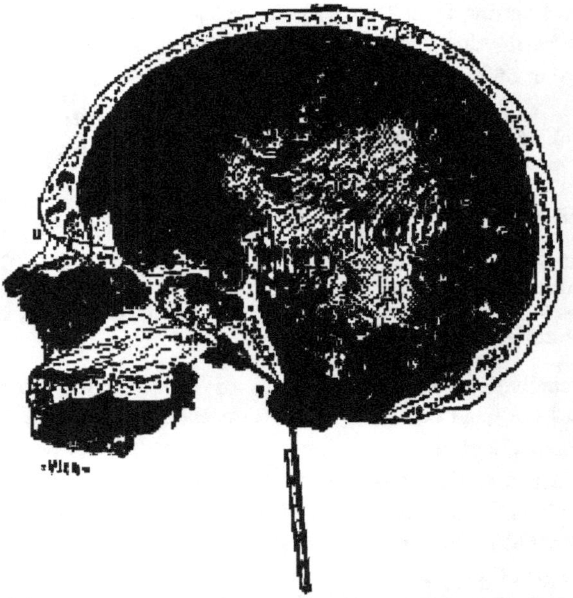

Fig. 37.—Median section of the skull. N B, Naso-basilar line; N S and S B, The two
sides of the sphenoidal angle; S, Ephippium, vertex of the angle where the point of the
sphenoidal ratchet, which is seen in position, ought to touch.

proceeding from the basion to the transverse ridge, which, in the
interior of the skull, separates the sella turcica from the optic
groove, and a line, S N, passing from this point to the naso-frontal
suture; the obtuse angle which they make looking from below and
in front is the sphenoidal angle or ephippium. If from this point
a circle is described, all which is above and behind belongs to the

cranium, all below and in front to the face—hence its interest
Subjoined are the measurements published by M. Welcker :

30 Germans (men)	...	...	...	...	...	134°
20 „ (women)	...	...	...	...	...	128
11 children from 10 to 15 years of age			...	...	137
6 new-born infants	...	...	...	...	...	141
6 negroes	...	...	...	...	...	144
1 chimpanzee	...	...	...	...	...	149
1 orang (old)	...	...	...	...	...	174
1 „ (adult)	...	...	...	...	...	172
1 „ (young)	...	...	...	...	...	155
1 baboon	...	...	...	...	...	170
1 magosin (adult)	...	...	...	...	...	174
1 „ (new-born)	...	...	...	...	...	140
1 „ (old)	...	...	...	...	...	160

Looking only at the adults in this table, it appears that the angle
is less in the white, more open in the negro, more still in the orang,
and that it increases still more in a pithecian ; which means that
a small face, and reciprocally a large cranium, are the characteristic
of superiority in the scale of Primates. But when we take the
various ages into consideration matters present themselves in a
different light. The sphenoidal angle is relatively a little larger in
infancy than in adult age, and notably smaller in monkeys, which
is in accordance with M. Welcker's statement that in Man the
cerebral cavity at birth is less, relatively to its maximum volume,
than at full age,[*] but that this cavity grows much more rapidly
(see page 131).

It has been asked what relation there is between the sphenoidal
angle, that is to say the straight and curved portion of the body
of the cranial vertebræ, and prognathism. M. Virchow asserts that
it diminishes when the latter increases. M. Welcker says the
reverse. M. Lucæ considers that they have no relation to each
other. The same comparison has been made with the naso-basal
angle, but improperly so, this only measuring a very small part of
prognathism, and that the least important part, which we have
called the nasal or supra-maxillary.

[*] "Mémoire sur les Microcéphales," by Carl Vogt. Geneva, 1867.

The sphenoidal angle is very objectionable, inasmuch as it can only be measured on a section, and necessitates the skull being divided. M. Broca has, to a certain extent, met the objection by his proceeding with the sphenoidal crochet, shown at Fig. 37, and one which he has recently successfully carried out.[*] Under the rather inapt title of the angle of the condyles, M. Ecker understands the obtuse angle, open above and behind, that the plane of the occipital foramen forms with the plane of the basilar groove, or clivus.[†] It varies from 100 to 125 degrees in negroes, and from 117 to 140 in whites; the mean being 119·5 in the former, and 128·2 in the latter. The difference, therefore, is so remarkable that this measurement ought to be maintained. It arises, according to the author, from the fact that the plane of the occipital foramen is lowered at its anterior border, as M. Broca has shown by the help of his occipital angles. But the strange part of it is—and it is not the first time that we have met with things of this kind—that this angle in anthropoids more nearly approaches that of the white than that of the black. It was 130 degrees in a young orang, 123 in a gorilla, and 128 in an old orang. Its diminution in negroes is not due, therefore, to the lowering of the occipital foramen, inasmuch as the latter is lower still in anthropoids. The variations of the angle of Ecker are dependent then on the inclination of the basilar groove.

Special Systems.

Under the title of special systems several topics might be considered which have not been noticed in the foregoing chapters. We shall only mention two of them—endometry and endoscopy.

If we attach importance to the external configuration of the skull, how much more should we do so to its interior or endocrane? M. Broca, having laid down certain rules for the measurement of the capacity of the cerebral cavity, proceeded without delay to

[*] See "Dict. Encycl. des Sciences Médicales," article "Angles Céphaliques," by M. Bertillon, 1866.

[†] "Ueber die Verschiedene Krümmung des Schädelrohres und über die Stellung des Schädels auf der Wirbelsäule beim Neger und beim Europäer," by M. A. Ecker, in "Arch. für Anthrop.," vol. iv.

study its form and configuration in detail. For this purpose he invented a series of instruments for measuring its diameter, for tracing its outlines, for making drawings, and lastly, for looking directly into it. Its results have not yet been thoroughly arrived at. As an example of what we may look for, we shall give the measurements of the trapezium and the surface included between the two optic foramina, and the two internal auditory foramina :

	Caucasian type. Millimetres.	Mongolian type. Millimetres.	Ethiopian type. Millimetres.
Bioptic distance ...	23·89	23·76	23·29
Diacoustic distance ...	65·66	62·00	68·00
Acute angle formed by the prolongation of the two other sides ...	71·1°	70·90	73·10
Surface of the trapezium ...	1787	1956	1888

Among the details, of which an impression has been taken across the occipital foramen, we may note the ethmoidal fossa, the form and depth of which correspond to the projection of the beak of the encephalon, which is more developed in the inferior races, less so in the higher.

The cranial net of M. Welcker, a system of triangulation of the external surface of the cranial ovoid, exclusive of the face, has not given results worthy of being recorded. It consists of—(a) A superior cranial quadrilateral, included between the parietal and frontal protuberances ; (b) A frontal quadrilateral, smaller, included between the frontal protuberances and the line uniting the external orbital processes of the frontal ; (c) An inferior quadrilateral, the anterior side of which is formed by that line, and the posterior by the line going from the point of one mastoid process to the other ; (d) A triangle having this latter line for a base, and the inion for its apex. A triangle with its apex still at the inion, but its base on the line of the two parietal protuberances, terminates the circle of the figures in pairs. Two quadrilateral and two lateral triangles complete the entire system. It is useless to proceed farther.

The system of Ihering is applied to the method of projections.

The author seems to have had a strong feeling against the doctrine of Oken on the vertebral constitution of the cranium, and in favour of that of Gegenbaur, maintaining that the cranium is formed in a manner independently of the vertebral column. There are no anatomical points, he says, upon which one can rely; that it is useless to search for the relations of the different portions of the cranium; and that it can only be measured as a whole, with the aid of maximum, and reciprocally perpendicular, lines. M. Ihering has consequently invented an apparatus for taking these maxima of height, breadth, and length, the skull being in its natural attitude. But here M. Ihering sets the rule he has laid down at defiance, and has recourse to anatomical points. In order to place the skull in proper position, he adopts, as a fundamental line, the line of Meckel, going from the centre of the auditory meatus to the inferior border of the orbit. Now this line, by which everyone is guided, is raised eight degrees in relation to the axis of the orbital cavities, or to that of vision, in order to give the skull the most appropriate attitude. In the *norma verticalis*, to which it gives rise, the most prognathous skulls become orthognathous. Moreover, M. Ihering has partly given up his system: in the table of measurements which he propounded at the Dresden Congress in 1874 he becomes quite eclectic.

The system of Antelme allows, with the aid of a special cephalometer, which is unfortunately very costly, of our determining with great exactness the reciprocal position of all the external points of the skull, and the distance from these points to the centre of the biauricular axis. Designed for use on the living subject, M. Bertillon has modified it so as to adapt it to the skull. For his description of it we refer the reader to the first volume of the "Mémoires de la Société d'Anthropologie," and for examples of its application to the memoir of M. Bertillon on New Caledonians, in the "Revue d'Anthropologie," vol. i. p. 284, 1872.

The system of M. Kopernicki also requires a particular craniograph, which must have been suggested by the physionotype of Huschke, and reminds one of the circular band used by hatters. Its object is, among others, to take measurements of the skull

which have been omitted by other methods of procedure. For a
description of it we refer the reader to the "Bulletins de la Société
d'Anthropologie," 2nd series, vol. ii., 1867; and for its application, to the memoir on Bulgarian skulls by M. J. Kopernicki, in
the "Revue d'Anthropologie," vol. iv. p. 63, 1875.

To sum up: the craniometer substitutes mathematical data for
the uncertain data founded on judgment and opinion. It studies
the skeleton of the head in its *ensemble*, the cranium and the
face separately, and then each of its parts, by methods which take
the head in its natural attitude, accept certain central points of
more or less physiological importance, or have to do directly with
absolute measurements apart from all preconceived theory. One
of its systems is specially fertile in good results, namely, the comparison of methods under the form of indices; but it requires a
large number of skulls in which individual marks of variation are
effaced. Characteristics hitherto left to chance investigation also
come within its province. It shows that the eye may be deceived,
and analyses as far as possible those variable impressions which we
term the beautiful. Although at first, and even now, encumbered
with materials many of which ought to be eliminated, it has enabled
us to recognise human types which without it would have remained
undetermined; and it bids fair one day to furnish a solid basis for
the classification of races into genera and species.

CHAPTER IV.

SKELETON: ITS DESCRIPTIVE AND OSTEOMETRICAL CHARACTERS—ITS
PROPORTIONS—THE VISCERA—THE BRAIN: ITS WEIGHT.

The other parts of the skeleton have been less studied than the
skull: in the first place because their importance was not understood; and in the second, because travellers and archæologists
neglected to take account of them. The characters which they
furnish are of two orders, some having reference to the configuration

of the bones themselves, and others to their respective proportions.
Among the former may be placed the perforation of the humerus,
certain forms of the femur, the tibia, the fibula, and the ulna; the
torsion of the humerus and the femur; the curvature of the latter;
the angle which its body makes with the diaphysis; the projection
of the calcaneum; the breadth of the olecranon, &c. We shall
only refer to some of these.

The perforation of the olecranon cavity of the humerus, first
noticed in some skeletons of Hottentots and Guanches, is also met
with in the negro and European. Its degree of frequency among
the races of France has been the subject of discussion of late,
and it is asked whether this character did not specially belong
to one of the most ancient. The subjoined table will in a measure
solve this question. We are indebted to the kindness of Dr.
Prunières de Marvejols, to whom anthropology owes so much for
his many valuable discoveries, for all that we know respecting La
Lozère. The results at the Pre-gallic station of Campons emanate
from MM. Broca and Millecamps; those on Parisians of the fourth
to the tenth century, and on the mountaineers of the Ain, from
ourselves. The others have been specially published in a note in
the "Mémoires" by M. Broca, vol. ii. p. 366. We shall only give
the cases in which the number of the humeri which have been the
subject of study has been furnished.

Number of humeri		Per cent.
66 Caverne de l'Homme Mort (La Lozère)...	...	10·8
368 Dolmens of La Lozère	...	10·8
128 Stations of Vauréal, Orrony, and Chamans (Polished Stone period)	}	21·7
44 Pre-gallic station of Campons	...	12·5
42 Mountaineers of the Ain (8th century) ...	...	27·7
69 French Basques	...	13·4
200 Parisians of the 4th to the 10th century	...	5·5
218 „ of the Middle Ages	...	4·1
160 „ anterior to the 17th century ...	...	4·6
1000 (?) Merovingians of Chelles	...	2·0

This shows that the perforation of the humerus as a common
character dates back to the Polished Stone period; that it was

frequent at that epoch; that it has continued among peoples placed
in conditions favourable to the resistance of inter-breeding; and
that it has diminished in frequency since the commencement of our
era. Its excessive rarity in the burial-places of individuals of the
higher ranks at Chelles seems to account for this diminution. The
following list of the variations at similar stations of the same
epoch shows, however, that we must accept the above with some
reserve. It has reference to the dolmens separately noticed by
M. Prunières de Marvejols.

Dolmen No. 1.—	27 humeri	...	7 perforated	...	26 per cent.
„ „ 2.—	65	„	... 11	„	... 17 „
„ „ 3.—	8	„	... 1	„	... 12 „
„ „ 4.—31		„	... 1	„	... 8 „
„ „ 5.—16		„	... 0	„	... 0 „

Lastly, it is well to remark—(a) That the perforation does not
always show itself on both sides at once, which lessens its value;
(b) That it is exhibited in various degrees; and (c) According to
M. Broca, that it is more particularly to be seen in women. The
character which the tibia sometimes presents, and which bears the
name of platycnemia, or sabre-like, is much more remarkable.
This bone is described in all works on anatomy as having a
prismatic or triangular diaphysis. Its anterior border, immediately
under the skin, is termed the crest of the tibia; its internal gives
insertion to an aponeurosis, which is applied to the fibula, and
separates the muscles of the anterior region of the leg from those
of the posterior. Its posterior surface is traversed above by an
oblique rough line, which serves for the insertion of the popliteus
muscle; and below by a longitudinal line, giving insertion to other
adjoining muscles. In platycnemia, the tibia has only two surfaces
in its three upper fifths, an external and an internal. The anterior
border is thin, the internal and external borders occupy the centre
of the two surfaces, and the new posterior border corresponds to
the above lines of insertion of muscles. Figure 35 shows a section
of the two sorts of tibia. Platycnemia is noticed here and there in
many of our graves, but with variable frequency. The first time

it was observed was in the tibiæ of the family buried at Cro-
Magnon, at the Ancient Stone period. It has frequently been described as existing in England, both at the Pre-gallic and the
Polished Stone periods. In 200 Parisian tibiæ, which we have
collected from the St. Marcel and St. Germain-des-Prés cemeteries,
dating from the fourth to the tenth century, 5·25 per cent.
were platycnemic, and 14 per cent. were bent. This latter peculiarity is not uncommon in old graves, as well as the channelled
fibula, that is to say, the fibula with enormously large longitudinal
grooves for the insertion of muscles, the ulna incurvated forwards
in its upper fourth, and the *fémur à colonne*. This last is worthy a
separate description.

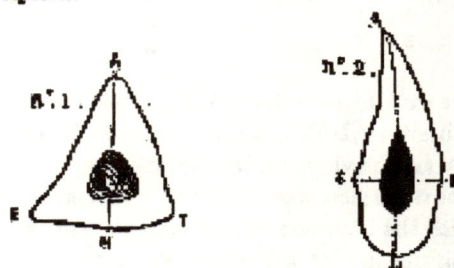

FIG. 33.—No. 1, Ordinary triangular tibia, the diaphysis divided on a level with the
nutritive foramen. No. 2, Platycnemic tibia divided at the same spot.

The muscles of the posterior part of the thigh are principally
attached to the two longitudinal lines which form the posterior
border of the femur, and together bear the name of *linea aspera*
(*ligne âpre*). These two lines are wanting in the anthropoid ape,
the border being round. In Man they are either blended together
so as to be scarcely visible, or they project, and are separated by a
rough interval. In the *fémur à colonne* they form a still greater
projection; they are wider apart, and the adjoining surfaces of the
bone being sunk in, make this projection appear still greater.
Hence their pilaster-like appearance extending along the middle
three-fifths of the bone. The femurs of Cro-Magnon are the most
striking examples of this, those of the Guanches, in the laboratory
of M. Broca, are very similar. Of 200 Parisian femurs obtained

from the cemeteries before referred to, in 6·5 per cent. the column was very marked, and in 36 per cent. it was so slightly. It seems, therefore, that these peculiarities of the tibia, femur, and fibula belonged to one and the same race in Western Europe. The 30 subjects from the cave at Sordes, in the Basque territory, belonging to the Polished Stone period, all exhibit them (*Hamy*). It is very remarkable, however, that they are rarely met with having perforation of the olecranon cavity. The two races which have bequeathed to us the two varieties are therefore distinct. We have observed platycnemia, the incurvated ulna, and the pilar-like femur in other races, notably in skeletons from Oceania. The complete obliteration of the *linea aspera* of the femur, one of the highest simian characteristics, is rare. It is observed in the skeleton of the Hottentot Venus, now in Paris.

Osteometrical Characters.

At page 81 we have shown the difficulties met with in at once determining the proportions of the body on the skeleton and on the living subject, and the two methods which are in favour with anatomists—one in which the length of the bones is compared with the stature of the individual, the other in which the bones are compared with each other. We have also given the general results arrived at on a comparison of Man and the anthropoids. It now remains for us to speak of the appreciable differences between races · first, of those which we notice directly on the skeleton; and then of those which are to be studied on the living subject.

The selection of osteometrical measurements and methods of proceeding varies according to the object we have in view. When we wish to calculate the proportions of the body, we are obliged to measure the bones in their normal position, the individual being supposed to be standing erect, and only to include that portion which contributes to the total length of the limb. At other times we are satisfied with their absolute length. For some, as the clavicle, the fibula, and even the ulna, this is generally sufficient. The bone is laid upon a graduated slab—the osteometrical slab of M. Broca

being preferred—and with a square we take the two most deviating
projections which it gives on this slab. Such is the usual mode of
proceeding. With the radius we do the same, having no choice in
the matter. The forearm really extends no farther than the convex
articular surface of the carpus, and consequently the articular cavity
corresponding to the inferior extremity of the radius; but no spot
on the circumference of this cavity furnishes any fixed measuring point, so that we are obliged to include the styloid process in
the length of the bone, consoling ourselves that the measurement
becomes easier to compare with that taken on the living subject.

In the humerus the natural obliquity of the bone is so slight that
we may leave it out of consideration, and we have no hesitation as
to the measuring points, except as regards its inferior extremity.
White measured the humerus from the border of the acromion to
the point of the olecranon. M. Hamy, when engaged on the
subject of the development of the bone, and looking for its maximum, took the internal border of the trochlea. M. Broca, wishing
to join the humerus to the radius, makes the former terminate at
their point of contact, at the condyle. In the tibia the superior limit
is, without doubt, the flat articular surface; while the inferior, if we
require the true length of the leg, is the cavity articulating with the
astragalus, and in practice one of the borders of this cavity; we
therefore do not include the internal malleolus, which is like a
supplementary bone. It certainly is not rational, when the proportions of the limbs are in question, to include the internal malleolus
with the leg, at the same time that we discard the styloid process
from the forearm; but in this latter case necessity makes the law.

The femur is the long bone, in which our methods of proceeding
necessarily vary according to the object we have in view. If we
want its length in proportion to the height of the body, we must
take account of its obliquity. For this purpose the bone is placed
on its posterior surface, so that the two condyles are square with the
vertical plane. The regular position of the bone on the living
subject is thus obtained; and it only remains to determine, with the
square, its superior maximum, whether at the top of its head or at
the point of the great trochanter—the former being the better for

getting at the general proportions. If, on the contrary, the absolute length is required, inclusively or exclusively of the great trochanter, we begin, as with the clavicle, by laying the bone on the outer side.

Proportions of the Skeleton.

White, as far back as the year 1794, remarked in the living subject, and demonstrated both on this and on the skeleton, that the forearm of the negro, compared with the arm, is longer than that of the European; but not going into the matter further, nothing was done up to the time of Lawrence in 1817.

Humphry, in 1858, was more explicit. He stated that the thigh and the arm of the negro are shorter than those of the white, while his superior extremity is longer; that there is but little difference between his arm and forearm; that his leg is of the same length, but longer as compared with the thigh; and that his hand is an eighth, and his foot a twelfth, shorter. The following are his measurements relatively to the stature, this being = 100 :

	In Europeans.	In Negroes.	Difference as regards the negro.
Humerus + radius	39·69	39·68	+ 0·99
Femur + tibia	49·66	50·63	+ 0·97
Radius	14·15	15·16	+ 1·01
Humerus	19·54	19·52	− 0·02
Tibia	22·16	23·23	+ 1·08
Femur	27·51	27·40	− 0·11

But the objection is (see page 82) that the correct stature cannot be ascertained on the mounted skeleton. Let us then take M. Broca's figures. In the following table the absolute lengths are compared together and added. We draw attention particularly to the first three relations :

	Europeans.	Negroes.	Diff. as reg. negro.
Humerus + radius : femur + tibia = 100	69·73	68·27	− 1·46
Radius : humerus = 100	73·93	79·40	+ 5·47
Radius : femur + tibia = 100	30·54	30·58	+ 0·04
Humerus : femur + tibia = 100	40·11	38·20	− 1·91
Clavicle : humerus = 100	44·63	46·74	+ 2·11

We gather from this—(a) That the clavicle in the negro is longer in proportion to the humerus. (*b*) That his anterior extremity, from the shoulder to the wrist, is a little shorter, which is an anomaly, when we remember that it is longer in the anthropoid; however, it may probably be explained. (*c*) That his radius is perceptibly longer in proportion to the humerus, thus approximating it to that of the ape; White, Humphry, and Broca are all agreed in this respect. (*d*) That his tibia is longer as compared with the femur, which, if our statement at page 58 is confirmed, would make it less simian than the European.' (*e*) Lastly, that his humerus is shorter, and this no doubt explains the above anomaly. The upper extremity of the negro is shorter than that of the European, not because his radius has been lengthened, but because his humerus has been shortened. A superior character has originated from the union of two inferior ones. The anomaly in M. Broca's table is perhaps accidental—Mr. Humphry's figures giving the relation to the height of the body, lead us to think so—it loses all its importance when, considering the diversity of races, we see the unimportant position which the proportions of the skeleton exhibit in the series.

The following are some relations calculated according to M. Broca's mode after measurements made by Barnard Davis,[*] Humphry, Broca, and ourselves:

	Hum. + radi. fem. + etc.	Radi.: hum.	Tib.: fem.
1 Esquimau	71·1 (100)	71·0 (100)	75·8 (100)
1 Aino...	68·4 ...	76·2 ...	76·6
1 Andaman	70·3 ...	79·3 ...	81·6
2 Javanese	66·9 ...	82·0 ...	68·0
4 Tasmanians ...	66·2 ...	98·5 ...	84·8
7 Australians... ...	66·4 ...	75·6 ...	84·2
8 New Caledonians ...	69·6 ...	77·5 ...	82·9
5 Borjeamans... ...	68·4 ...	75·5 ...	89·5

This table, which is somewhat similar to the foregoing, shows in the first column that we must not expect to find the position of a race in the scale in the proportion of the upper to the lower extremity. It is true the Esquiman and the Andaman have the

[*] "On the Osteology and Peculiarities of the Tasmanians," by J. Barnard Davis. Harlem, 1874.

longest upper extremity, and the four Tasmanians the shortest in
the list, the Europeans coming between them.　By far the longest
radius is seen in the Javanese and Tasmanians, and the shortest in
the Esquimau, while the Europeans are intermediate in length.
The tibia appears to be decidedly the longest in the inferior races,
and shortest in the Esquimau and the Aino.　As regards the
tibia, therefore, the balance is in favour of Mr. Humphry's views,
and contrary to the foregoing calculations.

It is clear thus far, without one's being able to account for it on
any definite principle, that the proportions of Man neither approximate to, nor are far removed from, those of the anthropoid in all
parts of the skeleton at once, but sometimes in one and sometimes
in another.　Nothing is more opposed to the monogenistic theory
of hierarchical gradation of races, and more conformable to that of
parallel formations.　A type is superior in one point, inferior in
another.　It is the same with the family of the anthropoids, there
is the same divergence of proportions between their genera and
species as between the human races.*

The proportions of the trunk, with the exception of the pelvis,
can hardly be studied except on the living subject.

The Pelvis.

The pelvis, formed by the two iliac bones and the sacrum, is
divided into two parts—the great pelvis, or wide upper portion, and
the small pelvis, or pelvic cavity, through which the fœtus passes
at birth.　Camper and Sœmmering observed that the pelvis of the
negro in its ensemble is narrower than that of the white.　Cuvier,
in his brilliant memoir on the Hottentot Venus, insisted on the
evidences of inferiority which he found in it.　Weber maintained

---

* See "Mémoires," by M. Broca, already referred to, page 85; "A Treatise
on the Human Skeleton," by Humphry, Cambridge, 1858; "Recherches sur
les Proportions du Bras et de l'Avantbras," by E. Hamy, in "Revue
d'Anthropologie," vol. i., 1872; "Observations on the Skeleton of a
Hottentot," by Jeff. Wyman, in "Anthropol. Review," London, vol. iii.,
1865, &c.

that the inlet, that is to say the upper opening of the cavity, exhibits four forms, which are met with in all races, but most frequently the oval form in the European, the square in the Mongolian, the round in the American, and the wedge-like in the negro. In 1826 Vrolik came to the conclusion that the pelvis of the male negro—from its strength and thickness—from the want of transparency of its iliac fossæ—from the higher projection of its superior extremity, and from the spinous processes of the iliac bones being less projecting and less separated from the cotyloid cavities, approximates to that of animals, while the pelvis of the negress maintains a certain slenderness. In 1864 Joulin asserted that the transverse diameter of the inlet is always greater antero-posteriorly in the female, and that as to configuration, there are only two human groups—the European and the Mongolian negro. In the negress, he says, the iliac bones are more vertical, the transparency of the fossæ, the capacity and depth of the cavity less, the pubic arch, as well as its angle, greater. But M. Joulin had only studied the female pelvis, and M. Pruner-Bey, the year subsequently, set to work to prove that ethnic differences ought rather to be looked for in the male pelvis.[*]

The most general of all the characters of the pelvis is the relation of its breadth to its length, which has been already described, page 67. In the subjoined table, where the sexes are given separately, the length being equal to 100, the breadth would be :

* On the pelvis, see "Considérations sur la Diversité des Bassins des différentes Races Humaines," by Vrolik, Amsterdam, 1826 ; "La Doctrine des Formes Primitives du Crâne et du Bassin Humains," by Weber, 1830 ; "Des Races de l'Océanie Française;" "Du Bassin Néo-Calédonien," by A. Bourgarel, in "Mém. Soc. d'Anthrop.," vol. i., 1860 ; "Anatomie et Physiologie du Bassin des Mammifères," by Joulin, in "Archs. de Médic.," 6th series, vol. iii., 1864 ; "Études sur le Bassin considéré chez les différentes Races Humaines," by Pruner-Bey, in "Bull. Soc. d'Anthrop.," 1864 ; "Du Sacrum suivant le Sexe et suivant les Races," by Hecrrisse, thesis, Paris, 1873 ; "Des Proportions Générales du Bassin chez l'Homme et dans la Série des Mammifères," by Paul Topinard, in "Comptes Rendus de l'Association pour l'Avancement des Sciences," vol. iii., 1874, Lille ; "Le Bassin dans les Sexes et dans les Races," by R. Verneau, thesis, Paris, 1875.

	Men.		Women.	
White races...	... 25	... 180·2	... 4	... 189·1
Yellow races	... 2	... 195·7	... 2	... 199·3
African negroes	... 17	... 121·3	... 8	... 159·8
New Caledonians	... 14	... 128·9	... 6	... 129·9
Bosjesmans ...	... —	... —	... 2	... 185·6

Other less important osteometrical characters are furnished by the skeleton, which want of space prevents us from entering upon, and which, moreover, are still under investigation. For example (a) The degree of curvature of the femur, that is to say the height of the diaphysis when the bone is placed on a horizontal plane; (b) The angle of inclination of the diaphysis upon the plane passing across the inferior surface of the condyles, that is to say, its normal obliquity in the standing position; (c) The angle of the neck with the diaphysis; (d) The angle of torsion of the humerus; (e) The antero-posterior and transverse diameters of the tibia, from which an index is formed for estimating platycnemia; (f) The breadth and thickness of the olecranon, which give another important index; (g) The length of the calcaneum behind the articular border of the tibia; &c.

Muscles,-Viscera, Vessels, and Nerves.

Their study, equally with that of the bones, forms part of the comparative anatomy of Man; but we can only give a brief sketch of the subject.

The anatomy in ordinary use with physicians has been acquired in our dissecting-rooms, on white subjects, of which there is always a plentiful supply. Some few negroes and Mongolians have also been submitted to dissection, but without much attention being paid to the subject. It is only now that this branch of anthropology is beginning to spring into life. We begin to find that there are as many reasons why we should search into the differences which exist in internal organs as into the features of the countenance. Some splendid works on the anatomy of foreign races have already appeared; anatomical variations, supposed anomalies, are no longer passed by as matters of no interest; and

x 2

the laboratory of M. Broca is so arranged as to furnish the amplest
materials for study, and bids fair one day to supply the deficiency
which has been so long experienced. One fact has been already
ascertained—namely, that the muscular system is the seat of
differences: some as to the nature of the characters which we
have termed unimportant; others produced by arrangements which
are found normally in various classes of the mammalia. The
variations exhibited by the cutaneous muscle, the muscles of the
face or of the ears, the adductors of the arm, the rectus abdominis
muscle, the muscles of the hand and foot, the glutei, and the triceps
of the calf of the leg are in this category. Some are even repeated
so frequently in certain individuals of the same race as to lead
us to ask if they are not the normal condition in that race, and
one of its characteristic features. The skeleton of itself recognises the existence of peculiarities of the muscular system, and
exhibits them in default of postmortem examination. Thus the
development of the temporal fossa, in extent and depth, shows
the degree of development of the temporal muscle which was
inserted there; the *femur à colonne* and the channelled fibula of
our ancestors of the Eyzies testify as to the strength and size of
their posterior femoral muscles, and of the external muscles of the
leg. All the internal parts of the body are subject to variety in
different races: the peritoneum, the ileo-cœcal appendix, the liver,
the larynx; and if the small number of cases observed did not lead
us to fear pronouncing as an individual variation one of an ethnic
character, we might mention many examples of them. No doubt
special peculiarities in the internal generative organs will be discovered. Mr. Bakewell at one time thought he had discovered
differences in the blood globules; they were attributable to acclimation. Nevertheless we hope he will continue to prosecute his
inquiries in this direction.*

* See "On the Various Forms of the Glottis," by Gibb, in "Anthrop.
Review," vol. ii., 1864; and "On the Larynx of the Negro," by the same
author, in "Anthrop. Review," vol. iii., 1865; "Dissection of a Bosjesman
Woman," by Flower and Murrie, in "Journ. of Anat. and Physiol.," London,
1867; "Observations d'Anatomie Anthropologique sur le Corps d'un
Nègre," by Kopernicki, in "Revue d'Anthrop.," vol. i., 1872; M. Chud.

The nervous system has been the subject of closer study. Soemmering, and after him Jacquart, demonstrated that the nerves of the negro, particularly those of the base of the brain, are larger than those of the European. It has been ascertained that his cerebral substance is not so white. With regard to the external structure of the brain and its convolutions, no fundamental difference between them has been as yet discovered; which was to be expected, inasmuch as there is none between Man and the anthropoid. Nevertheless there are gradations as regards the richness of the secondary convolutions. The convolutions are larger and less complex in the inferior races. The superior frontal was not unfolded in the Hottentot Venus; the *plis de passage* from the parietal to the occipital lobe are exceptionally less superficial on one side, so that the perpendicular fissure is more visible, and the occipital lobe better marked; there is in fact more or less want of symmetry between the two sides. But these are individual variations, and not characters of race.

The weight of the brain, one would suppose, ought to exhibit differences of a more important character. Nothing of the kind. Individual variations wholly prevail, and necessitate, more than in any other character, our carrying on our investigations upon an extended basis.

Now, if weighing the brain immediately after death had been practised on a sufficiently large scale either in Europe or America, it could hardly have been so in countries inhabited by the inferior races. The process of weighing requires the most minute care, and should, properly, be conducted when the brain is in a fresh state, and not after having been kept in spirit. Thus science has but few materials to work with. These variations depend on age, sex, stature, the disease which was the cause of death, the individual's amount of intelligence, &c. We have referred to this at page 120; we shall confine ourselves therefore to making an approximate

rinck's "Mémoires," already quoted; "De la Valeur des Anomalies Musculaires au Point de Vue d'Anthropologie Zoologique" by Samuel Pozzi, in "Comptes Rendus de l'Assoc. pour l'Avanc. des Sciences," vol. iii., 1874; &c.

estimate of the probable percentage in the form of a table similar to
that of Parchappe.

						Variations in the total weight.
As to sex	...	...	...	...	...	10 per cent.
„ age	...	...	...	...	...	4 „
„ height	...	...	...	...	...	4 „
„ mental disease	...	...	...	...	...	4 to 5 „
„ idiotcy	...	...	...	...	...	18* „
„ last illness	...	...	...	...	...	10 (?) „
„ intelligence	...	...	...	...	...	20 „

This shows that we ought to take brains in precisely identical
conditions, that is to say healthy ones of the same age and the
same sex, and to take care, following Huschke's example, not to
confound the cases of individuals who have died under ordinary
circumstances with those who have died suddenly in sound health,
such as suicides. The difference between them may be as much as
130 grammes, or as great as between the means of a superior and an
inferior race. But an entire security is afforded to the comparison
of the brain in different races by the individual variations, which
are so capricious, and are dependent on so many external circumstances of original or acquired intelligence, or more still on cerebral
activity, whatever its physiological manifestations may be. The
density of the cerebral substance increases probably, as well as
the total volume and richness of the convolutions, by intellectual
activity. The brain of an Australian, superior relatively to his
fellows around him, will be heavier and have more convolutions
than that of a Parisian of mere mediocre intelligence. The
deviation of 20 per cent. in the weight of the brain in the white
race is the difference between the average weight of this race and
that of the brains of Cuvier and Dupuytren. Supposing that these
two cases are anomalies, and reducing the deviation one half, it
would still be 130 grammes. Here, therefore, more than in any
other anthropological character, we must make our calculations
upon large masses, in which individualities are lost. Bearing these

* The average weight of the brain of idiots as taken by Mr. Ouchley
B. Clapham is 1158 grammes in the male, and 1057 in the female.

things in mind, we shall reproduce the following table of weights
of the brain in various races :*

	Men.				Grammes.
106	English and Scotch (Peacock)	...	...	...	1427
23	French (Parchappe)	...	...	...	1364
40	Germans (Huschke)	...	...	...	1382
18	„ (Wagner)	...	...	...	1396
60	Austrians (Wiesbach)	...	...	...	1342
1	Annamite (Broca)	...	...	...	1280
7	African Negroes (various authors)	...	...	1238
8	„ „ (Broca)	...	...	...	1289
1	Negro of Pondicherry (Broca)	...	...	...	1330
1	Hottentot (Wyman)†	...	...	...	1417
1	Cape Negro (Broca)	...	...	...	974

	Women.				
84	English and Scotch (Peacock)	...	...	...	1266
18	French (Parchappe)	...	...	...	1210
22	Germans (Huschke)	...	...	...	1244
13	„ (Wagner)	...	...	...	1209
18	Austrians (Wiesbach)	...	...	...	1160
2	African Negresses (Peacock)	...	...	...	1233
8	„ „ (Broca)	...	...	...	1067
2	Bushwomen (Marshall, Flower, and Marric)	...	974
1	Australian (Owen)	...	...	...	907

* See the "Mémoires" of Parchappe, already quoted ; "Schädel, Hirn, und
Seele des Menschen und der Thiere," by Huschke, Jena, 1854 ; "On the
Weight of the Brain, and the Circumstances affecting it," by J. Thurnam,
in "Journal of Med. Sciences," vol. xii. ; "Contributions towards deter-
mining the Weight of the Brain in different Races of Men," by J. Barnard
Davis, London, 1868 ; "On the Weight of the Brain of the Negro," by
Peacock, in "Mem. Anthrop. Soc., London, vol I., 1863–64 ; "Mémoires,"
by Wagner, Broca, Gratiolet, already quoted, in "Bull. Soc. d'Anthrop.,"
Paris, 1862.

† This exceptional weight in a negro is surpassed by one of M. Broca's
negroes, which is as much as 1500 grammes. May it not be asked whether
the free negro living among Europeans has not a heavier brain than if he
had remained in his own country, far removed from great intellectual excitement ? With regard to Wyman's Hottentot, his stature was 169 centimètres
which is sufficient to show that he was not a Hottentot but a Kaffir, or at
least a half-caste.

We have omitted from this list a series of weights taken during the American war, by Sandifort B. Hunt, which included 405 brains of whites, blacks, and half-castes. Mr. B. Davis finds fault with their author for not having indicated his method of operating. These weights, notwithstanding, are of considerable value for their reciprocal relations.

In the first place, the mean weight of 278 European brains was 1430 grammes; the extremes being 963 and 1842 respectively. This latter was evidently a case of disease, or belonged to some obscure Cuvier. In the second place, the mean weight of 141 negroes was 1331, and the maximum and minimum 1507 and 1013 respectively. The author divides the half-castes into white and black, according to the degree of mixture of breed. It is the method of determining this degree to which exception may be taken. *

							Grammes.
24	Whites	...	...	...	...	...	1424
25	Three parts white...	...	...	...	...	1390
47	Half white, or mulattoes...	...	...	...	1331
52	One quarter white	...	...	...	...	1919
95	An eighth white	...	...	...	...	1305
22	A sixteenth white...	...	...	...	...	1290
141	Pure negroes	...	...	...	...	...	1331

Does not this seem to show that the white blood where it predominates in a mixed breed exercises a preponderating influence in favour of cerebral development, while the inverse predominance of negro blood leaves the brain in a condition of inferiority approaching even that of the pure negro? This would lead us to believe that the mixed breeds assimilate the bad more readily than the good.

In default of being able to obtain direct weights of the brain in sufficient numbers in the various races, we must address ourselves to the cranial capacity. B. Davis, Wiesbach, and Welcker have endeavoured in this way to ascertain the probable weight, and have published long tables on the subject. Mr. Davis makes use, as we all know, of sand in making his calculations. From the total

* "The Negro as a Soldier," by Sandifort B. Hunt, "Anthropological Review," vol. vii., 1869.

weight of sand he subtracts 15 per cent. for the membranes, the
blood of the venous sinuses, and the serous fluid within the cavity
of the cranium. Others consider that 13 per cent. is nearer the
mark. As a matter of fact the waste varies extraordinarily between
one cranium and another.[*]

The specific weight of the dried sand being taken at 1425, and
that of the cerebral substance at 1040 (which also varies), the
calculation is very simple. The following are some results, selected
by Mr. B. Davis, from a list of 133 examples:

			No.		Grammes.		Weight		Grammes.
English	...	...	21	...	1425	...	13	...	1222
Chinese	...	...	25	...	1357	...	8	...	1208
Esquimaux	...	...	6	...	1396	...	6	...	1247
Negroes of Dahomey	...	9	...	1322	...	3	...	1249
Australians	...	...	17	...	1187	...	7	...	1169

M. Wiesbach has confirmed the value of this method. He
obtained the cubic measurement of 115 crania with sand, deducted
from it the probable weight of the brain, and then weighed this
organ. The following was the result, in grammes, in males below
80 years of age:

			Age.		Weight calculated.		Direct weight.		Difference.
5 Crania	...	10 to 19	...	1270·08	...	1225·63	...	45·21
76	"	...	20 „ 29	...	1355·11	...	1341·43	...	13·68
9	"	...	30 „ 59	...	1374·95	...	1330·12	...	44·83
11	"	...	60 „ 80	...	1349·44	...	1241·31	...	108·13

This approximation ought to suffice, for why should we go on
with so complicated a proceeding when, after all, we can only
substitute one figure for another, the relation remaining the same
in the different series? We cannot expect to compare this new
result with the weight obtained directly. One of the most certain
elements of divergence between one man and another is precisely
the density of the cerebral substance, which is here supposed to be
uniform. The operation of Mr. Davis really gives only the relative

[*] In eight negroes M. Broca found a difference of from 8 to 20 per cent.
between the weight of the brain and the cranial capacity.

volume, therefore we may as well confine ourselves to the cranial capacity itself.

Provided that all the conditions for weighing the brain properly are fully complied with, that the influence of the disease of which the individual died is taken into consideration, as well as the hypostatic accumulation of blood in depending parts at the time of death; that some form of wicker receiver is made use of in which to place the brain, for a given time, so as to allow it to drain, &c.— then the difference of weight, according to race, might be ascertained; in the same way, difference in the volume of the cavity, fluids and blood included, may be ascertained by regular cubic measurement. Consequently, until some better method has been suggested, we must rely more upon our tables of cubic measurements (see page 230).

CHAPTER V.

PHYSICAL CHARACTERS IN THE LIVING SUBJECT—ANTHROPOMETRICAL CHARACTERS—PROPORTIONS IN ART—STATURE—MEASUREMENT OF THE HEAD AND BODY.

THE physical characters, deduced from the examination of the internal organs, occupy the highest place in natural history, for the sole reason that the field in which they are displayed is more vast. But anthropologists and naturalists do not on that account neglect those which the external organs manifest, and which invite a much greater amount of attention. Among the latter some have reference to the envelope of the body itself, and its connections; such as the colour of the skin, the character of the hair, and whatever has reference to the external organs of sense and reproduction. They are ascertained by inspection, and are only exceptionally expressed by figures: these then will be our descriptive characters. Others are only the reflex of the internal conformation, and are obtained by systematic measurements: these are anthropometrical characters.

Such are the proportions of the body, which we may think ourselves fortunate—seeing the few opportunities we have of noticing them on the skeleton, and still less on the dead body—to be able to verify upon the living subject, and, even to do this, we have to appeal to the kindness of travellers.

Anthropometrical Characters.   Proportions of the Body.

The sculptors of antiquity were the first to make these their study. Certain canons, that is to say, conventional rules, based no doubt on observation, but more still on individual feeling, were adopted by them. Three of these were recognised among the Egyptians, and one among the Greeks—the famous statue of Polycletus. But they deviated from them according to the conception which they desired to infuse into their work. If they wished to represent a god, as Jupiter, for example, they developed the subject less by a rigorous adherence to nature than by selecting from those around them a form of forehead which suited them the best, or by cunningly bringing the ear lower, by which the facial angle was enlarged; if they aimed at nobleness and grace, the neck was bare, the limbs were made round and slim; if at the sublime, the head, the limbs, and especially the joints, were made larger (*Quételet*). Wide shoulders denoted strength; narrow shoulders youth, or effeminate character; the trunk all of one size, or drawn in at the waist, had also its signification. The pelvis was contracted when it was designed to awaken modest sentiments, or widened when intended to excite feelings of an opposite character. Rigorous exactness was so little sought after by the Greeks that they were not afraid to commit the most egregious errors in anatomy (*Gerdy*), and even to make the limbs unequal. In the Laocoon the left leg is longer than the right, and in one of his sons it is the reverse. The Pythian Apollo and the Venus de Medicis have each one leg longer than the other (*Audran*).

The various schools which have succeeded the Renaissance period have been inspired with the same ideas. In Italy, height of figure was expressive of dignity. In Spain, the figure was reduced in

size with a view to denote delicacy of form. In Holland, it
was made large to illustrate realism. In France, of late, the head
only has been exaggerated, with a view to its exciting greater
attention. The artistic and the anthropological conception therefore
are contradictory the one to the other : the one idealises the beautiful,
the other searches after the true. Art, then, ought to rest upon
anthropology, in that its whims are tolerated, though under the
express condition that they do not go beyond the individual variations which anthropometry reveals to it. If there is no art without
feeling, neither is there any without design and without truth.

It had not occurred to the ancients that there were differences in
the proportions of the various races of mankind, notwithstanding
which, as M. Edwards has remarked, the Greeks set before them
two types, the divine and the heroic. Almost involuntarily, the
Egyptians took as their model two indigenous types, not including
those of negroes and Jews, which figured more particularly among
their prisoners of war. But the sentiment which prevails throughout antiquity, and which is perpetuated throughout the Renaissance
period up to the present time, is, that unity of the human type
corresponds to unity of species. It was this which led Quételet
to affirm that ten individuals of the same age and of the same sex
were ample to exhibit the proportions of the body, and that all
deviations from them were only individual variations.

The opposite doctrine of the plurality of types did not begin to
be delineated until the time of Albert Dürer. Camper aided in
developing it. It is now generally admitted, and we look for the
negro ideal, or the Mongol ideal, as well as for the white ideal. It
is upon this conception that the science of the proportions of bodies,
as ascertained by anthropometry and by the method of averages,
rests. And in the first place let us give the terms of the modern
canon, as taught in the schools of art, where the white is the
standard for the anatomy of the figure, as it is in the dissecting-
rooms for ordinary anatomy.[*]

[*] " Les Proportions du Corps Humain mesurées sur les plus Belles Figures
de l'Antiquité," folio, by Gérard Audran, 1908 ; " Anatomie des Formes
Extérieures du Corps Humain," 8vo., by P. N. Gerdy, Paris, 1869 ; " Types

"The human body is equal to eight lengths of the head, divided thus: from the vertex to the chin, one; from the chin to the nipples, one; from these to the umbilicus, one; from the umbilicus to the genital organs, one; from these to the middle of the thigh, one; from this point to the spine of the tibia, one; from this spine to the middle of the leg, one; from this to the ground, one (*Gerdy*).

"The head is divided into four equal parts: from the vertex to the line of the hair; from this point to the root of the nose; from the root to the base of the nose; from this base to the chin (*Gerdy*).

"The space between the eyes, and the breadth at the base of the nose, are each equal to one length of the eye. The mouth and ear are each equal to two lengths of the eye.

"The length of the head and that of the face (from the line of the hair to the chin) are equal, and form the ninth part of the stature. The length of the foot and the circumference of the clenched fist are equal, and form the sixth part of the stature.

"But these are only approximations, and like all canons are only for the purpose of refreshing the memory. Let us see what the real dimensions are. As in the skeleton, there are two methods of ascertaining the proportions of the body: one consists in comparing the principal parts together, as the superior extremities to the inferior, the forearm to the arm; the other to reduce the dimensions obtained into thousandths of the stature. The latter is the better, and the readiness with which it can be had recourse to is precisely that which gives the advantage of the measurements on living subjects over those of the skeleton. The first thing, therefore, is to ascertain the stature."

Stature.

This is arrived at with difficulty on the skeleton, as we have shown at page 81. On the dead body when laid out straight it

Ethniques représentés par la Sculpture et Proportions du Corps." by Gerdier, in "Bull. Soc. d'Anthrop."; article "Anatomie des Beaux Arts," by Duchenne, in "Encycl. Sc. Méd., 1866; "Anthropométrie," by Quételet, Brussels, 1871; &c.

loses about 13 millimètres. The best way is to take it on the
living subject, which allows of our pursuing our investigations upon
large numbers, in whom the individual variations are lost.

The height or stature varies, like all the dimensions of the
various parts of the human body, according to age, sex, individual
peculiarity, external circumstances, state of previous health, and
race.

At birth man's height is about 50 centimètres, according to
Quételet; at 5 years of age, about 1 mètre; at 15, 1·50 mètre; at
19 years of age he wants 15 millimètres to complete his full height,
which is reached generally at or about 30 years of age, though this
varies. From 50 to 60 years of age the height always decreases,
according to Quételet, and at 90 years of age is less by 7 centimètres.
From our own personal observation we find that this is so almost
universally, and consequently, in order to get at the true stature, we
ought to confine ourselves to individuals beyond 30 years. The
woman is shorter than the man, on the average about 12 centimètres;
that is to say she is 7 per cent. less in height. Consequently, when
we wish to compare the measurements of both directly, we must add
to that of the woman, or deduct from that of the man, 7 per cent.
But this difference varies according to race. It is greater, cæteris
paribus, in tall men, and less in races of low stature. In the
former it reaches an average of 14 centimètres, or 8 per cent.; and
in the latter, 7 centimètres, or 5 per cent. Therefore, according as
we have to do with tall, medium, or short races, we add, when
making the comparison of the woman's with the man's height, 8,
7, or 5 per cent. to her measurement. Between individuals of the
same age, sex, and race, the height varies indefinitely. In fifty-five
series in which we made the comparison, the difference between the
maximum and the minimum was from 9 to 39 centimètres. The
difficulty is to distinguish those which are normal from those which
ought to be looked upon as dwarfs or giants, the transition is so
imperceptible. In more than 1,000,000 American soldiers, five
were above 2·032 mètres, and four below 1·244 mètre; but the
averages are not affected in consequence of this, because the
abnormal cases have in all probability been equally distributed at

the two extremities of the series. The only condition is that the series should be sufficiently numerous. External circumstances have a certain influence on the stature of the individual. Villermé brought forward evidence to show that the stature was much higher previously to the year 1813 in the arrondissements of Paris, in consequence of the prosperous condition of the population. M. Gould also showed that the stature of American sailors is less than that of soldiers of the same race, who were better fed. Drs. Bertrand, Peray, Morillé, and Léques point to poor countries where the stature is low, while close beside them, where the country is rich, it is high. D'Orbigny came to the conclusion, after examining a large number of Southerners of the United States, that the stature decreased with the latitude. Quételet found that in Belgium the townspeople are taller than the countryfolk; and Dr. Beddoe proves the contrary to be the case in England: two facts which may be explained differently by different people. M. Durand (de Gros) states that in chalk districts the inhabitants are taller than in the districts of the primary rocks. But all these matters require further consideration. Sufficient account is not taken of the races which have been intermingled with the population in towns, in a way sometimes the most unexpected, and under a great variety of influences. One of the causes which Dr. Beddoe brings forward, with a view to explain his statement above referred to, is the varied influences which are at work among the population of towns. We should also consider whether the acquired diminution or increase in stature is not purely individual, as well as under what conditions and after how many generations the change would become hereditary and permanent. To the influence of external circumstances, mode of physical existence, and food, may be added that of health. It is absolutely invariable, provided that the morbid agencies are at work before the period when the epiphyses of the long bones are entirely welded to the diaphysis. This period is indicated in the table at page 140, but growth ought still to continue slowly and within certain limits, subsequently to this. The tardy term of thirty years, which we have indicated as one of growth, proves it. We should moreover ascertain if, when the ossification and growth of the skeleton have been suspended, the work does not commence with renewed activity, and thus make up for lost time. The last influence which we shall notice is of more interest to us, namely, that of race. We shall confine ourselves to the male sex, on which our measurements are most usually made, and which furnishes us with examples in abundance. The extreme limit of stature among races, or rather among peoples, varies on the average from 1·40 mètre to about 1·80, which makes the general average 1·60. But tall races are the more numerous, and the two or three whose stature is below the above limit are isolated, and are fast dying out. We may look upon 1·65 as the average stature, taking the entire population of the globe. We in France are thus exhibited in a favourable light, inasmuch as this is precisely our own mean stature.

This being established, races or peoples may be divided into four groups. (1) Very tall, averaging 1·70 mètre and upwards; (2) Those above the middle height, from 1·70 to 1·65 inclusive; (3) Those below the middle height, from 1·65 to 1·60; (4) Those of low stature, below 1·60.

The following averages of stature are extracted from our "Étude" before referred to. They are sometimes those obtained from the traveller himself, sometimes from other sources, varying from 2 to 15. The number of individuals in each series varies from 14 to 30,000. 14 is certainly very few; but in one such as the Veddahs, we may consider ourselves fortunate to be able to give even this number.

MEN (AVERAGES).
Very tall—1·70 and above.

Tehuelches of Patagonia (6 series)	...	...	...	1·751
Polynesians (16 series)	...	...	...	...	1·702
Iroquois Indians (Gould)	...	...	...	...	1·735
Negroes of Galaos (4 series)	...	...	...	1·724
Amazons Kaffirs (Fritsch)	...	...	...	...	1·718
Australians (Topinard)	...	...	...	...	1·719
Scandinavians (3 series)	...	...	...	...	1·718
Scotch (2 series)	...	...	...	...	1·710
English (3 series)	...	...	...	...	1·708
Western Esquimaux (Beechey)	...	...	...	1·708

MEN (AVERAGES).

Above the middle height—from 1·70 to 1·65 inclusive.

Irish (2 series)	1·697
Doomhers and Vadagas of India (Shortt)	1·691
Danes (Hechine)	1·686
Belgians (Quételet)	1·684
Charrus (D'Orbigny)	1·680
Arabs (5 series)	1·679
Singhalese (La Pérouse)	1·678
Guaranis (2 series)	1·677
New Caledonians (Bourgarel)	1·670
Fuegterais of Tierra del Fuego (4 series)	1·664
Kirghis (Prichard)	1·663
Russians (4 series)	1·660
Roumanians (3 series)	1·657
Berbers (3 series)	1·655
Esquimaux, central (6 series)	1·654
Tribes of the east coast of India (3 series)	1·652
Aborigines of the Caucasus (Shortt)	1·650
French	1·650

Below the middle height—from 1·65 to 1·60 inclusive.

Negroes of Algeria (Gillabert d'Hercourt)	1·645
Dravidians and Hindoos (2 series)	1·643
Jews (Schultz)	1·637
Magyars (Bernstein)	1·631
Nicobarians (Navarra)	1·631
Chinese (Navarra)	1·630
British India beyond the Ganges (4 series)	1·622
Araucanians and Botocudos (D'Orbigny)	1·620
Sicilians (Lombroso)	1·618
Fins	1·617
Indo-Chinese (5 series)	1·616
Peruvians (4 series)	1·600

Low stature—below 1·60 exclusive.

Malays (11 series)	1·596
Australians of Port Jackson (Lesson)	1·575
Tribes of Orissa—Indians (3 series)	1·560
Kurumbas of the Nilgherries (Shortt)	1·539
Lapps (2 series)	1·536
Papuans (Mayer)	1·533
Veddahs (Bailey)	1·535
Negritos (4 series)	1·478
Boschismans (3 series)	1·401

Y

The extremes are thus seen to be Patagonians and Bosjesmans. Two series, however, are not in the table, which might show this not to be so. The first, that of Humboldt, who assigns to the Caribs of the Orinoco a height of 1·84 mètre; and the second, that of La Pérouse, which gives the height of the Orotchys of the river Amour as 1·38 mètre. But these extremes have not been confirmed by others, while those of the Patagonians and Bosjesmans have been so by a host of travellers.

In Africa two great negro races are distinguished by their height: one, the Kaffirs scattered at the south-east, and along the west coast of Congo to Senegal, and ... in America, to which they have been wafted by commerce; the other represented by the Bosjesmans to the north of the Orange River, the Obongos of Du Chaillu, and the Akkas of M. Schweinfurth—the first very tall, the last very short. Among those of middle height may be placed Hottentots, which are nearer to the Bosjesmans, and perhaps another negro race in the Sahara zone.

Oceania furnishes also some good examples of stature: on the east, the Polynesians are very tall; on the west, the Malays are short, and the Negritos shorter still; in the centre, the New Caledonians are much above the middle height. The Australians are divided into two races: the one short, which has disappeared; the other tall, which is fast dying out. In Asia the general character is that of low stature, or below the middle height. It decreases in the north in Siberia, and in the south as we approach the Malaccas; increases in the centre, in the Japan Islands, in China, and as we advance towards the Himalayas and Turkistan. In India, particularly, many varieties of stature are to be met with: (a) Tall tribes, some wandering, others settled in the plains at the foot of the Nilgherry Hills and about the north-west angle; (b) Tribes above and about the average, on the east coast; (f) The Dravidians, below the average; (d) Savage tribes, decidedly small; and lastly (e) In the Nilgherries and Ceylon, tribes still smaller, as though the three races had become intermingled: the first, of whose nature we are ignorant, and which is represented by

the Danubes ; the second of Mongolian origin ; the third black, and
probably aboriginal.

In America, at the extreme north, we notice the Esquimaux,
whose stature, we are told, is short in the east of Greenland, increases
as we go west, and is tall in the neighbourhood of Behring's Straits.
The inhabitants of both North and South America are generally
tall, which is not quite in accordance with the usually received
opinion as to the Asiatic origin of Europeans. Two orders of
peoples may be recognised among them, however : the one—and
this constituting the majority—being very tall, from Patagonia to
the River Mackenzie ; the other being below the average height and
thinly scattered, notably in Vancouver's Island, and among the
Crees in the north, and Peru in the south. In Europe the tallest
men are the Norwegians, and the smallest the Lapps and—if we may
include nurseries in our measurements—certain of the ancient
Guanches of the Canaries. In France two varieties of stature are
to be seen : the one very tall, in the north ; the other below the
middle height, in the south.

The stature has only been studied in a direct manner either in
individuals of all ages, or in those who have attained their maximum
of growth. The most numerous statistics in France have reference
to individuals under certain special circumstances, that is to say to
conscripts from 20 to 21 years of age, from which we must subtract
all those below 1·56 mètre, and the infirm. Hence we have two
kinds of averages which these statistics give, namely, the proportion
of those annually rejected, that is to say those of low stature, and
the average height of those remaining. M. Broca has published
them for the whole of France, for each of its Departments, and for
each of the Arrondissements of Brittany. He has given with his
results—which are of the greatest interest—variously-coloured maps.
Boudin, on the other hand, has prepared a map—which is less
exact, but very interesting nevertheless—of the proportionate
distribution of the statures of 1·732 mètre and upwards in the
various Departments. The researches of these two observers have
been corroborated, and show that everywhere the numbers of high

z 2

and low statures are in an inverse ratio, giving at the same time the distribution of the two races to which these extremes correspond.

In fine, the probable average stature, calculated with the greatest care, has varied in France annually, from the year 1836 to 1864, from 1·642 mètre to 1·649 mètre; the general average throughout the twenty-eight years being 1·646. This is somewhat under the mark, however, because the individuals to whom it refers had not reached their maximum. On the other hand, the proportion of conscripts rejected on account of being too short has varied, in the same years, from 101 to 162 per 1000 of those examined throughout the whole of France; and in the Departments, in the entire period, from 24 per 1000 in the Doubs to 147 per 1000 in the Haute-Vienne. The proportion of tall statures leads to the same result; the tallest in France amount to 156 per 1000 conscripts in the Doubs, and the shortest 31·6 in the Haute-Vienne. Now the Doubs, where there are so many tall statures and so few short, is the country of the ancient Burgundians; and the Haute-Vienne, where it is just the reverse, that of the ancient Celts.

At the bottom of the maps in question two distinct zones are drawn, which are separated by an oblique or curved line, going from the Department of the Ain to the bay of St. Malo. On the north and east are the short statures, on the south and west the tall: the former inhabited by the ancient Kymris, Burgundians, and Normans; the latter by the ancient Celts. Here and there, however, in the south and west, are portions of territory where the statures are tall. This is so in the neighbourhood of Toulouse, where the Volkian Tectosages of the race of the Kymris located themselves; and along the banks of the Rhone and the shores of the Mediterranean, where there was a constant interchange between the Gauls on the north and the cisalpine Gauls. The map of Brittany shows the tall statures predominating in the north, along the coast where the Bretons, the ancient Belgian Kymris, landed from the island of Albion about the fifth century of our era; and the low statures in the south and in the centre, where the Celts were previously repulsed.

Similar statistics of stature have been published in other

countries, as Italy, Spain, Bavaria, which have led us to the conclusion that the stature increases generally in Europe from the
north to the south, the two extreme points being represented by
Norway and the islands of the Mediterranean, not taking into
account the Lapps and the Fins, which form a distinct group.
Apropos of stature, a particular method has been employed which
many prefer to that of averages generally in use in craniometry,
namely, the method of seriation, in which the individual figures are
arranged in a scale, in groups from the minimum to the maximum,
and the number of times noted that they are repeated in each
group. Generally there is a regular increase from the extremities
of the series towards the centre, where the character is found expressed, not in the form of an average, but of a "medium." Sometimes there are two centres or two medians. M. Bertillon explains
them by the mingling, without the complete fusion, of two races
of opposite characters. Thus in the Doubs, where the position of
the stature in the series gives rise to two medians, one to 1·635
and the other to 1·732, the former would answer to the ancient
Celtic Sequanians, the latter to the ancient Burgundians. This
method, which indicates particularly the extent of individual
variations, is very much adopted in England, and has been maintained on the Continent by Quételet and Bertillon.[*]

Having now considered the stature, we may pass on to the
measurement of the several parts of the body. The methods
employed are similar to those in use for the skeleton, modified
according to the accessibility of the measuring points (points de
repère). We shall confine ourselves to the most important—to those
which travellers are recommended to adopt—and shall commence
with the head.

Measurement of the Head.

Here, as upon the skull, the measurements to be employed are
of three orders, namely—(a) By straight lines, which we take

[*] "De la Méthode en Anthropologie," in "Bull. Soc. d'Anthrop.," vol. iv., 1863; and article "Moyenne," in "Encyclopédie des Sciences Médicales," by M. Bertillon.

with the callipers and the sliding compass, and by curves, which
require the measuring-tape ; (b) By projections, which are taken
with the double square ; (c) By nught: cubic measurements of course
are not made use of. The following is a list of those measurements
which are absolutely necessary to be taken, and the figures are
those which we have recently obtained from an examination of a
Chinese of 23 years of age :

Maximum antero-posterior diameter, as on the skeleton, from the glabella to the maximum posterior point	196 mill.
Maximum transverse diameter, as on the skeleton, above the ears	·150 ,,
Length of the face from the inter-superciliary point to the superior alveolar point, between the middle incisor teeth, at their neck ...	91 ,,
Bizygomatic, or maximum transverse facial diameter	160 ,,
Height of the vertex above the ground (stature)	1·620 cent.
,, ,, auditory meatus	1·457 ,,
,, ,, chin	1·373 ,,
Distance from the auditory meatus to the posterior plane	87 mill.
Distance from the inter-superciliary point to ditto	192 ,,
,, ,, of the superior alveolar point to do.	227 ,,
Frontal minimum, as on the skeleton	103 ,,

The first two measurements give the cephalic index on the
living subject, which we must take care not to confound with
that of the cranium. M. Broca found [*] in nineteen subjects which
he measured, a difference in the former varying from – 0·66 to
+ 5·09, or an average of 1·68, which he attributes to the thickness
and resistance of the soft parts, by which each diameter is increased,
the transverse especially. He thinks that this difference ought to
be greater on the living subject, and comes to the conclusion that,
as a general rule, we should subtract two units from the index of
the living subject to get that of the cranium. The index in forty-

[*] " Comparaison des Indices Céphaliques sur le Vivant et sur le Squelette,
by M. Broca, in " Bull. Soc. d'Anthrop.," 2nd series, vol. III., 1868.

seven Basques from the neighbourhood of St. Jean de Luz, measured by M. Argelliès, being 83·1, it would be 81·1 on the cranium.

The following are examples of the cephalic index from various authors:

20	Negritos of Luçon (Micklocho-Macley)	...	88·6 (?)
300	Auvergnians (Durand (de Gros))	... ...	84·6
423	Bretons of the interior (Gaibert)	... ...	84·9
443	„ „ east „	... ...	83·0
8	Fins (Beddoe)	... ...	83·7
10	Ruthenians, or Little Russians (Kopernicki)	...	81·6
36	Danes (Beddoe)	... ...	80·5
10	English „	... ...	78·1
38	Swedes „	... ...	78·8
180	Berbers (various authors)	... ...	79·7
47	Arabs „	... ...	78·3
7	Dravidians (Rowland)	... ...	75·6
6	Black Mundas of India (Rowland)	... ...	75·6

The next two measurements in the list give the facial angle of M. Broca, that is to say, the relation of the simple length of the face to its bizygomatic breadth; the differences as regards this index on the living subject have not yet been determined.

A third index is the relation of the vertical projection of the head, expressed by the difference between the height of the vertex and the height of the chin to the same bizygomatic breadth. This is the general index of the head. (See p. 274.) It corresponds with that which travellers express by the terms "long head," or "broad head," "long face," or "broad face." If we take the length of the face as = 100, it is because it has been so taken in the ordinary facial index. The last six measurements are by projections in relation, not to the alveolo-condylean, or true horizontal plane of the skull, whose measuring points are out of reach, but to the plane of Camper, that is to say to the line passing over the auditory meatus and the base of the nares, which is the only convenient one, the one most easy to determine on the living subject. With the table at page 267, which gives the inclination of this plane in relation to the alveolo-condylean, it will always be possible to convert the projections, and even the angles relating to them, into equivalent measurements on the skull.

The general method of proceeding is shown in Fig. 39. The individual is in an upright position against a wall, upon which a measuring-tape or a graduated rule is applied, whose zero is on the ground. The head looks straight forward, so that the horizontal line of Camper, passing across the auditory meatus and the base of the nares, is exactly perpendicular to the wall. A large sliding-square is moved up or down until the various measuring

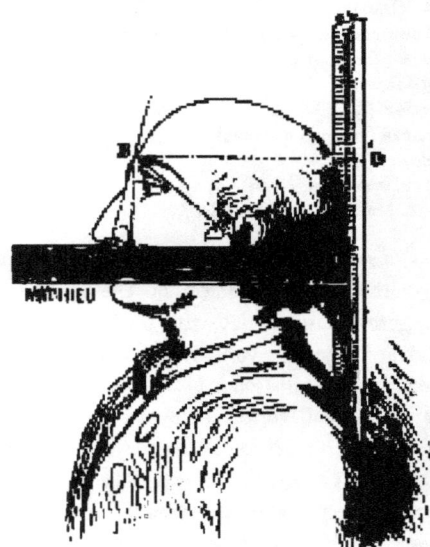

Fig. 39.—Position for taking projections of the head on the living subject. The line passing across the auditory meatus and the base of the nares, or Camper's line, represented by the upper border of the square, is exactly horizontal; that is to say perpendicular to the posterior plane. A D, Projection of the entire head; B D = B D, The projection of the entire cranium; C D, Projection of the posterior cranium; C E, Projection of the anterior cranium; A E, Projection of the nasal and supra-nasal portions of the face.

points, such as the top of the head, auditory meatus, &c., are reached; a second, smaller one, at right angles, is applied upon it at the measuring points which are otherwise inaccessible, as the supra-orbital, the alveolar, the mental points, &c. The heights above the ground are read off on the wall; and on the sliding-square, which is graduated, the horizontal distances in front of the posterior plane, these distances being directly visible, or indicated by the heel of the smaller square. In Fig. 39 the small square, which is held in the hand, has been left out so as not to interfere with the drawing. Should the posterior part of the head not touch the wall, something must be intervened, the thickness of which must be deducted from each horizontal measurement. It is absolutely necessary that during the various measurements the individual should be motionless, and that the auriculo-sub-nasal line determined by the large sliding-square should be perfectly horizontal. All the principal elements of the proportions of the head are then obtained: namely, the vertical projection of the entire head; the horizontal projection of the skull (B D′, Fig. 39); the particular projections of the posterior cranium (C D); of the anterior (H C); and of the nasal and supra-nasal portion of the face. In the same way we get the elements of the facial angle of Camper; that is to say the line H C, the line A H, the perpendicular B H to their intersection H, and consequently the position of the point B. We have then only to draw the triangle on paper and measure the angle D A C with the protractor.

It is needless to say that by this method of the double square in combination with the attitude indicated, we may take a number of other projections, according to the object we have in view. (Fig. 40.)

Other measurements in connection with the face are not without interest. Thus there are three for the nose, of which we shall speak when giving the descriptive characters of this organ. There are also several for the mouth, the eyes, and the ears. Subjoined are some obtained by Quételet on Belgians of the male sex, from 25 to 30 years of age, which may be usefully compared with those given at page 317. The stature is taken as = 100.

From the vertex to the line of the hair		...		...		2·5
„	line of the hair to the root of the nose		...			4·0
„	root of the nose to its base			...		8·0
„	base of the nose to the chin		...			3·2
Total from the vertex to the chin (head)		...				13·7
Length of the eye		...	...	...	...	...	1·6
Breadth between the eyes		...	...	...	...	2·4
„	of the nose at the base		...	...		2·1
Length of the mouth		...	...	...	...	...	3·2
„	„	ear	...	...	...	...	...	3·7

These are manifestly at variance with those laid down by Art, and we have been obliged to give them approximately only. But they refer exclusively to Belgians, and it would be necessary that the same proportions should be established with reference to all races as well as to their individual variations. Then artists should know the physiological limits beyond which they ought not to go.

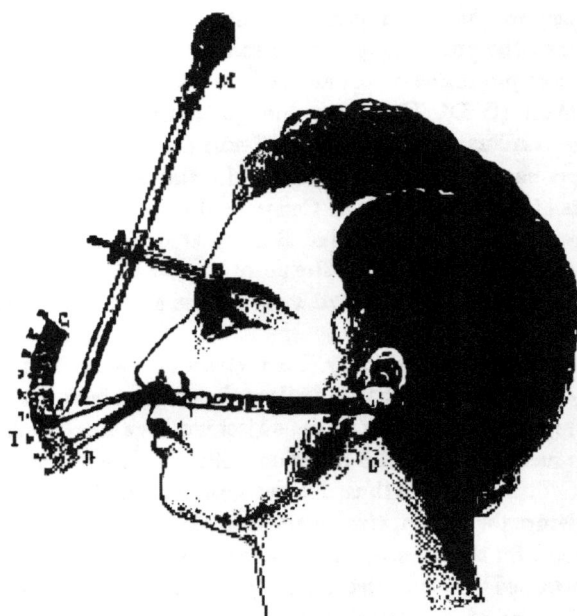

Fig. 46.—Median facial goniometer of M. Broca, in position for taking the facial angle of Jacquart, whose apex is at the subnasal point. The two circular pins, O, being in plum, the point A being on the superior alveolar point, and the branch H B being placed in its proper position, the instrument also gives the angle of Cloquet.

To speak only of the head: Gerdy asserts that its measurement is commonly limited to 1·11 and 1·33 per cent. of the stature : but he made his measurements in Paris, where there is a mixture of long and short heads ; while Quételet made them upon individuals of the Kymri race, that is to say on the long heads, proving the numerous types of proportions.

Measurement of the Body.

Measurements of the head and body so nearly correspond that, subject to certain corrections, we may generally make a direct comparison between them. It is not so with those of the body alone, which often differ altogether from those of the skeleton. Owing to the necessity there is to appeal to the kindness of travellers, and those sometimes not the most experienced, the *Instructions* generally prescribe, not the most logical measuring points, but those which are most easily found.

Thus in the wrist, in default of the articular line, the exact position of which requires some surgical knowledge, we require the point of the styloid process. At the inferior extremity of the humerus, in default still of the line of separation between it and the radius, we take the epicondyle. At the knee, in default of the same line of separation between the tibia and femur, most people are satisfied with the centre of the patella.

In order, therefore, that anthropometry on the living subject may be as practically useful as possible, it is necessary to have rules for converting the simple measurements recommended, into strictly anatomical ones. For example, by adding seven millimetres to the length of the hand, we should have its true length on the skeleton; by subtracting twelve millimetres from the length of the leg, stretched out in obedience to the *Instructions*, we get the length of the tibia without the malleolus; that is to say such as we make it in our calculations for determining the proportions of the skeleton. Again, one of the principal objections to the measurement of the thigh, or of the entire lower limb, is our inability to take its true upper extremity, that is to say the head of the femur, which lies out of reach in its cavity. In default of this we have occasionally taken the anterior superior spine of the ilium, the great trochanter, the pubis, and the perinæum; but it would not be difficult to correct these measurements. A series of investigations—which we do not put forward as being strictly accurate—have led us to think that in the adult European of the male sex and of

middle height, these various points and the head of the femur may
be arranged in the following order: From the spine of the ilium to
the head of the femur, 6 centimètres; from this to the great
trochanter, 2·3; from the great trochanter to the pubis, 2·0; from
the pubis to the perinæum, 4·7. The following are the rules for
converting each of the measurements of the thigh, or of the
entire limb, into anatomical measurements of the femur:

			Millimètres.
Commencing from the spine of the ilium, subtract	...	60
"	"	great trochanter, add...	...	23
"	"	pubis, add	...	...	43
"	"	perinæum, add...	...	90

These dimensions answer for statures of 1·650 millimètre. When
the individual or the race is taller or shorter, by a simple rule-of-
three sum we get the proportionate amount which should be added
or subtracted. Independently of the measuring points, which it is
recommended to look for, and to mark with coloured chalk before
commencing our operations, the calculation of the anthropometrical
measurements is simple enough. The individual is placed with his
back against a wall, in the same way as for the measurement of the
head, in the attitude of a soldier standing at attention, the feet
together, the arms hanging down, with the hands extended on the
thigh. By the double square we then take the height of each point
above the ground. The least asymmetry of the body, the slightest
separation of the limbs or unevenness of the hips would give rise to
considerable mistakes. The difference between the length of the arm
in the above attitude, and of the same in complete abduction, may be
as much as two or three centimètres, which arises from the head
of the humerus sinking deep into the armpit, and shortening the
limb that much. In the lower extremity, when the superior point
is taken from the pelvis, the difference is still greater. The em-
ployment of a tape for directly measuring the exact distance from
one point to another, by following the contour of the limb, is inexact;
the line is not only oblique, but also convex, owing to the projection
of the muscles; two causes which contribute to elongate it. The
following are the most important measurements recommended in the

" Instructions de la Société d'Anthropologie," and the corresponding
dimensions obtained by M. Gillebert d'Hercourt on eighteen Arabs and
ten negroes of Algeria.   To obtain the length of a part, one measure
must be subtracted from another.   The height of the epicondyle
being 1087 millimètres in the negro, and that of the styloid process
of the radius 795, the forearm will be 262 millimètres; which relatively to the total height will be expressed by 189·2, and would
then be compared with the same value in the Arab.

Height above the ground.					18 Arabs.		21 Negroes.
From the vertex (stature)	...	...	...	...	1·680	...	1·646
„ acromion (empula)	...	...	...	...	1·374	...	1·366
„ epicondyle (external tuberosity of the humerus at its inferior border)				...	1·087	...	1·087
„ styloid process of the radius	...	...	...	0·801	...	0·795
„ inferior extremity of the middle finger	...	0·619	...	0·601
„ great trochanter (superior border)	...	...	0·877	...	0·875
„ articular interspace of the knee (outside)	...	0·464	...	0·456
„ internal malleolus (point)	...	...	...	0·780	...	0·740
Breadth.							
Grande envergure	...	...	...	...	...	1·757	...	1·704
From one acromion to the other (point)	...	...	0·373	...	0·372
„ the crest of one ilium to the other (maximum)	0·261	...	0·255
Length of foot	...	...	...	...	...	...	0·269	...	0·253

We may add two other measurements, on account of their sim-
plicity and readiness of application.   The first is the length of the
trunk, one of the most important in anthropometry to determine.
We take the distance from the prominent spinous process of the
seventh cervical vertebra to the point of the sacrum or coccyx; or
that of the clavicle, or the sternal fourchette, to the pubis or
perinæum: but these present some difficulties.   By following the
" Instructions de la Société d'Anthropologie," this measurement is
indirectly obtained in many ways.   The method we recommend is
direct, and is easy of application among savages, who are not
frightened by it.   The second measurement was devised by the
Americans during the War of Secession, and was suggested by a
well-known comparison (see page 86) which Mr. Huxley makes
between Man and the anthropoids.   These measurements are : The

height of the fourchette of the sternum above the ground, the individual being seated on the ground with the trunk upright, and breathing quietly :

The distance of the extremity of the middle finger in the ordinary vertical attitude from the upper border of the patella, the muscles of the thigh being flaccid. Now let us proceed to the application :

The relative height of the head, of the length of the neck, and the height of the trunk, to the stature, are the three primary elements of the proportions of the body which we have to determine. Setting aside the essential proportions of the head and the pelvis, we shall presently have to speak of the dimensions of the various parts of the trunk. Then come the proportions of the extremities. There are two methods by which we may at once ascertain the relative length of the upper extremities: namely, the *grande envergure* (see page 84), and the distance from the middle finger to the patella.

The *grande envergure* is taken with two squares, the back of the individual resting against a wall. The following are some of its averages relatively to stature = 100 :

10,876	American soldiers (Gould)	...	...	...	101·8
908	English (Gould)	...	...	...	...	101·4
51	Scotch	,,	...	...	...	101·0
827	Irish	,,	...	...	...	101·6
663	Germans	,,	...	...	...	106·3
2020	Negroes	,,	...	...	...	106·1
869	Mulattoes	,,	...	...	...	108·1
817	Iroquois Indians (Gould)	...	...	...	108·9
30	Belgians (Quételet)	...	...	...	...	104·6
20	Berbers (various authors)	...	...	...	104·2
27	Arabs	,,	...	...	...	101·3

It follows then that the envergure is manifestly greater than the stature, except in individual cases, where it is frequently less, and also that it is notably greater in negroes, mulattoes, and Iroquois Indians, than in whites; this arising from the length of their upper extremities.

The distance from the middle finger to the patella is given in the four following series of Mr. Gould, the stature = 100 :

10,876 American soldiers	...	...	...	...	7·49
617 Iowpools Indians	...	...	...	...	5·36
2050 Negroes	...	...	...	...	4·57
868 Mulattoes	...	...	...	...	6·12

The more the distance diminishes in these cases, the greater is the length of the upper extremities. The arm then is shortest in whites, longest in negroes, and intermediate in length in mulattoes. This verifies Mr. Humphry's statement that the upper extremities of the skeleton of the negro are longer than those of the European. Now this result is clear from the above statistics, and does not vary in any of the seventeen series of whites and the eight of negroes of which they are composed. Frequently, in the latter, the extremity of the middle finger touched the patella; once it was twelve millemètres below its upper border, as in the gorilla.

With respect to the proportions of the extremities, there are three relations which have specially engaged the attention of authors: (1) That of the superior to the inferior extremity apart from the hand and foot; (2) That of the forearm to the arm; and (3) That of the leg to the thigh. We shall select some examples from the Novarra measurements, which were made by very experienced physicians, and on races very dissimilar to one another. There is only one fault to be found with them—namely, that they were taken with the measuring-tape:

	Forearm and arm to leg and thigh.		Forearm to arm.		Leg to thigh.
30 Germans	80·9	...	80·5	...	99·4
20 Slavs	80·7	...	86·8	...	89·8
10 Roumanians	68·4	...	89·3	...	99·4
26 Chinese	76·6	...	84·5	...	101·1
54 Nicobarians	70·2	...	83·8	...	111·1
8 Javanese	73·5	...	86·4	...	107·0
3 New Zealanders	75·9	...	85·9	...	96·6
1 Australian	78·3	...	90·3	...	109·0

This shows: (a) That in the first relation there are very decided differences, the three series of whites having the upper extremity relatively short, the three other series, especially the New Zealanders and the Australian, relatively long; (b) That the proportion between the forearm and the arm, contrary to what we should have expected, does not show any very sensible difference, except in the Australian, where the forearm is the longer, as in the African negro ; (c) That the relation of the leg to the thigh is found to possess great importance, the leg being short in the three series of whites and in the New Zealanders, and long in the others, except the Australian. We see the contrast between the New Zealanders and the Australian ; the latter being similar in all the three relations, if we accept Dr. Humphry's opinion as to the tibia, the former only being so as regards his upper extremity, and approaching the European as to his forearm and leg.

The proportions of the foot and hand will now engage our attention. In the following averages, the stature being = 100, the square has been employed by M. Gillebert d'Harcourt and others, and the tape by M. Wiesbach, of the *Novarra*, by Quételet and Bourgerel. We need not, however, take any account of the slight differences in consequence.

	Hand.		Foot.
10 Kouronglis of Algeria (Gillebert d'Harcourt)	9·9	...	14·2
10 Negroes of Algeria	10·8	...	16·3
27 Arabs of Algeria (various authors)	11·1	...	15·4
86 Berbers (various)	11·1	...	15·4
50 Belgians (Quételet)	11·5	...	15·4
20 Germans (*Novarra*)	12·8	...	16·1
20 Slavs	12·7	...	15·2
10 Roumanians	11·6	...	14·8
26 Chinese	12·8	...	16·9
58 Nicobarians	15·1	...	16·2
28 Todas, a superior tribe of the Nilgherries (Shortt)	11·8	...	16·1
80 Aborigines, inferior tribes of the Nilgherries (Shortt)	10·8	...	16·8
12 New Caledonians	12·6	...	15·6
10,876 White soldiers (Gould)	12·8	...	16·9
2020 Negroes	12·9	...	16·0
863 Mulattoes	12·9	...	16·7
617 Iroquois Indians	12·8	...	14·5

What conclusion are we to draw from this ? In the first place, that the hand and the foot of man, although shorter than those of the anthropoid ape, do not vary among races according to their order of superiority, as we should have supposed. A long hand or foot is not a characteristic of inferiority. One would say that the Germans and Slavs of M. Wieslach have a hand larger and more simian in character than the negroes of Algeria, and more nearly resembling that of the negroes of Oceania. Of the two distinct tribes inhabiting the Nilgherries, in Southern India, the inferior has the smaller hand. As regards the foot, it is true the negroes of America are between the whites and the anthropoids in the same way as mulattoes are between them and whites. We are unable to form any definite opinion on this point with respect to the Boskesman, the Negrito, and the Australian, from lack of documentary evidence. It seems that the Australian has the usual-sized hand, while the foot is extraordinarily long.

In default of a general character, this measurement gives us a special differential character between certain races. The Nicobarians have both upper and lower extremities very powerfully developed. The Arabs and Berbers have the same average hand, but the foot of the former is small, while that of the latter is large. The hand of the Koroughis is remarkably small, and the foot of the Todas monstrously large. It is curious to compare the two general averages of the same proportions of the stature as recognised in the Arts, which are expressed below in hundredths. That of Albert Dürer, it appears, was the nearest in results to our own.

					Hand.		Foot.
Our general average	...	...	...	...	11·7	...	15·4
Greeks	...	...	...	...	10·9	...	14·0
Vitruvius	...	...	...	...	10·0	...	16·7
Albert Dürer	...	...	...	...	11·1	...	15·2
Shadow	...	...	...	...	10·6	...	15·2
Caron	...	...	...	...	10·5	...	15·9
Gerdy	...	...	...	...	11·1	...	16·8

We are met at the commencement of our study of the proportions of the body with the fact that they differ considerably in each race, without the superiority of rank which such race takes enabling us to guess the meaning of such differences. Each race, M. Wiesbach says, has its share of characteristics of inferiority, and

the resemblance to the ape is not confined to any race in particular.
It is true that the learned anthropologist of the *Navarra* refers to
the proportions of the orang, and the question is whether some
races approximate in these to certain anthropoids and others to
others. It is certain that there are human types which differ in
the proportions of the skeleton, but these are not yet settled.

Besides the measurements of length, there are those of breadth,
and those of volume as estimated by the circumference. Thus (*a*) The
relation of the breadth of the foot and hand to their length (this
breadth being taken, in both cases, by projection with the square
commencing from the head of the fifth metatarsal or metacarpal
bone, and crossing the great axis of the organ at a right angle;
(*b*) The relation of the maximum breadth of the hips, at a level
with the great trochanter, to the maximum breadth of the pelvis
over the crests of the ilia; (*c*) The corresponding relation, at the
other extremity of the trunk, of the maximum breadth of the
shoulders at the external surface of the deltoid muscle to the
biacromial breadth; (*d*) The relation of these various diameters with
the breadth of the thorax from one armpit to the other (taken with
two squares).

The biacromial breadth, the measuring points of which are more
anatomical, has been measured with the tape, by passing it in front
of and behind the neck, and with the double square. Subjoined are
some averages obtained by the only exact method of proceeding.

		Stature = 100.
18 Arabs (Gillebert d'Hercourt)	... ...	21·1
13 Kabyles „	... ...	22·7
15 Negroes of Algeria (Gillebert d'Hercourt)	...	22·6
27 Annamites (Mondière)	... ...	21·0
14 „ women (Mondière)	... ...	20·4

In order to show the differences between them, we give the same
measurement by the tape.

		Stature = 100.
25 Belgians (Quételet)	... ...	23·4
25 „ women (Quételet)	... ...	22·0
25 Chinese (Navarra)	... ...	26·2
9 Javanese „	... ...	24·0
6 „ women (Navarra)	... ...	23·6

It will be observed that in the Belgians, the Javanese, and the Annamites, the biacromial diameter is smaller in the woman.

The circumferences are generally bad measurements, because they vary according to the development of the muscles, the fat, and the subjacent organs.   Moreover, the relation of the maximum circumference of certain articulations with those of the maximum enlargements of the parts situated above and below, shows whether the articulations are large or small. The relations of the minimum circumferences at the bottom of the leg, and the maximum above, gives the development of the calf, which is a characteristic of superiority in the white race relatively to the negro races, whose spindle leg resembles that of apes. The relation of the circumference of the hips or the chest with the circumference at the waist marks all the intermediate gradation between the wasp figure (*taille de guêpe*) of the women, and the trunk all of a size (*tronc tout d'une venue*) of the man in general and of the Andaman race in particular (*De Quatrefages*).

The circumference of the chest has received a considerable amount of attention, but more in reference to the capacity of the pulmonary cavity according to race.   It has an interest not only for art and for anthropology, but also for medicine, as a diagnostic of disease.   We shall again refer to this later on, when speaking of physiological characters.[*]

[*] See, for the measurements on living subjects, "Des Races de l'Océanie Française," by A. Bourgarel, in "Mém. Soc. d'Anthrop.," vol. ii., 1861; "Reise der Oesterreichischen Fregatte Novarra um die Erde in den Jahren 1857–59," "Anthropologischer Theil," by Drs. Scherzer, Schwartz, and Weisbach, Wien, 1867 ; "Investigation on American Soldiers," by B. Gould, New York, 1869; "L'Anthropométrie," by Quételet, Brussels, 1870; "Études sur Soixante-seize Indigènes de l'Algérie," by Gillebert d'Hercourt, in "Mém. Soc. d'Anthrop.," vol. iii.; "Rapport sur la Mensuration des Cent Indigènes de Biskra by Dr. Bériziat," by Dr. Topinard, in "Bull. Soc. d'Anthrop.," 2nd series, vol. v., 1870; "Sur les Kabyles du Djurjura," by Duhousset, in "Mém. Soc. Ethn.," 1872; "Note sur l'Anthropologie de la Race Annamite," by A. T. Mondières, in "Mém. Soc. d'Anthrop.," 2nd series, vol. i., 1878; &c.

CHAPTER VI.

DESCRIPTIVE CHARACTERS—COLOUR OF THE SKIN, EYES, AND HAIR
—CHARACTERS OF THE HAIR—PHYSIOGNOMY—FORM OF THE
FACE, NOSE, MOUTH, AND EARS—EXTERNAL GENITAL ORGANS—
TABLIER AND STEATOPYGA.

Descriptive Characters.

THE white races personally studied by anthropologists constituting
only a fraction of the human family, the description of outward
characters comes to us principally from travellers: they furnish the
details which we embody.   But accompanying their descriptions,
traced as they may be with a masterly hand, we too frequently find
simple detached phrases which must be explained, respecting which
opinions, varying according to the mood of the individual, have
been substituted for plain facts.   A traveller arrives in the midst
of a savage tribe, and depicts it in colours of the most hideous
kind; as he proceeds with his account, having become familiarised
with it, he looks at it in quite another light: the two descriptions
are at variance with one another.   One could hardly imagine the
contrary impressions given by the nude, hunchbacked, shambling
savage, like the Australians of Port Royal, which Péron and
Dumont d'Urville met with, and the same bold and menacing
creature, with head erect and cambered loins, armed with his
shield and lance.   You look at the former as a most disgusting
object, with his thin and lean and disproportionate limbs, and his
forbidding countenance; at the latter as the very impersonification
of the ancient gladiator, whose figure recalls the most beautiful
antique marbles.   This kind of contradiction, as found in the
traveller's diary, is not confined to individuals of the same race:
the Bosjesmans, the Esquimaux, the people of Tierra del Fuego,
come in for their share.   As regards the female it is worse still.
According to the mental impression created at the time, one will
be represented as having hideous simian features, another, of the

same age and of the same tribe, as having a pleasing countenance. The Bosjesman woman produces this kind of impression upon the European. Hence the anthropologist's earnest desire to be furnished with definite facts, and not with exaggerated descriptions.

In matters of detail it is the same, and one is deceived even as regards prognathism, the form of the nose, the colour of the skin, and the character of the hair. There is no doubt that the appellation "aquiline" has been given to flat noses, which when looked at in profile exhibited a slight convexity. It is thus that in Australia all imaginable types, even the Caucasian, have been described. After a most attentive perusal of accounts given of the hair, in which even its physical characters have not been neglected, we are often obliged to pause to inquire whether the hair, which has been spoken of a dozen times, is straight or woolly. Humboldt mentions that to those who had newly arrived in South America, all the Indians seemed to be alike, but that after a certain time their diversity of feature appeared as remarkable as among Europeans. In estimating colour, the most egregious errors are committed. In the midst of blacks the mulatto would appear white. It is not that the traveller is deceived in this matter; but he gradually alters his opinion, and his estimate from being relative becomes absolute. The French people look upon the English as fair, but they consider themselves dark; this is because the French compare the English with themselves, and we compare ourselves with inhabitants of the north. Dr. Beddoe has especially drawn attention to this kind of error. Dr. Livingstone, referring to the negroes of the coast, continually speaks of those to the west of Lake Tanganyka, and especially Cazembe, as having fair skin, but slight prognathism, and a Caucasian nose; in short, with as fine heads as are to be found among Europeans. For these numerous sources of error, we do not say for the practised anthropologist, but for the ordinary traveller, there is but one remedy, namely, not to trust to his own impressions, but to confine himself to making use of tables for the colour of the skin as well as for the hair, and as far as possible for measurements. The index of breadth of the nose gives us more information on the subject than all the roundabout descriptions. We return therefore to the anthropological instructions, circulated by various societies and printed in many languages.[*]

Lumbo-Sacral Ensellure.

Among the descriptive characters, some are only supplementary to the observations of the preceding chapter on the proportions of the body. (a) The development of the muscles, or of the fat, when it is peculiar to the race and not to the individual; (b) The development of the region of the buttocks, of which we shall speak presently; (c) The development of the abdomen, which may sometimes be a character of race, but is most frequently caused by living habitually on vegetable food, and by irregular diet; thus, savages go many days without food, or nearly so, and then for twenty-four or forty-eight hours gorge themselves to repletion; (d) Lastly, the degree of inflection of the two spinal curvatures, the one the lumbo-sacral, to which Duchenne de Boulogne gives the name ensellure; the other dorsal, each being compensatory to the other. The former, having the concavity posteriorly, is enlarged in certain races, and diminished in others. " I have seen," says Duchenne de Boulogne, " Spanish ladies whose lumbar incurvation was such, and the movement of the lumbar muscles so extensive, that they were able to throw themselves backwards so as almost to touch the ground.' He has met with the same thing among the women of Lima, and of Portel, near Boulogne.

Colour of Skin, Hair, and Eyes.

The colour of the skin, hair, and eyes is the result of a general phenomenon in the organism, namely, the production and distribu-

---

[*] See "Instructions Générales adressées aux Voyageurs," in " Mém. Soc. Eth. de Paris," vol. i., 1841; "Instructions Générales de la Soc. d'Anthrop. de Paris," drawn up by M. Paul Broca, Paris, 1865, 2nd edition in the press; "Notes and Queries on Anthrop.," published by the British Association for the Advancement of Science, London, 1874; "Anleitung zu Wissenschaftlichen Beobachtungen auf Reisen," Berlin, 1875, the anthropological portion by R. Virchow; "Instructions Générales aux Voyageurs" of the Geographical Society of Paris, 1875, anthropological portion by M. de Quatrefages.

tion of the colouring matter. The skin of the Scandinavian is white, almost without colour, or rather rosy and florid, owing to the transparency of the epidermis allowing the red colouring matter of the blood to be seen circulating through the capillaries. After haemorrhage or in anaemia, the amount of globules, which is normally rather over twelve per cent., may descend to two per cent., the smallest known ; the blood has then lost five-sixths of its colouring matter ; the surface of the body becomes pallid and has a waxy tint.

The skin of the negro of Guinea, and especially of Yoloff, the darkest of all, is, on the contrary, jet black, which is caused by the presence in the minute cellules on the deep surface of the epidermis of black granules, known by the name of pigment. The black layer thus formed by these cellules, which used to be called the *rete mucosum* of Malpighi, remains adherent sometimes to the dermis and sometimes to the epidermis on removing the latter, after previously submitting the skin to maceration. This pigment is found in all races, whether black, yellow, or white, but in very different quantity ; hence their various tones of colour, from the lightest to the darkest. Whites, who readily become brown on exposure to light, are undoubtedly provided with it. It is always more abundant in the scrotum and round the nipple. It is very visible on the mucous membranes of negroes, which are frequently surrounded by masses of it, notably on the vault of the palate, the gums, and the conjunctiva, which we have also met with in young orangs. The same pigment is found in all races on the internal surface of the choroid, sometimes in the lungs, and, among negroes, in the brain. The colouring matter of the hair resembles it very much. The disease described at page 161, under the name of "albinism," is owing to its diminished quantity in the skin, as well as in the choroid and in the hair. It may be seen in all races, but it is necessarily more observable in those in which the pigment is more abundant. Besides the red colouring matter of the blood, and the black colouring matter of the skin and the choroid, we must mention a third, biliverdin, which is secreted in the liver, and to which the yellow colour of the tissues in jaundice is due. This also gives the yellowish colour of the cellulo-adipose tissue, of the muscles, and of the blood, which is so often met with when making autopsies of negroes. In not this colouring matter a transformation, an altered condition of the colouring matter of the blood, or of the pigment? Chemists must answer the question. We may remark that the shades of colour in the mixed breeds, between the negro and the white, partake more of the yellow than the red tint.

The last vestiges of a mixture of breed returning towards the white, are the yellow colour of the sclerotic, and the lunula of the nails: the latter sign is well known among American Creoles.

There are then three fundamental elements of colour in the human organism; namely, the red, the yellow, and the black, which, mixed in variable quantity with the white of the tissues, give rise to those numerous shades seen in the human family, which it would be impossible to enumerate. We may, however, reduce them to four fundamental types, which the first anthropologists expressed in these terms: namely, the white in Europe, the yellow in Asia, the red in America, and the black in Africa. The white and black there can be no doubt about; they correspond to two of the primordial divisions of the human race. The two others are less definite, the red especially. From their mixture and the influence of external conditions issue all the shades of colour which we now see. In the white there is every variety of shade. The rosy complexion of Scandinavians differs from the florid complexion of the English and Danes. The dark colour of our French races to the south of the Loire is not that of Spaniards, nor of the bronzed Kabyles. There are at least two groups in the series: namely, those whose skin easily becomes dark, sometimes enormously so, from the contact of air and light, and is uniform; and those whose skin when exposed to the sun becomes brick-red, or covered with freckles. Among the former especially, this colour becomes less in winter, and disappears on a return to temperate or cold countries, readily making its appearance again in hot countries. In the latter a sort of burn is produced, the skin becoming chapped and excoriated. In either case, children are born white. The French in Algeria, and the English in India, furnish us with abundant examples of this. The yellow tint of eastern Asiatics varies even more. Sometimes it approaches that of the white, so as to be indistinguishable from it; at others, it is olive green, passing through all the intermediate shades from pale yellow to brown or gingerbread colour. Among the Chinese, those of the north more particularly, it becomes dark in winter, as in the first group above alluded to, and pale in summer (*Lamprey*).

The term "red" has been applied to the American Indians less on account of this being their ordinary colour than of their dyeing the hair and painting the skin red. All shades of colour are seen among them, from the light tint of the Antisians of the Central Andes to the dark olive of the Peruvians (*D'Orbigny*), and the negro black of the ancient Californians (*La Pérouse*). They are frequently, however, said to be copper or cinnamon coloured. This copper colour is common in Polynesia, whose very light yellow or brown tints are as frequently met with. In Africa, red and yellow are very common, particularly in the south, the centre, and towards the Upper Nile. The Foulbes are of a rhubarb-yellow colour, those of pure blood approaching to red. The Bisharis are very frequently of a mahogany red. We know that the ancient Egyptians were painted red on their tombs. The classification of olden times in which the red colour was said to be peculiar to the American Indians is therefore incorrect.

If negroes are, as regards colour, so widely separated from whites, they insensibly blend with the yellow or the red in many parts of Africa. The most decided blacks are those of the Coast of Guinea, but from the Yoloff to the Mandingo and the Ashanti there is every variety of shade. In South Africa, the Hottentots, and especially the Bosjesmana, are not black, but of a yellow-gray, like old leather. On the Gaboon, the Obongos seen by Du Chaillu were also of a dirty-yellow colour. We speak of the red Kaffers. Among the Mokololos of the Zambesi, and the Fans of Burton, many were the colour of *café au lait*. The expressions "light brown," "light colour," are frequently applied to the negroes of Lualaba in Livingstone's "Last Journal," but are they not so relatively to the surrounding peoples? The black colour of the skin is met with in other countries besides Africa, as among the Australians, and the straight-haired blacks of India—one of whom, of an intense black slightly mixed with red, was dissected in M. Broca's laboratory— also among the black Arabs of the Yemen, or Hymiarites, &c.   In the same way that whites become dark by being removed into hot countries, blacks become lighter in cold and temperate countries, as well as when suffering from illness.   Dark colour in the negro is a sign of health.

The colour of the skin is usually, we might say constantly, associated, if the races are pure, with a certain colour of the eyes and hair.   Thus, those with white skins of a rosy hue, which cannot bear the sun, have usually light eyes and hair.   Those with white skins, which readily tan with the sun, and those with yellow, red, or black skins have on the contrary dark hair.   Light hair and eyes are much more rare, although they are met with to some extent everywhere throughout the globe, except in Australia and in Central Africa.

It is not always easy to determine the colour of the eye, or rather of the iris.   The iris is formed of two circles, which are occasionally of different colours, the external being darker than the internal, and of an intermediate zone of a lighter hue.   Radiated striæ and spots are sometimes seen, which add to our difficulties.   It is desirable, therefore, to stand at about the distance of a centimètre in order to ascertain its general appearance, without going into minutiæ. We ought always to look with suspicion on an abnormally dilated pupil, as well as carefully to note the shadow projected by the eyebrows and eyelashes.   The "Instructions de la Société d'Anthropologie" recognize four shades of colour—brown, green, blue, and gray ; each having five tones—the very dark, the dark, the intermediate, the light, and the very light.   The expression "brown" does not mean pure brown, it is rather a reddish, a yellowish, or a greenish brown, corresponding with the chestnut or auburn colour, the hazel (noisette), and the sandy (roux), made use of by the English.   The gray, too, is not pure ; it is strictly speaking a violet more or less mixed with black and white (Broca).

Dark and light blue eyes usually belong to those which we

form fair people, and are more characteristic of a particular group of race than any other shade; they are commonly associated with fine, silky, and yellowish or flaxen hair; when associated with black hair, they are a sign of mixed breed. Gray, greenish, and neutral-tinted eyes is one of the characteristics of the Celtic race. They are very common in Russia in conjunction with a skin naturally marked with freckles, and appear to have been derived from an ancient race now extinct or merged into other races. It is nevertheless a question whether green eyes are not in certain cases a transformation of the blue by crossing. (See Chapters X. and XI., "The Fair and Fin Types.")

The colour of the hair may be classified as follows: The flaxen (approaching tint of Albinos), the flaxen (properly so called), the golden yellow, the sandy, the chestnut, the brown, and the various shades of black up to that of jet. Dr. Beddoe does not look upon sandy hair as ethnic, he considers it accidental. Have we not, on the contrary, ground for considering it as a vestige of an extinct race with green eyes, which might have advanced as far as England and the confines of the Rhine?

There is often an alteration in the colour of the hair on the surface of the body, especially in the folds about the joints, where it becomes reddish, owing to the acid which is there secreted. The inquiry is often made by travellers how it is that there are individuals with light or reddish hair in the midst of people with black hair. It is due occasionally to a complete or incomplete albinism, and more frequently still to the use of dyes. All the tones and shades of colour have been arranged by M. Broca in the "Instructions de la Société d'Anthropologie," under the form of a chromatic table, which has been reproduced by many of the foreign societies, and is now universally received. We thus get fixed data, upon which discussion is scarcely possible, instead of individual notions. Dr. Beddoe, in England, has given a considerable amount of attention to the colour of the eyes and hair in a large number of Europeans. Not being able in our limited space to reproduce his tables, even in part, or of giving a résumé of them, we shall only take into consideration one point, namely, the proportion of those commonly called fair, chestnut, and brown. Considering that light eyes and light hair, for example, are both well understood terms in pure races, and that we have nothing to do with mixed races, we have added (a) Those with black and fair hair and light eyes; (b) Those with chestnut-coloured hair and eyes of an intermediate tint; and (c) Those with dark brown and black hair and dark eyes. The sum is divided by two, and the quotient expressed in hundredths of the number of individuals examined. The following are our results in this most remarkable series:

	Sandy and Fair. Per cent.	Intermediate or Chestnut. Per cent.	Brown. Per cent.
29 Danes	76·5	17·9	5·5
400 Wallachians	62·0	22·2	26·2
1125 Scotch Highlanders ...	45·4	23·9	30·9
90 Irish	45·3	22·2	31·9
654 Normans	29·1	29·3	37·6
1250 Viennese	32·5	26·5	41·4
369 Bretons	20·0	22·7	57·3
518 Ligurians	17·0	16·0	67·0
103 Northern Jews	14·4	13·2	73·6
233 Southern Jews ...	12·5	14·7	73·1
180 Maltese	5·8	11·8	79·3

From this it appears—(a) That not one of these series is absolutely pure, and that, among the Jews more particularly, there are individuals with fair and chestnut hair; no one moreover would assert that this people marry exclusively with those of their own religion, and do not intermix with those of other creeds. (b) That the greatest number of fair people are met with among the Danes, then the Wallachians, and the largest number of brown-haired individuals among the Maltese, the Jews, and the Ligurians. (c) That the Southern Jews and the Northern Jews are almost entirely brown-haired, which is a certain argument in favour of the influence of external circumstances. (d) That the Bretons are essentially brown-haired. Moreover, the comparison is perhaps not altogether an impartial one as to the fair-haired, inasmuch as the chestnut-coloured are somewhat taken into account. The board, of which nothing is said here, is often light when the hair is brown, while the converse is rare. The following table, calculated in the same way as the American statistics of the War of Secession, also merits our consideration on account of the prodigious number of cases to which it has reference. The first five series relate to fair, and the last to brown races.

	Sandy and Fair.	Intermediate and Chestnut.	Brown.
English	48.9	26.9	23.4
Scotch	57.2	25.7	21.0
Irish	50.5	30.1	22.6
Germans	49.0	27.8	23.3
Scandinavians	66.4	19.5	14.8
Spanish and Portuguese	25.7	17.7	57.8

A map of the colour of the hair and eyes, similar to that which M. Broca has arranged for the stature, would be very desirable for any country.* M. Bernard, an army surgeon, has commenced one, but it has reference only to a few hundred soldiers. In his two most striking series, and at the same time those of the most opposite races—one being made up from the Kymric Departments (Nord, Jura, Bas-Rhin, Moselle, Haut-Rhin, and Meurthe), the other from the Celtic Departments (Corrèze, Haute-Loire, Aveyron, Indre, Cantal, Ardèche, Dordogne)—the percentage is made up as follows:

	Hair.		Eyes.	
	Fair. Per cent.	Chestnut. Per cent.	Blue. Per cent.	Brown. Per cent.
Kymric Departments	55.0	44.9	60.0	41.8
Celtic Departments	21.8	78.0	50.0	50.0

Unfortunately these distinctions of colour are not sufficient. Thus, in the first series, we have blue eyes, and in the second grey-blue; the altogether black-haired are not noticed at all except as regards Basques.

It is common for the hair, and in a less degree for the eyes, to become darker during the second period of childhood or later. The light hair becomes chestnut and chestnut dark brown. In a word,

* The Germans are preparing a map of this kind for their country.

colour is an excellent characteristic of race, but it should not be taken as a basis of classification. The division of the white races, these being subdivided into the fair and the dark, is the only established one. Yellow, red, and black have too many intermediate colours, and are not sufficiently characteristic. Taken in connection with others, this character becomes very valuable. The Boojesmen is distinctly separated from all the other negroes by a peculiar yellow tint, and the Australian from all the other straight-haired races by the black.

The Pilous System.

The Ainos, the Australians, the Tasmanians, and the Todas of the Nilgherries are, as regards the body generally, the most hairy. In the first in particular, the front of the chest, the back of the shoulders, and the limbs are covered with a thick fur, the skin not being visible. M. Roeory has met with a half-breed between the Ainos and the Japanese whose hair on the chest was 17 centimètres in length. We might mention, as examples of a very hairy race, the ancient Assyrians, and an extinct race, well-marked vestiges of which are found here and there among the brown races of southern Europe. Scarcely a trace of hair is to be found on the body among the negroes of Africa and the Mongolian races, in which we must include the American races. The ancient Egyptians are represented as beardless. The hair, both of the head and body, varies moreover as to quantity. In the Chinese, the hair on the head is straight, long, and moderately abundant, while their eyebrows and moustaches are reduced to a narrow pencil of stiff hair, and their beards and whiskers frequently to a few scattered hairs. Certain races are distinguished for the regularity with which the hair of the beard is implanted, while in others, as the Australians and Todas, it is scattered and tangled so as to deserve the epithet of bushy. The exact limit to which the beard and whiskers grow is a striking feature in some Orientals. The period when the hair falls off is taken notice of in the American statistics, to which we have already referred. From this it appears, contrary to what we

should have anticipated, that baldness takes place earlier in the
white than in the negro and the mulatto.

The conformation of the hair, whether straight or spiral, is also
of interest.

Bory de St. Vincent was one of the first to insist upon the two
great differences which it presents among races, which he has
divided into *leiotrichi*, or straight-haired, and *ulotrichi*, or woolly-
haired. His division therefore corresponded to the two species of
mankind of Virey: the white and the black. He has also made
divisions of the straight-haired.

To the naked eye, the hair is *straight* when the individual hairs
are straight throughout their entire length, *wavy* when they describe
curves, *curly* when at a certain distance from their extremity they
form large curls which are generally incomplete, *frizzled* when the
smallest of these curls occupy the whole length of the hair, and
woolly when these little curls are twisted in among those adjoining
them, thus forming tufts resembling wool. We may remark here
that the resemblance is only apparent, for the structure of human
woolly hair is altogether different from that of sheep's wool.

Crisp or woolly hair is fine or coarse, and presents itself in
various aspects. It is long, and falls down in twisted curls which
resemble thick fringes, as in certain Tasmanians; or long and
bristly, thus forming a round mass, which is as much as 30 centimètres in circumference, and which we term "mop-headed" (*en tête
de vadrouille*), as in Papuans and Kaffirs; or very short, sometimes
looking like a fleece, sometimes being distributed in little masses
like peppercorns (*en grains de poivre*), as in Hottentots. The way
in which the individual hairs are implanted tends to produce some
of these differences. The hairs are generally inserted obliquely.
In Hottentots, Papuans, and some other negroes, they are inserted
perpendicularly (*Pruner-Bey*). Generally, too, they are equally distributed on the surface of the head, but sometimes irregularly or
in straight lines or curves. In Hottentots and Papuans they grow
in little tufts, separated by bald patches, which, when the hair is
cut short, gives to the head the appearance of a brush with pencils
of bristles. Another character of woolly hair but little studied is

the width of the roll, which is more or less contracted, giving the
appearance of a spiral tower. In a collection of Hottentots' hair
belonging to the Société d'Anthropologie, the roll is not wider
than two millimetres. It is very narrow, and is sometimes less
than two millimetres.

Straight, wavy, and frizzled hair is sometimes soft and silky,
as in Scandinavians; sometimes glossy, as in the Malays; sometimes harsh and stiff, like horse-hair, as in Americans, and also,
though in a less degree, in the Mongolian races. Frizzled hair
is sometimes like the head of a mop, as in the Cafusos, a mixed
breed between Americans and negroes.

These differences take place in all parts of the body, and
probably woolly hair is even more persistent in the negro cross-
breeds on the unexposed parts, and especially on the pubis. All
depends on the microscopic structure of the hair.

M. Nathusius maintained that the hair was cylindrical in all
races, and that its spiral character depended on the form of the
secretory follicle at its root. M. Weber, and especially M. Pruner-
Bey, affirm that this form varies, and that its spiral appearance
arises from its flatness.

The hair consists of the root, including the bulb, and the stem.
In the centre of this is a sort of canal, transparent in Europeans
with light hair; more or less opaque, though still visible, in
Europeans with black hair, Mongols, and Americans; and invisible
in negroes, Papuans, and Malays. M. Pruner-Bey does not look
upon these appearances as constant, or characteristic in any race.
The size of the stem is of more importance; it is the cause of the
harshness and rigidity of the hair, or its fineness and flexibility.
The largest transverse sections are to be met with in Thibetans,
Polynesians, Santals of India, and Americans; and the smallest in
Fins. The shape of the section is decidedly characteristic: it is
cylindrical, ovoid, elliptical, or reniform, and is estimated according
to its width or length. The thinnest and flattest hair is that of
Boojesmans, Papuans, and negroes; the most cylindrical being
that of Polynesians, Malays, Siamese, Japanese, and Americans.
Europeans are between the two. Half-breeds present characters

intermediate between the two races from which they are derived,
or take the hair peculiar to either the one or the other race.*

The microscopic examination of the hair, easy enough when one
is satisfied with ascertaining the size, colour, or condition of the
medullary canal, is very difficult when we have to do with its
form. The smallest deviation of the instrument, the slightest
folding of the hair, converts a transverse section into an oblique
and elongated one. Then, again, the hair must be taken when it
is fully developed, that is to say, at about the period of the second
dentition; and after examining a great many specimens from the
same head, we must select the average.

From what has just been said, and particularly from the observations of M. Pruner-Bey, it is evident that the hair presents definite
anatomical characters, and that these alone might be taken as a
basis of classification for the races of mankind. Three groups
might thus be portrayed: (1) Flat or woolly hair, characteristic of
negroes; (2) Large and coarse cylindrical hair, belonging to
Mongols, Chinese, Malays, and Americans; (3) Hair intermediate
in shape and size, peculiar to European races. The first group
might be divided into two, according as the hairs are inserted in
tufts, as in Papuans and Bosjesmans, or in a continuous layer, as
in other negroes. The third might be classified according as the
hair is brown, as in our southern races, or light, as in the northern.
Lastly: by comparing the character of the straight hair with the
pure black colour of the skin in certain races, we might have a
further group, comprising the Australians, Hymiarites, &c. Thus
we should have six fundamental divisions bearing upon one and
the same organ.

The Features.

The features include the general form of the face, its details,
and everything contributing to its expression. The expression of

* See la Chevelure comme Caractéristique des Races Humaines d'après
des Recherches Microscopiques;" and "Deuxième Série d'Observations sur
la Chevelure," by M. Pruner-Bey, in "Mem. Soc. d'Anthrop.," vols. ii.
and iii.

7 A

the face arises from various causes, of which some are fixed and anatomical, others changing and physiological. There is nothing respecting which there is such diversity of opinion. The conformation of the forehead, the amount of projection of the eyeballs, the contrast between the hair and the eyes, the shape of the eyelids, the nostrils, the lips, the chin, are the elements upon which it is based. The injection of the capillaries of the skin, which is always more or less visible except in negroes, and the action of the subjacent muscles excited by the inner feelings, are still more essentially connected with it. One of the best and most brilliant lectures of the lamented Gratiolet was devoted to this subject.

With regard to general form, we have first to distinguish the two kinds of countenance as seen in profile; one evidently oblique or prognathous, in which the two jaws project in the form of a muzzle, and the lips are large and upturned. This is the negro type. The other, sensibly vertical or orthognathous, in which the lips are fine, straight, and small. This is the European type. There are also two kinds of countenance as looked at in front, the one developed and projecting in front of the median line, the sides receding and becoming narrower. This is also the European type. The other, in which the middle portion is flat, while the sides become wide and project out. This is the Mongolian type. The term "eurygnathous," applied to this by Isidore Geoffroy Saint-Hilaire, is in allusion to the prominence of the cheek-bones.

There are two other types, the one elongated, the other contracted vertically. Among negroes, the pure Melanesian element, which has contributed to form the New Caledonian race now in existence, is in the former category; the Tasmanians, now extinct, are in the latter. The Esquimaux and Patagonians have the long face, the Negritos the short face. M. Edwards was the first who established this distinction as regards the people of France. The men of Picardy, Champagne, and Burgundy have the long sharp face, with the cheek-bones scarcely visible, like the Gauls described by Roman historians; while those inhabiting the central districts have it more or less round. In short, there are regular countenances, of a fine oval, like that of the Arab, as well as those with irregular outlines, or angular, like that of the Australian, &c.

A straight and contracted forehead is a feature of inferiority, a broad ample one, a mark of superiority. There can be no doubt about this. The vertical high forehead, with the frontal bosses very marked, is met with in some men of genius, as Sir Walter Scott, and the same, only narrower, is commonly observed in the negro. All the Nubians of M. Brown have it. Nothing was more incorrect than the forehead of 90 and 100 degrees which the Greek sculptors gave to their divinities; it was by lowering the level of the ear that they obtained this appearance. A high and bulging forehead is an anomaly, reminding one of hydrocephalus in infancy. Microcephales and idiots have the receding forehead, with the frontal bosses scarcely visible, and very low. The happy medium is the best. A large full forehead, very slightly receding, describing an ample curve at the level of the moderately high frontal bosses, and from that point passing backwards, are the characters of the well-formed European. Our ancestor of Cro-Magnon was in this respect the very opposite of his predecessor of the Neanderthal.

The development of the superciliary arches in Man, and of the eyebrows which rest upon them, is the principal cause of the character which we designate by the name of "deep orbits" or "sunken eyes;" The depression of the root of the nose, the smallness of the eyeball, and the narrowness of the palpebral aperture, contribute to it. This aperture is shaped like an almond, with its external extremity tapering, in Semitic women, who enlarge its outline by means of sulphuret of antimony. It is wide in negroes, whose eyes are even with their head (*Lawrence*), and very small in Chinese and the majority of the yellow races, owing to the shortness of the upper eyelid, which is as if pinched outwards. The oblique direction of the eye, and the raising of its external angle, in the Mongols are partly due to these two causes, and are partly natural. However, these features are far from being constant in these races, although they are those by which we recognise them the best. King, in speaking of the eye of the Esquimau, which, with that of the Chinese, may be con-

2 A 2

sidered as the type of the race, says : " Its internal part is lowered,
while its external has an upward direction. The internal angle is
covered by a fold of loose integument. This fold is slightly
stretched over the angles of the eyelids, and covers the *caruncula
lachrymalis*, which is visible in the European, and forms as it were
a third eyelid, in the form of a crescent." That which tends to
exaggerate the impression of obliquity given by the Chinese or
Esquimau eye is a particular movement of the eyebrows, the two
internal thirds of which are lower, and the external third higher than
ours (*Broca*). The oblique eye, so called by travellers, is met with
also among the American Indians, and, according to Barrow and
others, among Hottentots. The reverse of this too narrow or too
short lid is the drooping lid, as though puffed or too loose, and
covering a portion of the eyeball. Something of this kind has
been noticed in certain Australians. So much has been said
respecting the malar-bones when describing the skeleton, that we
need not further refer to the projection of the cheek-bones, so
characteristic of all the native races of Eastern Asia. This prominence is sometimes so remarkable in the Esquimaux, that when
associated with a sunken condition of the entire nose, it enabled
King to place a rule on both cheek-bones at the same time without
its touching that organ.*

The morphological variations of the nose have not received that
attention which they deserve. Developed in an antero-posterior
direction in Europeans and North Americans, it is wide and flat
in the majority of Mongols—in our opinion, in all true Mongols
—and in negroes. Projection and width are generally in an
inverse ratio, and form the starting-point of a series of differences
with respect to the bridge and the base, which are principally
expressed by two indices, one of which corresponds very nearly to
the nasal index as taken on the skeleton. The following table
embraces the essential points bearing upon these differences :†

* "On the Physical Characters of the Esquimaux," by King, in "Journal
of the Ethnol. Soc.," vol. I. London, 1848.

† "De la Morphologie du Nez," by P. Topinard, in "Bull. Soc. d'Anthrop.,"
2nd series, vol. viii., 1873.

- Maximum height ......
- " breadth ...
- " projection ....

  { Transverse index.
  { Antero-posterior index.

- Base ......
  - Lobule ......
    - distinct (pinched, trilobed varieties).
    - non-distinct.
    - extending beyond the ears.
  - Alæ ......
    - near together.
    - divergent.
  - Nostrils ...
    - Shape ....
      - elliptical.
      - round.
      - special.
    - Their plane looking ...
      - downwards.
      - forwards.
      - backwards.
      - outwards.
    - Direction of their axis
      - antero-posterior.
      - oblique.
      - transverse.

- Bridge ...
  - Its angle of inclination.
  - Direction
    - rectilinear.
    - bent or dinted.
    - convex (aquiline variety).
    - concave (retroussé variety).
  - Shape ......
    - like a roof.
    - rounded off.
    - broad and flat.

The height is taken with the sliding compass, vertically from the root to the base of the nose, as on the skeleton; the breadth from the widest portions of the alæ, and the projection or antero-posterior diameter, from the point of the nose to the sub-nasal point, with a small graduated rule, which is held horizontally on the line of Camper, and at the same time pressed against the skin. The transverse measurement is common to the two indices. It varied from 29 to 42 millimètres in 75 Europeans which we examined, and from 40 to 52 in 18 busts of negroes and Mongols. Its relation with the height = 100, or transverse nasal index, averaged 68·14 in the first, 89 on a Cochin-China bust, 100 on a Papuan and an Australian, and was as high as 110, 112, and 115 on some African negroes. The extreme deviation was 75·00, so that a considerable margin is left for the apportionment of the averages

and of the individual cases. The transverse nasal index is therefore a valuable character in the living subject, as the corresponding
index of M. Broca is on the skeleton.

On looking from below upwards at the nose of the European, on
the one hand, and that of the negro and Mongolian, on the other,
we are struck with the difference in the shape of the little (sorcules
triangle formed by the septum in the middle and the nostrils at
the sides, and which has hitherto escaped the attention of Anthropologists.   The difference consists in the relation of the length
antero-posteriorly of the sub-septum, or rather of the entire projection of the nose at the above maximum breadth, otherwise
called the antero-posterior nasal index.   In our 76 Europeans, it
varied from 55 to 80, the mean being 86·6.   In the negroes and
Mongolians it was probably as low as 30.   Having measured but
a few living subjects, and principally busts, upon which no pressure of the lip could be made, we cannot speak with certainty.
We recommend this measurement to travellers as being easy to take.

Among other characters may be mentioned—(1) The depth of
the hollow at the root, which is not indicated in the table.   It is
considerable in Melanesians, who are thus distinguished from the
negroes of Africa.   It is also tolerably marked in the majority
of our European races, though generally less so in the female.
It is less marked in the Mongolian races, as also in the Arab,
and in what is commonly called the ancient Greek type, represented
by the Venus de Milo.   (2) The arching of the nose.   Exceptionally, as if broken or bent, as in Bourbons, more general and
more projecting in Americans (Catlin); it is altogether characteristic of the aquiline nose peculiar to the Arabs, Jews, ancient
Assyrians, Guebros, or ancient Persian fire-worshippers, &c.   Two
types of this feature ought to be distinguished : the one, thick—
in which the nose is large and rounded off at the back, big and
puffy at the point; the other, thin—in which the lateral planes
are well defined, the bridge sharp, and the median lobule distinct
from the alæ, and prolonged below the plane of the nostrils like an
eagle's or parrot's beak, whence its name, aquiline.   (3) The two
kinds of flattening of the nose, which may be distinguished by

the terms *épaté* and *busqué*; the former having reference to the
organ in its *ensemble*, and being equally applicable to the skeleton;
the latter to the peculiar depression of its lower half, owing to
a want of consistence of its cartilages. The Chinese have the nose
épaté, the Malays the *busqué*, negroes both *épaté* and *busqué*. It is
true that both these characters are very commonly found together.
(4) The form of the nostrils viewed from below. These are
elliptical from before, backwards in the white, more or less
diverging backwards, so as to become almost transverse, in the most
inferior races, their variations depending principally on the breadth
of the sub-septum behind. (5) The elevation upwards and outwards of the plane of the cutire base, or of the alæ separately, so that
the internal surface or side of the nostrils becomes more or less
exposed to view. The Bosjesmans, and the lowest-type negroes
approximate in this respect to the simian types. Among the
accessory features of the nose may be placed the variable development of its muscular apparatus. In Europeans, the nostrils are
only seen to dilate exceptionally, when the breathing is oppressed.
In a large number of individuals, and especially in the inferior
races, the movements of dilatation and contraction are very marked,
thus giving to the countenance a ferocious expression.

We have previously spoken of the harmonious or symmetrical
characters of the cranium and face; nowhere are they so striking
as in the nasal apparatus of the living subject and of the skeleton.
The width of the interval between the eyes, or rather the space
included between the external angles of the ascending processes
of the superior maxillary bones, is usually accompanied by flatness
of the same interval, and the obliteration of the glabella. The
width of the base of the nose and the anterior orifice of the nasal
fossæ in the skeleton corresponds not only with the two or three
preceding characters but also with the flatness of the entire nose,
both bone and cartilages. So with the nostrils, from being placed
antero-posteriorly, they become transverse. Any one of these
characters being given, we can at once determine the others.
The opposite conditions of contraction with counterbalancing projection of these different points are in the same category. According

to the rules of art, the space between the eyes = the base of the
nose; this is exactly so in the two opposite types of which we
are speaking. But there are constant exceptions in a race, as there
are in the harmony between the cranium and face, which thus
become valuable differential characters for certain sub-races. An
analogous harmony exists in the mouth and ear. Both characters
must be preserved, the harmonious as well as the incongruous.

Delicacy of shape of the lips, and smallness of the mouth are
European features, except in some individuals of the lymphatic
temperament, in whom the upper lip is decidedly the larger.
Sometimes immoderately thick lips are the ordinary accompaniment
of prognathism, especially of alveolo-dental prognathism, and arises
from the development of the orbicular muscle of the lips, and still
more from hypertrophy of their cellulo-adipose tissue. It is said
that Man alone has a chin. On the skeleton it is indicated almost
without exception by a small more or less projecting triangular
surface, such as that on the prehistoric Naulette jaw. On the
living subject it is represented by a rounded-off and well-defined
projection, which is very remarkable on the busts of Nero and
Napoleon. It is sometimes obliterated, which often arises from the
lower jaw being much smaller than the upper, and shrinking in.
Barrow says that the Boojesmans, although prognathous in the
lower jaw, have a projecting and pointed chin.

The ears have not been sufficiently studied, though furnishing
characters of considerable value. They are large or small. In the
Kabyles they project out; in others they are close to the side of the
head. The lobule is wanting in certain Chaouias or Kabyles of the
province of Constantine, in the religious fanatics of the Pyrenees,
and here and there in individuals of every race. In Europeans the
ears are oval and well defined; in negroes they are round or approaching to square. The ear without a folded margin behind or
above, an angle at the union of the superior with the posterior
border, as well as flatness, are important features, and somewhat of
a simian character. The varieties of configuration of this organ,
and of its folds and hollows, are very commonly hereditary.
It is modified by certain ethnic usages, such as the elongation

of the lobule by heavy earrings until it almost touches the
shoulders.

But little has been determined as to the value of certain dissimilarities noticed in the teeth. A more or less thick enamel, a
yellowish or bluish colour, variety in the number of the roots, as well
as certain particulars connected with the crown, have attracted
attention. In the negro races they are better set and more regular
than in the white races, in which they are small and close together.
Caries is more common in England, Ireland, and Germany than in
Canada, according to some American statistics, gathered from an
examination of a thousand soldiers. Certain ethnic customs leave
their traces upon them, which we sometimes utilise in craniology
for the purpose of ascertaining the source from which skulls are
derived. In Africa, as well as in Oceania, a considerable number
of the savage tribes extract or sharpen their front teeth at the
period of puberty. Malays have the front of the teeth corroded in
a transversely concave line, owing to their chewing the betel-nut.
On the anterior surface of the teeth of the Yucatan there is sometimes a point of enamel of a blue turquoise or greenish colour.
Their wear and tear, which in our races inclines inwards in the
upper jaw, in many foreign ones inclines outwards.

There are some other physiological features to be noticed. Thus
the skin of the negro is shining and velvety, and cooler than that
of the European, according to Prichard. Others have maintained
the contrary.

The odour of the cutaneous envelope, sui generis in each race,
would furnish important differential characters, if one could employ some definite re-agent as a substitute for the uncertain sense
of smell. The missionary Huc declared that he could recognise
the Negro, the Tartar, the Thibetan, the Hindoo, the Chinese, and
the Arab, by their effluvium, and added that although disguised
the dogs of the Chinese barked at him. The Peruvian, says
Humboldt, has three distinct words by which to designate the
odour of the European, the Indian, and the Negro, respectively.
Knegger states that mosquitos are attracted to certain races by
their peculiar odour. The characteristic effluvium from the bold

of a slave-ship can never be got rid of, and it is owing to this that
the blood-hounds of New Orleans were enabled to track the run-
away slave.

The external genital organs present very marked differences in
different races. In the male these are but slight. In the female,
the differences are very considerable. In the first place, it is certain
that the hemispherical, conical, and pyriform mammæ which
are now characteristic of the races which surround us, were
formerly peculiar to distinct races. So with the perforation of
the olecranon, or the platycnemic tibia. It is no less certain that
their exaggerated length, from the period when the female has
fulfilled her maternal functions, is an essential characteristic of
other races. We commonly meet with accounts by travellers of
negresses throwing their breasts over their shoulders to suckle
their infants hanging at their backs. A Boojesman woman, examined by Flower and Murie, could bring the two breasts together
behind, above the region of the buttocks.

Under the name of "steatopyga" is understood the development
in the female of enormous fatty masses, shaking like jelly at the
least touch, which are superposed upon the glutei muscles. This
character is met with here and there in Africa, among the Somalis,
Kaffirs, and Hottentots, and is constant in various degrees in
Boojesmans. There is no evidence of it either on the skeleton or
on the glutei. It is more than an hypertrophy of the adipose
tissue, it is almost a supplementary organ, as special as the
laryngeal sacs of the gorilla and the chimpanzee; nay, more so,
for these are only a progressive increase as age advances, and
more particularly in the male, of a cavity at the back part of the
larynx common to all the higher mammalia, while nothing in the
European has any resemblance in the slightest degree to steatopyga.
This strange organ, the particular use of which is not known, was
present, as well as the tablier, in a Bosjesman virgin of 12 years of
age.[*] The fat increases in size like the breasts.

* Review of a memoir of Flower and Murie, on "A Dissection of a
Bosjesman Woman," in "Anthropological Review," vol. v., 1867.

Everything tends to support the belief that a peculiar race, possessing these two characters, and of which the Bosjesmans are the closest representatives, formerly lived as a scattered people from the coast of Aden to the Cape of Good Hope. If we compare the yellowish colour of this people with other original characters which separate them from the negroes of the adjoining countries, this hypothesis becomes almost a matter of certainty. Hitherto we have met with many opposite characters in the human groups, but few so remarkable as these. We have seen the marked difference between woolly and straight hair, between the prognathous and the orthognathous, the jet black of the Yoloff and the pale complexion of the Scandinavian, between the ultra-dolichocephalic Esquimau or New Caledonian, and the ultra-brachycephalic Mongolian. But the line of separation between the European and the Bosjesman as regards these two characters is, in a morphological point of view, still wider, as much so as between each of the anthropoid apes, or between the dog and the wolf, the goat and the sheep.

CHAPTER VII.

PHYSICAL CHARACTERS—AGE—MENSTRUATION—CROSSES—SUCCESSION —CONSANGUINEOUS UNION.

IF the physical differences noticeable either on the dead body or on the living subject, are of the first importance as distinguishing races, the differences resulting from the function of organs have also their value. It is of importance to know whether the Australian lives, breathes, propagates his species, thinks and speaks like the European; whether the Hottentot is subjected to the influence of external conditions, inter-crosses, satisfies his wants, and is of sociable habits like the Chinese. All the subjects we have passed in review when comparing Man with animals, again present themselves to our notice when comparing men between themselves. This part of the science whose more general questions have scarcely yet been explored, would merit the title of *biology* as opposed to that which has been discussed in the preceding pages under the name of *anatomy*.

Duration of Life.

The duration of life is less at the poles among the Esquimaux and Lapps, and at the equator among the Negroes; but that may depend on climate and external circumstances. In Greenland, there are more women than men, because the men die from accident, and rarely reach 50 years of age. The women, however, attain to the age of 70, 80, and even beyond. Prichard has collected together cases of centenarians from every race. Nine English emigrants in America from 110 to 161 years; 10 or 15 negroes from 107 to 160; one Kaffir 109; many Hottentots of 100 (*Barrow*); two Indians of 117 and 143 respectively (*Humboldt*); 35 Egyptians above 100 (*Larrey*). Recently Sir Duncan Gibb mentioned the case of a Fin of 115 years. The mean duration of life in France, which was 33 at the close of the eighteenth century—and 39 from 1817 to 1831, increased to 40 from 1840 to 1859, thanks to the progress of sanitary science and civilisation. There are some reasons, however, for believing that apart from the influence of climate, and the power which Man has of dealing with the causes of disease, the mean normal longevity is not the same in all races.

So, decrepitude shows itself sooner in some races than in others. The Australians and Bosjesmans are old men at a period when the European is in the full enjoyment of his faculties, both physical and intellectual. The Japanese the same, according to Dr. Krishaber, physician to the Japanese embassy. Unquestionably the woman fades away much sooner in the negro races even from the first pregnancy. In the negro, the development of the body is generally in advance of the white. His wisdom teeth are cut sooner; and in estimating the age of his skull, we must reckon it as at least five years in advance of the white.

There are many points connected with this subject still unsettled. The successive dates of the eruption of the milk and permanent teeth, the period of growth of the body generally, and of the brain in particular, the period at which the epiphyses of the long bones become anchylosed to the diaphyses, the period of the commencement and cessation of menstruation, the period when the hair falls off and changes colour—all this would furnish more certain data for the solution of the problem than the average duration of life, which is too much dependent on external circumstances.

Whites lose their teeth much sooner than negroes, but this is owing to their bad quality and to their being too close together, which predisposes them to caries. D'Orbigny says that the Charruas never lose their teeth. They wear out however more quickly in savage races, from their masticating corrosive substances, as the betel-nut by the Malays or very hard matters by the Patagonians. The hair becomes white more slowly in the yellow races, and baldness is rarely seen among them. (See page 300.)

Menstruation.

Menstruation, and the periods at which it becomes established and disappears, have not yet afforded anything conclusive with respect to races. The influence of the duration of life upon the period of the cessation of the catamenia is a well-established fact, thanks to a work of Mr. R. Cowrie. In the Shetland Islands the period of the appearance of the menses is the same as in Scotland, but that of their disappearance is from 50 to 51 years of age, while in Scotland they cease at the age of 45 to 46. Now, in the Shetland Islands, longevity is considerably greater. There are 33 per cent. of old people from 70 to 80, and 20 per cent. from 80 to 90; while in Scotland there are only 18 per cent. of the former, and 7 of the latter. The influence of external circumstances also exerts its action. After comparing all the published statistics, Joulin came to the conclusion that in temperate countries the phenomenon makes its appearance at the age of 15, and in hot countries at 12½. In 6000 German girls, M. Meyer found that the first menstruation took place at 16·34 among the rich, and 16·50 among the poor; at 15·96 in the towns, and 15·20 in the country. Food, warmth, good air, and good sanitary arrangements, being all the vital functions into full play. According to M. Guérault, the catamenia are less abundant, or are altogether suspended among the Esquimaux during the winter, when food is less abundant, while they are copious in summer. In hot countries, among Europeans, they readily pass into true menorrhagia.

In making statistics with respect to menstruation, the difficulty is to divest the subject of that which has specially to do with the race. Two opposing influences are at work, and may apparently falsify the results. The following are the most important published statistics as to the average period of the first appearance of the catamenia in various races:

Christiania (Faye)	...	2801	...	14 years 0 months.
Copenhagen (Rawn)	...	3819	...	16 „ 0 „
North Germany (Laguean)	...	4024	...	16 „ 9 „
Russia (Lieven)	...	1000	...	16 „ 6 „
France (Laguean)	...	9081	...	15 „ 1 „
England „	...	3758	...	14 „ 11 „
Madeira (Robertson)	...	242	...	14 „ 10 „
Jamaica, Negresses (Robertson)	...	80	...	14 „ 10 „
Southern Asia (Laguean)	...	1140	...	12 „ 10 „

The races which it would interest us to know the most about are not in the list, as the Esquimaux and Lapps, Australians and Bosjesmans. The records respecting the former are very contradictory, and relate to but few examples; and as regards the latter, we have none.[*]

The duration of pregnancy, fecundity, the number of twin-births, &c., are so many questions of comparative anthropology, which come next to that of menstruation. With regard to the first point, we have little information beyond the French statistics. The facility with which child-bearing takes place among savage peoples, in spite of the want of the smallest care, depends altogether upon the anatomical and physiological arrangement of the parts, and on the degree of resistance to pain. There are undoubtedly very decided differences in these respects between one European race and another. An accurate estimate of fecundity is an exceedingly difficult one to determine. In France, three or four children is the usual number born in a family. In other countries of Europe this number is exceeded. In Iceland, according to Moser, it is as high as five. The hypoborean races are less fertile, the Slavs more so. Negresses readily conceive, and make excellent nurses. In Western Australia, 44 women beyond the middle age had 188 children, or 4·3 each—three had seven each, and one only was barren (G. Grey). But statements of this kind are frequently erroneous. With regard to multiple births, the information we possess scarcely extends beyond the French statistics. According to a table of Moser, the largest number of twin-births was in Dublin and in Russia. In Australia the number is about the same as in France: "I am acquainted with four cases" of twin-births, writes Sir G. Grey.

Crossing.

This is one of the most vexed questions in Anthropology. Under this title is understood in Natural History the union of two individuals whatever may be their supposed or actual zoological difference. Their progeny have the general name of hybrids, and in Man that of mongrels. The former of these terms is usually applied to the fixed or variable products of species between themselves, and the latter the products of varieties or races.

Between animals of classes differing widely we occasionally witness the most singular connections, as between the dog and the sow, but the generative impulse goes for nothing. It is stated

that individuals of different Orders have given birth to offspring, as
between the bull and the mare, whose progeny, or jumarts, inhabited
the Atlas mountains and the mountains of Piedmont. It is a
better authenticated fact that the phenomenon takes place between
different Genera. M. de Bouillé in 1873 described the offspring of
the cross between the ibex of the Pyrenees and the domestic goat.
The Peruvians in the Chilian Alps crossed this latter with the
sheep, and obtained a very vigorous breed called *chabins* (buck-
sheep), whose descendants, fertile through an indefinite number of
generations, are of considerable commercial value on account of
their skins and fleeces, known by the name of "pellons." Between
species the crosses are common and fertile, the mongrels themselves being either sterile, as mules—the offspring of the ass and
the horse—or fertile, as the progeny of the hare and the rabbit,
the dog and the wolf, the jackal and the fox, the camel and the
dromedary, the alpaca and the llama or vecuna, the horse and the
zebra or wild mule, the bison and the European ox, &c.

There is therefore no reason to suppose that we have been
deceived as to the reality of certain species, and that such were
only varieties. Two or three well-established facts out of many
will suffice. It is now certain that the limit of species is not
an absolute obstacle to fertility, and consequently that its circum-
scription has nothing decided about it, which puts us entirely at
our ease when discussing the question of human cross-breeds.
Whether races anthropologically distant from each other have or
have not indefinitely fertile offspring, is of little importance, the
simple question is whether they represent species or varieties.
(See page 193, et seq.)

Much mystery remains to be cleared up, however, relative to the
phenomena of hybridism in general. Why, for example, a male of
one species produces fertile hybrids with the female of another
species, while, inversely, a female of one with a male of another
is sterile (unilateral hybridism). Why a female savage in captivity
does not produce more fertile offspring with the male of her own
species, while captivity increases the fertility of other species;
why among dogs, or human beings, the germs being appa-

rently sound, there are some fertile unions and others not
so. We have only the simple facts before us from which to form
a judgment.

M. Broca has defined the various degrees of sexual affinity, which
he calls homogenesis,* thus:

Heterogenesis.

Homogenesis {
  Abortive ...
  Agenesic ...   } without offspring.
  Dysgenesic ...
  Paragenesic.. } with offspring.
  Eugenesic ...
}

In heterogenesis there may be intercourse without impregnation.
Abortive homogenesis is merely a matter of speculation; impregnation takes place, but the foetus does not arrive at its full term.
In agenesic homogenesis, or agenesis, there are offspring, but these
are absolutely sterile *inter se*, or with individuals of one or the
other mother-race. In dysgenesic homogenesis, or dysgenesis, these
mixed breeds are still sterile *inter se*, but they are fertile with individuals of one or other mother-race—their offspring, called hybrids
of the second blood, being nevertheless sterile, so that it cannot
again form a new race.

In paragenesic homogenesis, or paragenesis, or collateral hybridism,
the direct hybrids, or those of the *first blood*, are still sterile between themselves, or as far as the second or third generation; but
those of the *second blood* are indefinitely fertile, so that a race may
take its origin by collaterals. In engenesic homogenesis, or
eugenesis, or direct hybridism, the two orders of hybrids are now
indefinitely fertile, so that the new race makes its way directly and
without hindrance.

Heterogenesis is never other than individual in Man, nor consequently is agenesis. There was a disposition for some years to
believe in absolute dysgenesis between certain races. This must

* Mémoire, "Sur l'Hybridité," by M. Broca, "Journal de Physiologie,"
vol. i., 1858.

2 B

now be given up. The whole dispute concentres upon the two
latter kinds : Are there unions which could not give origin to a new
race except by collaterals, that is to say, by a reversion towards
the one or the other mother-races?

There are numerous species of human mongrels. There are
(1) Those of the first blood, including their direct offspring, and all
those which are derived from them by alliances with them ; (2)
Those of the second blood (first degree of reversion), including all
the offspring of the cross of the first blood with one of the two
mother-races ; (3) Mongrels of the third blood (second degree of
reversion), resulting from the cross of the second blood with one of
the mother-races, and so on. At the fifth or sixth reversion all
trace of hybridism has generally disappeared, the features of the
mother-men have reverted to the original type. That there is but
one species of mongrel of the first blood, but two species of the
second, of the third, of the fourth, each resembling more one of the
two original races, is certain ; and also that there are complex and
nameless cross-breeds resulting from the cross of mongrels of
different orders.

If we express by W, or white, and B, or black, the two races,
and by a fraction the amount of each according to its degree, we
shall have the following series of reversion towards W :

Mongrels of first blood	...	...	...	$= W\frac{1}{2}$	$+ B\frac{1}{2}$.
„ second blood	...	...	...	$= W\frac{3}{4}$	$+ B\frac{1}{4}$.
„ third blood	...	...	...	$= W\frac{7}{8}$	$+ B\frac{1}{8}$.
„ fourth blood	...	...	...	$= W\frac{15}{16}$	$+ B\frac{1}{16}$.
„ fifth blood	...	...	...	$= W\frac{31}{32}$	$+ B\frac{1}{32}$.

Homogenesis is absolute or eugenesic, and still more paragenesic,
between contiguous races. The peoples of Europe are a proof of
this. All, in various degrees, are the resultant of a series of crossings, one of the most striking products of which is the co-existence,
in one and the same individual, of light or dark blue eyes with
jet-black hair and beard. A friend of our own who traces back
among his ancestors elements on the one side reaching to the

Western Pyrenees and on the other to Lorraine, is an example of this. M. Broca found, when investigating the subject of stature, that nineteen-twentieths of the whole population of France presented, in various degrees, the characters of mixed races. The Bretons are one-fourth Kymris and three-fourths Celts, without including another element which is seen among them, and which dates back to a later period than the Celts. Up to the time of the French Revolution victors and vanquished lived apart; the former were the aristocracy, the latter the people. But since they have been brought more into immediate contact the population has largely increased, proving how valuable that union has been. The table which we have constructed with materials furnished by Dr. Beddoe, shows that everywhere throughout Europe, and even among the Jews, two elements must be taken into account, the fair and the dark, which are promiscuously intermingled.

The prosperity of the New American race is another example of eugenesis. Immigration into the United States, which has taken so considerable a flight during the last thirty years, has already been enormous. Every variety of cross has been going on between English, Irish, Germans, Italians, French, &c., with the greatest possible success. We may also mention numberless Spaniards from the Peninsula among whom are found the features of the Saracen invaders of the ninth century; then that population on the Barbary coast, called Moors, and which is a medley of races of every description, the Arab and Berber blood predominating. On tracing back the yellow races we also discover a perfect eugenesis. It would be difficult in the part of Asia which relates to them to mention a single race, or a single people, where crossing has not taken place. De Mas speaks in the highest terms of mixed breeds of Chinese and Mongolians, and MM. Mondière and Morice of those of Chinese and Annamites under the name of Minxongs. Dr. Bowring describes a race in the Philippine Islands, intermediate between the Malays and Chinese, as the principal agent of civilisation in these latitudes.

Their mongrels, which are said to be thriving but little in the Eastern Malacca Islands (*Waitz*) and those of Chinese and Cam-

2 B 2

logians but little fertile (*Gutzlaff*), are local exceptions, arising from the difficulties attending acclimatisation in these unhealthy countries. One of the first effects of the inability to become acclimatised is to diminish fecundity. The Mamelukes of Egypt during 500 years have had no children when married to women of their own race from Georgia, and have never established a branch in the Valley of the Nile. Such are some of the singular phenomena which everywhere present themselves when we have to deal with the question of reproduction. The failure of power to become acclimatised seems to attack the germ in its very earliest development. It is undeniable that in Africa the negro races do not cross to any great extent. The Kaffirs have carried their tall stature to a great number of points; the Bosjesmans have here and there left traces of their steatopyga and their small stature. On the present frontiers of the two races a number of cross-breeds are to be met with. Eugenesis still continues between races already somewhat separated from one another. The half-breeds between Indians and Europeans are very numerous both in North and South America. We ourselves have seen, in the United States, numerous families, the issue of the Italian and the Yankee, whose offspring were very fertile.

In the official report, in 1870, upon the Aborigines, it is stated that there exists in Kansas an entire nation of half-breed Osages. In Mexico the Spanish mixed breeds constitute two-thirds or three-fourths of the whole population. In Brazil, La Plata, and Chili, the Portuguese mongrels are also in the majority. In Lima there are twenty-three different names to designate the varieties of mixed breeds of Spaniards, Peruvians, and Negroes.

The children of the half-breed between the Chinese and the Spaniard are called *tornas atras*, according to Dr. Bowring. The facility with which the Chinese interbreed with every sort of race is well known. In the Antilles and in California, they are to be found everywhere, and they interbreed with the Indians and whites, thus producing many varieties of mixed progeny (*A. Maury*). The reason why these are not greater is that the Chinese marries and returns to his own country as soon as he has amassed a com-

potency. The inferiority of the mixed breeds between the Chinese and the Portuguese, so conspicuous at Macao (*Castano*), ought still to be attributed to acclimation, in the same way as the Lippladens, or half-breeds between the Malays and the Dutch, which have never succeeded in establishing themselves in Java, and whose progeny were sterile to the third generation (*Ivan*). In the French colony of Indo-China, M. Morice speaks of half-breeds of Europeans and Annamites as resisting exposure to the sun better than their European relations. Fitzroy describes the children and infants of the English and Malay, or Polynesians, as of a bright red-brown. The half-breeds of English and New Zealanders constitute a healthy and very muscular race, according to Waitz. Prichard speaks of marriages between the progeny of Europeans and aboriginal Samoans and Tongas as being as prolific as any other. The success of the Polynesian mixed breeds is no longer a matter of doubt. In 1769, nine English sailors, six male Tahitians, and 15 Tahitian women settled in Pitcairn Island, in the Pacific. In 1793 they were reduced to four white men and 10 Tahitian women. In 1846 the population of the island increased to 66, and in 1856 to 169. Moreover, at the termination of Cook's voyages, the Polynesian races were still unmingled with any infusion of white blood. Now, their mixed breeds are so numerous that it would be difficult to find among them any individuals of pure race (*De Quatrefages*).

In Africa, the Soudan is the great centre of mixed breeds between two races equally removed from one another. Here, in the tenth century, there appeared a red race with glossy hair, commonly known as that of the Foullas (*Barth*), which engrafted itself as a dominating race upon a previous negro stock with woolly hair, and giving origin to all sorts of mixed breeds, of which the Toucolors of Senegal are the most celebrated. The Somalis, the Gallas, and a score of other peoples of Eastern Africa, are, no doubt, mixed breeds between negroes and some red race or Arabs. On the Abyssinian plateau mixed breeds continue, but the Arab element is increasing. On the plain of Sennaar there are no less than six denominations between the more or less pure Arab and the pure negro: (1) The

El-Asfar, or yellow; (2) The El-Kat Fatclobem, analogous to the Abyssinians; (3) The El-Akder, or red; (4) The El-Asraq, or blue; (5) The El-Ahudar, or green; and (6) The Ahbits, or Noubas, whose hair is not absolutely woolly.

The mixed breeds between races more widely separated remain fertile; but to what extent do they remain so? Is the intermediate race produced directly or by collaterals? easily, or with difficulty, in the former case?

The mixed breeds of negroes and Europeans have various names, according to their relative proportion of blood. The first are called mulattoes, the second tierceroons, the third quadroons, the fourth quintroons, &c., without mentioning a number of local terms for mixed breeds of every shade. They form a peculiar race, and are pangenesic. There is no doubt about this; but are they also eugenesic? Nott made a comparison of the mixed breeds of Carolina, Louisiana, and Florida, and found a difference between them as regards fecundity; and came to the conclusion that the hybrids of the Anglo-Saxon race with the negro are sterile for the first or second generation, while the offspring of the brown race of Europe with the negro are of better constitution and decidedly fertile.

The observations of Long in the English colony of Jamaica, as well as examples of an opposite description in Cuba, Hayti, and Porto-Rico—French and Spanish colonies—go to strengthen this view.

Jaquinot, Waitz, Van Amringe, Hamilton Smith, and Seemann, on the other hand, speak of the fertility of negroes with Europeans of every description. There is considerable difficulty about the matter, there being no statistics establishing the distinction between the first and second blood. The white woman generally refusing to marry a mulatto, and the latter to marry a negress, it becomes necessary, notwithstanding, that the mulatto should find a wife, and this he can only do generally among his own people. Once only have we any record on the subject, namely, in North Carolina. There the caste of freemen was constituted entirely of mulattoes freed by their white fathers. The State, dismayed at

the important position which they assumed, put a stop to this
liberation. Left to themselves their number diminished 29 per
cent. The fact is the question has not yet been settled.

Now let us pass to the continent of Africa. One of the arguments of Prichard in favour of the unlimited fecundity of all the
human races was derived from a consideration of the Griquas, a
race the issue of the union, at the close of the last century, of the
Hottentots with the Dutch. Prichard was too dogmatical, and M.
Broca justly remarks that the number of bastards at first was small,
and was soon absorbed into the mass of Bosjesmans and Koranna,
with whom they became amalgamated, so that, in 1825, the Griquas
might be looked upon as having reverted to the aboriginal type.
If the experiment failed through the excess of reversions, it nevertheless succeeded at first. The English author also mentioned the
existence of Malayo-Papuans in the Malay Archipelago, on the
authority of Quoy and Gaimard. We think he was right, and the
existence of these mixed breeds seems to us demonstrated by
craniology, although some are now considered to be negritos.

One of the arguments in favour of dysgenesis was drawn from
a consideration of the Australians. Until within the last few years
only three or four instances were known of their interbreeding
with Europeans, and these were mentioned incidentally by
Freycinet, Quoy, Gaimard, and Lesson. Those mentioned by
Mackenzie and Robert Dawson had been unnoticed. The frequency
of the intercourse between whites and the Australian Gins was,
however, a matter of general notoriety. But subsequently Miles,
Murray (of Sydney), P. Beveridge, and D. Lee have stated that
they have seen them, and that they are common, especially on the
borders of the regions occupied by the squatters, to whom they
were of great service. An undoubted example has been given
by Stokes. From 1800 to 1805 some English seal-fishers settled
in Bass's Straits had exchanged, for the seals they had taken
on the banks of the Strait, some Australian and Tasmanian
women.

In 1846 they had given birth to a numerous progeny. On
Preservation Island alone there were 26 children, or rather grand-

children, seeing that the first unions had taken place more than 40 years previously. Mr. Stokes says they are excellent sailors. The fact that a great number of Australian mixed breeds are to be met with in the towns and plantations has lately been confirmed in a letter received by us from M. de Castelnau, French consul at Melbourne, as also at a personal interview with M. E. Simon, French consul at Sydney. We have yet to know within what limits the mulattoes are the more frequent, whether by collaterals or by the first blood.[*]

The accounts furnished by Prichard, in 1856, respecting the mixed breeds of the Melanesians of the Fiji islands, appear applicable to Australians. He says the half-blood mongrels are less fertile *inter se* than those of the original stock; in other words, their cross-breeds are eugenesic, but they thrive less than the paragenesic.

From the foregoing we must conclude that the rule as regards the human race is eugenesic, but that certain races are less fruitful between themselves by their first-blood mongrels than by their collaterals. It is only a question of degree. Consequently these may always be produced either directly or indirectly, a strictly intermediate race between two races as distant as any now existing on the globe. Frequently the race will become extinct before being fixed by a sufficient repetition of the laws of inheritance, or because external circumstances and acclimation will not favour it. Frequently, owing to the predominance of one or the other element, there will be a progressive reversion towards one of the mother-races, as in the case of the Griquas. But time and circumstances acting together, the product of that race will be inevitable. Let us suppose that the cross is only paragenesic, the result will be the same. Let there be two parallel and cross races, the one formed by a reversion of the mongrels of the first blood towards the white, the other by a reversion towards the black. Once established, their anthropological distance will be evidently less than between the two primitive mother-races. Supposing the cross *inter se*

[*] " 'Note sur les Métis d'Australiens et d'Européens,' in 'Revue d'Anthropologie,' by P. Topinard, vol. iv., 1876."

recommences, it will still form two new races inclining in the same way, the one towards the white, the other towards the black, but more nearly allied the one to the other than the preceding. Their establishment being produced in the same way, and the operation being repeated, the distance will be once more lessened, so that at a certain moment there will be none at all, and between the two original black and white races there will spring up a definite and strictly intermediate race. There is no other way of accounting for the infinite number of races now in existence, which have taken their origin from two neighbouring races, having all the appearance of comparatively pure races. In a series of 100 New Caledonian skulls, one-third represents a more or less peculiar and well-defined type, resembling no other with which we are acquainted, and which is the extinct Melanesian type—one-third is indistinguishable from the most characteristic Polynesian skulls—and one-third is the superposition, or mixture in various proportions, of the characters of the two other types.

In time the average type will be that of a New Caledonian race, and yet at a remote period there had been these two types profoundly different. Formerly, when seas and forests caused mankind to be more isolated, the accidental characters in a race were confirmed, their aspect remained unchanged. Now that immigration has assumed such vast proportions, the characters are less distinct. Crossing is the principal agent in the confusedness of races, as hereditary influence and external circumstances are the principal agents in their separation. The one will introduce unity in the future the others must have produced plurality in the past.[*]

Inheritance.

In every individual, or in every generation of individuals, there are two opposite tendencies : the one to divergence, or variability

[*] We are compelled to omit many notices of books for want of space. The reader is referred especially to the article "Métis," by Dr. Dally, in the "Encycl. des Sciences Médicales," 2nd series, vol. vii.

of characters; the other to concentration, or perpetuation of these characters. The force presiding over the latter is inheritance, which may be defined as the property of living beings of repeating themselves, or of reproducing themselves under the same forms and with the same attributes. A white man removed to a hot country assumes such a dark colour as to be almost taken for a black. His child, however, is born white, and continues so as long as he is not exposed to the same atmospheric conditions. The Jews of Cochin are generally darker in colour, nevertheless they are white; their children are born white, and their wives, being sheltered from exposure to the sun, are white. It is so with the Parsees and Arabs, who are often very dark. The reason of this is that the white colour is a fixed character of these races, that is to say dating back to the remote past. Thus from inheritance emanates the law of permanence of types, which show the identity between the ancient Egyptian type, as represented on monuments of five or six thousand years ago, and the type of Fellahs which still inhabit the banks of the Nile; the identity of the Jewish types of that period and of the present, and the persistence of character here and there of the Cro-Magnon man in the midst of peoples who have succeeded them, and into which they have become absorbed.

If physical characters, the existence of which is lost in the obscurity of past ages, are transmitted without appreciable change, is it so with characters acquired accidentally at a later period? If we look at the custom among the Chinese of squeezing the foot, which has been practised for a thousand years, without its size being diminished; at the use of circumcision among the Jews, as well as at the non-transmissibility of artificial deformations of the skull, we should be disposed to answer in the negative. But in the first two cases, and generally in the third, the deformation has only to do with one sex. Goss maintained, indeed, that the deformations of the skull practised on both sexes during many generations, became hereditary. The question is still an open one; but we must not conceal from ourselves the fact that the vertical flattening of the nucha among the Malays, the Syrians,

and many Americans,* favours this opinion. The inheritance of
polydactylia—a deformity which frequently takes place through
three or four or five generations simultaneously in many families—
also deserves consideration. In all those cases, marriages take
place outside the families predisposed. If they had had their
origin from within, who knows whether a new race of polydactyls
might not have been produced? It is true an objection may be
made to these cases, as well as to other hereditary deformities
mentioned by Scoutetten as hypospadias, and cleft palate, namely,
that the cause which at first engendered the anomaly spontaneously
is alone perpetuated; in a word, that there is only an hereditary
predisposition. But among animals in which selection practised
by Man's hand favours the development of a character, an accidental lesion has frequently become the origin of a particular race.
Thus the hornless oxen, or those with very rudimentary horns, of
Paraguay, the short-legged sheep of Massachusetts, the races of
tailless dogs. What has been produced by selection, cannot chance
perpetuate?

In a pure race all the individuals resemble each other as regards
their main features. The law of inheritance is that the son is the
reproduction of his father and mother. We are told that the
Andamans and the Todas are all alike. We can hardly say so of
the Greenlanders. M. Broca has in his laboratory five skulls of
Patagonians which are identical. But these are rarities. Among
the inscrutable influences which cause the child to put on such and
such characters, there is a conflict of all the elements which figure
in his genealogy. He resembles his mother during a portion of his
existence, at a later period he becomes like his father, and sometimes like some distant relative. We have seen that in a hybrid
we take into account the quantity of blood belonging to one or the
other side. So with respect to inheritance, there is a struggle
between the characters; some are added, others are neutralised,
while others have no reciprocal influence. The most remote ancestors have their share in it as well as the nearest relatives.
M. de Quatrefages knew a great-grandson of the bailiff of Suffren who
was a striking likeness of his ancestor after four generations, and

who, nevertheless, bore no resemblance either to his father or his mother. It is thus that we account for the horse unexpectedly presenting the characteristic stripes of the zebra, which might have formed part of his zoological genealogy. This phenomenon is termed atavism, and is common to Man. An individual presents the features of a past generation which has been absolutely forgotten. The appearance of such characters is therefore a matter of chance; or rather, there are in the germ certain latent influences which it is impossible to fathom. Certain characters retain their hold more firmly than others, such as the shape of the nose or of the ear. Everyone recognises the Bourbon nose. M. L. Rousselet met with it at the Bhopal court in Central India, in a direct descendant of Francis I. Waitz says one of the most frequently quoted examples is that of the thick lip of the house of Hapsburg since its alliance with the ancient house of Jagellon.

Intellectual qualities are transmitted, as well as physical characters. In the family of Bach there were thirty-two musicians. It is the same as regards morbid affections. In all these there is a transmission of anatomical forms, either original or acquired by no matter what process, and by education among others. In the law of inheritance, as in all the other laws of the universe, there is nothing of an occult kind. Here like begets like. The following are the principal forms of inheritance: (a) *Continuous* inheritance, when the son resembles the father and mother, and these resemble their parents; (b) *Interrupted* inheritance, when, without resembling either father or mother, he is like his grandfather: this is very remarkable as regards the transmission of disease, and is frequently alternating; (c) *Collateral* inheritance, when the child resembles an uncle or a great-uncle; (d) *Atavic* inheritance, when the resemblance goes back still farther. We need not say that the accounts of resemblance to a stranger who might have struck the attention of the mother during pregnancy are fables. So we must only accept with reservation those cases where the child might have had the features of its mother's first husband.

The characters which mongrels exhibit are only applications of the law of inheritance, the consequences of which are reduced to a

calculus of probability. Sometimes the mongrel of the first blood is
exactly intermediate between the two parents as regards the colour
of the skin and the character of the hair, as M. Pruner-Bey has
shown, or as regards the proportions of the skeleton, as M. Broca
has stated. One of the varieties of Zambos, or mixed breeds of
negroes and Americans, is the Cafuso, in whom the hair is very
curly, and coarse enough to form a huge bristly wig. Sometimes
this mongrel embodies in himself a portion of the characters of one
or other parent; for example, as in the mulatto mentioned by
M. de Quatrefages, the intelligence of the father and the features of
the mother. In this group are the piebald mongrels, whose skin is
black in some places and white in others, or white on the whole of
the lateral or upper half of the body and black on the other.
Sometimes the child possesses altogether the character of one or
other parent: for example, the child of a European father and a
Chinese mother, Dr. Scherzer says, is altogether a European or
altogether a Chinese. A Berber with blue eyes and with the lobule
of the ear absent, married to a dark Arab woman with a well-formed
ear, had two children, one like himself, the other like his wife.
An English officer, fair, with blue eyes and florid complexion, had
several children by an Indian negress. Some were the image of the
father, others exactly like the mother. Lucas mentions the case of
a negress who had three children at a birth; one was white, one
black, and one fawn-coloured; that is to say of the colour of a
quarter-blooded hybrid between a negro and a mulatto (De Quatrefages).

Examples of interrupted, collateral, and atavic inheritance are
numerous among mixed breeds, and it is then in fact that they are
the most striking. A decided negro having had a white among his
ancestors has unexpectedly a child with a white skin by a negress.
Instances of this have been repeated regularly every second generation: this is alternate inheritance.

The peculiarities of one or the other race are more particularly
apt to be retained. The coarse hair of the American, or the woolly
hair of the negro, for example. The most persistent character of
the reversion from the negro to the white is the yellow colour of the

nails, and the want of firmness of the cartilages of the nose. The child of a negro father and a white mother will be more like the father than the child of a white father and a negro mother will be like his father (*Waitz*, *Fitzroy*). Pallas relates that the mongrel produced by the alliance of the Russian with the Mongolian will be more like the latter than the former. Others maintain the reverse.

It is asked whether crossing produces an improvement or deterioration of races in an intellectual point of view, and whether they ought to be encouraged. But the external conditions in which the new race is found have been too much overlooked, as when considering their degree of vitality we lose sight of their acclimation. Half-castes are often excluded from the society into which they are thrown. So they readily adopt its vices, and use them against it by way of retaliation. The majority of the examples which we have are rather favourable to them. The Griquas, if they are not equal to the Dutch, are superior to the aborigines. The mongrels of Java are better, according to Dr. Yvan, than the Malays. It is impossible to doubt but that the Polynesians have gained by crossing with whites. The Australian mongrels of Bass's Straits were very clever, according to Stokes. The highest encomiums were passed upon the *boundary-riders*, who were Australian half-breeds. If, in America, the Zambos occupied the prisons of Lima and Mexico, the Cafusos are described in most glowing terms by Spix and Martius. Mulattoes in the United States are exempt from yellow fever the same as negroes. Their mongrel reversions towards the white have, in various degrees, a similar immunity.

M. de Gobineau attributes to crossing the disasters of empires and the degradation of races. Nott maintains that if it were general it would lead to the extinction of the human race. Knox and Périer did not believe that civilisation could make progress except with pure races. M. Dally thinks that in an equal struggle, the superiority would remain with the pure races. Bodichon, on the other hand, declares that the era of universal peace and fraternity will be realised by crossing; and Thévenot, Deschamps, Serres, Waitz, and De Quatrefages hold a similar opinion.

Dare we say, after these authorities, that the problem is nevertheless a simple one? Two pure races will have a better progeny; two impure races a worse. Two races, the one pure, the other impure, will have an impure progeny relatively to the superior race, and pure relatively to the inferior. The law of inheritance is exerted with rigid exactness, but a multitude of other conditions are mingled with it, which we cannot separate from it—such as the action of external circumstances, acclimation, morals, education, and social laws.

The number of mongrels on the face of the globe has been estimated at 12 millions, of whom no fewer than 11 millions are in South America, 3000 in Oceania, &c. But has a computation been specially made of those of Europe? Gerdy states that there are no pure races in Europe. Does crossing increase fecundity? This is the really important question. We reply: Certainly not between races anthropologically very remote from each other, but probably so between contiguous races. M. de Quatrefages, however, thinks that even in the former case fecundity is increased. M. Broca remarks that in France the population has increased since the Revolution, owing to the intermingling of the classes which were originally constituted of victors and vanquished.

Consanguineous Unions.

Our conclusion on the subject of crossing was that the more nearly allied the races, the greater were the chances of fecundation between two individuals. Carrying this out to its logical sequence, the result would be that in the same tribe or in the same family the most nearly related ought to be the most fertile. But it seems that in this case we must distinguish between the number and the quality of the progeny. Breeders who select their subjects with a definite object to breed in and in, that is to say between near relations, rapidly obtain excellent results. They know, however, that fertility then diminishes, and that it will cease altogether if they do not have recourse from time to time to crossing, in order to strengthen the race.   Extreme fecundity and superiority of race would therefore be two contradictory terms, which may be a consolation to those who maintain, though improperly, that the fecundity of the French is diminishing.   But is it with Men as with animals?   The question of consanguineous unions has been discussed at the Société Anthropologique, by Boudin, Dally, and De Ranse.   It is said that blindness, pigmentary retinitis, albinism, epilepsy, idiocy, mental aberration, sterility, scrofula, abortion, hare-lip, and deaf-muteness are more frequent after unions among kindred.   It is necessary to produce facts in support of this statement. Dr. Voisin went to pursue his studies in the borough of Batz, in the peninsula of Croisic, among an isolated population who only married among themselves.   As the result of 45 marriages between first cousins or second cousins, he found 174 children not one of whom exhibited either of the above ailments.   The conclusion was obvious, viz. that consanguineous unions, even if closely allied, were not attended with hurtful consequences.   Other facts have been observed by M. Ferrier at Pauillac (Gironde); by M. Gabler at Gavat, in the Pyrenees; by M. Dally in the island of Bréhat (Côtes-du-Nord); by Dr. Duchenne, of Boulogne, at Portel.   All are agreed upon the matter.   Beyond the seas, one example alone will suffice.   The Todas of the Nilgherries are endogamous.   They all marry among themselves, and are all related to one another in some way.   Their wives are polyandrous, and have sometimes four or five brothers for husbands ; and notwithstanding all this, the race has for ages been one of the finest in India.   Out of 198 individuals, Mr. Marshall found only two suffering from any infirmity.

In conclusion, it seems clear that unions between cousins and second cousins are followed by excellent results when both are healthy, and that, on the contrary, morbid predispositions being afloat, their effects are proportionately felt by the offspring.   As to alliances between direct kindred and blood-relations, the question is yet sub judice.   We may remark that the laws of civilized countries have only forbidden them on moral and social grounds.

CHAPTER VIII.

INFLUENCE OF MILIEUX—ACCLIMATION—WEIGHT OF THE BODY
—MUSCULAR FORCE—PULSE—RESPIRATION—INTELLECTUAL
FUNCTIONS—PATHOLOGICAL CHARACTERS.

Influence of Milieux.

In antagonism with inheritance, which preserves the characters, and the crosses, which bind them together, there is, as we have said, the variability which multiplies them, and tends to make them diverge. Varieties are produced under two influences. (1) During intra-uterine life, spontaneously and as it were by accident; (2) In the course of existence, by external circumstances, or milieux. The doctrine of Darwin rests entirely on the former, that of Lamarck and Geoffroy Saint-Hilaire on the latter. At present we shall only examine facts respecting these latter, without reference to theories.

Under the name of milieux, M. de Quatrefages includes "the assemble of conditions or influences of every kind, whether physical, moral, or intellectual, which may act upon organised beings;" in a word, all the external causes capable of producing, either directly or indirectly, a change in living organs. We shall confine ourselves to the most manifest characters, relative to which there has been the greatest difference of opinion.

The colour of the skin, it is said, is variable, and results from atmospheric causes. Races are regularly distributed from the equator to the poles—the darkest in hot countries, the lightest in cold. Let us see if this is so at the present time, for those of the orthodox school make no allusion here to the past, it is already known to them; this is the Adamic version.

The peoples nearest to the north pole are the Esquimaux, the Samoiedes, and the Lapps, with tawny complexions, black hair and

2 c

eyes, and have dwelt in these icy latitudes from the most remote
periods. Let us remember that there is a general harmony between the colour of the skin and that of the hair and iris, which
colour depends on the increase or diminution of pigmentary
matter in the organism. At a lower latitude, in a country with a
relatively elevated temperature, are the Scandinavians, in Europe,
a race with a lighter skin, hair, and eyes than perhaps any in the
world, and the Finn, with fair complexion, chestnut or red hair,
and grey or greenish eyes. In Asia there are whole populations
with black hair and eyes, but with yellow complexions, and in
America, Indians with complexions of a reddish hue.

The doctrine is at fault from the very beginning.

At the south pole the first habitable regions that we meet with
are at about 34 degrees south latitude, and are peopled by the
Peschereis, with olive or tawny complexion, next to which are the
Patagonians, whose complexion is darker, and the Charruas, whose
complexion is analogous to that of mulattoes, if not darker. In
the other hemisphere there are the Tasmanians, with a complexion
as black as soot, with a slightly yellowish tinge in it, and the yellow-
tawny Hottentots, close to the Kaffirs, who are entirely black.
Nothing is as yet favourable to the doctrine of which Prichard was
the interpreter. If we go to the equator we meet with facts
equally contradictory. In America the ancient Indians of California were as black at 42 degrees north latitude as the negroes of
Guinea, while farther south there were tribes of an olive or reddish
complexion, relatively light. So in Africa, the darkest negroes are
at 12 or 15 degrees north latitude, while their colour becomes
lighter the nearer they approach the equator.

"The Yoloffs," says Golberry, "are a proof that the black colour
does not depend entirely on solar heat, nor on the fact that they
are more exposed to a vertical sun, but arises from other causes, for
the farther we go from the influence of its rays the more the black
colour is diminished in intensity." In the tropics, among the
Tawareks of the Sahara, the Afghans of India, and on the banks
of the Orinoco and the Amazon, in the midst of a dark population,
we meet with whole tribes with fair complexion, light hair, and

blue eyes. But it is said these irregularities are due to local circumstances, such as altitude. Prichard says fair complexions are to be seen more in mountainous districts, and dark in the plains. Thus the Swiss, in the lofty mountains of Lombardy, have brown or red hair, while the Milanese, in the plain, have black hair. The Berbers, of fair complexion, are seen principally in the Aurès mountains, and the dark in the plain. The negroes of the table-lands are less dark than those of the low plains near the shores of the Gulf of Guinea, &c. In the higher regions of Estates and Kaffas, in Abyssinia, we find the natives are of a lighter complexion than in Europe, &c. All these are examples upon which we can rely, but we might mention some of an altogether opposite character. M. de Quatrefages states that the Abyssinians become black on leaving the plains for the heights, which he attributes to the more direct action of the sun's rays. The Antisian race of the low plains of Peru is white in comparison with the Aymaras and the Quichuas of the high table-lands (*D'Orbigny*). Humboldt says: "The Indians of the torrid zone, who inhabit the most elevated plains of the Cordillera of the Andes, and those who are engaged in fishing at the 50th degree of south latitude, in the islands of the Chonos Archipelago, have the same copper colour as those who, under a scorching climate, cultivate the banana in the deepest and narrowest valleys of the equinoctial region." He adds that the tribes of the Rio Negro have a more sunburnt complexion than those of the Upper Orinoco, notwithstanding that the banks of the former are cooler than those of the latter.

The smooth or crisp character of the hair would be equally due to climate, according to the doctrine of the influence of external circumstances (*milieux*). Heat and dryness cause the hair to roll into spirals, but it will not produce flattening to the same extent. Is it not the reverse as regards animals? The woolly fleece of the sheep of temperate countries would be transformed into a fleece with straight hair towards the equator. Moreover, there are negroes with very woolly hair even in Tasmania, at a latitude of 45 degrees south, and we know that in the southern hemisphere the temperature is much colder than in similar latitudes in the north. On the

contrary, in the tropics, there are blacks with smooth straight hair,
as the Australians, the blacks of the Deccan, the Himyarites of the
Yemen, &c.   How is it, according to the above hypothesis, that
the heat has exerted its influence on the skin and not on the
hair?   The stature has also been attributed to the influence of
external circumstances, especially to food, to differences of temperature, and to altitude.   We have referred to this at page 319.   We
only remark that if the Peruvians are small on the most elevated
table-lands of the globe, the Malays, called *Orangs laut*, on
the coast of the peninsula of Malacca, and the Andamans, at sea-
level, are still more so ; which subverts the opinion of D'Orbigny,
that the tall Kaffirs and the diminutive Bosjesmans live side by
side in the same forests of southern Africa; that the Todas at
the top of the Nilgherries are tall, and live only on pulse and
milk-food, while the Irulas and the Krumbas on either side of them
are comparatively short, and live on the flesh of the buffalo ; that
the Scandinavians in their cold countries, the negroes at the
equator, the Redskins in the Rocky Mountains, the Tehuelches in
the sands of Patagonia, and the Polynesians in the low islands of
the Pacific, are all very tall under the most opposite conditions.
" I have observed," says M. Broca, " that the stature of the French,
generally speaking, does not depend upon altitude or latitude, is
not a question of poverty or riches, of character of soil or of food,
nor is it the result of any other external condition; but I have been
led to believe it to arise solely from a *general* influence, that of
ethnic inheritance."

We have no proof, indeed, that in the present state of things,
and in the very short time during which our observations have
extended, there has ever been produced an important and hereditary change of a physical character under the influence of external
circumstances.   Whenever we meet either with Arabs or Jews,
their type is the same, as we learn from Egyptian monuments.
At Leyden, the Jew is said to be simply a little lighter, at Algiers
of a yellowish tint, in India to be dark.   There is no doubt as
to the last.   At Cochin, on the coast of Malabar, there are—(1)
Black Jews ; these are native converts ; (2) White Jews, who

came there at the period of the destruction of Jerusalem, and
whose history can be traced back at least six centuries. Now
these have remained white, or rather brown, from the climate, and
as compared with ourselves, but white as compared with the surrounding nations. Their children are born white, and their wives
when not exposed to the sun remain white.

Notwithstanding all we have said, external circumstances have
an undeniable influence certainly. Vegetables become white when
excluded from the light, and not only on the surface but throughout
their entire substance, and it even affects their flavour, and extends
to other properties of the sap. The animals of the polar regions
become white on the approach of winter. The small and puny
oxen of the Sologne when transported to the valleys of the Loire,
in one or two generations assume an entirely altered appearance as
regards their size and quality. Peasants and sailors become tawny
on exposure to the open air and in hot countries, on the uncovered
parts of the body. But in the last-mentioned case the influence is
confined to the individual, it is not hereditary; it is also different
in different races. We have said that dark and fair Europeans do
not tan equally when exposed to the air; the former readily become
black, the latter become sunburnt, and of a brick-red hue, or
assume a yellowish tint, which Monrad considers as the first
evidence on the coast of Guinea of having become acclimatised.
This yellowish colour passes into that of copper, and becomes
darker in each succeeding generation. The Chinese also become
black on exposure to the sun during the summer, and light in
winter. There is a vast distinction between this and the individual's
transmission of an acquired character to his posterity. The
individual becomes black as he becomes fat. If excluded from
exposure to the sun, and his food is scanty, he becomes pale and
thin.

In the Sandwich Islands an opposite phenomenon takes place
(*Choris*). The children when first born are black, the people
of distinction dark brown, and the labouring people of a lighter
tint, or orange colour. But this is a different matter; one
ought perhaps to look upon the two classes as two distinct races,

Nevertheless we admit that modifications of physical characters might be produced, if not under our very eyes, at least in the course of time, and might be added to from age to age. We must admit that these things might be explained physiologically according to this hypothesis.

Stature, for example, is the result of two influences. (1) Of the race, or rather of the predominance of action of such race whether a paternal or maternal; and (2) Of a concurrence of hygienic circumstances. According as the nutrition of the skeleton goes on properly or not, its ossification is or is not regular—the epiphyses are united to the diaphyses soon or late—so will the individual be either tall or short.

Let the accident be repeated, let the phenomenon go on in the same way during many generations, it will become a habit (in medicine we recognise pathological as well as physiological habits, and their tenacity and hereditary character are truly remarkable), and soon a regularly transmissible character. We cannot therefore be surprised to see the persistence with which travellers, those in Australia for example, assert that individuals of low stature in that country, are badly fed, poorly clad, and miserable, while tall statures are characteristic of the natives of the interior, who are strong and healthy, having every resource within their reach. Individual varieties unquestionably depend partly on external circumstances, and partly on the state of the health. M. Broca himself allows this as regards certain differences between the sexes. Some statistics of Quételet relative to healthy and diseased children prove it.

The increase of the pigmentary matter might also be easily explained in this way. The cutaneous system, excited by contact with the air, heat, and light performs its functions more readily, its glandular apparatus secretes more, and the black matter is deposited in greater abundance in the cellules beneath the epidermis. From this cause, and probably by reflex action upon the supra-renal capsules or the liver, the hypersecretion would be diffused through the entire organism, and the colouring matter derived from the blood, from the biliary matter, or from elsewhere, would increase.

Peculiarities proper to each race would be that one would become
decidedly black, another yellowish or olive, a third reddish. An
objection of this sort might arise : Why the parts exposed to the air
are not the only ones black? The opposite phenomenon, a want
of excitation, would, on the contrary, produce pallor, that is to say
a sort of anæmia, as in miners. The white Antisians of Peru, says
D'Orbigny, live at the foot of perpendicular rocks, under enormous
trees, the branches of which form a vast arbour impenetrable to the
rays of the sun; where the atmosphere is humid, and the vegetation
luxuriant. Their five tribes live there enveloped in darkness, and
are of lighter complexion than the Moxos of the adjoining open
plains, and the Aymaras on the elevated plateaux. As regards the
increase of the volume of the skull and all the craniometrical
characters which result from it, the explanation would be no less
easy. The more the brain works the more does it continue to
increase beyond its ordinary term of growth, and the sutures are
closed later. The small size at the present day of the skull of
women relatively to that of man, as compared with that which it
was at the prehistoric period represented by the two beautiful
series from the cavern of L'Homme Mort and the Baye caves in the
department of La Marne, would arise from an opposite cause. The
variations of the forms and proportions of the skeleton might be all
explained in the same way, by virtue of the physiological law, that
the function makes the organ. The more work a limb, or an
organ, or a muscle does, the more it increases in volume; changes
at the same time taking place in the parts with which it is connected. The fémur à colonne, the platycnemic tibia, the large chest
of individuals compelled to take deep inspirations, the corpulence
of persons who confine themselves principally to a vegetable diet,
and whose meals are irregular, and sometimes very large in quantity,
are accounted for in this way.

No explanation can be given as to the varieties of the hair in
its fundamental types. For example, the straight and round, the
woolly and flat hair, as seen under the microscope. In this lies the
most serious objection to the theory of the derivation of characters
from one another. In the present state of science we have no

explanation to give on the subject. Individuals experience the
influence of external conditions under our own personal observation,
but they do not visibly transmit the changes so made—there is no
authentic instance of it. The distribution of characters according
to altitudes and latitudes has exclusively to do with the fortuitous
migration of peoples. In the present state of science, and as far as
our limited investigations extend, the law of permanence of types
remains intact. Moreover, physiology enables us to understand the
mechanism by virtue of which new characters might take their
origin. Under what exceptional conditions, at present unknown
to us, may not hereditary influence, that great conservative force,
depart from its extreme strictness? This is the question. It is
quite clear that the variations of climate and conditions of life are
very slight now in comparison with what they necessarily were
formerly. The fact is that Man has not always known how to
guard against the preponderating influence of external agencies,
nor has he always been able to leave the country under every
change of circumstances. No new race, having characters other
than those of the mixed races produced from crossing, has been
created within our knowledge; and moreover, everything compels
us to believe that there was a greater tendency to change at a
remote period in the past than there is at present, and this belief
has found a support in the law of hereditary influence.

It is one of two things: either races have been created originally
in infinite number, and have since become diminished by natural
extinction or by crossing, or they have been multiplied under the
influence of climate and external circumstances.*

Acclimation.

There is but a step from the influence of climate and external
conditions to acclimation. Man, unlike the anthropoids, is found
in all climates, and conforms himself to every condition of life; but

* See the articles "Altitude," by Leroy de Méricourt; "Méologia," by
Bertillon; "Climat," by Fauvelgrives; "Atmosphère," by Gavarret, &c.,
in "Encycl. des Sciences Médicales."

he owes it to his intelligence, and pays the penalty. Let us examine the question more closely.

The words *acclimation* and *acclimatisation* are not synonymous. The former is understood of the spontaneous and natural accommodation to new climatic conditions, the latter of the intervention of Man in this accommodation. The one is the fact, the other the knowledge of the conditions and phenomena of accommodation; the one is a physiological property of Man, and concerns anthropology, the other is in the domain of hygiene, of medicine, and of the schools. M. Bertillon has treated of them, from every point of view, with his usual critical acumen, and it will suffice for us to analyse his article, " Acclimatement," in the " Encyclopédie des Sciences Médicales." M. Bertillon commences with a comparison of the statistics of births and deaths. He finds differences between one race and another, either in their general faculty of acclimation or in their capability of living in some latitudes in preference to others. He discovers differences even between European races. Thus the English become habituated to the climate of the United States, the island of St. Helena, and the Cape of Good Hope, but they fail to do so in the Antilles and in India. In the same way the Germanic race thrives in the United States, but dies out in the tropics, and even in Algeria. The Dutch likewise. Under the name of Boers they continue to live under the most favourable conditions in the colony of the Cape, the climate of which is very similar to that of our own country, while they perish under the scorching climate of the Malay peninsula. The French do well in Canada, in Nova Scotia, in the United States, in the Mauritius and the Friendly Islands, but as they approach the tropics their faculty of adaptation decreases. In the Antilles they succeed in making a first branch, but they do not increase, and require to receive fresh blood by crossing with foreigners up to the third or fourth generation. In Algeria the French belonging to the northern departments do not thrive, while those of the south make progress. In Madagascar, and especially in Senegal, no European race can hold out long. In New Caledonia the mortality among French emigrants is less than in France. The Spaniards, in whose blood there is much of the

Berber, adapt themselves wonderfully to the climate of the southern part of the United States, of Mexico, the Antilles, and South America. These, with the Maltese and Jews, are the most favoured of Algerian colonists. The Portuguese share with them the same privileges.

The Tschinghani, Gipsies, or Bohemians, are, of all peoples, those whom we meet with most universally. In the waste lands of Brazil, on the summit of the Himalayas, in Moscow, Madrid, London, Stamboul, at 30 to 35 degrees centigrade above zero, in the torrid zones of India and Africa, they are to be found everywhere. The Israelites also possess a remarkable aptitude for becoming acclimatised; but they do not advance so much towards the north, they proceed step by step, cautiously feeling their way, and follow the course of civilisation. The Arabs readily become acclimatised, but they remain in hot isothermal zones, and venture but little into the temperate zones. M. Bertillon does not speak of the Chinese, but everyone knows that they are much esteemed as labourers in Malacca, Australia, California, and the Antilles. Since the abolition of slavery in America, they are gradually taking the place of the negro, owing to their soon becoming accustomed to the climate; but we have not seen them emigrate into cold countries.

Australia, although having the most opposite climates, is very suitable to Europeans of every nationality, while the Malay Archipelago, more especially the northern part, is very fatal to them; Cochin-China the same. In Java and Sumatra the Dutch do not become acclimatised, and this no doubt is the cause of the sterility of certain of their mixed breeds with the aborigines for a definite number of generations. India is also fatal to Europeans, but the low plains situated on the sea-shore, and the banks of the great rivers, must be distinguished from the elevated plateaux of Central India. The English have established sanitaria in the mountains, where they go to recruit their health. Egypt is no less remarkable for its insalubrity. Its present population is the same as it was in former days. It has never been maintained without being incessantly renewed by immigration. It is very fatal even to the negro. The Mamelukes have had sway there for 560 years, and not one has been able to keep up a persistent race. The rate of mortality among the negroes of Africa, even in their own country, is considerable. The birth rate however is very high; but for this they would become extinct. This mortality seems to be consequent on their indolence, and on their using too exertion for their well-being. We must not therefore be astonished at their success in America, where, particularly in the Antilles, and in the United States previously to the war, they were taken care of like valuable merchandise. In 1808, the period when the importation to that country ceased, they were 400,000, in 1860 their number increased to 4,000,000. Since the war they have been compelled to look after themselves, and have returned to their natural indolence; thus their number is diminishing. So much for emigration into hot countries. In cold regions, Europeans do not readily become acclimatised, and negroes especially die rapidly. The fair population of Iceland is visibly decreasing, which is to be attributed to the island becoming progressively colder. The Esquimaux, who on their first arrival in Greenland found a climate which was more supportable than now, decreased for the same reason. At St. Petersburg the deaths exceed the births; and if the Slavs are masters of the northern part of the continent, they owe it to their crossing with the Finns, and perhaps more to the west, with the Samoïedes. Thus it appears that extremes of climate are not suitable to any race, and that if Man transports himself from one part of the globe to another, and settles down there, it is frequently at his peril, notwithstanding the resources with which his intelligence furnishes him. The fair races are especially adapted to temperate and cool regions, and the south is looked upon as almost forbidden ground. The brown races, on the contrary, have a remarkable power of becoming acclimatised. In the north they are represented by the Laplanders. They stretch away as far as the equator, the most characteristic of them especially. But when considering the question of removing from one climate to another, we must distinguish between slight and important changes, between those which are sudden and those which are progressive. M. Bertillon divides the accidental circumstances due to sudden acclimation in a new isothermal region, and are produced upon the individual and his progeny, into four groups or phases. (1) Sudden diseases; (2) Chronic consecutive anæmias, which place the individual in an unfavourable condition to resist accidental diseases, or make him quickly look old; (3) Diseases of early infancy in offspring born in the country; (4) Physical and intellectual degeneration, and the infertility of the second and third generations. (See page 372.)

Very different are the circumstances connected with acclimation on a small scale. A family incapable of being suddenly transported from Paris to Senegal is well able to bear removal to Pau. In succeeding generations it will be able to go to Cadiz, many generations afterwards to Morocco, and so on. It is thus that the slow immigrations from Central Asia have been accomplished—not the invasions of the barbarous tribes which rushed down upon Europe at the commencement of our era. Some of these migrations bearing off to the north-west would have reached comparatively cold countries, and others going south would find India, where at the present time some fair people are to be met with in a country where the English could not settle. The Esquimaux, before becoming acclimatised in their country of eternal snow, lived in Asia, at about the 40th degree of north latitude. All parts of a country are not equally unfavourable for acclimation. Without speaking of a swamp here or a desert there, which increases the mortality among new-comers, there is the altitude to be taken into consideration. A family will not be able to become acclimatised at the level of the sea, and will thrive by ascending the course of a river or the sides of a mountain. High table-lands are in much request in all hot countries. The contradictory opinions of Jourdanet and Coindet relative to the residence of Europeans in elevated parts of Mexico, leave the question undecided. But in a French territory the experiment has been made. Whilst Bertillon and Ricoux come to the conclusion that the Germanic race, in a general way, does not become acclimatised in Algeria, we find in the entire province of Constantine, and on the whole line of the

Atlas, from the Aurès mountains to Morocco, a large number of fair people, who have existed there for four or five thousand years. A circumstance favourable to permanent acclimation is the crossing, however little, with the native race, or with other races which have settled in the country at the same period with it, but with a greater power of acclimation. A small quantity of negro blood lessens the tendency to contract yellow fever. So at the Cape of Good Hope, in the United States, in Australia, and also in Algeria, the emigrant races must not be designated by their particular name, but must be looked upon as now mixed races, having their own special characters. Under these conditions the influence of climate and external circumstances appears even more marked, the same as in chemistry certain re-agents act more readily when bodies are brought into contact in the nascent state. After the greatest mortality, a few of the survivors are sufficient to serve as a starting-point for a new population. In a word, Man's restricted faculty of acclimation may favour, within certain limits, the diffusion and mixture of races on the face of the globe, and even the formation of new races; but it is also an obstacle to their diffusion and transformation. It tends to allot them a place at the period which is the most suitable to them. This is why we see the negro races generally predominating in some zones, the brown or yellow in others, and the fair races in others. Having the minimum mortality in these zones, the race is kept up. The fair races, for example, far from being so on account of climate, as Prichard would have it, would only conform themselves to it in the same way as the prehistoric animals which went northwards or southwards in the course of ages, according to the changes of temperature and vegetation. If we did not know that the climatic conditions of all parts of the globe have radically changed over and over again, we should deduce from this that the negro races took their rise on the continents of the inter-tropical zone, while the fair races originated in the cold or temperate regions of the north. It is thus that the faculty of accommodation to climate or acclimation, which varies according to race, furnishes an argument for the polygenistic doctrine. The two questions of crossing and of

inheritance are connected with the functions, so mysterious, of
reproduction; those of external conditions and acclimation, to the
more general function of nutrition. The two characters which
exhibit the amount of vital energy in individuals, as well as in
races, are the weight of the body and muscular strength.

The Weight of the Body,

Studied in its relation to age, profession, and stature, by Quételet,
Hutchinson, and Gould, does not possess the interest which has
been extended to it. Its causes are various, such as hygiene, food,
character of occupation, temperament, and race. The probable
connection between these last two makes it the more difficult
to consider the question of race by itself. The cases of exceptional
obesity, due to high feeding or to indolence, are observed in all
races from the Englishman to the Hottentot, and ought to be at
once set aside, as well as those cases of extreme emaciation, consequent on habitually insufficient food, or continued exposure to the
sun. The Arab, shrivelled up in the desert, becomes fat in the
towns, especially his half-breeds. The Mongols, the Chinese, and
the Polynesians readily become obese.

The following averages of weight are only interesting as a matter
of curiosity :

		Kilogrammes.
607 Iroquois Indians (Gould)...		78·5
680 Musketoes (Gould)...		65·8
12,740 Bavarians (Bernstein)		65·5
400 Frenchmen (Bernard)		61·9
1775 Negroes (Gould)		64·0
617 Englishmen (W. S. Thomson)		68·8
9157 American soldiers of all nationalities (Gould)...		64·4
150 New Zealanders (W. S. Thomson)		63·9
373 Magyars (Bernstein)		60·7
860 Roumanians (Bernstein)...		58·4
50 Hindoos, high caste (Shortt)		58·2
60 Natives of the Caucasus (Shortt)		50·0
50 Hindoos, low caste (Shortt)		48·7
60 Natives, low casts, of the Nilgherries (Shortt)		44·6
69 „ low class, of the Madras coast (Shortt)		42·7

Muscular Strength.

Muscular strength is a more important subject, although we must consider it in its connection with the individual's state of health, food, age, and sex, as well as with the power acquired by the continued use of the muscles. The dynamometer, by the aid of which the experiments which we are about to mention were carried on, was invented by Regnier, at the close of the last century, at the suggestion of Buffon. Chaussier was the first to make use of it, then the travellers Péron, Freycinet, Quoy, and Gaimard, and lastly, Forbes, Quételet, and the anthropologists of the *Novarra* and of the war of American secession, who modified it. It gives, at will, the force of *pressure of the hands*, and the force of *vertical traction* from below upwards, the two hands acting together in both cases; that is to say the *manual strength* and the *strength of the back or loins*, of authors.

The following are some averages at five different periods to show the influence of age in two very opposite races. They are borrowed from Mr. Gould:

			Number of whites.	Strength of the back, Kil.	Number of negroes.	Strength of the back, Kil.
17 years	...	...	171	114	44	131
20 "	...	...	543	150	140	140
25 "	...	...	293	166	124	155
30 "	...	...	171	160	89	158
35 "	...	...	271	160	81	166
50 " and upwards	...	94	146	11	132

According to Mr. Gould, the maximum of muscular strength in both cases is at 31 years, and according to Quételet at 25. It is evident that we must take the former. The following table, which it would have been easy to enlarge, has reference to races. It is derived from various sources, and where not specially mentioned from Péron, Quoy, Gaimard, and the *Novarra*:

		Manual strength. kil.	Back strength. kil.
122	French	61·0	160
23	Hawai Islanders	60·1	171
64	Micronesians	56·9	150
26	Tongolans	52·4	118
12	Tasmanians (Péron)	50·6	118
30	Australians	48·0	100
57	Chinese	46·9	111
816	French seamen (Bansonnet)	46·9	142
5391	White soldiers (Gould)	46·8	155
1141	„ seamen	46·8	130
1600	Negroes	45·8	146
704	Mulattoes	46·8	156
600	Iroquois Indians	46·3	160

Péron and Freycinet at first came to the conclusion that savage races were inferior in point of strength to the European races. But

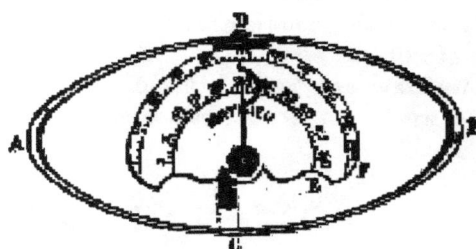

FIG. 41.—Mathieu's Dynamometer.

the aborigines upon whom their experiments were made were not in their own native forests, and were no doubt frightened during the experiment. The above averages clearly show that the Australians are very defective in manual strength, but that the Chinese are still more so. Those with the greatest amount of strength in the back, on the other hand, are the Iroquois Indians, and after them the natives of the Sandwich Archipelago. Negroes are undoubtedly stronger in the back than whites, but mulattoes are stronger than either. The muscular inferiority of the white seamen of Bansonnet and Gould clearly proves that the physiological condition surpasses in all cases the anthropological condition. In his statistics Mr. Gould has separated the delicate from those in perfect health, the difference between them being considerable. Thus, in white soldiers of delicate constitution the strength of the back was 127 kilogrammes, and in those in health 155 kilogrammes.

Another and more portable dynamometer is recommended in the "Instructions de la Société d'Anthropologie," that of Mathieu, figured in the preceding page. It measures the force of pressure with one hand, and the force of vertical traction, as with the instrument of Regnier. In twenty-four Frenchmen, from 20 to 60 years of age, the mean manual strength was 51·6 kilogrammes with the right arm. But it would be better to ascertain correctly the force of horizontal traction, as, according to M. Broca, it is this which gives more reliable results as between one race and another.[*]

To the functions of nutrition indirectly belong those of the circulation, respiration, and digestion. All have reference to organic life, and cannot materially differ between one race and another.

The Circulation of the Blood.

The circulation of the blood may be summed up in one single phenomenon—the beating of the heart, as indicated by the pulse at the radial artery. But more than any other phenomenon it is subject to transient or permanent influences foreign to Anthropological notions. The pulse varies with age, sex, individual peculiarity, stature, and also with the size of the body, before and during digestion, in the morning and at night, after exercise of any kind, and under the influence of emotion, even that caused by the examination of the individual. We cannot therefore deduce much

* "Description et Usage du Dynamomètre," by Regnier, in "Journal de l'École Polytechnique," vol. ii., Prairial year 6; "Voyage autour du Monde de l'Uranie et de La Physicienne, de 1817 à 1820," two vols., by L. de Freycinet; J. Forbes, in "Proceedings of Royal Society of Edinburgh," Jan. 16, 1837; Quetelet and Gould, op. cit.

from its study, and give the following averages for what they are worth:

						Pulse.
8284	White soldiers (Gould)		...	...	...	74·8
1505	Negroes	..	...	...	...	74·0
705	Mulattoes	,,	...	...	...	76·9
500	Iroquois Indians	,,	...	...	...	76·5
1080	Englishmen (Hutchinson)		...	...	...	80·0
30	Belgians of 30 years of age (Quételet)				...	71·0
250	Mexicans (Coindet)	...	...	...	...	80·3
24	Chinese (Nostrra)	...	...	...	...	77·0
34	Nicobarians	,,	...	...	...	77·0

The Respiration.

The respiration presents considerable diversities in different individuals; some of these are of a radical character, others are consecutive to the action of *milieu*. The movements of the chest concerned in inspiration are three in number—namely, an upper costal, a lower costal, and an abdominal or diaphragmatic. We have yet to know whether either of them may or may not be peculiar to certain races. The rhythm of the respiration may also vary, although it usually bears a definite relation to the pulse, there being one inspiration to four beats of the heart. Quételet found that in the Belgians in the above list, the inspirations were 18 in the minute, and Hutchinson that in the English there were 20. According to Coindet, the respiration increases the higher one ascends. Supposing, in 250 Europeans, the number of inspirations were 19·2, in the same number of Mexicans, at an altitude of 2277 mètres, the number would be 20·3—the correctness of which statement M. Jourdanet questions. The difference, however, is scarcely appreciable, and the number of individuals too few to enable us to form a definite opinion on the matter. The capacity of the thoracic cavity is a subject which has received a considerable amount of attention. It is ascertained with the spirometer. The individual makes a full expiration and then a full inspiration, three times in

succession, when the mean is taken. Of all the physiological
causes which tend to make it vary, like every other animal function, the most important is the stature. In 1080 Englishmen
Mr. Hutchinson found, with a stature of 1·52 mètre, a capacity of
2·842 cubic mètres, and with an addition of one inch in height,
namely, 2·64 centimètres, an increase of 131 cubic centimètres,
so that with a stature of 1·82 mètre, the capacity is 4·260.
M. Schreevogt finds it less in the German race—namely, 52 cubic
centimètres for every centimètre of height. The following table,
having reference to healthy adult men, shows that there are
material differences between races :

					Cubic mètres.
8395 White soldiers (Gould)	...	...	...	...	2·954
1631 Negroes	,,	...	...	...	3·700
671 Mulattoes	,,	...	...	...	2·620
604 Indians	,,	...	...	...	3·022
1080 Englishmen (Hutchinson)	...	...	...	0·602

From this it appears that the chest capacity is less in negroes
than in whites, and especially in the English. Now the stature of
the former averages 1·70 mètre, and that of the latter about 1·71
in the corresponding statistics, so that negroes maintain their
inferiority. With regard to mulattoes, it is with them as with
their brain—(see page 312)—they seem to appropriate the worst
character pertaining to the two races of which they are the issue.
Their chest capacity is even less than in pure negroes.

The Circumference of the Chest.

The circumference of the chest is connected with the study of the
respiratory functions, as well as with that of the proportions of the
body ; it has even to do with that of the reproductive functions in
the female : hence it presents differences according to race. We
shall only speak, however, of the measurement in the adult man.
The works which have been written on the subject are numerous,

and have an equal interest for anthropology, medicine, military
enlistment, and the Arts.   When measuring a man's chest the tape
is passed round under the armpits, or, what is better, over the
nipples. The individual should stand upright, should be calm, his
respiration being carried on quietly, the mouth open, the arms
above the head, and the hands joined, unless we want to take the
mean circumference during inspiration and expiration.   As the
capacity of the chest increases with the stature it is necessary to
take account of this.   In the following table the first column shows
the absolute circumference, and the second the same circumference
relatively to the stature = 100 :

		Absolute circumference.	Relative to stature.
5738 Scotchmen (Quételet)	100·0	...	60·7
508 Indians (Gould)	98·5	...	85·5
1080 Englishmen (Hutchinson)	89·9	...	54·0
468 Germans (Gould)	91·2	...	55·8
4660 Russians (Seeland)	86·7	...	52·4
400 Frenchmen (Bernard)	87·9	...	52·0
1792 Negroes (Gould)	88·0	...	52·9
719 Mulattoes ,, ...	86·7	...	52·1
151 New Zealanders (A. S. Thompson) ...	89·9	...	51·4
25 Todas of the Nilgherries (Shortt) ...	81·8	...	50·9
60 Interior tribes of the Nilgherries (Shortt)	76·6	...	42·9

All the European races in this list have the circumference of the
thorax decidedly greater than the inferior races.   What Mr. Gould
calls the play of the chest, that is to say, the difference between
the two circumferences taken during inspiration and expiration, is
also much greater in them. The first column below shows this
difference in centimètres of length, and the second the volume in
cubic centimètres of the thoracic capacity to which it corresponds,
according to Mr. Gould's calculation.

		Centimètres.	Cubic centimètres.
2471 American soldiers	6·0	...	44·5
1792 Negroes	4·1	...	26·4
719 Mulattoes	4·0	...	26·7
508 Iroquois Indians	4·5	...	30·0

Digestion.

The digestion also varies, if not according to race, at least so far as to produce certain effects which may become permanent. It is influenced by certain habits. Thus, according to the regularity or irregularity of the meals, a redundance or insufficiency of food, a herbivorous or a carnivorous regimen, the stomach will become distended and deformed, as is the characteristic of many inferior tribes, or be retracted. The lumbo-sacral curvature also will be more or less hollowed. The teeth will become worn, horizontally, almost down to the gums, as in the Patagonians, or obliquely, as in our prehistoric races. In truth, in anthropology we must study all the functions of the body exactly as we study the corresponding organs; and these functions may exhibit differential characters between races which we least expected, or throw some light on the problem now under consideration with reference to the influence of external conditions and habit. Next to respiration and digestion, therefore, come the functions of the larynx, of the senses, &c.

The Voice.

The voice varies in its quality and tone in different races, and may even be characteristic of certain human groups, according to the statement of travellers. The tenor or bass voice is frequently associated with a certain physical type. This subject belongs more particularly to linguists, whose attention is specially directed to differences of pronunciation. Much has yet to be done in this direction.

Vision.

Vision may be studied with respect to its extent. According to Mr. Gould, the white, the negro, and the Indian see at the greatest distance at from 17 to 28 years of age, after which the distance progressively diminishes. The following interesting statistical table has been drawn up by this author. The first column gives the distance of clear vision of type corresponding to No. 11 of Jaeger. The three following columns indicate the proportion per cent. of short-sighted persons, of those of intermediate vision, and of the long-sighted, the first seeing the type at less than 50 centimètres, the second at from 50 centimètres to 1·50 mètre, the third above 1·50 mètre.

| | Mean distance. | Proportion per cent. of | | |
		Short-sighted.	Intermediate.	Long-sighted.
White soldiers	1·20	2·7	80·9	16·4
„ sailors	0·92	8·3	87·7	4·0
Negroes	1·15	2·0	84·8	13·2
Mulattoes	1·13	2·4	81·0	16·6
Indians	1·31	0·9	88·5	10·6

It is singular that as regards the greater number of physiological characters, for example weight, muscular force, vision, chest capacity, and even stature, sailors are inferior to soldiers in Mr. Gould's statistics, these being confirmed in many particulars by other observers.

Cerebral Functions.

The cerebral functions are to be examined in the same way as all the others. Intellectual phenomena are the expression of the activity of the brain, while their external manifestations are its product. Both the one and the other are consequently included in the category of physiological characters which we are now studying. They present the greatest anomalies, because this is precisely the general characteristic of the human family, but they also exhibit marked differences, which doubtless were more considerable at first when races were in a condition of isolation. There are two characters common to the whole human race: the faculty of imitation and the faculty of improvement. The ape repeats that which he sees done, and goes no further. Man profits by what he sees, and is more or less capable of being educated. Hence the difficulty, when analysing intellectual traits, to distinguish that which appertains to the race and to the individual from that which is the result of education and of training. Not only a victorious tribe, but a single individual starting up as if by chance, may so transform the customs and modify the characters of a people as, after a brief period, to render them unrecognisable. The ancient Peruvians owe most of the intellectual traits which distinguish them from neighbouring races to Manco-Capac, the first of the Incas. Who knows whether the Australians might not have become elevated in the social scale, if they had met with a man who knew how to deal with them? This proneness of Man to appropriate to himself that which he can make subservient to his wants and desires, and to transform himself intellectually, is not equally developed in all. In some it is acquired rapidly, in others slowly. We know that the Andamans and Australians, brought up according to our ideas of civilisation, cast off their clothing on the first opportunity, and resume their savage mode of life; notwithstanding this, these same savages quickly learn to read and write, and are very observant. Hence we must distinguish between the rough-and-ready education of an individual, and the lengthened and progressive education of a race. In spite of this tendency to intellectual uniformity in the human family, certain differences persist, each corresponding to certain peculiar anatomical conditions of the brain, which they denote as surely as though demonstrated by the most delicate microscopic examination.

Among those properties inherent in the structure of the brain, the faculty of language occupies a prominent place. Linguists have come to the clearest conclusions on this point. A certain number of languages irreducible from one another have had an independent origin. At that remote period the corresponding primitive races lived distinct in a state of nature. Has chance then presided at the early development of a few articulate sounds, which have become the point of departure of so many root-words?

or has the brain become previously modified in order to render this development possible? What interests us here is that there are languages profoundly different from one another, which require organs of a special construction to pronounce them, and special powers of intellect to comprehend them. In the same way we must view the various methods of appreciating the musical gamut in the several quarters of the globe. That which is harmony to the auditory fibres of the brain in some races, is not so in others. Education here has nothing to do with it; the thing has been so from the first, and is, therefore, an anatomical fact. The varieties of arithmetical systems are in the same category. The races termed Aryan are acquainted with all of them, and have considerable aptitude for mathematics. Other races, styled inferior, cannot count above two, or three, or five; any numbers above these are altogether incomprehensible to them, and in spite of all our efforts we can seldom give them any higher notion of number: this was the case with a Damara mentioned by Lubbock. As regards drawing, there are differences in the same way. There is a race, the existence of which can be undoubtedly traced back to the earliest period, only capable of making circles and straight lines, and certain of its representatives cannot even distinguish the difference between a drawing of a head and a tree or a ship. The Chinese, after a social existence probably equal to that of the ancient Egyptians, and, although advanced in many other respects, have not the slightest idea of perspective.

Other races, on the contrary, and these the most ancient and the most savage, as our ancestors of the Reindeer Period, have exhibited almost from the first, a thoroughly artistic taste. The marvellous difference in the systems of writing testifies also to the primitive isolation of races and to their various degrees of aptness and impulse. The perfection which some seem to have attained almost from the first, whilst others have remained in *statu quo*, is well worthy our consideration. Races are still more distinguished from one another by their mode of life and social condition. From the earliest dawn of tradition, and even previously, when all our information is derivable only from prehistoric archaeology, we see tribes settling down peaceably, engaged in fishing and barter, as well as those of a warlike and turbulent spirit. The former soon become amenable to the softening influence of civilisation, the latter, on the contrary, are proof against it, and prefer a rough and savage life. The former are sceptics, or indifferent to religious forms ; the latter recognise a protecting Providence, and have a settled faith. Some are naturally inclined to a sedentary life, while others seem to be always on the move, like the Tschinghani, the Jew, and the Arab. The Tschinghani have no religion, and wander about in the midst of civilised peoples without allowing themselves to be influenced by them in any way. The Jew, now a wanderer, and then a sojourner, from the time of Joshua to that of Titus, has again become a wanderer, as far as the customs of the peoples among whom he dwells will permit. The Arab also retains his old habits, only he does not adapt himself to them. He moves away to India, into Central Africa, in search of fresh moorings, but does not remain long anywhere, like the Anglo-Germanic race.

No one doubts the value of intellectual characters. It would be commonplace to say that they continue for ages in the same way as physical characters. The Spaniards of the time of Scipio Æmilianus are still those of to-day. Fighting in ambush, long patient endurance, and hatred of the foreigner are always their distinguishing marks. The predominating character of the French race is still that of the Gauls described by Cæsar. In Algiers, the Berbers are distinguished from the Arabs more by their disposition, their temper, and their sociability than by their features of countenance. The contrast between the Anglo-Germanic and the dark southern race is also very striking. The impulses inherent in the cerebral matter are so tenacious, in spite of education and civilisation, that they still continue after crossing and mixture of races, and are of assistance to us in recognising them. Mr. Brace depicts the character of the French in these terms.* " In character and genius the French show the evidences of the three powerful races which have constituted the nation—traits which sometimes seem

* " The Races of the Old World : a Manual of Ethnology." By C. L. Brace. London, 1863.

contradictory, and which only those familiar with the French
people can fully understand. In their brilliant martial character,
their love of display and effect, their sudden enthusiasm and as easy
discouragement, their readiness to be governed by military leaders,
their fondness for ornament and art, and their gaiety, fickleness,
and amorousness, they are thorough Kelts; but in the sober devout-
ness of a large mass of the people, in their seriousness, in their
personal sensitiveness and personal independence, in their spirit of
sceptical inquiry and the thoroughness of their scientific research, they
are Teutons; while their marvellous talent for organisation, and
their tendency to centralisation, are Roman. The French race,
with its genius, its science, its grandeur, its faults—which are the
scorn of mankind; its misfortunes—which afflict the world; its
magnificent past, its uncertain present [the author wrote under the
Empire], and mysterious future, is a unity, a new and living force
entering into the life of mankind, and henceforth as distinct as any
of the great races of antiquity."

The points of view from which one might treat the vast subject
of primitive cerebral differences are infinite. Each fundamental
race would require to be submitted to minute analysis, and everything eliminated from it which is due to a natural state of perfect-
ness, to accidental occurrences, to the influence of other races, and to
historical circumstances. The power of each faculty, feeling, or
instinct would have to be taken into account. Superstitious
tendency, religion, family history, individual peculiarity, degree of
sociableness, aptness for civilisation, preference for this or that kind
of life. All these would have to be examined. What the varied
amount of cerebral activity in the so-called higher races, as compared with the torpid condition of those regarded as inferior, &c.
It seems, says Sproat, speaking of the Ahms of North America
(*Lubbock*), that the intellect of the savage is in a half-sleepy state.
If we hold conversation with him for however brief a period, he
becomes fatigued, especially when his replies require some effort of
thought and memory. The savages of the interior of Borneo (*Dalton*),
as well as some from Western Australia (*Scott Nind*) live in a state
of the most absolute indifference, like animals. Their sole business

is to eat and drink. There are numerous examples of savages, as
the Bosjesman described by Lichtenstein, in whom there is nothing
either in features of countenance or in their actions indicative of the
least glimmer of intellect.

A subject, almost a new one, has for some years excited much
attention : namely, the history, based on facts, of the steps whereby
the most favoured of the human races have arrived at their degree
of intellectual development. In our opinion it is one intimately
connected with ethnology or general ethnography.   Mr. Tylor has
written a work under the title " Primitive Culture ; or, The early
History of the Human Race," and Sir J. Lubbock one on the " Origin
of Civilisation." The former clearly shows, just to take one example,
that morality is synonymous with general conduct, that it is always
utilitarian, that it varies in different peoples, conformably to their
wants, that originally restricted within the narrow limits of the
family, then of the tribe, it has extended to greater confederacies ;
that, in a word, it is progressive. Suffice it to say that ideas of
morality may give ethnic characters but not differential physiological characters between races, at least until a new order of such
should arise. The knowledge of religious beliefs advances in the
same way. By the comparison of the fables and allegories upon
which all systems of mythology are based, it traces back its inquiries,
as is done with regard to language, to the remote period when
peoples came in contact with one another, and consequently
separates the acquired character from that which is inherent. It
has a still wider range : it takes a retrospective view of the various
phases of those intellectual qualities of which races have mutually
become the possessors, as well as of that which they have acquired
by the simple and natural development of the faculties inherent in
Man generally. The problem of the differential characters of
human races dependent on their special cerebral organisation, will
be in this way simplified, and then no doubt we shall be able really
to say that the modes of activity of the brain furnish distinctive
characters, in the same way as the shape of the skull or the
character of the hair. The only objection would be that their
varieties could not be measured with the compass.

The "Bibliothèque des Sciences Contemporaines" has in the press a volume by M. Girard de Rialle, which treats on Comparative Mythology. We doubt not that the subject of the successive and mutual phases of perfection through which the human races have passed, both intellectually and socially, will be fully considered in this volume.

Pathological Characters.

Pathological characters are a deviation from the physiological, and, like them, have to do with the living subject. All morbid peculiarities which certain races, to the exclusion of certain other races, present, may be classed under this head. It is not our present intention to treat of this subject, which has rather to do with medicine. We should have to consider, at the outset, the progress and the development of diseases, depending, on the one hand, on telluric and atmospheric conditions, and, on the other, on race. With respect to the former, we enunciated, some sixteen years ago, a fact which was more or less confirmed by others, namely, that the mortality after capital operations in the English hospitals was less by one-half than in the French. We attributed it to a better diet, to their better sanitary arrangements, and to their superior management. There was but one serious objection offered to our statement. M. Velpeau, with his wonderful acumen, made reply, at the Academy of Medicine, that the flesh of the English and of the French differed; in other words, that the reaction after operations was not the same in both races. It is, in effect, an anthropological character. The immunity of negroes and their cross-breeds from yellow fever; the few cases of hepatitis in Senegal as compared with those among Europeans; their greater predisposition, on the contrary, to plague, are other examples of the same kind. According to M. Obédénare, the inhabitants of Rome are almost proof against malarial fever, while Germans residing there are very sensitive to its influence. These pathological characters form an entirely new subject, to which we beg to direct the attention of our naval surgeons. In treatises on pathology we find much as to the influence of age, sex, and temperament on disease, as well as concise descriptions of affections peculiar to certain countries, but almost nothing as to the influence of race properly so called. This is a gap which must be filled up.*

Apropos of the skin of the negro, discussion has arisen with regard to the colour of cicatrices after wounds. The question has now been settled. After deep wounds the cicatrices are whitish, and when superficial they are blacker than the adjoining skin.

The causes of the extinction of races may be considered here. Whether rapid, slow, or scarcely perceptible, this progressive extinction in the presence of new races, relatively superior, and differing in morals and civilisation, is an acknowledged fact. That it should be so in tribes as truly savage as the Obongos of Du Chaillu, and the Australians of Port King George, described by Scott Nind, is not surprising; but that the phenomena should be repeated among the Polynesians, who are far from being an inferior race, in the North American Indians, and in the Arabs of Algeria, is very remarkable. The same influences, however, are at work in each case; some morbid, others physiological, all capable of being summed up in one word. Among morbid causes are included diseases new to the country, and more or less contagious, which Europeans bring with them in the same way as they did the dog.

---

* A volume might be written respecting the comparative pathological characters of the two races, the negro and the white, as seen in the United States. Official documents might be furnished for the statistical part of the work. Thus, as regards the relative frequency of mania and idiocy, tables like the following are full of interest:

		Proportion per 1000.	
		Mania.	Idiocy.
19,556,000 Whites	...	0·78	0·72
434,000 Freed negroes	...	0·71	0·61
3,204,000 Negro slaves ...	...	0·10	0·37

It proves that social influence predominates over the influence of race; a brain having nothing to think about is less exposed to insanity than one having to battle with the necessities of the social condition. This is quite natural; an organ which has much work to do is more likely to become deranged than one which does not work at all.

grass to La Plata, and as the Americans recently gave France the phylloxera. For example, the small-pox, imported into St. Domingo in 1518, into Iceland in 1707, into Greenland in 1732, into the Cape of Good Hope in 1748 (*Boudin*), and which, when it first made its appearance in Australia, in 1788, almost annihilated the curious tribe of Port Jackson, now called Sydney; the measles, which has just destroyed half the population of the Fiji Islands; scarlatina, syphilis, the severity of which, however, has been exaggerated; alcoholism, in all its forms, which is propagated by imitation, and easily assumes an epidemic character.   Among physiological causes are a sudden change of habits, the impossibility for the native, under these circumstances, to supply his necessities as heretofore, and nostalgia combined with anæmia, which are the results of this change.   Before the arrival of Europeans, the Australians were in possession of immense territories, where game was, as it were, preserved, and where food was always at hand. The kangaroo occupied the same place as the reindeer did formerly among our own ancient populations of the Périgord, or as the horse among those of Solutré.   They had, moreover, vast natural pastures and cultivated grounds, the harvest from which they gathered regularly every year.   They were agriculturists and sheep farmers, without having the cares and anxieties of those occupations.   All at once they were driven from their hunting-fields and pasturages, the kangaroos were put to flight before the musket, and before a generation had passed they were compelled altogether to change their habits and mode of life (*Report of the Adelaide, South Australia, Commission*).   Their life was an easy one when they had a vast extent of country at their command; but when it became circumscribed in extent, and they had to contend with all the obstacles of civilisation, it became insupportable.   With insufficient food, they in their naked state were unable to withstand the cold, in addition to which, dejection and sadness at finding themselves under subjugation in a country of which they had been the sole proprietors, opened the door for the ingress of every kind of disease, as well as for every sort of vice.   Under these circumstances they were generally carried off by phthisis.

Now, in Australia, as in so many other places, the population was sparse in proportion to the extent of the country. The scarcity of women, the regular practice of infanticide, and the frequency of accidents which are inseparable from savage life, together with circumstances we have already mentioned, helped to keep it down.

Moreover, there are two influences at work in producing disease : an external, morbid or accidental, and an internal, caused by a want of power of resistance in the system. It is this latter which plays the principal part among savages. There is therefore nothing mysterious in this extinction of race. An old Namaqua woman, to all appearance a centenarian, when asked by Barrow if she remembered the period prior to that when the Dutch took possession of the country, replied : "I have good reason to remember it, for at that time we did not know what it was to have an empty belly, now we can hardly get a mouthful." Under a less cruel form the cause of the progressive diminution of a race is always the same. That portion of the race which secures the better part of the resources of the country has the advantage over the other which does not follow the movement. The Arabs are long lived in Arabia, because they are in undisputed possession of the country ; they decrease in Algeria, because they meet with opposition, and therefore cannot enjoy their pastoral life uninterruptedly. They instinctively retrograde in the Desert of Sahara, like the Americans in the Rocky Mountains. The Berbers, on the contrary, with whom our civilised mode of life thoroughly agrees, thrive well there. In fine, it is the law of adaptation to external conditions, whatever they may be, whether physical or moral, and the mechanism of progress.

The regular and progressive increase of the populations, such as we see now going on in Europe, is not noticed in the savage state, as among the negroes of Africa, nor in the barbarous state, as it was in Europe before our present era. In both these cases, the number of premature deaths by murder and accident, as well as by preventable disease, has considerably increased, and the balance as between births and deaths remains in reality stationary, barring certain oscillations annually, either upwards or downwards. In Africa at the present time, where the influence of the European has not yet been felt, there are negro tribes which are becoming extinct without any apparent reason, without any change in their external condition, and almost without having become reduced in number by war. It is not surprising therefore, another unfavourable condition being added, such as the necessity of suddenly changing their habits of eating, sleeping, walking, method of clothing, &c., that the equilibrium should be destroyed, and that death should get the upper hand. At the present rate of increase of European population and of emigration, the earth will soon be overcrowded, to their advantage.

There are, however, causes which tend to the rapid destruction of races. The Tasmanians have been exterminated to the last man, and their half-breeds alone remain. The English die out in India, and the Dutch in Malacca, because they are unable to acclimate in those countries. The Esquimaux in the northern part of America are becoming extinct because their country is gradually becoming colder, and existence in it is becoming impossible. Captain Hall says the Esquimaux die more from phthisis than from all other diseases put together. Among the most celebrated races which have become recently extinct from natural causes, we may mention the Charruas, the Caribs (?), the blacks of California, and among the first to disappear, the natives of Easter Island, the Kamskatdales, the Esquimaux, and the Makololos, &c.

CHAPTER IX.

ETHNIC, LINGUISTIC, HISTORICAL, ARCHÆOLOGICAL CHARACTERS:
THEIR VALUE—PREHISTORIC RACES—OUR ANCESTORS OF THE
ROUGH AND POLISHED STONE PERIOD.

THE two series of anatomical and physiological characters which
we have been describing are really the only ones belonging to the
province of Natural History, the only ones upon which one can
directly rely in order to determine the number as well as the
nature of the principal divisions of the human family. Those of
which it remains for us to speak, to which we shall continue to
give the name of *characters*, are of an entirely different order.
They are indications derived from various sources, and may be
compared with those which one would seek from a breeder in
order to establish the genealogy of a breed of dogs or cattle. But
as regards Man, the sources are more varied and of a nobler
character. His customs, his language, his migrations, the relics of
his remote industry—all these are to be considered before we can
solve the problem of the relationship of each of his races.

In a certain point of view, the characters included under the
terms "ethnic" and "linguistic" should have found a place in the
previous chapter, under the title of simple intellectual manifestations of the physical organisation of the individual regarded as a
type of the race. But if mode of living, laws, and language are
inherent in the men, they depend much more on such an union as
the chance of events establishes. Race and people are, in fact,
two terms having no relation to each other; the former is an
anthropological group, the latter a social group. Hitherto we have
only considered races; now we shall speak of peoples, and shall
begin with ethnic characters *par excellence*.

Ethnic Characters.

By ethnic characters are understood all those things which result
from the association of men with each other, whatever their cause,

2 E

such as want of society, interest, caprice, or warlike passion.
National unity, as we see it realised in the highest degree in
France, and the federation of autonomous provinces, as in the
United States, are the highest forms of this enlightened association.
The small tribes of Todas, in which all the members are united by
ties of kindred, and where association is synonymous with family,
are an example of the lowest degree of an opposite character.
In each case a greater or less share of liberty is left to the in-
dividual, and authority is confided to a chief or to an assembly of
delegates.

The democratic organisation of the Kabyls of Algeria, the
authoritative institutions of the nomad Arab, the system of the
Australians, who settle their disputes in assemblies periodically
called together, termed corrobories, are other examples of this.
Very rarely is there any trace of organisation of any kind, as
among the Australians of Port King George, described by Scott
Nind, and the Obongos of Du Chaillu. The object of association
is defence against the common enemy, and mutual support in the
battle of life. Its result is the establishment of customs, regu-
lations, and subsequently of laws, written, or transmitted verbally
from generation to generation. The idea of an equal participation
in the expenses and pleasures of life comes at a later period,
tardily followed by a notion of morality, as the term is understood
by Europeans, namely, the protection of the weak and the infirm,
and the equal right of all to the "banquet of life." It, however, continues everywhere among pariahs, the oppressed, the
down-trodden, and perhaps among civilised nations—but with
them more as a matter of habit. The principal object of democracy,
the highest conception of morality, is to dispel these inequalities.
As a sequel to laws and customs, and with a view to public utility,
there become developed—we know not how—a number of customs,
either of a rational or a ridiculous character, corresponding to some
innate weakness of the human machine. Such are the rites
associated with the great epochs of life, with birth, puberty,
marriage, parturition, and death; the custom of tattooing, of
mutilating the teeth, the nose, the ears, the feet, the body,

the head, &c.; the ceremonies pertaining to religion, to memorials, whether of glory or calamity, &c. It is to the social state again that all our inquiries are directed respecting implements, arms, methods of navigation, the character of dwellings, and the kind of food selected by different peoples. It is here also, as well as in reference to intellectual capability, that we place the description of the pursuits of fishing, hunting, agriculture, trade, and commerce; and lastly the literary, artistic, and musical productions characterising each nation. If races are naturally predisposed to a particular mode of life, peoples do not often adopt it unless to follow the example of, and owing to their contact with, other peoples.

Such are the materials which ethnography has to employ. *Ethnography*, then, is the description of each people, as now existing, or in the successive phases of its development, of its laws and customs, its language, its origin, and its relationships. *Ethnology* treats of the same subject, but from a higher point of view, by attaching itself to ordinary traits of character, and seeking to determine the laws which preside over the relations and changes of peoples, and the development of their customs and institutions. Both the one and the other powerfully contribute to the progress of Anthropology, but should, strictly speaking, be separated from it. (See page 7, *et seq.*).

Among these ethnological, or, for greater brevity, ethnic characters, some have but little importance when taken together, while others possess an individual value, and are useful as affording us a knowledge of past, and consequently of present, ties of kindred, and a power of determining the anthropological elements which enter into the composition of each people.

Cannibalism, for example, has existed almost universally among races living in a savage state, sometimes as a means of subsistence, as among the Monbouttons and some other African tribes—among whom shambles for human flesh are openly kept; sometimes with the idea of appropriating to themselves the qualities of the deceased. It is practised after a battle as a religious ceremony, or spontaneously in time of peace. Cannibalism therefore, by itself, does not furnish us with any means of discovering the pacific arrangements which have taken place at a certain moment between two peoples; but from the circumstances which have occurred, and from subsequent proceedings, it may go some way towards it.

So the custom of erecting rough stone monuments as records of important events, or for the purpose of receiving the remains of those to whom honour has been paid when living. Stones set upright, or placed one upon another, or forming chambers, have been met with in almost every country. They are still constructed in India. The present race of Kabyls of the Djurjura sometimes set up stones in a circle on the spot on which they hold their great federative assemblies. The marble slabs which we place in our cemeteries are a relic of this natural disposition in Man to appropriate that material which appears to him to be the most durable for the purpose of making of it a commemorative memorial. According to the peculiar form of these constructions, so are they classed under different groups. It is quite clear that the dolmens and cromlechs of Denmark, France, England, Portugal, and Algeria have been the conception of one and the same period of civilisation, while those of the Deccan, the Assam, and the provinces to the south of the Brahmapootra have been that of another.

In all countries of the world Man made use of flint weapons for purposes of warfare, before he became acquainted with metals. In Patagonia, in the Sahara, in Oceania, as well as in Europe, they are found in great numbers, either on the surface or embedded in the earth. Frequently even their shapes are alike in countries which, as far as we know, have not been in communication with each other from the remotest periods. Moreover, from the particular way in which these flints are worked we are able to form a judgment as to the relations which have existed between tribes far removed from one another. Even the substance of the flint itself furnishes useful sources of information. The use of the bow and arrow, the lance, the shield, as observed in various parts of the globe, is simply a question of ordinary

interest. So with the boomerang, which has been met with almost
identical in shape both in Australia, in the Deccan, in Egypt, and
in America. It is in use throughout the entire extent of the first-
mentioned country; but it is not found either in New Guinea or in
Polynesia; while the bow and arrow, so common in these latter
countries, have disappeared in Australia, proving that the natives
have not been in contiguity sufficiently long for the industry of
either one to have become influenced by that of the other. In the
Deccan, the bow and arrow are in use at the present moment,
whence we come to the conclusion that the Australians must have
brought it from that country, at least, that the reverse is not the
case. Various considerations make us lean to the former hypothesis.
It must be thoroughly understood that these circumstances in no
way establish a relationship between two races. They simply
indicate that two peoples, having the same custom or the same
industry, have probably been previously in contact. Consequently
they may be derived the one from the other, have descended from
one and the same stock, or have crossed.

The Todas of the Nilgherries live an altogether exceptional life :
they have a special worship ; they subsist on milk and pulse ; and
transform their dairies into temples. It is the duty of the priest to
perform the operation of milking the buffaloes, and to look after
the apportionment of the milk ; and the little bell hung round the
neck of the principal cow is a sacred symbol. As far as we know
no similar kind of worship has been found anywhere ; but it is
evident that it might be discovered among some other solitary
people of India or of distant parts of Asia. It would then become
probable that they had lived together, and possible that they
might be of one and the same race.

The *artificial deformation of the head* shows also how much may
be gathered from ethnic customs. From the Caucasus to France
we come on the track of peoples who practised it after one particular
fashion. On the other hand, in America, previous to our era, we
see a people who also practised deformation of the head of so
special a character, that we are able to trace all the spots at which
it sojourned in its journeyings through both North and South

America. We frequently discover a deformation produced in another way alongside of, and even among, this same people. What relation is there between the two races, both having one and the same custom, but that custom modified in two altogether different ways? By supposing them to be the issue of one and the same stock at a very remote period, would there be any relation between this stock and the European part of the Caucasus? The question cannot be solved; but further researches may clear up the matter. Already in Asia we see other deformations showing themselves, as if to establish another link between Europe and the Americas.

The practice of *scalping* is one very extensively carried on in North America, where each tribe of Indians has its special method. Duncan also found it employed in Africa in 1845. The ancient Scythians (*Burton*), the ancient Germans, the Anglo-Saxons, and even the French in 879, according to the Abbé Domenech, had recourse to it.

The institution of *caste*, regularly established in India, and found in Australia in a rudimentary state, as well as in some parts of the Malay peninsula; the custom of *tatooing* with the needle in some countries, and by scarifying in others, as well as the different marks adopted by each tribe; the *taboo*, so national among the Polynesians that it makes one suspicious whence this custom originated; the universal practice of chewing the betel-nut in the Malay archipelago—are so many ethnic characters for our consideration. There are a number of most singular practices connected with the period of puberty, or adopted in infancy, and which are designated by the general term *ethnic mutilations*.

But of all customs, the most varied have reference to the method of *disposing of the dead*. Besides the dolmens, there are the tumuli of ancient Siberia, of North America, and of the Gauls of the Bronze Age; the canoes of the Patagonians; the practice of embalming of the Peruvians, the Guanches, and the Egyptians. Sometimes the corpse is burnt, or simply smoked, or eaten by the relatives. Sometimes it is allowed to putrefy on the branch of a tree, or left to vultures on a lofty wicker structure or,

on an exposed tower, as among the Parsees, &c. Sometimes we
see the bones prepared, and hung round the necks of relatives,
as among the Andamans; or the head only, with the face preserved with its usual expression (*tsantsas*), as among the Jivaros
Indians.

But it is not our purpose to describe the general subject of
ethnic characters. This sketch, therefore, must suffice, inasmuch as
a treatise on ethnology about to be published in the "Bibliothèque
des Sciences Contemporaines" will, no doubt, treat of them in
detail.

Linguistic characters are one of the most valuable sources of
information connected with Anthropology.

Linguistics is the comparative study of the elements of each
language, as *philology* is the comparative study of the literary
productions of a language. The two fundamental points upon
which the former bears are the vocabulary and the grammar—their
present state, their derivation, their origin. Every language has
passed through three conditions, has had three phases, before its
arrival at completeness.

Some languages have passed through these rapidly; others, after
continuing for a lengthened period, have stopped at the first or
second stage of their development. Hence we have three types of
language—monosyllabic, polysyllabic or agglutinative, and inflective
languages. The first are represented by the Chinese and its
dialects; the second by the idioms of the American, Basque,
Berber, Mongolian, Finnish, &c.; the third by the Semitic and
Aryan languages. Our European languages belong, with about
two exceptions, to this last class.

By an analysis of vocabularies and especially of root-words, by a
comparison of grammatical forms and constructions, one of the first
results of linguistics has been to divide the eight hundred known
languages, whether dead or living, into families; these again being
subdivided into genera and species according to their degree of
resemblance and affinity. Some of these families include but one
known genus, as the Basque; in others there are a great number of
genera, as in the Uralo-Altaic or Turanian, which is divided into the

Samöyed, the Fin, the Turk, the Mongol, and the Tungus languages, and each of these into different dialects. Some are so perfectly distinct in their mechanism and in their constituent elements—as the Indo-European or Aryan, and the Syro-Arabic or Semitic, in spite of all the attempts of specialists to find in them points of contact—that they give one the idea that at the time of their formation the races which spoke them lived absolutely separated, without having any communication with other races. M. Renan states the fact, and goes no farther. M. Chavée is more definite. He says: "We might put Semitic children and Indo-European children apart, who had been taught by deaf-mutes, and we should find that the former would naturally speak a Semitic language, the latter an Aryan language." Whence the conclusion that the type of language is independent of the will of Man, and the inevitable product of his cerebral organisation.

The argument is considerably in favour of the polygenistic doctrine. At the moment when Man acquired the dignity of Man by the acquisition of language, he was dispersed in groups or distinct races on the surface of the globe. Now the number of these irreducible languages is enormous, without speaking of those which have become altogether extinct. The question as to the precursor of these races remains untouched, and does not belong to linguistics. Another result of the distribution of languages by families, is its application to the classification of races. We must not lay too much stress on this.

Languages, like systems of mythology, methods of numeration, and all ethnic customs, often continue in the centre whence they have taken their origin, and have greater chances of being perpetuated in such centre, though they frequently change it. They are transmitted from one race to another, or from one people to another, in whole or in part, especially when the language of the invader is a more perfect one, and corresponds better with his new habits. Words having relation with ideas recently acquired are the first to pass away, the old ones become modified, then changes in the grammar take place.

Some groups of the vanquished people resist more. Protected

by their customs, their spirit of independence, or by their settling
down in obscure places, they retain their idiom for a long period;
but foreign influence continuing, whether friendly, hostile, or
enlightened, their language in time yields and becomes absorbed.
There is in fact a struggle. The Franks of Neustria, less civilised
than the Gallo-Romans, were not able to force their language upon
them; on the contrary, they lost their own. The soldiers of Rollo,
less than a hundred years after the cession of Normandy, spoke
nothing but French. Their descendants were unable to communi-
nicate the French language to England at the time of the invasion
of William the Conqueror. The Saxons, on the contrary, five or
six centuries previously, not only had taken possession of England,
but had forced their language on its semi-barbarous inhabitants,
upon whom the Romans had only made a passing impression.
In these cases, number was everything. With us, on the contrary,
as regards the influence of the Romans, it was their civilisation
which decided the point. The Celtic language has been progressively latinised throughout. We do not now find traces of it
except among the peasants living out of the usual path of civilisation. The Celtic language itself was not autochthonous in
Gaul, it had been brought from the East by a different race. That
which had preceded it was the Euskarian language, vestiges of
which are found in the geographical names dispersed through
Spain in ancient Aquitania, and as far as into Corsica, Sardinia,
and Sicily, according to Humboldt; this is the present Basque
language. M. Broca is disposed to think that its area extended
at a remote period over the whole of Western Europe up to the
point towards the east where it meets with the Fin languages.
The languages now used by the peoples scattered over the globe
are not therefore necessarily those which they spoke originally.
The community of language between two peoples, or even between
two races, determined by their physical traits, does not show that
there was any kindred or connection between them, but simply
that they had participated in the same lot. The Yakuts of the
banks of the Lena in features pass for Mongols, and speak a Turk
language. The Voguls and the Hungarians both speak a Fin

language; the former, as to physique, are Mongols, and the latter
Europeans, among the upper classes. The Belgians speak Latin,
and have remained Kymric. Linguists include under the name
of Kaffirs all the peoples speaking the Bantou languages, as the
Amaxulos of Kaffraria, the Makololos of the Zambesi, the Mpon-
gwes of the Gaboon; their types however are different. Evidently
a conquering people, speaking the Bantou, has become scattered
through the whole of these various negro tribes, and has bequeathed
to them their language. It is for Anthropology to separate them.
In short, the characters derived from linguistics furnish only
"indications, and not positive information," to quote M. Broca.
They are not permanent, and simply teach us one of the phases
which the history of races has passed through. They are valuable
in the same way as ethnic and archæological characters, but are
not to be placed in the same category as anatomical and physiological characters, which are perpetuated in spite of crossing and
the influence of external conditions. In a word, they frequently
concern peoples and not races. Certain of their elements more
or less resist absorption however. The vocabulary is the first
altered, grammatical forms and all that which might be called the
genius of the language remain to the last. For further detail we
would refer to the classification of races according to linguistics,
published by Fred. Müller in his "Ethnographie Générale," and
especially to the volume "Linguistique" (2nd edition) of the
"Bibliothèque des Sciences Contemporaines," the author of which,
M. Hovelacque, holds similar views to those we have enunciated.[*]

Historical and Archæological Characters, &c.

If ethnic and linguistic characters are useful in enabling us to
retrace the past histories of races which have become united to

* See also "La Linguistique et l'Anthropologie," by Paul Broca, in
"Bull. Soc. d'Anthrop.," vol. i., 1st series, 1862; "L'Origine et la Répar-
tition de la Langue Basque," by the same author, in "Revue d'Anthrop.,"
vol. iv., 1874.

form present races, those of which we are about to speak are still
more so. In what way have these races been brought into close
contact with one another or succeeded at one particular point?
What struggles have they had to sustain, what examples to follow,
how have they become commingled, and what remains of the most
ancient of them? Such are, in effect, the problems which are
incessantly presented to the anthropologist when called upon to
settle the physical and even the biological characters of races.
Direct sources of information are happily sufficiently numerous.
Besides those we have already examined, we have written history,
tradition, and all connected therewith — heroic poems, books
of devotion, songs, &c., inscriptions on rocks, as in India and
Algeria, or buried; as at Nineveh; and lastly, prehistoric archæology, which furnishes more than mere information on the subject,
namely, the relics belonging to populations which have disappeared.

History.

History, as connected with our present subject, concerns peoples
in nearest connection with ourselves ; it teaches us their migrations,
their passions, their intellectual manifestations, their customs, looks
back some three or four thousand years, and thereby enables us to
trace the obstacles to which they were subjected at their origin.
The information indeed which we derive from the Greek and
Roman historians scarcely extends beyond the sixteenth century
before our era. If at that period, which to some would seem
far distant, we were adequately enlightened, and we knew
exactly the races which inhabited the globe, and how they were
distributed — suppose we could look forward for a moment to a
corresponding period in the future, crossing will have diminished
the number of pure types; the native race of America will have
entirely disappeared—there will be no Esquimaux, or Ainos, or
Australians, or Bosjesmans; and anthropologists will only have
whereby to recognise them, exhumed skeletons here and there, in the
same way as we now have those which come to us from Egypt.

Imagine their situation if it were possible that there were no
printed records, no monuments of any kind, and we ourselves had
no existence. They will judge of the present period as we do that
of three or four thousand years ago. The question of inferior
races will no longer be in doubt, the intermediate races between
Man and his nearest allies will have disappeared; there will be no
linking threads, no beings occupying a transition state; Man will
stand out alone and resplendent to the view of delighted philosophers. Well, changes such as we are supposing must have been
taking place in the three or four thousand years of ancient authors.
History which would carry us back to that period would be of the
greatest assistance to us. Africa of itself alone would give us probably the key of the problem of Man, the connecting link which has
disappeared between the Bosjesman and some other zoological
being. Whether assisted or not by archæology, history narrates
that, under the twelfth dynasty, about 3300 B.C., the Egyptians
consisted of four races: (1) The *Rot*, or Egyptians, painted red, and
similar in feature to the peasants now living on the banks of the
Nile; (2) The *Namu*, painted yellow, with the aquiline nose,
corresponding to the populations of Asia to the east of Egypt;
(3) The *Nahsu*, or prognathous negroes, with woolly hair; (4)
The *Tamahou*, whites, with blue eyes. It tells us that seventeen
centuries before our era, Thothmes III., of the eighteenth dynasty,
carried his victorious arms over a multitude of peoples, among
whom are recognised existing types of negroes of Central Africa,
and that in the year 1500 B.C., a swarm of barbarians, blonds with
blue eyes, came down upon the western frontier of Egypt from the
north, while in Europe, at the same moment, an invasion had
leaped over the Pyrenees, and banished the Ligurians and Sicanians
into Italy, and the Iberians beyond the Ebro into Africa.

In another part of the world, in Asia, history shows us, on the
frontiers of Persia, two rival nations, one to the south-west, in Irân,
the other to the north-east, in Tûrân (a Persian word signifying
"the country of enemies"). Farther off, from B.C. 1500 to A.D. 250,
many nomad peoples, one of which, the Hiung-Nu, encamps to the
north of the Celestial Empire, and obliges the Chinese to build

the celebrated Great Wall. In India, a yellow people passing round the foot of the Himalayas, and coming in contact with a black people. Lastly, in France, a secular struggle between a brown group, which resists, and a succession of invasions of blondes from the extreme end of Europe—a struggle of which the previous passage into the Iberian peninsula was but an episode. We also learn from history that more recently 38,000 Franks invaded the Gauls, substituting their own for the Roman sway, which five centuries previously had conquered the Kymris and the Celts leagued together under the name of Gauls ; that the Hungarians came from the banks of the Obi to establish themselves, after various revolutions, in the country where we now find them ; that the Parsees fled from their country during the seventh century, dividing into two groups, the one going to the Caucasus, where it is almost extinct, the other to Bombay, where it now prospers, numbering some 49,000 souls. History speaks also of the Malays making their appearance in the island of Sumatra in 1160 ; of Manco-Capac, founding during the eleventh century the dynasty of the Incas of Peru ; of the Nahoas, who emigrated from Florida before the Christian era, leaving Mexico in A.D. 174, some following the Mississippi towards the north, others going to the Isthmus of Panama towards the south.

But it is necessary that we should inquire as to the results of the wars and migrations of peoples, the number of the invaders and their characters, whether they consisted exclusively of warriors, or whether women were associated with them. In one place, where a countless horde like the Huns, under Attila, in Western Europe, or the Gauls, under Genseric, in the Atlas mountains, passes like a hurricane, without leaving a trace ; a continuous current, like that of the Kymris in Gaul, the Saracens (Arabs and Berbers) in Spain, or the Portuguese in South America, modifies the physical type. Elsewhere a handful of individuals makes a good deal of noise, gives its language, as well as its religion and its civilisation, to the vanquished, and has no other influence on their type. The Phœnicians have long been in relation with the coast of Barbary, as well as with the sea-coast generally, and, with the exception of

two or three colonies, have not left a particle of their blood among
their dependents. The name by which the peoples are called is
no proof of their real origin. The English derive theirs from a
Germanic tribe, the Angles, who inhabited the country to the
north of the Elbe; the French, from another Germanic tribe, the
Franks; the Russians, from Rossi, a Scandinavian whose family
governed for many ages at Moscow; the Bulgarians, from a
Finnish tribe, who made their conquest about the seventh century.
Each historical datum requires, like linguistic and ethnographic
characters, to be carefully weighed; and conquest, however prolonged, does not imply a fusion between the victors and the
vanquished.

The question is of direct interest to us, especially with reference
to the Aryans. Linguists, finding that all the European languages,
with the exception of the Basque and the Finnish, are derived
from the Sanskrit—that before the dispersion of these languages in
Central Asia, they possessed words for the metals and for the
various implements of husbandry—mythologists also recognising a
reciprocal relation between the various religious myths of the
peoples of the West and those of the East, came to the conclusion,
the former especially, that the large mass of the peoples of Europe
were Aryan, and had come from Central Asia. A reaction has
now set in against this belief. A comparison of the remains of
ancient races found embedded in the earth in our own country
with those of the populations which have succeeded them, shows a
continuity of type more or less persistent, which the infusion of
foreign blood from time to time alone interrupted, with here
and there a mongrel, or disappearing altogether.

But there has been no positive proof that the Aryans of the East
carried with them into the West any thing beyond their civilising
influence, their language, and their knowledge of the metals. It
may be questioned whether this influence has not taken place in
consequence either of a succession of direct emigrations, by a sort
of infiltration, or by commerce. In France, on the other hand, we
are not Aryans by blood, but by a superposition of various races,
the majority of which are Kymric in the north, Celtic in the

contre, and no doubt bearing the nearest analogy to the aborigines, at least to the ancient people whose relics have been discovered in the caves of the Pyrenees and the Périgord, in the south.

Tradition.

Tradition frequently steps in where history is at fault. History at first was simply tradition committed to writing. Such were the sources whence the first historians, Herodotus, Moses, &c., drew their supplies. The 20,000 verses of the Fin poem, "The Kalavala," were for long ages preserved orally, before they were brought together and written down by E. Lonnrot in 1850. Again, the various pieces which enter into this compilation are slightly anterior to the introduction of Christianity into the northern countries (ninth to the twelfth century).

The "Iliad" was founded on some tradition respecting the connection of the Greek ancestry with Asia Minor, towards the close of the Bronze Period. The "Ramayana," and still more the "Mahabharata," rehearse the exploits of the first conquerors, when India was peopled by a native race represented with heads like an ape. The migrations of the Polynesians, from the island of Boroto or Bouru to the various islands of the Pacific, are only known to us by the national songs and the local traditions gleaned from each island and put together. Traditions ought on no account to be despised. When the Ainos represent themselves as coming from the West in company with a dog, and the Tehuelches of Patagonia also affirm that they sprang from the West, in spite of the enormous distance which separates them from any other land in that direction, this ought to make us reflect seriously on the subject. The most astonishing migrations moreover are quite possible. Lyall maintained that Man, however savage, transported to any part of the globe, would at last bring it entirely under his subjection. By land there can be no doubt of this; rivers, mountains, forests, swamps, deserts, he leaps over them all, either in masses or in groups, whether for his own pleasure or by accident. M. de

Quatrefages, in his lectures, tells of the exodus of a horde of Kalmucks, who, to the number of 400,000, including women and children, and in spite of the most incredible obstacles, made a remarkable migration from the banks of the Volga to the eastern confines of China. Voyages by sea, under favourable circumstances of one kind and another, are no less possible. Islands frequently bring into connection the most distant points, like those stepping-stones which we threw into the stream to enable us to cross to the opposite bank. It is thus that by Kamschatka, the Aleutian Islands, and Alaska, or directly from one side of Behring's Strait to the other, the Esquimaux have easily been able to reach America. In this way, from Asia to the centre of Oceania there are two natural roads, the one by the island of Formosa, the Philippines, and the Moluccas, leading to the Fiji Islands, by passing along the chain of the Solomon Islands; the other by the peninsula of Malacca, the Sunda archipelago and Timor to Australia, and on to Tasmania. Independently of the various islands scattered about, the wind and currents lend their aid. The most contrary winds, blowing almost constantly from one particular quarter, change at certain periods of the year; and close to the strongest current running in one particular direction there is always a counter-current. The Gulf Stream of Mexico, and the Equatorial Current of the Pacific, are no exceptions to this. They pursue their course in one direction for a great distance, but by counter-currents they absolutely return again, as we notice in some of our rivers. So, however inaccessible or lost in mid-ocean a solitary island may appear to be, chance as well as man's will, however inexperienced he may be, may always bring visitors to it. This is how vessels coming from the Marianne Islands made the Carolines, which were situated at a distance of 600 kilomètres. Tradition, even more than history, furnishes a multitude of similar examples.

Archæology

Makes its appearance when history and tradition are both at fault; not the archæology whose aim is to discover the traces of known events, like the Retreat of the Ten Thousand in Asia Minor, the sojourn of the Romans in Great Britain, or the passage of the Red Sea by the Israelites; but that which belongs to populations of which no history has come down to us, whether written or oral, and which inquires into their customs, their industry, their commerce, and even their objects of thought. This we term *prehistoric archæology*. This science makes us acquainted with the dolmens, their contents, and the sepulchral object for which they were designed. It shows them to us in every direction from the north and west of Europe as far as Algeria. It examines the caves which are used as a substitute for them, in places where they are found naturally, and in countries where, owing to the chalky nature of the stone, they were easily excavated. The tumuli which are seen from east to west across the middle of Europe from the Caucasus to the plains of Champagne; those of Siberia, for example, examined by Meunier and Eichthal, and afterwards by M. Desor; those of the northern part of America; the constructions called Pelasgic, in the Mediterranean, Kaffraria, and Arabia; the monoliths of Easter Island, representing human figures; the refuse-heaps of Italy; the kjökken-möddings, or kitchen-leavings, close to the sea-shore, in Europe, in Patagonia, as well as in the Andaman Islands; the pile-villages of Switzerland, &c.

To archæology in general we refer all that specially has reference to the Metal Age, and to prehistoric archæology that which concerns the two Stone epochs, the neolithic and the palæolithic.

We were just now contemplating with wonder the changes which will probably take place in three or four thousand years to come in the races now existing, and we were picturing to ourself those which have possibly been produced during the last three or four thousand years. This lapse of time is, however, but a trifle as compared with the ages which have preceded it. One of the first

2 F

dates of history fixed by Mr. Henry Martin, is about the year
1500 B.C. The Egyptian annals make mention, at this period, of
the advent of a blonde people from the north, whose appearance is
coincident with the passage of the Celts into Spain. It, however,
was doubtless merely one of the last efforts of the same people to
spread towards the south. The dolmens of Algeria and Morocco
testify that at a previous period invasion after invasion of the same
populations had taken place. Some of those dolmens contain iron,
and even historic medals; others, and these the larger number,
contain only polished-flint implements. It is therefore presumable
that the conclusion of the Polished Stone epoch in Algeria occurred
about the period of the last invasion of the blonde people described
by the Egyptians. This might be fixed in Africa about the year
2000 B.C. But Africa was nearer some of the commercial sources from
which iron came, and it is very likely that the exact termination of
the Polished Stone epoch in Western Europe ought to be put farther
back still. Whenever it may have terminated, there is no doubt
that the duration of the *Polished Stone, or Neolithic epoch*, was a
very lengthened one. It was of sufficient duration to cover Europe,
from Scandinavia to Gibraltar, with megalithic monuments, with
grottoes used for purposes of burial, as well as for dwelling-places.
Great events, such as wars and invasions, took place during the
period. New races sprang up which had time to cross with
the aboriginal races, and to form almost as many mixed races as
exist at the present day. The duration of this period, however, is
as nothing to that of the *Rough Stone, or Palæolithic period*, which
preceded it. At the commencement of this latter, the cavern-bear,
the mammoth, the rhinoceros with partitioned nostril, inhabited
the whole of France. A considerable diminution of temperature
had favoured their emigration from the north, no doubt, and driven
them towards the south, or had been the means of destroying some
of the species which had preceded them. At one time, the glaciers
had become greatly extended in our country, a relative elevation
of temperature followed, and assisted in the development of the
fauna and Flora. A second cooling and a second extension of
glaciers then supervened. Man hunted the great animals above

referred to; this was the Mammoth Age. But they began to
diminish in number, with the exception of one of them, the reindeer, which, on the contrary, multiplied *ad infinitum*. This was
the Reindeer Age. Civilisation and the taste for art became
developed, particularly in the Périgord and the Pyrenees. Man
was passing a sedentary life and had nothing, consequently, of the
Mongol men about him, all these things betokening his physical
character. Then the earth became progressively warmer, the reindeer reached the north, the ibex and the marmot were to be seen
on the mountains.

During this considerable phase, and especially at its commencement, our valleys were formed. The bed of the Seine, of which some
remains are still visible at Montreuil, was fifty-five mètres in height,
and consisted of those deposits which are termed the ancient sea-
levels. Later on, the bed became about twenty-five mètres lower, the
lowest alluvial deposits of Grenelle were formed, and then slowly
became filled up, forming the banks as we now see them. How
can we possibly determine the interval which must have elapsed
between these various deposits?

At the Mammoth period, distinguished more particularly by the
fossil bones of animals and the rough flints left in the alluvia
of rivers, Man constructed only coarse stone implements, and
especially those of the shape called *St. Acheul*, so abundant in
the valley of the Somme. At the following period, intermediate
between the Mammoth and the Reindeer, he preferred these forms
termed *Du Moustier*. Later on, that is to say at the Reindeer
epoch proper, in the valley of La Vézère, we find him taking
regular steps in the path of progress. Instead of the heavy massive
implements, flakes of flint were used for javelin points, or fixed
in handles after the fashion of our graving tools. Man soon
utilised the bones and horns of the reindeer for the purpose of
constructing implements of every description, even needles and
fish-hooks. In other parts of France, as at Excideuil, at Solutré
in the Pyrenees, the method of working the flint continued to
improve, and implements in the shape of laurel leaves, with finely
sharpened borders, became common. It was then that the art of

polishing the flint must have commenced, one possibly imported by
some conquering nation, but probably also by the application to the
stone of the process which had already been practised upon bone.
This double epoch of the Mammoth and Reindeer was therefore a
considerable one, and yet from the Mammoth period to the present
time the interval is almost nothing as compared with the period
during which Man previously existed. The temperature in Europe,
contrary to that of the succeeding period, was hotter than it is
now. Man, whose flint implements have been found in the
Pliocene formation of St. Prest, hunted the *Elephas meridionalis,*
the *Rhinoceros etruscus,* the *R. Merckii,* and the *R. leptorhinus.*

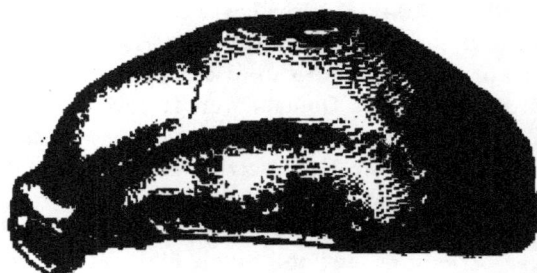

Fig. 42.—Neanderthal skull in profile (Mammoth epoch).

At the close of the Miocene epoch, when we have the shell
heaps of Pouancé, Man was in conflict with the mastodon and
the halitherium, and he possessed a knowledge of fire. We are
less acquainted with his ancestors who worked the flints found by
the Abbé Bourgeois at Thenay, in the lower Miocene, below the
La Beauce chalk. But his existence at that epoch—one but little
distant from the period at which are deposited the Meudon millstone
or the Fontainebleau sandstone—is a clearly revealed scientific fact.
We possess his implements : they indicate a tolerable amount of
intelligence : but his remains are wanting. Up to the present
moment archæologists, or rather geologists, have never found the
smallest fragment of a human bone. All these questions will be
considered in detail in the volume of the "Bibliothèque des

"Sciences Contemporaines," now in the press, entitled "Archéologie Préhistorique," by M. Gabrielle de Mortillet.

Prehistoric Races.

Human palæontology commences with the Post-pliocene or Mammoth epoch. Examples of it are few in number, and are not readily capable of classification. De Quatrefages and Hamy, however, have not flinched from this difficult task.* By joining together fragments of male skulls from Canstadt, Eguisheim, Brux, Denise, and the Neanderthal, and female skulls from Staengenæs, L'Olmo, and Clichy, they succeeded in discovering in them certain common characters; that is to say, dolichocephaly, a remarkable sinking of the vault of the skull, or platycephaly, a great recession of the frontal bone, and a very marked development of the superciliary arches. Of all the specimens the most remarkable are the calvarium of the Neanderthal and the jaw of La Naulette. Anyone accustomed to handle the skulls of the anthropoid apes will be immediately struck with the great resemblance between them. The Neanderthal especially reminds one of the calvarium of the female gorilla, which is similarly staved in as it were, or of the skull of a hylobate. The superciliary arches are altogether simian, although the skull is clearly human. Its capacity, estimated at 1200 cubic centimètres, dissipates all doubt on the subject. The jaw of the Naulette is not less remarkable by the obliteration of the tubercles géni, and of the projection of the chin; there is complete prognathism of the body of the bone, analogous cases of which are seen in races now existing, although not to the same extent. We are unable to come to any decided conclusion upon the matter however.

The characters of the Neanderthal are found, though in a less degree, in the majority of the other specimens collected by MM. de Quatrefages and Hamy, to which the generic name of *Canstadt Race* has been given. It is not impossible, however, that

* "Crania Ethnica. Les Crânes des Races Humaines, décrits par MM. de Quatrefages et E. T. Hamy." Paris, 1873-79.

this type was an exceptional one, and that these were cases of atavism, and represented less a race belonging to the Mammoth Age than one of the Pliocene or Miocene epoch. This is, no doubt, the case as regards the famous Namaqua skulls in the Museum, whose prognathism is most remarkable, although they came from the midst of a Hottentot race. They might be the representatives of a previous African race which had become extinct. From the meteorological and geological changes which took place at the close of the Miocene and Pliocene epochs, we can easily understand how it was that the majority of the inhabitants of Thenay and Pouancé succumbed, and that only a small number, namely, those who were able to escape from the destroying causes, survived. Now the inferior races disappear, while the superior increase in number. This fact, however we may explain it, is one against which it is impossible to contend. At that prodigiously remote period there were necessarily inferior as well as superior races. The same law was doubtless in existence then as now. It is possible, therefore, while admitting that the Neanderthal was an exception, that it represents one of those inferior races which has disappeared. It would be at the Mammoth period, in relation to anterior races, as a tribe or an individual, whether Indian or Negro, will be in three thousand years in relation to ourselves.

Admitting that the Neanderthal belonged to a race of the period, or to an anterior race, is it the skull of a man in the sense in which we use the term ? In other words, Had he or his ancestors to answer for it ? We know that the man of the upper Miocene period was acquainted with the use of fire. In point of fact, Was the Neanderthal race more nearly allied to the Anthropoids, whether known or unknown, or to ourselves ? We simply ask the question.

The palæontological remains of the succeeding epoch, or Reindeer Age, in Western Europe, have been studied by the authors of the " Crania Ethnica," by whom they have been termed the Cro-Magnon Race, taking as its type the subjects exhumed from the cave of that name in the Périgord, by Christy and Lartet. As compared with the Constadt race, they seem but of yesterday. After an examination, in 1872, of several parts of the Cro-Magnon cave previously

untouched, we were of the same opinion. Their essential characters
are as follows, according to De Quatrefages and Hamy : They are
dolichocephalic, like the skulls of the Canstadt race. They have a
high forehead, broad, and well developed above the superciliary
ridges, of average size, the vault being rather high, with a fine curve
continuing regularly from the forehead to the obelion, where it
bends down to form an oblique flat, which is continued on into the

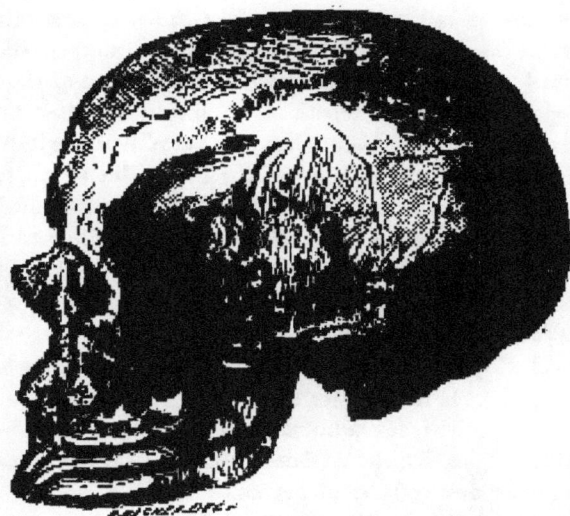

FIG. 41.—Skull of the Old Man of Cro-Magnon, Eyzies (Reindeer epoch).

supra-occipital region. The frontal bosses, which are as though
flattened in the preceding race, are in this high and projecting.
The face is broad and short in relation to the maximum length of
the skull, the orbits are deep, in the form of a parallelogram, having
a minimum index of sixty-one, the smallest on record.   There is
considerable prognathism at the sub-nasal portion in the old man of
Cro-Magnon, namely, 62·6° according to one measurement, as much
as in the most prognathous negro.   In looking at this last trait of
the corresponding prognathism presented by the other specimens of

the same group collected by De Quatrefages and Hamy, we are nevertheless inclined to think that this old man was an exception. One of the Cro-Magnon skulls, on the contrary, exhibits one of the weakest prognathisms we have examined, namely, 86·7°. The projection of the mental eminence of the lower jaw is considerable, and is in strong contrast with the absolute obliteration of the same part in the Naulette jaw.

The Cro-Magnon race, if we may judge of it by the bones in our possession, was of tall stature, robust, the skeleton presenting the characters we have described above, namely, the platycnemic tibia, the anteriorly-channelled fibula, the thick *linea aspera* of the femur, and the curve of the upper fourth of the forearm. After the Cro-Magnon race, the authors of the "*Crania Ethnica*" describe in Western Europe certain less frequent types of the Palæolithic epoch, namely, the brachycephalic type, represented by the skull discovered at La Truchère, near Lyon, close to the *Elephas primigenius*, and by two or three other skulls found at Grenelle, near Paris, in the alluvia of the middle levels above the dolichocephales of the previous races, the Mesaticephalic and the Sub-brachycephalic type described under the name of *Furfooz Race*, and found in the strata posterior to those of Cro-Magnon. It remains for us to make a *résumé* of the results to which the various communications of M. Broca have led with regard to the region which at those epochs has greater interest for us, namely, our own country of France.

When the admirable discoveries of linguists had established the kindred and relationship of the Indo-European languages, we were led to believe that Europe had been peopled, as we said just now, by immigrants from that region of Asia in which we might discover remains nearest akin to the common linguistic stock. Various considerations, moreover, led us to suppose that these immigrants carried with them the use of metals, religion, &c. But two languages, which two small groups of peoples spoke, escaped the general law—namely, the Fins and the Basques. Retzius, ascertaining that the former were brachycephalic, thought that the latter were so likewise; and noticing that the Swedes around him were dolichocephalic, formulated his celebrated pro-

position, that the autochthonous race of Europe was brachycephalic, and that which came after dolichocephalic.   Gradually,
however, M. Broca was enabled to prove from abundance of facts
that the Basques are dolichocephalic, and that the proposition of
Retzius ought to be reversed, the most ancient inhabitants of
Europe being dolichocephalic, and those coming afterwards brachycephalic.   Thus the most ancient race of France represented by
the three Cro-Magnon skulls, the two of Laugerie, the three of the
middle and lower levels of Grenelle, had a dolichocephalic index
of from 73 to 75.   So the race from the cavern of l'Homme Mort,
which has all the appearance of that of Cro-Magnon, has an average
index of 73·22°.

The precise period when the brachycephales penetrated into
Western Europe has not been determined.   Certain little tribes
with round skulls have possibly made their appearance here and
there since the Paleolithic epoch, but they have only done
so in large numbers at a later period.   At the close of the
Rough Stone epoch, at Solutré for example, M. Broca proves the
existence of two races united together, the one dolichocephalic,
having the appearance of the race of l'Homme Mort, the other
sub-brachycephalic, approaching nearer to the Furfooz race.

In England the facts are determined in a precise manner.   There
exist in that country two sorts of dolmens, the long, called *long
barrows*, containing only polished-stone implements, and skulls for
the most part thoroughly dolichocephalic; the others round, and of
a different construction, the *round barrows*, containing metal, and a
great number of brachycephalic together with dolichocephalic skulls
of the preceding race, as well as mesaticephalic, the issue no doubt
of crossing between the two.

The date of their first appearance in England is therefore fixed.
They came in at the close of the Polished Stone period, at the
same time as the metals.   But did they arrive directly, or by
passing through France?   The track left by the brachycephales
on the Swiss frontier, at the extreme point of Brittany, would
incline us to the latter view.   It must be admitted—(1) That
the most ancient inhabitants of France were dolichocephalic;

(2) That a small number of brachycephales afterwards crept in among them, but without changing their ethnic basis; (3) That the immigration of these latter towards the close of the Palæolithic epoch was remarkable from the fact of its limiting itself to certain points of territory, as the Mâconnais; (4) That an invasion must then have been made from the north, bringing with it the custom of burying in dolmens or grottoes, but which being dolichocephales, or numerically very inferior, bequeathed to the population its dolichocephalic character, though somewhat lessened (indices in the dolmens in the neighbourhood of Paris 75·01; in the grottoes of La Marne, where it is less pure, 77·78); (5) That, lastly, the invasion of the brachycephales already commenced in the east, and probably passing by two currents, the one below, the other above the Alpine range, assumed greater proportions at the close of the Polished Stone period, traversed through the centre of France, and there crossed with the ancient aboriginal race, giving origin to the new historic race, which we shall describe further on, under the name of Celtic type. All these questions have to do with Anthropology pure and simple, and especially with craniometry; but the inquiry as to their elements, the determination of the age and circumstances of strata, the discovery of relics of industry, and other memorials of that remote past, are in the domain of prehistoric archæology and geology; for what, after all, is geology, but the archæology of the earth and its inhabitants?

CHAPTER X.

ANTHROPOLOGICAL TYPES—BLONDE AND BROWN EUROPEAN TYPES—
HINDOO, TROGLODYTIAN, IRANIAN, CELTIC, BERBER, SEMITIC,
ARABIAN TYPES.

The four orders of characters which we have been describing are not, as we have said, of equal value. If the races now in

existence were pure and homogeneous, such as nature made them,
it would suffice to sum up their differences and their resemblances,
to take account of their individual varieties and pathological deviations, and to proceed to give them their most natural position. But
the ground is altogether different—unity is wanting. Races have been
divided, dispersed, intermixed, crossed in various proportions and
in all directions, for thousands of ages. The greater part of them
have relinquished their language for that of their conquerors, or for
a third or even for a fourth; the principal masses have disappeared,
and we find ourselves no longer in the presence of races, but of
peoples, the origins of which we have to trace or to make a direct
classification of. In other words, there are two orders of classification, which we must not confound, namely, the classification of
the masses of human beings, such as the flux and reflux of time
have left us; and the classification of races such as we are able
to arrive at after a most minute process of analysis. The former is
ethnological, the latter, anthropological. Their point of departure
is the same, the point at which they meet, different. The most
important classifications of the human race have, as their basis,
physical characters, such as the nature of the hair and the colour
of the skin, and then immediately diverge in every direction.
They agree however in details, when they concern some tribe
isolated, owing to exceptional circumstances, like the Esquimaux in
Greenland or the Tasmanians in Van Diemen's Land. But beyond
that the ethnographical point of view is alone apparent, and the
use of the word race is most unfortunate. We speak of Anglo-
Germanic and Latin races, of German, English, Slav races, as
if these epithets had anything more than a political signification, a
fortuitous aggregation of anthropological elements from various
sources. In France, where the nation is so homogeneous and
unity so complete, there are the French people but not the French
race. We find in the north the descendants of the Belgæ, the
Walloons, and other Kymris; in the east, those of Germans and
Burgundians; in the west, Normans; in the centre, Celts, who at
the same epoch at which their name took its origin consisted of
foreigners of various origins and of the aborigines; in the south,

ancient Aquitanians and Basques; without mentioning a host of
settlers like the Saracens, which are found here and there,
Tectosages which have left at Toulouse the custom of cranial
deformations, and the traders who passed through the Phocæan
town of Marseilles. In Asia, where the peoples have been tossed
about from east to west and from west to east, in so prodigious
a way that the most characteristic race is found perhaps on
the other side of the Pacific, in the polar zone; in Africa, where
a similar-movement has taken place at different times; in America,
where great convulsions in historic epochs have taken place—we
no longer meet with primitive races, but with the resultants of
repeated crossing, of close contact, of mixture of every kind.
Classifications with elements such as these are little more than
ethnographic.

Gerdy rightly affirmed that there are no longer any pure races.
Our illustrious master, M. Broca, however, allows that there are
some, and M. de Quatrefages a short time since published a long
list of those "regarded as pure." Doubtless, if we are satisfied
with a small number of individuals or of skulls, we may discover
in them, or unite them into, an identity of type. "Whoever has
seen one Toda," says Mr. Marshall, "has seen the whole race."
Be it so, we will record his statement.

Of all races, we are told, there is not a more homogeneous
one than that of the Esquimaux, thanks to their isolation, which
has been maintained in consequence of geographical and atmospheric circumstances. There are about a dozen skulls in the
Museum, all from Greenland, forming the most homogeneous
series in the collection. But in the Denmark collection, from
which some specimens were brought to the Geographical Congress
at Paris, this unity of type is not perfect, and we discover in
them indications of hybridity. In Mr. Davis's collection, from
the shores of Baffin's Bay, the differences are still more marked.
Travellers speak of similar and equally important differences as
existing at the present time. Variations in stature are very
common. At Morton's Strait the stature is 1·82 mètre; at
Barrow Point, 1·64. In one tribe the average stature of the men

is 1·714 mètre, in another 1·584. Greenlanders are looked upon as one of the smallest of the human races. At Hotham Harbour, an Esquimau "was exactly like a negro," at Spafarist Inlet, "like a Jew" (*Seemen*). "The oval face, associated with the Roman nose," is by no means rare (*King*). The complexion is sometimes very fair, sometimes very dark. In the series of Malay skulls, one of the most homogeneous in the Museum, there are at least two types. We think we have shown that there is no unity among the Australians. In Patagonia, the skulls of the ancient Paraderos are of two very opposite types, one being dolichocephalic, the other brachycephalic. Among the Japanese there are three distinct types noticeable in the living subject (*Roang*), and a fourth which we may gather from an examination of skulls. Among the Ainos, in the same country, there are certainly two. Along the coast of Guinea the tribes vary, even at short distances from one another; and travellers describe altogether different characters in one and the same tribe, according to the particular individuals upon whom they happen to have fixed their attention. Among Hottentots it is even worse.

We are not aware but of one example of perfect identity of type in a human group, namely, that of the Andamans. We have had an opportunity of seeing twenty-two photographs of this race, and in all, the heads appear as if cast in the same mould. Colonel Man, however, affirms that there are two different races in the Andaman archipelago. We may remark that Mr. Owen, on measuring ninety-six skulls of negroes of the Gaboon, was astonished at their remarkable resemblance to each other, which was even greater than we notice among Europeans. In a word, the greater number of classifications of any extent are only anthropological as regards their basis. As soon as we enter upon secondary divisions they become ethnographic, and have not so much to do with races as with peoples. The true classification of the divisions and subdivisions of the human family has yet to be made, and cannot be entered upon until we know the real component elements of peoples now in existence. Given a certain

group, the following questions will arise for our consideration:
(1) What, in a physical and physiological point of view, is its
average, that is to say, the type? (2) Are the variations from
this average so slight as to enable us to look upon the type as
pure? (3) Are the variations so divergent, and are the average
secondary groups sufficiently definite to enable us to recognise in
them one or many types? (4) Has there been a close fusion of
these types? in other words, has the race crossed, or have the
types remained distinct, or is the race only a mixed one? By this
means we at last separate the characters of one, two, or more types
successively. Ethnography gives us valuable aid as regards the
majority of these questions; linguistics equally so; and more than
all, the study of the characters of ancient human remains found
embedded in the earth. It is thus that M. Broca has succeeded
in eliminating the Celtic element, which has contributed to form
the Breton group, and thus that he hopes eventually to trace
the original elements of which the Celtic group itself is composed.
A sufficient number of the most characteristic of the first, second,
and third order being thus determined, it will be necessary to
search for their kindred, and to classify them. We should only
then have seriously to inquire whether they belong to genera,
species, or varieties. The task is a long and laborious one.
Science is in a transition state on this matter. Some general types
have been already acquired, although we cannot always affirm
which human group expresses them the best. Others have only
been accepted provisionally, while of others we have a preconceived
idea, and are nevertheless unable to determine them even with
the specimens before us. In the résumé that we are about to give
we must therefore only look upon them as one series of land-
marks, indicating one of the stages at which anthropology has
arrived.

By *human type* must be understood the average of characters
which a human race supposed to be pure presents. In homogeneous
races, if such there are, it is discovered by the simple inspection of
individuals. In the generality of cases it must be segregated. It
is then a physical ideal, to which the greater number of the

individuals of the group more or less approach, but which is better
marked in some than in others. Frequently in one series it is
associated with some other type. Sometimes at its extreme
boundaries it is amalgamated with the type of another group.
Of course community of type implies a relationship of some sort.
There are general types, then types and sub-types of these, and in
each of the latter, other divisions. When once fixed by science,
they will even form bases of classification.

Let us take an example : the Berber people is formed—(1) Of a
brown autochthonous groundwork, that is to say of the most
ancient of which we can find any trace ; (2) Of blondes from the
north, Arabs from the east, and negroes from the south. The
Berber type is the ensemble of the characters which must have belonged exclusively to the autochthonous stock : its sub-types are
the Tawásek, the Kabyl, &c. It is itself the offspring of some
other more general type of which we are still ignorant.

We shall now have to describe types which are altogether
relative, such as the Celtic. This is one of the constituent
elements of the ethnographic French race, and is itself composed
of many original types, which we ought to be thoroughly acquainted with. The first types for our consideration correspond to
what anthropologists call, according to their several notions, species,
races, trunks, or branches. These are the European, the Mongolian,
the negro of Africa, the Hottentot. We shall separate the
American from the second, and add a red type in Africa. We shall
give a separate paragraph to the Fin, the Lapp, the Australoid, and
the two negro types of Oceania ; and then notice some others of
less importance, without concerning ourselves about those of a
subordinate character.

The European Type.

The European type is very defined, although its title is hardly
an exact one. Even by leaving out of consideration all the
emigrations posterior to the sixteenth century, we meet with it in

all four quarters of the globe. In Europe, with the exception perhaps of the Lappa and the Fin races, it is general. In Asia it is largely represented by the Semites, the Persians, the Affghans, the Hindoos, and doubtless also by the Ainos, the Miaotsé, the Todas. In Africa it is represented by the Barbers; and in America the existence of natives which are considered to belong to it has been frequently noticed. Its characters may be thus summed up :

The complexion is always fair among the children. The pilous system is moderately developed. The beard, the moustache, and the whiskers are abundant. The hair is straight, wavy, or undulated, long and flexible. The top of the head is round. The *norma verticalis* of the skull is oval, with a regular outline, the zygotic arches being unnoticeable. The anterior cranium is very developed relatively to the posterior. The capacity of the cranial cavity reaches the highest amount recorded, namely, 1523 cubic centimètres, in the Celtic type. The cranial sutures are very complicated. The greater wings of the sphenoid are articulated with the parietal to a considerable extent. The curve described by the temporal line is not a large one. The forehead is broad below, well developed, the summit being neither receding nor projecting. The frontal bosses on each side are moderately distinct. The superciliary arches vary, never exhibiting, in the male sex, the large size which we notice in the Melanesian races, nor the obliteration peculiar to the majority of Mongolian or negro skulls. The face, looked at in front, describes rather a long oval, the malar bones, or the maxillary apparatus, not being particularly marked, as in the Mongolian type or the Negro types. The median projecting portions present, when developed in their highest degree, what is familiarly termed the face like the blade of a knife. The nose is highly characteristic in the European type, and projects in front at the expense of its transverse diameter. Its two lateral surfaces are united at an acute angle. Its point is firm, and the two nostrils, situated on the same horizontal plane, are elliptical, directed from before backwards, and almost parallel. The skeleton of the nose is leptorhinian or mesorhinian, never

platyrrhinian. Its anterior aperture has the shape of an ace of
hearts reversed, its point being very long, its base being formed
by the nasal spine, frequently very long, and by a simple sharp
border. The ensemble of the two jaws and the teeth, in profile,
is almost a right line. It is to the European type that we apply
the term "orthognathism," to express the minimum of prognathism
observed in Man. This minimum varies from 82° to 75·5°. The
mouth is small, the lips bright red, well formed, never thick,
except in individuals of a certain temperament. The teeth are
straight, close together, bluish white or yellowish white, and
subject to caries. The chin is projecting. The shape of the ear is
that of a long oval, with folds above and behind, the lobule being
well formed. Lastly, the plane of the prolonged occipital foramen
meets the face above the middle of the nose, and frequently at its
root. Beauty of form does not specially belong to the European,
and many savages would surpass him in this respect. Most commonly, however, he is well-proportioned, tall, or of medium
height; his neck is large and finely formed, his chest broad,
shoulders wide, the bend of the back well marked, the muscles of
the buttocks strong, the calf large, and reaching below the middle
of the leg, the foot well arched, and he seldom exhibits those
deformities of the abdomen and limbs noticed by the early navi-
gators in the inferior races. The European becomes decrepit less
quickly than the negro, the breasts in the woman retain their
firmness and proper form for a longer period, and the articulations
of the joints are rather small. For a description of the proportions
of the body, see pages 315, 331, et seq.

The two most natural divisions of the European type are the
blonde and the brown.

The Blonde Type.

The *blonde type*, in its highest expression, is marked by three
special characteristics: namely, blue eyes, fair hair, and light rosy
or florid complexion, which becomes of a uniform red-brick colour
or freckled under exposure to the sun.

The eyes assume various shades of green, gray, yellowish, light brown, &c., according as they are associated with one of the two other characters. The reddish colour of the eyes of the albino must be considered as quite distinct. Yellow-golden hair, or reddish and chestnut, are in the same category. These last, however, have less value, inasmuch as on the one hand they frequently correspond with a first degree of crossing of the blonde with the brown type, and on the other are characteristic of other types than the blonde and brown. Dr. Beddoe does not give any particular significance to red hair. We think, however, that in the generality of cases it is a form of light hair, and sometimes is characteristic of a distinct type, of which we shall speak presently. With regard to the shades of colour of the skin, they have less value, inasmuch as they are more easily affected by crossing and external circumstances. Blue eyes are after all the most certain element upon which to fix, on looking at a single individual, or in the absence of a sufficient description of other characters, the actual or past existence of the blonde type in the blood.

This type, whether complete or incomplete, has spread over four out of the five portions of the globe. The peoples belonging to it possess in a high degree the faculty of emigration and colonisation, without being indebted for it to a very highly-developed faculty of acclimation. The natural centre whence it has shed its lustre seems to be the north of Europe. The purest example of the blonde type is in Iceland, in the Scandinavian peninsula, Lapland excepted, and Denmark. Then Holland, North Germany, Saxony, Belgium, and the British Isles. In France it is less pronounced, and stops at about the position of an oblique line passing from Granville, on the coast of the British Channel, to Lyon. Here and there, however, it is found more to the south, particularly in the Basque territory, and in the south of Spain. The populations belonging to it are tall, stout, and square-built, or slim; the face is long, the nose large and straight, the point extending slightly beyond the nostrils. They are of lymphatic temperament, the passions not very strong, and individuality very marked. The shape of the head is difficult to determine, owing to the numerous

crosses here and there which have caused a change in it. The
Danes are brachycephalic, the Normans mesaticephalic, the Norwegians, Swedes, Belgians, and English dolichocephalic. With
regard to the Germans in the extended sense, they present every
form imaginable. For our part we are convinced that the primitive blonde type was dolichocephalic.

In another race, that of the Irish in Dublin, Dr. Beddoe
found in 1900 individuals 54 per cent. with fair hair, of whom
6 per cent. were red, 13 flaxen, and 36 chestnut—or rather
more than half blondes, according to the hair. Dr. Wilde, on the
other hand, found in 1200 other Irish, 34 per cent. with blue
eyes, 9 brown, and 66 decidedly dark. The Dutch are therefore
much purer as blondes than the Irish. Again, in the Basque
provinces, Dr. Argelliès found light eyes in 23 out of 47 individuals, of whom 14 had blue and 35 brown eyes, while there
was not a single example among them of flaxen hair, only 2 of
red, some few of dark chestnut, and the rest black. It follows
from this that the present Basque race is formed of two elements—
the brown and the blonde; that it is decidedly brown if we
are to judge by the hair, at least in the localities observed, and
that the blonde type is to be traced in the colour of the eyes
and not in that of the hair. The Irish statistics indicate, on the
contrary, that of the two elements, the more persistent is that
of the hair. We refer the reader to page 348 for other important
details, and to the tables at pages 343 and 349 for the relative
proportion of flaxen, chestnut, and brown in different races, the
two elements, the hair and the eyes, being associated together.
The blonde type, with its three fundamental characters, is met
with in other parts of the world, but seeing the difficulty of being
guided by descriptions derived from the hair and skin, we shall
only consider the question as regards blue eyes.

In Asia, we at once notice the blonde type on the banks of
the river Amour (Klaproth, J. Barrow, Castren). "We saw
Mantshú Tartars," says Barrow, "who accompanied Macartney's
embassy to Pekin, men as well as women, who were extremely
fair and of florid complexion; some of the men had light blue

2 G 2

eyes, a straight or aquiline nose, brown hair, and a large and bushy beard." Among the Miáu Tsz of the south-east of China there are tribes which pass for the aborigines of the Celestial Empire. We find it in India, notably among the Katices, who have sometimes "light hair and blue eyes" (Prichard and L. Rousselet), and even in Ceylon, among the Cingalese (Davy). The Bussahirs of Rhaenpoor, not far from the sources of the Ganges, are frequently of very fair complexion though tanned by the sun, with blue eyes, hair and beard curly and of light colour, or even red (Fraser). (2) The Paians or Affghan soldiers are commonly brown, and of the Iranian race, but a large number have "red hair and blue eyes, and a fair and florid complexion" (Fraser). But the most celebrated example is that of Siah Posh of Kaffristan, at the junction of the Himalaya and the Hindoo-Koosh. The majority are tall, have Caucasian features, fair complexion, blue eyes, and chestnut hair. According to their traditions they came from Affghanistan; they speak a language derived from the Sanskrit, and have burial rites which remind one of those of the Parsees. We may add, according to Mr. G. Hayward, that light chestnut hair is more common than black among the inhabitants of Darnistan, that the eyes are gray, chestnut, and occasionally blue, and that the women remind one very much of the English. Some of the Kirghis of Turkestan, and the Tadzhiks of Persia, have "blue or gray eyes," and among the Ossetians, the Abassians, and the Swanethians of the southern side of the Caucasus, there are individuals with "flaxen hair, fair complexion, and blue eyes," whom we must not confound with the recent German immigrants. These examples show that the blonde type has to a certain extent prevailed in Asia, but they are not such as to induce us to suppose that it was cradled in this part of the world. It has been satisfactorily shown that the blonde type exists in the north of Africa. In Tunis, in Algeria, in Morocco, in the Canary Islands, and in the Sahara, it exists everywhere. It is derived from a Tamahou people, who, about the year 1500 before our era, made their appearance on the frontiers of Egypt, coming from the north. The blondes which we meet with in the Basque territory, and near the Strait of Gibraltar in Spain, are probably descendants of theirs.

Dr. Schweinfurth remarked, in Central Africa, in the Monbouttous' country, the frequency of light or reddish hair. The greater number are complete albinos, as he has taken care to tell us. Others are only so in a slight degree. Others may hold to the practice, so common in Africa, of dyeing or colouring the hair. In the present state of science, it must be allowed that in really Negro countries blondes are never met with unassociated with albinism.

The facts mentioned with respect to America should be looked at differently. They arise no doubt from blondes imported from Europe, to whatever remote period this importation may be referred, and whatever the course they may happen to have followed. A tradition of this kind exists among the Boronos of the eastern chain of the Chilian Andes, among whom we find blue eyes, associated sometimes with black, sometimes with light or red hair, and with the ordinary features of the American races. Another remarkable example is that of the Mandans, mentioned by Catlin, who have "hair as light as the mixed breeds, with chestnut, gray, or blue eyes." The Athapascans have also been described as having among them individuals with gray eyes (*Mackenzie*). Light hair is also seen among the Lee-Pangwes (*Pike*), and people with very fair complexion among the Antisians (*D'Orbigny*) and the Koliches (*Dixon*).

The Brown European Types.

The *brown European types* are characterised by dark eyes, absolutely black hair, and fair skin, which readily becomes a warm bronze tint by exposure to the sun. Were we to leave out the blonde races, which have manifestly crossed, it would be difficult to separate some sub-types from the general blonde type of which we have just spoken. The Scandinavian and the Dane would perhaps be the only ones. The brown types, on the contrary, are very numerous. It is usual to divide the fair races into two branches, the Hindoo and the European. This is a linguistic division only; the first term however must be retained in order that we may find in it an anthropological type. After this, we must accept the Tschinghanian type, on account of the probable hypotheses to which it has given rise. If we suppose an Aryan migration from the east to the west, we must equally admit an Iranian type for those remaining behind, which we still find on the spot. Having disposed of the blonde types seen in Europe, we have yet to speak of the most remarkable brown types, namely, the Circassian, the Pelasgian or Albanian, the Ligurian, the Basque, &c. &c. Then, as we pass round the Mediterranean, the Berber and the Semitic, which are most certainly allied to the European types.

In this enumeration no Slav or German type appears. The reason is because there is no such. In Russia in Europe, for example, the populations are Finnish, or a mixed race of Fins from the north, more or less Mongolian here and there, and having some ill-defined brown element in the south. Among the peasants, who, as everywhere, more properly represent the primitive element, we find countenances which remind us of those of the pure Alans and the Todas. Where then are we to get the Slav type? This name appeared in history with the Wendes, the Antes, previously called by the Greeks Serbs, and the Sclavons (*Jornandès*). In 552 the Sclavons are before Constantinople. From the sixth to the seventh century the Wendes advance as far as the banks of the Elbe. But whence has originated the Slav language, which alone justifies its pretension to a corresponding type? We know not. Now the peoples which speak it, or its derivatives, are divided into two groups: the western, including the Poles or Laschs, the Bohemians or Tchechs, of which the Slovaks form a part, and the Wendes of Lusatia; and the south-eastern, divided into Great Russians or Muscovites, Little Russians, Ruthenians or Russniaks, White Russians, Bulgarians, and Serbs—these last including Croatians, Dalmatians, Bosnians, and Slovenians, &c. The only character which is common to them all, besides language, is brachycephaly. Roumanians and Hungarians are also brachycephalic, as well as a large number of Germans, Italians, and French.

Mr. Edwards describes, in the following terms, a type which he has noticed as predominating among Poles, Silesians, Moravians, Bohemians, Hungarians, and Russians : " The outline of the head looked at in front appears square, because the height somewhat exceeds the breadth, and the top is sensibly flat, and the direction of the jaw horizontal. The length of the nose is less than the distance from its base to the chin. It is almost straight, that is to say without any decided curve, but if this is at all appreciable it is slightly concave, so that the end has a tendency to turn up. The lower part is somewhat wide, and the extremity rounded. The eyes, somewhat sunken, are exactly on the same line, and if they have any peculiarity, it is that they seem smaller than they should be relatively to the size of the head. The eyebrows are scant, very near together, especially at the inner angle ; they are frequently directed obliquely outwards. An additional character to the preceding, and which is very general, is to be noticed, namely, the small size of the beard, except on the upper lip." He looks upon it as a Slav peculiarity, but is it not rather that of some anterior prehistoric race belonging to this region of Europe ?

In Germany it is still more difficult to get at a German type. The course of all the invasions into this country has been from east to west, including those which terminated in the north or centre of France. Neither its prehistoric constitution nor these continual surgings of invasion have in the slightest degree succeeded in constituting it a homogeneous type. In the south and centre it is brachycephalic, in the north dolichocephalic. The primitive Germans were dolichocephalic, while the Bavarians and the Badois, on the other hand, were brachycephalic. The colour of the eyes and hair gives evidence in the same way of the mixture of manifold races, judging from the statistics of Virchow, Mayr, Saśse, &c. The Germans moreover resign their pretensions to being a distinct type ; they have discovered that after all they are no exception to the other populations in Europe, and that if they are a federation of peoples, they are not an anthropological race.

In France there is no longer the French type only : there are many types, of which one is sufficiently characteristic, as to

physique as well as historically, for us to give it a place under the
name of Celtic type among the brown Europeans that we are now
examining, without being satisfied however that this position is its
true one.

The Hindoo Type.

The *Hindoo type* is but faintly represented in India by the
Rajpoots, and especially by the most venerated Brahmans of Mattra,
Benares, and Tannesey, in Hindostan. The population of the Indian
peninsula is composed of three strata: namely, the Black, the
Mongolian, and the Aryan. The remnants of the first are at the
present time shut up in the mountains of Central India, under the
name of Bhills, Mahairs, Ghonds, and Khonds; and in the south
under that of Yenadis, Maravers, Kurumbas, Veddahs, &c. Its
primitive characters, apart from its black colour and low stature,
are difficult to discover, but it is to be noticed that travellers do not
speak of woolly hair in India. The second has spread over the
plateaux of Central Asia by two lines of way, one to the north-
east, the other to the north-west. The remnants of the first
invasion are seen in the Dravidian or Tamul tribes, and those of the
second in the Jahts. The third, more recent and more important, as
to quality than as to number, was the Aryan.

"The Brahmans of the banks of the Ganges," says M. Rousselet,
"have the high well-developed forehead, oval face, the eyes perfectly horizontal, the nose projecting, *busqué*, and slightly thick at
the extremity, but having delicately-shaped nostrils. They are fair,
but more or less bronzed by the sun. Their black pilous system
seems abundant."[*]

The Tschinghanian Type.

Does this type belong to the preceding? The terms Bohemians,
Gitanos, Gipsies, Zingaris, Tschinghani are applied indiscriminately
to one and the same nomadic population scattered over Europe and

---

[*] "Tableau des Races de l'Inde Centrale et de l'Inde Septentrionale," by
M. L. Rousselet, in "Revue d'Anthrop.," vols. ii. and iv., 1873 and 1875.

Asia, and having a language presenting the greatest analogy to the languages of Hindostan.   Some say this people must have left their native land at a very remote period; F. von Miklosich says at an epoch when the modern dialects were already formed, about the year 1100.   It probably descended from one of the numerous wandering tribes that we see in India.   Its type is undoubtedly Caucasian.   The complexion of the Tschinghanians is more or less tawny, the hair jet black, the eyes a rich black, the face long, narrow across the cheek-bones, the forehead narrow and receding, the nose moderately projecting, its bridge sharp, never flat, the space between the eyes rather narrow, slight prognathism, the mouth small, and the teeth white and not subject to caries (*Blumenbach*).   They are on the confines of mesaticephales and sub-dolichocephales, and are leptorrhinians.   Their cerebral capacity is feeble.   M. Kopernicki compared the Tschinghanian and Hindoo skulls, and found but slight difference between them, though many points of resemblance.   M. Abel Hovelacque recognises two types, the one refined, with the face more elongated and more oval, the features more compact, the nose more aquiline.   The other coarse, with the features more closely set, the countenance more penetrating, eyes more sparkling.   He considers that both may have been existing from their point of departure in Hindostan.[*]

The Iranian Type.

The *Iranian type* is represented by the Tadjicks of Persia, the Parsees, the Armenians, the Kurds, the Georgians, the Ossetians, and the brown Affghans.   Its highest expression is met with in the first of these.   The Tadjicks are of medium height, with a long oval face and regular features.   The forehead is broad and high, the eyes large and shaded with black eyebrows, the nose prominent and straight, or bent round, the mouth large, and the lips thin, the complexion fair and rosy, the pilous system over the whole body abundant, the hair straight and black, the beard and moustache also black, long, thick, and well placed.   Authors, with the exception

[*] See " Revue d'Anthropologie," vol. II. p. 161, and vol. III. p. 224.

of Chardin and Tavenier, agree in considering it a beautiful type. They appear to be dolichocephalic.[*]

The Celtic Type.

The *Celtic type* is thoroughly recognised by the universal testimony of ancient authors. The name Celts has been taken in four different acceptations, thus causing much confusion. Linguists understand by it the ancient peoples speaking the Celtic language,

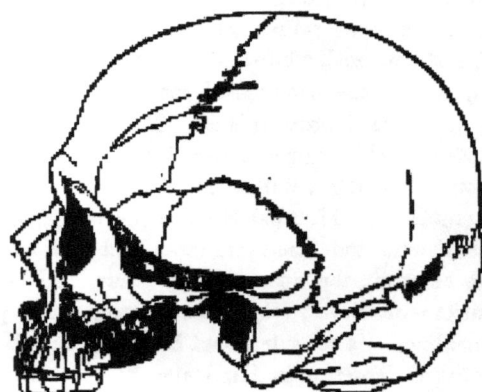

Fig. H.—Celtic type: Skull of an Auvergnate, from the Mémoire of M. Broca on the Celtic race.

such as we now find it in Ireland, in Cornwall, in Wales, in the Isle of Man, in Scotland, and in Brittany, but which was very widely diffused at one time, and was the first detached from the mother-stock of Asia. Archæologists, on their side, call by this name the dolmen builders during the Polished Stone epoch, and the importers of bronze into Europe. Both linguists and archæologists think that the Celts form the first migration of the invaders from the East. A certain number of ancient historians again confound under this name all the peoples of Western and Central Europe, including those of the British isles among them, the Galli, the Goëls, the Gauls,

[*] "Ethnographie de la Perse," by M. de Khanikoff. In 4to. Paris, 1866.

the Galatians, the Kymris, the Belgæ, the Cimbri, the Cimmerians, the Caledonians, the Firbolgs, the Bretons, &c. Lastly there is the precise geographical term, the only one to be preserved. " The title Celts," says Diodorus Siculus, " belongs to the peoples who inhabit the interior of the country above Marseilles." " Gaul," says Cæsar, " is divided into three parts, one part being occupied by the Belgæ, another by the Aquitanians, and a third by peoples who call themselves Celts." This last has been called Celtica by nearly all historians, and is a circumscribed territory included between the Seine, the Garonne, the sea, and the Alps.

Of what elements was this population of Central Gaul composed? In the first place, of the contemporaneous race of the Rough Stone period, very few in number, and of that coming afterwards, and which we find in the dolmens of La Lozère. Both are dolichocephalic, the latter less so than the former. In the second place, of the last invaders who had come from the East in sufficient number for their types in some places to become predominant. The Celts, thus understood, were different to the Gauls, who had become concentrated in the north, and better known to the Romans on account of their turbulence. These were moreover the people who held firmly aloft the banner of national independence on the heights of Gergovia and Alesia, and it is there that its descendants must be looked for. Another consideration proves it, namely, that the language of the Celts is scarcely spoken anywhere at the present time in France, except in Brittany, under the name of Armorican, Bas-Breton, or Broyzel. "The inhabitants of Celtica," says Strabo, " are distinguished from those of Aquitania by their language as well as by their physical characters." Anthropologically, therefore, there is some reason for considering the Bas-Bretons as Celts. The skull has really the same characters as that of the Auvergnians, and the living representatives of the type are similar, although somewhat modified by contact with the Gallo-Bretons, who consist, for the most part, of populations who came over from Great Britain about the fifth century; and of natives of Belgium, who came over some centuries previously. We are indebted to M. Broca for this information. The name *Arverne*

Vercingétorix is Celtic. The type of the Auvergnians of the present day is that of the Bas-Bretons, though more pure, and may be looked upon as that of the people of Celtica at the time of Cæsar and Strabo.*

The Auvergnians are less tall than the Belgæ and other Gauls of the north; their hair is brown or dark chestnut; the eyes gray, greenish, or of a light shade. Their brachycephaly is on the average 84·07 in the series of St. Nectaire studied by M. Broca. Their cranial capacity is considerably greater than that of Parisians. Their forehead is wide and full, although the anterior cranium is less developed relatively to the posterior than in Parisians; the occiput, although well rounded, falls straight. The superciliary prominences are very much developed. The zygomatic arches, examined according to the norma of Blumenbach, are among the least prominent to be met with, hence in a great number there is a negative parietal angle. The face is large in proportion to the cranium, and they are leptorrhinian and orthognathous. In the living subject the face appears decidedly flat and of rectangular shape, the cheek-bones are occasionally large and wide, the lower jaw square. The bridge of the nose is somewhat concave, and inclined to turn up, projects but little, and is as if buried in a depression in the middle of the face. Taking it as a whole, the head is large, the neck being so narrow in proportion that the angles of the jaw project considerably beyond it. The Auvergnians are robust, very muscular, their limbs being thick and short.†

So in France we meet with—(1) In the north, a blonde type,

---

* It is important to distinguish here between the people and the chiefs. These latter conducted the expeditions to Delphos, to Rome, and into Galatia, and particularly excited the attention of the Romans. These were the powerful and fair-complexioned Gauls, the latest arrivals in the country at the fifth century before our era, who bore the name of Belgæ and Kymris. But below them there were the people over whom they had dominion, namely, the Celts proper.

† "La Race Celtique Ancienne et Moderne: Arvernes et Armoricains, Auvergnats et Bas-Bretons," by P. Broca, "Revue d'Anthrop.," vol. ii., 1873.

more particularly represented in Picardy, and extending itself
into the Ardennes (Walloons) on the Belgian frontier, in Champagne and Burgundy. The Gauls represented on the Roman
tomb of Jovian near the cathedral at Rheims are a good example
of this type. (2) In the centre, the Celtic type above mentioned.
(3) In the south, several types—a very brown and complex one,
reminding us of the ancient Phocæan colony of Marseilles; another,
which is the Basque type; and a third, which has however its
highest expression beyond our frontiers, perhaps about the Canary
islands. Let us follow it from this side.

The Berber Type.

The *Berber type* is scattered throughout the whole of the north
of Africa, from the Gulf of Tripoli to the ocean, from the southern
confines of the Sahara to the Mediterranean, and is there represented by the Tawáriks, the Kabylæ, the Berbers, the M'zabites,
and the Shulus. It extended at one time as far as the Canaries,
under the name of Guancha. There is every reason to believe
that it intrenched upon Southern Europe, and that the oldest stock
of the Iberian peninsula, the basin of the Garonne, and the islands
of the Mediterranean is Berber. The stature of this type is
above the average. He is well-proportioned, but less shrivelled,
more muscular, and less shapely than the Arab. His skin is fair
in childhood, and readily bronzes on exposure to the air. His
hair is black and straight, and tolerably abundant. His eyes
are dark brown. He is dolichocephalic (74·4°), leptorrhinian,
though not excessively so (44·3), and moderately orthognathous
(81·8). His face is less long, and its oval outline less regular
than that of the Arab. His forehead is straight, and has at
its base a transverse depression. The superciliary ridges are
moderately developed. The nose, deeply sunk in at the root, is
frequently *busqué* without being aquiline, sometimes oblique
in front and turned up at the base, so as to allow the nostrils
to be plainly seen. The ears are set out from the head. His
moral characters are a strong feeling of equality, of benevolence,

of his own dignity, and of his individual freedom; a great want
of activity, love of work, economy, fondness for his home. He
is a Mussulman by accident.

The Moors are the result of complex crossing between the

عرفش بني مراش

Fig. 45.—Berber type: A Kabyl of the Djurjura (collection of Colonel Duhousset).

Berber and every sort of ethnic element in which the Arab
predominates. One of their characters is a tendency to obesity.

The Semitic Type.

The *Semitic type* is one of the most wide-spread, by a process
of infiltration as it were. The ancient Assyrians, Syrians, Phœni-

cians, and Carthaginians, and the modern Arabs and Jews are
ranged under it. The language is polysyllabic, with a power
of inflection without relation either as to vocabulary or grammar
with the Aryan languages, its principal ethnic connection being
that of form. Rawlinson, in the following terms, describes the
type represented on the Assyrian monuments : "The forehead
straight but not high, the full brow, the eye large and almond-
shaped, the aquiline nose, a little coarse at the end and unduly
depressed, the strong firm mouth with lips somewhat over thick,
the well-formed chin, the abundant hair and ample beard, both
coloured and black, all these recall the chief peculiarities of the
Jew, more especially as he appears in southern countries." The
moral traits of the Semite are equally characteristic—a marvellous
activity, as exemplified on the sea by the Phœnicians, and on
land by the Israelites ; the love of gain, which engenders the
commercial spirit ; a disturbed nomadic life, among the Hebrews,
from the taking of Jericho to the destruction of Jerusalem, and
which is still kept up, though modified by the necessities of social
life, egotism of sect, attachment to old institutions, the want of a
God peculiarly and nationally their own, of which this proverb
is the echo—Out of the Church, no salvation—Hors l'Église,
point de salut.

The Arabian Type.

The *Arabian type* will serve as an example of the modern
Semite. The Arabs made their appearance in the night of time,
under the name of Atila, and more especially of Adites. The
Koran mentions their Cyclopean buildings in Arabia. Later on,
they form two great families, Jectanides in the Yemen, and the
Ismaelites in the north of the peninsula. In 622 of the Hegira
of Mahomet their nationality is planned out, they commence a
movement, and either by conquest, or infiltration from time to
time, they at last spread over the greater part of Africa, and half,
at least, of Asia. They are now to be met with, in greater or less
number, from Egypt to Morocco, especially in Algeria, where they

are diminishing, from Abyssinia to the Fellatah country, from the
Gulf of Aden to Kaffraria, even beyond Lake Tanganyka, where
they were before Livingstone; from the Mediterranean and the
Red Sea to the Bolor Mountains on the one side, to the mouths of
the Ganges and Cambodia on the other. With the exception of
Malaisia and Madagascar, they have always kept to countries
bordering on the tropics. Even in Spain they have left traces of
their lineage. In the south-east of France some vestiges of them
are described under the name of Saracens. The Arabian type is
one of the finest in the world, says Larrey. The skull, seen from
above, describes a perfectly regular oval. The face, which is long
and thin, forms another oval, with a no less regular outline. The
complexion continues perfectly fair as long as it is not exposed to
the action of the air, but becomes bronzed very quickly. The hair
and beard are glossy and jet black, the limits of their implantation
being very defined. The eyes are black. The palpebral apertures
almond-shaped, and fringed with long black eyelashes. The forehead is not very high, the curved nose and receding chin, however,
give to the profile rather a round than straight form. The superciliary arches, as well as the glabella, are only slightly developed.
The root of the nose is somewhat sunk in, so that the forehead and
the bridge of the nose are almost in a direct line. The nose is
aquiline, and the point is separated from the alæ, and descends
below them, curving down like the eagle's beak. The cheek-bones
do not project, the mouth is small, the teeth are white and vertical,
the ears are well shaped, rather small, and close to the head. The
stature is slightly below the average in Arabia, and a little above it
in Algeria. The Arab is shrivelled and nervous, his neck is well
placed upon the shoulders. He is dolichocephalic (76·3 on the
living subject, 74·0 on the skull). Moderately leptorrhinian (45·5),
and the orbital index mesoseme (88·6). There exists however a
type slightly differing from the preceding, and which we may term
coarse. The skin is less smooth, the nose thicker, its extremity
being in a round mass and somewhat depressed, as Rawlinson says.
The general shape of the body is rather lumbering. Were not
this the description of the ancient Assyrians we might suppose

that this was a cross-breed. One of the results of crossing with the Arab is the tendency to corpulence.

The moral traits of the Arab are those of the Semite in general, modified by an enervating and fatalist religion.[*]

Our object not being to give a description of every type, but simply to give a few examples of each, we shall omit the Jewish type, which is well known, as well as the Etruscan and Albanian types, respecting which we have but little information, and pass on rapidly to another group.

CHAPTER XI.

FINNISH AND LAPP TYPES—MONGOLIAN, ESQUIMAU, AND SAMOYED TYPES—MALAY AND POLYNESIAN TYPES—AMERICAN AND PATA-GONIAN TYPES—RED-AFRICAN TYPE.

The Finnish Type.

THE *Finnish type* forms, as it were, the connecting link between the blonde types of Europe and the brachycephalic types of Asia. It extends from Lapland and the country of the Samoyedes, from the confines of Sweden and the Baltic to the river Yenissei, from the White Sea to the middle course of the Volga, as far as the 53rd degree of north latitude. It includes the Ostiaks of the Obi, the Tchuvatches, the Tcheremisses, the Morduins, the Votiaks, and Permians of Central Russia, and the Finlanders, Esthonians, and Livonians of the Baltic. The Fins have long hair, usually reddish or yellowish, of a flaxen or whitish hue, and more rarely chestnut. The Finlanders, the Tcheremisses, the Tchuvatches, the Ostiaks of the Obi, and especially the Votiaks, have red hair. The fiery red colour is not as frequent among other people as these last (*fists*). Their beard is moderately full, and is generally

---

[*] For the parallel between the Arab and the Berber, see "Anthropologie de l'Algérie," by General Faidherbe and Dr. P. Topinard. Paris, 1874.

red. The eyebrows are thick, the eyes sunken, of a blue, greenish gray, or chestnut shade. The palpebral aperture is narrow. Their complexion is fair and usually covered with freckles. The nose is straight, the nostrils small. The cheek-bones are prominent, owing to the thinness of the face, the lips small. The teeth rapidly wear away; the chin is round, the ears are high, broad, and flat. In eight individuals measured by Dr. Beddoe the cephalic index was 8·37. The craniology of the Finnish type has only been studied on a few specimens. Five skulls of Finlanders, measured by M. Broca, had an average index of 83·7; and those of four Esthonians an index of 80·4. Their mesorhinia and their sub-nasal prognathism approximate them to the yellow races. It would be interesting to know if their orbital index is megaseemic as in these. The stature of the Fins is below the average,* and consequently higher than that of the Lapps. Their neck is small, the chest narrow and flat, the arms long, the hands broad, the pelvis broad in proportion to the trunk, the legs short, slim, and tapering, the feet flat.

The Fins are of simple manners, of sedentary habits, and of spiteful disposition. They are a hunting and fishing people. They have a national poem, the Kalevala, fragments of which have been transmitted orally from generation to generation. Their name appeared in history about the first century before and the second after our era (*Pliny, Jornandes*).

The Finnish type is clearly separated from all the surrounding types, and without being European, it is more nearly allied to it than to the Mongolian type. It is this which partly gives to the Russians of the north their physical characters. When we see in the blonde type fiery-red coloured hair, with freckles, we may fairly attribute them to this fact. It would not be surprising if we were so to regard similar cases of this kind observed both in England and France. Moreover, there has hitherto been no proof that the Finnish type really existed in Western Europe, but it is probable that a certain number of Fins were among the invaders who laid it waste. Neither in the description of Attila by Priscus nor in that

* Six hundred and eighty-two Fin soldiers, however, measured by Bous-dorff, had an average stature of 1·714 mètre (?).

of the Huns can their type be recognized; and yet bands of Fins, without a doubt, accompanied that warrior.[*]

Among the Fins, nevertheless, exceptional characters are to be found—as low stature, black hair and eyes, flat nose, high cheek-bones, &c., which must be attributed to crossing with the Lapps, and more frequently with the Mongolians. The Morduins in particular, the least pure of the tribes mentioned, have a considerable mixture of Mongolian blood in them. The Voguls, who speak a Finnish language, have the same; Pallas says they resemble the Kalmuks.

The Hungarians, or Magyars, are changed in another sense by their mixture with Turks, Khazars, Bulgarians, and Roumanians. Historians make them to be descended from the Ostiaks, or rather to have come from a country beyond the Ural mountains, called Ugria. Linguists speak of them as having a Finnish language, and ethnologists take note of certain of their ethnic traits, which recall their tent life and their skill in the saddle. At the present day, among the upper classes, they form one of the most beautiful types in Europe. Of a stature below the average, they have regular features, a coarse (âpre) or fair complexion, black hair and eyes, a full and dark beard. The slight obliquity of the eyes, and rather high cheek-bones among some of them, remind one, not of the Finnish type, but of a Mongolian influence. The ancient Hungarian type is only met with among the lower classes.

With this Finnish question is connected that of certain mysterious tribes of ancient Asia. To the west of the Hiong-nu,[†] whose incessant incursions, from the second century before our era to the second century afterwards, compelled the Chinese to build the Great Wall, there existed, says Matuanlin, the Chinese historian, another tall people, with green eyes and red hair, who from being under subjection to the Hiong-nu became independent, namely, the

* See "Des Tribes Mongoles," by Pallas, in " Mém. du Museum d'Histoire Naturelle," vol. xvii.; and " Voyages dans l'Empire de Russie," by the same author; translated into French by G. de la Peyronie, Paris, 1788-96.

† Hiong-nu, Hiong-nou, Hiung-nu, Hioung-nou, or Heoung-noo. M. Maury also writes Chiong-nou.

On-sioan. Another people, the Ting-ling, with green eyes and red hair, is mentioned at the same epoch, as existing beyond the Altai mountains, in the countries of the Yenissei. A third inhabited—from 648 to 874—the north of the Chinese Empire, near the Obi or the Irtish, namely, the Kieham, the issue of the Kiangkuans, or Kakas of Klaproth. They were tall, and also had red hair, fair complexion, and green eyes; "black hair was looked upon as a prodigy." Lastly, contemporaneously with Matouanlin, that is to say about the twelfth century, barbarous tribes presenting these characters occupied the same regions. He considered them to be the descendants of the Kiang-kuans.

The existence, formerly, in the centre and in the north of Asia of a race with green eyes and red hair is therefore established. But whence did it come? That all the populations of the region at the present time have black hair and eyes, and that the Samoyedes, to whom one would imagine they might belong, are in this category, and are of short stature, with a smoky-yellow complexion, is a fact well worthy of our attention.

Desmoulins professed to have found it in the Baskirs, many of whom have red hair; in the Kirghis; in the Yakoutes; in a word, in the whole Turkish race. But red hair and green eyes are altogether exceptional in these different groups, which are distinguished, on the contrary, by their black hair and eyes.[*]

Another solution to the question presents itself. The fundamental traits indicated, with the exception of the stature, are those of the great majority of the Fins. Green eyes are less common, it is true, among these than blue eyes, but we may consider that a change has taken place in them by crossing. Our own opinion is that the peoples of ancient Asia, with green eyes and red hair, ought to be looked upon as the progenitors of the Ostiaks, Tchuvatches, &c.[†]

We have just spoken of the Turks; it is necessary to say a few

[*] See "Histoire Naturelle des Races Humaines," by A. Desmoulins, Paris, 1826.

[†] A translation of the annals of the Hiong-nu was published last year in the "Journal of the Anthrop. Institute," with annotations from "Deguignes

words further respecting them. They have been also designated
by the name of Turanians, under the supposition that Turin,
whose struggles with Iran are mentioned by the Zend-Avesta, was
occupied by populations having this origin. Linguists make them
enter into their Tátár branch of the Uralo-Altaic family, whose
other branches are the Samoyedes, the Finnish, the Mongolian,
and the Tungusian. In the same branch they range the Yakuts,
the Kirghis, divided into Bourontes and Kaïsaks, the Turcomans,
the Uzbeks, the Nogays, the Osmanlis, or Turks proper, &c.

The descent of the Turks has been fully established by Klaproth. The name is derived from the Tho-kin, who inhabited the
Altaï about the sixth century, not far from the famous tribe of the
Ouïgours, both being descendants of the Hiong-nu, at the time
of their dispersion in 263 of our era. In 1034, one of their
bands, the Ghaznecides, broke through into Western Turkestan.
At the close of the eleventh century they were before Constantinople. An important group under the name of White Huns had
made the conquest of India, and are the ancestors of the present
Jähts.* The Yakuts, now between the Yenessei and the Obi, were
then more to the south, and were separated from the principal
mass at the time of the dismemberment of the empire of Gengis-
Khan. The Kirghis and the Uzbeks are looked upon as the more
or less changed remnants of the Ouïgours, whose language the
Bourontes still speak. The actual existence of a particular group
designated by the name of Turks, and in subjection to that portion
of the Mongolian race to which has been given that of Turanians,
is therefore certain. But are there any remains of them, and what
is their type? The Tchuvatches of whom we thought, speak a
Tátár language, but as regards physique they are Finn. The
Yakuts are absolutely Tongooses; the Turcomans, the Uzbeks, and

Vocabulary and Handbook." The tall people to the west of the Hiong-nou
bear the name of Woo-sun, and have the same complexion as the Ting-
ling. We find there, also, the Koon-kwan, whose ancestors, in the year
200 B.C., were the Hakkas.

* The White Huns, or Ephthalites of M. Vivien, of St. Martin, must not
be confounded with the Huns of Attila, who are true Mongolians.

the Kirghis are also Mongolians in various degrees. The Osmanlis have so crossed with the Circassians and the Greeks that they have become Europeans. The Tatars of Kashan and of the Crimea are intermediate as regards their physiognomy. To sum up : a primitive Turk must have existed, but it is impossible to determine at what period. It is probable that it approximated to the Mongolian type.

The Lapp Type.

The *Lapp type* is well known, but its parentage is not so. It is confined to the parts of Norway, Sweden, and Russia which border upon the North Cape, and formerly went down more to the south, from whence it has been expelled by the Fins. Linnaeus describes it in these terms: *Lappones corpore parvo; capillis nigris, brevibus, rectis; oculorum iridibus nigrescentibus*; and thus speaks of the Fins as compared with them; *Fennones corpore toroso; capillis flavis, prolixis; oculorum iridibus fuscis*. The Lapps are very short of stature, and ill-looking. The head is thick, the chest broad, the figure slim, the legs short and slender. The forehead is broad and low, as well as the face. They have large brown hollow eyes ; the nose is short and flat, and very wide at the root. The hair is hard, short, and of black colour, and they have but little beard. The complexion is pale, according to some, yellowish-brown according to others. The cheek-bones are prominent, the chin pointed. The eyelids are oblique, according to M. Vanderkindere. Their cephalic index is 85, the highest average brachycephaly yet observed. They are less mesorrhinian and less prognathous than the Fins. Their characters, in short, separate them from the latter race, and bring them nearer to the Samoyed races. Their mesoseen orbital index, however (87.5), is not that of the yellow races. Reduced in number to 9000 (*Guillard*), they have continued the only nomadic European race. The reindeer occupies the whole of their time and attention.* We

---

* See "Lapons," by Léon Guillard and Hertillon, in " Encycl. des Sciences Méd., 2nd series, vol. i.; "Parallèle des Lapons et des Esquimaux," by H. Guérault, in " Mém. Soc. Anthrop.," vol. i.; "On the Laplanders," by F. Campbell, in "Trans. Soc. Ethnol.," 1866, &c.

might here be tempted to describe the Samoyed type, but as it is clearly Mongolian, we shall hold it in reserve to speak of it in its proper place.

The Mongolian Type.

The *Mongolian type* corresponds to that of the yellow races in general. Its name is derived from a small tribe to the north of the desert of Gobi, near the Kara-korum mountains, so sadly celebrated by Gengis-Khan at the commencement of the thirteenth century. It has not been shown that the traits of this horde, now designated by the name of Mongol-Kalkas, best exhibit those of the Asiatic races scattered to the east of the Obi, the Caspian Sea, and the Bay of Bengal; but custom, whether rightly or wrongly, has adopted the name. The general characters of the type are the following: The skin is of a pale yellowish colour, more or less tawny, not mixed either with red or brown. The hair is straight, stiff, somewhat long and black, its transverse section being more or less round and large. The beard is scanty as well as the whiskers, and the hair on the upper lip consists of two delicate pencils, which are sometimes long. The body is more or less bare. The head is thick, sometimes high, sometimes short, its cranial capacity being between that of the negro and that of the European. Its summit is sometimes flat, sometimes raised into a crest antero-posteriorly, corresponding to the sagittal suture. The superciliary arches and the glabella are very slightly marked, the interval between the orbits is considerable. The face on the whole is flat, as if crushed in everywhere, and broader about the situation of the cheek-bones, the external and anterior borders of which look upwards and outwards. We shall not reiterate the description of the Mongolian skull, as given by Prichard, nor that of Blumenbach, respecting the prominence of the zygomatic arches, and shall confine ourselves to stating that the characters designated some years ago by the name of *Mongoloid*, upon which a doctrine now settled was based, are only met with exceptionally. The parietal angle in particular is one half less in Mongols than in New Caledonians. (See pages 246, 247.)

The following traits have more value: Flatness of the skeleton of the nose in its *ensemble*, flattening and widening of the interval between the orbits, mesorrhinia, obliteration of the inferior border of the anterior nasal aperture, its folding over into two lips: by this mark alone we were able to recognise the upper jaw of a Chinese skull. In the living subject, the nose is broad and flat (*épaté*), concave, round at the back, and very similar to that of the negro in the disposition of the nostrils and the slight consistence of the cartilages of the lobe; but it is small and generally delicate, while that of the negro is thick. Another series of characters is derived from the eyes. The axis of the eyelids is directed obliquely upwards and outwards. At the internal angle is a vertical falciform fold, at the external, a sort of transverse duplication of the upper eyelid, which slightly covers the eye, and appears to be due to the small size of the palpebral aperture; the eyes with their black irides thus appear smaller. The orbits give indication of this; in other types their great axes are united at an obtuse angle, open below. In many of the Mongols there is scarcely any angle, or rather the axes are perfectly horizontal (see page 355).

M. Broca has demonstrated quite unexpectedly that one of the least variable attributes, not only of the most typical Mongolian races, but also of all those, with the exception of the Esquimaux, that we usually associate with them, is megaseme in of the orbital index, and in the Chinese it is 93·8 (see page 359).

The yellow races are generally very prognathous (76 to 68 degrees). The Esquimaux, the Chinese, and the Malays are more than this, and approximate to the negro type. True Mongols and other Western tribes, and undoubtedly also the Thibetans, are much less so. Their stature is below the average, their neck is short, their limbs are short and thick, and they have a tendency to corpulence. The ability to bring the toes together in such a way as to take hold of objects is somewhat common among them.

Of the three fundamental types, the European, the Negro, and the Mongolian, the last exhibits the least homogeneity as regards details. Asia, of all parts of the world, must have been the most violently convulsed as regards its populations. Its prehistoric

revolutions previously to its having any geographical communication
with Europe must have been very numerous. The hordes which
have come forth from it, as from a crater, have all been nomads
and warlike. We find numerous evidences at the present time
of these convulsions: foreign races absolutely dissimilar as to type
enclosed in the midst of surrounding average types. Instead of
the flat nose, looked upon as characteristic of the yellow races, is
frequently seen a prominent nose, of firm construction and arched.
The oblique and small eye is found replaced by a horizontal eye
like our own, the almost invisible superciliary arches by prominent
ones, the scant and paltry pencil of hair on the upper lip, by a thick
bushy moustache. There is frequently no prognathism at all, the
face becoming almost rounding, while the head of the Kalmuck of
the Altaï, or the Mongol of Gobi, is a combination of the two
characters of which we have been speaking with an external
brachycephaly, and a no less remarkable shortness of all the vertical
diameters of the cranium as well as of the face. The head of the
Esquimaux, with the same characters, is the most dolichocephalic
in the world, and has the greatest vertical diameters of the cranium
as well as of the face. These are two sub-types which are contradictory in some respects. In describing the foregoing under the
name of Mongolian we had the former rather in mind—brachycephaly; we lay more stress now on the latter—dolichocephaly.
Prichard, moreover, considered the face of the Esquiman as the
best expression of the type of the yellow races.

The Esquiman Type.

The Esquiman type is found in its highest expression in Greenland. Dolichocephaly and extreme height of the skull become less
as we approach Behring's Straits. The Aleutians and Kalushes
would form the passage between it and the Samoyed or Mongolian
type. The Esquimaux have received this name from the Mohicans
(Seemeen), and call themselves Innuit. About the twelfth century
they may have reached the Potomac and the Delaware; at the
fourteenth they penetrated into Greenland. Previously we find

them in Asia. They are now rapidly decreasing in numbers (*Hall*, *Hayes*).

They are of low stature, fat, squat, with wide shoulders and large heads, large limbs, but with small well-made feet and hands. The face is flat, and even hollowed out about the region of the nose; the cheeks are full, the cheek-bones extremely prominent; the nose is broad, small, and projecting but little; the palpebral aperture small, the eyes black and sunken; the mouth small, round, with a large under lip. The teeth are regular, and are worn down to the gums at an early age, owing to the custom of employ-

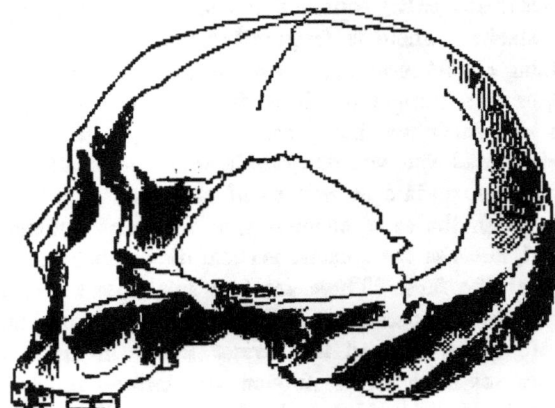

Fig. 40.—Esquimau type: Skull of Greenlander (Copenhagen Museum).

ing them in preparing skins. The hair is jet black, long, hard, and scanty, and on a transverse section is more round than elliptical. The beard is almost absent. "On the upper lip of one," says Hayes, "some coarse black hairs were growing like the whiskers of a cat, and also on the chin." The complexion is light, or dark-gray, showing the redness of the capillary vessels beneath. The skull of the Esquimau, which is a pure dolichocephalic, gives an index of 71·4 (*Broca*), 71·8 (*Virchow*), 71·3 (*Retzels*). It forms a long parallelogram, the sides of which fall down vertically, and in some skulls the sagittal crest is so marked that they seem, physiologically, scaphocephalic. They are the most leptorrhinine known

(42·2). Their prognathism (71·4) corresponds to the average degree observed in all the yellow races. The direction of the occipital plane very nearly approaches that of the Chinese. The bones of the nose proper are the narrowest known, the orbita are round, the maxillary bones are so enormous, and the molar bones so large and thick, that, out of a number of skulls, we are able to identify the Esquimau skull without hesitation.*

The nomad character of the Esquimaux in summer allies them to the Lapps and Samoyedes, from which they are separated by their making use of dogs for sledging.

The Samoyed Type.

The *Samoyed type* is scattered from the Mezen, an affluent of the White Sea, to the river Khatanga in Siberia, and from the Arctic Ocean to the vicinity of the Altaï and Lake Baïkal. The Khasovo in the north, and the Soiony in the south, are its principal groups in Asia. Between them there are a number of Finnish or Mongolian tribes. The Samoyedes make their appearance in history in 1096. The following description specially applies to those of the north-west, who are the best known: Their stature is below the average, if not diminutive, but greater than that of the Lapps. They are fat, squat, with short legs, the knees turning out; the feet are small. Their hair is long, harsh, jet black and glossy. They have very little beard. Their complexion is of a smoky-yellow tint. The face is wide and flat; the cheek-bones are prominent. The nose is very depressed, and on a level with the cheeks; it is broad and flat at the root; the nostrils are wide and gaping. They have black eyes, long, narrow, and slightly oblique palpebral apertures, large mouths, the lips being small and turned up (*retroussées*).†

* See "On the Esquimaux," by King, first memoir in the "Journal of the Ethnological Society," London, vol. I, 1848; "On the Esquimaux," by Sutherland, in "Journal of the Anthropological Society," London, vol. III., 1865; &c.

† See Latham's drawing of the Samoyed in his general treatise on Ethnography.

A drawing of the skull of a Samoyed has been given by Blumenbach, and the description of one by Mr. Busk. The bones are narrow in the former; the latter is brachycephalic (80·3)[*] and platyrrhinian; the inferior border of the malar bones and zygomatic arches turns outwards, there is a slight crest at the vault of the cranium, the orbital axes are almost horizontal, the vertical diameter of the cranium is short and that of the face long. It evidently follows from this that the Samoyed sub-type assimilates the general Mongolian type proper, and that it comes very near to the Esquimau sub-type. In its *norma verticalis* it recalls the Lapp tribe. From want of space we must pass over the Tungusian type, to which the Mantshú belongs, and which differs in some respects from the Mongolian sub-type proper; the various types in Japan, with which the Corean is allied; the Kamtchadals, but imperfectly known; the Thibetan, to which the Chinese, the Birmese, and the Annamites are allied, and which establish the transition between the Mongol and the Malay. The Ainos of Japan, the Miao Tsz and the Lolos of the province of Yunnan, in our opinion belong to the European group.

The Malay Type.

The Malay type embraces the whole of the territory called Malaisia.

According to M. Maury, the cradle of the Malays was the mountains of Thibet, whence they passed by the rivers of Indo-China. Others make them come from Borneo. Mention of them is made for the first time in 1160, from which it appears that they left the Palembang country in the island of Sumatra, and were the founders of Singapore in the peninsula of Malacca. Their skin is light brown, sometimes copper coloured. The hair is straight or wavy, standing on end when cut about two inches from the head, long, abundant, and jet black. They have very

---

[*] Many dolichocephalic skulls have been collected in the Samoyed territory, but they may belong to other races. If the Esquimaux, so dolichocephalic, have ascended, as it is said, the southern confines of Siberia, they must necessarily have left a train of dolichocephales behind them.

little beard. The nose is short, wide, and flat, thin at the extremity, the nostrils being dilated. They are mesorhinians (51·47), and have an arrangement of the lower border of the nasal aperture and of the vomer which is almost characteristic. The cheek-bones are wide and prominent, and the face is almost as broad as it is long (Van Leent). The profile is straight, the interval between the orbits wide and flattened, the superciliary arches united, and almost imperceptible.

The forehead, says Pickering, is depressed and receding in the Mongols, high and well formed in the Malay. The occiput, on the contrary, is flat, vertical, and does not pass beyond the line of the neck. The mouth is large, the lips are thick, and their prognathism is the greatest that has been met with in the yellow races (69·5). The teeth are of a bluish-black colour, and corroded from chewing betel, of which they make constant use. They are brachycephalic. In twenty-nine Javanese examined by M. Broca, the mean index was 81·0. Lastly, they are very short of stature, slim, and moderately muscular.

M. Van Leent speaks of two sorts of Malays, some similar to the yellow races we have described, others being a mixture of Caucasian features. The Battaks of Sumatra, from whom this sub-race is named, the Macassars and Bugis of Celebes, the Dyaks of Borneo, &c., are among the latter. The Battaks are better built, more muscular, and taller than the Malays previously spoken of. Their skin is of a lighter brown, the hair fine and black, sometimes chestnut, the beard moderately thick, the nose straight, rather thin, less flat. The cheek-bones are less prominent, the face long, the mouth somewhat small, the lips less thick, the occiput round. It would be interesting to know whether this particular type corresponded with those dolichocephalic skulls which we find labelled in our collections under the same name as the Malays before spoken of. It would also be desirable to find out whether it is not derived from India.*

* See "The Malay Archipelago," by A. R. Wallace, 2 vols., London, 1869; "Géographie Médicale des Possessions Néerlandaises des Indes Orientales," by Van Leent, in "Arch. Méd. Nav.," Paris, 1867, &c.

Polynesian Type.

The Polynesian type approaches the Malay, and must be separated from the Micronesian type. It extends from the Tonga Islands and New Zealand to Easter Island in the Pacific. The Kanaka or Polynesian race originated, according to M. de Quatrefages, in the island of Boeroo, situated to the west of Ceram, one of the Moluccas. Its first station was the Tonga and Samoan Archipelago, whence it was dispersed. It made its appearance at the beginning of the fifth century in the Marquesas Islands—in 1100 at Tahiti, in 1200 at Rarotonga, in 1500 in New Zealand, and in 1700 in the Chatham Islands. Its first known migrations took place therefore into Malaisia a thousand years before any mention is made there of the Malays. The two races are looked upon as one by linguists, who speak of them as the Malayo-Polynesians. Moreover there is much reason for believing that the South Americans have some relation to the Polynesians.

The Polynesian should be studied in the Eastern Islands, where he is more detached from the Melanesian element. He is mesaticephalic. The *norma verticalis* of the skull exhibits an oval, swelling out on a level with the parietal bones. The vault is generally occupied by a crest, the two sides of which incline like the roof of a house, or are hollowed out in wide channels, after which come the parietal protuberances; this latter arrangement is termed keel-shaped (*en carène*). His megaseemic orbits place him in the same group as the Chinese, the Malays, and Americans. The Kanakas of the Owhyhee Islands have the highest orbital index that M. Broca has observed (95·4). He is mesorrhinian (49·3). His sub-nasal prognathism of 68 degrees in New Zealand, 70·9 in the Marquesas Islands, and 75 at Tahiti, is evidence of the influence of the yellow and black populations with which he has been mingled. But as these crosses would only increase his prognathism, and as we cannot find any neighbouring race which could cause it to diminish, we must come to the conclusion that the principle of this diminution is to be found within himself. The primitive Polynesian, therefore, was not prognathous; at least the accepted minimum index of 75 places him on the confines of the White type.

The nose of the Polynesian, called by some travellers short, and by others projecting, is sometimes straight, sometimes aquiline, and more nearly approaches the American than the Mongolian type; it is wide only at the nostrils. The molar bones are large, not very wide, and the face is oval, not coming within the category of those decidedly flat. The superciliary arches project but little, and the falling in of the root of the nose is not very deep, which clearly distinguishes him from the Melanesian type. The eyes are black, large, and well formed, more or less full, and not oblique. The complexion is very variable. According to some it is of mahogany colour, of others of a dull copper colour. M. Bourgarel says it is of a yellowish-olive hue, lighter sometimes than that of the Malays, especially at Tahiti. Jacquinot says it is generally tawny-yellow, mixed with more or less dark bistre. The hair is black, thick, and harsh occasionally, becoming beautifully curly by crossing with the European. The beard of the Polynesian is scant. He is of tall stature, well built, slight, but with some tendency to obesity.

The American Type.

The *American type* is that which was most commonly met with both in North and South America previously to the arrival of Europeans, the Esquimaux being put aside. We shall describe it according to the best authors, especially Morton. The average colour of the skin is olive-brown, variously mixed with white and red, and sometimes amounting to a cinnamon colour (*Nott*). The hair is long, glossy, black, and stiff like horsehair. The eyebrows and eyelashes are thick, but the hair in the beard, the moustaches, and on the surface of the body is scant. The eyes are small and sunken, and the eyelids exhibit all the varieties observed in Asia, being sometimes contracted and oblique, at others horizontal as with us. The superciliary arches are more developed than in the Mongolian type. The nose, sometimes Asiatic, is more frequently large, prominent, bridged, and even aquiline (*Coffin*). The nostrils are dilated. The cheek-bones are prominent, the face is round or triangular, the jaws are heavy and slightly prognathous (*Nott*). The mouth is large, and the teeth are vertical, strong, and but little liable to caries. If we are to rely on the method of cubic measurement, followed by Morton, the American skull is one of the least capacious of the whole human race. It is more frequently dolichocephalic than brachycephalic, judging from the collection at Philadelphia. That at the Museum, on the contrary, is mesaticephalic, being caused by the mixture of brachycephaly and dolichocephaly in equal proportions. The Mexicans have an index of 78·1, the Peruvians of 78·7 (*Broca*). Dolichocephaly is more extensive in the north, according to Morton, among the tribes that originally inhabited the east of the Alleghanies, and brachycephaly among those to the west of the Mississippi. The same thing occurs on the coasts of South America. The Peruvian skulls are distinguished by their quadrangular form.

A common characteristic of the Mexican populations is flattening of the posterior part of the skull which is vertical. The vertex is often pyramidal, especially when looked at from behind. The forehead is moderately broad, but low and receding, upon which Humboldt laid some stress. The orbits are quadrangular and megaseme, which is an important fact. The skeleton of the nose is mesorrhinian. Their stature is generally very much above the average of Americans, although there are some tribes in South America, as the Patagonians of the south, and the Assiniboins in the north, who are very tall, and others, as the Peruvians and some tribes in the island of Vancouver, that are rather short, proving the existence of divers elements in the American type.[*]

To sum up : the American in his ensemble approximates to the type of the Yellow races in many important particulars. Thus : his face and nose are sometimes flat, the colour of his skin, the nature of his hair, the colour of his eyes, the slight development

[*] See "Crania Americana," by Morton, Philadelphia, 1839; "Types of Mankind," Nott and Gliddon, Philadelphia, 1854; "L'Homme Américain," by A. d'Orbigny, 2 vols., Paris, 1839; article "Américain," by E. Dally, in "Encycl. des Sciences Médic.," vol. iii., 1865; &c.

and harshness of his pilous system, his small eyes with narrow palpebral apertures, his orbital megasemia, &c. Flattening of the occiput is met with also in some races of Asia. But he also exhibits marked differences, such as his projecting, convex, and comparatively narrow nose, his very tall stature, the small capacity of his cerebral cavity, and his slight prognathism. These are characteristics of races which have crossed, one of the elements being clearly Asiatic, and the other altogether special—dolichocephaly, the European nose, &c. The above description applies rather to North Americans. Nevertheless the Toltec sub-type, to which Morton refers the natives of Mexico, Peru, and New Granada, differs but little from them. The difficulty of American craniology arises from the fact of the existence of such extensive cranial deformations. By basing it upon them, and setting aside some mere deformations, we might however, we think, take out from the mass of Americans two ancient peoples who practised deformation of the head—the one in the method employed by the Nahuas, the other in that by the Aymaras. (See p. 163.) The Tehuelche or Patagonian type should also be set aside, and then we might take account of those singular differences of complexion, pale in the Botocudos and in the Guarani race, almost black in the ancient Californians and the Charruas of Uruguay, which are now extinct.

"The Californians," says La Pérouse, "have a similar complexion to that of the negro whose hair is not woolly. Judging simply by their colour, one would imagine oneself amongst negroes in a plantation in the island of St. Domingo." "Their hair," says Rollin, "is long and very tough. Their forehead is low, the eyebrows are thick and black, the eyes black and sunken, the nose is short, and depressed at the root; the mouth large, the molar bones are prominent, the lips thick, and the teeth beautiful." "The Charruas," says Prichard, "belong by their colour to the Black races, or those which are nearly black, with scarcely any mixture of red tinge in them. They are upright, well-proportioned, and active; they are of middle stature, and about an inch taller on the average than the Spaniards. They have a straight head and

2 i

open forehead, regular features, although the nose appears narrow and as though sunken between the eyes; the eyebrows are scant, they have no beard, and very little hair on other parts of the body. The hair of the head is thick, very long, glossy, and always black. Their hands and feet are smaller than those of Europeans, and the neck of the women is less full than that of the Indian." The characteristics of these two races therefore partake more of the American Mongol element than of the one having projecting features, which we are about to describe.

The Patagonian Type.

The *Patagonian type*, or rather a certain ancient Patagonian type, requires that we should speak of it by itself. The whole population being confined to one extremity of the continent, where it is shut up among mountains, there is greater probability of its being the remains of some primitive race. The Patagonians, or Tehuelches, are exactly in these conditions. Their characters, as obtained from a study of living subjects, are the following: They are very tall, the limbs and the trunk being in proportion; the head is large, the face a long oval, the complexion olive brown, or a tone that Fitzroy compares to old mahogany; the nose is short, broad, and flat; the forehead bulging (*bombé*) and prominent, the superciliary arches are moderately pronounced, the chin projecting, the beard and moustaches scanty. Up to this point there is but little difference between it and the average American type, but it specially belongs to the present race of Patagonians. Five skulls procured from the ancient encampments, or prehistoric *paraderos* of Patagonia, and brought to the Museum of the Laboratory of Anthropology belonging to the Ecole des Hautes Etudes, by M. Moreno, present an appearance totally distinct from all the other American skulls in the collection. At first sight one would think they were the skulls of Esquimaux. The narrowness of the forehead, its height, its bulging at the level of the frontal bosses, the antero-posterior elongation of the cranium, its posterior part in the form of an inclined plane, and then curved round; the height

of the vertical diameter or acrocephaly, the vertical direction
downwards of the sides, the elongation of the face, the projection
forwards of the malar bones, the degree of prognathism, the narrowness of the interval between the orbits, the harmony of form
between the cranium and the face—all this is Esquimau. The
teeth themselves are worn down horizontally as in this race. But
it is wanting in many of their characters. Their malar bones,
looked at in profile, project forwards, and fall straight, as in the
Esquimau (compare Figs. 46 and 47); but looked at in front they
do not project outwards, and are not unusually large : whence the

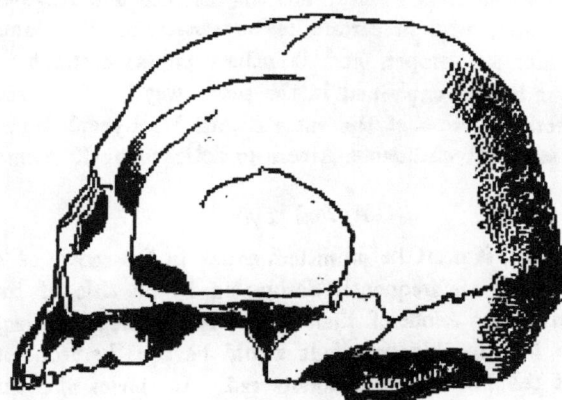

FIG. 47.—Patagonian type: Skull from the guardaros, from the collection of M. Moreno
(Museum of the Laboratory of Anthropology of the École des Hautes Études)

oval shape of the face, described by Lieutenant Musters as that of
the present Patagonian race, while the Esquimau has a full face
and has very wide cheek-bones, and the American, barring his
prominent nose, generally has it both broad and flat. The cephalic
index of these five skulls is 72·92, that is to say they are the most
decidedly dolichocephalic in the world, after those of the Esquimaux, and their prognathism is 69·4, or less than the American,
and as much or more than the Esquimaux. To make up for this, they
are mesorrhinian, very nearly approaching to platyrrhinian, while
the Esquimaux are the most leptorrhinian on the face of the globe.

2 I 2

There is no unity of type, it is true, among the skulls from the paradeoe; there are brachycephales to be found among them, some with deformations, and some without, showing that at that epoch the races of Patagonia were already numerous. But the type that we select from them must have predominated, for the average of the twenty-seven normal skulls of M. Moreno are dolichocephalic, 75·02. However this may be, this unexpected approximation to the Esquimaux suggests some curious questions for consideration. Are the Tehuelches the autochthonous dolichocephalic element, which, by its crossing with a race of Asia, has given origin to the present American type? May not the craniological singularity of the Esquimaux, who in certain respects resemble the Samoyedes and the Mongols proper, and in others are as distinct as it is possible to be, be explained in the same way? They would be another form of cross of the same Asiatic brachycephalic element with the same autochthonous American dolichocephalic element.[*]

A Red Type.

A *Red type*, it must be admitted, exists in the centre of Africa. The Americans are frequently designated by the title of Red, not on account of the colour of their skin, but because they frequently paint the face in this way. It would be equally proper to call certain of the Polynesian Islanders red. In Africa also this tint is very common in the centre of the continent, from the Red Sea to Senegal; but it is separated in so decided a way in the midst of the surrounding black populations, that it is necessary to look upon it as a particular type.

The Red African type is associated with black and glossy hair, and unfortunately is found everywhere mixed, or in close contact, with the negro populations. Here and there, however, it is sufficiently isolated, among the Foulbas for example, for its independent character to be demonstrated. Let us consider first the colour of the skin.

---

[*] See "At Home with the Patagonians," by G. C. Musters, London, 1871; "Des Cimetières et Paradoros de Patagonie," by F. P. Moreno, jun., in "Revue d'Anthrop.," vol. III., 1874; &c.

Although it is stated that the red colour adopted by the ancient
Egyptians in their representations of themselves on their monuments was merely arbitrary, it may be asked whether they had not
some motive for this. A portion of the present race of Barábras
of the valley of the Nile above the First Cataract are still of this
colour, which they themselves compare to polished mahogany. In
the plains of Sennaar, Cailliaud has described the El Akmar, or
Reds, as half-breeds, or of a peculiar caste. A considerable number
of Danakil negroes on the banks of the Red Sea are of a red
copper-colour (Rochet d'Héricourt). The ancient inhabitants of the
Straits of Bab-el-Mandeb are called Himyarites, which signifies red
(Maury). Among the southern Tawáreks, and the Tibboo Indians,
they speak also of reds. The Ronga, Dor, Bongo, Kredj, and
Nyam-Nyams of the western affluents of the Bahr-el-Ghazal have a
more or less reddish complexion mixed with black. The ancient
Egyptians moreover were not ignorant of the existence of red
people in the centre of Africa. Negroid people of a reddish
colour are depicted on the monuments of Thebes of the 18th
dynasty. At the present time negro tribes are spoken of on the
banks of the Zambesi, and as far as the Congo, with this shade of
colour. But the most important consideration is the fact that the
Foulbe people are now flourishing in the Soudan. Known by the
name of Peuls in Senegal, called Foulahs by the Mandingoes,
Fellani by the negroes of Howssa, Felfatahe by the Kanori of
Bornú, and Foellan by the Arabs, they came from the east, according to Dr. Barth, at a very remote period. They do not however
appear in history until about the tenth century. At that epoch
they constituted the " pale " element, which was predominant in
the Ghanata kingdom to the south-west of Timbuctoo. In 1500
they were powerful in the west and south of the Songay kingdom
to the east of Timbuctoo; in 1600 they appeared in Howssa; in
1700 in Beghanni. They are shepherds and nomads, and continue
to spread and propagate Islamism, without forming distinct
nationalities. It was only in 1809 that Othman dan Fodie, one of
their chiefs, on his return from a pilgrimage to Mecca, united them
into a community, and by force of arms imposed his authority over

the greater part of Soudan. In this vast territory, which is to a certain extent civilized, Dr. Barth met with three principal races : (1) The autochthonous Negroes, constituting the majority, the vanquished people of the country ; (2) The Foulahs, or Foulbes (native name), the conquerors, with red complexion and straight hair ; (3) The Arabs, traders or shepherds, who, two centuries ago, came from the east into Bornú.

This close contact everywhere of the Foulah with the negro, explains why travellers describe them sometimes as slim and well-proportioned, with glossy hair—(Mungo Park on two occasions writes "silky hair")—sometimes as squat and short, with woolly hair. They often indeed take wives from among the negresses, while the reverse is rare (*Barth*). Among their half-breeds are noticed the Toucolors of Senegal, the Black Pauls, the Toródes, and the Susus, these last belonging to the Mandingoes.

The colour of the purest-blood Foulahs is sometimes coppery-red, sometimes of a rhubarb shade. In the country, where the natives go naked, the contrast between the two types—the one reddish yellow, the other negroid—is very striking. The characters of the type may be specially gathered from the western Foulahs. The face is oval, the nose long and arched, the teeth vertical, the lips somewhat thin, the figure slim and tall, the limbs well-proportioned, the extremities small. Dr. Barth thus describes those to the east of the Niger : "They have small, sharp, and open features, they are lively and intelligent ; the face is long as compared with the round negro face ; the lips not thick, the complexion copper-coloured, the hair black, long, reaching sometimes to the shoulders ; the figure upright and slim, the extremities slender, moderate corpulence." In a word, we must, in the Anthropology of Africa, take into account a special Red type with smooth hair, approximating to the European type. Being now closely intermingled with the negro races, it is no longer represented but by the pure-blood Foulahs.[*]

[*] "Travels and Discoveries in North and Central Africa," by Dr. Barth, in 1849–55. London.

CHAPTER XII.

NEGRO, KAFFIR, HOTTENTOT TYPES—PAPUAN, NEGRITO, TASMANIAN
TYPES—AUSTRALIAN TYPE—CONCLUSION OF THE SUBJECT OF
HUMAN RACES.

The Negro Type.

THE *Negro type*, understood in its more general acceptation, is
met with in Asia, near its south-eastern angle, in Oceania, where
it exhibits two distinct types, the Papuan and the Negrito, and
in Africa, where it is divided into the Guinean, Kaffir, and
Hottentot types. We take the Guinean as best representing the
most ancient and the most classical Negro type.

The northern limit of the most characteristic negro tribes extends from the river Senegal, inclines to the east as far as the
10th degree of north latitude (*Maury*), and is lost in the region
visited by Speke and Baker, where there are different tribes whose
parentage is not as yet thoroughly determined. Above this line,
however, in the Desert, we find an isolated negro tribe, the Tebous,
or Tibboos. On its confines we meet with a regular succession
of other tribes, interrupted here and there by the Foulahs, namely:
The native negroes of Adamawa, Massina, Howssa, Bornú, Beg-
harmi, and Dar-Fúr; the Nubians of Kordofan; the Shilluchs,
Fungi, and Schangallas, close to Abyssinia; and the Nouairs,
Bari, and Sere of Bahr-el-Ghazal. The western limit of the Negro
type is formed by the sea. Its principal tribes are from Senegal
to Benguela, as if they had been driven to the coast, namely: The
Yoloffs, Sereres, and Mandingoes of Senegambia; the Feloupas
of Sierra Leone; the Kroumans of Liberia; the Fantis, Accras,
and Ashantis of the Gold Coast; the Mahis and Dahomeys of the
Gulf of Benin; the Ibos, Makos, and Calabar of the mouth of
the Niger; the Douhis, Bakalais, and M'pongwes of the Gaboon;
&c. Behind them are grouped other tribes of a better type, with
somewhat clearer complexion, or slightly mixed with red. Certain

Peuls of Senegambia, the Bambarras of the Upper Niger, and certain tribes of Fans, or Pahuins, of the Gaboon are of this number. The following description specially relates to the Guinean sub-type, but may be considered as that of the Negro type in general. The skin of the negro is velvety, cool to the touch, glossy, varying from a reddish, yellowish, or bluish black to jet black. His hair and eyes are black, the sclerotic dark or yellowish, black spots are seen on the tongue, the roof of the mouth, and even under the conjunctiva. The palms of the hands and soles of the feet are lighter in colour than the rest of the body. The beard is scant, and is developed late. The body is destitute of hair, except on the pubis and in the arm-pits. The skull is dolichocephalic (73·0 on the west coast of Africa), occasionally mesaticephalic, and even sub-brachycephalic. Its capacity, in eighty-five Western negroes, measured by M. Broca, was 1372 cubic centimètres, or 151 cubic centimètres less than in the natives of Auvergne.

The norma verticalis is of an elliptical shape. The supra-iniac portion of the occipital is frequently projecting, its lateral portions are flat and vertical, the curved temporal lines describe an arc corresponding with the mass of temporal muscles which are inserted beneath them; the temporal shell itself is larger than that of the white. The frontal is articulated frequently with the temporal; the greater wings of the sphenoid are consequently not articulated with the parietal. The cranial sutures are more simple than in the White type, and are obliterated sooner (Gratiolet). The squamo-temporal, and the spheno-parietal frequently form a horizontal straight line. The forehead is narrow at the base, sometimes receding and rather low, sometimes straight and bulging (bombé) at the summit. The frontal bosses are often confluent, or replaced by a single and median protuberance. The superciliary arches project but little, and are smooth, very different from the Melanesian negro, so much so that by this the two sexes tend to resemble each other. As a result of this, the orbits are less deep, which contributes, with the slight depression of the root of the nose, and the less marked general appearance of the face, to give to the negro of Africa a less

ferocious aspect than to the negro of Oceania. The orbits moreover
are microsèmes, that is to say short from above downwards, but
much less so than in the Melanesian negroes, thus helping still more
to distinguish them.

The eyeballs are close to the head, and the palpebral apertures
are nevertheless small and are on the same horizontal line. The
space between the eyes is less flat and less large than in the
Mongolian type, but more so than in the European type. The
nose is developed in width at the expense of its projection; its base
is large and crushed in, owing to the softness of the cartilages, and
spreads out into two divergent alæ, with elliptical nostrils more or
less exposed. This extremity is sometimes trilobed. The skeleton
of the nose is platyrrhinian (54·76); the two bones proper are
occasionally united, as in apes. The inferior border of the anterior
aperture is obliterated, or replaced by a sort of platform, the
boundary between the nasal fossæ and the sub-nasal region being
undefined in proportion to the very slight development of the
median spine.*

The face as a whole is usually long, like the cranium, but it is
sometimes short and round, and then it is frequently flat. The
zygomatic arches, and the malar bones have only a slight lateral
projection; the former are more frequently cryptozygous,† according to Blumenbach's method, than in the White type, and less
frequently than in the Mongolian type. The prognathism of the
negro extends within certain limits to the entire face. All the
parts of the superior maxilla contribute to it, and even the pterygoid processes, which are drawn forward by the development of the
jaw; but it is only really characteristic and considerable in the sub-
nasal region, and in the teeth. It frequently exists also in the
lower jaw, that is to say the chin recedes, and the teeth project

---

* Loc. cit., in "Revue d'Anthrop.," vol. i. p. 667.

† When making use of the expressions "cryptozygous" and "phœnizy-
gous," as synonymous with the less or greater development of the zygomatic
arches, it is well to remember that, with very few exceptions, when the
parietal angle is negative these arches are always visible, according to the
norma verticalis.

obliquely forwards. The teeth themselves are wider apart than in the white races, beautifully white, very firm and sound. Lastly, the ears are small, round, their border not well curled, the lobule short and scarcely detached, and the auditory opening wide. The neck is short.

M. Pruner-Bey speaks of two important characters which remind one of the ape. The three curvatures of the spine are less pronounced in the negro than in the white; his thorax is relatively flat from side to side, and slightly cylindrical. The shoulders, he adds, are less powerful than in the European; the umbilicus is nearer the pubis; the iliac bones in the male are thicker and more vertical; the neck of the femur is less oblique. With respect to the proportions of the extremities, we refer the reader to pages 303, 304, et seq. The femur is less oblique, the tibia more curved, the calf of the leg high and but little developed, the heel broad and projecting, the foot long, but slightly arched, flat, and the great toe rather shorter than in the white. Negresses age very rapidly, their breasts elongate after the first pregnancy, and afterwards become flabby and pendulous.

The Kaffir Type.

The *Kaffir type*, one of the highest expressions of the general Negro type, extends from the Zambesi to the Hottentot territories, and from the coast of Mozambique to the Atlantic Ocean. Its principal tribes are: On the west coast, the Damaras or Ovahereros; on the east, the Amakosah; near Cape Colony, the Ama-Zulus and the Mamias; in the interior, on the western declivity of the chain of the Maloutus, the Bechuanas, and the Bassoutos; and on the Zambesi, the Makololos. Linguists, however, relying on the extension of the Bantou language, extend their boundaries, on the one side to the Congo and even beyond, and on the other to the coast of Zanzibar, among the Suahilis. The raids made continually by the Kaffirs against the Cape Colony, and traditions according to which they are said to have come from the

north at a remote period, testify to their warlike spirit, and to the
possibility of their previous influence at some former time. But it
does not follow that they should have left their physical traits in
their course. We confine ourselves, therefore, to the best recognised tribes of the south-east. The Kaffir type bears a general
resemblance to the Guinean or Ethiopian, but it is a degree less
bestial. The face is longer and of somewhat oval figure, the outlines of the head are more decided, its muscular attachments and
processes more marked, the maxillary bones larger. The skin
exhibits various shades of blackish brown. The hair is thick,
harsh, and woolly. The nose is broad and flat (épaté), the lips
thick. The palpebral openings remind us sometimes of those of
the Yellow races. The odour exhaled from the skin in all the
negro tribes is stronger in the Kaffir. They are very tall, slim, and
well made.

Seven Kaffir skulls measured by M. Bertillon showed an average
capacity, enormous for negroes, of 1455 cubic centimètres. "Their
vertical diameter is considerable," adds this author. In eight
similar skulls examined by M. Broca, the mean cephalic index was
72·5, being slightly less than in the Guinean negroes. The
platyrrhiny of the two types is sensibly the same (54·99 in Kaffirs).
The prognathism, according to our own tables, is a little less in
Kaffirs, 68·01.

It would be very desirable to ascertain the type of the
Makololos of the Zambesi, whose language approximates them
to the Kaffirs, but who appear to differ from them in physique.
Perhaps they may be the remnants of some ancient type. Unfortunately they are rapidly decreasing.*

The Hottentot Type.

The *Hottentot type*, now confined to the extremity of Southern
Africa, formerly extended quite as far as the 10th degree of south

* See article, "Cafres," by Ch. Létourneau, in "Encycl. des Sc. Médic.,"
2nd series, vol. II.; "Die Eingeborenen Sud Africa's Ethnographisch und
Anatomisch Beschrieben," by G. Fritsch, Breslau, 1873.

latitude. As evidence of this, the geographical names in Kaffraria
are still Hottentot. The type includes the Hottentots of the
Colony, the Korannas, the Namaquas, the Griquas (see page 382),
and the Bosjesmans. We shall specially have in view the first
three. The Hottentots, or Koï-Koïn, have a yellow-brown or
gray skin. This character is almost an invariable one. Their
long woolly hair, which is inserted obliquely in very small tufts,
approximates them to the Papuans. Their thick, broad, and
prominent cheek-bones, and their small and oblique palpebral
apertures, on the other hand remind one of the Chinese races
(*Burrow*); their eyes are dark chestnut or black, and very wide
apart. Their cranial capacity is 1290 (*Broca*), that is to say
82 cubic centimètres less than in the Western negroes; they are
more dolichocephalic than these. Their narrow forehead is com-
pensated for by its height, and it is frequently bulging at the
height of the frontal bosses. The nose is frightfully broad and
flat, the nostrils are thick, very divergent, and exposed. Their
prognathism is generally enormous, though it varies. The mouth
is large, with thick projecting and turned-up lips. The chin is
pointed, although supported by a receding jaw. The ears are
large, and without lobule. The Hottentots have but little beard,
and the body is destitute of hair. Their stature is below the
average, at least in the three tribes in question, the Korannas
being not quite so small, which may arise from a cross with the
Kaffirs. Their joints are thick; some of them have broad and
heavy feet, but in the majority the feet and hands are somewhat
small. Some are of weak frame, others squat and very muscular.
Steatopyga, which is somewhat common among the women, increases with puberty. It is met with, here and there, throughout
the whole Hottentot group, and, as we have said, as far as the
regions occupied by the Somalis, where the Hottentot race is no
longer to be seen. In a case mentioned by Burrow, the tremulous
mass passed 14 centimètres beyond the line of the back (see page
362). This character, as well as the tablier, is only constant and
of any extent in the Bosjesman tribe.

The Hottentot type is, in other respects, without unity; one would call it an agglomeration of ancient races driven down into this extremity of the globe. Thus, fifteen of their skulls in the Museum have a sub-nasal prognathism of 73·5, and yet we find among them three marked as Colonial Hottentots, in which it is only 80, and this one of the most favoured of the Yellow races. There are two examples of Boajesmans, where it is 63·4, and two of Namaquas, as low as 58·3 and 51·8 respectively. Such differences are certain evidences of crossing. So with platyrchinia—M. Broca found the nasal index varying from 48 to 72.

Travellers agree in considering the greater number of the Boajesmans, and some of the Namaquas, as forming a distinct type. Three characters in the former seem to favour this view: (1) The large steatopyga, which is the exception among the Hottentots and the rule with a very large number among the Boajesmans; (2) The tablier, in the same way; (3) The stature, which is much smaller than that of Hottentots. Livingstone imagined that he had seen a Boajesman 1·83 mètre in height, but he was no doubt deceived by a stray Kaffir. It is certain that the Boajesmans are the smallest race in the world, and that it is a stretch to put their mean stature at more than 1·40 mètre. Many traits in their skeletons have also attracted attention, such as the welding of the two bones proper of the nose into one—the obliteration of the *linea aspera* of the femur, as in apes. In other respects their characters and those of Hottentots are alike. For example: the hair growing in tufts of closely-twisted spirals, some millimètres in diameter, the skin of a yellowish colour, or like dirty varnished oak, &c. Their facial angle varies from 64 to 70, according to Fritsch; it is 64 in one of the Namaquas in the Museum, this being the lowest known in Man. The Boajesman woman, known by the name of the Hottentot Venus, who died in Paris, and whose full-length portrait in the Museum is an excellent example of this race, was considered tall by her own people. Cuvier has given a good description of her: "She had a way of pouting her lips," he says, "exactly like that we have observed in the ourang-outang." To anyone who has seen these anthropoids the simile is very expressive. "Her movements had something abrupt and fantastical about them, reminding one of those of the ape. Her lips were monstrously large. Her ear was like that of many apes, being small, the tragus weak, and the external border almost obliterated behind. "Those," he says, after having described the bones of the skeleton, "are animal characters." Again: "I have never seen a human head more like an ape than that of this woman." What we said before relative to the Hottentot type throughout the whole of Southern and Eastern Africa is still more true with respect to the special Bosjesman type. The Obongos, near the banks of the Gaboon, have the same old yellow, femme brown complexion, the same growth of the hair in tufts as the Hottentots, and a character which is par excellence that of the Bosjesmans—smallness of stature. From the coast of Aden, among the Somalis, to the mouth of the Ogobai on the west, we find races of the Bosjesman type—the lowest of the human race. The fact escaped Cuvier that this type is the most animal known, and diminishes the distance which separates the European from the anthropoid ape. What should we say if the type were a pure one?

In concluding our remarks concerning the Negro types of Africa[*] it should be noticed that the several divisions we have admitted among them are altogether insufficient. We have been studying the Negro as compared with the White, but without taking any great account of the distinctions between them, which are as palpable as between White or Yellow races. Thus, among the black tribes of the West Coast that we have associated together under the name of Guineans, there are evidently two very distinct types—one ugly, diminutive, with large and squat limbs, and with a round or short face; the other comparatively handsome, tall, with slender and well-proportioned limbs, and with a long face. Thus we shall have to give up the Hottentot type, and after perhaps separating the Namaquan type, keep to that of the Bosjesman. So among the Kaffirs, or rather those sprung from them, extending from the

[*] See "Travels in the Interior of Southern Africa," by J. Barrow, 2 vols. London, 1801; "Mémoire sur la Femme Hottentote," by Baron Cuvier, in "Hist. Nat. des Mammifères," by G. St. Hilaire and F. Cuvier, 2 vols. in 4to, Paris, 1824; &c.

Zambesi to Bahr-el-Ghazal to the west of the great lakes, there are very many types, which are at the same time very characteristic ones. The collection of busts of M. de Froberville is sufficient of itself to prove that the description of the Negro races of Africa must be altogether remodelled.*

The Papuan Type.

The *Papuan type* is distributed throughout the whole geographical area called Melanesia, except in Australia. It appears to be most pure in the Solomon Isles and the New Hebrides. In the Fiji Islands, and even in New Caledonia, it is mingled with the Polynesian type. Its characters are the following:

Ordinary stature, but relatively taller than the Negrito and Malay types; the skin is black or of a chocolate colour; the hair is black, harsh, frizzled, growing in distinct tufts, which are short and thick in early life, and at a later period assume a bushy character, or like the head of a mop (*tête de escroudille*), measuring thirty centimetres on each side. The beard, as well as the hair on the body, grows in the same way in tufts, but these are farther apart. They have a very dolichocephalic skull, with the lateral walls vertical, and frequently exhibiting a median crest commencing behind the bregma, or going beyond as far as the middle of the forehead. The eyes are sunk, the sclerotics dull; the nose is thick and wide at the base, but projecting and turned up, it is said, at least in New Guinea, with the median lobule extending beyond the nostrils (*Wallace*). The sub-nasal prognathism is considerable, the lips thick and projecting, the jaw receding, and the face, on the whole, rather long.†

The New Caledonians.

The New Caledonians are generally associated with the Papuan type. In reality, they are a mixed race formed of three elements:

* See "Die Nigritien," by R. Hartmann.   Berlin, 1876.
† See "Indian Archipelago—Papuans," by J. W. Earl. London, 1850.

a Polynesian ; one whose name, Melanesian, it would be as well to allow to remain, which leaves us in no doubt as to its relationship ; and an intermediate or cross race. Out of a large number of skulls it is easy to select them ; the half-breeds are in greatest number, the Melanesians tolerably numerous, and the Polynesians rare. M. Bourgarel arrives at the same result on the living subject, and describes two varieties—the black and the yellow. The former is characterised, he says, by the very dark colour of the skin, the short hair, flocculent rather than woolly (*Forster*), short stature, slender limbs, flat foot, very considerable dolicho-cephaly, marked prognathism, enormous superciliary arches, vertical direction of the two lateral planes of the skull, &c. The latter has the same characters, though attenuated ; among others, taller stature, limbs better proportioned, olive-yellow complexion, longer and less woolly hair, sometimes frizzled, sides of the head round, &c. However this may be, the present mixed or crossed race presents the following characters on examination of skulls which have been brought to Europe, and which, for the most part, are those of the original inhabitants of the Island of Pines :

The cranial capacity in the adult man is 1460, and in the woman 1428, and is greater than that of the Australian and the negro, but much less than that of the White and Yellow races, especially in the man. The cephalic index of 71·78 is as small as that of Australians, Esquimaux, and the Veddahs of Ceylon. The forehead of 93·0 is much narrower than in the negroes of Africa, but less than in Australians. The nasal index clearly places it apart from all the Black races ; it is 53·00, that is to say very nearly mesorhinian. The orbital index of 80·6 approximates it to the Australians and the prehistoric races, and separates it from the Yellow races. The prognathism is 69·8, and a little less than in the Australians and negroes of Africa, though in all it is considerable. Simply by the arrangement of the inferior border of the nasal aperture one may always distinguish a New Caledonian from an African negro. In the former it is absolutely obliterated, and replaced by two channels of an altogether simian character, which pass down on each side in the direction of the alveolar border. In the latter it is blunt but tolerably distinct, or replaced by a sort of platform. The facial angle is the smallest in our tables (see

Fig. 48.—A New Caledonian half-breed; Yellow variety of M. Bourgarel, from M. de la Richerie's collection.

page 286). Daubenton's angle is that of the Black races, the parietal angle the smallest known. The superciliary arches are more prominent according as the individual is more Melanesian—a

remarkable difference from the negro of Africa, in whom they are
small and flat. But what strikes one at a cursory glance in the
principal type of the Island of Pines, is the coarseness of the
features, and the contrast between the hollows and prominences of
the face, which gives it a ferocious appearance. The integuments
would however modify these characters, as in the Tasmanian, to
judge by the very beautiful photographs forwarded by M. Simon,
French consul at Sydney, and unless they represent another altogether
contemporaneous type, the face would be, on the contrary, full,
round, moderately long, the features, as it were, pasty, and without
animation. The hair forms a thick and continuous fleece ; the nose
is large, broad, and flat, the lips large and pouting, &c. Figure 48
represents a half-breed, no doubt one of the Yellow variety.
From her tall stature, her slender limbs, and her comparatively
light complexion, she is Polynesian. From her deeply-sunken
eyes and overhanging eyebrows, her long forearm, her slender and
high calf of the leg, her projecting heel and flat foot, she is
Melanesian ; from her frizzled rather than woolly hair, she is a
cross-breed.[*]

It must be admitted, in short, that the present New Caledonian
race is principally Melanesian, as the hair, as well as the features
generally, testify, but that the Polynesian influence has made itself
apparent, especially in the stature and the nasal index. It is to
this we have alluded whenever we have been comparing the
negroes of Oceania with those of Africa.

The Negrito Type.

The Negrito type has been carefully defined by M. de Quatrefages.
Its present representatives are the Mincopies of the Andaman

* "Des Races de l'Océanie Française et en particulier de celles de la
Nouvelle Calédonie," by A. Bourgarel, in "Mém. Soc. d'Anthrop. ;" first
Memoir, vol. i. ; second, vol. ii. ; "Étude des Crânes Néo-Calédoniens du
Musée de Caen," by Bertillon, in "Revue d'Anthrop.," vol. I., 1872 ;
"Présentation de Photographies de Néo-Calédoniens et d'Australiens," by
Topinard, "Bull. Soc. d'Anthrop.," 2nd series, vol. xi., 1876.

Islands, the Semangs of the interior of the peninsula of Malacca, the Aëtas of the Philippines. Their fundamental characters are low stature, woolly hair, black skin, and sub-brachycephaly. This last character is the most prominent. The cephalic index of five of their skulls is 82·54. The stature of five individuals collected by M. Hamy from various authors, is, on the average, 1·47 mètre. The hair of the Andaman is black, woolly, and grows in spirally-twisted tufts, like that of Papuans, Tasmanians, and Hottentots. They have but little beard, and the skin, the reverse of the Tasmanian, is glossy and jet black. The following characters also belong to them: The forehead is full and projecting, wide as compared with that of negroes, but less so than that of Tasmanians. The face is round or quadrilateral, and rather short, the cheek-bones broad and somewhat flat. The eyes are large and round, that is to say not very well formed, and horizontal, with thick eyelashes. The nose is broad at the base, but slightly crushed in, and the nostrils are round. The sub-nasal prognathism of 70·2 in the two specimens in the Museum is about the average of Yellow races. The lips are moderately large, and appear but little turned up for negroes; the face is round at the bottom, and not receding. The Andamans are short and squat, though the Luzon girl, according to the drawing of Choris, is slim and well-proportioned. They have square shoulders, well-developed chest, the trunk the same all the way down, without the slightest figure, the feet and hands moderately large, the fingers long, the heels not projecting, the toes spread out when standing on the ground. There is but little difference in the figure between the two sexes. In fact, were it not for the hair and the complexion, the negritos would, on the whole, be moderately negroid. They at one time occupied Malacca, and probably New Guinea, and the southern extremity of Asia. But it has not been shown that the black populations of India mentioned in the Mahabharata were negritos. Up to that time no positive statement has been made as to the presence of woolly hair in that peninsula with regard to absolutely inferior simian types. The descriptions of them given by Piddington, Rousselet, and Blond are very meagre. The only argument in favour

2 K 2

of the negrito nature of the autochthonous stock of India is the
existence, here and there, especially in Ceylon and the adjoining
part of India, of black tribes of very low stature.[*]

The Tasmanian Type.

The *Tasmanian type*, now extinct, is separated in a most remarkable manner from all the neighbouring types, negroes or others.
While the fifty-four New Caledonians in the Museum have a cephalic
index of 71·7, and the twenty-seven Australians of 71·4, that of the
forty-one Polynesians is 76·3, and that of ten Tasmanians, 76·1.

Then the *norma verticalis* of Blumenbach leads to a similar
result; the vault of the cranium of Tasmanians is characteristic—
it is of the keel-shaped type (*en carène*), at least in the skulls in
the Museum; in other words, it has a median sagittal projection,
bounded by two lateral depressions, beyond which are two enlargements, like the sides of a ship. The Polynesians exhibit this also,
especially those in the east, although less marked, while it never
exists either in Australians or New Caledonians, who are the
most Melanesian. Again, while the angle of alveolo-nasal prognathism is 69·8 in New Caledonians, 68·2 in Australians, 73·8 in
two Andamanese, and 75·0 in Polynesians, it is 76·2 in six Tasmanians; in other words, they are scarcely more prognathous than
Europeans. With regard to the direction of the plane of the
occipital foramen, a character of the first importance, we have the
same result; they must be grouped with Corsicans and Berbers, the
very opposite of the Oceanic races. Notwithstanding this, from
their complexion, their hair, their platyrrhinia, their retroussés
lips, and their little cranial capacity, they are negroes. Their other
craniometrical characters are these: Greater development of the
posterior cranium, which places them among the occipital races of
Gratiolet; swelling out of the temporo-zygomatic regions; forehead

[*] See "Étude sur les Microcies et la Race Négrito en général," by
A. de Quatrefages, in "Revue d'Anthrop.," vol. i., 1872; "On the Andaman
and Andamanese," by O. E. Dobson, in "Journal of the Anthropol. Institute," April, 1875, &c.; "Les Noirs de l'Inde," in "Revue d'Anthrop.,"
vol. iv. p. 507.

broad at its lower part (94 millimètres), superciliary arches and glabella very projecting; orbits deep, small, microsemic; root of the nose considerably crushed in; face broad and contracted, at the expense especially of the superior maxillary, though also of the inferior; some flattening of the face otherwise; the malar bones of the usual dimensions. With regard to the characters in the living subject, they are: A chocolate-black complexion, a little less dark perhaps than that of the Australian, and less than that of the negro of Guinea; woolly hair, growing not in one continuous fleece, but in spiral tufts, which fall down in long ringlets; the beard and the hair on the rest of the body very abundant, as in Australians, the hair being flat in sections under the microscope; small eyes, sunken, with dull sclerotics; nose broad and flat (*épaté*), not projecting, thick, and puffy at the base; mouth large, lips thick, the upper especially, and turned up; chin small and receding; ears oval, with a thick lobule. Their stature exhibits nothing particular to remark upon, and is below the average. From this it will be seen that the Tasmanian type is absolutely *sui generis*, and exhibits anomalies which cannot be otherwise accounted for. We have stated elsewhere that their skulls in the Museum appeared to be the product of a cross between the Melanesian and the Polynesian, but that they had a special physiognomy of their own. By their manners and customs, the Tasmanians have some points of resemblance to the Andamanese.[*]

The Australian Type.

The *Australian type*, geographically allied to the preceding, is no less paradoxical, but in another sense. It is characterised by the combination of smooth hair with negroid features. On comparing some Tasmanian and Australian skulls, we at first came to the conclusion that the former race were physically superior. On

[*] See "Étude sur les Tasmaniens," by Dr. Paul Topinard, in "Mém. Soc. d'Anthrop.," vol. iii., meeting of the 18th Nov., 1869; "Examen des Mesures Craniométriques des Crânes Tasmaniens" of Mr. Barnard Davis, in "Revue d'Anthrop.," vol. ii., by the same author; "On the Osteology of the Tasmanians," by Mr. Barnard Davis, Haarlem, 1874.

making some further measurements, which have been since published by M. Broca and ourselves, we thought the same; but judging by their characters on the living subject, it is just the reverse—the Australians are superior.

But is the Australian type a pure one? Commissioned by the Société d'Anthropologie to deliver certain "Instructions" to travellers in Australia, we were all at once struck with the differences between the Australians of the coast, of the low plains, and some isolated spots in the bush, on the north-west more especially, and the Australians en masse of the interior, of the high lands, and especially those of the north-eastern region. We therefore called the attention of travellers to this point, and, in particular, as to the existence of woolly hair here and there, as mentioned by Hombron, Pickering, and Stokes. We thought that before the present race of Australians there must have existed on their continent a race much inferior still, of whom the individuals with woolly hair and the ugly deformed tribes were the descendants. From other considerations relating to the ethnic customs described by Mr. Staniland Wake, we were confirmed in this opinion. It is clear that the Australians might very well be the result of the cross between one race with smooth hair from some other place and a really negro and autochthonous race. The opinions expressed by Mr. Huxley are in harmony with this hypothesis. He says the Australians are identical with the ancient inhabitants of the Deccan. The features of the present blacks of India, and the characters which the Dravidian and Australian languages have in common, tend to assimilate them. The existence of the boomerang in the two countries, and some remnants of caste in Australia, help to support the opinion. But the state of extreme misery of the inferior Australian tribes may equally explain some of the physical differences which they present. Woolly hair appears to be now but seldom seen. A few examples of it have been noticed in the York peninsula and the north-west point, which might be accounted for by the immigration of Papuans from New Guinea, and in the south by the passage over to the other side of Behring's Straits of some Tasmanians to the continent

On the other hand, on studying the Australian skull, we notice tolerably-marked differences of type, and it is certain that the Polynesians landed at some period or other in the north-west, and the Malays in the north-east.   Lastly, if the Australians are thorough Hindoos as regards their hair, they are Melanesians, or if you will, New Hebrideans, New Caledonian negroes, in every other respect.   The question may therefore be left.   We are still in ignorance as to whether the present Australian race took its

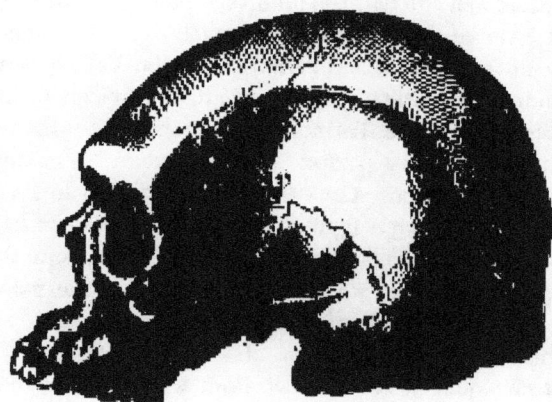

Fig. 43.—Australian type: One of its forms.

origin on the spot, with the characters that we admit as belonging to it, or whether, on the contrary, it was altogether constituted in Asia, or whether it is a cross race, and in that case, of what elements it is composed.

However it may be, the present men of Australians have the pilous system very developed over the whole body, the hair and the beard long, tufted, black, and straight.   Their complexion is a dark-chocolate black, with sometimes a tinge of red in it.   They are slight, well made, and if there are travellers who have only seen caricatures of them, there are sailors who describe them as perfect models for the sculptor.   The Australians have one of the smallest cranial capacities known among mankind (1·347); they are among the most dolichocephalic (71·4), the most prog-

nathous (48·2), and are platyrrhinian (53·4); their angle of
Daubenton (direction of the plane of the occipital foramen) of 0·8°
approximates them to the negro, and separates them, on the contrary, from the Tasmanians (2·6) and the White races. They have
frequently the "mître-like" shape of the vault of the cranium,
a narrow forehead, sometimes straight, sometimes receding (two
forms opposed to each other), the superciliary arches very projecting, the superior border of the orbit jutting out above the inferior,
the eyes black and sunken, the nose very hollowed out at the root,
thick and broad at the base, but less crushed in than the negroes
and Hottentots of Africa, and perhaps than the Yellow races.[*]

But the most important character of all, that which warrants our
setting them apart as a distinct type, is their smooth hair, con-
trasted with all the most perfect negro characters. The microscope
confirms this distinction. On a transverse section it holds a middle
place, in M. Pruner-Bey's figures, between the more or less round
shape peculiar to the Yellow and American types, and the somewhat elliptical form that we meet with in the Semitic races. It is
therefore far from being of the long, elliptical, and flat form
peculiar to the negro of Africa, the negrito, and the Papuan.
Their stature would be sufficient of itself to prove that the present
race is composed of two ancient races, whose stature might have
been—the one about 1·600 mètres, the other above 1·700. The
maximum and minimum observed in the male have been 2·130 and
1·447 respectively. Those which we might consider in India as of
the same race are—(a) The Bhils, "black, with small horizontal
eyes, and with hair in long straight skeins;" (b) The Ghounds,
"black, with flat nose, thick lips, and tufted, black, shining hair,
falling down in straight skeins;" (c) The Khounds, more or less
black also; (d) The Maloirs, "very black, superciliary arches

* See "Journal of Discoveries in Central Australia in 1840-41, with an
account of Aborigines," by Eyre, London, 2 vols., 1849; "Discoveries in
Australia," by Stokes, London, 2 vols., 1848; "Exped. in North-West and
West Australia," by G. Grey, London, 2 vols., 1840; "Voyage au Port du
Roi Georges," by Scott-Nind, in "Journal Royal Geograph. Soc.," vol. i.,
1881; "On the Aborigines of West Australia," by A. Oldfield, in "Trans.
Ethnol. Soc. London," vol. iii., 1865; "Études sur les Races Indigènes de
l'Australie," by P. Topinard, in "Bull. Soc. d'Anthrop.," 1872; &c.

projecting, small eyes, and flat nose;" (e) The Varalis, &c.
(L. Rousselet); (f) The Morudas, described by Roulland, who have
the forehead low and receding, the nose thick and flat, the iris
dark brown, the face wide and flat, the cheek-bones prominent, the
incisor teeth vertical, a cephalic index of 78·6, and a stature of
1·61 mètre; (g) The Yenadis and Manvers of the coast of Coro-
mandel; and (h) The Veddahs of Ceylon, whose dolichocephaly of
71·7 is equal to that of the Australians, and whose stature is 1·58.
Last year a black of this group, a native of Pondicherry, was dissected in the Laboratory of Anthropology; his black complexion,
slightly tinged with chocolate, and his smooth, long, and shining
hair, were very remarkable. His skeleton, as well as his bust, are now
in the collection of M. Broca. Among the Todas of the Nilgherries,
and, strangely enough, further on towards the north, among certain
of the Ainos, two of the fundamental Australian traits are met
with; namely, the very projecting superciliary arch and the
abundant hair over the whole body—characters the more remarkable from the fact that the reverse is the rule through the whole of
Eastern and Southern Asia. In the same Nilgherry hills, situated
at the junction of the western and eastern Ghauts, towards the
southern extremity of the Deccan, in the desired conditions for
concealing the remnants of ancient races, two of the above-mentioned tribes especially afford matter for reflection, namely, the
Kurumbas and the Irulas. The former have a black complexion,
the hair long and wavy, black, and in tufts, the conjunctiva often
injected, the iris dark brown (No. 1 in M. Broca's table of colours),
the root of the nose hollowed out to the depth of 5 millimètres, the
bridge of the nose depressed, the alæ wide, the nostrils gaping, the
jaw and the teeth prognathous. Is not this an accurate portrait of
the Australian? We may add that they are of low stature, like
the Australians of the coast. It is true the beard is scanty, but
exceptionally it is very abundant.*

* See John Shortt, "Memoirs on the Savage Tribes of Southern India,
particularly those of the Coast and of the Nilgherries," in "Transactions
Ethn. Soc. London," vols. i. ii. v. and vii.; Roer King, "Ser les Tribus des
Nilghiris," in "Revue d'Anthrop.," vol. ii.; W. F. Marshall, "A Phreno-
logist among the Todas," 1 vol., London, 1873.

Lastly, in the west, about Madagascar, and the point of Aden,
in Africa, there are black tribes with smooth hair, or, at all events,
large numbers of individuals who have it, mingled particularly
among the Somalis and the Gallas, in the region where M. Broca
has an idea that some dark and not negro race, now extinct, once
existed.   The Himyarites, in common with the Australian type,
are black, with straight hair; but the face is long, the nose aquiline
and well shaped, and the lips thin and small: these are black
Arabs. With regard to the Charruas and the ancient Californians of
America, Mr. Huxley himself would not wish to make Australoids
of them.[4]   (See pages 431, 432).

Conclusion.

Our task is completed. We have passed in review the differential
characters of the Human Races, we have pointed out their most distinctive types; we must now return to the question which was
proposed at the close of our remarks on zoological anthropology.
Is the human family composed of genera, of species, or of varieties?
In other words, what interval separates its most natural divisions?
We must state, at the onset, that a classification of these divisions
and subdivisions would be premature. Classification supposes a
science completed, and anatomical anthropology is almost in its
infancy. A certain number of groups of races which merit the
title of branches, and some particular races, are thoroughly defined,
but this is all.   Happily it is not necessary, for the solution of our
problem, that we should know their value and their dependence the
one upon the other. Some being well determined under conditions in
which they now present themselves to us are amply sufficient, and
we have our choice in this respect. The sole difficulty arises from
the confusion created by intermediate types, some due to crossing,
others natural, and in a state of transition, such as we meet with
in every degree in the animal series. Such are the Malays, the
Chinese, the Dravidians, the Hottentots of the Cape, the Himyarites,

<hr>
[4] "Les Peuples de l'Arabie Méridionale," by Maltzan, in "Zeitschr. für
Ethnol.," 1873.

the Abyssinians. Let us take, then, simple general types, as the White, the Yellow, and the Black with woolly hair; or particular ones, such as those of the Scandinavian, the Semite, the Esquimau, the Mongol, the Kaffir, the Bushesman, the Negrito. What is the distance separating them? Let us leave the less palpable physiological traits, forgot that we have to do with Man, and proceed with physical characters as a naturalist would with a mammifer. We take up a treatise on Natural History. The genus Ursus comes before us; it belongs to the family of Plantigrades, order Carnivora, and is composed of fifteen or sixteen species. But, as in Man, many of these divisions are doubtful, or in a state of transition; let us put them aside in the same way, and attach ourselves to the well-recognised types. Cuvier, the great authority in such matters, describes six principal species. The most common are the brown bear of Europe, or *Ursus arctos*, the black bear of North America, or *Ursus Americanus*, and the white Polar bear, or *Ursus maritimus*. We exclude the prehistoric Cavern bear, or *Ursus spelæus*, from our consideration altogether. The first, says Cuvier, has the forehead convex, the hair brown, and more or less woolly in the young animal, becoming smooth with age. Its colour varies, as well as the relative length of its limbs. The second has the forehead flat, the hair black and smooth, the muzzle fawn-coloured. The third has the head long and flat, and the hair white and smooth. According to other naturalists, the bear of Europe has the trunk shorter than that of America, the soles of the fore and hind feet shorter; and the Polar bear, the hind-quarters higher, the muzzle tapering, and the claws less incurvated and shorter. If we are not very much mistaken, these characters neither belong to another order, nor are they more defined than those which we employ to distinguish the human types; not only those the most widely separated from each other, but those which approximate sufficiently to induce us at once to consider them as secondary types. The long head of the white bear is our dolichocephaly. The convex, flat, or concave forehead (*Ursus spelæus*) corresponds with the oblique forehead of the Neanderthal, the straight one of Cro-Magnon and Engis, or the high and bulging forehead of the

CONCLUSION. [CHAP. XII.

Nubian, three distinct races. Black, brown, or white hair: Is it
not thus that we separate our blonde, brown, or red types? The
pointed muzzle is the analogue of our prognathism, or our small
and narrow jaws as compared with the large and square ones.
Differences of stature, and in the proportion of the body, are met
with in the human race as well as in the bear species. In a
word, there is less interval, as regards characters, between the white
and the brown bear than between the European and the negro.

Let us take another example: The genus *Bos*, in which the
commonest species are the ordinary ox, or *Bos taurus*; the auroks,
or *Bos urus*; the bison, or *Bos Americanus*; the buffalo, or *Bos
bubalus*, &c. The specific character of the first, says Cuvier, is
a flat forehead, longer than it is broad, and round horns placed
at the two extremities of the projecting line which separates the
forehead from the occiput. The second has the bulging forehead,
broader than it is high, the horns inserted below the occipital
crest, the limbs tall, a pair of supplementary ribs, a sort of crisp
wool which covers the head and neck of the male, and forms
a short beard under the throat. The third resembles the auroks,
but its limbs, and especially its tail, are shorter. The fourth has the
forehead bulging, longer than it is broad, the horns directed sideways, and showing in front a projecting longitudinal crest, &c.

These are characters of the same order as our own: The shape of
the skull, the abundance of hair on such or such region, its smooth
or woolly nature, the mode of growth of the horns—organs similar
to the hair—the proportions of the skeleton. The most important
difference is in there being in the auroks and the bison a pair of
supplementary ribs. But steatopyga in the Bushwoman is an
equivalent thing. A supplementary rib is not more astonishing,
in an anatomical point of view, than that exaggerated mass of fat
on the buttocks, and which corresponds, not absolutely, but to
a certain extent, with the callosities of apes. Between the various
species of anthropoid apes, between those of the genus chimpanzee
for example, the differences are less pronounced than between
the principal human races. Between the orang and the gorilla
there is less distance than between the Australian and the Lap-

lander. We cannot say more. The distinctive characters of the jackal and the dog, the wolf and the fox, the horse and the mule, the zebra and the quagga, the camel and the dromedary, are scarcely more divergent, and are frequently less, than those of our types. The blonde Swede, with fair rosy complexion, light blue eyes, slender figure, orthogonathous face, and large cranial capacity, is at a prodigious distance from the negro, with the sooty black complexion, the yellow sclerotic, the short and woolly hair, the prominent muzzle, and the projecting turned-up lips—from the Papuan, with similarly woolly hair, but long, growing in tufts, sometimes dishevelled, and forming a globular mass, much larger comparatively than the mane of the bison—or the Bosjesman, with the yellow complexion, with lips of the orang, as Cuvier says, with nymphæ reaching almost to the knee, and with deformed buttocks. On a single geographical point, a little island, what a difference there is between the Aino, with the projecting nose and long tufted hair over a great part of the body, and the Japanese, with the flat nose and smooth skin! It is from skulls that we obtain the most startling evidence. Compare the skull of a New Caledonian of the Island of Pines, who has been exempt from crossing, one of the Namaquas of Delalande in the Museum, a certain Mongol skull brought by Dr. Martin from the desert of Gobi, a certain supposed Uzbek skull presented by M. de Khanikoff to the Société d'Anthropologie, any Esquimau skull you please, and particularly one of those brought from Denmark to the Geographical Congress—compare any of these with the skulls of Nubians, of Guanches, of Arabs, or those from the Caverne de l'Homme Mort. The differences are frequently most surprising, and greater than those recognised generally by naturalists between simple varieties; they are even more in number than those which they admit between species.

If it is so in mixed types, crossed by chance in every direction, and influenced by the external circumstances which have been bequeathed to us after fifty or a hundred thousand years perhaps, what shall we say of the pure types, when men lived in an isolated state, like the anthropoids of the Gaboon and of Borneo, and only

crossed in-and-in? The forehead of the Neanderthal, and the jaw
of La Naulette speak more eloquently than the flattening looked
upon by Cuvier as a mark of separation between the bear of
Europe and the bear of America. The platycnemic tibia, the *femur
à colonne*, and the perforated humerus, were the appanage of prehistoric men which have disappeared, swallowed up, as it were, in
Western Europe. The sagittal crest, which made its appearance
sporadically among the primitive races of the south-west of Asia,
as well as steatopyga among the Somalis, is the vestige of an
arrangement which has been characteristic in some ancient race
absorbed about the same period. The most animal-like example of
the skulls of the Island of Pinos, so different from that which we
now find among the negroes of New Caledonia, and that of certain
Tasmanians, are a record of themselves. But enough for the
present. Without the labour of analysis and reconstruction, it
shows us directly that the anatomical and physiological contrasts
between human types are greater than those admitted by naturalists
between varieties, and as great as between species. The interval
appears even to be greater in some cases, and to extend to that of
genera. Thus, the four characters which distinguish the goat from
the sheep are no other than those which separate certain great
branches of the human family.

We would not deduce from this that certain human groups are
genera—this is for future consideration; but we come to the conclusion that at any rate they are species. The three following are
in this category: (1) Brachycephalic, with low stature, yellowish
skin, broad and flat face, oblique eyes, with contracted eyelids,
hair scanty, coarse, and (on section) round; (2) Dolichocephalic,
with tall stature, fair complexion, narrow face, projecting on the
median line, hair abundant, light-coloured, soft, and of somewhat
elliptical form under the microscope; (3) More dolichocephalic,
with black complexion, hair flat, and rolled into spirals, very
prognathous, the radius long, the buttocks prominent, the breasts
(in the female) elongated, &c.

One objection alone arises, namely, that all men are eugenesic,
and certainly paragenesic; in a word, that they may give origin to

time to a fixed intermediate race, whilst in order to answer the
classical definition of species, they ought to be agenesic.   (See page
195.)   But in face of the fact that certain species of animals are also
eugenesic and undoubtedly paragenesic, the objection falls to the
ground.   We confess that before coming to the conclusion that
there is eugenesis between certain genera we must wait,* but between
certain species it is beyond a doubt; they give birth to offspring indefinitely fertile, without the reversion towards one of the two primitive
races having yet been established.   It is of little consequence,
therefore, that the Negro and White species are more or less homo-
genesic; they are no less species; for the sole reason that their
differential characters have the value of those upon which we
establish a basis in natural history for the creation of species.   With
regard to the question of monogenism or polygenism, in the signification given to it at the present day, it is absolutely foreign to the
subject in debate.   To sum up: The HUMAN FAMILY, the first
of the ORDER of Primates, is composed of SPECIES, or fundamental human races, whose number and primordial characters form
the subject of this the Second Portion of Anthropology.

* We have spoken, at page 195, of a case of hybridity between genera,
which might have occurred in the Department of Aisne.   We had reason to
speak with reserve.   From positive information we have since received, we
find that the thing did not take place.

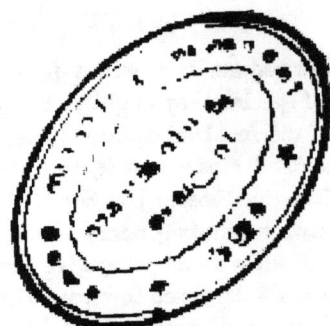

THIRD PART.

ON THE ORIGIN OF MAN.

CHAPTER I.

MONOGENISM OF M. DE QUATREFAGES—POLYGENISM OF AGASSIZ—
TRANSFORMISM OF LAMARCK—SELECTION OF MR. DARWIN—
THEIR APPLICATION TO MAN: HIS GENEALOGY, HIS PLACE IN
NATURE.

WITH regard to the position of Man in the Mammalian series, and
the dignity of his races, we come to the general conclusion that
they are distinct from the other problems which the knowledge of
that Man implies. It matters but little whether at a particular
moment, sooner or later, the physical types had been *genera*, *species*,
or *varieties*, and whether it is still so. What philosophers are
curious to know is how they took their origin, whether suddenly
and spontaneously at all points, or progressively and naturally
from things which had pre-existed.

At first naturalists and anthropologists took but little interest in
all these questions. They worked without listening to dogmas
taught outside their own sphere, their methods of investigation
were carried on in temperate regions. According as the science of
facts progressed, it became impossible for them any longer to be un-
interested in the lofty views which gave to Newton and Humboldt
so great a reputation, and which is not forbidden in any other
branch of human knowledge.

Two currents therefore are established regarding the Origin of
Man leading to two different doctrines—the one orthodox, monogenistic, affirming that all the human races are derived from one
and the same stock, and have been produced by the influence of

2 L 2

climate and external circumstances in the brief space of time that
has elapsed since the creation of the world, according to the biblical
version; the other revolutionary, polygenistic, maintaining that
this lapse of time is insufficient, that the types are permanent under
present conditions and as we now see them, and, consequently, that
they must originally have been multiple. But the horizon has now
changed; it is no longer a question of 5877 years, but of an
incalculable number of ages, and what was false in the former case
may be true in the latter. It is with the telescope that we must
now search for the origin of man. Let us then look at the doctrines
before us. We shall be brief, this work professing merely to be a
résumé of facts and of the methods of study relating to Anthropology. This Third Part does not strictly come within our plan,
and is only supplementary.

We shall say nothing respecting the dissertations of meta-
physicians on the essence of Man, the pre-established harmony
between the body and mind, or the intelligent intervention of
nature; nor as regards the philosophers of a higher order. The
following quotation will form the exception: "In the necessary
course of things," said Epicurus and Lucretius, "all possible com-
binations take place, sooner or later, in the midst of complex
conditions, which sometimes are more or less favourable to them,
and sometimes contradict them, so that the results are as variable
as can be according to the conditions of times and places, and
the combination of those conditions."[*]

We would willingly pass over in silence the explanations which
we find at the foundation of all religious systems, if one of them—
our own—had not been disputed by eminent anthropologists. In
that concerning the book of Genesis, such as we find from the
compilation of Esdras after the Babylonian captivity, two opinions
present themselves to our notice. Some, believing themselves
to be thoroughly orthodox, affirm that it is merely a question
relating to the Semitic peoples, and particularly to the Jews; they
revive the arguments upon which, in 1655, Isaac de la Peyrère

* "Sur la Transformisme," by Paul Broca, in "Bull. Soc. d'Anthrop.,"
2nd series, vol. iv., 1870.

founded his doctrine of the Pre-Adamites,* and bid us to remember,
for example, that God "set a mark upon Cain, lest any finding
him should kill him," and go on to remark that, in chapter vi.,
the "sons of God" are represented as races of Adam, and the
"sons of man" as non-Adamic races. Others, radical in their orthodoxy, declare, on the contrary, that all races originally descended
from a single pair—Adam and Eve—and consecutively from the
three pairs saved from the Deluge; that all the animal species are
derived in the same way from pairs saved at the same time; that
the influence of climate and external circumstances soon manifested
itself, and that subsequently came the diversity of languages.
That Linnæus had some doubts on the subject; he was dissatisfied
with regard to the exceptional character of the country which had
supplied the wants of zoological species as opposed to one another
as the polar bear and the tropical hippopotamus. Prichard replied
that it had to do with the supernatural, and hence, that a little
more or a little less made no difference. This must be repeated to
those who inquire whether Adam was white, black (*Prichard*), or
red (*Boudin de Sallex*), or who make him a dolichocephale, while
the Pre-Adamites should have been brachycephalus (*Stanikowl
Wake*).

We pass on to the scientific doctrines. In the first place, we
have that of M. de Quatrefages, who, without allowing himself
to be disturbed by influences foreign to science, strongly defends
the doctrine of the unity of the human species, while thoroughly
acknowledging its very great antiquity. He considers that zoological species are unchangeable in their physical type, and circumscribed by their character of homogenesis within their own area,
and of heterogenesis outside it.† Human races are only varieties
arising from the influence of climate and external circumstances
(*milieux*), and of crossing, and may be reduced to a small number,

* "Præadamitæ," by Isaac de la Peyrère: Ed. Elzevior, Amsterdam, 1655.
† "De l'Unité de l'Espèce Humaine," 1 vol., Paris, 1869; "Rapport sur
les Progrès de l'Anthropologie," Paris, 1869; "Leçons Professées au
Muséum," in "Revue des Cours Scientifiques," 1864-65, 1867-68, &c.; by
M. de Quatrefages.

all of which come from one and the same stock. Man was created in the beginning, in conditions to us unknown, by the intervention of an extraneous force, or by a supreme will. M. de Quatrefages, therefore, recognises but one human species, and in deference to man's elevated rank, and his character for religiousness, he concedes to him a place apart in the zoological series, under the name, proposed by Isidore G. Saint-Hilaire, of *régno humain*.

The various arguments in favour of this doctrine have been examined in the course of this work. We merely remark that religiousness is not really peculiar to Man; and that among men, whether individuals or races, many do not possess it; that the influence of external circumstances is but little, and does not—as far as we can see, and in the present state of things, as Geoffroy Saint-Hilaire said—succeed in producing a new physical character indefinitely transmissible; that fecundity exclusively taking place between individuals of the same species is not the criterion of the species; and, lastly, that the interval which physically separates the principal human types is equal to, if not sometimes greater than, that which separates and determines zoological species. The origin of species, Agassiz maintained, is lost in the obscurity of the first establishment of the present state of things. Species are not strictly fixed within certain limits, nor determined by the faculty of individuals of being fertile only *inter se*. Human races differ as much as certain families, certain genera, or certain species. They were produced, in some independent way, on eight different points of the globe, or centres, which are as distinct in their fauna as in their flora. Agassiz admitted, nevertheless, the intervention, at every phase of the history of the world, of a superior will, operating by virtue of a preconceived plan.[*]

The third of these propositions, coming from a naturalist of such world-wide renown, has considerable weight; and agrees with our own conclusions as anthropologists. As to his centres of creation, which he calls realms (*les royaumes*), their particular localization is only justified, as regards some of them, by the flora and fauna

* "Sketch of the Natural Provinces of the World," by Professor Agassiz in "Types of Mankind," by Nott and Gliddon.   Philadelphia, 1854.

generally, but not by Man: the Australian realm for example. To his Arctic realm, apparently so proper, it may be objected that it is now entirely peopled by men and animals which have been imported there, and that their conditions of existence were precisely identical at one time in the centre of France. The doctrine of M. de Quatrefages is classical monogenism, which must be distinguished from the new monogenism of which we shall speak presently: that of Agassiz is a special polygenism. Both are allied to each other, in that they search into the secret of the formation of Man outside the known natural laws which regulate the universe. It is otherwise with the doctrine we are now about to speak of, namely—

Transformism.

This is of French origin. The entire honour of its introduction is due to A. Lamarck, although De Maillet and Robinet had previously sketched out some of its traits. A species, Lamarck wrote in 1800,* varies infinitely, and, considered as regards time, does not exist. Species pass from one to the other by an infinity of transitions, both in the animal and vegetable kingdom. They originate either by transformation or divergence. By going back for ages, we thus come to a small number of primordial germs, or monads, the offspring of spontaneous generation. Man is no exception to this; he is the result of the slow transformation of certain apes. The ladder to which we before compared the organic kingdoms only exists, he says, as regards the principal masses. Species, on the contrary, are, as it were, the isolated extremities of the branches and boughs which form each of these masses.

This striking hypothesis was the offspring of Lamarck's brain, at a time when the knowledge of natural history, palæontology, and embryology was very imperfect, and upon which so vivid a light has since been shed. Nothing has been added to its principle: the ways and methods of transformation have been discussed, facts of observation have been supplied, genealogical tables of animated

* "Philosophie Zoologique," by J. B. A. Lamarck, Professeur de Zoologie au Muséum, Paris; 1st edition 1809, 2nd edition 1873, in two volumes.

beings have been proposed; but the foundation has remained intact both in France, in Germany, and in England. Lamarck, in that he was in advance of his time, and stood forward firmly in advocacy of his theory, showed himself to be a man of genius. The ways and methods of Lamarck may be summed up in a single sentence—the adaptation of organs to conditions of existence. Change in external circumstances, he says, obliges the animal placed in the presence of animals of greater strength, or in new conditions of life, to contract different habits, which produce an increased activity in certain organs, a diminution, or a want of exercise, in others. By virtue of the physiological law inherent in every organism, that the organ, or a certain part of the organ, diminishes or increases in proportion to the work that it performs, these organs become modified when submitted to new conditions. The internal power of the organism, dependent on the general function of nutrition which is called forth, is immense. The wants induced by external changes brought it into play.

The doctrine in its entirety was too far in advance of the age to have the success which was its due. Cuvier, the advocate of the orthodox opinions of the time, had but little difficulty in stifling it in the cradle—Cuvier, who ridiculed the idea of the foundation of the Normal school, as well as the honorary title of *hero* granted by the Convention to Lacépède. Notwithstanding this, however, the doctrine had its adepts. In France—Poiret, Bory de Saint-Vincent, Geoffroy Saint-Hilaire; abroad—Treviranus, Oken, Goethe. From the year 1818 Geoffroy Saint-Hilaire became its champion, and laid particular stress on the immediate effects on the body of external circumstances. Cuvier a second time resumed the discussion, and, in opposition to him, propounded his own doctrine on the periodical revolutions of the earth, of the renewal each time of the Flora and Fauna, and of the incessant and miraculous intervention of a creative will. The contention between these two powerful geniuses had to do with the movement which ended in the Revolution of 1830. Authority at last had the advantage, and in France *transformism* was vanquished. But the number of its proselytes increased from far and wide. The last

work of Goethe was favourable to it. Botanists, especially, accepted
the new doctrine—W. Herbert, P. Matthews, Lecoq, Hooker, Raf-
nesque, Naudin. Then the geologists—Omalius d'Halloy, Keys-
erling, and other savants. L. Buch, Schaffhauser, Herbert Spencer,
and Lyell had already cleared the way, by sapping at the foundation
the theory of the periodical catastrophes of Cuvier, when Charles
Darwin made his appearance, in 1859.

This great naturalist was not vividly impressed by the views of
Lamarck. His own ideas passed through his mind during his
voyage round the world in the *Beagle*.* On his return to
London, six years afterwards, he studied the results which were
obtained by breeders on animals, and he devoted himself to make
experiments, especially on pigeons. The subject of artificial selection most occupied him, when one day he stumbled on the work
"On Population," by Malthus. This was a streak of light; the
word which was to make the fortune of his theory was found—
"the struggle for existence."

By a singular coincidence, another English savant, Richard
Wallace, who had taken up his abode in Malasia, forwarded to
him at that moment a memoir, supported by facts, in which the
same ideas were set forth. But Mr. Wallace, with his task hardly
entered upon, recoiled before the consequences of his labours when
he perceived that they, of necessity, applied to Man. Charles
Darwin, on the contrary, persevered, and it is with justice that his
countrymen gave to his theory the name of Darwinism, a theory
which should be thus defined: "Natural selection, by the struggle
for existence, applied to the transformism of Lamarck."

We know that breeders and horticulturists obtain, almost at will,
the new forms which they desire, by first selecting from one and the
same species, then from the offspring of a first cross, then from
those of the next crosses, and so on, individuals possessing in the
highest degree the variety required. A new species is thus developed, and by dint of perseverance, fixed. The divergences from

* "Voyage d'un Naturaliste autour du Monde, à bord du Navire le
Beagle, de 1831 à 1836," by Charles Darwin. Traduction de E. Barbier.
Reinwald.

the primitive type which are obtained are very strange. They have to do with colour, form of the head, the proportions of the skeleton, the configuration of the muscles, and even with the habits (*mœurs*) of the animal. Sir John Sebright undertook to produce in three years a certain feather in a bird, and in six years a certain form of beak or head. In this consists "artificial selection," as it is effected by the intelligent hand of Man on animals in a state of domestication. But is not the same result sometimes produced naturally in wild animals? Mr. Darwin affirms it, by substituting for the hand of Man the chance circumstance derived from vital competition (*concurrence*).

Competition is a general law of the universe,—it is exerted between physical forces, between beings of the two kingdoms, between men, between peoples. Under the name of "struggle for existence" it is even useful; without that, there would soon be a retardation of everything upon the face of the earth. It has been calculated that a single pair of elephants—the slowest of all animals to breed—would produce, barring all restraints, fifteen millions of young in five hundred years. Darwin, quoted by Boudin, speaks of a woman, who died at 93 years of age, as having 1396 children, grandchildren, and great-grandchildren. Malthus has proved that population increases in a geometrical ratio, while the resources of that population only augment in an arithmetical ratio. The law of the stronger predominates everywhere—the large devour the small; those the best protected by their organization, the best provided with means of attack or of resistance to external agencies, survive the longest; the more numerous they are, and the longer they live, the more they multiply and establish a stock in preference to those who are less favoured.

Spontaneous variability is another element of the Darwinian theory. Two individuals of the same species, or of the same family, do not resemble each other in every respect; they differ by characters of no value, or by characters which give them an advantage in the struggle over those whose wants, or conditions of climate, food, and external circumstances of every sort are the same. The animal with a protective-coloured skin, that is one

like the ground upon which he is moving, will better escape his
enemies. In one of Darwin's works there is a very curious example of this kind in butterflies. The animal with the thick fur
will be under more favourable circumstances at the poles, the one
with the sleek skin at the equator. Every advantage acquired
from birth, and therefore more easily transmissible in consequence,
places the individual in a better condition for resistance to causes
of destruction and to sterility. It follows, then, that certain
individuals are, as it were, selected, chosen by a natural process
which replaces the agency of Man in artificial selection; and that
these individuals are precisely those who are separated the most
from others by some new character. The thing being repeated for
many generations, the divergences become marked, the tendency
to inheritance increases, and new types are formed, farther and
farther removed from the point of departure. It follows, also,
that wherever an ensemble of conditions exhibits itself, which
allows a divergence to be developed without being stifled by rival
divergences, it will take its place in the series of beings, and
possibly form one for the occupation of a zoological species. One
difference between artificial and natural selection is in the time
they require for a transformation to become confirmed. In the
former nothing is left to chance; matters progress rapidly, but the
types are not thoroughly fixed, and readily revert to the primitive
type. In the latter we must reckon by ages, chance also inter-
vening, for the destruction of that which has commenced only to
be completed. The results once obtained are more stable. Between the methods set forth by Lamarck and those of Darwin
there are important differences. As regards the former, the point
of departure of transformation is in the external circumstances
which modifies the way of living and creates new habits, new
wants, which induce a change in the nutrition and structure of
organs. For the latter, the point of departure is in the superiority
that procures for the individual some advantage in the daily
struggle. Lamarck considers that variation is effected gradually in
the course of existence. Darwin, that it appears spontaneously at
birth or rather during embryonic life. To the process of selection

by vital competition, Mr. Darwin adds selection by sexual competition, which depends on the will, on the choice and vitality of the individuals, and especially affects the males.[*]

The Germans, who have vigorously espoused the cause of transformism, particularly Haeckel, recognise two orders of methods. They give to those of the French school, including changes of life and habits, of food and climate, training, the excess or want of use of organs, the name of *phenomena of direct adaptation*; and to those of the English school, that is to say, to congenital characters, the name of *phenomena of indirect adaptation*. Endeavours have been made to see whether there may not be other processes of formation of species. According to the doctrine of Darwin, the new character pre-exists in the germ, and depends on the influence of the parents even before conception. According to Geoffroy Saint-Hilaire, the action of climate and external circumstances is not confined to its exercise upon the individual in the course of existence, it may equally make itself felt in the germ in progress of development, and produce varieties, sometimes monstrosities. Such would be the origin of the race of goats oxen of La Plata. In the above processes it is only a question as to slow transformations. We might also have sudden transformations. "An accident which it is not necessary to mention," writes E. Geoffroy Saint-Hilaire, "trifling at its origin, but of incalculable importance in its effects, has been sufficient to change the inferior type of oviparous vertebrata into an ornithological type. The process of M. Kölliker would be equally an accident, taking for his *point de départ* the various degrees of genæogenesis and the succession of forms in the development of the embryo. He thinks that beings may produce other beings separated from their parents by characters of species, genus, and even of class. He bases his theory on that which takes place sometimes in inferior forms, and supposes, as regards the superior, that a normal egg may

* "La Descendance de l'Homme et la Sélection Sexuelle," by Ch. Darwin; translated into French, 2nd edition, Paris, 1873. See also "L'Origine des Espèces et de la Variation des Animaux et des Plantes sous l'Action de la Domestication," by the same.

go past the period of its ordinary development, and give origin to a higher organisation. These theories and processes concern the two organic kingdoms. The limits of this work do not allow of our entering into the subject farther, and we must confine ourselves to Man. Do they apply to Man, as well as to animals? Evidently they do, or they are false: laws are uniform. As we said in the early part of this work, the Primates form the first natural group of the order of Mammalia, thanks to a certain number of characters common to them and to the succeeding orders. Moreover, this group presents numerous points of contact with the latter, and, in the series of families of which it is composed, an ascending gradation of types is observed, becoming more and more perfect. Thus, at the bottom of the scale we have the Lemurs, some of which are allied to the Insectivora, others to the Cheiroptera, and even to the Marsupialia; above them the Cebians, many of whose genera are lemurs in a state of transition; then the Pithecians, some species of which seem derived from Cebians. Afterwards, the anthropoid apes make their appearance, separated by a sensible interval, if one of them, the Gibbon, did not diminish it, owing to his numerous features of resemblance to the Pithecians. At the summit is Man, many of whose types approximate in many of their features to the Anthropoids.

Their differences, indeed, may be thus summed up: (1) There are modifications of form connected with the decidedly vertical attitude of Man and the oblique attitude of the Anthropoid; (2) The more perfect adaptation of the foot and hand to their respective functions of locomotion and prehension in Man; (3) The volume of the brain, which is three times as large, or more, in Man, thus causing a corresponding activity of the organ, and a proportionate development of all its functions; namely, language, observation, judgment, &c. The continuity, on the one hand, of the inferior order of Mammalia with the superior order of Primates, and in this latter of its inferior family of Lemurs with its superior family of Man passing through the Anthropoids more nearly akin to Man than to the Pithecians; and, on the other hand, the continuity of certain human races with others rising higher and higher in-

the scale are clearly the result of this. Moreover, between one
type and another, sufficiently recognised for naturalists to make
them the representatives of special groups, whether of order,
family, genus, or species, some variation of the organ, or some
bastard species, almost always comes in to establish the transition. *Natura non facit saltum.* It might be said that a creative
force had been at work, step by step, leaving its track behind
it, and that groups are due to the periods of repose during which
that force was in operation on a certain spot, with a view the
better to increase the number of forms. When Lamarck supposed
that Man was the issue of the chimpanzee, his mind was atten-
tively engaged in observing both the family of Primates in
particular and the animal kingdom in general. The rudimentary
organs in Man, or vestiges of perfectly useless organs—like the
ilio-cæcal appendix—which are well developed in other species
among the Mammalia, and the unusual appearance of organs, like
the supplementary mammæ, or conformations peculiar to other
animal species, furnish so many arguments in favour of transformation. On no other hypothesis are they to be explained. They
may be phenomena of atavism, of remote reminiscence, of facts of
reversion. (See page 127.) Embryology would also be favourable
to the doctrine. (See page 129.) "The series of diverse forms
which every individual of a species passes through," says Haeckel,
"from the early dawn of his existence, is simply a short and rapid
recapitulation of the series of specific multiple forms through which
his progenitors have passed, the ancestors of the existing species,
during the enormous duration of the geological periods."[*] A
series of teratological cases, entering into the arrests, and even into
the perversions of development, of the embryo, are thus explained.
Hare-lip, polydactylin, microcephaly, are, as it were, hesitations of
the principles of evolution, attempts on its part to stop at points
where it had rested in anterior forms, or to progress in other pre-
viously-followed directions. Human palæontology does not reach

[*] "Histoire de la Création des Êtres Organisés d'après les Lois Naturelles,"
by E. Haeckel. French translation. Paris, 1874.

back sufficiently far for us to found any arguments upon it; it should pass beyond the last or quaternary period. The most ancient human fossil of this period, however, is favourable to the idea of a derivation of man from the anthropoid.

Direct proofs as to transformism are not wanting. In so far as Man is concerned, the matter is clear; but rational proofs, as Geoffroy Saint-Hilaire said, are abundant. Transformism imposes itself as a necessity: everything is as if things had thus taken place; or man was created out of nothing, by enchantment; or he proceeds from that which existed previously. But what are we to think as to the mode? Those of direct adaptation of organs to life are so rational, they are so conformable to the general laws of physiology, that it would be unwise to reject them positively. Of course we have never seen a White changed into a Black, nor smooth hair into woolly; but in time, by passing through intermediate races produced by crossing, there is no proof that the phenomena might not have taken place. We are too exacting. Prichard was anxious to prove that Whites might make their appearance spontaneously among Negroes. All his arguments were wrong, in that he entirely left out of sight the way in which races have become removed from place to place. But we are not at all sure that his aspirations, if better supported, might not now triumph. The brain increases in volume, and its convolutions increase in richness, in proportion to the degree of activity of which they are the seat, bringing in their train a series of subordinate craniological characters. Nutrition and external circumstances may in the same way cause the stature and colour of individuals to vary as well as the proportions of the body. *La fonction fait l'organe* of Lamarck is a demonstrative fact. When a muscle is paralysed, it becomes atrophied, the osseous eminences in which it is inserted disappear, the skeleton becomes deformed. In persons who have lost a limb by amputation, the nerves, having become useless, progressively become atrophied from their extremity to their central point in the brain (*Luys*). The digestive tube is dilated, and the belly becomes large in those who are large eaters of vegetable food. All the difficulty is in the transmission of

the acquired individual character; clearly, facts are at fault here.
There is no proof, however, that the tribe of Akkas is not indebted
for its diminutiveness to the fact of inheritance fixing accidental
characters. If the albinos are as common among the Monbuttous,
as Dr. Schweinfürth states, the question is, whether circumstances
being favourable, a new species may not some day start up. Supposing in that country, through some catastrophe, the temperature
and radiation should be suddenly lowered, many would die, but
the survivors would have a better chance of thriving. In poly-
dactilia, supposing crossing outside the family did not counteract
inheritance, transmission, now limited to five generations, according
to the facts hitherto mentioned, would certainly go beyond.

Let us pass on to the methods of indirect adaptation of Mr.
Darwin. Vital competition is a thing which must not be confounded with selection. It exists, no matter how we apply it,
between individuals, as between societies and races. We have
before us the fact of races inferior in the struggle becoming extinct.
The Charruas, the Caribs, the ancient Californians, the Tasmanians,
no longer exist; the Australians, the Negritos, the Esquimaux, are
fast following them. The Polynesian, the American Indians, will
soon be in their wake, if they have no chance of surviving except
by crossing. The superior races, on the contrary, thrive and increase. It is easy to foretell the moment when the races which now
decrease the interval between the White man and the Anthropoid
shall have entirely disappeared.

There is nothing mysterious in this extinction; its mechanism is
altogether natural (see page 413). The result will be the survivance
of those most adapted to benefit the superior races. But at one
time, in Australia, in Malaisia, in America, and in Europe it was
not so. These very races which now are succumbing, were superior
relatively to others which no longer exist. The Australians of the
present, whom we look upon as savages, have a civilisation conformable to their external condition, a certain social organisation—
in relation to the Negritos of the interior of the Philippines, for
example. We think we have proved that they have ejected a
negro race inferior to themselves, as we now eject them. The

wandering aborigines of Western Australia, described by Scott
Nind, are the remnants of this race.   In our own country, the
races of the Périgord, which have disappeared before, or become
absorbed into, the brachycephalic races from the East and the
Bondes from the North, have played the same part before the races
anterior to the Neanderthal as these probably did to the Miocene
races of Thenay and Saint-Prest.   In these successive extinctions,
which exhibit to us series of generations, strata of more and more
perfect races succeeding and replacing each other, do we not recognise the selection by vital competition of Mr. Darwin?   But where
is the character which gives the advantage in the struggle?   Among
animals, and during the first ages of the human race, the power
which enabled them the better to defend themselves against other
living beings, and against changes of climate and external conditions, was necessarily of a physical kind, such as quick-sighted-
ness, more acute smell, more vigorous muscles, a constitution better
adapting itself to cold or heat, to marsh miasm, or to certain kinds
of diet.   If Man acclimates tolerably well now, it must not be forgotten that he owes the power, in a great measure, to the processes
which he makes use of.   Formerly he must have succumbed, or his
constitution must have been modified.   We speak here especially of
sudden acclimation.   But from the period when societies were
formed, and moral force took its legitimate supremacy over brute
force, the advantage remained with the most skilful, the most
industrious—in a word, with the most intelligent.   Selection, from
henceforth, was made to the advantage of a single organ.   The
largest brains—those with the richest convolutions, and with the
most delicate structure, with the most appropriate histological
elements—were the most favoured.   Hence a state of progress
which is undeniable.   The process of Mr. Darwin has, therefore,
had its effect in the past, as it has now in the present.   With
appropriate institutions we might direct it, and accelerate its already
so remarkable results.

The external circumstances of Lamarck must, in fact, have an
action of whose mechanism we know nothing.   The selection of
Mr. Darwin has one of which we are certain.   With the latter we

reckon by strata of races, with the former we must do the same. The characters which we now see permanent in a given race are not the more so when we compare a succession of races.

Absolute immobility nowhere exists, and fixity of species is only relative. May there not be other processes contributing to gradual transformation? Certainly not. There are three orders of characters which *transformism* explains, says M. Broca, some of *evolution*, others of *improvement*, a third *serial*. But there is a fourth, the unimportant, the key to which he does not give. Such are the presence of the *os intermedium* of the carpus, the absence of a nail on the great toe, and the absence of a round ligament in the hip-joint, peculiar to the orang-outang among Anthropoids. Why, how, and when, did these characters take their origin?

Another objection is that, in going back in the past, we do not find human races differing much from the races of the present; that we do not find, for example, men with half the cranial capacity of those of the present. But do we discover the Pliocene Man and the Miocene Man by the flint implements of Saint-Prest and Thenay? The former made use of fire, the latter did not: is not this a reason for suspecting that the fact of the volume of his brain being less was the cause? If he was unacquainted with fire he ought not to have the sense to bury his dead. The Anthropoids are in this condition, and we have none of their remains. Probably also, human bones do not last for so immeasurably prolonged a period. However, on surveying the road travelled over, and the discoveries made during the last fifteen years, we must not despair. Is it not by chance, when making a road or a railway cutting, or after a land-slip, or an earthquake, that discoveries of this kind are made? Here a man of intellect, and one interested in the subject, should be at hand.

Now, Africa, Asia, Oceania, and even the greater part of Europe, are still as it were virgin soils. Perhaps, also, the stratum in which is now lying the *precursor*, not possessing language, announced by G. de Mortillet and Hovelacque is at present submerged; perhaps he has only existed on a very limited point of the globe. Some day or other he may present himself before us under the form of a skeleton stranded upon some bank of mud, as at Grenelle; crushed under a rock, as at Laugerie-Haute; or embedded in lava, as at Denise.

The derivation of Man from some previously-existing form being admitted, the question is what this form may have been. Lamarck believed it to have been a chimpanzee. We have seen that each of the three great Anthropoids approaches more or less to Man in certain characters, but not one possesses them all. So in the inferior races; no one race, not even the Bosjesman, is specially marked out as descending from an anthropoid—they are only made to approach more or less by such or such a character. The precursor of Man, then, is only analogous to the Anthropoids. The human type is an improvement upon the general type of their family, but not of one of their known species in particular.

M. Haeckel does not express an opinion on this point. He asks whether the dolichocephales of Europe and Africa are not derived from the chimpanzee and the gorilla of the coasts of Guinea, both of which are dolichocephales; and whether the brachycephales of Asia do not descend, on the contrary, from the brachycephalic orangs of Borneo and Sumatra. Many reasons lead to the belief, indeed, that all the dolichocephales are originally from Europe and Africa, and the brachycephales from Eastern Asia, not to speak of the old continent of Asia. M. Vogt thinks otherwise. He thinks that Man is only cousin-german to the anthropoid, and that the ancestor common to them both is further off still. Here M. Haeckel speaks positively. He says that this very remote ancestor is an ape of the old continent, a Pithecian, which was itself derived from a Lemur, and this in its turn from a Marsupial. He even gives it the name of *Lemuria*—a term borrowed from Mr. Sclater; and, as the focus of this series of transformations, a continent now submerged, of which Madagascar, Ceylon, and the Sunda islands are the remains.

But what becomes, in all this, of the old dispute between monogenists and polygenists? It no longer has any interest, and, to be brief, may be summed up as follows: As to the question of the most elementary human types to which we might go back, types

utterly irreducible, whatever their value of genera or species, in the
sense usually applied to those words, are they the issue of many
Anthropoid ancestors, Pithecoids or others ; or are they derived from
a single stock, represented by a single individual of their genera
now known, or not ? The anthropological data given in this work
appear to us more favourable to the former opinion, if we accept
the transformation theory. The most characteristic races, whether
living or extinct, do not form one single ascending series, such as
may be compared to a ladder or a tree, but, reduced to their simplest
expression, to a series of frequently parallel lines.

We shall conclude by giving a *résumé* of the possible genealogy
of Man, according to Haeckel. Equally relying on comparative
anatomy, palæontology, and embryology, the learned professor of
zoology at the University of Jena thus gives his views on the
subject of *evolution* :

At the commencement of what geologists call the *Laurentian*
period of the earth, and of the fortuitous union of certain elements
of carbon, oxygen, hydrogen, and nitrogen, under conditions which
probably took place only at that epoch, the first albuminoid clots
were formed. From them, and by spontaneous generation, the first
cellules or *cïtarogénenses* took their origin. These cellules were
then subdivided and multiplied, and arranged themselves in the
form of organs, and after a series of transformations, fixed by
M. Haeckel at nine in number, gave origin to certain vertebrata of
the genus *Amphioxus lanceolatus*. The division into sexes was
marked out, the spinal marrow and *chorda dorsalis* became visible.
At the *tenth* stage, the brain and the skull made their appearance,
as in the lamprey ; at the *eleventh*, the limbs and jaws were
developed, as in the dogfish : the earth was then only at the
Silurian period. At the *sixteenth*, the adaptation to terrestrial
life ceased. At the *seventeenth*, which corresponds to the Jurassic
phase of the history of the globe, the genealogy of Man is raised
to the kangaroo among the Marsupials. At the *eighteenth*, he
becomes a Lemurian : the Tertiary epoch commences. At the
nineteenth, he becomes Catarrhinian, that is to say an ape with a
tail, a Pithecian. At the *twentieth*, he becomes an Anthropoid

continuing so throughout the whole of the Miocene period. At the *twenty-first*, he is the man ape, he does not yet possess language, nor, in consequence, the corresponding brain. Lastly, at the *twenty-second*, Man comes forth, as we now see him, at least in his inferior forms. Here the enumeration stops. M. Hæckel forgets the *twenty-third* stage, that in which the Lamarcks and Newtons make their appearance. Although having attained so lofty an eminence, Man must have had a very low origin, in no way differing from that of the first and most simple organic corpuscles. What he is now in the womb, he would have been permanently on making his appearance in the animal series.

This theory is painful and revolting to those who delight to surround the cradle of humanity with a brilliant aureole; and if we were to boast of our genealogy and not of our actions, we might indeed consider ourselves humiliated. But what is this new restraint to our *amour-propre* in comparison with that which astronomy has already imposed? When the earth was fixed in the centre of the system, and it was thought that the universe was created for the earth, and the earth for Man, our pride ought to have been satisfied. This doctrine, called by the Germans "geocentric," as applied to the earth, and "anthropocentric," as applied to Man, was perfectly co-ordinate; but it fell to the ground the moment it was demonstrated that the earth is only the humble satellite of a sun which itself is but one of the luminous points in space. It was then, and not now, that Man was truly recalled to humility. It was no longer for him that the sun rose each morning, that the celestial vault was nightly bespangled with innumerable resplendent orbs. Out of all this Macrocosm there was but one lowly planet left to Man. Like that peasant who dreamt that he was ruler of the world, and woke up to find himself in a simple cottage, it was not without regret that he saw himself thus degraded. Long the remembrance of his vanished dream troubled his thoughts; but he was obliged to be resigned, to become accustomed to the reality; and now he consoles himself, as he is no longer this monarch of creation, with the thought that he is really sovereign of the earth. This undoubted royalty he has a right to be proud of. But in what way is it threatened or diminished by the *transformation theory* ? Would it be less real if he had brought it under subjugation by himself or inherited it from his first ancestors? Far from depreciating Man and his origin, the doctrine of Lamarck dignifies and ennobles them, by substituting for the theory of the supernatural the theory of the mutability and natural evolution of organic forms.

But, after all, what matter to science the regret or complacency of some people? Its aims and designs are beyond their comprehension. Man is not at liberty to put or not to put a curb upon the functional activity of his brain; his spirit of inquiry is the most noble, the most irresistible of his attributes; and as M. Gabriel de Mortillet said at the meeting of the Association for the Advancement of Science, his characteristic is here, and not in religiousness. For want of knowledge the imagination muses upon the unknown, and forms it to our own ideal. But to true observers the reality is sufficient; they contemplate the magnificent spectacle which is opening out before them; they even worship nature in its beauty, its grandeur, its harmony, and its thousand varieties of form and movement. The animal has the simple notion of cause and effect, and sees that the boundary of his faculties and senses is limited. Man alone investigates and wills; his horizon is indefinite, like his intellectual faculties when they are exercised without trammel.

Let us not, therefore, seek to contract the circle of knowledge. Is it not knowledge which has conducted us step by step, age after age, to the degree of prosperity we now enjoy? Is it not this which engenders civilisation, which adds to our well-being, brings to us the purest satisfaction, instructs us in philosophy, and secures our supremacy over everything on our planet? Each one has his task to perform in this immense sphere. To some is given subjects of study relating to the progress of life; to others its realities. Let the former have for their object the development in society of ideas of justice, honour, and morality, without which it cannot exist. The means are within their power. Our part is to ascertain facts, to deduce from them laws, and to look at them calmly, without allowing ourselves to be carried away by our feelings. Whatever may be his origin, whatever his future destiny, Man, to the anthropologist, is but a Mammifer, whose organization, wants, and diseases are in the highest degree complex; whose brain, with its admirable functions, have reached the highest development. As such, he is subject to the same laws as the rest of the animal creation; as such, he is a participator in their destinies.

THE END.

INDEX.

www.ingramcontent.com/pod-product-compliance
Lightning Source LLC
Chambersburg PA
CBHW022127020426
42334CB00015B/788